A Companion to the Study of Virgil

A Companion
to the Study
of Virgil

Nicholas Horsfall

BRILL

LEIDEN · BOSTON · KOLN

This journal is printed on acid-free paper.

Design: TopicA (Antoinette Hanekuyk), Leiden

On the cover: The Wounded Aeneas from the Casa di Sirico, Pompeii, Italy. reproduced with permission.

Library of Congress Cataloging-in-Publication Data

The Library of Congress Cataloging-in-Publication Data are also available.

ISBN 90 04 11870 5

© Copyright by Koninklijke Brill NV, P.O. Box 9000, NL-2300-PA Leiden, The Netherlands

PRINTED IN THE NETHERLANDS

CONTENTS

Introduction and editor's note vii

Short-title list xi

Chapter One: Virgil: his life and times
N.M. Horsfall 1

Chapter Two: *Bucolics*
A. Perutelli (Translated by the Editor) 27
Title 27; Date 28; Arrangement 31; Numerology 33; The genre of pastoral 34; Poetic tradition 37; Bucolic characters 42; Countryside and setting 45; Language 47; Metre and Prosody 51; Narrative and dramatic structure 53; Dominant motifs 54; Allegorical interpretations 58; The interpretation of the fourth *Eclogue* 60

Chapter Three: *Georgics*
N.M. Horsfall 63
The dating of *G.* 63; Publics, politics and agriculture 65; Town/country: a false polarity 70; *Uidi:* observation and tradition 71; The *Georgics* as a 'traditional' poem 72; Structure 73; The excursus or digression 75; Sources—prose 77; Hesiod 78; Alexandrian Poetry 79; Cato and 'Cato' 81; Lucretius 82; Catullus and the Neoterics 83; Varro 84; Homer 84; *G.*4, Gallus and the 'second edition' 86; Language 89
Appendix 1: War; peace; *princeps* 93
Appendix 2: The actual readership/intended
audience of *G.* 95
Appendix 3: The prooemium to *G.*3 96
Appendix 4: The prooemium to *G.*1 99

Chapter Four: *Aeneid*
N.M. Horsfall 101
Book 1: Myth, history, and the subject of the *Aeneid* 101; Book 2: Points of view; symbolism and imagery 109; Book 3: Character and development 118; Book 4: Love and ethics 123; Book 5: Structure and architecture; gods 135; Book 6: History and philosophy 144; Book 7: Motivation and responsibility 155; Book 8: Historical allegory; incompleteness 162; Book 9: Emotions and evaluations 170; Book 10: Battle-scenes; poetic sources 179; Book 11: Rhetoric 186; Book 12: Justice and judgement 192

Chapter Five: Style, language and metre
  N.M. Horsfall 217
    Introduction   217; Language   219; Prosody and morphology;
    metre and rhythm; sounds and alliteration   222; grammar and
    syntax; oddities and ambiguities   225; Sentence-structure and
    relation to verse and rhetoric   231; Development   232; *Buc.*9.
    56–65   237; *G.*4.405–14   239; *G.*4.490–8   241; *Aen.*11.378–
    91   244

Chapter Six: Virgil's impact at Rome:
  The non-literary evidence
  N.M. Horsfall 249

Chapter Seven: Virgil: The literary impact
  W.R. Barnes 257
    Ovid, *Metamorphoses*   257; Lucan   268; Valerius Flaccus   273;
    Statius, *Thebaid*   279; Statius, *Achilleid*   285; Silius Italicus   287

Chapter Eight: The transmission of Virgil's works
  in Antiquity and the Middle Ages
  M. Geymonat (Translated by the Editor) 293
    The publication of Virgil's poems and the earliest phase of their
    diffusion in Rome and in the Empire   293; Devotion to Virgil
    in late antiquity and its swift decline in the early middle
    ages   303; The renewal of interest in Virgil from the Carolingian
    period to the Renaissance   310

Appendix
  W.V. Clausen   The 'Harvard School' 313

Index 315

Addenda 327

INTRODUCTION

This is not intended as a conventionally impersonal manual, in the tradition of PW, TSK or Sch.-Hos. These days, Virgil excites strong passions: *G.* and *Aen.* in particular have become ideological and methodological battlefields. I am not a neutral (though the device on my shield may not always be the same!), and I have tried (with the kindly but judicious support of Mr. Julian Deahl, our editor at E.J. Brill) to discourage too much cold impartiality in the other specialists who have contributed to this volume. What follows will probably leave the reader convinced of the incontestable validity of one particular critical position uneasy, to say the least. I have myself been lumped with the New Augustans (D. Fowler, *GR* 37 (1990), 106) and defined (rather better!) as a cheery pragmatist (P. Hardie, *CR* 44 (1994), 42). Perplexity may after all be forgivable: I cherish an instinctive (and probably excessive) reaction against dogmagogues and their jargonauts; in this I am not, I discover, alone.[1] In reviews, in particular, I am driven to extremes by extremists, if only in the interests of reasserting the multiplicity of (more or less) legitimate positions and methodologies in Virgilian studies.

If an approach, carefully applied, repeatedly produces credible results, it is probably worth using and may tell us something worthwhile about one or more aspects of what Virgil was doing, or saying. That is all: I can only offer experience; I am a part of all that I have read. But some acquaintance with Virgil and Virgilian studies (I had best come clean and say that I began seriously ca. 1965) and a working knowledge of Latin poetic usage may at times serve as counterweights to the overenthusiastic application of more exciting (but at the last, less convincing) techniques. And even a retrograde pragmatist can perceive that of course Virgil unquestionably and often pulls his readers in several directions, at several levels, at the same time. But the quicksands of indirection, ambiguity, polyvalence, etc. do not always seem to me quite bottomless. Ingenuously, I must voice the suspicion

---

[1] R. Glei, *Der Vater der Dinge* (Trier, 1991), 41, T. Eagleton, *Literary Theory* (Oxford 1983), J. Griffin, ap. V. Mehta, *Up at Oxford* (London 1992), 332f., W.R. Johnson in *The interpretation of Roman poetry* ed. K. Galinsky (Frankfurt 1992), 200–14 (cf. Galinsky, ib., 21–7).

that the centre holds. What follows is not systematic polemic, nor do I (or the other contributors) offer an overall *prise de position*. A certain fondness for allusion may even be taken as indicating that *de facto* I am closer to Conte, Lyne and Thomas (e.g.) than our divergences of ideology and method might seem to suggest. No clear answers, then, to be found here about what Virgil is, does, and says. At most I try to react, and have urged my colleagues to do the same, with due discretion, against what I (and not I alone) see as in some ways a loss of equilibrium and proportion.

The collaborators in this volume were chosen, I freely admit, because their positions were not incompatible with my own, but no attempt has been made to drive them into offering an unbroken shield wall against some common foe! I have myself tried hard not to repeat what I have written elsewhere, nor to presuppose too much of a recent (but inaccessible) small book of mine, written in Italian, about some of Virgil's methods and techniques in the *Aeneid*.[2] Now that we have the bibliographies of Briggs and Suerbaum to the whole *opus*,[3] the entire *Enciclopedia Virgiliana*,[4] and the yearly bibliographies in *Vergilius*, in addition to *Ann.Phil.*, it is very easy to drown in detail or in the history of your problem. I recently, quite by chance, noted three (or was it four?) new items just on the end of *Aen.*12 in a single fortnight. Let us therefore be clear: the bibliographical guidance here offered is neither comprehensive nor totally up-to-date; that would be neither feasible nor even necessarily desirable. I am, though, grateful to the friends, librarians and review editors who have permitted me to keep more or less abreast of the current,[5] and in particular to my friend Christina Huemer, librarian of the American Academy in Rome. One learns that completeness is a mirage and constant updating in the end a sacrifice to fashion[6] I know perfectly well that my notes are not completely up-to-date, but I have done all that I could! We shall be selective and shall cite what we have ourselves found most helpful and stimulating. We do not even offer a systematic doxography on all the main Virgilian problems, above all when it has been done

---

[2] *Virgilio: l'epopea in alambicco* (Napoli 1991).

[3] *Buc.*: W.W. Briggs, *ANRW* 2.31.2 (1981), 1265–1357; *G.*: W. Suerbaum, ib. 395–499; *Aen.*, *id.*, *ib.*2.31.1. (1980), 3–358 with 2.31.2, 1359–99 (index).

[4] In six volumes, Rome 1984–91.

[5] Cf. S. Timpanaro, *Nuovi Contributi* (Bologna 1994), 265 on the mirage of completeness.

[6] Bibliographical amplitude is much in vogue these days; it has little if anything to do with scholarship and is here cut to the very minimum.

well elsewhere. Thus, for example, not a word here on epithets: there is ample bibliography; I know of no interesting open problems or burning unresolved issues. Silence seemed therefore the sanest solution. And rather than offer highly abbreviated surveys of all major issues currently under discussion among scholars working on the *Aeneid*, I have preferred to concentrate much more specifically on each book successively, as exemplifying one, or two, of those issues. I have tried to uphold the cause of realistic accessibility in the bibliography here offered. It is not helpful to cite continually very rare books and articles (though it is sometimes inevitable and essential); it is our purpose to help serious readers of Virgil, not to encourage a general persecution of library assistants. Rather than offer prolonged and systematic polemic against all those Virgilians from whom we—severally—differ, we have tried to provide relatively uncluttered accounts of the major issues and to relegate dissent, where possible, to the footnote. That does not mean simplification of those issues which remain genuinely open and unresolved. But however much fun it might have been to offer an *Index Librorum Prohibitorum*, we have tried to concentrate both on the positive results of the best scholarship (so that silence, in respect of a relatively accessible book, may be taken as indicating some degree of dissent!) and on those problems which, strangely enough, remain relatively unexplored. There is still a great deal of work to be done, at least on the *Aen.*; I shall be at pains to suggest areas for exploration that seem to me promising. That may be taken as a statement of faith, that Virgil is alive and well and amply worth studying. Readers of this book are not geese to be force-fed with an indigestible concentrate of Virgil scholarship: we have tried, rather, to suggest what information and methods may be relevant to their enquiries, how they may acquire fuller detail, and where indeed they may find themselves on their own.

I am much indebted to Wendell Clausen for sending me his brief historical account of the misnamed 'Harvard School' (cf. pp. 313–4); he and I speak with two voices, but that does not exclude friendship or cooperation! Sarah Spence has most kindly cast herself in the role of 'intended reader' and as such has offered much trenchant comment. To the summary account (n. 2, 13) of those who have contributed most to my development as a Virgilian, I should like to add Elisabeth Henry, in whom commonsense and a deep love of poetry coexist happily, and in whom friendship is not suffered to temper honest criticism, and Julia Budenz, scholar and poet: it has been the

very greatest help to me to be able to talk about Virgil to a practis-
ing (learned, allusive) poet, remarkably well-read not only in Virgil,
but in Servius, Dante and others. Mrs. Henry and Miss Budenz are
not supposed to concur with my contributions (though I hope they
will, here and there!), but I offer them what I have written with
grateful thanks.[7]

Nicholas Horsfall

Editor's note:
The contributions of Profs. Perutelli and Geymonat I translated from
the Italian, editing a bit as I went. In Prof. Geymonat's chapter, I
have indicated my more obtrusive interventions by [Ed.]. Dr. Barnes'
chapter I have altered hardly at all. I have tried in general to avoid
duplication and to achieve uniformity in modes of citation and in
internal references.

It was never part of the original scheme that I should write the
section on *G.*, but when it became apparent that those plans could
not remain unaltered, I decided (with much constructive support from
Mr. Julian Deahl) that, so as to avoid any deleterious delays to the
project as a whole, I had better go ahead and do it myself, even
though my lack of convictions as to the *Georgics'* deeper meaning
may be regarded as a disqualification by some! I am most grateful to
Alessandro Biotti (cf. 91) for having induced me to begin writing on
G. a couple of years ago. Books and articles available to me in Rome
up to Christmas 1994 are mentioned as appropriate; a very few more
recent items have been inserted in proof (see p. viii with nn. 5, 6).

---

[7] Prof. Harry Gotoff kindly read about a third of my own contribution in ms.; I
wish he had had the time for more benign surgery (and post-operative rehabilitation).

SHORT-TITLE LIST

This list does not cover all the abbreviations used in the pages which follow. The conventional systems of *Ann.Phil.* (periodicals), LSJ (Greek) and TLL (Latin) are presupposed, as in all serious works of classical scholarship! Occasionally references may be given in ampler form. Here are included those references which belong to the convenient jargon of professionals and may therefore create initial perplexity, along with a few specifically Virgilian works more conveniently cited in shorter form. Inclusion and exclusion here have nothing to do with merit; only convenience counts! We offer no general bibliography; in some cases short bibliographies are appended to individual chapters, but in general each chapter's notes aim at providing sufficient bibliographical assistance, and I have tried therefore to avoid unnecessary duplication. Some of the works here cited run to many volumes and/or editions; only enough information to help the reader get started in a library is cited.

Aen.	*Aeneid*
Buc.	*Bucolica*
G.	*Georgica*
Ind.Serv.	*Index Servianus*, eds. J.F. Mountford and J.T. Schultz, Cornell Studies in Classical Philology 23 (1930)
Serv.	Servius
SDan or Serv.Dan.	Servius Danielis (Th.-H. indicates a precise reference to the edition of Thilo-Hagen)
TCD	Tiberius Claudius Donatus (cited in Georgic's edition)
VSD	Vita Suetonii/Donati
Ann.Phil.	*Année Philologique* (Paris 1928–)
ANRW	*Aufstieg und Niedergang der röm. Welt* (Berlin 1972–)
CHCL	*Cambridge History of Classical Literature* 2 (Cambridge 1982)
CIL	*Corpus Inscriptionum Latinarum* (Berlin 1863–)
CLE	*Carmina Latina Epigraphica* (Leipzig 1895–1926)
ILS	*Inscriptiones Latinae Selectae* (Berlin 1892–1916)

KS	R. Kühner, C. Stegmann, *Ausführliche Grammatik; Satzlehre* (repr. Darmstadt 1962)
LHS	*Lateinische Syntax und Stilistik*, eds. M. Leumann, J.B. Hofmann and A. Szantyr (München 1965)
LIMC	*Lexicon Iconographicum Mythologiae Classicae* (Zürich 1981–)
LSJ	*A Greek-English Lexicon*, by H.G. Liddell, R. Scott, H. Stuart Jones (Oxford, ed. 9, 1949, etc.)
MGH	*Monumenta Germaniae Historica* (Berlin 1877–)
NW	C.F. Neue, C. Wagener, *Formenlehre der lat. Sprache* (Berlin 1877–1905)
OCT	Oxford Classical Text
PW	A.F. von Pauly, G. Wissowa, W. Kroll, *Realencyclopädie der classischen Altertumswissenschaft* (Stuttgart 1893–)
RAC	*Reallexicon für Antike und Christentum* (Stuttgart 1950–)
RVV	*Religionsgeschichtliche Versuche und Vorarbeiten* (Giessen 1903–)
Sch-Hos.	M. Schanz, C. Hosius, *Geschichte der röm. Literatur* (ed. 4, München, 1927–)
TSK	W.S. Teuffel, L. Schwabe, W. Kroll, *Geschichte der röm. Literatur* (ed. 6, Leipzig 1913–6)
Bennett	C.E. Bennett, *Syntax of Early Latin*; 1 *The Verb* (Boston 1910); 2 *The Cases* (Boston 1914)
Ernout-Thomas	A. Ernout, F. Thomas, *Syntaxe Latine* (Paris 1953)
Gotoff	H.C. Gotoff, *Cicero's Caesarian Speeches* (Chapel Hill 1993)
Helbig	W. Helbig, *Führer durch die öffentlichen Sammlungen. . .in Rom* (4 vols. ed. 4, Tübingen 1963–72)
Hof.-Ric.	J.B. Hofmann, revised L. Ricottilli, *La lingua d'uso latina* (ed. 2, Bologna 1985)
Onians	R.B. Onians, *The Origins of European Thought* (repr. Cambridge 1988)
Otto	A. Otto, *Sprichwörter der Römer* (repr. Hildesheim 1965)
Wissowa, RKR	G. Wissowa, *Religion und Kultus der Römer* (ed. 2, München 1912)

Commentaries

Coleman	Vergil, *Eclogues* (Cambridge 1977)
Clausen	Virgil, *Eclogues* (Oxford 1994)
Mynors	Virgil, *Georgics* (Oxford 1990)
Thomas	Virgil, *Georgics* (2 vols., Cambridge 1988)
Benoist	Virgil (3 vols., Paris 1884–90)
Conington	Virgil (3 vols. ed. 4, rev. H. Nettleship, London, 1881–3)
Forbiger	Virgil (3 vols., Leipzig 1836–9)
Heyne	Virgil (4 vols.; in many edd. including that revised by Wagner. I cite London 1793, unrevised)
Page	Virgil (3 vols. London, many eds. and reprints)
Austin	*Aen.*1 (Oxford 1971), 2 (ib., 1964), 4 (ib., 1955), 6 (ib., 1977)
Williams	*Aen.*3 (Oxford 1962), 5 (ib., 1960)
Pease	*Aen.*4 (Cambridge, Mass. 1935)
Butler	*Aen.*6 (Oxford 1920)
Norden	*Aen.*6 (ed. 4 repr. Stuttgart 1957)
Fordyce	*Aen.*7–8 (Oxford 1977)
Gransden	*Aen.*8 (Cambridge 1976)
Eden	*Aen.*8 (*Mnem.* Suppl. 35, 1975)
Harrison	*Aen.*10 (Oxford 1991)
Gransden	*Aen.*11 (Cambridge 1991)
Commager	*Virgil. A Collection of Critical Essays*, ed. S. Commager (Englewood Cliffs 1966)
Harrison	*Oxford Readings in Vergil's Aeneid*, ed. S.J. Harrison (Oxford 1990)
McAuslan	*Virgil*, ed. I. McAuslan, P. Walcot (Oxford 1990)
Robertson	*Meminisse Iuvabit* ed. F. Robertson (Bristol 1988)
Vergiliana	ed. H. Bardon, R. Verdière (Leiden 1971)
Alambicco	N. Horsfall, *Virgilio: l'epopea in alambicco* (Napoli 1991)
Atti	*Atti del convegno mondiale scientifico di studi su Virgilio* (Milano 1984; 2 vols.)
Bailey	C. Bailey, *Religion in Virgil* (1935, repr. New York 1969)
Binder	G. Binder, *Aeneas und Augustus* (Meisenheim 1971)

Buchheit   V. Buchheit, *Vergil über die Sendung Roms* (*Gymnasium Beiheft* 3, 1963)

Büchner   K. Büchner, P. Vergilius Maro, Stuttgart 1966 (the PW article on V.)

Cairns   F. Cairns, *Virgil's Augustan epic* (Cambridge 1989)

Camps   W.A. Camps, *An Introduction to Virgil's Aeneid* (Oxford 1969)

Clausen   W. Clausen, *Virgil's Aeneid and the Tradition of Hellenistic poetry* (Berkeley 1987)

EV   *Enciclopedia Virgiliana* ed. F. Della Corte (6 vols., Roma 1984–91)

Feeney   D.C. Feeney, *The Gods in Epic* (Oxford 1991)

Heinze   R. Heinze, *Virgils epische Technik* (repr. Stuttgart 1965). The Eng. trans. (H. and D. Harvey, F. Robertson, Bristol 1993) retains the German pagination (which I use) in the margin. After 90 years, still the best introduction, and now fully accessible!

Henry   J. Henry, *Aeneidea* (4 vols., Dublin 1873–92)

Highet   G. Highet, *The Speeches in Vergil's Aeneid* (Princeton 1972)

Knauer   G.N. Knauer, *Die Aeneis und Homer* (Göttingen 1964)

König   *Die Aeneis und die griechische Tragödie* diss. Berlin 1970

Lyne *FV*   R.O.A.M. Lyne, *Further Voices in Vergil's Aeneid* (Oxford 1987)

Lyne *WP*   *id., Words and the Poet* (Oxford 1989)

Mackie   C.J. Mackie, *The Characterisation of Aeneas* (Edinburgh 1988)

Otis   B. Otis, *Virgil. A Study in Civilised Poetry* (Oxford 1964)

Putnam   M.C.J. Putnam, *The Poetry of the Aeneid* (Cambridge, Mass. 1965)

Quinn   K. Quinn, *Virgil's Aeneid* (London 1968)

Warwick   H.H. Warwick, *A Vergil Concordance* (Minneapolis 1975): for almost all purposes, by far the most useful Virgil concordance now available

Wigodsky   M. Wigodsky, *Vergil and Early Latin Poetry* (*Hermes* Einzelschr. 24 1972)

Williams   G.W. Williams, *Technique and Ideas in the Aen.* (New Haven 1983)

CHAPTER ONE

VIRGIL: HIS LIFE AND TIMES

N.M. Horsfall

Sixty years ago Tenney Frank entitled an article[1] "What do we know about Vergil?"; ten years ago, Heinrich Naumann[2] asked again "Was wissen wir von Vergils Leben?". The answer was very different. It is worth putting the question a third time, not merely for the fun of seeing whether an even more minimalist position than Naumann's is justifiable (it is!), but to clarify an argument carried on with unusual savagery since ca. 1938,[3] mostly in German and Italian (often, too, in rare journals) and to set the debate (as has hardly been done) in the context of work on ancient literary biography in general. If we turn out to know next to nothing of Virgil's 'life and times', that matters little if at all to our understanding of the poetry.[4]

In recent years, Mary Lefkowitz and Janet Fairweather[5] have analysed with sober scepticism the methods and reliability of Greek poetic biography (with, understandably, no more than a few glances at the Roman material): they have defined and documented numerous types of conventional invention which unsurprisingly recur with equal frequency in the lives of the Roman poets.[6] Suetonius' famed devotion to archives and rare sources[7] does little to save him, we shall see, from his predecessors' romanticisings and embroideries. Very slowly, rigorous analysis is spreading to the biographies of Roman authors and we are getting rid of the comfortable accretions which clutter many literary historics:

For Juvenal, Terence and Horace, the bulk of the work has been

---

[1] *CJ* 26 (1930–1), 3ff.

[2] *Das altspr. Unterricht* 24.5 (1981), 5ff.

[3] A dismaying bibliography, *EV* v*, 585–8; add Jocelyn (n. 137), 271f.

[4] H. Cherniss, *UCPCP* 12.15 (1943), 279–92, "The biographical fashion in literary criticism" (esp. 286–7) = H.C., *Selected Papers* (Leiden 1977), 1–13 (esp. 8–9).

[5] Mary R. Lefkowitz, *The lives of the Greek poets* (London 1981), J.A. Fairweather, *Anc.Soc.*5 (1974), 231ff., ead., *PLLS* 4 (1983), 315ff.

[6] H. Naumann, *Sileno* 2 (1976), 35ff., id., *WS* 92 (1979), 151ff.; Rostagni's ed. of Suet. *De poetis*, though convenient, appeared first in 1944 and is in most respects quite inadequate.

[7] J. Gascou, *Suétone historien* (Rome 1984), 463ff., A. Wallace-Hadrill, *Suetonius* (London 1983), 88ff., B. Baldwin, *Suetonius* (Amsterdam 1983), 101ff.

done;[8] on Virgil, the earliest extended expression of scepticism that
I know is dated 1911[9] and it is interesting to contrast the more credulous Nettleship (1879).[10] We may feel dismay that classicists have lagged
so far behind scholars in comparable fields; on the lives of the Saints,
rigorous analysis begins in 1607[11] and in biblical criticism little later.[12]
But it is not my purpose to explain why it seems harder to write
sensibly about Virgil than about Christ.

Our sources for the life of Virgil consist of

(i) The testimony of contemporary authors in prose and verse, of
which convenient collections exist.[13] We should not forget that the
Vergilius of Hor. *C*.1.3.6 and 1.24.10 is identified with the poet only
by general and justified agreement,[14] while scholarly consensus tends
rightly to exclude his homonym at *C*.4.12.13. *P.Herc. Paris* 2 is now
to be added to the list:[15] Philodemus on *kolakeia* lists Plotius (Tucca),
Varius (Rufus), Virgil and Quintilius Varus. In *P.Herc.*1082, Virgil's
name was not certain; here it is.[16] As Augustan testimonia we should
not forget (i) a detail (15f. below) attributed to Varius by Quintilian
10.3.8, (ii) a fragment of Maecenas' *Symposium* (in which V. features),
quoted by Serv. *ad Aen*.8.310 and (iii) several fragments of letters by
both Virgil and Augustus,[17] not necessarily precious rarities in the
imperial archives and quite possibly in general circulation.

(ii) The testimony of writers between the death of Augustus and
the 'publication' of Suetonius' *de Poetis*,[18] listed by Götte-Bayer 412–20
and in EV 5**, 429–33. Gellius 17.10.2 speaks of the *amici familiaresque*

---

[8] Juv.: the comm. by E. Courtney (London 1980), 1–10; Terence, A. Gratwick,
CHCL 2, 814–6; Horace: E. Fraenkel, *Horace* (Oxford 1957), 1ff.

[9] E. Diehl, *Die Vitae Vergilianae und ihre antiken Quellen* (*Kleine Texte* 72, Bonn 1911).

[10] *Ancient Lives of Virgil* (Oxford 1879).

[11] H. Delehaye, *Les légendes hagiographiques* (Bruxelles 1906), 14ff. summarises three
centuries of progress since Rosweyde's *Fasti Sanctorum* (Antwerp 1607); cf. further
D. Knowles, *Great historical enterprises* (Edinburgh 1963), 1ff.

[12] W. Neil in *Cambridge history of the Bible* 3 (Cambridge 1987), 238ff.

[13] Vergil, *Landleben* ed. J. and M. Götte with *Vergil-Viten* ed. K. Bayer (München
ed. 2, 1970, ed. 3, 1977), 406–12, *EV* 5**, 429–30.

[14] Hor. and Virg. were old friends: Hor. *Serm*.1.5.39–44, 47–9, 6.54–5. The voyage
to Greece to which *Carm*.1.3 refers cannot be Virgil's last for chronological reasons.

[15] M. Gigante, M. Capasso, *SIFC* 3.7 (1989), 4.

[16] Cf. further, M. Gigante, *Cron.Erc*.3 (1973), 86f.

[17] Götte-Bayer (n. 13) 412: Augustus cited by Priscian (10.43) and VSD (*infra*),
Virgil by Macr.1.24.11 (twice); cf. E. Malcovati, Imp.Caes.Aug. fragmenta, *Epist*.
frr. xxxv, xxxvi, *Epistologr.Lat.Min*. ed. P. Cugusi, 2.1.349, 395.

[18] Not to be dated accurately on the evidence of Plin. *Ep*.5.10.1; cf. Baldwin
(n. 7), 16f.

of Virgil who *de ingenio moribusque eius memoriae tradiderunt* stories about him: the unwary used this passage as evidence for a 'liber amicorum', which was then exalted into a prop of Suetonius' reliability.[19] There is a vital distinction here: of contemporaries who knew Virgil, only Augustus wrote an autobiography (cf. Naumann 1981, 17): the rest, apart from poems, letters, wills and a few scattered references, is, or is claimed to be, oral tradition, not necessarily good just because early.[20] When Suetonius says *dicitur*, or the like, he may mean no more than that 'I do not know quite who actually said this'; a great mass of '*traditur*-material' is transmitted, transposed, altered, invented even by (for the most part) schoolmasters and grammarians.

(iii) The Vita Suetonii/Donati (VSD). This biography is formally and explicitly the work of Aelius Donatus (mid-c. 4 master of Servius and St. Jerome).[21] Only in Paris BN 11308 does a dedicatory letter from Donatus himself precede the unsigned *Vita*.[22] This dedication and the preface to the commentary on *Buc.* are all that survives intact of Aelius Donatus' commentary on Virgil.[23] The *Vita*, however, in all probability is not his, with the exception of §§37–8 (*heredes fecit. . . huiusmodi versus*), but rather Suetonius', essentially unaltered: the prefatory letter declares Donatus will follow all who have written on Virgil; only Suetonius had written systematically on Virgil's life[24] and it is Donatus' stated policy (*etiam verba servare*) to follow his source to the letter. *Admixto etiam sensu nostro* remarks Donatus; that leaves the door open only to the microscopic analysis of possible c. 4 additions.[25] Donatus had no sources unavailable to Suetonius, nor had biographical writing meanwhile improved in sophistication. Even if the question

---

[19] Cf. Naumann (n. 6, 1976), 45f., *EV* 5*, 574, (n. 2), 15. Berres, 7ff. is ill-informed and credulous.

[20] Gell. l.c., Serv.Dan. *ad Buc.*4.11, VSD 10, 16, 29, 34, 42; cf. the anonymous *tradiderunt*, VSD 1, *ferunt*, VSD 4, *vulgatum est* VSD 9; Berres, 24 unfortunately believes that *aiebat* etc. indicate a real oral source: see rather Neumann (n. 2), 7f., Fairweather (n. 5, 1974), 246, n. 71.

[21] Brugnoli, *EV* s.v. *Donato, Elio*, R.A. Kaster, *Guardians of language* (Berkeley 1988), 275–8.

[22] B. Munk Olsen, *L'Etude des auteurs classiques latins. . .2* (Paris 1985), 819.

[23] *Buc.praef.*: Götte-Bayer (n. 13), 228–40, Diehl (n. 9), 22–6, *Vitae vergilianae* ed. I. Brummer, 11–9, etc.

[24] Thus Donatus records at the end of the life of Terence which prefaces his commentary to the plays (§8) *haec Suetonius Tranquillus*.

[25] Cf. H. Naumann, *HSCP* 85 (1981), 185–7, id. (n. 6, 1979), 159f., id., *EV* 5*, 572–3, id. *RhM* 118 (1975), 178, id. *RhM* 87 (1938), 374, E. Norden, *Kl.Schr.* (Berlin 1966), 469f., G. Brugnoli, *EV* 2, 126, 5*, 576.

'who wrote the bulk of the *Vita*?' were in truth open, it would make little or no difference to our analysis of the 'facts'. What follows will respect the order of VSD; so little that we think we know does not depend on that text, and only by understanding VSD can we unlearn our ideas on the 'life of Virgil'.

(iv) There is no call to examine minutely the later ancient lives of Virgil—though there are scraps in Servius' life not in VSD, of little moment[26]—not to mention the numerous mediaeval and humanistic versions.[27] The information they contain is not reliable, independent, authoritative.[28]

(v) Virgil's own works.[29] Does *G*.4.125–7 mean that Virgil really saw an old man with a little garden near Tarentum? I once thought so,[30] and autopsy is not necessarily excluded by the complex literary tradition behind the passage.[31] *G*.4.564 is firmer evidence for the poet's links with Naples (cf. 7 below). Dedicatees in *Buc*.[32] hint at the range of the young Virgil's friends and protectors. Elusive indications of a 'poetical autobiography' lurk in *Buc*.6.1–8, *G*.2.173–6, 3.1–48, 4.559–66. To Virgil's relations with Maecenas, formally addressee of each book of the *G*., we shall return (94, 97f.); the poet's own definition of the level of amity and the degree of pressure (3.41–2) is remarkably, and one supposes deliberately, impalpable.[33]

(vi) All else, as we shall soon see, is not biographical fact, as we understand it, but either explication of V.'s text in biographical terms or defence of the poet against criticism.[34]

---

[26] Götte-Bayer (n. 13), 697–8, Naumann, *EV* 5*, 575.

[27] Now conveniently available in *EV* 5**, 437ff.; the edd. by Bayer, Diehl, Brummer and (OCT) Hardie will serve for consultation, though many minor lives are omitted.

[28] Naumann (n. 2), 6, id. *EV* 5*, 573, 575, Götte-Bayer (n. 13), 697–8, 761–3.

[29] Cf. the passages gathered at Götte-Bayer (n. 13), 422; cf. 11ff. for the difficulties and dangers involved in using the *Buc*. and 10f. for the problems of *Catal*.5 and 8.

[30] *PLLS* 6 (1990), 52f. and *CR* 34 (1984), 134.

[31] R. Thomas, *Lands and Peoples. . . PCPhS* Suppl. 7 (1982), 56f., id. comm. on *G*.4.116–48, id., *MD* 29 (1992), 35ff. I do not so much believe that Thomas is right as that I myself used invalid evidence!

[32] 4.11f. Asinius Pollio, 6.7 Alfenus Varus, 10.2 Cornelius Gallus; cf. 9.35–6 on Varius Rufus and Helvius Cinna.

[33] Cf. J. Griffin in *Caesar Augustus* ed. F. Millar and E. Segal (Oxford 1984), 195, P. White, *Promised Verse* (Cambridge Mass. 1993), 175ff.

[34] Naumann (n. 2), 15f., Brugnoli, *EV* 5*, 577–9, Hardie (n. 27), xiii–xxiii, Diehl (n. 9), 58–60.

That Virgil was born on 15 Oct. 70 B.C. should not be questioned: the cult of the birthday, in life and posthumously[35] is security enough. That he was a native of Mantua is a deduction from the text (Brugnoli 578): Cf., leaving aside for now *Catal*.8.6, *Buc*.9.27–8, *G*.2.198–9, *G*.3.1–12, *Aen*.10.198–203. The claims of Andes (VSD 2), 30 MP from Mantua[36] might (Naumann 1981, 11) be embroideries on the ground of *Buc*.1.34, 9.6, 64. Mantua is accepted by the literary tradition[37] but we should not accuse the poets of sharing the accuracy of a census-return. The poet's *parentes modici* are conventional;[38] that his father was a bricklayer (*figulus*) and his mother was named Magia Polla[39] might[40] be an ingenious fantasy extrapolated from the source of Jerome's '*Nigidius Figulus; Pythagoricus et Magus*' (after Suetonius). That his father bought woodland must derive from *G*.2.426–33; that he kept bees is a transparent theft from *G*.4. Study of the three birth-miracles (VSD 3–5) should help us evaluate the text justly; the mother's dream (§3)—and the credulity of Suetonius was notorious (cf. Plin. *Ep*.1.18 and Suet. *Aug*.94)—develops from the association of laurel and poet. §4 expands on *Buc*.4.60, while §5 grows out of a play on *virga*–Vergilius, enhanced by a characteristic allusion (cf. Suet. *Aug*.6) to 'local superstition'. The childhood spent at Cremona (also in Jerome from Suetonius) expands *Buc*.9.28 (with its earliest exegesis) and *Catal*.8.6 (cf. 10). That an element of actual truth might also be involved cannot be sustained, or denied. Virgil 'reached the *toga virilis* the day Lucretius died, under the same consuls as in the year of his

---

[35] A. Stuiber, *RAC* 9, 220f., W. Schmidt, PW 7.1, 1142.5ff., id. *Geburtstag im Altertum, RVV* 7.1 (1908), 21ff.

[36] 30, rather than 3 is pretty clearly what 'Probus' wrote (L. Lehnus, *Scripta Philologa* 3 (1982), 200f.) but the detail is anyway not even remotely reliable; Lehnus 197, after G. Jachmann, *Klio* 35 (1942), 85f.

[37] Mart.14.195.2, Ov. *Am*.3.15.7. See W.J. Watts, *GR* 18 (1971), 91–101 for the non-Roman origins of Latin authors; for the cultural life of the Po valley in Virgil's youth, cf. S. Mratschek, *Athen*. 62 (1984), 154ff. On the names Vergilius and Maro, see too Mary E. Gordon, *JRS* 24 (1934), 1ff. Analysis does not prove that the poet was either Etruscan or Etruscologist: cf. my discussion at *BICS* Suppl. 52 (1987), 100ff. Prof. Giuliano Bonfante points out to me that Vergilius is of certain Celtic origin: cf. J. Whatmough, *Dialects of Ancient Gaul* (Cambridge, Mass. 1970) 591 on Vergobretos, Caes. *BG*.1.16.5.

[38] Brugnoli, *EV* 5*, 577 compares Homer, *vit. Hom*. 11; note similar tales at the beginning on the *vitae* of Sophocles and Euripides; cf. Fairweather (n. 5, 1974), 268f.

[39] Magia: *Vita Servii*; Magia Polla: Focas, 'Probus'. Magus is given as the name of Virgil's father's employer in VSD!

[40] G. Brugnoli, *Maia* 19 (1967), 387–8.

birth'. The double synchronism is an overenthusiastic display of the biographer's technical virtuosity (cf. Fairweather (n. 5, 1974), 261ff.), involving numerical error (Virgil accepted the *t.v.* aged 17 (53), but Pompey and Crassus were consuls again in 55),[41] while underscoring the 'miraculous' element.[42]

From Cremona, Virgil passed (VSD 7) to Milan (confirmed as Suetonian by Jerome) and then to Rome. Rome one might wish to impugn as a 'factual' explanation of *Buc.*1.19ff.: schol. Bern. *Buc.*9 *praef.* might lend substance to such scepticism. That Virgil and Octavian were fellow-students of the rhetor Epidius (*vit.Bern.*1) is a fancy of a type dear to biographers (Fairweather, n. 5 (1974), 261f.), and a chronological impossibility long since exploded. The details in VSD 7 are not in themselves incredible, but if we wish to accept them, we are in no position to explain how they were preserved, recorded and transmitted. The progression from Mantua (not to speak of Andes!) to Rome is at once entirely credible, enticingly persuasive, and eminently fragile.

§8 describes Virgil's physical appearance (tall, dark and rustic) and health (variable; weak stomach, throat, head...). The *facies rusticana* may derive from Hor. *Serm.*1.3.31, which was thought[43] to refer to Virgil. That editions of Virgil with portrait prefaced circulated (Mart.14.186) is no guarantee of accurate knowledge of the poet's physique. Stomach trouble might be a deduction from Hor. *Serm.*1.5.49 (Brugnoli, *EV* 5*, 578). Frugal in food and drink? Possibly a deduction from (e.g.) *Buc.*1.80f. or 2.11; frugality anyway appeals to the biographer: Suet. *Aug.*76, 77.

The poet liked boys, particularly Cebes (also a poet) and Alexander, called Alexis in *Buc.*2 So §9. Literary biography entails a paragraph of innuendo (Fairweather, n. 5 (1974), 263f.): such inventions on a ground of the text of *Buc.* are old (Mart.8.56.12, Juv.7.69); allegorical exegesis, here fired by a long tradition of traducing Virgil, encourages extravagances of pedophile prosopography (Naumann 1981, 8f., Brugnoli *EV* 5*, 580). For Alexis, cf. Serv. *ad Buc.*2.1; for Cebes the poet, Naumann points to *Buc.*2.15 and *Buc.*3. The homoerotic element in *Buc.* and *Aen.* is no proof of the poet's inclinations; noth-

---

[41] Naumann, *WS* 92 (1979), 162, Brugnoli, *EV* 4, 1090.
[42] See Naumann (n. 41) for full bibliography. That Suet. could not do his sums is no reason for changing the poet's birth: it has been tried!
[43] Ps.Acr. *ad loc.*; Brugnoli, *EV* 5*, 578.

ing whatever, though, suggests that he was a *tombeur de femmes*. Worse follows: VSD records a story (*vulgatum est*) that Virgil slept with Plotia Hieria too, while Asconius said that the lady (whom he could not really, on chronological grounds, have known) liked to relate that Varius (? her husband; Serv. *ad Buc*.3.20 mentions Varus not Varius)[44] invited the poet to share her, whether simultaneously or sequentially is not clear (cfr. Naumann 1981, 15, Brugnoli, *EV* 5*, 580). The woman's name is no more encouraging than her morals: Plotia suggests Plotius Tucca; a marriage between Varius and Tucca's sister would be a guess worthy of VSD, if it is indeed implied. Hieria is Greek 'priestess': an attested name (Suerbaum (n. 44), 510), but also one fitting the partner of a *Musarum sacerdos*. Names are favourite toys of the biographer-romancer, as Syme so brilliantly showed for *SHA*.

But for the rest, continues VSD, the poet was so proper that he was generally called Parthenias at Naples and when on rare visits to Rome he was seen in public, he hid from his fans *in proximum tectum* (so the story in VSD 11). 'Parthenias' is ambiguous: possibly because of the connection with Naples (Parthenope),[45] possibly because of an astrological link with the constellation Virgo (Brugnoli, *EV* 5*, 577). The timidity may come out of *G*.4.564–5 *me. . .dulcis alebat/Parthenope, studiis florentem ignobilis oti*; equally, defence of Virgil against his *obtrectatores* (which did not begin only with Asconius' *contra obtr. Vergilii*)[46] entails the development of stories in illustration of his *fama* and *verecundia*. Such 'Virgil and his fans' stories hit both targets (cf. also the exegesis of *Buc*.6.16; Brugnoli, *EV* 5*, 580). That Virgil lived for choice on the Bay of Naples is suggested by Aug. *Ep*. fr.xxxv Malc. and by *G*.4, 564–5 and is now confirmed by *P.Par.Herc*.2 (supra). It may be further reinforced by his unquestioned burial there.[47] Let us leave Nola (a late embroidery) out of consideration.[48] Studies with the Epicurean Siro (linked independently with Naples)[49] are indicated explicitly only by *Catal*.8, and implicitly by *Catal*.5. Significantly, not a word in VSD (though Serv. *ad Buc*.3.16 and *ad Aen*.6.264 knows

---

[44] W. Suerbaum, *Festschr.R.Muth* (Innsbruck 1983), 510ff.

[45] F. Hornstein, *WS* 70 (1957), 148–52.

[46] W. Görler, *EV* s.v. *Obtrectatores*; S. Costanza, *Mnemosynum, Studi in onore di A. Ghiselli* (Bologna 1989), 103ff.

[47] Brugnoli, *EV* 5*, 578, Plin. *Ep*.3.7.8, St. *Silv*.4.4.54, Mart.11.48.

[48] A. Barchiesi, *ASNP* 3.9.2 (1979), 527ff., L.A. Holford-Strevens, *CQ* 29 (1979), 391ff.

[49] *P.Herc*.312; cf. the bibliography in nn. 15, 16, F. Sbordone, *Atti* 2, 113ff.

the story; cf. 11). Epicureans are well-known on the Bay of Naples;[50] once Epicurean elements are suspected in the text of Virgil,[51] the desire to close the circle by biographical means will have been irresistible;[52] the papyri have not yet linked Virgil and Siro.

Virgil 'preferred not to accept' (VSD 12) the property of an (unnamed) exile, offered him by Augustus; the lack of detail is striking and the anecdote is a minor exemplification of the poet's *verecundia* (Naumann 1981, 14; the relation of this yarn to the 'loss of Virgil's farm' (infra) is uncertain). He was worth ten million sesterces: the sum may well (so even Naumann (1981, 16) be based ultimately on the poet's will (cf. 21f.) and is very large, twenty-five times the property qualification of an *eques* (but was V. ever formally an *eques*?).[53] He reached such wealth *ex liberalitatibus amicorum* (VSD, *ib.*). That does not make V. the paid spokesman, the mercenary mouthpiece of an imperialistic regime. Suetonius' language is not reliable in such matters,[54] but *amicus* is not used here (as often) deprecatingly, of an inferior.[55] *Liberalitates* cannot be large and frequent cash handouts:[56] that would have been rank bad manners at Rome, for donor and recipient—at least at that date. Inheritances, then, are the obvious source, though we remain ignorant of who these wealthy, deceased, generous friends might have been.

Virgil had a house on the Esquiline, but spent most of his time in the *secessus* of Campania and Sicily (VSD 13); the poet's house is a regular element in the biographical tradition[57] and the Esquiline might be suggested by the *horti Maecenatis*; cf. Suetonius' account of Horace's tomb, (*Vit.Hor.*16). The *secessus Campaniae* has just (7f.) been considered. Cf. *Buc.*2.21 for how Virgil's links with Sicily might have been created (see Brugnoli, *EV* 5*, 578–9).

---

[50] M. Gigante in *Virgilio e gli Augustei* (Napoli 1990), 9ff., id. *Virgilio e la Campania* (Napoli 1984), 74ff., J. D'Arms, *Romans on the bay of Naples* (Cambridge Mass., 1970), 56ff.

[51] L. Alfonsi, *EV* s.v. *Epicureismo* and V. Mellinghoff-Bourgerie, *Les incertitudes de Virgile* (*Coll.Lat* 210, Bruxelles 1990), (maximalists); H. Naumann, *Sileno* 1 (1975), 245ff. (sceptic): Lucretian echoes do not prove committed Epicureanism.

[52] Cf. the methodological scepticism of G. Brugnoli, *EV* 5*, 578.

[53] L.R. Taylor, *TAPA* 99 (1968), 483f. is not overwhelmingly convincing.

[54] Fraenkel (n. 8), 364.

[55] P. White, *JRS* 68 (1978), 80f.

[56] ib. 86f., 90; cf. my n. on Nep. *Att.*2.6, P. White in *Literary and artistic patronage* ed. B. Gold (Austin 1983), 52, Griffin (n. 33), 192.

[57] Suet. *Vit.Hor.*11, id. *Vit.Ter.* id. (on Enn.) ap.Hier. *Chron.*, Ol.135.1; ample bibliography collected by W.M. Calder, *GRBS* 23 (1982), 281, n. 1.

Virgil was *iam grandis* when he lost his parents as well as two full brothers, the young Silo and the grown-up Flaccus, mourned under the name of Daphnis (VSD 14): Flaccus suggests Horace's *cognomen* (vd.Serv. *ad Buc.*5.20 for growing confusion), while Silo is a *cognomen* borne by several minor literary figures familiar from Seneca Rhetor: Arbronius (father and son), Gavius, Pompeius.

The poet studies (§15) *medicinae ac maxime mathematicae*: this last word can indicate either mathematics or astrology; the commentaries attribute omniscience to Virgil, frequently;[58] Servius attributes to Virgil a certain amount of astrological wisdom and its place in the interpretation of the text was discussed in a *quaestio* attributed to Probus.[59]

Virgil only ever pleaded a single case in court: Melissus, a freedman of Maecenas relates that Virgil was *in sermone tardissimum et paene indocto similem*. A silly joke from Melissus' *Ineptiae* (Naumann, 1981, 7), based on *G.*2.508? Or does *(alii) orabunt causas melius* (6.849) enter into it? Is there any inconsistency with VSD 28–9 (on V's great skill as a reader of his own poetry)? The techniques are after all very different (cf. too Sen. *Contr.*3.*praef.*8). Was Virgil an orator or a poet? The topic was debated eagerly in c. 2 A.D. schools and a scrap of discussion by 'Florus' survives.[60]

Virgil began writing poetry as a *puer* with an epigram against one Ballista and went on to write *Catalepton Priapea Epigrammata Dirae Ciris* and *Culex*. Fairweather helpfully compares the accretion of *opuscula* around the author of *Il.* and *Od.* (n. 5 (1974), 259–60). So VSD 17; also, *de qua ambigitur, Aetnam* (ib. 19). Ballista is described as a *ludi magister*, the boss of a gladiatorial *ludus* (Lehnus, *EV* s.v. *Ballista*), or a schoolmaster, fitly punished, as occurs indeed in Suet. *Gramm.*[61] Here chastisement is *ob infamiam latrociniorum*. The name B. is not itself rare; here, though, the 'siege engine' dies *coopertum lapidibus*. Thus the pun has swollen to fill the couplet and the couplet finds shelter at the head of a whole gaggle of pseudepigrapha, of varying date and importance; for Horace, cf. Suet. *Vit.Hor.*12, where the list of authentic

---

[58] Cf. n. 128.

[59] Serv. *ad Aen.*10.18; medicine in V.: F. Stok, in *EV* s.v. *medicina*, id. *Percorsi dell' esegesi virgiliana* (Pisa 1988), 63ff.; astrology and the interpretation of V.: C. Santini in *EV* s.v. *astrologia*. Vd. *Index Servianus* s.v. *mathematici, mathesis, astrologia*.

[60] G. Highet, *The speeches in Virgil's Aeneid* (Princeton 1972), 3f., C. Di Giovine, *EV* s.v. *Floro*.

[61] H. Naumann (n. 25, 1938), 362.

works has dropped out.[62] As a poet, Virgil begins late: that is a boon to biographers and fakers.

This is not the place to offer a full discussion of the *Appendix Vergiliana*: at almost all points (but see (viii) below) a degree of unanimity has been reached among serious scholars. J.A. Richmond, *ANRW* 2.31.2, 1112–1154 offers a convenient survey; A. Salvatore, *EV* s.v. *Appendix* still tries to sustain authenticity, but here the case will not be (and need not be) argued. Only *Catal.* still enjoins circumspection.

(i) *Priapea* = The first three poems of *Catal.*

(ii) *Epigrammata*: for title and content, Richmond has surveyed thoroughly and repeatedly that which may legitimately be suspected.[63]

(iii) *Dirae*, possibly between *Buc.* and *G.* in date.[64]

(iv) *Ciris*, later than Ov. *Met.*8, perhaps not by much.[65]

(v) *Culex*: Tiberian, and widely believed in the c. 1 A.D. to be by Virgil.[66]

(vi) *Aetna*: late Augustan/post-Augustan.[67]

(vii) Donatus (VSD 48), not Suetonius, attributes Varius' *Thyestes* to Virgil (it was also wished on to Cassius of Parma).[68] VSD 17 omits *Copa*,[69] *Moretum*[70] and the *Elegiae in Maecenatem*.[71]

(viii) *Catalepton*: there is widespread agreement that *Catal.*5 and 8 could be Virgilian;[72] Richmond has recently concluded in favour of the authenticity of the whole collection.[73] Difficulties remain: Naumann, for example, was right to point out[74] that *Catal.*8 would ring truer if we had independent testimony to Virgil's links with Siro, and if it did not mention Cremona, hallmark of the biographical tradition, not home of the (Mantuan) poet. Had the author of *Catal.*8.2 read *Buc.*1, 68–9, and is 8.6 a re-hash of *Buc.*9.28? Worse, the author of

---

[62] Cf. W. Speyer, *Die lit. Falschung* (München 1971), 124, n. 1.
[63] l.c. 1143, *Herm.*102 (1974), 300–4, *Atti* 1, 50f., *EV* 1, 698.
[64] E. Fraenkel, *JRS* 56 (1966), 142–55, F.R.D. Goodyear, *PCPhS* 17 (1971), 30ff.
[65] Goodyear, *EV*, s.v., Richmond, *ANRW* 1138–40.
[66] Richmond, *ANRW* 1126f.; see St. *Silv.*1, proem.2, 2.7.73f., Mart.14.185, Lucan ap. Suet. *Vit.Luc.*
[67] ed. Goodyear, 59.
[68] Porph. *ad* Hor. *Ep.*1.4.4, cf. *EV* 5*, 441 (Cova).
[69] Goodyear, *EV* s.v., id. *BICS* 24 (1977), 117ff., R.J. Tarrant, *HSCP* 94 (1992), 331ff., P. Cutolo, *PLLS* 6 (1990), 115ff.
[70] *EV* s.v. (Perutelli) and recent edd. by Perutelli and Kenney.
[71] Richmond, *ANRW*, 1135, *EV* s.v.
[72] For a tabulation of views, Richmond, *EV* 1, 699.
[73] *Atti* 1, 50–65.
[74] *RhM* 121 (1978), 78ff.

Catal. knows too little about Virgil, and invents ineptly; I am nagged by the suspicion that the author has heard the first exegetes of *Buc.* (taught soon after publication, 250), for analogies with Serv. are numerous and point towards the schoolroom.

Virgil knows Tucca (1.1) and Varius (7.1); his friends and heirs (cf. 21f.). Virgil and Varius were pupils of Siro according to Serv. *ad Buc.*6.13. *Catal.*14 begins with a mythological flourish out of *Aen.*1 (415, 681); 14.3 echoes *G.*2.176; the thought of vv. 3–6 presupposes the proem. to *G.*3; enough. *Catal.*8.6 smacks not only of *Buc.*9.28 but of Serv.Dan. *ad Buc.*9.7. 11.1 is wittily parodic of *Buc.*1.6 (with play on Octavius/Octavianus). What of the Musa of 4.6, 8 and the Octavius of 11.1? Octavius could be identified with the O. *optimus* of Hor. *Serm.*1.10.82 or with the historian M. Octavius cited at *OGR* 12.2 and 19.5, but the parodic manner of his appearance has already made us wary, just as the proximity of *Clio* (4.10) might make one wonder about Musa at 4.6, 8. Worse, an individual named Octavius Musa appears in the note Serv.Dan. *ad Buc.*9.7 already cited. D'Anna (*EV* s.v. *Siro*, 894) is right to point out that *Catal.* makes the young Virgil meet Maecenas' friends (Varius, Tucca) too long before he met Maecenas himself (39–8; Hor. *Serm.*1.6.54ff.: in the interval between *Buc.* and *G.*). But I am far more disquieted by the realisation that the writer of *Catal.* does so very clearly seem to use the text of V. (and the schoolroom exegesis thereof) as a quarry for facts and names. Once a faker reveals his methods (vide Syme and the *SHA*) the game is up; *Catal.* does not even invent cunningly!

VSD 19 continues *mox cum res Romanas incohasset, offensus materia ad Bucolica transiit.* Serv. on *Buc.*6.3 suggests that Virgil was put off by the metrical difficulties of a poem on the Alban kings, and Serv.Dan. sees a reference to the *Ciris* (cf. also Serv. *ad Aen.*6.752). All of which amounts to literalist exegesis of *Buc.*6.1–5 (cf. Jocelyn, *Atti* 1, 437). We remain unable to attribute poetry to Virgil before the earliest *Bucolica.* So Asconius: he published the *Buc.* aged 28.[75] The 'three years' of composition of *Buc.* (VSD 25) are not altogether clear and comprehensible.[76] "Three" may be inexact schematisation; that Virgil

---

[75] 'Probus', *praef. ad Buc.*3.2.329.5ff. (Th.-H.), Brugnoli, *EV* 5*, 577.

[76] Thus (e.g.) 41–39 (Cupaiuolo, *EV* 1, 542–3), 42–39 (Götte-Bayer (n. 13), 493); 42–38/7 (Coleman, ed., p. 16). I am not convinced by the 'late' dating of *Buc.*, advanced by G. Bowersock: see J. Farrell, *CP* 86 (1991), 204ff., R.G. Mayer, *BICS* 30 (1983), 21ff., V. Tandoi in *Le Bucoliche* (ed. M. Gigante) (Napoli 1981), 268ff.; cf. further 29.

began in 42–1 seems likely. Asconius should probably have written 'incohasse' not 'edidisse': that would square well with the accepted facts. Virgil wrote *Buc. maxime ut Asinium Pollionem Alfenum Varum et Cornelium Gallum celebrarent.* Suetonius' mechanical and anachronistic approach to dedications, patronage and the like has been noted;[77] cf. the composition of the *Georgics in honorem Maecenatis* (VSD 20; an extreme contrast with the recent comm. of R. Thomas on *G*.3.41). VSD, not satisfied with the references to Pollio, Varus and Gallus in *Buc*.4, 9 and 10 (I repeat, Suet. had the text, biographical exegesis of details, and little else) goes on 'because in the distribution of lands, which after the victory at Philippi were divided out to veterans in Transpadana by order of the triumvirs, they had kept him out of harm, *indemnem se praestitissent.* Virgil himself openly invited the readers of *Buc.* to some degree of allegorical exegesis (5.86f., 6.3f.): that was indeed how they were read by contemporaries (Prop.2.34.67ff.) and during the first century A.D. (Mart.8.56.8, Quint.8.6.47, etc., Naumann, *EV* 5*, 574). The question, especially in the case of *Buc*.1 and 9, was where to stop.[78] Coleman and Wilkinson[79] still assume, as, it seems, did the author of *Catal*.8.5–6, that *Buc*.1 and 9 are essentially autobiographical (that is, that V. really did lose land in the redistributions, which was won back for him by influential friends). P. Veyne ingeniously removes the element of personal involvement while retaining a belief in the historical reality and local detail of the confiscations.[80] Once we are rid (well rid, indeed)[81] of bucolic autobiography, we may still wish to study the growth of the biographic-allegorical scholia.[82] We have seen that the damage wrought by allegorical exegesis spread to §9 (6f.); it is also visible at §20: Maecenas saved V.—whom he can hardly have known as early as 42–1 (11)—from the violence of a veteran (unnamed) who nearly killed the poet *in altercatione litis agrariae:*[83] the scholiasts' attempts to name this veteran

---

[77] Cf. n. 54 and the discussions by Peter White (nn. 55, 56).

[78] Götte-Bayer, 396–400 offer an anthology of 'scholia de agris distributis'.

[79] Coleman (n. 76), 30ff., L.P. Wilkinson, *The Georgics of Virgil* (Cambridge 1969), 24ff.; cf. id., *Herm*.94 (1966), 320ff.

[80] *RPh*.54 (1980), 233ff.

[81] Cf. G.W. Williams, *Tradition and Originality in Roman Poetry* (Oxford 1968), 45f., 311f., M. Winterbottom, *GR* 23 (1976), 55ff. = McAuslan, 65ff.; note that Griffin (n. 33), 192 retains a curious residual faith in the autobiographical character of *Buc*.1 and 9.

[82] Diehl (n. 9), 51ff. is still fundamental; Naumann (n. 2), 9f. offers a terse orientation.

[83] Naumann (n. 2), 9f., Diehl (n. 9), 57ff.

founder in chaos.[84] 'The total sceptic has to explain where the names came from' (Jocelyn, *Atti* 1, 437). Wordplay, transference from other spheres and stories, guesswork; we have already looked at some cases in greater detail (5, 9); study of the *SHA* and Syme's analysis should shake remaining doubters. *Buc.*1 and 9 of course reflect a real rural tragedy—the confiscations, and in this they are not alone in Augustan poetry.[85] What must necessarily remain unknown is where Virgil was and what he did (apart from write poetry) in the years after 42 B.C.

Poetry brought Virgil immediate and lasting fame: cf. 249f. for first reactions to *Buc.*; cf. Hor. *Serm.*1.6.54f. for the significant fact that ca. 38 Virgil knew Maecenas well enough to introduce Horace to him, with a hand from Varius; in spring 37(?) Horace and Virgil accompanied Maecenas and Cocceius on the *iter Brundisinum*.[86]

The chronological problems raised by VSD for *Buc.* also apply to *G.*: Virgil wrote the *G.*, as we have seen (12), in honour of his 'saviour' Maecenas, over a period (VSD 25) of seven years. The *termini post quos* are (i) the completion of *Buc.* by 38 at the latest cf. 11, and the 'publication' of Varro, *Res Rusticae*, one of Virgil's principal prose sources,[87] firmly datable to 37; cf. 2.161, the building of the *portus Iulius*, also in 37. Indications of internal dating (e.g. 1.509, 2.171, 496, 3.25, 27) are tantalisingly imprecise: the *sphragis* (4.559–566) points firmly to Octavian's settlement of the East in 31–30.[88] 37–30 gives us seven years, plus not only 38–7 unexplained but 30–29 unaccounted for (cf. Jocelyn, *Atti* 1, 431); the story in VSD 27, possibly based on Augustus' autobiography, presupposes *G.* in definitive form and fit for imperial ears in summer 29 (cf. below 87). Did Virgil spend a year on revision? Had he already begun the *Aeneid*?[89] The spans at VSD 25 do not square with absolute chronology, cf. 63–5.

It is perhaps as well to mention here the story told by Serv. at

---

[84] Serv.Dan. *ad Buc.*9.1, *Schol.Bern.Buc.*9 praef., 'Prob.' *ad Buc.* praef. p. 328.4 (Th.-H.), Serv. *ad Buc.*3.94, Vit.Don.Auct.63, Naumann, *RhM* 87 (1983), 349ff., id. (n. 25, 1979), 158. On Serv.'s accuracy, cf. J.E.G. Zetzel, *CP* 79 (1984), 139ff., White (n. 33), 145ff.

[85] Hor. *C.*2.18.26ff., *Serm.*2.2.127ff., *Dirae, passim.*

[86] P. White, *JRS* 68 (1978), 76ff., id. (n. 56), 59, id. (n. 33), 28, Horsfall, *Anc.Soc.* (Macquarie) 13 (1983), 163f. White (n. 56), 59 well says that 'poets were able to improve the leisure of the rich'.

[87] Cf. 84 below (with bibliography). The dramatic dating of individual books should never have been used to confuse the simple question of the date of publication: see J.S. Richardson, *CQ* 33 (1983), 463.

[88] T. Rice Holmes, *Architect of the Roman Empire* 1 (Oxford 1928), 159f.

[89] Cf. *G.*3.1–43 with V. Buchheit, *Der Anspruch des Dichters* (Darmstadt 1972), *passim.*

*Buc.*10.1 and at *G.*4.1 that after the disgrace and death (27 B.C.) of Cornelius Gallus,[90] Virgil excised the *laudes Galli* from *G.*4 and replaced them with Aristaeus/Orpheus.[91] Two chief lines of attack lie open: (i) the stylistic: Virgil's use of Homer in *G.*1–3, 4 and *Aen.* shows a regular and uninterrupted development;[92] (ii) the historical and evidential.[93] We have learned to view with deep suspicion the validity of historical and biographical statements in the ancient Virgil commentaries: confusion with Gallus present in *Buc.*10.72–4 (and indeed in all *Buc.*10) is explanation enough for Servius' notes at *Buc.*10.1 and *G.*4.1. One could dwell on the inconsistencies and crudities of language in Servius' two notes, but, more to the point, ancient scholars wondered what a mythological *fabula* was doing in a didactic poem (Serv.3.1.118.8, 12 Thilo-Hagen) and quite what bees had to do with Orpheus (Serv. *ad G.*4.1, Naumann 1981, 14f.). The questions in themselves are good and important (Naumann, *Sileno* 4 (1978), 12), but we are best off without the ancient answer![94] (Cf. 86f.)

Lastly, (VSD 21), Virgil began the *Aeneid*, which (§25) he completed in eleven years. We shall return to VSD 21's interesting statement of the *Aeneid*'s intent (162). In VSD 35 and 41, the unfinished state of the *Aen.* is acknowledged; in §25 it is described, for the sake of symmetry, as completed (*confecit*), over the eleven years 29–19, on the ancient inclusive calculation. There are some further indications of chronology, both internal and external.

8.714ff. the Actian triumph of 13 Aug. 29 B.C.; 6.860ff., the death of Marcellus (late 23); 7.604ff., the gates of war opened with hostile intent against Getae, Hyrcani, Arabs, Indians, and *Parthosque reposcere signa*, presumably but not necessarily before the return of the standards in 20;[95] references to Augustus under that name (6.792, 8.678) are necessarily later than 16 Jan., 27.

---

[90] R. Syme, *The Augustan Aristocracy* (Oxford 1986), 32.
[91] Champions of two editions of the *G.* are also to be found: Büchner, 293.31ff., Jocelyn, *Atti* 1, 431ff., S. Koster in *Pratum Saraviense (Festgabe P. Steinmetz)* (Stuttgart 1990), 133ff.
[92] G.N. Knauer, *ANRW* 2.31.2, 871ff. Cf. 86.
[93] W.B. Anderson, *CQ* 27 (1933), 36ff., Wilkinson (n. 79), 108ff., H. Naumann, *Sileno* 4 (1978), 16ff.; here particularly I have tried to keep references to a minimum (for a fuller discussion, see below, 86–9). Note the brief but acute remarks of R.G.M. Nisbet, *JRS* 77 (1987), 189.
[94] Jocelyn, *Atti* 1, 431ff. offers the only detailed defence of the Servian story by a serious scholar in recent years known to me.
[95] Gates: Berres 11ff. is confused; the passage in *Aen.*7 can be anticipatory just as

Prop.2.34.61–6 expects the *Aen.* and alludes both to *Aen.*1.1–2 and to the Actium-scene in bk. 8; there are some echoes of Horace in the *Aen.* and since the poets were friends, dating depends on individual poems, books or passages, not on formal 'publication';[96] a link between Livy 1–5 and *Aen.* exists[97] but, given the difficulty of dating the two editions of the first pentad,[98] priority cannot be determined and the coincidence is interesting but unhelpful.[99] Analogies with the *Paneg.Mess.* are unconvincing.[100] The correspondence between Augustus and Virgil[101] belongs in all probability to the princeps' absence in Gaul and Spain (May/June 27–June 24).[102] It is likely that Virgil read *Aen.*2, 4 and 6 to Augustus, his sister Octavia, and others, in 22 (VSD 32; cf. 19).[103]

Both haste[104] and slowness[105] in poetic composition accumulate anecdote and elaboration. When Virgil was writing *G.*, it is therefore no surprise to be told (VSD 22) that he is said (*traditur*) daily to have been in the habit of dictating *plurimos versus* in the morning, to have worked on them (*retractando*) all day and to have reduced them *ad paucissimos*. He said that he gave birth to the poem like a she-bear, bringing his cub into final shape by licking.[106] *Traditur* perhaps indicates the absence of a precise written source (Naumann 1981, 8); Gellius (17.10.2f.) cites the poet's *amici familiaresque* (cf. 2f.) for the poet's use of the same expression (perhaps also implied by Quint.10.3.8 citing

---

well as commemorative. For the facts see R. Syme in *Studies in Latin literature and its tradition in honour of C.O. Brink* (Cambridge 1990), 113ff. = *Roman Papers* 6 (Oxford 1991), 441ff. R.G.M. Nisbet and M.E. Hubbard, Comm.Hor. *Odes* 1, xxvii–xxxviii offer a useful chronology of Augustan foreign policy during this period.

[96] Nisbet-Hubbard, xxxv.

[97] A.J. Woodman in *Studies...Brink* (n. 95), 132ff.; notably 139 on Liv.5.47.2 and *Aen.*9.373.

[98] R. Syme, *HSCP* 64 (1959), 27ff. = *Roman Papers* 1 (Oxford 1979), 400ff., R.M. Ogilvie, Comm.Liv.1–5, 2, J. Gagé, Liv.1 (ed. Budé), xviff.

[99] Cf. my remarks, *CR* 40 (1990), 448.

[100] Horsfall, *CR* 37 (1987), 16.

[101] Bibliography, n. 17.

[102] H. Halfmann, *Itinera principum* (Stuttgart 1986), 157.

[103] A. Gercke, *Die Entstehung der Aeneis* (Berlin 1913), 71ff. and G. D'Anna, *EV* 2.239ff. provide summaries of the evidence for dating in the *Aen.*; that here offered is, though, quite independent.

[104] Plut. *Cic.*40, Hor. *Serm.*1.4.9f., Cic. *Arch.*18.

[105] Isocr.: 10 years for the *Panegyricus* (Quint.10.4.4); nine years for Cinna's *Zmyrna* (Cat.95.2, Quint. l.c., cf. Cinna fr.11.1f.; 'nine' becomes swiftly proverbial, Hor. *AP* 388).

[106] Naumann (n. 2), 15, *EV* 5*, 574, (n. 6, 1976), 47f.; Berres 7f., 14f. fails to see that there is a basic problem about the evidence for V's methods of composition.

Varius). But one might wish that the dictum was not so close to
*Aen.*8.634 (the she-wolf, foster-mother of the Twins, *corpora fingere lingua*) and was not in content a commonplace of peripatetic zoology,[107]
prettily though it exemplifies the *labor limae* so esteemed in Virgil's
day, and indeed practised by him with such masterly refinement.[108]

The Aeneid (VSD 23) was first formed (*formatam*) in prose and
arranged in twelve books; Virgil began to write it in bits (*particulatim*)
as the fancy took him (*prout liberet quidquid*) and in no order (*nihil in
ordinem arripiens*). And so that nothing should delay his *impetus*, he passed
over *quaedam imperfecta*; other bits he so to speak propped (*veluti fulsit*)
with very insubstantial (*levissimis*) verses, which he used to say jestingly were put in as props (*pro tibicinibus*) to hold the work up until
the massive columns got there. Some details of VSD's account of
composition, incompleteness and the poet's will might in theory derive from Varius' edition of the *Aen.*; much else belongs to the defence against the *obtrectatores*; so already Hyginus fr.7 *GRF*: 'Virgil
would have corrected this (or that)'. The account in VSD 23 indeed
opens three lines of defence to Virgil's admirers: either a passage
may be '*quoddam imperfectum*', or 'these are *levissimi versus* inserted as a
tibicen' or indeed 'this was written *particulatim* without definitive adaptation to its present context'.[109]

Buchheit (n. 109) collects interesting modern analogies for the 'prose
sketch', but nothing ancient. I have wondered not only about the
relationship of 'divided into twelve books' to ancient accounts of
Homeric book-division[110] but also about Callim. *Aet.* fr.112.9, Pf.: it
is easy to see how *pedester* in the Horatian sense[111] might have been
confounded with actual prose. Fragile, weakly-based and open to attack
on all fronts as the account in VSD is, it is not incompatible with

---

[107] PW s.v. *Bär* 2759.62ff. (starting from Arist. *Nat.Hist.*6.30), S. Zenker, *RAC* s.v.
Bär, 1143–4, O. Keller, *Thiere des Altertums* (Innsbruck 1887), 122f., Bömer on Ov.
*Met.*15.379f.

[108] Cf. Thomas' commentary on *G.* (1988) and W. Clausen, *Virgil's Aeneid and the
traditions of Hellenistic poetry* (Berkeley 1987).

[109] The bibliography on Virgil's methods of work is vast; the list in Berres, 322ff.
is imposing but partial. See Brugnoli, *EV* 5*, 580, V. Buchheit, *Nachr.Giess.Hochsch.*33
(1964), 132; Sparrow (n. 146) is provocative but often acute. Some of the statistics
collected in ch. 5, and in particular the table for the frequency of elision do
seem at first sight to favour the book as a unit of composition, rather than VSD's
particulatim.

[110] R. Pfeiffer, *History of classical scholarship* 1 (Oxford 1968), 115f.

[111] *AP* 95, with Brink's note.

the evidence of text and scholia and is accepted fully (and without question!) by Geymonat in the latest detailed survey of the problem known to me.[112] The image of *tibicines*[113] and *columnae*, possibly from Virgil via Varius, is not, like the bear-cub dictum, a variation on Virgil's own text, but an expression of a relatively common type of architectural metaphor applied to literary composition,[114] while *tibicen* is itself a Catullan word (63.22).

At §26 VSD passes to the fame of Virgil's works: the *Buc.* were so successful *ut in scaena quoque per cantores crebro pronuntiarentur*. The anecdote reported by Serv. *ad Buc.*6.11 cannot be cited in support,[115] but pantomimes on Virgilian themes and public recitals of the text are well-attested (*Atti* 2, 49 (Horsfall); cf. 249 below) while the suitability of *Buc.* for dramatic performance is evident.[116] Serv.'s information may be true but anachronistic; its source is not clear, but the detail in itself is entirely credible.

The *Georgics* Virgil recited to Augustus after his victory at Actium (VSD 27; in fact shortly before 13 Aug. 29 B.C.) when he stopped at Atella to recover from throat trouble, over four days without a break: Maecenas took over whenever Virgil was interrupted by throat trouble of his own. Naumann (1981, 11f.) suspects the influence of *G.*2.39 *tuque ades. . .Maecenas. . .ades* (44) *et. . .lege* (though in a very different sense!). The poet's laryngitis is already mentioned at §8; both might derive from Augustus' own, which might have been recorded in the *de vita sua*. 'Four books in four days, unbroken' is disquieting; this is an exceedingly gentle pace, to be borne by the most enfeebled reader, involving less than an hour 'on stage' per day.

Virgil delivered poetry with charm, indeed with remarkable allurements (VSD 28). So Seneca Rhetor recounts that Julius Montanus the poet used to say that he'd lift (*involaturum*) bits from Virgil, if he could also lift voice, expression (*os*) and delivery (*hypocrisin*), for those same verses sounded well when Virgil delivered them; without him

---

[112] *EV* 2, 286ff.

[113] Serv.Dan. *ad Aen.*1.560 equates *hemistichia* and *tibicines*: gravely misconceived, misunderstanding the sense of *t.* and undervaluing the half-lines; cf. Berres, 16f., Sparrow (n. 146), 9 and infra, 23f.

[114] Cf. ἀστήρικτα at Longin.2.2 (with Russell's note), Arist. *Rhet.*1415a13; for the poet as architect, cf. J. Taillardat, *Les images d'Aristophane* (ed. 2, Paris 1965), 438f.

[115] For the chronological inconsistency, cf. M. Bonaria, *EV* 1, 576, K. Quinn, *ANRW* 2.30.1, 153.

[116] G. Wille, *Musica Romana* (Amsterdam 1967), 115f.

they were void and dumb (*inanes. . .mutosque*). The context in Seneca (fr.3) is lost; he cites a poet of a younger generation, Montanus.[117] We may compare Montanus again,[118] ap.Sen. *Contr.*7.1.27 who said that Cestius tried to imitate *Aen.*8.26–7, but that it was Virgil who brought off the imitation, having transformed fr.8 of Varro Atacinus. Montanus could have heard Virgil, while Ovid did not (*Tr.*4.10.51). The judgement could, that is, be that of an eye-witness: the context of the first Montanus-story is more interesting as it implies *obtrectatio*: some weak writing in Virgil redeemed only by incomparable delivery.

So great was the fame of the *Aeneid* when hardly begun (VSD 30) that Propertius had no hesitation in proclaiming (2.34.65–6; 26 B.C.) the birth of a work greater than the *Iliad*. So Augustus too,—perhaps, notes VSD, rightly (15 above), absent on the Cantabrian campaign,— *efflagitaret*, enjoined Virgil in a letter both beseeching and jokingly threatening '*supplicibus atque etiem minacibus per iocum* to send him a first ὑπογραφή' (sketch) of the poem (could this remark indicate independent knowledge of the prose sketch, or could it be the expression that led to that sketch's invention?) or some κῶλον (limb, member). *Efflagitaret*, pregnant with imperial menace is Suetonius' word (common in the *Caesares*; cf. n. 54: Suet., as so often, gives a false tone from his anachronistic view of the Augustan principate) not Augustus'; yet Suetonius' definition of Augustus' manner could be applied equally well to the fragments of Augustus' letter to Horace, cited in Suetonius' own *Vita* of that poet—even if the jesting threats are absent from the letter to Virgil here discussed. That we have two citations from Virgil's reply (ap.Macr. *Sat.*1.24.11) seems likely: Augustus' letter was one of many (*frequentes a te litteras accipio*); Virgil would gladly send him something 'of my Aeneas', had he anything worthy of Augustus' ears.[119] But he does not; the task is vast, undertaken *paene vitio mentis*, requiring other and much weightier *studia*. The poet's 'omniscience' (n. 128) encourages the biographer (VSD 15, 35 for amplification); the range of Virgil's learning is now adequately recognised in our studies of *Buc.* and *G.* and is slowly emerging in work on the *Aeneid*.[120] What is important, though, is not that Augustus has told Virgil to write the

---

[117] Julius M.: cf. Ov. *Tr.*4.6.11; elegiac and epic poet (Sch.-Hos.2, 271).

[118] *Comes Tiberii; egregius poeta*: Sen. *Contr.*7.1.27, Naumann (n. 2), 7, *EV* 5*, 574, J. Fairweather, *Seneca the elder* (Cambridge 1981), 311f.

[119] Cf. Suet *Aug.*89, Hor. *C.*1.6.12, Griffin (n. 3), 201. White (n. 33), 115f. is not persuasive.

[120] Horsfall (Introduction, n. 2) summarises much earlier work.

Aeneid? (did he? did they talk about it? did Maecenas drop heavy hints? We have truly not the faintest idea)—or indeed to write it in a certain way, but that he wishes urgently, because of his literary expectations, to enjoy a preview, and, perhaps yet more important, that the poet can deny him even this much.[121] Pressure to produce there is, but it remains resistible.

However (VSD 32) much later (hardly more than four years, though: p. 17) and when the content was finally brought to perfection, Virgil recited to Augustus bks. 2, 4 and 6: 6, however, so affected Octavia (who was present) that when the poet reached 6.883, *tu Marcellus eris*, she is said (*fertur*) to have fainted and to have been revived with difficulty. *Fertur*, we recall, is an ambiguous confession of inexactitude (Naumann 1981, 8); the information reached Servius (*ad Aen.*6.861) in a rather different form, just as Serv. also may have related that the books read were 1, 4, 6: see C. Murgia *HSCP* 72 (1967), 334.

Virgil also recited[122] (VSD 33; cf. 43 *recitante eo*) to larger numbers but not often and generally those passages about which there was doubt, so that he could make better trial of human judgement. They say that Eros, his clerk and freedman used in advanced age to relate that Virgil once completed two half-lines extempore. To *Misenum Aeoliden* (6.164) he added *quo non praestantior alter* and roused by a similar warmth he added to *aere ciere uiros Martemque accendere cantu* (6.165). He gave instructions that (Eros) should write both down in the roll. Unable to cite exactly (*tradunt*) his source for a 'tale told by an old man',[123] Suetonius stands throughout but a step from unabashed fantasy. Pliny the Younger says that he recited himself, but does not know whether Virgil, Nepos, Accius and Ennius did so too (*Ep.*5.3.7). Pliny has therefore forgotten (or never knew) the story told here. Not proof enough of post-Suetonian interpolation. Pliny also tells us that Silius (3.7.5) *non numquam iudicia hominum recitationibus experiebatur*; the practice had been no less common in Augustan times.[124]

---

[121] Cf. Hor. *Epod.*14.5, Nisbet-Hubbard (n. 95), 81ff., Griffin (n. 33), 190f.

[122] Not the only poet for whom recitations are attested in the biographical tradition: cf. E. Rohde, *Die griech. Roman* (ed. 3, Leipzig 1914), 327, n. 1, G. Funaioli, PW s.v. *Recitationes*: Xenophanes (DL 9.18), Philoxenus of Cythera (DS 15.6); Antiphanes (Athen. 13.555a), A.R. (*vita*). For V. himself, see now G.P. Goold, in *Author and audience in Latin literature* ed. T. Woodman and J. Powell (Cambridge 1992), 110ff.

[123] Cf. my remarks about old men used thus, *Athen.*66 (1988), 33.

[124] Quinn (n. 115), 158ff., R.J. Starr, *CQ* 37 (1987), 213ff., Hor. *Serm.*1.10. 76–90, *AP* 438–9 with Brink's note, *Ep.*1.19.39, 47, 2.2.97; cf. Plin. *Ep.*6.17.2,

Suetonius is therefore innocent of anachronism but guilty of simple stupidity: two successive hemistichia would have left a text incoherent and unreadable: the hemistichia were a source of fun for the ingenious or mildly dishonest;[125] the Eros-story probably reflects tinkering and quibbling over 6.164–5 (Serv. applied the story only to the second line).[126] That a *volumen* of text (in some definitive sense) is implied will rapidly (n. 138) become significant in another context.

In the 52nd. year of his life (VSD 35), being about to put the final touches to the *Aeneid*, he decided to go to Greece and Asia and for three years unbroken only to correct (*emendare*), so the rest of his life should be free for philosophy alone. But when, on his way, he met Augustus on his way back to Rome from the East, he decided not to leave him, and even to return with him. While visiting nearby Megara under a very hot sun, he collapsed and so worsened his condition by not breaking off his journey that he put in at Brindisi a good deal worse and there died on 21 September when Cn. Sentius and Q. Lucretius were consuls (19 B.C.).

To continue to impugn Suetonius' account of a story so famed, tragic, nay sacred may seem the step from mere heresy to actual blasphemy. But all is not well (Naumann 1981, 12). 'Three years' we have met already, a stock figure (VSD 25: composition of *Buc.*). Devotion to philosophy is likewise familiar (11 on *Catal.*5), and regularly attributed to Virgil by the ancient critics,[127] perhaps to excess: note the learned *otium* of *G*.4.564, the *locus* of intellectual *secessus* (cfr. Hor. *Serm.*2.3.11f., *Ep.*1.18.109), and a general tendency to elevate the poet's wisdom in all disciplines.[128] Three years for revision is in keeping with VSD's emphasis on Virgilian *labor limae* (24, 33): exquisite perfectionism is the essence of Virgil's neoteric inheritance (p. 16) and likewise an anecdotal commonplace. Did Hor. *Carm.*1.3 refer to an earlier journey by Virgil or was it a source for this one? Did SD have in mind similar stories (Nep. *Att.*4.2: Sulla asks Atticus

---

A.-M. Guillemin, *Pline et la vie littéraire de son temps* (Paris 1929), 44–6, W. Kroll *Studien zum Verständnis der röm. Literatur* (repr. Stuttgart 1964), 122.

[125] Sen. *Suas.*2.20, Sen. *Ep.*94.28, Geymonat, *EV* 2, 287.

[126] Berres, 18. Austin *ad loc.* Cf. Brugnoli, *EV* 5*, 579 for doubts on the structure of the three *recitatio*-sections.

[127] E. Thomas, *Essai sur Servius* (Paris 1880), 259f., M. Squillante Saccone, *Le Interpretationes Vergilianae di Tiberio Claudio Donato* (Napoli 1985), 20.

[128] Cf. Quint.1.7.18, Macr. *Somn.*1.6.44, *Sat.*1.16.12, Serv., *Aen.*6 praef., Squillante Saccone (n. 127), 19ff., Servius index s.v. *Vergilius, peritus antiquitatis; philosophia; Epicurei*, etc.

to return to Italy with him)? Had SD really considered whether a stay in Athens and Asia Minor might have helped revision more than three months (or years) in a quiet Italian library? Had Suet.'s thoughts strayed to his own account of the death of Terence, contaminated as it is by details of the life of Menander, and revealing the grave anachronism of Italians going on long cultural visits to Greece?[129] Had SD pondered constructively the near-synchronism of Virgil's death and Augustus' return to Rome from the East,[130] both known dates? Unfortunately VSD ends (46) with the words *et tamen destinasse secedere*, he determined to withdraw to decide everything to the satisfaction of the *malevoli*, that is, the *obtrectatores*, which suggests that Asconius' *contra obtrectatores* is VSD's source here. But there could have been no *malevoli* in respect of the *Aeneid* until 17 B.C., the probable date of Varius' posthumous publication,[131] when at last there was free access to the text (Naumann, *EV* 5*, 574). At this point the text of VSD must stand as a touchstone of the reader's credulity or scepticism.

Virgil's bones, continues VSD, were carried to Naples and placed in the tomb which stands on the Via Puteolana, before the second milestone. He wrote the couplet on it:

> Mantua me genuit, Calabri rapuere, tenet nunc
> Parthenope; cecini pascua rura duces.

Without foreknowledge of death at Brundisium and burial at Naples,[132] Virgil could not have written this couplet, which was possibly transmitted with the so-called *Epigrammata*.[133] The epitaph was known early and widely;[134] Date of death and site of tomb are unassailable (Naumann 1981, 16; cf. n. 47 for literary confirmation).

His heirs (VSD 37) he made, to one half of his estate, Valerius Proculus, his half-brother, to one quarter Augustus, to one-twelfth

---

[129] A. Gratwick, *CHCL* 2, 814ff., E. Rawson, *Intellectual life in the late Roman republic* (London 1985), 6f.

[130] 12 Oct.; Halfmann (n. 102), 157f.

[131] In Jerome's *Chronicon*, Varius and Tucca *habentur illustres* in 17 B.C.; this has been taken with some credibility, as dating Varius' 'publication' of the *Aeneid* (cf. Berres, 31).

[132] On V.'s tomb, cf. J. Trapp, *PVS* 18 (1986), 1ff., *JWCI* 47 (1984), 1ff., *EV* s.v. *sepolcro*.

[133] J. Richmond, *Atti*, 1, 50f., *EV* 1, 698, M. Bettini, *Dial.Arch.*9–10 (1976–7), 439ff., C. Murgia, *CSCA* 7 (1974), 204.

[134] Ov. *Am.*1.15.25 may allude (Naumann (n. 2), 13); for inscriptional evidence, cf. Bettini (n. 133), 441, n. 4, H. Armini, *Eranos* 26 (1928), 256f., R. Hoogma, *Der Einfluss Vergils auf die CLE* (Amsterdam 1959), 222.

Maecenas, to the rest Varius and Plotius Tucca. At Rome at this
date wills were not systematically preserved,[135] nor is the text here
reminiscent of testamentary language (Suet. *Aug.*66, Naumann 1981,
7). The exact detail contrasts, moreover, with the utter confusion
surrounding the rest of the will. This is not to deny (cfr.8 for the size
of V.'s estate) that some kind of archival information was available
to Suetonius here: did Augustus perhaps keep some kind of register
of those who had made him their heir (Naumann 1981, 7)? It would
be very rash to claim that Suetonius had actually seen Virgil's will.

The rest of chs. 37–8 are not Suetonian: so much is admitted
even by the keenest supporters of his authorship of the *vita*.[136] If the
Sulpicius Carthaginiensis of VSD 38 is indeed Sulpicius Apollinaris,[137]
Suetonius would not have cited him, as a contemporary. But numerous other arguments, unnecessary to repeat here, consign this passage to a later date.

VSD continues (39): Virgil had settled with Varius, before he left
Italy, that if anything should befall him, he (Varius) should burn the
Aeneid.[138] But Varius refused flatly (*pernegarat*) to do it. Therefore in
the last extremity of his illness he called repeatedly for his book-
boxes, to burn them himself; but as no-one brought them, he made
no specific disposition about it (sc. the *Aen.*).

Gellius (17.10.7) relates that Virgil, dying, *petivit oravitque a suis
amicissimis impense* to burn the *Aen.*, *quam nondum satis elimavisset* (following upon *G.*'s version of the bear-cubs story, 15). In the verses by
Sulpicius (VSD 38), Virgil had ordered the burning of the *Aeneid*:
Varius, Tucca and Augustus forbade it. Part of this story is old: Plin.
*Nat.*7.114 says that Augustus forbade the *carmina* of Virgil to be burned,
contra testamenti eius vececundiam. So too the lives by Servius and 'Probus',
as well as Macr.1.24.6 *qui enim moriens poema suum legavit igni*. Incen-
diarism, intended or accomplished, is a commonplace of poetic biography:[139] it is possible that some such tales were true, but that is
more than we can say.

---

[135] M. Kaser, *Das röm. Privatrecht* 1 (München 1971), 692f.

[136] H. Naumann (n. 25, 1981), 185ff., *EV* 5*, 574, (n. 25, 1938), 364ff., *Phil.*118
(1974), 133ff., G.P. Goold, *HSCP* 74 (1968), 123f.

[137] Brugnoli, *EV* 5*, 577 and s.v. *Sulpicio Apollinare*, L. Holford-Strevens, *Aulus Gellius*
(London 1988), 61f. See now H.D. Jocelyn, *Sileno* 16 (1990), 263ff.

[138] How many copies were there? Did V. carry a master-text with him? Did
Varius hold a duplicate? To such questions, our answers are but guesswork.

[139] W. Speyer, *Büchervernichtung...*(Stuttgart 1981), 93ff., citing e.g. Schol. *Il.*17.263
(Plato), Plut. *Lys.*18.8 (Antimachus), Ov. *Tr.*1.7.15ff. (Ov. *Met.*).

VSD 40 continues: but to the said Varius and also to Tucca he left his writings on condition that they should not publish anything that had not been published by him (*ne quid ederent quod non a se editum esset*).[140] But Varius (41) published the text on Augustus' authority, corrected, however, lightly (*summatim emendata*), in as much as he left any half-lines (*versus imperfectos*) as they were. Note the distinction: both Varius and Tucca were heirs; only the former edited the *Aeneid*.[141]

Attempts have been made to disentangle this shambles in terms of Roman law.[142] The problem is, though, primarily one of source-analysis:

(a) According to one account Virgil made no specific provision in his will (VSD 39).

(b) Virgil had laid down that the *Aen.* was to be burned in the event of his premature death (VSD 39, Pliny, Sulpicius, Gell.17.10.7).

(c) VSD 40: Virgil left the *Aeneid* for Varius to publish, on certain conditions.[143] These three versions conflict with each other and their discord conflicts with the precise information on Virgil's estate and heirs. The inevitable conclusion is that Virgil's will did not survive, that the financial information derives from another source (22), which had itself in some way had access to the will, while the three versions of what was to happen to the *Aeneid* rest on nothing except speculation, intended (cf. Plin. *Nat.*7.114) to exalt the poet's *verecundia* or to defend his text against captious critics and illicit tinkerings:[144] so already Hyginus fr.7, 8 GRF: 'he would have corrected this' (cf. Brugnoli, *EV* 5*, 580).

Ch. 41 continues: many tried to complete the half-lines, but failed because of the difficulty, since all, excepting 3.340, were complete in

---

[140] Had this provision any bearing on *Buc.* and *G.* too? What exactly did it mean? Cf. Berres 22. I have no answers.

[141] Varius alone was mentioned by Suet.; Varius and Tucca together appear in Jerome, Donatus, Servius and much later scholarship: F. Leo, *Plautinische Forschungen* (Berlin 1912), 40f. reached the answer; cf. Goold (n. 136), 128f., S. Timpanaro, *Per la storia della filologia virgiliana antica* (Roma 1986), 18, n. 7, Berres 21f., 29f., Naumann (n. 6, 1979), 160. Jocelyn (n. 137) does not quite persuade me that Tucca merits a return to favour.

[142] *EV* s.v. *Testamento di Virgilio* (Guarino), V. Scialoja, *Athen.*8 (1930) 168ff., R. Scarcia, *RCCM* 5 (1963), 306f., with n. 3, W.T. Avery, *CJ* 52 (1956–7), 225ff.

[143] Cf. *Vit.Serv.*29–31 *hac lege iussit emendare* (sc. Augustus), *ut superflua demerent, nihil adderent tamen*; Jerome (*Chron.*17 B.C.) has only *ut nihil adderent*. See Berres, 24–6, J. Perret in *Recueil...Collart* (Paris 1978), 405ff., Jocelyn (n. 137), 269ff.

[144] Cf. Naumann, *EV* 5*, 574, (n. 2), 12ff.; I am grateful to Profs. E. Champlin and T. McGinn for clarification of the legal issues.

sense.[145] 'Half-lines' renders *hemistichia*; cf. *dimidiatos versus* 34, and *versus imperfectos* 41:[146] not all such lines in fact end half-way (at the third or fourth foot caesura) and their 'imperfection' lies in form not sense. It is likely that the *quaedam imperfecta* (24) left by Virgil so as not to delay his *impetus* refer only to the half-lines.[147] Cf. further 293ff. on the textual history of the *Aen.* in antiquity.

Nisus the grammarian used to say (42; N. belongs to the mid-c. 1 A.D.) that he had heard from his elders that Varius had moved what was then book 2 into third place. In its present form, textual problems aside,[148] this information is confused, senseless, possibly corrupt.[149] Nisus (l.c.) also repeated a story that Varius had 'corrected' the beginning of *Aen.*1 by the removal of the *ille ego* verses. These were never written by Virgil:[150] if Nisus had at least honestly reported an older story, then we are back in the age of Tiberius, one of the golden ages of faking at Rome,[151] when the characteristically Ovidian collocation *ille ego*. . .(Gamberale 260) had had time to take root. We note that Varius' name is used to lend spurious glamour to fraud and foolishness. The rest of VSD is best discussed (268ff.) in the context of the *fortuna* of Virgil in the c. 1 A.D. It may now be apparent that very little external information indeed may legitimately be used in the understanding of Virgil and his work.

---

[145] See M. Geymonat, *EV* 2, 287, W. Suerbaum in *Studien. . .S. Lauffer* 3 (Roma 1986), 981ff.

[146] Pace Servius on 6.186, *tibicines* are quite another matter (cf. n. 113): see J. Sparrow, *Half-lines and repetitions in Virgil* (Oxford 1931), 9, Berres, 16f., B. Baldwin, *SO* 68 (1993), 144ff.

[147] But not formally certain, Sparrow (n. 146), 17.

[148] I read, with Hardie, *tunc* not *nunc*; the *nunc* printed by Bayer raises even graver difficulties.

[149] But see Serv.1.4.16f. (Th.-H.); cf. Naumann (n. 6, 1979), 158, Berres, 24, Murgia (n. 133), 205, n. 5, Jocelyn (n. 137), 265f.

[150] R.G. Austin, *CQ* 18 (1968), 107ff., Goold (n. 136), 126ff., *EV* s.v. *Preproemio* (Gamberale), id. (a fuller version) in *Studi. . .G. Monaco* 2 (Palermo 1991), 963ff.

[151] O. Skutsch, *Phil.*103 (1959), 153, E. Fraenkel, *JRS* 42 (1952), 8 = *Kl.Beitr.*2 (Roma 1964) 194f.

Bibliography

I know of no recent work in English on Virgil's life of which I am able to speak well, though there are excellent discussions of the methods of ancient literary biography (n. 5). The articles by Naumann and Brugnoli in *EV* 5* s.v. *Vitae Vergilianae* contain much of value. Naumann, from 1938 on (as recognised by G.P. Goold, *HSCP* 74 (1968), 123) has revolutionised our understanding both of VSD and of the life of Virgil, though his writing is often repetitive and acrimonious. Cf. nn. 25, 6, 93, 51 for a selection of his publications; the most useful (called above Naumann 1981) is not easily found (n. 2). Almost all the evidence one could wish for is in Götte-Bayer (n. 13). T. Berres, *Die Entstehung der Aeneis* (*Hermes* Einzelschr.45, 1982). I cite only to show what can still happen to those who fail to realise that Virgil's life is a problem not of facts but of sources.

CHAPTER TWO

BUCOLICS

A. Perutelli (Translated by the Editor)

Title

Our earliest explicit evidence for the title *Bucolica* derives, if not already from Suetonius (VSD 19), then from Macr.5.17.20 *maluit inscribere Bucolica*,[1] but Colum.7.10.8, who introduces a citation of *Buc.*7.54 with the words *ut Bucolicum loquitur poema* and even *G.*4.565 *carmina qui lusi pastorum* (the exact equivalent of the Greek title)[2] let us return to a far earlier date. But indirect testimony may weigh even more heavily: thus Numitorius (VSD 43) wrote *Antibucolica* against Virgil's work.[3] Still, the term *ecloga* is current from the late c. 1 A.D. on (VSD 9, 43), to designate, like the Greek ἄνθος, the individual poem that forms part of the *liber*.[4] It has at the same time been noted[5] that early on, perhaps even earlier than the general title and in any case in rivalry with it, there developed the usage of giving the individual *eclogae* a title which referred to the poem's content. Don. *praef.Buc.*[6] already lists the ten *eclogae* with their individual titles, normally the name of a character.[7] But much longer titles, which offered a short description of the content, are also found. Recent papyrological discoveries, such as *P.Narm.*66.362,[8] offer some evidence for calculating the overall length of the text copied: they seem to indicate that the individual poems circulated separately, with pretty substantial titles related to their use for live performance.

The facts do not seem irreconcilable: we have two ways of entitling

---

[1] The earliest ms. evidence, in P, M and G all probably belongs to the late c. 5 (or perhaps even slightly later): M. Geymonat, *EV* s.v. *Codici*, A. Petrucci, in *Virgilio e noi* (Genova 1982), 64ff., Clausen, xx n. 23.

[2] F. Della Corte, *EV* 1, 541.

[3] Horsfall, *BICS* 28 (1981), 108f.

[4] A. Traina, *Latinitas* 15 (1967), 97ff., Horsfall, l.c.

[5] M. Geymonat, *BICS* 29 (1982), 217f.

[6] 316ff., ed. Bayer/Brummer (cf. 3).

[7] 1 *Corydon*; 2 *Alexis*; 3 *Palaemon*; 4 *Pollio*; 5 *Daphnis*; 6 *Varus* or *Silenus*; 7 *Corydon*; 8 *Damon* or *Pharmaceutria*; 9 *Moeris*; 10 *Gallus*. Could this nomenclature be related to performances on stage (cf. 249) by particularly favoured actors?

[8] C. Gallazzi, *ZPE* 48 (1982), 75ff.

the work, which exist in function of two ways of enjoying it: *Bucolica*, which takes up the title of Theocritus' collection, refers us to a reading of the *liber* as a whole, while other titles of individual poems, all of them quite long, were used for performance, normally not of the whole collection, but of one, or of a selection.[9]

Date

Our ancient sources offer precise information on Virgil's age at the composition of *Buc.*[10] PsProbus' information has at least an air of greater exactitude and we may add that, according to VSD 25, Virgil *Bucolica triennio perfecit.* That would mean that Virgil wrote *Buc.* between 45 and 42 (date of publication).[11] There is good reason to reject this hypothesis:

4.11 gives us just about our safest starting-point: that is, the reference to Pollio *teque adeo decus hoc aeui, te consule, inibit.* Pollio was consul in 40, but the use of the future gave rise to some uncertainty: was Pollio already consul, or was he still consul designate (which would put us in 41)? Both dates have been propounded energetically and other indications have been adduced, such as 4.17 *pacatum. . . orbem,* an expression which, some maintain, must refer to the peace of Brundisium (Oct., 40).[12] But the essential point seems to be the fact that the composition of the individual *eclogae* could not coincide with their publication, or at least with their final publication in the *liber*: in the *liber*, if there are precise references to current events, they may therefore have been updated, modified, or added.[13] Thus everything points to the fourth *Eclogue* as having been written if not in late 41, when Pollio was consul designate, then not later than early 40, at the beginning of his consulship. That is the most satisfactory interpretation of the references to the future, which extol the consul's office, though we would do well not to exclude altogether

---

[9] Cf. 250; the evidence from Pompeii suggests that the homosexual *Buc.*2 was specially popular.

[10] Serv. *praef.Buc.*3.23.26f. Th.-H. *sane sciendum Vergilium XXVIII annorum scripsisse Bucolica,* Ps.Prob.323.13 *scripsit Bucolica annos natus VIII et XX*; 329.5f. *cum certum sit, eum, ut Asconius Pedianus dicit, XXVIII annos natum Bucolica edidisse.* Serv. and PsProb., though, are quite capable of confusing date of starting and date of conclusion!

[11] Della Corte, *EV* 1, 542.

[12] J. Carcopino, *Virgile et le mystère de la IV Eglogue* (Paris 1930), 107f., Clausen 125f.

[13] As was undoubtedly the case with several passages in *G.*, 63ff., 93.

the hypothesis that, as often happens in ancient poetry, the celebration was written later than the occasion to which it refers.[14]

Eclogue 8 is also dedicated to Pollio: here 6ff. express the expectation of his triumphal return from Illyricum and anticipate the celebration of that triumph. The repeated attempts to identify the dedicatee of the poem with Octavian are not convincing,[15] particularly on account of v. 10 (the dedicatee's literary output) *sola Sophocleo tua carmina digna cothurno*. Tragedy, that is, and hardly appropriate to Octavian's attempt to write an *Ajax*,[16] but much more in accord with Pollio's literary production.[17] The date (Pollio's proconsulship in Macedonia) must (*MRR* 2, 387f.) be 39. On the other hand, *Buc*.6 is dedicated to (P. Alfenus) Varus and alludes (5–6) to the dedicatee's campaign. This must, apparently, refer to his proconsulship (38; *MRR* 2, 386). At this point, we have clearly gone beyond the period of three years and the discrepancies between our ancient sources become quite marked.

In fact, *Vita Serv.* (26ff. Bayer) adds a further detail: *tunc ei proposuit Pollio ut carmen bucolicum scriberet, quod eum constat triennio scripsisse et emendasse.* Such a period cannot refer to the composition of a single *ecloga*,[18] but it is beyond question that some of the *eclogae* have nothing to do with Pollio[19] and cannot conceivably have been written at his behest or inspiration. Should we wish in some way to save Servius' credit, despite the clearly mechanical structure of his notice, then[20] the solution might seem to be that of an early version of the *liber*, containing a smaller number of poems, all of which depend in some way on Pollio's patronage.

Another historical reference is the first solemn celebration of Julius Caesar's birthday since his death,[21] to which *Buc*.5 alludes, in all

---

[14] Ed. Coleman, 15.

[15] Cf. in particular G.W. Bowersock, *HSCP* 75 (1971), 73ff., D. Mankin, *Herm*.116 (1988), 63; against, V. Tandoi, in *Le Bucoliche* ed. M. Gigante (Napoli 1981), 268ff., R.G. Mayer, *BICS* 30 (1983), 17ff., J. Farrell, *CP* 86 (1991), 204ff. Cf. now Clausen, 233–6, eloquent but unpersuasive.

[16] So, well, R.G. Tarrant, *HSCP* 82 (1978), 197ff.

[17] Cf. *Scaen.Rom.Frag.* 1, ed. A. Klotz, 308; J. André *La vie et l'oeuvre d'Asinius Pollion* (Paris 1949), 31ff.

[18] The exact parallelism of *carmen bucolicum. . .Georgica. . .Aeneiden* suggests in fact that Servius' words refer, however awkwardly, to the *Liber* as a whole. That is not to say that behind this confusion there may not lurk a hint at the earlier 'edition'.

[19] Servius is a prisoner of the schematic sequence Pollio-Maecenas-Augustus.

[20] Coleman, 19, a lucid exposition.

[21] S. Weinstock, *Divus Iulius* (Oxford 1971), 206f. Clausen, 152 n. 4 is overly sceptical.

probability. But—and this is beyond any doubt—the same *ecloga* contains citations from *Buc*.2 and 3, which must therefore be earlier than 5 (and likewise 4 and 8) and thus probably the earliest of the entire collection. Supposing we were to grant that there was a first 'Pollio' collection,[22] it would have contained, in chronological order *Buc*.2, 3, 5, 4, 8: it is 8 that refers to Pollio's proconsulship in Macedonia, in 39, the last year of the triennium to which the Servian life refers.[23]

In general, we may allow that the composition of those *eclogae* which do not belong to the early, 'Pollio' group may be a year or two later. To 6, dedicated to Varus, I have already referred. W.V. Clausen suggested[24] that 1.42–3 might allude to the Hellenistic practice of monthly celebrations of the ruler's birthdays, an honour which could have been bestowed on Octavian not earlier than 35.[25] As for *Buc*.1 and 9, once their non-autobiographical nature is accepted (cf. 11ff. for full discussion), they refer simply to the redistribution of land after Philippi (42), which continued for some years.[26] We cannot date the definitive edition of *Buc*., in the order which we have, and we have not found any reason to look later than 38.

Other criteria for establishing the relative dating of individual poems have been suggested. That of style is not only subjective and impressionistic, but shows itself to be false on account of the variety of tone and function within *Buc*. For example, the spondaic rhythm of 4 does seem to be influenced by the seriousness of the content, as expressed clearly in the first verse. Another internal element which has been considered is the relationship of the text to Theocritus. One could in theory reconstruct a line of development from close imitation in the early poems (an actual repetition of Theocritean themes); next, as the work proceeds, a greater tendency to variation

---

[22] Let us remember that only 4 and 8 are actually dedicated to Pollio and that his credit here is gravely weakened by his schematism.

[23] While we may thus have managed to explain the 'three years' as applicable to the 'first edition', that edition was not identified by Serv. as such, while he was taken in altogether by the dangerous tale of the 'second edition' of *G*.4 (cf. 86ff.)!

[24] *HSCP* 76 (1972), 201ff.

[25] But cf. App. *BC* 5.541 and R. Syme, *Roman Revolution* (Oxford 1939, etc.), 233f.: it is not in Appian's ample list. If Theoc.17.126f. is not Virgil's actual source, it still demonstrates that real Hellenistic usage, known from literary texts, could have influenced Virgil just as well as Roman practice.

[26] 42 was perhaps a familiar date used to fix the incipit or completion of the whole collection; the 'autobiographical' reading of 1 and 9 clearly favours this possibility. Cf. Clausen, 29–33.

in close echoes and a greater liberty in the choice of themes and motifs. But this criterion likewise, as soon as we realise that within the same poem different procedures stand side by side, reveals its own weakness.[27]

Other proposals verge on the comic, such as those of L. Herrmann[28] and G. Ruelens,[29] who claim to organise the poems in chronological sequence on the basis of the references to the seasons which they contain!

On the evidence that we have (not all cited here), a possible order of composition would be: 2, 3, 5, 4, 8, 7, 6, 9, 1, 10. But it would be presumptuous to defend to the end such a claim. E. Coleiro[30] provides schematically an ample list of the sequences proposed by various scholars: the divergences that emerge are only too visible.

Arrangement

There is also a text of some interest which bears on the arrangement of the individual *eclogae*: Don. *praef.Buc.*336ff. *sed sunt qui dicant initium bucolici carminis non 'Tityre' esse, sed: 'Prima Syracosio dignata est ludere uersu'*, whence, more or less directly, it appears, Serv. *praef.Buc.* (3.1.3.19f. Th.-H) *alii primam illam uolunt 'prima Syracosio dignata est ludere uersu'*. What to make of this uncertainty?[31] That the order was, from a very early date, that which we now have is guaranteed both by *G.*4.566, which cites 1.1 to designate *Buc.* as a whole, and by Ov. *Am.*1.15.25 *Tityrus et fruges Aeneiaque arma legentur*.[32] At most, behind VSD and Serv. may lurk a moment of hesitation, the order of a first collection or even of a provisional collection (were all the poems included? or only some? was *Buc.*1 not yet written?), soon modified in favour of the order we have. This hypothesis is reinforced by the fact that *Buc.*1 has nothing of the character of a prooemium: remarkable in

---

[27] Cf. 3.44ff., where the description of the cups (*pocula*) is, by comparison with Theocritus, strongly innovative, while in the rest of the *ecloga* there are almost literal renderings of Theocritus. Cf. Clausen xxiii.

[28] *Humanitas* 5 (1930), 179ff.

[29] *AC* 12 (1943), 79ff.

[30] *An introduction to Vergil's Bucolics with a critical edition of the text* (Amsterdam 1979), 93.

[31] We should note that the ancient Virgil-commentators had observed the anomaly of prooemium-features in the 6th. poem of the *liber*; we are not compelled to accept their explanation! Cf. Clausen xxii–iv.

[32] Cf. also Calp.Sic.4.62.

the structuring of a book so much indebted to Alexandrian poetics. On the other hand, *Buc*.6 (*recusatio*. . .) is a perfectly suitable prooemium to the *liber* and that should make us take seriously the information found in VSD/Servius. In other more or less contemporary collections, the *recusatio* of epic is found at the centre or at the beginning, as in Ov. *Am*.1.1: there too a divinity, Cupido, intervenes to prevent the poet from attempting heroic themes, just as Apollo does in *Buc*.6. Why was the original order modified? So as to have the chance to place first the one poem in which Octavian was mentioned, and not one dedicated to a minor patron such as Varus (Coleman).[33]

Apart from the position of the first *ecloga* and that of the farewell to pastoral (10), which was pretty much predetermined, the problem of whether or not a criterion of arrangement is recognisable remains. Here too there are innumerable interpretations, based on the most varied criteria (subject-matter; form; numerical correspondences of various kinds): sometimes such criteria overlap or combine.

But agreement on some secure conclusions can, I believe, be reached.[34] *Buc*.1, as I have said before, refers to the help given by Octavian and that gives the poem its position of prominence: 6 too, placed at the opening of the second half of the collection, seems to be an internal prooemium with its *recusatio* and declaration of poetic principle.[35] If then we omit 10, and take 5 as a 'hinge', quite credible correspondences between the other poems emerge. 5 was probably placed at the centre on account of its (probable) celebration of the death of Caesar.[36] The correspondence between 1 and 9 is clearly apparent: both 2 and 8 contain monologues on hopeless love. Likewise 3 and 7: both are contests of song. The link between 4 and 6 is rather less clear but may be found in the cosmological element. The factor of alternation is also important: we may also note that usually *eclogae* which are primarily in dialogue form alternate with those that are primarily monologues.

---

[33] Coleman, 19f. We have seen (11) that Virgil was associated with Maecenas by 38. By 35, Octavian had begun to take on the air of the eventual winner (Syme (n. 25), 227ff.) but we do not have to suppose that Virgil necessarily waited that long, far less until Actium, before paying Octavian the compliment of honouring him with the first poem of the collection. Cf. now Clausen xxivf.

[34] I follow the general lines of the discussion in A. La Penna, *Virgilio e la crisi del mondo antico* in PVM ed. E. Cetrangolo (Firenze 1966, etc.), xxiii.

[35] Cf. G.B. Conte, *Il genere e i suoi confini* (Milano 1984), 121ff.

[36] So the majority of interpreters from Serv. *ad Buc*.5.20, 29 to I. Du Quesnay, *PVS* 16 (1976–7), 31f., *EV* s.v. *Dafni*, A. Salvatore in *Bucoliche* (n. 15), 216f.

The division in two (1–5; 6–10) is less clear. B. Otis[37] in particular has emphasized the difference between the first five, more 'peaceful, conciliatory and patriotic' and the remainder, 'neoteric, ambiguous or polemic, concerned with the past and emotively dominated by *amor indignus*'. The generalisation does not work perfectly but has been attacked with perhaps too much rigour.[38] Note the implicit relationship between 1 and 9: optimistic and pessimistic views, respectively, of the same problem. The monologue of the hopeless lover in 2 is consistently less dramatic than 8; optimism for the world's future is expressed, unquestionably, in 4. In short, while details have been adduced against this division, it does in general bring out elements of a real variation between 'halves'.

Numerology

Research into arithmetical sums or ratios which regulate the structure or arrangement of *Buc.* are quite another matter. An article published by P. Maury in 1944[39] was the first piece of work clearly aimed in this direction: the key number is 333, sum of the verses in 1–4 and 6–9, as also in 3 + 7 + 2 + 8. Further calculations do not yield exact correspondences. In any case, the criterion for grouping the poems to be added up is—roughly—by content, but is really so fragile that it may easily be refuted. Number-plays were nevertheless then taken up, especially by American Virgilians, who have repeatedly either amplified Maury's theories or simply developed similar correspondences. I refer in particular to E.L. Brown, B. Otis and J. Van Sickle.[40] This series of studies, which displays escalating audacity and complexity in the fine mesh of mathematical correspondences laid over the text of *Buc.*, nonetheless ended up by convincing one of the scholars most opposed to such approaches, Otto Skutsch,[41] who criticised energetically earlier proposals, but still advanced one of his own, perhaps the most credible so far: 5 (allegorical commemoration

[37] B. Otis, *Virgil. A study in civilized poetry* (Oxford 1964), 128ff.

[38] O. Skutsch, *HSCP* 73 (1969), 153ff.

[39] *Lettres d'humanité* 3 (1944), 71ff.

[40] E.L. Brown, *Numeri Vergiliani* (*Coll.Lat.*63, 1963), Otis (n. 37), 128ff.; on this topic Van Sickle has written a great deal, but cf. in particular *The design of Virgil's Bucolics* (Roma 1978), *ANRW* 2.31.1 (1980), 576ff., *EV* 1, 549ff.

[41] Cf. n. 38.

of the death of Caesar) serves as fulcrum and 10 is excluded from all calculations: 4 + 6 (149) and 1 + 9 (150) are almost equal; 3 + 7 and 2 + 8 exactly so (181). So, according to Skutsch, the book's structure acquires a mathematical rigour.

Hitherto criteria for selecting texts to stand in correspondence or contrast have been heterogeneous, involving now verbal echoes, now content. Such heterogeneity has increased and indeed raised to the level of a key element by Van Sickle, in his most complex examination. Taking up the various previous studies, he observes that as the discourse unfolds, it brings into play both whole *eclogae* and single passages and develops at three levels: (i) quantitative, that is, in the amount of text considered (usually the number of verses); (ii) qualitative, that is, in the key motifs of form or content; and (iii), functional, that is, in special relationships between passages or whole *eclogae* on the basis of (i) or (ii). Once this basic classification is established, various structures are offered for each level under consideration. For example, the division of individual *eclogae* into constituent elements is driven to yield correspondences both internal and external. The structures which contain references to the other levels become extremely complex. Within individual *eclogae* a division into segments comes into effect: these 'segments' contain (more or less) balancing numbers of verses. Thus *Buc.*1 breaks down into 5:5:29:5:1:28:5:5. It is unnecessary to add that the criteria for delimiting these 'segments' range from the obvious to the improbable. But once we pass to the 'qualitative' and 'functional' levels, chaos ungovernable reigns.[42]

Among other attempts, the most credible would seem that of G. Brugnoli:[43] he confirms the division of the *liber* into two by his observation of a series of correspondences between the central *eclogae* of the two halves, 3 and 8 starting from the (perfect) correspondence of both theme and number between 3.84–8 and 8.84–8.

The genre of pastoral

Our ancient sources[44] offer two distinct origins for pastoral: from the Peloponnese or from Sicily. Perhaps the fullest and most systematic

---

[42] For a summary, cf. *EV* 1, 549ff.
[43] *Linguistica e letteratura* 10 (1985), 47ff.
[44] DS 4.84, Athen.14.619ab, Ael. *VH* 10.18, Schol.Theocr., *Prolegomena* 2f. Wendel,

treatment is Don. *praef.Buc.*230ff. The 'Peloponnese' tradition speaks
of the second Persian war, when the country was invaded by the
enemy and the virgins could not perform their usual songs in honour
of Diana: then it was the shepherds who celebrated the rites for the
goddess with their own pastoral songs. The Sicilian story, on the
other hand, advances the flight of Orestes from Tauris, with his sister Iphigeneia and with a statue of Diana. The statue of the goddess
was hidden in a bundle of wood (whence the goddess' epithet, Fasc-
elina). Iphigeneia performed an expiatory sacrifice for her brother:
whence *id genus carminis Dianae redditum.* Other versions identify the
origins of pastoral in songs offered to Apollo, while he pastured the
flocks of Admetus, others in songs dedicated to Mercury, father of
Daphnis, others in songs in honour of Pan, Silenus, and the Fauni.
Other versions again mention that pastoral songs were introduced
with the rites in honour of Diana to procure release from a pesti-
lence that was afflicting the island. The rites were annual and were
performed by singers called *bucolistae* (Diom. *GL* 1.487.5), who went
from house to house carrying tokens of the earth's fertility. If we
look to the historical facts, we find a literary genre 'codified' only in
the Hellenistic period. Its underlying causes sprang from the first signs
of unease aroused by city life: whence a desire for escape, expressed
in exaltation of the countryside.[45] The 'codification' of bucolic is
brought off by means of a mixing of genres, according to normal
Hellenistic practice. The metre is epic (hexameter), but the structure,
with refrains, has something of the manner of lyric, while the dialogue form and the contest suggest mime.

   Predecessors can naturally be sought: they have even for some
time been given names, like Anyte of Tegea or Mnasalcas of Sicyon,
already discussed from Reitzenstein on[46] as poets who anticipated
the taste for vignettes of rural life, though certainly not authors of
bucolic. Recently, there has even been an attempt to gather convincing indications in favour of Philetas as Virgil's partial model for poetry
in a pastoral context, with reference to the *Corycius senex* in *G.*4.[47] All
the same, these hints do not add up to much: we have not identified

---

Don. *praef.Buc.*221ff., Diom., *GL* 1.486.17f.; Ps.Prob. *praef. ad Buc.*, Th.-H 3.2.324ff.,
Philarg., Th.-H. 3.2.10.4ff., F. Graf, *ZPE* 62 (1986), 43f.

   [45] A. Perutelli, *ASNP* 3.6.3 (1976), 788.
   [46] R. Reitzenstein, *Epigramm und Skolion* (Giessen 1893), 123ff., 193ff., Clausen xv–xx.
   [47] R.F. Thomas, *MD* 29 (1992), 35ff. On Philetas, see too E. Bowie, *CQ* 35 (1985),
67ff.

other pioneers in the bucolic genre as we understand it—apart from
Theocritus. Recent criticism has done well to underline more closely
the dependence of Theocritus on mime and to hint at doubts of his
having been aware of his role as codifier of a new genre. D.H.
Halperin in particular[48] has demonstrated, from a purely formal point
of view, how Theocritus' bucolic idylls are not sufficiently differentiated—terms of specific factors—from the other poems of the corpus
to permit the delineation of a genre really independent from that of
epos. According to Halperin, Theocritus' intention was simply to
compose narrative poetry distinct from traditional epos. Since the
characters of epic were outstanding heroes, pastoral's choice had to
fall instead upon modest figures, whether rustics or city-born. On
the other hand, it has also been observed that there really is a close
affinity between pastoral and urban mime. As is well-known, Theocritus wrote both, and in that case, the real mark of his novelty is
not so much the bucolic mime as the mime (of whatever environment) with humble characters.[49] Early developments in the ms. tradition likewise show that Theocritus' bucolic poetry was not recognised
as an independent genre: his bucolic poems were linked with other
poems from his hand, or even to poems by others, such as Moschus
and Bion, certainly authors of epyllia as well as of pastoral poems.[50]
Overall, we may accept a revised form of the 'sociological' view of
urban unease in the birth of bucolic poetry, but should, however,
avoid the opposite excess of studying it from a purely formal point
of view. That, above all, has not managed to account for the presence of many elements, such as the presence in the corpus of poems
of hymnic character. From the viewpoint of Virgilian studies, such a
picture of the Theocritean corpus better explains the presence of
non-bucolic motifs.

When Virgil, in the sixth eclogue, claims to be the first bucolic
poet at Rome, his claim, so far as the available evidence goes, is
perfectly true: we have no basis for postulating earlier bucolic verse
in Latin. The evidence has been tested;[51] Virgil was right. Nonetheless, there are signs that motifs connected with bucolic poetry did
spread: thus Suet. *Gramm.*3.5 has been thought to allude to an event
in the circle of 'preneoteric' poets which flourished in Rome ca. 100

---

[48] D.M. Halperin, *Before pastoral* (New Haven 1983), 217ff. et passim.
[49] B. Effe, *Die Genese einer literarischen Gattung: die Bukolik* (Konstanz 1977), 19.
[50] Excellent discussion of the whole problem by M. Fantuzzi in *Lo spazio letterario della Grecia antica* 1.2 (Roma 1993), 192ff.
[51] B. Luiselli, *AFLC* 28 (1960), 23ff.

B.C.: *pretia uero grammaticorum tanta mercedesque tam magnae ut constet Lutatium Daphnidem quem Laeuius Melissus per cavillationem nominis Panos agasma dicit, DCC milibus nummum a Q. Catulo emptum ac breui manumissum.*[52] If Laevius(?) jestingly called a slave of Lutatius Catulus 'Panos agasma', then, evidently, among those men of letters there was some familiarity with the characters and motifs of bucolic poetry. But we know of course that within the Theocritean conventions Daphnis was the rival, not the beloved of Pan,[53] while Pan's relations with Daphnis were erotic in the love epigrams of the Hellenistic period.[54] This was exactly the genre practised by the 'preneoterics' and Laevius'(?) joke is therefore best attributed to the generic context of love-epigram and not to that of bucolic. But the textual foundation of this story is sadly weak.

Poetic tradition

Just as the *Buc.* are quite new in Latin poetry, so there is a corresponding novelty in the link between them and Theocritus (a corpus perhaps very similar to that we have today and one that already contained apocryphal texts). In place of the learned approach of the late c. 19 which aimed basically to collect and list all the imitations of Virgil to be found in Theocritus' text,[55] scholars have long since passed to an attempt to understand Virgil's original features and to a careful study of how the model is handled and how changed. The most specific examination[56] of the problem, now twenty-five years old, still offers us, though only as a useful tool, tables[57] of all Theocritean echoes. So we discover that, of the corpus we have, only *Id.*14, 19, 21, 27, 28, 29, 30 are not taken up in *Buc.*: Theocritus is omnipresent in Virgil's collection and influences both themes and modes of expression.

---

[52] Text as restored in G. Brugnoli's Teubner ed. But note *Gaius Melissus* printed by Kaster (1995).

[53] Reitzenstein (n. 46), 246ff.

[54] For such a relationship, see e.g. *AP* 7.535, 9.341, 12.128.

[55] For *Buc.*, a series of works by Paul Jahn are specially significant: *Die Art der Abhängigkeit Vergils von Theokrit*, Progr. des kölln. Gymn. Berlin, 1897, 1898, 1899. Cf. Jahn's own revision of the Ladewig-Schaper-Deuticke commentary to *Buc.* and *G.* (ed. 9, 1915), or that of C. Hosius.

[56] S. Posch, *Beobachtungen zur Theokritnachwirkung bei Vergil* (*Comm.Aenip.*19, Innsbruck 1969), R.W. Garson, *CQ* 21 (1971), 188ff.; cf. now Clausen xv–xx.

[57] (n. 56), 15ff.

A preliminary question to put is that of what sort of edition of Theocritus Virgil used. In truth, the history of the transmission of the text of Theocritus poses several questions not easily answered.[58] Thirty poems, twenty-four epigrams and a figured poem (*Syrinx*) have come down to us under his name. Separately, we have fragments of another poem (31 Gow), on an Antinoe papyrus (c. 5–6 A.D.), while Athenaeus (7.284A) preserves five hexameters from Theocritus' *Berenice* (fr.3 Gow). Some poems (19, 21, 23, 25, 27) and probably a couple of epigrams are spurious: so too now by general agreement *Id.*8 and 9, but Virgil probably knew them as Theocritus'.

This state of affairs led Wilamowitz[59] to formulate the hypothesis that Theocritus did not publish his own poems in a corpus but rather issued them separately: they were then gathered some little while later in a collection which included other poems, bucolic or at least of similar character (e.g. Moschus and Bion); the grammarian Artemidorus of Tarsus (active at Alexandria, c. 1 B.C.) made this collection; in some of our mss., an epigram (whose author claims that he has gathered the straying Muses of bucolic) precedes the poems and this epigram appears in the Anthology attributed to Artemidorus (*AP* 9.205); later Artemidorus' son Theon separated the Theocritean poems from the rest and equipped them with a commentary, the basis of our corpus of Theocritus-scholia; this explains why we only have scholia to the authentic poems, plus the two (8, 9) which were already attributed to Theocritus in antiquity.

Wilamowitz' reconstruction has been exposed to various criticisms,[60] both on account of the weakness of the evidence on which it is based and because the papyri since discovered are of Theocritus proper (plus the usual *Id.*8 and 9) but not of the other bucolic poets; so there is no evidence for a collected edition of all bucolic poetry. But more recently, Wilamowitz' theory has been readopted and updated: particularly thanks to codicological considerations, the hypothesis[61] of an edition of Theocritus, containing all the authentic poems, plus 8 and 9, has been advanced. It is therefore at least likely (if very far from certain) that Virgil had an edition of Theocritus of this kind.

---

[58] Cf. the up-to-date remarks of G. Serrao, *EV*, 5*, 110ff.; cf. Clausen, xx.

[59] U. von Wilamowitz-Moellendorff, *Bucolici Graeci* (Oxford 1905), iii and following; id., *Die Textgeschichte der griechischen Bukoliker* (Berlin 1906), 102ff.

[60] In particular those of two later editors of Theocr., Gallavotti (Roma 1946) and Gow (ed. 2, Cambridge 1952), 1, lix–lxii.

[61] J. Irigoin, *QUCC* 19 (1975), 27ff., C. Meillier, *REG* 94 (1981), 315ff.

Theocritus' presence in the *Buc.* is not uniform but reveals peaks, especially in *Buc.*2 and 3. This has led some critics to formulate the hypothesis that the poems which display most imitations of Theocritus are the first to have been composed,[62] as though Virgil wanted to 'free' himself step by step from the canonical model as composition advanced. *Eclogues* 2 and 3 are in fact two poems which, for other reasons can be attributed to a first phase of composition.[63] But a regular line of development away from Theocritus is not to be traced. In these same two eclogues, there are many fundamental departures from the model. The character of Corydon, protagonist of 2, is as distant as may be imagined from the grotesque Polyphemus of Theocr. 11: Theocritus' Polyphemus derives from the portrait in satyr-drama, while Virgil's shepherd, though he descends into the realism of his rustic world, shows elegiac sensitivity in the description of his unhappy love.[64]

Similarly, in *Buc.*3 (36ff.) we find the description of the cups, perhaps the passage most closely based on its model, in Theocr.1.27ff. But Virgil reveals directly features quite distinct from his model[65] and this not so much because two cups replace the Theocritean κισσύβιον, as because the content of the reliefs is completely altered. Those of Theocritus, in three distinct scenes, are a true masterpiece of Alexandrian realism applied to description. The border is of ivy and helichryse. In the first scene, there is an elegant woman, wearing peplos and diadem, wooed by two men; she smiles now at one, now at the other, while they 'labour to no purpose'. In the second, an old fisherman, still fit and muscular, strains to draw in his catch. In the third, the boy and two foxes: one of them preys on the ripe grapes, while the other lies in wait for the boy's lunch, while he hunts grasshoppers. All quite different in Virgil, where the ekphrasis begins with the frieze of grapes closely interwoven with ivy, a description difficult and almost obscure in its syntactical developments, perhaps with the aim of suggesting the closeness of the interweaving. Secondly, the two astronomers depicted *in medio*: apart from the difficulties raised by its actual place on the cups, the scene is altogether

---

[62] Cf. E.A. Schmidt, *Poetische Reflexion. Vergils Bukolik* (München 1972), 57ff.

[63] Cf. 30f.

[64] Cf., in particular, J.J.H. Savage, *TAPA* 91 (1960), 353ff., A. La Penna, *Maia* 15 (1963), 484ff., E.W. Leach, *AJP* 87 (1966), 427ff., M. Geymonat in (n. l.), 107ff. On elegiac elements in *Buc.* in general, cf. E.J. Kenney, *ICS* 8 (1983), 44ff.

[65] La Penna in *Bucoliche* (n. 15), 140ff. is particularly helpful.

different and is rendered in the unusual guise of a riddle. One of the astronomers is actually Conon, well-knonwn to the Roman literary public because celebrated in Catullus 66 as the discoverer of Berenice's lock; Menalcas seems to have forgotten the other's name (*et-quis fuit alter*). Apart from conjectures as to the second astronomer's identity (perhaps Archimedes, a name *contra metrum*, or Eudoxus), the subtle play thus introduced by Virgil is of interest: by means of his suggestion that Menalcas has forgotten the name, he presents the shepherds as uneducated and at the same time he anticipates the riddles which the poem will set. Furthermore, the second astronomer is indicated by means of a periphrasis,[66] almost identical to that used by Callimachus at the beginning of his *Coma Berenices* (πάντα τὸν ἐν γραμμαῖσιν ἰδὼν ὅρον),[67] while 42 *tempora quae messor, quae curuus arator haberet* seems both to allude to the content of Aratus' work and in some way to foreshadow the *Georgics*. Damoetas responds (44ff.), describing *his* two cups, likewise Alcimedon's work, and apparently more sophisticated than Menalcas'. The frieze is of acanthus leaves and the character depicted is none other than Orpheus, symbol of song, at whose miracles the text hints.

The comparison between Virgil and his model leads us to the discovery both of a lesser ability and interest in realistic description but likewise of myriad networks of references and meanings which go far beyond those in Theocritus' text. Furthermore, in *Buc.*3, as elsewhere, we find contamination of various models, both Theocritean and attributed. The description of the cups points to Theocr.1, while the beginning of *Buc.*3 takes up Theocr.4.1–3 Damoetas is the name of the shepherd who competes with Daphnis in Theocr.6; Menalcas appears in the 'spurious' Theocr.8 and 9. From this we gather that for Virgil the corpus of Theocritus, whatever its form, was a single text of reference: to imitate it was, as Virgil says in the opening of *Buc.*6, to declare adhesion to the genre of bucolic. The special relationship to Theocritus naturally does not exclude others, whether to bucolic texts or not. Above all, Moschus, with at least two significant references,[68] and Bion (with at least three),[69] but we should not exclude other unattributed Hellenistic bucolic texts, like the apocryphal

---

[66] V. 41 *descripsit radio totum qui gentibus orbem.*

[67] Cf. A.C. Cassio, *RFil* 101 (1973), 329ff.

[68] *EV* s.v. *Mosco* (Perutelli).

[69] Bion fr.2.17 imitated at *Buc.*3.56; Bion, *Adonis* 32ff. at *Buc.*3.56; the *formosus...
Adonis* of 10.18 imitates the καλὸς Ἄδωνις of the refrain of the *Epitaphium.*

poems in the Theocritean corpus and others such as the *Epitaphion Bionis*. All these texts were complementary to Virgil's relationship with Theocritus: in the texture of the *liber*, reference to the bucolic genre was fundamental precisely because Virgil was the first at Rome to write such poetry.

This need to proclaim adhesion to the genre affects the imitative technique of the whole *liber*, which, overall, displays much less in the way of imitations, allusions and reminiscences of the Latin poetic tradition. References to archaic Latin are decidedly scattered and sporadic: cf. *Buc*.3.47 *numquam hodie effugies: ueniam, quocumque uocaris*; as Macr. (6.1.38) tells us, this evokes (parodically, to be sure), Naev. *trag*.15R(ed. 3) *numquam hodie effugies quin mea moriaris manu*. Cases such as this may lead to the conclusion that Virgil in his paratragic vein was sometimes influenced by comedy.[70] As we shall see, he derives elements of style and also features of content from comedy, while it is hard to trace precise references. On the other hand, the colloquialisms which *Buc*. share with comedy must also take us back to Latin neoteric poetry, which envisaged the contribution of comedy in the formation of a new poetic language.

Most of the imitations and of those learned plays which allude to Latin poetry refer back to the verse of the Caesarian period, hardly a generation ago. To give an idea of the range, I offer a few examples:

Servius tells us that the apostrophe to Pasiphae at *Buc*.6.47 *a, uirgo infelix* comes from Licinius Calvus' epyllion, *Io* (fr.9 Morel). All the passage that follows, above all from the repeated apostrophe at 52, *a, uirgo infelix, tu nunc in montibus erras* on, suggests aimless wandering, a traditional motif attached particularly to the figure of Io. The 'play' will probably have lain in the transfer to the story of Pasiphae of hints from Calvus' poem.[71]

Calvus' influence has not always been fully recognised by scholars, while that of Catullus has been stressed, particularly in the acclaim paid to the New Age in the 4th. eclogue. Whatever the meaning of this most problematic poem,[72] the hint comes from the prophecy made by the Parcae at the wedding of Peleus and Thetis in Catullus

---

[70] La Penna in *Bucoliche* (n. 15), 144.

[71] Cf. R. Thomas, *CP* 74 (1979), 337ff., V. Tandoi, *EV* 1, 624.

[72] Pre-eminent, for its survey of the problem and for the distinctions it draws between Roman and oriental elements, R.G.M. Nisbet, *BICS* 25 (1978), 59ff. Further updating in J. Van Sickle, *A reading of Virgil's Messianic Eclogue* (diss. Harvard, repr. New York 1992). See now Clausen, 119–29.

64. Among the few points on which an almost unanimous agreement has been reached among interpreters is that the poem is at once a reworking and a reversal of Catullus' epyllion: this ended with a pessimistic vision of the spread of vices and crimes in the world after the gods' departure, while *Buc*.4 advances the rise of a new age of gold: the detailed references make the relationship almost too obvious.

Virgil drew close to Calvus and Catullus by poetic temperament, by kinship of taste and above all because he was himself at the outset a neoteric poet, though later by a generation. The place of Lucretius amid his *auctores* was from the beginning different and more arguable: specific references to his poem are quite numerous, starting from 1.2, where for the first time (cf. also 2.34, 10.25f.) the hint of Lucr.4.580 is taken in (belief in rustic deities subjected to rationalist criticism; it is due to echo-effects alone). Just as in Catullus' case, a model is used so as to invert its content and ideological line. Lucretius too is employed in *Buc*.4. (40f.): here again an inversion of rationalistic pessimism occurs. It is important that we take note of Virgil's antiphrastic relationship to his immediate predecessors: to begin with, no more than the construction of a conventional imaginary world (like that of bucolic) as an alternative to Lucretius' and Catullus' pessimism; steadily, Virgil's poetry improves and develops its own content, which becomes the voice of the new age.

Bucolic characters

Our statistical basis for evaluating the role and the character of the individual figures in the *Buc*. comes from lists drawn up ca. 1900. Wendel analysed the relationship with Theocritus, on the basis of Jahn's material.[73] Various modes of treatment emerge:[74] (i) in an imitation of Theocritus, the name present in the model is preserved Theocr.3.3f. = *Buc*.3.96, 5.12, 9.23f. (Tityrus); Theocr.4.2 = *Buc*.3.2. (Aegon); Theocr.9.2 = *Buc*.3.58 (Menalcas); (ii) instead of the name in the passage of Theocritus, Virgil uses another, but one which still belongs to Theocritus' onomasticon (nine instances); (iii) instead of the name in the passage imitated, Virgil uses one which does not

---

[73] Cf. n. 55, n. 75.
[74] Formulated by F. Michelazzo, *EV* 1, 570ff.; cf. Clausen, 33f.

belong to Theocritus' onomasticon (five instances). Overall, we note a tendency either to alter the model (rather than to reject it), or to work out elaborate plays of interchange, whereby, in place of Theocritean characters of the same name, there often appear in Virgil either characters differently named (but with the same personality), or characters similarly named (but with a different personality)! If we look away from Virgil's precise references to his model to the more general picture, he introduces by name in *Buc.*33 characters: 17 are present in the corpus of Theocritus; the other 16 may have been Virgilian coinages, even if they are Greek, according to a procedure already known in comedy and epigram. The old hypothesis that they came from Cornelius Gallus lacks, in most cases, any solid support.[75] Even if we restrict the field to the 13 characters who have a really active role in *Buc.* and are not merely named or brought on in bit parts, we get (proportionately) similar results: more than half[76] were already there in Theocritus. Alphesiboeus too is in essence Theocritean (cf. the Ἀλφεσιβοίας at Theocr.3.45), while the rest leave us amid hypotheses. With the exception of Daphnis, you do not get the same characters in more than two idylls of Theocritus, while in *Buc.* usage is much freer and reappearances obviously more numerous: Corydon, Menalcas and Meliboeus each appear as protagonists in two *eclogues*.

The decision on whether there is (or is not) coherence in the characterisation of individual figures within the *liber* is a problem largely misstated by critics, who, from antiquity on, have sought equivalences with real characters. But to leave aside for the moment this aspect of the problem, even if we read the text in a non-allegorical light, serious inconsistencies emerge. For example, in *Eclogue* 7 Corydon is called goatherd, and in 2 a Sicilian shepherd. Clearly, two separate characters, but is the homonymy accidental? Surely not, if we look generally at the similarity between the two delicate and sensitive figures, but a link also emerges specifically in the refined literary play of 7.37–40, where Corydon sings of his love for Galatea. This clearly takes up Theocr.11, model of *Eclogue* 2, where the other Corydon sings of his love for Alexis.[77] The characterisation of Amaryllis, mentioned in several poems, is more complex: she is represented as ready to anger both in 2.14 and in 3.81; further elements

---

[75] *RFil* 118 (1990), 267; Gallus: C. Wendel, *Jhb.kl.Phil.* Suppl. 26 (1901), 1ff.
[76] Corydon, Damoetas, Daphnis, Lycidas, Menalcas, Thyrsis, Tityrus.
[77] Coleman, 25.

'enrich' her, like her visual charms (1.5), her association with the
magical arts (8.77), her role as object of pastoral passions (2.52, 3.81,
9.22) and so on. Perhaps one of the richest and most varied pictures
of the collection, broken up into numerous brief allusions, which fit
together with marked credibility. It is the Meliboeus of *Eclogue* 1 who
reveals the most serious discrepancies: he seems to have no links
with the Meliboeus of 3.1 or 7.9; likewise the Daphnis of *Eclogue* 5
has little to do with the Daphnis apostrophised at 9.46ff. Faced by
such inconsistencies, critics waver between the extremes of a drastic
scepticism towards attempts at coherent characterisation[78] and of the
attempt to allow the various inconsistencies on the basis of the 'development' of the individual characters.[79]

However, Daphnis is the only bucolic character who, in keeping
with his Theocritean backgound, reveals, at least in *Buc.*5, a stature
of his own, markedly superior to that of the other shepherds and
one defined sharply by his apotheosis (5.57ff.). His role goes back to
an Indo-European cultural prototype, an inventor of new rites and
introducer of magical songs.[80] To this 'type', we may refer various
mythological figures, such as Gilgamesh in Mesopotamia, or Orpheus
and Dionysus himself in Greece. The references to Dionysus are very
striking, reaching virtual identity at 5.29ff.

For the rest, figures such as Meliboeus (1) or Menalcas (9) seem to
all effects Roman citizens, who undergo the consequences of those
events through which such citizens must pass. As happens with many
other kinds of characterisation, the name guarantees the conventions
of the bucolic genre, but behind the name there stands an individual
solidly inserted in the real Roman life of the period.

The social status of the characters, whether slaves or owners, is
not always made clear in the poems in which they appear. Some
have thought that status is recoverable in certain cases, where it might
have a certain dramatic importance, like Tityrus and Meliboeus (1)
or Corydon and Alexis (2). But in *Eclogue* 2 the 'references' to servile
status are pretty obscure and may easily be refuted.[81]

---

[78] Wendel (n. 75) already takes this position.
[79] E.g. E.A. Hahn, *TAPA* 75 (1944), 196ff.
[80] W. Berg, *Early Vergil* (London 1974), 15ff., Clausen, 151–3.
[81] Cf. the attack by R.G. Mayer, *CQ* 33 (1983), 298ff.

Countryside and setting

In Theocritus, not all the *Idylls* had the same geographical setting
(Sicily, Cos, etc.); so too in the *Buc.*, where mythological and pastoral
references are overlaid by apparent autobiography in often perplexing modes and variations. After Theocritus, Sicily appears (4.1, 6.1),
but only in *Eclogue* 2 is the island really the poem's setting. On the
other hand, the countryside round Mantua, the background of *Buc.*1
and 9 in particular, will have been associated with the poet's Mantuan
origin and with a legitimate and widespread wish to sing of his own
land. But Virgil, even when he introduces this new setting, repeats
what Theocritus does, in setting several idylls in his own homeland,
Sicily. Though the country round Mantua has likewise been subjected to a profound mutation into lyric terms, it is still, in the end,
tied essentially to an historic fact, the confiscations of land after the
battle of Philippi. Thus Virgil adds a new level of reference, beyond
Theocritus, that to historical events, which he transforms into a source
of pathos. The confiscations of land introduce and explain suffering,
sorrow and the sense of an end which in Theocritus' pastoral world
was only aroused by the natural cycle of life and death. If, as seems
likely, *Buc.*1, 9 (and 7 too) are not among the first to have been
written (cf. 30), we may think of an extension of the bucolic landscape in a late phase of composition, though the addition of the
countryside round Mantua.

From *Buc.*4.58ff. on, Virgil refers to Arcadia, a region not named
in the Greek bucolic poets; some have thought Arcadia a Virgilian
innovation, while others claim to have found its origins.[82] In particular, discussion turns on an epigram of Erucius,[83] where the shepherds Glaucus and Corydon are called Ἀρκάδες ἀμφότεροι, calque of
Arcades ambo at *Buc.*7.4. Erucius was a contemporary of Virgil and
though in the past different views were offered, there is now a definite
inclination to the conclusion that the epigrammatist imitated *Buc.*7.[84]
From various Greek sources, notably Plb.4.20f. (cf. n. 44), we gather

---

[82] The two positions, after Reitzenstein (n. 46), 121, who believed in a debt to
epigram prior to Theocr., have been maintained above all by B. Snell; (against
Snell, cf. now R. Jenkyns, *JRS* 79 (1989), 26ff.) *Discovery of the Mind* (various eds.) ch.
13 (Virgilian invention) and G. Jachmann, *Maia* 5 (1952), 161ff. (debt towards post-
Theocritean bucolic poetry). Cf. also Clausen xxvi–xxx.

[83] *AP* 6.96.

[84] Cf. R. Keydell, *Kl.P.*2.365, after C. Cichorius, *Röm.Studien* (Leipzig 1922), 304ff.;
cf. G.W. Williams, *Change and Decline* (Berkeley 1978), 125f.

that, historically, Arcadia was a land of primitive shepherds, set apart in isolation from the rest of Greece. It was, moreover, in traditional mythology, the home of Hermes, inventor of the lyre and of the pipes, and in some texts the father of Pan. The myth of Arethusa, who, in flight from Alpheus, an Arcadian river, was changed by Artemis into a spring in Sicily, hints at a link between the two regions. Virgil will have invented or taken up the localisation in Arcadia, putting together various elements derived from both history and myth. However, prior to *Eclogue* 10, the references are not precise:[85] at 4.58 Arcadia is named home of Pan; at 8.17ff. Damon's song seems situated in Arcadia, but the description of the landscape is rather vague and only in *Buc.*10 do the references become striking. In *Buc.*7, the presence of two Arcadian shepherds who sing beside the Mincio (13) offers an idea of how mythical a character Virgil gives this land. Whence various interpretations of Arcadia, not only those of the critics of Virgil, but above all those of all later literature. What has emerged ever more clearly is the link of this geographical indication with Gallus, to the point that it is thought to be almost a metaphor for the poetry of Gallus and Virgil.[86]

The bucolic landscape is therefore an ideal one, freed from precise references in place and time; here hints drawn from various traditions and moments converge. That we have no longer to do with the realistic landscape of Theocritus emerges from several clear contradictions in the text.[87] The words used by Meliboeus at 1.47ff. to describe Tityrus' farm seem in open conflict with what follows shortly (51–8). First a realistic description, then a sort of idealisation of the same spot, according to the scheme of the *locus amoenus*. Similar contrasts in *Buc.*2, where Corydon describes (46 55) the gifts of flowers and fruit which the nymphs will carry to Alexis if he deigns to frequent their *sordida rura*. In reality, the various gifts cannot coexist at the same season and the ensemble is therefore product of a free imagination, unfettered by reference to a real countryside. Yet Virgil shows an apparently contradictory tendency—that of augmenting the realistic details offered by Theocritus' text. A whole string of such details turns out to be altogether new, even in cases where the reference to Theocritus is very close. Thus the insistence on the dan-

---

[85] Cf. Coleman, 22.
[86] D.F. Kennedy, *Hermath.*143 (1987), 47ff.
[87] Coleman, 23.

gers which the kids run in the river at 3.94ff.; the references to the market at 1.34f.; some details of cattle-raising, like the mating of the bull (1.45). These observations do not alter our picture of the Virgilian landscape and its idealisation as a whole, but show rather that Virgil imitates his model even in seeking out more precise details, in the description of pastoral *realia*. To fill them out, it was also opportune to introduce explicit references of a specifically Italian character—Ambarvalia (3.76f.), Pales (5.35), Silvanus (10.94), etc.—and they tend, from *Buc.* on to introduce that Italian element which will return as almost an ideological feature in the whole of Virgil's poetry.

Language

There is a fundamental question of language in our study of *Buc.*, raised by Virgil's striving after, if not realism proper, then an impression thereof; that requires a study of the shepherds' language and proper attention paid to their *rusticitas*. Theocritus' task was easier: he could make use of the Doric dialect, already well-tried in the Greek poetic tradition. But there were no Latin literary dialects, and Virgil sometimes met the challenge by means of spoken language (cf. 237–9) or rustic terminology. Sometimes, but not always, because elsewhere the shepherds use a rather more elevated language: the level varies from poem to poem. Thus in language, as in pastoral setting, we encounter tendencies both to realism and to idealisation, alike features of the *liber* as a whole.

In his pursuit of the 'realistic' solution, Virgil appears to follow the line of neoteric poetry. In the list of words which appear only in *Buc.* and not thereafter in Virgil's opus[88] we may easily distinguish (i) technical terms, (ii) expressions from spoken language, and (iii) a number of diminutives, typical of affectionate colloquial usage. If we consider these three groups, the obvious relevance of the first we may take for granted, while (ii) and (iii) correspond precisely to the stylistic texture characteristic of neoteric poetry.[89]

Latinists have tried to overvalue single aspects so as to apply an

---

[88] Cf. the list at *EV* 1.572 (Cupaiuolo).
[89] The fullest treatment of neoteric style is still A. Ronconi, *Studi catulliani* (ed. 2, Brescia 1971).

exaggerated assessment to the book as a whole. Thus J. Hubaux,[90] starting from the vulgar adj. *cuius* (3.1 = 5.87) and from a few other vulgarisms, played up the realism of the shepherds' language. But over all it is far more varied and the few vulgarisms and archaisms fit in with the experiments and innovations of the tradition of neoteric poetry. So too the use of Grecisms,[91] particularly justified by the special relationship with Theocritus: the Greek element is most clearly visible in the frequent use of Greek names and words. Proper names[92] have Greek endings in *-os* in the nom. sing. (*Hesperos*, *Tmaros*, etc.), masculines in *-as* and fem. in *-e*, voc. sing. masc. and fem. ending in a vowel (*Alexi*, *Amarylli*, *Damoeta*, etc.), acc. sing. masc. and fem. in both *-n* (*Alexin*, *Daphnin*, *Alcippen*, etc.) and *-a* (*Nerea*, *Orphea*, *Pana*, *Phyllida*, etc.), gen. sing. in *-os* (*Amaryllidos*, etc.), dat. sing. in *-i* (*Orphei*), acc. plur. fem. of 3rd. decl. in *-as* (*Dryadas*).

The question of nom. and voc. plur. in *-es* (short e) is rather more tricky: metrical necessity has been adduced, for only so can *Arcades*, *Libethrides*, *Naides*, *Proetides* be introduced into the hexameter. The same ending in an ordinary noun, *grypes* (8.27), when there is no question of metrical necessity, shows that the choice is essentially a stylistic one.[93]

More problematic are the cases in which Greek forms of proper names no longer appear in the tradition and editors are divided between preserving the Latin form, and normalising, in the Greek form (e.g. 3.81 *Amaryllidis/-os*, 6.30 *Ismarus/os*).[94]

Moreover, in the case of masc. nouns of Greek origin, the acc. plur. ending in *-as* (*crateras*, *delphinas*, etc.) has been preserved. But we note a marked Hellenizing *color* in well-known verses such as 2.24 *Amphion Dircaeus in Actaeo Aracyntho*, an apparent transliteration of a Greek verse, with Greek rules of metre and prosody. At the same time, the verse, though spoken by the shepherd Corydon, corresponds, on account of its numerous mythological and geographical references, to the most learned Alexandrian poetic usage: proof that in the matter of linguistic choice, realism rubs shoulders with artifice.[95]

To go beyond these blatant cases, there are imitations of Theocritus which, without display of lexical or morphological Grecisms, reveal

---

[90] *Le réalisme dans les Bucoliques de Virgile* (Liège 1927), 98ff.
[91] So already Macr.5.17.19.
[92] Vd. infra.
[93] Cf. Cupaiuolo (n. 88), 574.
[94] See most recently Coleman, 39, in favour of normalisation (against previous editors).
[95] Vd. supra 47f.

stark Grecisms of syntax and a sort of trans-lingual slide in verbal usage, like that demonstrated by Timpanaro at *Buc.*8.41 where *ut uidi, ut perii* renders Theocr.2.82 χὼς ἴδον, ὡς ἐμάνην, forcing the use of the second *ut* in a correlative sense.[96]

A solidly established feature of Theocritus' language is verbal repetition. From the simple *a Corydon, Corydon* (2.69), imitating Theocr.11.72 ὦ Κύκλωψ, Κύκλωψ, we pass to more complex instances, where (e.g.) the repetitions involve first and fifth feet (e.g. 1.74 *ite meae, felix quondam pecus, ite capellae*, after the repetition present in e.g. Theocr.1.64 ἄρχετε βουκολικᾶς, Μοῖσαι φίλαι, ἄρχετ' ἀοιδᾶς), or where there is epanalepsis of the subject in first and fifth feet (though that is not an exclusively bucolic phenomenon). Finally we reach rather more complex sequences, familiar not only in bucolic, but in Alexandrian poetry in general.[97] Thus cf. Theocr.1.4ff. αἴ κα τῆνος ἕλῃ κεραὸν τράγον, αἶγα τὺ λαψῇ / αἴ κα δ᾽ αἶγα λάβῃ τῆνος γέρας, ἐς τε καταρρεῖ / ἁ χίμαρος· χιμάρω δὲ καλὸν κρέας, ἔστε κ᾽ἀμέλξῃς, and Call. *H.Apoll.* 29ff.; the Virgilian equivalent appears in a short account of Medea's guilt (8.48ff.): *crudelis tu quoque, mater./crudelis mater magis, an puer improbus ille?/improbus ille puer; crudelis tu quoque mater.* Further research on word-order can likewise point to the Greek model's influence. Thus the exact correspondence at 7.61ff. between the competitors' sets of four is not just a matter of general structure, but goes further into detail:

> Corydon: **populus** *Alcidae gratissima,* **uitis** *Iaccho,/formosae* **myrtus** *Ueneri, sua* **laurea** *Phoebo./Phyllis amat corylos: illas dum Phyllis amabit,/nec* **myrtus** *uincet* **corylos,** *nec* **laurea** *Phoebi.*
> Thyrsis: **fraxinus** *in siluis pulcherrima,* **pinus** *in hortis,/***populus** *in fluuiis,* **abies** *in montibus altis/saepius at si me, Lycida formose, reuisas,/* **fraxinus** *in siluis cedat tibi,* **pinus** *in hortis.*

A similar careful patterning is to be found at e.g. (Theocr.) 8.41ff.

> παντᾷ ἔαρ, παντᾷ δὲ νομοί, παντᾷ δὲ γάλακτος / οὔθατα πιδῶσιν κὰι τὰ νέα τράφεται/ἔνθα καλὰ Ναὶς ἐπινίσσεται· αἰ δ᾽ἂν ἀφέρπῃ / χὼ τὰς βῶς βόσκων χαὶ βόες αὐότεροι.

Even though it is probably exaggerated always to try to attribute this sort of stylistic refinement to Virgil's model,[98] when there already existed marked traces in neoteric poetry. More Virgilian is the intro-

---

[96] S. Timpanaro, *Contributi di filologia* (Roma 1978), 219ff.
[97] R.G.M. Nisbet, *PVS* 20 (1991), 3ff.
[98] Id., 5ff.

duction of those shadings of sense which create minor but visible semantic variations between repeated words.[99]

Still on word order, certain recurrent features have been noted. The sequence *raucae, tua cura, palumbes* (1.57), was first defined *schema Cornelianum*, from its alleged origin in Cornelius Gallus;[100] it was then fortunately assigned to a poetic ancestry which reaches back to early Greek lyric![101] The placing of the vocative in *Buc.* has been noted as particularly mannered, or refined, so as to obtain, from time to time, special effects: e.g. 6.10f. *te, nostrae, Uare, myricae,/ te nemus omne canet*),[102] a mannerism, which, however, seems to go back to neoteric poetry.

Some syntactical features too have been attributed to Greek influence,[103] such as the use of plain infinitive in place of the usual more complex constructions (1.55 *suadebit inire*, 5.9 *certet. . .superare*, etc.); the use of *certare* with dat., calque of μάχεσθαι, infinitive dependent on adjective (5.1f. *boni. . ./tu calamos inflare leuis, ego dicere uersus* etc.), accusative of respect, etc. Even more, however, than in the case of verbal repetitions, these features of syntax should make us think not of the direct stylistic influence of Theocritus but of tendencies already well-developed in neoteric poetry.

The other aspect which work on *Buc.* has sometimes stressed is colloquialisms, found above all in Virgil's choice of words: thus, apart from *cuius* already noted, cf. *magis* = *potius* (1.11), *da* = *dic* (1.18); some paired adverbs such as 3.49 *numquam hodie*, 9.7 *certe equidem*. Other instances are less clear-cut: 9.16 *hic* is probably nom. sing., a usage both colloquial (Plaut., Ter.) and grecising (cf. ὅδε).

Some colloquialisms of form are more uncertain: e.g. 3.102 *his* = *hi*, which is at least supported by Ael. Donatus (on Ter. *Eun.*269), though another interpretation of the line is possible;[104] or 5.36 *hordea*, used as plural, not singular, a barbarism, by ancient definitions,[105] but metrically most convenient.

The vulgar spelling of various words is well-attested in the ms. tradition,[106] but over all there is not evidence enough to introduce

---

[99] H. Offermann, *GB* 3 (1975), 275ff.
[100] O. Skutsch, *RhM* 99 (1956), 198f.
[101] By J. Solodow, *HSCP* 90 (1986), 129ff.
[102] By A. La Penna, in *Mnemosynum: studi. . .A. Ghiselli* (Bologna 1988), 338f.
[103] Cupaiuolo (n. 88), 574.
[104] With the following punctuation: *his certe neque amor caussa est; uix ossibus haerent*, in which case, *neque* is still to be understood as *non* (archaic usage): cf. Coleman, 124f.
[105] Quint.1.5.16. Cf. also Clausen, index, s.v. *Colloquialisms*.
[106] Coleman, 40.

them into the text. Colloquialisms of syntax are likewise doubtful. They almost always coincide with grecisms. In any case, the omission of the verb at 3.7–9, 25, the lively parataxis of 28–30, 32–4, the aposiopesis of 40, the use of expressions such as *si quid habes* (52), *quamuis* + indic. (84), *parco* + infin. (94), etc. make *Buc*.3 the poem richest in colloquialisms (but cf. 237–9 on 9.56ff.); to be sure, they do accompany one of Virgil's rare moments of comedy.[107] This is perhaps the clearest sign of stylistic differentiation within the collection.

Metre and prosody

For Virgil, the hexameter is an inescapable choice, bound as it is to the bucolic genre. In Theocritus, or at least (cf. 38) in Virgil's Theocritus, the choice was not quite as clear, in as much as in the *agon* of *Id*.8 there appears a sequence of elegiac couplets.[108] In Alexandrian poetry, the fact was not specially significant: the metres were interchangeable, as the use of both in Call. *Hymns* shows. But Virgil, imitating precisely (Theocr.) 8.41–8 at *Buc*.7.53ff., naturally renders the whole in hexameters, thus showing he views his model's metre as almost a mistake.[109]

Servius[110] saw clearly the main divergences from Theocritus in the structure of Virgil's bucolic hexameter. According to what Aelius Donatus had laid down, the bucolic hexameter required a pause after the (preferably dactylic) fourth foot (the so-called bucolic diaeresis), but the first foot too should be dactylic. But if we go back to Servius' probable source, Donatus,[111] it is also early laid down that (i) the first foot should coincide with the end of a part of speech, (ii) the third trochee should coincide with a caesura, and (iii) the fourth foot should coincide with the end of a part or speech, while the 5th. and 6th. feet should constitute a self-contained group of words. Donatus adds directly that Theocritus *saepe* observes these rules, while Virgil more often neglects them. These statements have been checked statistically[112]

---

[107] La Penna (n. 15), 161f.

[108] Verses 33–60.

[109] F. Jacoby, *RhM* 65 (1910), 69, n. 1. Cf. also Clausen, index, s.v. *Metre and Prosody*.

[110] *Praef.*, 3.1.2, 5ff. Th.-H.

[111] Don. *Praef. ad Buc*.343

[112] E.A. Schmidt (n. 46), 45, n. 137.

and they are correct enough. In the first 100 lines of his corpus, Theocritus observes the first rule 37 times (25 in Virgil), the second 49 (17 in V.), the third 78 (18 in V.).

Virgil is also freer,[113] as Cat.64 had been, in respect of another rule of Alexandrian poetry, 'Hermann's bridge': when the fourth foot is a dactyl, the two shorts should be separate (as in 3.8 *transuersa tuentibus*). He treats other 'rules' similarly. Thus 'Fraenkel's law' (in a verse without pause at $1\frac{1}{2}$, a word that begins at ltr. must end at $2\frac{1}{2}$, 6.1 *prima Syracosio*) is often violated, from 1.31 *namque, fatebor enim* on (Cupaiuolo l.c.). As a whole, we see that Virgil, while remaining within the wider context of Alexandrian technique, is subject to the general tendency of Latin metre towards greater freedom, by comparison with Greek.

Signs of an attempt to create a more regular hexameter, freed from certain Alexandrian features, may also be noted. The clearest case is the presence of only three fifth-foot spondees. But, rare though they are, there are monosyllables at line-end without obvious emotive intent, as there will be, under Ennian influence, in the *Aeneid*.

An examination of the movement of the Virgilian bucolic hexameter in comparison with that of his closest contemporaries[114] led to the conclusion that the rhythm is quite distinct from that of Lucretius and Catullus 64, but closer to that of Cicero's *Aratea*. Of the sixteen possible combinations of dactyl and spondee in the first four feet of the hexameter, *Buc.* display ten metrical patterns, clearly more numerous than Catullus (6), the same as Lucretius (10) and hardly less frequent than Cicero (11). The detailed comparison of these samples allows us to establish the nature of the new musicality of Virgil's line, which eliminates a certain weightiness present in his predecessors in particular, the molossic word (three long syllables) after $2\frac{1}{2}$ caes. is eliminated: 4 cases in Lucretius, 9 in Catullus, only two in Cicero, both proper names.[115] These figures lead us to the conclusion that the hexameter of the *Buc.* is far more innovative than Catullus'.

Elision (a regrettable and improper term; called 'synaloepha' by all serious students of the subject), as is well-known, is used in *Buc.* rather less than in Virgil's other works 234f. with, predictably, the effect of a smoother and cleaner movement of the verse.[116] Polysyl-

---

[113] Examples in Cupaiuolo (n. 88), 575.
[114] G.E. Duckworth, *Vergil and classical hexameter poetry* (Ann Arbor 1969), 46ff.
[115] Coleman, 148.
[116] Cupaiuolo (n. 88), 575.

labic words ending with a long vowel in hiatus are rare: apparently a Grecism, as 2.24 *Actaeo Aracyntho* shows. A single case or a short vowel not *in arsi* in hiatus before the principal caesura occurs in a metrically exceptional verse (2.53).[117] Elsewhere, there is hiatus with the vowel shortened and with monosyllabic words (2.65, 8.108), or to introduce, in the Alexandrian manner, a prosodical variation in a repeated word (3.79, 6.44).[118]

The so-called lengthening *in arsi* of final syllables is to be thought of as an archaism, certainly so in the case of 3rd. person singular verbal endings (1.38 *aberat*, 3.97 *erit*), where the original quantity of the vowel reappears, as in (10.69) *Amor*. The prosodic explanation of *puer* is less clear (9.66): we should perhaps think or an archaic form **puerr*.[119] The lengthening of the first *–que* at 4.51 *terrasque tractusque maris* involves two phenomena: (i) the common variation of quantity in. . .τε. . .τε and (ii) the syllable closed after mute and liquid for metrical convenience, according to Latin poetic usage (cf. 4.5 *integro*).[120] There is synizesis of Greek endings (e.g. 6.30 *Orphea*); the contraction of forms such as *deerrauerat* (7.7) is normal in poetry.

Narrative and dramatic structure

In his note on *Buc*.3.1 Servius recalls the Platonic distinction between three *characteres. . .dicendi* on the basis of the room conceded in the text to the narrator's voice: (i) that in which only the narrator speaks; (ii) the dramatic, in which only characters introduced speak and (iii) the mixed, with both the narrator and characters introduced speaking. Servius hastens to specify that in *Buc.*, all three types occur.[121] This is, of course, a feature which Virgil derives from his model Theocritus, and it corresponds perfectly to the Alexandrian tendency to ποικιλία, variety. But Virgil displays a number of significant variations from his model. In particular, Virgil shows himself concerned to introduce the monologue (2, 6, 8) with a kind of prologue,

---

[117] Coleman, 103.

[118] In this verse of Greek flavour (*clamassent, ut litus 'Hyla Hyla' omne sonaret* the first *Hyla*, with long final vowel, is in hiatus; in the second, hiatus again, but short vowel.

[119] Discussion in Coleman 272.

[120] Coleman, 146.

[121] Cf. too Serv.Dan. *ad Buc*.6.1 and 9.1; Ps.Prob.3.2.329.10ff. Th.-H., Diom. *Gramm.Lat*.1.482.14ff.

while *Buc.*1, 3, 5, 7 and 9, where dialogue dominates, open pretty much directly. It has been shown in detail[122] that Virgil adopts large-scale innovations: for example, he declines to follow Theocritus' direct introduction of the shepherd's lament in *Id.*3 or the use of the narrative 'I' as a linking element in a largely dramatic poem, like *Id.*7. The markedly dramatic form of *Buc.* is to be interpreted in the context—already extant in Virgil's time—of their dramatic performance.[123]

Dominant motifs

Once it was agreed that the point of the *liber* was not the realistic description of the pastoral world, research turned to the true key motifs and to the nature of the collection's main theme. On the basis of references in the text (notably 6.31ff.) and of (e.g.) the 're-construction of Virgil's spiritual biography' (for the Epicurean element in his Neapolitan young manhood, cf. 7f.), the presence of Epicurean doctrine was proposed. Such doctrine would be quite compatible with Tityrus' choice of an almost contemplative life in 1 or with the exaltation of the rustic world's tranquillity in 2.[124] However, traces of a real choice of Epicureanism appear too rarely in the work as a whole; theirs is not a widespread presence and they are negated by the many references to the divine, present in a variety of forms.

Philosophy aside, love has been proposed as the guiding thread of the whole collection, still present in the last *ecloga*, dedicated to Gallus.[125] But the theme of love, though more widespread and persistent than that of Epicureanism (and recognised explicitly in the ancient world, 250), has on occasion only a marginal role, one secondary by comparison with an ideal of pastoral life, which seems quite distinct from it.

That brings us to the view that what really matters about the bucolic content is the characters' apparently remarkable privilege—of song![126]

---

[122] Schmidt (n. 62), 45–57.

[123] G. Rosati, *EV* 2.63f. The dramatic side of *Buc.* is emphasized above all by P. Steinmetz, *AuA* 14 (1968), 115–25. Cf. 249 for actual performances.

[124] Coleiro (n. 30) 37ff., A. Traina *AR* 10 (1965), 72–8 = *Poeti latini* 1 (Ed. 2 Bologna 1986), 163–74.

[125] Coleiro (n. 30), 34ff.

[126] The basic assumption of E.A. Schmidt's book (n. 62).

Daphnis, most famous of the shepherds, is exalted as sublime singer, to the point of apotheosis. Song is represented and ennobled in almost all the poems of the *liber*. And song, discussed in *Buc.*6 and 10, even reaches a metapoetic dimension. In the case of 6, Virgil, by the exclusion both of high epic poetry—there is an explicit *recusatio*[127]— and of love poetry (too 'low'),[128] probably expresses his choice of a middle ground.

Though the complex problems of interpretation raised by this poem still leave room for some element of doubt, what is certain is that the discussion of poetic theory here and in 10 involves Gallus directly. Certainly the dialogue with a poet friend derives from the neoteric custom, above all when questions of poetic theory are raised, of referring to other poets of the group,[129] with direct citations. Gallus' place in 6 and 10 evokes the characteristics of such gestures,[130] but the language and imagery is more veiled, in keeping with the idealisation of the pastoral world. For us, Gallus is complicated by much research and speculation: the man and the poetry are so often cited by Virgil, and we have lost them almost entirely, perhaps on account of the emperor's condemnation.[131] Hence the hunt for points of contact. Speculation reached a peak in the work of Franz Skutsch at the beginning of the century;[132] it was he above all that started off the passion for reconstructing bits of Gallus from the *Buc.* In particular he wished to explain the unexpected reference to Gallus in Silenus' lines[133] by the notion that the poetic themes listed up to line 63 had already been handled in Gallus' poetry. This thesis, already fully answered by Skutsch's contemporaries,[134] is to be rejected for a number of reasons—e.g., the resulting inconcinnity in the text as a whole and the unlikelihood that Gallus ever wrote *epyllia* of an Hesiodic character. Moreover, the recent discovery of the largest piece of Gallus that we have (ten rather mutilated lines on a papyrus)[135] has if anything

---

[127] *Buc.*6. vv. 3–5.

[128] Cf. most recently E. Courtney, *QUCC* 63 (1990), 99–112.

[129] 'Circle' is a most unhappy metaphor, P. White, *Promised Verse* (Cambridge Mass. 1993), 36ff.

[130] G. D'Anna, *EV* 1.895.

[131] R. Syme (n. 25), 309f., *Augustan Aristocracy* (Oxford 1986), 32.

[132] *Aus Vergils Frühzeit* (Leipzig 1901), *Gallus und Vergil* (Leipzig 1906).

[133] 64ff.: *tum canit errantem Permessi ad flumina Gallum.*

[134] E.g. R. Helm., *Woch.klass.Phil.*22 (1902), 204.

[135] Ed. princ., with commentary, R.D. Anderson, P.J. Parsons, R.G.M. Nisbet, *JRS* 69 (1979), 125ff. Note in particular the apparent echo of Gallus fr.4.2 *quae*

made Gallus into more of a problem. These lines, which mention Lycoris and include certain obscure historical references, are not terribly good.[136] The discussion is far from finished and Virgil scholars have had little joy of it.

The main point of *Ecl.*6 is that Virgil invites his friend to abandon elegiac poetry for higher, perhaps narrative, forms. Whether the invitation involves life as well as poetry is still very much an open question,[137] but we all know well that for the elegiac poet, by convention, life and poetry are reciprocally identifiable[138] and that means that the substance of Virgil's utterance must be about poetry.

Criticism of *Ecl.*10 is moving along similar lines;[139] 10 Virgil certainly wrote last and added to close his collection. Here the introduction of Gallus into the idealised world of Arcadia is even more explicit: a real, contemporary figure takes on, in the bucolic world a role and attitudes typical of traditional bucolic figures. Thus nature's lament for the poet's unhappy love (9ff.) certainly takes over nature's lament for Daphnis' death, described at Theocr.1.66ff., and already used at *Buc.*5.20ff. This bringing of the bucolic world into the actual present day is Virgil's boldest innovation. But about the new Daphnis, symbol of poetry and at the same time dying Arcadian victim, there is gathered the outline of a poetic discourse essential for Virgil's work. It is the love celebrated in his elegies that provokes Gallus' grief. For him to emerge from his tragic situation, his poetry must change genre; he must turn to bucolic and thus his suffering will be assuaged. If we read *Ecl.*10 as a discussion of poetry, it leads to the praises of bucolic as a model form.

---

possem domina deicere digna mea at *Buc.*10.2f. *sed quae legat ipsa Lycoris, cum domina carmina sunt dicenda.*

[136] [A remarkable accusation, that the lines are a forgery, was put forward by F. Brunhölzl, *Codices Manuscripti* 10 (1984), 33ff. Two of the editors I have known for nearly thirty years; the accusation is grotesque and tasteless. The hypothetical faker, if not Prof. Parsons himself, would be necessarily his superior in palaeography—and who, one might wonder, could that be? If the verses were faked, they would be more interesting and stylistically more exciting. Their mediocrity is the best guarantee of their authenticity: B. never realised how much more elegant is the writing of the best English Latinists. Cf. F. Graf *Gymn.*94 (1987), 177, and the valuable remarks of A.M. Morelli in *Disiecti membra poetae* ed. V. Tandoi 3 (Foggia 1988), 104–19. See now E. Courtney *Fragmentary Latin Poets* (1993), 259–68, R.G.M. Nisbet, *Coll. Papers* (Oxford 1995), 432. Ed.]

[137] D'Anna (n. 129), 894.

[138] A. La Penna, *L'integrazione difficile. Un profilo di Properzio* (Torino 1977), 33ff., 49ff.

[139] That Gallus' role is to be interpreted in metapoetic terms has been suggested

This metapoetic *sphragis* closes off the book and in all likelihood gives us a basic clue to the sense of the whole. Virgil's exaltation of his own bucolic poetry thus becomes a central theme of the book; it dominates the other themes, without crushing them.

The critics' uncertainty when it comes to identifying the continuing presence of key elements in the *Bucolics*' poetic character itself indicates deep inconsistencies and contradictions which mark all this first phase of Virgil's poetic production. The theme of Silenus' song in 6 certainly does not gybe with the proclamation of the new world's coming in 4; no more do Tityrus' satisfaction in 1 and the pessimism of 9 with respect to the land confiscations; in 5 Daphnis dies and attains apotheosis while at 9.46ff. he is addressed and bidden to pay attention to the arrival of the *Caesaris astrum*; that complicates yet further the allegorical interpretation of the figure of Daphnis in 5. Further examples might be adduced; over all, they tend to define the nature of the collection as a whole as neither single nor unified.[140]

The *Bucolics* are poems written independently from each other: though they hearken to the same literary genre and to some degree fulfil a structural role in the *liber* as a whole, each reflects distinct requirements, poetic stances, and contexts. These uncertainties and contradictions lead us to perceive, even through the somewhat clogged filter of the bucolic world, the swings in the period's public life in which no firm political situation had yet been established. We are also led to glimpse the poet's hesitations in setting his career under way and in effecting those choices which would be decisive for his poetry. Always through the pastoral transmutation, we perceive the poet's first uncertain steps towards the discovery of a poetic principle and of topics which are to develop far beyond the neoterics' range of choice. On the journey, still hesitant as it is, Virgil hits upon certain forms and values which seem for a moment to have won him over; then, in a later poem, a discussion which had seemed closed is re-opened. Despite the pursuit of structural effects in the *liber*, effects which Virgil sought at least at a late stage of composition, the *Bucolics* are revealed as a collection of poems and not as a strongly defined unit.

---

above all by G.B. Conte, *The rhetoric of imitation* (Ithaca 1986), 100ff., whose interpretation I follow here briefly. Cf. now Clausen, 288–92.

[140] Rightly emphasized by Otis (n. 37), 142f.

Allegorical interpretations

The concept of 'allegory' was already well-known to ancient commentators; it was derived from the Alexandrian interpreters of Homer, but, more to the point, was also applied to Theocritus: many (162 n. 4) believed that Simichidas concealed the poet himself. In his note on 1.1 Servius notes: *et hoco loco Tityri sub persona Vergilium debemus accipere; non tamen ubique, sed tantum ubi exigit ratio.* The basic elements of allegorical interpretation are thus laid down: autobiographical references to events in the poet's life and the irregular presence or such elements in the course of a whole poem.[141] On 2.1 Servius notes: *Corydonis in persona Vergilius intellegitur, Caesar Alexis in personis inducitur.* Under the *lemma* Alexis Servius introduces other allegorical interpretations: some say that Alexis is Alexander, a slave of Pollio, and Virgil's beloved, others that he is a slave of 'Caesar's', whose praises would have been much appreciated.

Discussion of *Buc.*5 is particularly warm; critics are still divided over the ancient interpretation, which saw in Daphnis the commemoration of Julius Caesar, deceased.[142] The poem's central position in the *liber* clearly assigns it pre-eminence, which might though be simply dictated by the praises of Daphnis as mythical shepherd and symbol of pastoral song. But Serv. on 5.20 (*alii dicunt. . .*) sees *extinctum. . .crudeli funere*[143] as referring to mourning for the dead Caesar.

On 6.13, Servius declares: *. . .quasi sub persona Sileni Sironem inducit loquentem, Chromin autem et Mnasylon se et Varum vult accipi.* That means a reference to the Epicurean school at Naples where Siro taught and Virgil and Varus were pupils (cf. 11; note Varus, not Varius; cf. *EV* s.v. *Alfeno Varo*). This interpretation has been followed and developed by various modern scholars, who have seen in the poem Virgil's thanks to Varus and Gallus for the recovery of his farm:[144] this produces a triple allegory, in which Chromis, Mnasyllos and Aegle correspond to Varus, Gallus and Virgil, all of whom are pupils at Siro's school(!).

---

[141] Systematic discussion, *EV* 1.105ff. (Della Corte); cf. 12f. for *Buc.*1 and 9; 162–7 for *Aen.* and allegory in the ancient commentaries.

[142] Summary of the *status quaestionis*, A. Salvatore in *Bucoliche* (n. 15), 215ff.

[143] Serv. ad loc.: *alii dicunt significari per allegoriam C. Iulium Caesarem, qui in senatu a Cassio et Bruto viginti tribus vulneribus interemptus est: unde et 'crudeli funere' volunt dictum.*

[144] E.g. D.E.W. Wormell, in *Virgil*, ed. D.R. Dudley (London 1969), 19, Coleiro (n. 34), 206.

Again, Servius on 7.21 reports the old interpretations of the figures in *Ecl.*7: *et multi volunt in hac ecloga esse allegoriam, ut Daphnis sit
Caesar, Corydon Vergilius, Thyrsis vero, qui vincitur, Vergilii obtrectator, scilicet
aut Bavius aut Anser aut Maevius poetae.* In this instance, modern critics
have not followed faithfully their ancient forbears, but have rather
concentrated on the definition of poetry enunciated by Corydon,
winner in the contest.

The usual identification of shepherds and historical figures is
offered—in the case of *Ecl.*8—by Philarg. on 8.1: *Damonis idest Cornificii.
Alphesiboei Virgilii. musam pro carmine posuit.* This time, little effect on
modern scholars.

The identifications proposed of the figures in *Ecl.*9 are rather
complex; most of them appear in Serv. and Serv.Dan. on 9.1: Moeris
becomes a *procurator* of Virgil who hastens to warn him of the dangers which menace him on account of the disputes caused by the
confiscations; Menalcas is identified with the poet himself, who is
warned of the danger.

In modern discussions the fullest range of reactions to the ancient
commentators' allegories has been contemplated. Some interpreters
have flung themselves into an unchecked contest to fix the correspondence between each and every bucolic character and an historical
personage,[145] but there are also those who maintain a position of
almost total scepticism; in between, various degrees of accord with
allegorical interpretation. In this context, Servius' first remark quoted
remains sensible: allegory does not always work: Virgil fills his poems with allusions that are always exceptionally subtle in reference
to the 'real world'. It is reasonable and inevitable to suppose that
when shepherds compete in song or discuss poetry there are references to poetry and to Virgil's own ideas—and that in some way,
and sometimes, an historic figure lies behind a bucolic character.
But it is altogether more difficult to suppose a real, full-scale allegory—that is, a mechanical correspondence of figures historical and
pastoral; that would be an entirely un-Virgilian procedure.

---

[145] On these lines, the fantasies of L. Herrmann, *Les masques et les visages dans les
Bucoliques de Virgile* (Bruxelles 1930) are unmatched.

The interpretation of the fourth Eclogue

This poem was of course the most famous of the collection, thanks above all to the Christianising interpretation, which, from Constantine on, saw in the birth of the *puer* a prefiguration of Christ's coming. Today, though the theory still finds occasional champions, attempts to identify the *puer* concentrate in other directions, and the attention of scholars in focused on Virgil's illustrious contemporaries and their offspring. A systematic list of proposals for the identification of the *puer* contains seven candidates.[146] Against each hypothesis it is easy to advance objections:

(i) A son of Pollio: Servius mentions two sons of Pollio, Saloninus and Asinius Gallus (cf. Syme (n. 25), 500, (n. 131), 132f. et passim); the latter was born in 41, too early for the probable date of the poem. Given the actual role of Pollio in the negotiations for the Peace of Brundisium, the reference would be out of proportion.

(ii) A son of Mark Antony. Or rather the twins, Alexander Helios and Alexandra Selene, born to Cleopatra. Were Virgil an Alexandrian court poet, this might work. But at Rome, this birth could only be seen as an outrage against Roman tradition (not to mention the rumours that Julius Caesar (Suet. *Caes.*79.3) had intended to transfer the capital to Alexandria or Troy).

(iii) A son to be born of the marriage between Antony and Octavia. Not the faintest hint at this marriage in the text; given that male offspring from this alliance seemed, on account of their age, unlikely and in fact did never materialise, such an allusion would have been imprudent. On a possible hint of Antony behind v. 17. cf. Clausen, 122.

(iv) A son to be born of the marriage between Octavian and Scribonia. Equally imprudent. They married in the summer of 40. Julia, of future ill fame, was their daughter and Octavian divorced directly after her birth.

(v) Marcellus, son of Octavia and Marcellus, her late husband: to be sung by Virgil at *Aen.*6.855ff. after he had been adopted by Augustus and had died prematurely. But he had no comparable importance ca. 40 B.C.

(vi) Augustus (so, the *Scholia Bernensia*). Unworkable, because the

---

[146] Coleman, 150ff., Clausen 126.

puer is not yet born; many of the *puer*'s attributes Augustus only acquires at a much later stage.

(vii) Christ. So first explicitly, Constantine[147] and St Augustine (*PL* 35.2089).[148] Augustine himself says that the Sibyl had likewise sung of Christ's coming (l.c.).[149]

Taken together, these difficulties lead us in the end to see in the *puer* not a real child, but rather a metaphor for the birth of a new era. Cf. e.g. Coleman, 152.

The interpretation of the prophecy is linked with a further problem—that of the relationship of *Ecl.*4 and Hor. *Epd.*16. The *Eclogue* is in all probability earlier.[150]

*Ecl.*4, despite a widely held opinion to the contrary, is not one of the most beautiful poems of the collection[151] and still divides the critics: at opposite extremes are those who want to hive it off completely from the western poetic tradition,[152] at the other those who cling to the eastern messianic view[153] long since propounded by Eduard Norden.[154]

Bibliography

Commentaries

R. Coleman (Cambridge 1977) has now been superseded, largely, by W. Clausen (Oxford 1994), but not even Clausen is magisterial, in the same sense as Mynors' *Georgics*. Coleman is still perhaps stronger on small questions of language; curiously, though, cf. 237–9: for this sort of minute stylistic commentary, neither Clausen nor Coleman proved very useful! E. Coleiro, *An introduction to Vergil's Bucolics with a critical edition of the text* (Amsterdam 1979) is a strange uncritical collection of information, sometimes of use.

---

[147] A. Wlosok in *2000 Jahre Vergil. Ein Symposion* (ed. V. Pöschl, Wiesbaden 1983), 68ff. = ead. *Res humanae-res divinae* (Heidelberg 1990), 444ff., Clausen 127f.

[148] H. Hagendahl, *Augustine and the Latin classics* 2 (Göteborg 1967), 442ff.

[149] Cf. the admirable synthesis by R.G.M. Nisbet (n. 72), which maintains the balance between East and West, and accounts soberly for analogies between poet and Isiah.

[150] Cf. N.M. Horsfall, *RFil* 119 (1991), 357 for a summary of the (very strong) case for Virgil's priority, by at least four years. S. Costanza, *Atti Acad.Pelor.Peric.* (1991); 147ff. reconsiders the issue at great length! Clausen 147–51 is not persuasive.

[151] So, explicitly, A. La Penna (n. 34), xxi.

[152] Cf. most recently W. Clausen in *Poetry and prophecy. The beginnings of a literary tradition* ed. J. Kugel (Ithaca 1990), 65–74.

[153] Cf. most recently L. Nicastri, *Vichiana* 18 (1989), 221–61.

[154] *Die Geburt des Kindes* (Leipzig 1924).

It would be easy to list several dozen recent books and articles on *Buc.*, but the notes *supra* indicate what the author finds most valuable. What follows is therefore kept to a minimum; inclusion in the notes, be it repeated, is a surer indication of approval.

Bibliography: W.W. Briggs, *ANRW* 2, 31.2, 1267–1357.

T. Fiore, *La poesia di Virgilio* (Bari 1930, 1944, 1946).

H.J. Rose, *The Eclogues of Vergil* (Berkeley 1942).

K. Büchner, *P. Vergilius Maro* in the reprint from PW VIII A, (Stuttgart 1959, etc.), 160–243.

F. Klingner, *Virgil. Bucolica, Georgica, Aeneis* (Zürich 1962).

F. Cupaiuolo, *Trama poetica delle Bucoliche di Virgilio* (Napoli 1969, etc.).

D.E.W. Wormell in *Virgil* ed. D.R. Dudley (London 1969), 1–26.

M.C.J. Putnam, *Virgil's pastoral art* (Princeton 1970).

B. Otis, *Virgil, a study in civilised poetry* (Oxford 1964), 97–143.

V. Pöschl, *Die Hirtendichtung Virgils* (Heidelberg 1964).

E.A. Schmidt, *Poetische Reflexion. Vergils Bukolik* (München 1972).

W. Berg, *Early Vergil* (London 1974).

E.W. Leach, *Vergil's Eclogues* (Ithaca 1974).

J. Van Sickle, *The design of Virgil's Bucolics* (Roma 1978).

Lecturae Vergilianae i, Le Bucoliche ed. M. Gigante (Napoli 1981).

CHAPTER THREE

GEORGICS*

N.M. Horsfall

The dating of G.

The question, important for Virgil's available sources, patronage and poetic development, raises some unexpectedly complex problems,[1] to some extent irresoluble. *Buc.* we have seen (28–31) belong to the years 42/1–39/8, nearly but not quite compatibly with the three years assigned to them by VSD and Serv. That leaves 20 (or 19) years until the poet's death: 7 for *G.* and 11 for *Aen.* (VSD and Serv.) Two or three years for recuperation? Or unexplained (cf. ch. 1, 13). This seeming inconsistency militates against the establishment of a firm absolute chronology.

We have four other chronological indications of importance:

(i) The appearance of Varr. *RR* in its author's 80th year (37/6). There is not much Varro, though, in *G.*1, apart from the prooemium (cf. 84), in any case perhaps later than the rest of the book (74, 99).

(ii) The Britanni of *G.*3.25:[2] the island is under marked Roman influence during this period, but we know of no real (far less, datable) invasion projects. Islands in the Ocean are anyway stock elements in Hellenistic ruler-panegyric.[3]

(iii) 1.509. Virgil is not a poet in whom precise references to real events can often be identified with confidence. Unfortunately, J. Bayet (*infra*) made a determined attempt to establish an early dating for this line: Ventidius' campaign against the Parthians (39/8) and Agrippa's in Germany. But the geographical names (Euphrates,

---

* For abbreviated titles of books of *G.*, cf. Bibliography, p. 91.
[1] Cf. also Horsfall in Biotti (1994), 14ff.
[2] Cf. R. Syme, *Roman Papers* 6 (Oxford 1991), 386, P.A. Brunt, *Roman imperial themes* (Oxford 1990). 103, 438, E. Gruen in *Between Republic and Empire* ed. K. Raaflaub and M. Toher (Berkeley 1990), 410.
[3] F. Christ, *Die röm. Weltherrschaft in der ant. Dichtung* (Stuttgart 1938), 52f., Verg. *G.*1.30, Vell.2.46.1 (with Woodman's note), Sen. *Ep.*119.8, Sen. *Suas.*l, *passim* (with the commentary of W.M. Edward), Nisbet-Hubbard on Hor. *C.*1.35.29f., Hor. *C.*3.5.2f., 4.14.47f., A.D. Momigliano, *JRS* 40 (1950), 39.

Germania) are typical and their polarity of a familiar type[4] Wilkinson
(159f.) makes an eloquent attempt to date 1.498–514 rather later
than the defeat of Sex. Pompeius in 36. But the marked lightening
of the heavy clouds of war which followed that campaign (cf. App.
*B.C.*5.132) is not visible in these lines, as far as I can see; they only
indicate (what we knew anyway from Hor. *Serm.*1.6.55) that Virgil
was an early follower of Maecenas (and, by implication, follower of
Octavian). Even if *G.*1.498ff. was as late as 36/5 (and I cannot see
why it should be), it could well be a late insertion in the book and
does not serve to date the whole. Of Virgil's movement away from
the (?) patronage of Pollio and from association with the other dedicatees of *Buc.*, we know nothing at all.[5]

(iv) The *sphragis* of the *G.* (4.559–66) is firmly datable to 30.[6] Cf.
appx. 1 (93f.) for a list of historical references in the whole text. There
are several references to events in the years 30–29; they serve only
to prove that Virgil added in the course of composition, as he is said
to have done in the *Aen.* too (but cf. 147f. on Marcellus). That is not
evidence for any sort of 'second edition'. Livy did the same, though
in his case the issue of a second edition of the first pentad is far
likelier.[7] We have, therefore, no precise internal indication, except
for the *terminus ante quem*, which we knew anyway (on VSD 27, cf.
ch. 1, 17). That, alas, leaves room for theory, or fantasy:

(1) J. Bayet wanted[8] to see Virgil begin *G.* the minute *Buc.* were
finished, in 39/8, before the publication of *RR.* The chief example
of Varronian imitation in the book is very striking (on the proem.,
cf. 99), but could so easily, as I have said, be a later addition.
There is indeed a marked lack of Varronian echoes in the book as
a whole,[9] but that is hardly significant, given how very little overlap
of subject matter there is between *G.*1 and *RR.* We are hardly at
liberty to think of the independent publication of *G.*1; it is simply
too short for a separate 'book', by the conventions of the time.[10] No
case, therefore, for a *Georgicon liber* or for some sort of ed. 1, prior to

---

[4] Cf. *G.*3.33 (see appx. 2 below), Christ (n. 3), 53ff., Thomas *ad loc.* on the literary reference in *Euphrates*.
  [5] P. White, *Promised Verse* (Cambridge, Mass., 1993), 45.
  [6] T. Rice Holmes, *Architect of the Roman Empire* 1 (Oxford 1928), 170f.
  [7] T.J. Luce, *TAPA* 96 (1965), 211ff.
  [8] *RPhil.*56 (1930), 128–50, 227–47, = *Mél. de litt. latine* (Roma 1967), 197–242.
  [9] *EV* 2.667.
  [10] Th. Birt, *Kritik u. Hermeneutik* (München 1913), 294.

RR. It seems, therefore, likely that part of *G.*1 is earlier than *RR* and part later.

(2) R. Martin[11] manages little better with his ed. of *G.*1–2. Granted that there is a strong closure of *G.*2 (458–end), granted that 3.40–1 marks a passage away from agri-culture, strictly speaking, granted too that on a very narrow interpretation (but cf. 97 below!), the *haud mollia iussa* of Maecenas appear to refer (though, clearly, in reality they do not) to the content of bk. 3 alone, does that add up to evidence for a real separation of the first two books? Certainly not, except on an erroneous view of the structure and subject matter of the whole[12] and on a misunderstanding (there are many!) of the proem. to *G.*3. Martin's further arguments, based on the pre-proem. to *Aen.* 1[13] are of no importance; those lines are most certainly not Virgilian. At least such hariolations have the merit of making us look more closely at the text; they do not have the power to seduce the relatively sane and sober. Thus chronology, both absolute and relative, leaves us perplexed and it remains to look a good deal more closely at the *G.* and their public, at public affairs and at the agriculture of the period.

Public, politics and agriculture

Discussion of the public of *G.* has long floundered[14] thanks to a failure to distinguish between an actual public (the intended readership) of educated men of letters,[15] well able to comprehend and evaluate the complex texture of *G.* and an imaginary audience of farmers of one sort or another, whom the poet treats in the Hesiodic tradition (cf. 78f.) as disposed to heed his instruction. This distinction you may find quite explicitly in the text: *omnia iam uulgata: quis aut Eurysthea durum/ aut inlaudati nescit Busiridis aras?* (3.4–5) Virgil is evidently talking about the learned reader, familiar with the subject-matter of centuries of mythological poetry. Not, as used once to be supposed, a public of veterans watching anxiously over their first crop of millet

---

[11] *EV* 2.666f.; cf. the bibliography at ib. 669.

[12] I note e.g. the perfect symmetry of the references to Maecenas (cf. Thomas on 1.2).

[13] L. Gamberale, *EV* s.v. *Preproemio*, id. *Studi. . .G. Monaco* (Palermo 1991), 963ff.; it has long been hard for a serious scholar to maintain belief in the authenticity of these verses; it is now surely impossible.

[14] R. Syme, *Roman Revolution* (Oxford 1939), 450, M.S. Spurr, *GR* 33 (1986), 182 = McAuslan, 87.

[15] This difficult poem was never very popular, Horsfall, *Atti*, 2.51f.

on their new allotments.[16] Some had indeed come originally from
the land, and some indeed truly knew well how to cultivate it.[17] Yet
it is grotesque to imagine scarred old soldiers battling with the complexities of Callimachean allusion. But the poem's imagined readership too reveals itself easily enough:[18] when Virgil writes (1.176) *possum
multa tibi ueterum praecepta referre* or (1.210) *exercete, uiri, tauros, serite hordea
campis*, who is envisaged, and what do we know about him (or indeed
her)?[19] There are two sides to the problem, one stylistic and one
agricultural:

Let us distinguish first (and I only do so in detail here because it
seems not to have been done!) those passsages where, as at 1.50
scindimus, the poet identifies with the farmer: a quite common stance
(cf. e.g. 1.204 *nobis*, 253 *possumus*, 351 *possemus*, 2.186 *solemus*, 249
discimus, 2.393f. *dicemus. . .feremus* 3.325 *carpamus*). These first-person
plurals are an extension of those few passages where the poet in-
structs in the first person, as agricultural preceptor: 3.295, *edico. . .*(300)
iubeo. . .(329) *iubebo*. Predictably, Virgil goes to great lengths to vary
the stilemes of instruction. Note:

(i) passages where Virgil distances himself from workers and work
alike by the description of farm operations in the third person:
2.74–7, 3.123–37, 158f., 446–8, the whole description of the plague
in Noricum, and perhaps most strikingly 4.295ff., instructions for the
bugonia.

(ii) those passages where he does the same thing in the 3rd. person singular, often after (e.g.) *si quis* (2.49, 105, 265, 3.141f., 453,
474, 4.6, 281) or as the subject of a jussive subjunctive (1.345, 2.54,
3.51, 188, 4.113ff.).

(iii) the use of impersonals, gerunds and gerundives (1.80, 160, 177,
313, 2.365, 371, 399, 419, 3.305, 4.8, 37, 267), the use of nouns
such as *tempus, cura, labor, studium, mos* (2.195, 397, 3.179, 224, 286,
288) and even of adjectives, as in the phrases (2.319) *optima satio* or
(1.373f.) *numquam imprudentibus imber/obfuit*.

---

[16] Heitland, 273, Syme (n. 1), 450f., J.E. Skydsgaard, *PCPS* Suppl. 6 (1980), 69f.,
E. Gabba, *Republican Rome: the army and the allies* (Oxford 1976), 47, P.A. Brunt, *Fall
of the Roman republic* (Oxford 1988), 272, L. Keppie, *Colonisation and veteran settlement*
(London 1983), 123, Wilkinson, 51.

[17] Cf. Varr. *RR* 3.16.10 and the fascinating *CIL* 11.600 from Forli.

[18] Though it is a pity that C. Perkell, *The poet's truth* (Berkeley 1989), 30 never
went into any sort of detail.

[19] Cf. *ILS* 7459, Hor. *C.*3.6.40, Colum.12.1.

That leaves us with those few passages where the verb is in the second person and Virgil specifies the subject:

1.100 *orate agricolae*
  210 *exercete uiri*
  343 *tibi*, on whom there depends a *pubes agrestis*.

At 1.299, the farmer of clearly Hesiodic inspiration takes his coat off and ploughs in person: *nudus ara, sere nudus*. None of the many second-person precepts[20] give us any help towards a more precise identification of the sort of farmer involved. We should look, therefore, first at the types of farm-staff that Virgil mentions, and, secondly, at the sort of farming that the poem envisages: Hesiod (*WD* ed. M.L. West, Oxford 1978, 33–40) lets Perses fade out of the *Erga*, so that second-person references in the second part of the poem are certainly not to the poet's brother; Virgil likewise does not have a unitary view of the work-force his text entails:[21] *colonus* (1.507, etc.; cf. Mynors on 1.299), *agricola* (1.317, etc.), *arator* (2.207, etc.), *putator* (2.28), *agitator aselli* (1.273), *pastor* (3.455, etc.), *messor* (1.316), *fossor* (2.264), *uiri* (1.210), *socii* (2.528), *puellae* (1.390); cf. the farmer's wife at 1.294, 2.524.

Some of these passages may refer to the *bonus agricola* in secondary or occasional roles, or to his slaves, or to poor free farmhands. We are slowly learning that the sharp distinction between free farmer and slave-gang is misleadingly simple: we should have recognised long ago, along with tenant-farmers such as Horace's Ofellus (*Serm.*2.2.133–5), who often paid with a share of their crop, the evidence for poor free (hired or seasonal) labour, labourers brought in by contractors, labourers working off debts, even poor free townspeople acquiring seasonal income.[22] In Virgil, the picture is predictably unclear: are the spinning *puellae* of 1.390 the farmer's daughters or are they slaves? The *fossor* of 2.264 Spurr (n. 14, at n. 46) asserts is a slave. But there is no reason why he must be. As Spurr himself points out, Columella (11.1.12) envisages an *optimus fossor* who could easily be a poor free specialist, working to hire. At 1.316f., the *agricola* directs the *messor*,

---

[20] 1.56, 63, 72ff., 100, 155ff., 167, 220, 221, 229, 267, 277, 299, 338, 343, 394, 425, 459—to give a sample of the material from one book.
[21] Cf. though Spurr (n. 14), n. 46 and Heitland, 227f.
[22] D. Flach, *Röm. Agrargeschichte* (München 1990), 157f., J.K. Evans, *AJAH* 5 (1980), 159ff., P.W. De Neeve, *Colonus* (Amsterdam 1984), 134f., Skydsgaard (n. 16), 65–72, P.D.A. Garnsey, *PCPS* 25 (1979), 4ff.; see e.g. Plin. *Ep.*9.37.3, 10.8.5, Varr. *RR* 1.17.2., Col.1.7.1, 3, Cato *Agr.*1.3, 2.6, 5.4, 14.1, 16.1, 21.5, 144.1ff., 145, 146.3.

at 2.230 'you' give orders for a pit to be dug, presumably by hired
fossores, at 2.529 *ipse*, on a holiday, has competitions for the *pecoris
magistri*. Virgil refers to the farmer's *pubes agrestis* at 1.343. Slaves,
then, or no slaves? On 1.286, *nona fugae melior* Mynors comments 'he
mentions slaves nowhere else' and that, if we are looking for explicit
references, is surely right.

We are even less clear than we were about the sort of farm that
Virgil envisages. Twice, Virgil hints at the existence of large estates
(2.412, 468), but no reader of *G.* would imagine that they are written about *latifundia*.[23] More interesting is the observation that some
of the farming operations described in *G.* are more appropriate to
the large holding—e.g. 2.177–258, on the varieties of soil a single
owner may encounter (Spurr (n. 14), 171f. = McAuslan, 76f.). So
too (Spurr 171 = 76) rotation of crops (1.71ff.), the use of plough-
oxen (1.43ff.), or oxen to pull wains of corn to bursting granaries
(1.49, 2.205f., 518); Spurr has done well to draw out attention to
these (and similar) passages. But even if we leave the beekeeper and
the *Corycius senex* out of consideration, Virgil's small farmer scares
birds and scythes undergrowth (1.156f.), roasts the husked grain (1.267),
ties vines to elms (2.221), brings down wicker baskets from store (2.242).
And a good deal else. For two simple reasons: the far greater suitability—as matter for poetry—of the small farmer, who has to diver-
sify to survive (Frayn, (1979), *passim*, Evans (n. 24), 134–59)—so agricultural diversification leads to poetic *poikilia*—, and the great antiquity
and spiritual significance of the myth (cf. 78f; 81 on Hes. and Cato)
of the *autourgos*, the man who tills his own land. But not altogether
a myth: we are slowly learning that another distinction, that between
the small holding and the vast estate, is equally false. A vast amount
of information has come to light from aerial photography, field-
surveys, studies of centuriation, neglected literary texts (notably
the *agrimensores*) and archaeology about the diffusion of the small
farm in late republican and Augustan Italy, and not just in the Po
valley and Campania, where Virgil might even have *seen* them!
(cf. 71f. on Virgilian 'observation').[24] Especially interesting is the in-
creasing range of possibilities that emerges for the size of veteran

---

[23] Cf. Wilkinson 57f. on *WD* 643 and *G.*2.412; cf. also *G.*2.468.
[24] Cf. Garnsey in *PCPS* (n. 16), 34ff., (n. 22), 1ff., Skydsgaard (n. 16), 65ff.,
Flach (n. 22), 157f., De Neeve (n. 22), 134, Evans (n. 22), 19–47, 134–73 (especially
159–62).

allotments.[25] Horace's Sabine farm is on a larger scale (*Ep.*1.14.2f.) than that worked by the Virgilian *autourgos*, bating those passages where the poet or his source strays into large-scale agri-business.

Now that we have destabilised certain traditional beliefs and false antitheses about late c. 1 B.C. agriculture, it becomes easier to dismiss the 'propaganda value' of *G.* with unprecedented vigour.[26] There was no 'Augustan agricultural policy', or rather, if there was, we have no evidence for it. Maecenas ap. Dio 52.28.3 is strikingly appropriate to the circumstances of Dio's own day.[27] The *rediit cultus agris* of Vell.2.89.4 belongs to an elaborate rhetorical development (note for a start the use of *re-* prefixes), perfectly in accordance with the analysis offered by Menander Rhetor.[28] And there is nothing else. At least, not directly. When *RR* appeared (cf. appx. 2) and when Virgil began *G.*, famine in Italy was endemic;[29] that continued until the defeat of Sex. Pompeius, 3 Sept. 36 B.C. Apart from the widespread and varied effects of war, plunder and devastation,[30] banditry remained.[31] But Virgilian/Hesiodic *autourgia* cannot have been seriously intended as an answer to national famine: only *latifundia* on the vastest scale could ever have remedied the interruption of trade-routes to Sicily and Egypt. The revival of hope at the defeat of Sex. Pompeius, which we see (93f.) reflected in gratitude expressed to Octavian, is context enough for Virgil at least to begin working on *G.* The *laudes Italiae*, at this date, are mere fantasy.[32] They express, rather, faith and hope.

It is the countryside viewed ethically,[33] not agriculturally, that represents what may be taken as the 'contemporary relevance' (distasteful

---

[25] See Keppie (n. 16), 91–6 on Augustan and triumviral veteran settlements, and further, ib., 58ff. with P.A. Brunt, *Italian Manpower* (Oxford 1971), 326ff.

[26] White (n. 5), 107 for c. 18 views; Woodman on Vell. 2.89.4, M.I. Rostovtzeff, *Social and economic history of the Roman empire* (ed. 2 Oxford 1957), 63f., Syme (n. 14), 450f.

[27] F. Millar, *A study of Cassius Dio* (Oxford 1964), 102ff., E. Gabba, *Del buon uso della richezza* (Milan 1988), 189ff., M. Reinhold, P. Swan in *Between republic and empire* (ed. K. Raaflaub, M. Toher, Berkeley 1990), 164.

[28] Men.Rhet.377.13; cf. Hor. *C.*4.5.17–20. But Suet. *Aug.*98.2 shows that here rhetoric and reality are not polar opposites.

[29] Brunt (n. 25), 290.

[30] Brunt (n. 25) 285–93; Spurr (n. 14), 176ff. = 82ff. misstates the matter gravely. This was (ch. 1, n. 85) a matter for serious poetry.

[31] Cf. my n. on Hor. *Ep.*1.7.86 for simple *abigeatus*; graver, Suet. *Aug.*32.1; cf. R. MacMullen, *Enemies of the Roman order* (Cambridge, Mass. 1975), 266–8.

[32] Brunt (n. 25), 129f.

[33] Wilkinson, 153ff., Syme (n. 14), 448ff.

expression!) of *G*. That does not make Virgil a 'spokesman' for some sort of 'New Catonism', but he may well be suggesting that the moral and religious values that attached to the countryside, at least in an earlier and idealised Italy, are not inappropriate to an age of reconstruction and renewal, in which notable weight is laid upon republican usage and precedent.[34]

Town/country: a false polarity

We should not suppose that with a sharp separation between intended reader and imagined addressee we have solved the problem(s) for good and all. The learned reader was a good deal nearer the land than might seem at first sight likely to the modern scholar. Thus Pliny on his visits to Tifernum, *Ep*.9.15: plagued by petitions, and with no time to work: he 'plays the part' of landlord and travels about his estate 'for the ride'; five letters on: *uindemias. . .colligo, si colligere est non numquam decerpere uuam, torculum inuisere, gustare lacu mustum*. Lastly, 9.36: still busy with his tenants, but now able to work: indeed he takes his notebooks out hunting (as in the fully-developed scene, 1.6). Now multiply those scenes by all the proprietors listed in Shatzman's *Senatorial wealth* (n. 150). Add the country properties of rich equestrians like Atticus (cf. my nn. on Nep. *Att*.13.6, 14.3). Add Hor. *Ep*.1.14.39 *rident uicini glaebas et saxa mouentem*. Allow for owners who farm seriously, like Turranius Niger, Varr. *RR* 2; offset the ones who barely pretend, like Pliny. Bear in mind the owners of villas near enough to Rome for short visits:[35] Cicero at Tusculum, Atticus at Nomentum (a working farm; cf. my n. on Nep. *Att*.13.6). Nor is the physical break between town and country at all sharp:[36] working farms within an hour's brisk walk from the Capitol; there still are a few, for those who know where to look! And one should even think of businessmen, who required an expert knowledge of prices and yield for trade in foodstuffs, rents and evaluating collateral for loans. It might not have been very easy to find a Roman innocent of country connexions (but cf. Hor.'s Volteius Mena, *Ep*.1.7.77f.)—or relatives. The persistence

---

[34] Cf. 166, nn. 35, 36.

[35] J.P.V.D. Balsdon, *Life and leisure in ancient Rome* (London 1969), 210ff., L. Casson, *Travel in the ancient world* (London 1974), 138ff.

[36] For this aspect of the Roman *suburbium*, cf. N. Purcell's admirable discussion in *Ancient Roman villa gardens* (Dumbarton Oaks 1987), 187–203.

of such connexions has a profound bearing on language, knowledge, diet, *mores*, lore and outlook; hence too on the degree of familiarity at least with terminology that Virgil can presuppose in his intended readership. Nor should we forget the growth of an 'ideal' country-side in Roman thought, from Cato on (81), where moral values sprout beside the cabbages.

Uidi: *observation and tradition*

But though we have sketched an ampler countrified background for the intended readership of the *G.*, the poet's own position remains obstinately and typically elusive. Expressions of the type *fama est* are, as I hope to have shown,[37] ambiguous; they can refer to tradition, or to innovation, or they can serve as non-committal distancing mecha-nisms. So it was good to see[38] a convincing demonstration that *uidisse* (*G.*4.127) refers to literary tradition and not to autopsy (cf. ch. 1, n. 31). That, as Thomas recognises, is part of a larger problem (nn. on 1.316–8, 451). We should compare *uides* (1.56, 3.103, 250), *uideas* (1.387), *uidebis* (1.365, 455), *uidemus* (1.451, 2.32), *uidi* (1.318), *uidimus* (1.472); cf. too 2.186f., 1.391 (the visual experience of the *puellae*). Such remarks are still sometimes taken as literal statements of obser-vation, as real claims to autopsy.[39] But already Hesiod appeals to experience shared with his brother or with the reader,[40] and such language is firmly anchored in the tradition of didactic.[41] Notably (so, rightly, Thomas), Lucretius.[42] That should make us pause before claiming a literal sense for the Virgilian *uidi*. Some indications that Virgil records in particular the agricultural usage of the Po valley and Campania have been noted[43] and we have no means of decid-ing whether that again is literary (from some lost source) or 'autoptic'. The appearance of precise observation is itself a literary inheritance

---

[37] *Alambicco* 117–33 is a marked improvement upon *PLLS* 6 (1990), 49–63.

[38] R. Thomas, *MD* 29 (1992), 44–51.

[39] Spurr (n. 14) 170, 172 = McAuslan, 75, 77, Mynors on 1.193–6.

[40] *WD* 569, 633, 680 (e.g.).

[41] Arat. *Phaen.*727, 733 (with Martin's note), 752. Cf., for that matter, Opp. *Cyn.*1.198, 239, *Hal.*2.657.

[42] Cf. C. Bailey's ed., 1, 99, D. West, *The imagery and poetry of Lucretius* (Edinburgh 1969), 14f. See e.g. 2.768, 4.61, 262, 353, 460, 577, 598, 5.460, 6.1044.

[43] Spurr, *EV* 1.61–4, Wilkinson 156f., 228f., n., Mynors on 1.215, 216 (cf. on 2.161–4).

(West (n. 41), 14), though clearly some poets (Lucr., Calp.Sic.) are more inclined to it than others.[44] Clearly, we should be cautious in claiming extensive and minute powers of observation for Virgil without hedging such claims about with proper caveats. Virgil's errors[45] offer an analogy; they may be inherited (and literary) or the result of faulty information and understanding, or even the consequence of the difficulties (e.g. of terminology) inherent in stepping from the farmyard to Parnassus and back again. Error, however generated, is of course compounded by omission, lack of system (which Virgil shares with Varro!), allusivity and the imprecision imposed on technical material by literary tradition, the conventions of linguistic choice (cf. 90f.) and generic mannerisms. This long series of 'filters' set up between *rus* and cultured *otium* should never be underestimated. If we still, despite everything, find it necessary to consider whether some farmers might have opened a roll or rolls of *G.*, we might for a moment contemplate the practical effect of the poet's declared haste and selectivity (2.42, 3.284f., 4.147f.) and of the substantial categories of farm work omitted, more or less totally, by the poet: asses, donkeys, mules (see 1.273), poultry, pigs (1.399f., 2.520, 3.255), dogs (3.345, 404–13).

The Georgics *as a 'transitional' poem*

Whatever the difficulties of chronology we have encountered, *G.* belong solidly between *Buc.* and *Aen.* and we need so see how, a little more closely. Style, metre and language help really very little (cf. 236–6); generic differences are too strong to permit us to analyse (let alone quantify) stylistic growth. But we should be in no doubt that V. senses growth as a poet: he chafes already at the modest bounds of pastoral (4.1, 6.3), and once embarked on *G.*, after the anxieties of 2.44 (with

---

[44] W. Kroll, *Studien zum Verständnis der röm. Literatur* (Stuttgart 1964), on *Die Unfähigkeit zur Beobachtung* (280–307) is masterly, though it does not touch directly on the 'real world' of these observations.

[45] Spurr (n. 14), n. 18 much understated the scale of the problem: cf. Mynors on (e.g.) 4.38–41, Wilkinson, 225f., 235, E. De Saint-Denis in *Vergiliana*, 335f., R.T. Bruère, *CP* 51 (1956), 228–46, White (1970), 40, id., *PVS* 7 (1967–8), 11–22, id. *EV* 1.65, Horsfall, *RFil.* 119 (1991), 212. Spurr may have saved Virgil from Seneca's criticisms (*Ep.*86.17–9), but there remain those of Col. (De Saint-Denis, 335–7), and Plin. *Nat.* (Bruère, cit., Venini, *EV* 4.144). Contrast Col.9.2.5 and Sen. *Ep.*86.15 on Virgil's public!

Farrell, 244–6), at a certain point (*G*.3, proem. cf. appx. 3) looks forward to epic. In the countryside of *G*. there is no more time for piping and flirtation; hard work has—Orpheus apart—taken over (though cf. 1.293, 350, 2.383f., 388, 394: music indoors or at festivals). Aeneas too has a great deal less fun than Homeric heroes; Dido is (cf. 123–33) scarcely 'fun'; Virgil's moral earnestness mounts. One way in which this 'transitional' status[46] has been analysed successfully is through the small-scale (though hardly simple) imitations of Homer down to 4.314; thereafter, his first extensive imitation of Homer, whether or not we can really speak of it as a rehearsal for *Aen.* (cf. 85f.).[47]

Structure

We have seen (15f.) that the composition of *G*. attracted VSD's attention: whether it is true that Virgil systematically began the day by dictating a few lines and then turned to their revision and whether he ever compared his methods to those of the she-bear (15f., 22; N. O'Sullivan, *Vergilius* 35 (1989), 55ff. is most unlikely to be correct) maybe questioned, or, depending on your attitude to VSD, even maintained! But if we wish to know more of how *G*. were composed, we must turn to internal evidence.

The suggestion that the 'digressions' were composed later seems profoundly infelicitous (75), once their integral relationship to the text is recognised. We should acknowledge, though, unhesitatingly, that certain passages were added at a late stage: the proem. to *G*.3 (cf. appx. 1 for the historical references it contains); exactly the same goes for the *sphragis* (4.559–66), the *Corycius senex* proclaims its lateness (4.115); *G*.1.1–4[48] and 5–42 are not necessarily of the same date; the bulk of the proem. to 1 is surely later than the victory over Sex. Pompeius (99f.). But there is no serious objection to the hypothesis that the bulk of the text was composed in pretty much the order in which it stands (cf. 93 for the end of *G*.4). The unwarlike Indian

---

[46] Cf. C.G. Hardie, *The 'Georgics': a transitional poem* (Jackson Knight Lecture 3, Abingdon 1971): note e.g. 15f. on myths from *Buc*.6 which reappear in *G*., F. Klingner, *Virgils Georgica* (Zürich 1963), 140.

[47] G.N. Knauer, *ANRW* 2.31.2 (Berlin 1981), 870–918, with the critiques of Farrell, 207–72; see 84–6.

[48] E. De Saint-Denis, *REL* 16 (1938), 297ff. was quite wrong to suggest (see J.G.F. Powell, ed. Cic. *Sen.*, 217) that V. owed the poem's structure to Cic. *Sen.*54, though there is (81) much of value in his article. Cf. Farrell, 155f. on Varr. *RR* 1.14–6.

(2.172) from whom Octavian protects Italy does not involve dating the whole *laudes* to the period of the Actium campaign; poetically, 'India' is but a suburb of 'Parthia'. Ample revisions and additions at a late stage seem likelier than not; 2188 lines in seven years allows abundant time for ample tinkering and serious revision.

If we now look at further principles of structure and organisation, we may begin with *uariatio*, long acknowledged as fundamental: SDan on 2.195: *uarietatis causa*, Serv. on 4.136: *mira uarietas*. The range of *uarietas* (Lucretian in origin)[49] detected is almost limitless—look for example at the structure of the references to the content of each book at 1.1–4 or at the geographical variation in the vine-names at 2.89–102.[50] In some sense, stylistic variety is a reflection of the variety of nature herself (1.53 with Thomas' note, 2.109–35).[51] And for the erudite reader, endless *uariatio* in the employment, or deployment, or interaction of sources.[52] There are also very remarkable instances of regular arithmetical balance between sections.[53] That at times might be pure chance, but the bulk of secure examples allows us to infer a poet with a formidable sense of order and equilibrium and one prepared, during revision, to work at his text, at least at times, with precise numerical correspondences in mind.

Thematic and emotional balances, contrasts, correspondences and the like have been dear to many recent students of *G.*,[54] and the hunt (cf. 89), in terms of death and rebirth, becomes positively fevered when we turn to *G.*4.[55] Perhaps more objective, if less 'interesting', is the balance by recognisable sources.[56]

---

[49] Farrell, 191ff., E. Burck *Herm.*64 (1929), 293 = *Vom Menschenbild in der röm. Literatur.* (Heidelberg 1966), 98.

[50] Farrell, 192f. I add (and it is hard to know where to stop!) Thomas on *G.*3.322–38 (winter>summer; torrid Libya and icy Scythia); id. on 4.125–48 for the relationship with 1.125–49; id. on 1.2 for the references to Maecenas; 4.363ff. and 467ff. (descents of Aristaeus and Orpheus), Horsfall in Biotti, 24 (structure of bk. 4), balance of the laments of Orpheus (507–10, 523–7) and Aristaeus (321–8).

[51] See further Wilkinson, 71f., G. Ramain, *RPhil.*48 (1924), 117–23.

[52] A remarkable case: 3.146–8 and R. Thomas, *HSCP* 86 (1982), 81–5.

[53] Thomas 1, 12f., n. on 2.83–108, index s.v. Structural arrangement, B. Frischer, *EV* 2.688–9; the fractions in K.-H. Pridik, *ANRW* 2.31.1 (1980), 500ff. do rather reduce his credibility.

[54] G.E. Duckworth, *AJP* 80 (1959), 232f., C.P. Segal, *AJP* 87 (1966), 308, Otis, 151f., Wilkinson, 325ff., B. Frischer, *EV* 2.690f. For divisions and developments of the argument, cf. still E. Burck, (n. 49), 279–321 = 89–116.

[55] Otis, 199, Segal (n. 54), 310ff., Griffin, *GR* 26 (1979), 71f. = *Latin poets and Roman life* (London 1985), 163f.

[56] Frischer, (n. 53), 690, after D. Wender, *Ramus* 8 (1979), 59–64; cf. now Farrell, 185–8 on *G.*1 and 131–4 on *G.* as a whole (admirable).

Thomas' commentary maintains a largely successful equilibrium between artistic microstructures and thematic or emotive mega-structures. It is as well not to forget that Virgil tells us *nec sum animi dubius uerbis ea uincere magnum/quam sit et angustis hunc addere rebus honorem* (3.289f.). *Angustae res* are what he calls his theme and that is no bad reason to concentrate on the corresponding small balances and contrasts in the wake of the admirable Ramain: that is an art perfectly and entirely compatible with the Hellenistic techniques revealed by Farrell and Thomas.[57]

The excursus or digression

Under *Georgiche*, s.v. *Digressioni* (*EV* 2.678–86), Francesco Della Corte listed 46 'digressions', totalling 812 lines, or nearly 30% of the entire text. That verges on the comical, listing as it does virtually everything in the *G.* not directly relevant to the declared subject-matter, on the narrowest view, of the several books! The topic is, however, serious, and has wide implications. It is, first, almost impossible to approach it via formal criteria of particles, resumptive formulae and the like (cf. 1.63 *ergo age*, 466 *etiam*, 2.177 *nunc*, 346 *quod superest*, 4.149 *nunc age*), of which Virgil, in contrast to Lucretius is quite sparing. He is aware of the dangers of excessive detail (3.284f.), of the limitations of space (4.147f.), of the sense of haste towards the end of his work (4.116f.), but that is no invitation to generalise and certainly no excuse to speculate that the digressive passages were written after the technical (*pace* Wilkinson, 70). I suggest elsewhere (90f.) that stylistic analysis might prove a fruitful approach, but recognise the complete lack of stylistic unity at least within Della Corte's catalogue: both Aristaeus (Homeric) and Orpheus (neoteric) (239–44), both the *Corycius Senex* (4.116/25–148),[58] full of technical language (cf. a fair quantity in the corresponding 1.118–54), and the *laudes Italiae* (2.136–76), where perhaps only *aconita* (152) checks the torrent of high language. Contrast 1.466–97; Virgil exploits richly the macabre possibilities of the battlefield revisited and *pinguescere* 492 reaches a

---

[57] But Wilkinson, 72f. is as alarmed by small details as I am by sweeping definitions!

[58] Beyond Thomas, Mynors and Biotti, see now R. Thomas. *MD* 29 (1992), 35–67 (fascinating reconstruction of Virgil's antecedents; generally convincing if not comprehensively mandatory). Cf. C.G. Perkell, *TAPA* 111 (1981), 167–77 and R. Thomas, *PCPS* Suppl. 7 (1982), 57 on thematic relationships between the *Corycius senex* and *G.* as a whole.

climax of nastiness. Given the inherited link between 'digression' and a pathetic/descriptive use of higher language (v. infra), however, the connexion, in general terms, between 'excursus' and the grander registers of language is secure; Virgil even hovers on the brink of euphuism at 2.143 *Bacchi Massicus umor* and 4.125 *Oebaliae turribus arcis*.[59]

Central to a clearer understanding of the 'excursus' in Virgil is an understanding of what happens in Lucretius and of how Virgil differs.[60] Once the straitjacket of the equivalences exposition :: bitter cup and excursus :: honey is ejected upon the refuse heap of bygone opinions, we begin to realise that the ampler exegesis permitted in the 'excursus' has itself a profound didactic function, in as much as the reader reaches a deeper understanding of a dense problem through a less dense and more spacious illustration. We are a very long way from the set-piece *laudes* analysed by Menander Rhetor.

The situation in Virgil is complicated by a peculiarly unhelpful and superficial discussion[61] of whether the *G*. are better described as 'descriptive' or 'didactic'; that is, are the digressions therefore intensifications or sources of alleviation? Since such 'problems' were seriously proposed, I do believe we have learned to read *G*. more seriously! It may also be helpful to look at 'digressions in the context of what has been said (73f.) about the structure of *G*. 'Digressions' supply variety; their *largior. . .aether* excites both poet and reader; they introduce changes of pace, level, language; they permit general reflection upon other 'digressions' and encourage meditation upon the wider sense of smaller and drier details.

This is hardly the place to undertake a full discussion of the relationship between 'digressions' and didactic text: the bibliography, 'digression' by 'digression' in Della Corte cit., is of some service to that end (and cf. n. 58 on 4.116/25–48). The *laudes Italiae*, to the historian, are mere fantasy (Brunt (n. 25), 129f.); 'serious deficiencies' rasps Thomas (n. 58, 49); 'Virgil tells lies' complains Ross.[62] But the

---

[59] Cf. Horsfall, *Maia* 41 (1989), 251ff. and Russell on Longinus 43: the description of low subject-matter in high language created a marked and peculiar incincinnity. Cf. noticeably in the description of primitive life at 1.118–54. That may indicate another piece of work to be undertaken.

[60] Lucr. ed. C. Bailey, 1, 33f., Farrell, 98, E.J. Kenney, *Lucretius* (*GRNSC* 11 1977), 33–6, id., ed. Lucr.3, 17, 26–9.

[61] Wilkinson, 4, 71, A. La Penna, *Convegno. . .Bimillenario. . .Georgiche* (Napoli 1977), 37f., Della Corte, cit., 678.

[62] D.O. Ross, *Virgil's elements* (Princeton 1987), 110.

Italy of *G.* is ideological as well as photographic (cf. 69f.); the *laudes*
serve, *inter alia*, for all that Virgil has said heretofore and will say
hereafter of his country; they enucleate the emotive charge of every
native place-name and personal name in the poem. What is truth?
At all events, I venture to protest against unequivocal ideologised
interpretations of passages so complex in function and texture.

Sources—prose

We are beginning to understand a good deal better Virgil's use of
prose sources—not only Roman, as we have long known, but Greek.
It is significant that Mynors' 'Appendix of Greek material' contains
three pages of Aristotle (330–3). The hard work of identifying the
actual passages was done by Paul Jahn in the years 1903–6,[63] and
Virgil's use of Aristotle, PsAristotle,[64] Theophrastus, and PsTheo-
phrastus, *De Signis*[65] requires only much fuller clarification along the
lines of R. Thomas, *HSCP* 91 (1987), 253–6, which studies Virgil's
use of Thphr. *HP* 2.1.1: a summary of how plants originate.[66] Virgil
knows, that is, technical treatises in Greek prose, metaphrasts (e.g.
Aratus, Nicander), who versify such works, and Greek nonmetaphrastic
didactic poetry (Hesiod and perhaps Empedocles, though 2.483–4 is
hardly enough to prove direct use). If this seems complex, that is
because it truly is so: read *G.*1.351–464 slowly, with the commentaries of Mynors[67] and Thomas,[68] for it is there that the complexities of
Virgil's technique in the use of inherited material are perhaps most
strikingly visible.

---

[63] Cf. Mynors' bibliography, xi, Suerbaum, 482, Jahn's own summary in Bursian
130 (1906), 41–115 and his revision of the Ladewig-Schaper-Deuticke comm. to *G.*
(e.g. ed. 9, 1915).

[64] *HA* 8/9; see Balme's preface to his Loeb ed., 1991.

[65] Easily available in the Loeb ed. of Thphr. *HP*, second vol., but not by Thphr.:
see O. Regenbogen, PW Suppl. 7.1412.55ff. Aratus did not, though, use the *De
Signis*; both texts reflect a source now lost; cf. id., 1413.37ff.

[66] Cf. too Thomas, 236 on 2.130 and Thphr; cf. too his comm., 1, 10–11.

[67] Mynors' articles in *OCD* ed. 1 (1949, etc.) s.v. *Didactic poetry, Greek, Latin* are a
useful introduction. Cf. now B. Effe, *Dichtung und Lehre* (*Zetemata* 69, München 1977),
E. Pöhlmann, *Charakteristika des röm. Lehrgedichtes, ANRW* 1.3 (Berlin 1973), 813–901,
EV s.v. *didascalica (poesia)* (2.47f.)

[68] Cf. also R. Thomas, *HSCP* 90 (1986), 188–9, Farrell, 221ff., L.A.S. Jermyn,
GR 20 (1951), 26–37, 49–59, G.W. Williams, *Tradition and Originality* (Oxford 1968),
255–60.

Hesiod

A poet widely read and imitated at Alexandria,[69] hence already
important for Virgil (as too clearly, for Gallus, *Buc.*6.70) in *Buc.*,[70]
like his follower Aratus (La Penna (n. 69), 226). The founder of didactic poetry, itself often viewed as a subdivision of epic (Horsfall in
Biotti, 13, n. 4), and honoured as such by Virgil, himself importer of
agricultural didactic poetry to Rome, at the close of his continuous
presence in *G.* (2.176, Farrell, 59f., a remarkable discussion).[71] Quant-
itatively, there is strikingly little Hesiod in *G.*, in contrast to the com-
positional homage at 1.1f.: *quid faciat laetas segetes* (*Works*) and *quo sidere*
terram/uertere (*Days*) (Farrell, 134, Thomas ad loc.) anticipating strikingly the allusion (101f.) to *Il.* and *Od.* in *Aen.*1.1 and at 2.176 (supra).
But what there is is handled with minute and conscious attention
through a delicate and complex inversion of the sequence in the
original text (Farrell, 136–42, with a useful chart at 141). Hesiod
writes for those already expert in the basic techniques of farming;
Virgil's instruction is, rather, a matter of form.[72] Recent analysis of
Virgil's debts, which reveal already an unswerving mastery of the
great range of techniques of allusion,[73] with inversion, correction,
combination with other authors, etc., increasingly familiar to serious
readers of the *Aeneid* (Farrell, 151–5, Thomas (n. 68), 171ff.), is itself
ample and of strikingly high quality.[74] Thus discussion here may be
kept to a minimum: freed of the confusing notion that either *WD* or
G. were actual manuals of agricultural instruction,[75] we may now

---

[69] Cf. Call. *Epigr.*27, on Aratus, significantly translated by Helvius Cinna, fr.11,
Euphorion fr.22 Powell, Effe (n. 67), 40ff., Farrell, 31, A. La Penna, *Entr. Hardt* 7
(1962), 237.

[70] Cf. Clausen's index, s.v.; on *Buc.*4, cf. La Penna (n. 69), 225f., on *Buc.*6, La
Penna, 218; see too Wilkinson, 57.

[71] Cf. the indices of Mynors and Thomas, La Penna, 234f.

[72] Farrell, 137f., West, (p. 67), v, 52.

[73] Note e.g. what happens to Hesiod's account of the Golden Age (109–26), sharply
altered by Virgil in the aetiology of *labor* (1.125ff.) and fleetingly present in Virgil's
idealisation of Italy (2.173) and account of the Golden Age at 2.536–40 (Farrell,
145f.).

[74] La Penna (n. 69), 225ff., id. *EV* s.v. *Esiodo*, Thomas 1.6, et passim, Farrell,
131–57, Wilkinson, 56–60, id. *CQ* 13 (1963), 73–84. Ross (n. 62), 11 is provocative.

[75] Cf. n. 72. The plough is a case in point: in Hes., for part of the work you call
in a joiner (*WD* 430 with West's note); in Cato, you buy one (*Agr.*135); in Varro
you do not make it on the farm (*RR* 1.22.1); Virgil (*G.*1.169–75), like Hes. (427–31)
offers skeletal information on how it is actually made: in neither world is it really
part of the farmer's tasks!

look at more significant links between the two works. It is of basic importance to recognise that Virgil finds in Hesiod the classic statement of the dignity of toil and the theological basis of the need to work;[76] not exclusively Hesiodic, however (cf. Wilkinson, 59f.), for Cato's position, so far as we can see (81) was not far different. The Virgilian *autourgos* is Boeotian, seen through a Sabine filter!

Alexandrian poetry

The *Georgics* are a profoundly Alexandrian poem in learning,[77] in artistry and technique and in the passion for the allusive reference (so already 74 above), in the sense that scientific fact was fit matter for poetry,[78] in the employment of certain narrative features,[79] in a particular curiosity about certain types of mythological figure,[80] in the mythological riddle or challenge,[81] in the occasional subtle mythological invention.[82] This is no challenge to Thomas' entirely successful championship of *G.* as an Alexandrian poem (with his article (n. 68) of 1986 as battle-cry): that was a crusade, but there is also an element of sporting challenge, of clues to unravel, even of a sort of learned fun that I find in the Alexandrianism of the *Aeneid* (*Alambicco*, passim, and see n. 81), in Virgil's erudition at times, whose existence Thomas and Farrell perhaps tend to overlook.

We should look briefly at four of Virgil's leading Alexandrian sources

(i) Eratosthenes, *Hermes* (see Fraser (n. 78), 623f.). Of prime importance at 1.231–56 (cf. Mynors, 53f., 325f.). For detailed comparison,

---

[76] Wilkinson, 76, Farrell, 142–5. The author recalls with gratitude Wilkinson's admirable exegesis of 1.118–46 (n. 74, 1963), in the days before Thomas and Mynors. Now, cf. too Farrell, 147, 185f.

[77] On myth, W. Frentz, *Mythologisches in Vergils Georgica* (Meisenheim 1967) is very useful; on ethnography, R.F. Thomas, *Lands and peoples in Roman poetry* (*PCPS* Suppl. 7, Cambridge 1982), 45ff.; for geography, R.G. Mayer, *GR* 33 (1986), 47–54, Horsfall, *RFil*.119 (1991), 214f.

[78] Because we still have a fair quantity of Alexandrian didactic poetry, we tend to overestimate its importance; cf. the corrective offered by P.M. Fraser, *Ptolemaic Alexandria* 1 (Oxford 1972), 623f.

[79] Cf. Thomas' index s.v. *aetiology*; for discoveries in agricultural science, cf. the next note.

[80] On the *inventor*, cf. the indices of Thomas and Mynors s.v. πρῶτος εὑρέτης, Horsfall in Biotti, 23.

[81] 1.14, 3.1, 4.283, Horsfall, *Vergilius* 37 (1991), 31ff.

[82] The link of Orpheus and Aristaeus (Horsfall, *Athen*.56 (1988), 36, n. 35), but not the story of Orpheus as a whole: C.M. Bowra, *CQ* 2 (1952), 113–26.

cf. Thomas (n. 68), 195–7; this is a passage in which V. integrates seven literary antecedents (cf. Farrell, 174–6, 208). It is significant (cf. 84) that Varro of Atax had already rendered these lines of Eratosthenes.

(ii) Nicander: followed by Virgil, according to Quintilian (10.1.56): Virgil may have used his *Melissourgika* in *G*.4, though that is quite uncertain; that Nicander gave him the title *Georgica* is at least likely (we have no other instance).[83] Not only a digestible source for herpetology, but very probably a provider of occasional nuggets of mythological learning,[84] and perhaps also a model for the structuring of the *sphragis* (cf. Mynors on 4.559f.). We should not suppose, therefore, that a technical poet, such as Nicander, was only open on Virgil's desk while he composed the directly relevant lines of *G*.[85]

(iii) Callimachus. Fundamental: in erudition (vide supra), in literary polemic (cf. 96f. on the proem to *G*.3), in occasional precise allusions,[86] and very noticeably in the structure of the whole in four books with reference to the *Victoria Berenices* at 1.24–42 and 3.1–48.[87]

(iv) Aratus. Keystone of any serious work on Virgil's use of sources (cf. n. 68). Alexandria balances Ascra (in the Hesiodic/Aratean structure of *G*.1), and Alexandria is heir to Ascra, and (n. 69) knew it.[88] For the second half of *G*.1, we have *Phaen.*, the copious scholiasts thereto, the Theophrastean *De Signis* (cf. 77), Cicero's translation, and a very little of Varro Atacinus' (cf. 84). That Virgil used the commentators to Aratus as Cicero had done[89] is likely, but not, I think, proved. But it would be quite wrong to limit the influence of Aratus to a single passage: thus cf. Farrell 161f. on *Phaen.*112f. and Iustitia in the Virgilian countryside and id., 162 on Aratean influence in the Virgilian Golden age at 1.136–8.[90]

(v) We should not suppose that that is the end of the matter: note

---

[83] The ed. by A.S.F. Gow and A.F. Scholfield (Cambridge 1953) is standard.

[84] Cf. Mynors on 3.391–3, Frentz (n. 77), 129f.

[85] On Nic. and Virgil in general, cf. *EV* s.v. (Gualandri), Farrell, 208, n. 5, Thomas 1, 8 and on 3.414–39.

[86] E.g. 3.36; cf. Thomas 1, 8, Farrell, 165f., 242f.

[87] Cf. Thomas on 3.19f., id. *CQ* 33 (1983), 92ff

[88] Cf. Farrell, 160, n. 42 and especially 163f. on the literary sense of the pairing of Hes. and Arat. See too Farrell, 217–25 for Homer behind Aratus.

[89] J. Soubiran, ed. Cic. *Aratea*, etc. (Budé, 1972), 93, A. Traina, *Vortit Barbare* (Roma 1970), 86, n. 1, J. Martin, *Hist. du texte des Phénomènes d'Aratos* (Paris 1956), 19ff. Certainly Cic. knew of Boethus of Sidon (*Div*.1.13., 2.47), author of a *Peri Aratous* (cf. Farrell, 217). Cf. further E. Maass, *Aratea*, (*Phil.Unt.*12, Berlin 1892), 156ff.

[90] For V. and Aratus in general, cf. Thomas 1, 7, Mynors, 326–30, Farrell, 157–

for example Thomas' argument (*MD* 29 (1992), 51ff.) for Philitas as inspiration for the *Corycius senex* (cf. further, Biotti, 120–3). Even on the basis of the meagre scraps that survive, we can show how rich *G.* is in allusions to Latin neoteric poetry (cf. 83f.); we should not expect Virgil to limit his Alexandrian allusions to the four (? five) authors named, either, and indeed he does not.[91]

Cato and 'Cato'

Direct debts to Cato's *De agri cultura* are few,[92] though Virgil does at times (89f.) evoke the abruptness of manner common to Hesiod and Cato. But Cato's importance is very great, as man and as legend.[93] Cato, that is, as seen in his writings (*orat.* fr.128 Malc. for his skills as farmer), as eulogist of agriculture (praef. 2 *uirum bonum quom laudabant, ita laudabant, bonum agricolam, bonum colonum*) and of the virtues of the farmer-soldier (ib.4): *at ex agricolis et uiri fortissimi et milites strenuissimi gignuntur.*[94] The Roman myth of the moral superiority of the countryside—in national, even in patriotic terms—is born with Cato, both man and myth.[95]

The notion that Cic. *Sen.*51–60 might have something to do with *G.* (so in passing Horsfall in Biotti, 18) was dismissed energetically by J.G.F. Powell (ed. Cic. *Sen.*, 206). It should not have been; let us leave structure out of it (n. 48) and observe (i) *G.*2.362–70, on the growth of the vine, with Cic. *Sen.*52 and De Saint-Denis (n. 48), 312f. (less striking *Sen.*53, *G.*2.335–68 and id., 313f.); (ii) the soil as cradle of Rome's old soldier-heroes (*G.*2.169f., *Sen.*60f.), though Virgil's heroes are not identical with Cato/Cicero's;[96] (iii) the *Corycius senex* is after all a *senex*, like Cicero's Cato. Further enquiry is called for.

---

62. Note the confusion caused by the different names used in antiquity for various parts of *Phaen.*: Horsfall, *PLLS* 7 (1993), 2f.

[91] For Theocr., cf. Thomas on 1.332, 3.338, 351!

[92] Thomas, index, s.v., id. *HSCP* 91 (1987), 238–41 on Cat. *Agr.*91 *si ita feceris neque formicae nocebunt neque herbae nascuntur*, 129, Varr. *RR* 1.51.1f. and *G.*1.176–86. See too *EV* 1.708 and note the useful general survey of Cato's work by K.D. White, *ANRW* 1.4 (1973), 440–58.

[93] A.E. Astin, *Cato the Censor* (Oxford 1978), 295ff., F. Della Corte, *Catone Censore* (Firenze 1969), 125ff.

[94] Horsfall, *Lat.*30 (1971), 1112.

[95] Cf. Thomas and Mynors on 2.412f., Wilkinson, 132.

[96] They derive from a standard list: Horsfall (n. 94), 1112, expanded without proper acknowledgement, M. Dickie, *PLLS* 5 (1985), 190.

Lucretius

The depth of Virgil's personal commitment to Epicureanism remains altogether a mystery. That he studied with Philodemus seems now clear (2), but we are as far as ever from understanding his beliefs, and the degree of Epicurean thought reflected in the text (cf. 149–54 on *Aen*.6, 199–203 on 12). At least we should distinguish as clearly as we can between Lucretian echoes in the text and some kind of philosophical *prise de position*.[97] In *Buc.*, we have seen the very limited impact of Epicurean thought; in *G.*, the picture is more complicated[98] and the impact of Lucretius has to be evaluated on the planes of style (cf. 90), of delight in the minute observation of the natural world (cf. 71 on *uidi*),[99] along with its intensification through personification and of a seriousness of moral and philosophical outlook[100]—creeds, be it noted, I do not mention—far different from the metaphrasts' elegant detachment and reminiscent rather, it has been suggested, of Empedocles (see 77). Virgil had not found minute and delighted (if not always scientifically exact) observation in Lucr. alone (note Cicero, in the wake of Aratus, 80), but the combination of an argument articulated somewhat after the Lucretian manner[101] with the formal tribute at 2.490ff. *felix qui rerum potuit cognoscere causas/atque metus omnis et inexorabile fatum/subiecit pedibus strepitumque Acherontis auari*[102] and with a common characteristic love of detail involves a good deal more than formal adherence (which is anyway most marked in *G.*2 and 3) to a poetical or intellectual master or to the generic tradition of Latin didactic poetry.[103] If I am right in (still!) seeing the *G.* as in some sense a plea for a renewal of faith in Italy (and particularly in the

---

[97] Cf. A. Traina, *RFil*.121 (1993), 86ff. on V. Mellinghoff-Bourgerie's *Incertitudes de Virgile* (Coll.Lat.210, 1990). On 4.564 *studiis florentem ignobilis oti* (at Naples!), contrast L. Alfonsi, *EV* 2.330 with the sceptical commentaries of Thomas and Mynors.

[98] The rejection of Lucretian influence by Ross (n. 62, 25ff.) and Thomas (1, 4) I have never clearly understood; no more has Farrell (277, n. 6).

[99] M. Gale, *CQ* 41 (1991), 418.

[100] Cf. Farrell 169–206 (169–172, a markedly useful survey of earlier work), *EV* s.v. *Lucrezio*, Wilkinson, 63–5, Gale (n. 99), 414–26.

[101] Pridik (n. 53), 508 on articulation; but see Farrell, 170 for the sparing way in which Virgil in fact uses such stylistic devices.

[102] See Farrell, 178 and Mynors' notes. The matter is certain: 491–2 summarised Lucr.3.

[103] Cf. Mynors, 251, Farrell, 202–6, Gale (n. 99), 414, 422 on the apogee of Virgil's transmutation of Lucr. in the description of the plague of Noricum.

land) (69f.), then Virgilian description acquires a Lucretian type of protreptic function, and more should be said on analogies with the Homeric simile,[104] as interruption and intensification of the narrative.[105] From his model/master, Virgil inherits a sense of the passion which the desire to convince or convert can arouse, quite irrespective of where one might wish to set Virgil on some sort of scale between Epicurean pessimism and Stoical pragmatic vigour,[106] even supposing that the widely (or wildly) varying impressions offered by individual passages ever permitted one to reach convincingly an overall verdict.[107] My own sense of wonder at the splendours of the parts is far stronger than my desire to reach a general ethical verdict upon the whole and hence I offer here no answer to this passionately debated (but in the end perhaps unhelpful and pretty clearly unanswerable) question.

Catullus and the Neoterics

Commentators have noted a fair number of imitations of style (cf. 241–4 for V. writing in the 'neoteric' manner) and phrasing.[108] Far more important, though, and very generally recognised, is the debt of the 'in-setting' of Orpheus to that of Theseus and Ariadne in Cat. 64.[109] Note that Virgil knew Cicero's version of Aratus, *Phaen.*[110] Debts

---

[104] Farrell, 94–104, 190, 197f.

[105] Gale (n. 99), 416, W.W. Briggs, *Narrative and simile* (*Mnem.* Suppl. 58, Leiden 1980), 91f.

[106] On the proportion of habitable land on the earth's surface, contrast Lucr.5.200–17 with *G*.1.231–43. Cf. Farrell, 172–4. Note 3.339 (*pastores Libyae*)—345 and 3, 349–83 (shepherds of Scythia): tributes to human adaptability in zones which might have seemed uninhabitable. A precise, visible distinction of position: Virgil is less pessimistic than his model. Cf. Farrell, 180f. for a similar observation on *G*.1.122 and 147f.

[107] Cf. Farrell, 184 on similar view of *labor* in Virgil and Lucr.; cf. too J. Griffin, *CR* 31 (1981), 26 *et passim*.

[108] Thomas 1, 8, nn. on 1.206, 3.352–3, index s.v. 1.50 (ploughing) *ac prius ignotum ferro quam scindimus aequor* could, as Thomas points out, but for *ferro*, refer to seafaring, like Cat.64.12 *quae simul ac uostro uentosum proscidit aequor*.

[109] For verbal echoes, Thomas, 1, 8; for structural inconcinnity, Horsfall in Biotti, 24; in general, A.M. Crabbe, *CQ* 27 (1977), 342–51.

[110] Thomas on 1.244–6, 378.

to Calvus,[111] Helvius Cinna,[112] Varro Atacinus[113] and Varius[114] have
also been noted. It appears that Virgil twice (? at least) borrowed
lines of Varro Atacinus unaltered, most unusually.[115]

Varro

For date and public, cf. 63, 95. Let us be clear: however we solve
the chronological problem, the text was itself a considerable influence on Virgil: first in the proem. to *G*.1, which, like *RR* 1, begins
with an invocation to twelve rustic deities (cf. appx. 4 for a comparison), and secondly in a number of technical details:[116] as in the case
of Hesiod, a debt formally underlined, but actually not notably copious.[117] This is not the technique of the metaphrasts, as Aratus (e.g.)
rendered Eudoxus, nor that of the translator, as Cicero rendered
Aratus. Rather, radical selectivity. So why the bow in the proem. to
1? A tribute to the author's age and eminence? To his love for Italy
(*RR* 1.2.3ff.)?[118] To his undiminished faith in Italian agriculture, before there was any sign of the civil wars ending?

Homer

While it has become clear that we are perhaps only now reaching a
proper understanding of Virgil's use of Homer in the *G*., recent work

---

[111] Thomas on 3.152f., id., *HSCP* 86 (1982), 81–5.

[112] Thomas on 4.465–6 (possible).

[113] Thomas 1, 8f.; for the *Ephemeris* (the likely title: E. Courtney, *The fragmentary Latin poets* (Oxford 1993), 244), cf. Mynors on 1.375f., Thomas on 1.374–87, 397, Farrell, 223, Courtney, 244–6; on *Chorographia*, Mynors and Thomas on 1.237f., Courtney, 250; on *Argonautica*, Thomas on 1.14f., 2.404, Courtney, 241f., *EV* s.v. *Varrone, Publio Terenzio*.

[114] Mynors and Thomas on 2.506; cf. Courtney (n. 113), 272; 79 on Eratosthenes; Thomas on 3.116f. with Courtney, 273, Thomas and Mynors on 3.253–4 and 467, with Courtney, 274, *EV* s.v. *Vario Rufo*. Note that Virgil also borrowed from another friend, Horace: Mynors and Thomas on 3.537f.

[115] Thomas on 1.377, 2.404.

[116] Instructions on the summer pasturing of sheep and goats: 3.322–38, *RR* 2.2.10f., R. Thomas, *HSCP* 91 (1987), 233–5; gadflies: *G*.3.143–56, *RR* 2.5.14, Thomas, 241f.: developed by Virgil in a passage of bravura Hellenistic learning, that owes nothing to the sage of Reate: Thomas, again, *HSCP* 86 (1982), 81–5.

[117] Wilkinson, 65–7, 223–5, Farrell, 154–6, Thomas (n. 116, 1987), 229ff., *EV* 5*, 446, indices to Mynors' and Thomas' commentaries, s.v.

[118] See J. Geffcken, *Herm*.27 (1892), 381–8, S. Bauck, *De laudibus Italiae* (diss. Königsberg 1914).

on the adaptation of *Il.* and *Od.* to a context both agricultural and
didactic has paradoxically, done a good deal to confirm the rightness
of the 'orthodox' explanation of why Virgil concludes the poem with
an aetiological epyllion with inset secondary narrative. While Knauer
(*ANRW* 2.31.2, 890–918) was perhaps too ready (Farrell, 210ff., 225f.)
to play down the use of Homer in *G.*1–3, and his very attractive
notion that Homeric adaptation in *G.*1–3 was a sort of 'dress-
rehearsal' for the far vaster imitation in *G.*4 (912) is dismissed (Farrell,
256) as 'plausible but simplistic', it remains perfectly clear that the
case of Homer in the Aristaeus-episode represents a marked and
decisive advance of scale, if not of technique (Farrell, 253). We have
now ample analysis of the details of Homeric allusion and adaptation in a non-narrative, though not, formally, non-epic (n. 67; cf.
Horsfall in Biotti, 13, n. 4) context: the reader in a hurry (the very
worst way to understand *G.*!) will go to the (excellent) summary at
Thomas 1, 5f.[119] In *G.*3, Homer is woven into (Farrell's metaphor,
237) a seamless robe (my own, *Athen.*66 (1988), 37): integration (cf.
Farrell, 225) into a context whether Hesiodic, Aratean, or Lucretian
is perfect (i.e. invisible, except to the reader or scholar actually looking minutely at the texts with the reworking of Homer as a principal
interest). Homer (both *Il.* and *Od.*; Knauer, 912, Farrell, 208 cf. W.J.
Verdenius, *Homer, the educator of the Greeks* (Amsterdam 1970), 21, 25)
had served to lend grandeur to agriculture. That remains true of the
bees (Farrell, 239–58), though apparently not of their battle (4.67–
87): perhaps that is significant; certainly I do not see the passage as
lighthearted (cf. Farrell, 239, n. 68), though it would be as grave an
error to claim that Virgil saw nothing droll whatever in the equiva-
lence of human and bee (whence the great importance of ethno-
graphical elements in Virgil's description; for bibliography, cf. Horsfall
in Biotti, 20, n. 34), or in the mighty enterprises of the tiny insects
(ib., 19f.). From bees, then to aition and inset narrative.[120] Bees, after
all, are not 'just' insects: they lead the reader to song, to the souls of
the dead, to human society, to the divine presence in the natural
world.[121] The subject matter of *G.*4 is thereby heightened (and
Aristaeus' feat in consequence reaches far beyond apiculture), while

[119] But cf. rather id., *HSCP* 90 (1986), 171ff., Farrell, 207–72, and in particular
214ff., building on Knauer; some of the *problemata* had been unravelled much earlier, such as that at *G.*2.528; cf. Knauer, 907, with further bibliography.

[120] Wilkinson, 113ff., Mynors on 281–314, Farrell, 253ff., Horsfall in Biotti, 23ff.

[121] Horsfall in Biotti, 19 for bibliography; cf. D.E.W. Wormell in *Vergiliana*, 429ff.

at the same time Homer had long been interpreted allegorically as a
poet of natural philosophy,[122] and therefore far closer to *G.* than might
at first sight appear. Thus what is new about Homer in 4.315ff. is
above all the scale (and note the variety of the Homeric passages
integrated, Knauer, 911, Farrell, 105–13). Is it therefore altogether
simplistic and teleological (Farrell's words, 256) to think of the poet's
'growth' towards the *Aeneid*? Less so, I would suggest, if we bear in
mind how close in time the composition of the proem. to *G.*3 (appx.
3; contrast *G.*2.39, with Farrell, 245f. Is this not too 'growth'?) might
be to that of the Aristaeus-episode—and for that matter to the end
of the *G.* and to Virgil's first detailed thinking on the structure and
methods of the new epic.

G.4, Gallus and the 'second edition'[123]

We have already noted (ch. 1, 13f.) the presence of a strange tale
reported by Servius:

> *ad Buc.*10.1 (a friendship between Cornelius Gallus and Virgil so close) *ut
> quartus Georgicorum a medio usque ad finem eius laudes teneret: quas postea iubente
> Augusto in Aristaei fabulam commutauit.*
> *ad G.*4.1: *sane sciendum, ut supra diximus, ultimam partem huius libri esse mutatam:
> nam laudes Galli habuit locus ille, qui nunc Orphei continet fabulam, quae inserta
> est, postquam irato Augusto Gallus occisus est.*[124]

From (e.g.) Sebastiano Timpanaro[125] we have learned that it is less
easy than it might once have been to write Servius off as a fool and
a blunderer, but we have seen (ch. 1) both that he is usually incapable of critical analysis of the 'facts' of Virgil's life and that he often
reveals himself a more or less helpless victim of earlier commentators' tinkering with the text in the interests of exhibitionistic ingenu-

---

[122] Farrell, 257ff.; cf. 151 on *Aen.*6.
[123] The same main lines of discussion will be found ap. Biotti, 21–6.
[124] Belief in the tale(s) recounted by Serv. often rests either on credulity (or on
the desire to fill gaps with *something*), or on the wish to find a few more rude things
to say about the tyrant Augustus, or on the desire to make something startling out
of a few small inconsistencies in the text. The only modern scholar of repute to
offer a proper defence is Jocelyn, *Atti*, 1.431–48. Cf. rather Mynors, 296, Thomas,
1, 13–6, Wilkinson, 108–13, H. Naumann, *Sileno* 4 (1978), 7–21, W.B. Anderson,
CQ 27 (1933), 36–45, E. Norden, *SBBerlin* 1934, 626–83 = *Kl.Schr.* (Berlin 1966),
468–532.
[125] *MD* 22 (1989), 123–82 = *Nuovi contributi* (Bologna 1994), 405–58.

ity and biographical romanticising.[126] No *prima facie* reason for believing the texts here cited therefore exists; we have to see how they stand up to criticism. We are not even quite sure from Serv. whether he thought "Gallus" occupied all of 281ff. or was only uncomfortably embedded in the midst of Aristaeus.

It was suggested (Anderson, n. 124) that someone, possibly Serv. himself, or possibly his source, confused the last *Buc.*, where Gallus is amply present with the last *G.* (where he is not) and invented a tale to explain Gallus' absence in the later passage. With the language used by Serv., Anderson ingeniously compared Amm.17.4.5: *Gallus poeta, quem flens quodam modo in postrema Bucolicorum parte Vergilius leni carmine decantat.* Now, R.G.M. Nisbet[127] suggests that the scholiasts might have been confused by an attempt to explain Orpheus as an allegory for Gallus.

There are of course some real critical difficulties present in the second half of *G.*4; Serv. knows that: he would like to explain the link between bees and Orpheus (*ad G.*4.1) and he is worried about a mythological *fabula* in a didactic poem (3.1.118.8, 12, Th.-H.). His answers are not as good as his questions.

We have just seen that Virgil's extensive use of Homer in *G.*4 is part of a development in his technique (85f.); attempts to see parts of *G.*4 as a reworking of lines in the *Aen.* are profoundly improbable.[128]

Wilkinson (110f.) evoked a scene of memorable embarrassment: Octavian, Maecenas and all the court gathered at Atella in the summer of 29; they hear, as climax to the new poem, a panegyric, not of the victor of Actium—but of Cornelius Gallus. An outrage, also, to the structure of the poem: allusions to Maecenas and Octavian coexist in perfect harmony and a heavy dose of Gallus-eulogy, in whatever form, would have damaged this balance irredeemably. Octavian was not to turn to book-burning and to the exiling of men of letters for a generation, but so grave a lapse of taste and discretion could never, in 29, been contemplated by a poet of intelligence and high political understanding. Some have asked (e.g. Wilkinson 111f.) whether a smaller tribute to Gallus and to his province of Egypt (cf. 4.287ff.) might once have existed in the text, a tribute

---

[126] Cf. ch. 1, n. 48, Geymonat, 299f.

[127] *JRS* 77 (1987), 189, Farrell, 255, n. 102.

[128] Otis, 408–13 (an excellent discussion), G.N. Knauer, *ANRW* 2.31.2 (Berlin 1981), 910–4.

which would have created a less stark division between the first and second halves of the book. An unnecessary compromise; no need to work that hard to save Servius' credit.

Is Egypt itself significant? Hardly: an inevitable consequence of the Aristaeus-Proteus episode's indebtedness to *Od*.4 and of the association (Mynors on 4.287f.) of the bugonia with Egypt, in the tradition of ethnographic writing about marvels (Thomas on 4.287–94). Is the nymph Lycorias significantly named (339), in view of the poetic name (Lycoris, Ov. *Tr*.2.445, etc.) of Gallus' mistress Cytheris? Both poets (cf. Mynors and Thomas ad loc.) have Call. (fr.62 Pf., *Hymn.Ap*.19) in mind. Does Orpheus' doom suggest Gallus' (Griffin (n. 55), 62 = 164)? Both after all are poets. Only, though, if, after all that has been said, we are still looking for Gallus! There are those indeed who believe that we indeed have him (cf. Thomas 1, 15f. after R. Coleman, *AJP* 83 (1962), 55–71), under cover of Orpheus. Some irregularities of form are—we should be ready to admit—present,[129] but may yield readily to the application of commonsense and an understanding of the complexities of aetiological narrative.[130] Now that we have the commentaries of Thomas, Mynors and Biotti, those readers who (Thomas 1, 23), not finding enough emotional satisfaction in *G*.4 as it stood, turned to embroidery where Servius had stitched before, will now find exquisite art in abundance, though that may not be enough!

Let us think, lastly, of the two years[131] which elapse between the reading at Atella and Gallus' suicide: long enough for the text to be read and copied widely. Gallus is then disgraced: could Augustus ever have managed to have all copies of the text withdrawn and destroyed, so that no trace survived? With Ov. *AA*, he of course achieved nothing of the kind.[132] No trace of the Gallus-eulogy survives: it would, I submit, have been an irresistible temptation to the many fakers of pseudo-Virgiliana under the early Empire (24), had the story been known. So perhaps it appeared on the scene at a later stage. A final thought: were our present text in truth the ed. 2,

---

[129] Wilkinson, 112–3: two introductions (283ff., 315ff.), two bugoniae (538–43, 295–314).

[130] Wilkinson, l.c., Mynors on 4.530; cf. Horsfall in Biotti, 24. On the dislocation of verses—of no real relevance to our problem at all—cf. Mynors on 291–3 (very nearly conclusive).

[131] R. Syme, *Augustan Aristocracy* (Oxford 1986), 32.

[132] Cf. W. Speyer, *Büchervernichtung und Zensur des Geistes* (Stuttgart 1981).

written in haste under pressure, could it possibly have turned out so infinitely complex, mature and refined a piece of writing? But I have read enough to realise that upon some Servius' few words exercise an insuperable fascination, and with that sort of conviction, there is no arguing!

The plague of Noricum, the Bugonia, the loss of Eurydice have led most modern critics to a philosophical/theological reading of *G.*3–4, though there are still some satisfied by the formal perfections of the story as it stands (Mynors, on 4.293–6, Horsfall in Biotti, 23ff.). To vaster perspectives, Griffin (n. 55) 61ff. = 163ff. and Thomas 1, 21–4 (cf. now id. *CP* 86 (1991), 211–8) offer useful introductions, though both are convinced 'pessimists'. Contrast e.g. Otis, 210–4 and P. Johnston, *Vergil's agricultural golden age* (*Mnem.* Suppl. 60 Leiden 1980), 90–129, though the 'optimists' have yet to find a champion who combines eloquence and rigour at their adversaries' level. If my (or Dr. Thome's) reading of *Aen.*12, though (206), has anything to commend it, we should be looking for equilibrium, not polarity. Equilibrium seems to have gone out with Wilkinson (118ff.; cf. 1982, 329–31), and while waiting for its rebirth in *G.*, I have stuck to the cautious certainties of observable detail, encouraged by the luminous discussion at Mynors 293–6.

Language

We understand the language of *G.* far less well than we do that of *Buc.*(47–51) or *Aen.*(217–48).[133] Perhaps the subject's extreme complexity and variety has discouraged research; certainly it is a very promising field for future enquiry. Let me—to give some idea of the breadth of the issues involved—indicate, *exempli gratia*, ten features of the style of *G.* which need to be explored further:

(i) The 'recipe' manner, evocative of Cato, and indeed Hesiod: 'if you want to. . ., do this and this'; cf. Thomas on 2.227–37. A stileme, therefore, evocative of the earliest strata of the Greek and Roman didactic tradition. A sort of archaism of form, and a gift to the parodist;

---

[133] Mynors' commentary is rich in passing observations; cf. also Thomas 1, 24–8. Huxley too is sometimes helpful. Suerbaum, 449–51 confirms how neglected the subject is. A. Salvatore *EV* 2.691–5 is not very satisfactory.

thus at 1.299 Serv. quotes (note the paratactic form): *nudus ara, sere nudus; habebis tergore febrem!*

(ii) Given that W.A. Merrill, *UCPCP* 3.3. (1918) gives the raw material (more raw than you would believe possible!), and Farrell (n. 101) now challenges the conventional view of the 'Lucretian' use of particles in the articulation of Virgil's argument, it would be very useful to have a full study of the question.

(iii) The use of Ennian and Lucretian language in general.[134] Contrast Grecisms of grammar, morphology, lexicon, syntax, manner (on which Thomas' commentary is usually very useful; cf. too Farrell, 61ff.). It is a pity that *EV* treats the style of *G.* (n. 133) much less satisfactorily than that of *Aen.* (226).

(iv) The presence of colloquialisms and vulgarisms is much understated by Salvatore (n. 133); cf. my remarks in G. Bonfante, *La lingua parlata in Orazio* (Venosa 1994), 18f. on *G*.1.388f., 3.256. Note Virgil's use of *siccus, spissus, subito, serpens, bracchium, crassus, dorsum, facies, grandis, imus, inuenio, lassus, nato, lauo, ostium, pauor*, with Bonfante's remarks on each.[135]

(v) The high language of epic.[136] 4.170–5 Virgil will re-use in 8.416–53 (and cf. further n. 128 above); though his closest source here is probably Callimachus, the verbal effects are eminently suited to an epic context.[137] Cf. 239–41 on the Homeric manner of the Aristaeus episode. At the opposite extreme, the much-disputed problem of technical language: cf. 225–6 for ancient criticism of Virgil's usage.[138]

(vi) What we might wish to call neoteric mannerisms, especially strong in the Orpheus-story (241–4); cf. Thomas, index, s.v. neoteric (and cf. ib. s.v. elegiac language), *EV* s.v. *Neoterismo*, A. Salvatore ed. *Aen*.1 (Napoli 1947), xxiff. The topic is not limited to stylistic features shared between *Buc.* (a major neoteric *liber*, 41) and *G.*, but includes significant echoes of neoteric poets in *G*.(ib.). But Italia is not Arcadia. Bucolic *mollitia* is now (cf. 96–8 on *G*.3, proem.) out of favour.

(vii) While Kenney analyses two distinct Lucretian styles ('expository' and 'pathetic') in his commentary on Lucr.3 (26–9), Thomas is reluctant to attribute a similar polarity to Virgil (1, 24); cf. 75–6 on

---

[134] Cf. also G.N. Knauer, *ANRW* 2.31.2, 908f.

[135] *EV* s.v. *Parlato, Volgarismi* does not help much.

[136] Knauer (134), 890ff., Farrell, index, s.v. Epic.

[137] Briggs (n. 105), 13ff., Knauer (n. 134), 993ff., Farrell, index s.v. *Similes*.

[138] H.D. Jocelyn, *PLLS* 2 (1979), 115ff., A. Ernout, *Philologica* 3 (Paris 1965), 128–35, C. De Meo, *Lingue tecniche del latino* (Bologna 1983), 25ff.

the difficulty of applying stylistic discriminations to the so-called digressions.[139] A lot more work is called for.

(viii) The techniques of style and language involved in turning prose sources into poetry.[140] Virgil, in short, as metaphrast.

(ix) Metaphor and transference: the language of war used of farming, the emotions of man applied to animals and the natural world, the metaphors used for poetry itself, for toil, and for decay in nature: a lot of attention has been paid of late to individual topics, but (cf. 115-7 on *Aen.*2); there is no general survey, historically directed.

(x) Cf. above (74 n. 53) on the arithmetical aspects of structure; such enquiries can lead (cf. 33-4 on *Buc.*) to conclusions altogether subjective and dotty, but some of the material gathered on both *Buc.* and *G.* is undeniably arresting and a cautious analysis of secure examples would have much to teach us.

Bibliography

Commentaries

Those of R.A.B. Mynors (Oxford 1990) and R.F. Thomas (2 vols., Cambridge 1988) are to some extent complementary (cf. Horsfall, *AR* 38 (1993), 121-3, *RFil* 119 (1991), 211-7): M. is indispensable for style, language and agricultural detail, T. for use of sources and allusion. The existence of two such valuable aids to the serious reader is the principal justification of the brevity of what precedes! W. Richter (München 1957) will now be consulted less often. H. Huxley's modest commentary on *G.*1 and 4 (London 1963) reveals much good sense. For *G.*4, see too A. Biotti (Bologna 1994) (with introduction by NMH): by no means just an Italian version of recent work in English! Note that the Penguin translation (L.P. Wilkinson, 1982) is excellent.

Handbooks

Note ample prefatory discussion in *EV* s.v. *Georgiche*; for bibliography, W. Suerbaum, *ANRW* 2.31.1 (1980), 395-499, with index, ib. 2.31.2, (1982), 1359-99.

Books

L.P. Wilkinson, *The Georgics of Virgil* (Cambridge 1969) is exemplary; you need to know *G.* very well before you recognise where the years reveal its

---

[139] However wrong Della Corte (*EV* s.v. *Digressioni*) may be about the definition of 'digression' (cf. 75), he is right to sense their stylistic unity with the text as a whole.
[140] Thomas 1, 25f., id. *HSCP* 91 (1987), 229-60.

weaknesses. There is a little updating in *id.*, *CHCL* 2 (Cambridge 1982), 320–32. Of many more recent works, it is difficult to speak with great enthusiasm: cf. J. Griffin, *CR* 31 (1981), 23–37, for a comprehensive hecatomb. But J. Farrell, *Vergil's Georgics and the traditions of ancient epic* (Oxford 1991) is (difficult but) excellent (cf. Horsfall, *CR* 43 (1993), 44–7) on allusive reference to sources and treatment of those sources.

Articles

Articles found useful appear in the footnotes above. Though it will be seen that I am not much in sympathy with R.F. Thomas' reading of Virgil's pessimism (a reading that stems from D. Ross, *Virgil's Elements* (Princeton 1987), a book that I find, quite literally, very hard to understand), I have learned a great deal from his many discussions of Virgil's Alexandrian sources and techniques, even when they are not absolutely convincing.

The agricultural background

EV is notably disappointing here. For animals, U. Dierauer, *Tier und Mensch* (Amsterdam 1977) rather than S. Rocca, *Etologia Virgiliana* (Genova 1983). On soil, trees, crops, techniques and the like, Mynors is nearly definitive, but (cf. 65–9, 72 above) it is still worth consulting K.D. White, *Roman Farming* (London 1970), id., *Agricultural implements of the Roman world* (Cambridge 1967), id. *Farm equipment of the Roman world* (Cambridge 1975), J. Frayn, *Subsistence farming* (London 1979), ead. *Sheep-rearing and the wool-trade* (Liverpool 1984), M.S. Spurr, *Arable cultivation* (*JRS* Monographs 3, 1986). W.E. Heitland, *Agricola* (Cambridge 1921) remains very useful.

APPENDIX 1

WAR; PEACE; PRINCEPS

The *G.* are to the highest degree a mirror of their age and of its remarkable changes. In outline, therefore (and I know of no such list elsewhere):

1.466–88 portents of the death of Caesar (44)

2.198 the confiscations (43–2)

1.489–97 Philippi (42) and (490f.) Pharsalus (48)

1.24–42 later than the deification of Caesar (1 Jan. 42), but so mannered as to be undatable[141]

1.2, etc. perhaps as early as 38 (cf. 13) Maecenas is assembling about him compatible poets; V. may be between *Buc.* and *G.*

2.161–4 Agrippa's engineering works at the Lucrine lake (37)

1.505–14 civil war still unchecked on all sides

1.498–508 the *iuuenis* Octavian as the potential saviour of the age[142]

2.497 the Dacians serve as emblematic of the risk posed by civil war to the security of the frontiers. Cf. 63f. on 1.509 (Germans and Parthians).[143]

The *G.* as a poem of all Italy; particularly compatible with the political circumstances of the years directly before Actium[144]

2.506 may well derive from adverse criticism of Antony[145]

4.88–95 just might be in part allegory of the struggle between Octavian and Antony[146]

3.26–9 Actium (31); cf. 97.

3.19f. Ludi (?) Actiaci

Octavian's settlement of affairs in the East, 30–29: 2.170–2; 3.12 (?) (cf. 96f.) 4.561; 3.30f., campaign against the Parthians anticipated.

3.32f. Octavian's triumphs, not necessarily the historical ones of 29; cf. 96f.

3.26 etc. (cf. 97), the temple of Palatine Apollo, vowed in 36, dedicated 9 Oct. 28.

Whatever Octavian's methods and principles, he represented the best chance for peace in Italy and the Mediterranean, at least from the end of 36, and arguably from the peace of Brundisium (Sept. 40). *Buc.* and *G.* alike view civil war and the concomitant confiscations as uniquely inimical to farming

---

[141] Wilkinson, 162–5, White (n. 5), 173–5.

[142] On 1.41, cf. Wilkinson, 52; after the defeat of Sex. Pompeius, I do not see that the *regna* were any longer to be viewed as actually *peritura* (cf. 64 for the dating of this passage).

[143] Vd. Mynors *ad loc.*; the material he collects indicates the entire imprecision of the reference.

[144] Wilkinson, 174, Syme (n. 16), 76–93

[145] Cf. Courtney (n. 113), 272f.

[146] Wilkinson, 180–2.

(69). Virgil's support for Octavian[147] is therefore not servile toadying, but a real, realistic, sensible decision, however hard we may find to swallow the Alexandrian rococo into which he plunges in the proemia to bks. 1 and 3. Maecenas' invitation[148] demonstrates an exquisite sense of timing and an admirable judgement of the compatibility of poet and theme, though we should always be careful not to interpret the harmony between Virgil's poetical growth and the political changes of the age non-teleologically and without suspicion of intentionality!

---

[147] Little though (e.g.) R.F. Thomas likes it; his comments are significant in the reception of *G*!

[148] White (n. 5), 266–8, 135–6; sensible and perspicuous.

THE ACTUAL READERSHIP/INTENDED AUDIENCE OF G.

Discussion of the actual readership/intended audience of G. is bedevilled by general incomprehension on two other scores:

(i) 'Real farmers could not of course read'. No, far from it; cf. my discussion at *JRA* Suppl. 3 (1991), 65f. Note petitions to Pliny the younger, ample references in the technical literature to written instructions for *uilici*, *dispensatores* or even head shepherds, not to mention anecdotal evidence and the odd rural graffito, hinting at the aleatory element in the survival of evidence for rural literacy. Add the existence of agricultural calendars, i.e. rudimentary instructions in chronological sequence (J.E. Skydsgaard, *Varro the Scholar* (Copenhagen 1968), 43ff.).

(ii) Is Varro, *RR*, then, a 'real' farming manual? The author's wife Fundania has just bought a farm and Varro says he will keep an eye upon it; reasonably, his wife wants it well-tilled and profitable (cf. Brunt (n. 16), 247). But the text is markedly disorganised and unsystematic.[149] Especially in bk. 3, Varro writes for the luxury market (aviaries and fishponds) and is concerned in particular with profitability;[150] profit there was, even in small-scale beekeeping (*RR* 3.16.10). But Varro includes ideological 'uplift' too, as in the praises of Italy (1.2.3), no less fantastical than Virgil's (cf. 69f.). I suspect (*RFil.*119 (1991), 212) that the *RR* stands in the tradition of those books (like Frontinus on aqueducts) written to help owners or administrators, particularly those new and inexperienced (dare one, in the case of *RR*, think of those who guessed right during the civil wars, proscriptions and confiscations? Cf. Shatzman (n. 150), 37–44), otherwise at the mercy, no less than Frontinus or his successors, of their permanent staff. Farm-owners otherwise risk not having the language, the terminology, the technical tricks, the profitable 'wrinkles' to be able to talk to their overseers and *RR* helps in an amusing and unsystematic way. Recall (70) the difficulties of the younger Pliny at Tifernum.

---

[149] E.D. Rawson, *PBSR* 46 (1978), 12–34 = *ead. Roman culture and society* (Oxford 1991), 324–51.

[150] T. Frank, *Econ. Survey* 1 (Baltimore 1933), 358–65, I. Shatzman, *Senatorial Wealth and Roman politics* (*Coll.Lat.*142, 1975), 24–9.

THE PROOEMIUM TO *G*.3

One of the most dense and satisfying of early Augustan poetic texts.[151] Virgil will now sing of Pales, patroness of *pastores* (sheep and goats included; cf. *G*.3.294), of Apollo Nomios (horses and cows)[152]—the exact content, that is, of bk. 3. The stock themes of mythology are exhausted (Call. *Aet*.1.27f.); Busiris and Hylas are Hellenistic, Eurystheus and Pelops (Virgil evoked Pind. *Ol*.1.27) classical, and the central *Latonia Delos* universal.[153] Virgil will therefore try a new *uia*, the conventional language of originality[154] and as *uictor* (*acer equis* suggests that this will be polyvalent) will be able *uirum uolitare per ora*.[155] Virgil will bring back—*deducam*, the language of the *triumphator*[156] but also (*Buc*.6.5) of the refined poet—from the Boeotian home of the Muses (Call.fr.572; cf. Thomas) *primus* (a classic Augustan vaunt, Horsfall (n. 154), 63) the Muses to his homeland, a matter for peculiar pride among Augustan poets (Ovid, Propertius and particularly Horace *C*.3.30.10–12). He will bring back Idumaean palms (the biblical Edom),[157] symbolic of the athletic victor, of the poetic victor and of the triumphator. He will build a temple by the river Mincio, a temple of song,[158] which will prove to have much in common with that of Palatine Apollo, shrine of Augustan poetic originality (Horsfall (n. 154), 58–67). In its centre (not so much premature deification as poetic centrality)[159] will be Caesar (Augustus) like Berenice (in the *Victoria*) in the *Aetia* and like Augustus in *Aen*.8 (675). *Modo uita supersit* and *interea* (40) refer to a work not yet undertaken. Virgil may be pondering

---

[151] Cf. the commentaries of Richter, Mynors and Thomas, V. Buchheit, *Der Anspruch des Dichters in Vergils Georgika* (Darmstadt 1972), 92–159, Wilkinson, 165–72, 323–4 and id., *Forschungen z. röm. Lit...K. Büchner* (Wiesbaden 1970), 286ff., R. Thomas, *HSCP* 87 (1983), 179f., White (n. 5), 135f., 175ff.

[152] Call. *HAp*.47 (horses); also (Mynors) cattle (Eur. *Alc*.8); for the anonymous form of reference, cf. 99 on *G*.1 proem.

[153] Cf. Horsfall in *Mythos in Mythenloser Gesellschaft, Colloquium Rauricum* 3 (Stuttgart 1993), 137.

[154] Horsfall, *GR* 40 (1993), 64, D. Steiner, *The crown of song* (London 1986), 76ff., Call. *Aet*.1.27f.

[155] Enn. *Epigr*.18V; Homer's winged words must be implicitly in play.

[156] Buchheit (n. 151), 100 on Lucr.1.72–9 (poet as victor); *deducere* triumphal: Hor. *C*.1.37.31.

[157] Hypothetically Callimachean (Thomas); just the area, though, in which, as Virgil wrote, Octavian was restoring to Herod lands in general and palm-groves in particular, after they had been appropriated by Antony and Cleopatra: cf. E. Schürer, *History of the Jewish people* (rev. F. Millar, etc.) 1 (Edinburgh 1973), 298–302, Jos. *BJ* 1.361, 398.

[158] Pind. *Ol*.6.1ff.; possibly Callimachean (Thomas).

[159] White (n. 5), 175–7, Thomas (n. 151), 179.

his prose sketch (cf. 16) of the *Aen*.! The survival of the idea that these lines might refer to the *G*. is depressing. As *triumphator*, Virgil, garbed in purple, will drive a hundred chariots[160] of song (Steiner (n. 154), index, s.v.) to the river. For Octavian (*illi*) all Greece will come to the contest (not just e.g. *Ludi Actiaci* but the conscious rivalry inherent in all Augustan poetry, Mynors, ad loc., Horsfall, n. 154), leaving Olympia (Call. *Aet*.3. fr.76–7) and Nemea (Call. *Suppl.Hell*.256ff.) even though the fight be with the Roman *caestus* (cf. *Aen*.5.410!).

Garlanded as victor, Virgil will dedicate gifts. Even now, with Palatine Apollo yet incomplete, Virgil delights in procession and sacrifice, and in the theatrical displays there will be, *uersis. . .frontibus* (24)—the scene changes in more ways than one; on the curtain will be depicted[161] the conquered Britons (cf. 63); this is (cf. 63 n. 3) panegyric language in the Alexander-tradition. On the doors (we think of Palatine Apollo, very different though those doors will be)[162] will be (cf. *Aen*.8.675ff.) Octavian's victory at Actium (cf. Buchheit (n. 151), 137ff.). A notable rejection of Callimachean themes, though in Callimachean language and imagery. Virgil will represent the *urbes Asiae domitas*[163] and even now in the best Augustan manner anticipates vengeance against Parthia[164] and triumphs in West and East (unspecified traditional polarity; cf. 1.509).[165] Had Virgil here inserted a reference to Octavian's triple triumph, a few days after the reading at Atella, he would have sunk to the level of the toadying court poet; note, though, that he mentions two, quite distinct from the actual, historical, three. There will also be statues, Palatine and poetical (Pind. *Nem*.7.70–9), anticipating the parade of heroes in *Aen*.6. The Trojan ancestors of Aeneas and Octavian—lynchpin of the *Aen*.—are here represented (Buchheit (n. 151), 143). *Inuidia*, foe alike of statesman and poet, and therefore not exclusively Callimachean (Buchheit n. 151, 142, n. 600) will be shown fearing the punishments of Hell (*Aen*.8.669, 6, *passim*).

In the mean time, the poet will continue to write of woods and pastures (*G*.3), *tua, Maecenas, haud mollia iussa*.[166] The *saltus* are *intactos*, uncut, and a fresh theme for poetry. Maecenas' *iussa* are *haud mollia*, not so much insistent as difficult of fulfilment and different from the *mollitia* inherent in bucolic. Maecenas is essential to Virgil's poetic endeavour[167] and Virgil invites him to speedy presence (*en age, rumpe moras*). On hand is the excitement of the hunt, integral element of pastoral and georgic life,[168] given here a Laconian context, though the horses are from Epidaurus.[169] Soon (as soon as *G*. are

---

[160] Typical Roman visual propaganda: Plin. *Nat*.35.22–5, E. Zinserling in (ed. H.-J. Diesner) *Sozialökonomische Verhältnisse* (Berlin 1961), 346–54.

[161] Cf. 63 for this passage as a non-chronological indicator.

[162] For the actual doors, cf. Horsfall (n. 154), 65, n. 3 for recent bibliography.

[163] A firm dating indicator; cf. 93 on 4.560f.

[164] Nisbet-Hubbard 1, xxxii, Syme (n. 14), 384, 441ff., Brunt (n. 2), 104ff., Gruen (n. 2), 396ff., R. Seager., *Athen*.58 (1980), 103–18, summarised, *PLLS* 1 (1976), 155f.

[165] F. Christ, *Die röm. Weltherrschaft*. . .(Stuttgart 1938), 53ff.

[166] White (n. 5), 135f., Horsfall, *Poets and Patron* (North Ryde 1981).

[167] Nisbet-Hubbard on Hor. *C*.1.12 is flawed by cynicism; cf. White (n. 5), 17f.

[168] Cf. 3.371–5, *EV* 1.590.

[169] Strab.8.8.1, E. Courtney, *AJP* 110 (1989), 488.

finished) Virgil will write of the *pugnas/Caesaris* and grant them eternity (Tithonus is conveniently not only a symbol of time but also a Trojan, indeed brother of Priam): Aeneas' victories are to some extent allegorical of Augustus' (cf. 163) and the latter anyway figures in *Aen.*1, 6 and 8; the reference is unambiguously to the epic we have.

THE PROOEMIUM TO *G*.1

We open with a formal statement of content, typical of prooemia (cf. 102f.), *Aen.* 1.11, 7.37f.), expressed in dependent clauses. With the invocation to Maecenas balancing that at 4.2, vv. 1–4 summarise the whole four books (cf. 74), but do not therefore necessarily belong to a late stage in composition, for they could reflect the moment when V. first had a clear view of the structure of the whole. There is exquisite balance (cf. Thomas ad loc.) between the space allotted to bks. 2 and 4 and between the words which describe 1 and 3. There follows (5–42) the longest sentence in Virgil, perhaps in all Latin poetry. The twelve gods of Virgil's invocation recall arithmetically and in occasional detail those of Varr. *RR* 1 praef. 4–6. Virgil starts with Sun and Moon (Varro's second pair, named, unlike Virgil's); his second pair, Liber and Ceres (developed more fully) are Varro's third (and they are Lucretian too, 5.14f.); next, the Fauni, and subordinate Dryads, anticipating 3.40; the dancing rhythm of v. 11 relieves the majestic tone, as do the parenthesis in 11–12, and the pause at *cano*, 12. Neptune follows, from 12 caes. (2½) to 14 (pause after elided first foot): note that Virgil is very sparing with the characteristic relative clauses of prayers and prooemia, and is careful to vary their grammatical form. Aristaeus (14f.), anticipating bk. 4, is not named,[170] in the Callimachean manner, while his home in Cea/Ceos alludes to both Apollonius and Callimachus (Thomas). The invocation to Pan runs to a pause at 3½ in its third line and is visibly richer in the conventional formulae of prayer. Minerva, discoverer of the olive, is paired with the nameless (and Callimachean) inventor of the plough (Triptolemus);[171] loosely, Silvanus follows them. Enough; Virgil masks the risk of limp disorder and breaks off with a general invocation in the manner of Roman prayer-formulae (the generalisation from fear of omitting the minor but appropriate deity; cf. Mynors): one short relative clause, and two solemn *quique*...which occupy entire lines. 5–23 balance exactly 24–42 (Octavian).[172] Again a towering periodic structure (main verb at 40). This invocation begins (cf. 12) *tu*...but it is not yet clear (*quem*..., just in the manner of a conventional invocation) what sort of a deity he will be and 'Caesar' is not named until the end of the second line devoted to him: cities and lands (25 from caes.–28), the sea (39–31), or the zodiac (32–5): whatever sort of deity Octavian will be (corresponding to 21ff.), he will of course not rule in Hades, whatever that region's mythological importance (36 from 1½–39). A due disproportion of scale corresponding to the distinction in public roles between Maecenas (one word) and Octavian (nine-

---

[170] Cf. Horsfall (n. 81).

[171] Frentz (n. 77), 7ff.

[172] Not so much specifically a reference to Oct. and the *cena dodecatheos* (Suet. *Aug.*70.1) as to the frequent association in the Hellenistic world of ruler and twelve gods: S. Weinstock, *Divus Iulius* (Oxford 1971), 185, 285.

teen lines!). Here Octavian is invited *da facilem cursum* (:: 3.42, Maec.) *atque audacibus* (cf. 565) *adnue coeptis*. Both princeps and poet shall pity the *miseros agrestis* (a Lucretian didactic pose: Thomas); one, with divine authority and knowledge, shall bring peace to the land. By way of climax, Octavian is to enter his new sphere of activity and even now become used to being invoked in prayer.[173]

---

[173] Cf. White (n. 5), 173–5: the poet anticipates Octavian's versatility and superiority among the Olympians as though such abilities were transferable from this world to a Higher Sphere! It is essential to note that (White, 170f.) the poet is extemporising, far ahead of any developments in actual ruler-cult, or indeed of the conventional Romulus/Hercules analogies of poetry: cf. A. La Penna in *Hommages Le Bonniec*, (Coll.Lat.201 (1988), 275–87).

CHAPTER FOUR

AENEID

N.M. Horsfall

Book 1: Myth, history, and the subject of the Aeneid[1]

'His epic is the unique history of his own unique people';[2] 'this neglect endemic to the imperial ideology of the human wastage generated by the mission it inspires'; 'the *Aeneid*'s failure was a condition
of its truth';[3] 'the struggle and final victory of order—this subduing
of the demonic which is the basic theme of the poem';[4] 'the more
Virgil appeals to our moral sense, the more that sense is outraged'.[5]
Well may Quinn ask 'What is the *Aeneid* about?'.[6] The question can
perhaps be answered better at the end of the poem, but it may prove
helpful to air it at the outset, in as much as the poet seems, if (conventional or traditional) critics have read the text's explicit rhetoric
in lines (say) 1–296 with some degree of insight and understanding,
to have been exceptionally generous with his indications of the levels
at which he proposes to write and the manner in which he wishes—
or so it would appear—to be understood. If that remark is in itself
now, in some eyes, a critical fallacy, then I can only say that here I
am writing about what I (and the scholars I cite) have seen and
heard in the prooemium. I am only seeking to disentangle elements
in a complex text, and do not wish to impose any reading—let alone
any dominant and unequivocal reading—of my own.

It is perhaps no longer necessary to explain the relationship of

---

[1] The poem's title, *Aeneis* has been discussed, not altogether satisfactorily *EV* 2,
236f. (Della Corte), and (better) J. Mantke, *Klio* 67 (1985), 238ff. Let us be clear;
titles matter. *Aeneis* is that used by Augustus (*Epist*.fr.xxxvi Malc. = VSD 31) and by
Ovid (2.533). That it could also be called *arma uirumque* is not here relevant. But
Virgil, ap. Macr.1.24.11 calls the poem 'my Aeneas' cf. Ov. *Ars* 3.337, Carv. Pictor,
GRF p. 543 (VSD 44, where in fact the mss. divide between *Aeneomastix*. and
Aeneidomastix). For the easy passage between formal title and economical description
of subject-matter, cf. *BICS* 28 (1981), 105, and for Greek antecedents (*Geryoneis*, *Heracleis*,
Theseis), cf. Mantke, 240. Cf. further n. 27.
[2] B. Otis, *Phoen*.20 (1966), 60.
[3] A.J. Boyle, *The Chaonian Dove* (*Mnem.* Suppl. 94 (1986), 146, 176).
[4] V. Pöschl, *The art of Vergil* (Ann Arbor, 1962), 18.
[5] K. Quinn in *Cicero and Virgil* ed. J.R.C. Martyn (Amsterdam 1972), 206.
[6] *Virgil's Aeneid* (London 1968), 23ff; cf. A. Primmer, *WS* 93 (1980), 83ff.

arma uirumque. . . .and the following lines to *Iliad* and *Odyssey*,[7] nor to examine the remarkable structure of the prooemium,[8] nor to examine *cano* in its place in the history of epic prooemia,[9] nor even to explain certain elements of scholarly polemic which Virgil nails to the poem's masthead.[10] Let us distinguish ten 'strands' in 1.1–11:

(1) *Arma* (1.1): Aeneas' (Iliadic) wars, by no means the Trojans' first (3 *terris iactatus*, 23, 30, 94ff., 238, 284ff.); there are, though, more to come: 5 *multa quoque et bello passus dum conderet urbem*, anticipating bks. 7–12. Note that *arma uirumque* anticipates chiastically 1–6 and 7–12.

(2) The hero, *uirum* (Odyssean), more precisely defined, in a new light, as (10) *insignem pietate uirum*; cf. 38 and §9 below. The 'new' style of hero is not characterised exclusively by *pietas*; he is also cast explicitly in the mould of Hector (cf. 1.99, 273).[11]

(3) The Trojans' sufferings, on sea (85ff.), on land, at war (3–5), which lead them to Italy (2), and in particular to Latium (6, 205) and the *Lauina. . .litora* (2f.). Note 31: the distance Aeneas has to travel augments Juno's opportunities for chastising Aeneas; *multum iactatus* is not only geographical but (31, cf. 47) temporal. Contrast 278. Future sufferings, too, are anticipated: the *contra* of 13 is not only geographical (cf. §§, 4, 5, 6). Aeneas' wars are in some sense allegorical of those that Rome will have to fight.[12]

(4) Carthage, over against Rome (13), rich and warlike (14; cf. 21, 445). The *fato* of 2 (cf. 258) is balanced by *fatis* 32 (cf. 205, 258); cf. Cic. *ND* 2.165f. for the doctrine of the *fata* of individual cities.

(5) Note the founding of Carthage from Tyre (cf. the *altae moenia Romae* from Troy): 12, 20. Leading to future rivalry (19ff. 33).[13] For above all Aeneas is a founder too:[14] cf. 5–7, 33, 258. Of a nation of rulers (7, 21, 253, etc.).

---

[7] Buchheit, 13ff., Austin, ad loc.

[8] 1–11 is exactly half the bulk of 12–33; within 1–11, note the climax at 7 taken up at 33; cf. further the next note.

[9] Further to n. 7, cf. *EV* s.v. *Proemi*, Knauer, 220, n. 3, Hardie 303, Quinn 40f.

[10] On *fato profugus*, cf. F. Bliss in *Classical and renaissance studies in honor of B.L. Ullmann* 1 (Roma 1964), 99ff.; on *Troiae qui primus ab oris* cf. G.K. Galinsky, *Lat.*28 (1969), 3ff.

[11] Horsfall, *Vergilius* 32 (1986), 16f., and *EV* 2, 221f. Cf. G.K. Galinsky, *ANRW* 2.31.2 (1981), 985ff.

[12] Pöschl (n. 4), 13ff., Hardie, 302ff.

[13] Horsfall (n. 30), 1ff. = 127ff. Cf. further 106 on Dido and the Punic wars.

[14] Horsfall, *Vergilius* 35 (1989), 8ff.; cf. P. McGushin, *Lat.*24 (1965), 411ff. E.D. Carney, *Coll.Lat.*196 (1986), 422ff. is not satisfactory.

(6) And Aeneas' foundation(s) will lead to that of Rome: 7, 33, 258ff. The 'political' simile of 148ff. is a famous inversion of Homer, heavily influenced also by Hes. *Theog.*81ff., a passage often cited in literature on the 'good king'.[15] We should probably not be looking for a reference to a specific episode in Roman history. But the simile's placing makes explicit (i) the central place of politics and order in any sane reading of the poem, (ii) the symbolic sense to be attributed to the calming of the storm[16] and (iii) the unmistakable invitation to the reader to apply a symbolical reading to some (?many, ?all) events in the text.[17]

(7) Aeneas will suffer much *ui superum* (4; cf. 5, 9, 10, 11, 29, 33, 207, 241). And because of the *fata* (32). His chief enemy is possessed of a *memorem. . .iram* (4; cf. 25ff., 36, 251, 10.61).

(8) The need to explain why Juno is so angry (8, 17ff.).[18] She is enraged historically, on account of Rome's future threat (19–22) to her beloved Carthage (12–8) and (*ueterisque* 23) also mythologically, both in the Trojan war (23f.) and on account of yet older causes (25–8). Her rancour and her sense of the power and privileges due to her[19] have driven her to (cf. 37; note *inimica*, 67) war. Aeneas is himself guiltless (231), but because of his destined goal, *cunctus terrarum clauditur orbis* to him (233, 251). Venus knows (234) that a better future is to come: not only fate (239, 261, 262), but Jupiter's promise (237; cf. 250, 258, 260) have reassured her (237ff.). The question is, when will the improvement begin (contrast 35 and 241f.)?

(9) Aeneas is from the first *insignem pietate uirum* (10; cf. 151, 220, 253); he is also bearer of Troy's gods (6). His sufferings therefore are particularly unmerited. But (cf. n. 28, and 68, 279ff.) reconciliation with Juno will come.

(10) The extraordinary, cosmic dimensions of the opposition to Aeneas. Juno's appeal to Aeolus presupposes her freedom of action. But Aeolus (60, 65; and Juno knows, 78) is subordinated to a higher order. The limits to his ability to provoke a global upheaval do not

---

[15] Cairns, 93f., Otis, 229f., S.J. Harrison, *PCPhS* 34 (1988), 55ff, Feeney (n. 22), 137.

[16] Cf. n. 12 and Otis, l.c.

[17] Cf. Buchheit, 183ff., and Pöschl, Otis and Hardie (nn. 12, 16). In general, Cf. 111ff. (on bk. 2).

[18] Cf. H. Kleinknecht, *Herm.* 79 (1944), 108f. = *Wege zu Vergil* ed. H. Oppermann (Darmstadt 1963), 484f., P. McGushin, *AJP* 86 (1965), 267ff., Harrison (n. 29), 106f., A. Wlosok, *Die Göttin Venus* (Heidelberg 1967) passim.

[19] Feeney (n. 22), 129ff., Heinze, 96ff., Wlosok (n. 18), 55f., Buchheit, 59ff.

become apparent until 124ff.[20] And it turns out (199, 258) that other deities will succour the Trojans.

In addition to key themes, key words such as *pius/pietas, labores, ira, urbs/moenia, condere, laeti, furor*. Key words, though, have come to exercise a certain tyranny over even the best modern writing on the *Aeneid*. When the individual word (very carefully selected) becomes more important than the whole verse, than the context, than the narrative, then perhaps it may be time to express anxiety, without wishing to question the need to study most minutely words such as those just listed. A sense of the whole tends to be lacking in rigorously word-based studies, and that is why I propose to offer rather examinations of the text which owe more to the old *lecture raisonnée*.

My admiration for books on Virgil's Venus, cosmology, sense of politics etc. does not divert me from maintaining that we can understand the text best by reading it, even, sometimes, as a whole, in the order in which it stands, rather than by microscopic analysis of selected details. Or rather, the one system should be used to reinforce the other!

In these opening lines, then, the lexical and rhetorical emphasis is not, except perhaps retrospectively, or by manipulation of the term 'ironical',[21] ambiguous:[22] if the poem is to be read as inimical to a patriotic view of Rome's history and destiny,[23] then such a reading necessarily entails a poet also committed to the subversion of all his own rhetorical strategy as presented in the programmatic texture of his prooemium. That is perhaps not entirely inconceivable, even in an author studied as a model in the rhetorical schools,[24] but such subversion implies a poet committed from the outset to toying, Juno-like, with his reader.

To 'disentangle' ten 'strands' in the ideas expressed in Virgil's prooemium is of course an entirely artificial *modus operandi*, undertaken only for the sake of clarity in exegesis; it bears stressing that these 'strands' are not separate in the text, that their interweaving presents us with an opening of quite exceptional density, and that within the almost impenetrable texture of 1.1–296, the various 'strands'

---

[20] Feeney (n. 22), 133, Hardie, 90, Buchheit, 63ff.

[21] Cf. M. Di Cesare, *The altar and the city* (New York 1974), 3.

[22] Cf. D.C. Feeney, *The gods in epic* (Oxford 1991), 140f. on 285 *seruitio*.

[23] A difficulty not missed by Quinn (n. 5).

[24] Cf. Highet, 3f., *EV* s.v. *Seneca, Quintiliano, Retori Latini Minores*, etc. Cf. further Bk. 11, n. 5.

react continually upon each other. The battles of the elements, of Jupiter and Juno, of Juno and Venus,[25] of Aeneas against his enemies, elemental, divine and human, and the struggles of Rome against her enemies, notably Carthage[26] are in continuous interaction. The *Aeneid* is both heroic and historic.[27] We should note that the programmatic emphasis on Rome's conflict with Carthage (cf. p. 106) not only defines and enlarges the poem's historic scope, but, over and above the allusions to *Iliad* and *Odyssey* just noted in *Aen.*1.1 and elsewhere in 1.1–11, in some way relates the poem to the work of Naevius and Ennius (cf. 124, n. 7 and note the sly use of *annales* at 1.373!).[28] I do not understand how Virgil can be accused of playing down the Punic wars by comparison with other episodes in Roman history:[29] the narrative of *Aen.*1 and 4 is in frequent dialogue with the history, especially of the second Punic war.[30] It is also noteworthy[31] that the *Aeneid* is seen as 'breach' of current dogma, as laid down in the prooemium to Callimachus' *Aetia* on the 'obsolescence of epic'. If in *Aen.*1.1–33, Virgil can engage in allusive discussion with Ennius, Naevius, and Homer, then his technique is flawlessly Callimachean, even if his subject-matter, formally, is not.[32] The *Aeneid* is both embedded in its poetic past and continuously inventive. Nor should it be thought that I wish to read bk. 1 as setting a dominantly national, patriotic and upbeat tone for the poem. By way of contrast, it is worth looking at 1.441–93. Allusively, the scene has already been set, not only for history (373), but also for tragedy.[33] Let us now look at the pictures in Juno's temple:[34]

---

[25] Feeney (n. 22), 130ff.

[26] Cf. bk. 4, n. 9.

[27] Serv. *ad Aen.*6.752 refers to the *antiqui* who called the poem *gesta populi Romani*. An exemplary description of the poem's subject-matter, if most unlikely ever to have been used as an actual title.

[28] Cf. bk. 4, nn. 7, 64. On Naevius and Virgil, cf. further *EV* s.v. *Nevio,* Horsfall, *GR* 38 (1991), 205. Feeney (n. 22), 138f., 148 is slightly overoptimistic Cf. further bk. 4, n. 7. On Ennius, cf. *EV* s.v. *Ennio,* Feeney (n. 22), 125f., 130f. and *CQ* 34 (1984), 179ff., Wigodsky, 55ff.

[29] E.L. Harrison in *Poetry and politics in the age of Augustus* ed. T. Woodman and D. West (Cambridge 1984), 102ff.

[30] So Feeney (n. 22), 130f.; my own position *PVS* 13 (1973–4), 1ff. = Harrison, 127ff.

[31] Otis, 5ff., Quinn, 34ff., etc.

[32] Cf. bk. 6, n. 45.

[33] E.L. Harrison, *PVS* 12 (1972–3), 10ff. = Robertson, 197ff., id., *Eranos* 77 (1979), 52ff. and *EMC* 33 (1989), 5, 7f. In the text, then, not only Venus' boots (1.337) but cf. also 1.427 *theatris* and 4.471 *scaenis*.

[34] On the pictures in the temple, Horsfall, (n. 30), 7f. = 136f., F. Muecke, *AJP*

When Aeneas arrives at the site of Carthage,[35] he sees, with wonder, the city being built. Contrast Troy's destruction and his own
false starts narrated in bk. 3. He has no idea that his descendants
will fight the Carthaginians three times, until 146 B.C. (cf. 1.22).
Against *moenia Romae*, the new *moenia* of Carthage (437); in his ignor-
ance, Aeneas calls their builders *fortunati*, in that they at least have a
city; he even wonders (454) *quae fortuna sit urbi*. Invisible, he reaches
the grove where the city's foundation-portent was discovered.[36] Here
Dido had built a temple to Juno, Aeneas' enemy and Rome's, as we
have been told repeatedly, and as Aeneas himself (cf. 2.612ff., 3.435ff.)
knows, in part. Here he does not perceive, or understand the dedication. We do, or should. That Aeneas takes comfort from what he
sees should not lead us automatically to share that solace. That Aeneas
hic primum. . .sperare salutem/ausus et adflictis melius confidere rebus should
perhaps suggest that we 'know' more than he does. Historical irony.[37]
He has heard the bloody story of the house of Belus (340ff.), obeys
his mother (387ff.) and heads for the city, whose queen, *fati nescia*
(299) has been induced, by a visit from Mercury, sent by Jupiter
himself, to welcome the visitors.[38] Aeneas does not know what will
happen; the gods do not care. Only the reader should perhaps grow
anxious, with historical retrospect. Let us return to those pictures in
which Aeneas finds solace:

He weeps for the knowledge that the Trojans' *labor* (cf. 102) is
known even here (460); as he tells Achates, he sees Priam, *sunt hic*

---

104 (1983), 152, R.D. Williams, *CQ* 10 (1960), 145ff. = Harrison, 37ff., W.R. Johnson,
Darkness Visible (Berkeley 1976), 99ff., K. Stanley, *AJP* 86 (1965), 267ff. (acute; cf.
further, 182 n. 26 on the war in Latium and the war at Troy). On ekphraseis in
general, cf. A. Laird, *JRS* 83 (1993), 18ff., D.P. Fowler, ib. 81 (1991), 25ff. Fowler
seems rather too ready to associate the ekphrasis here with Dido's own view of
Trojan history, as she had learned it from Teucer (623, 625f.)—a bitter enemy of
Troy (Horsfall (n. 30) 8 = 137). The 'focalisation' here is surely distinct, since we
have not yet heard of Dido's presumed source (nor have we taken into account his
peculiar enmity towards Troy). Fowler makes many acute remarks, but my polemic
of twenty years ago, though crude, still seem closer to Virgil's complex strategy of
mythological allusion than Fowler's! Cf. now A. Barchiesi *AuA* 40 (1994), 119.

[35] The chronological leap this entails long worried critics, unnecessarily.

[36] The portent (441–5): cf. E. Kraggerud, *SO* 38 (1963), 32ff. and E.L. Harrison,
PLLS 5 (1985), 131ff., which does not quite convince me: see *Vergilius* 35 (1989), 13.
uictu (445) from the noun *uictus*; not a supine ('ready to conquer'), a bad old idea
well crushed by Henry.

[37] Aeneas cannot place 339 *genus intractabile bello* in an historical context. He knows
(384: but how?) that he is in Libya, but not what that name will mean for his
descendants.

[38] On the Belidae cf. Harrison (n. 33, 1989), 14; cf. further Feeney (n. 22), 141.

etiam sua praemia laudi/, sunt lacrimae rerum et mentem mortalia tangunt.[39] Aeneas comments on what he sees: in his distress, depiction entails sympathy, and (461) merit in battle entails representation in art (*sunt hic etiam sua praemia laudi*). Even at Carthage *mentem mortalia tangunt.* Thus, Aeneas concludes, the Trojans' *fama* will save them (463, cf. 457). So he continues to weep at what he sees, and *animum pictura pascit inani.*[40] In the scenes described in specific detail, we should note:

(i) Rhesus, newly arrived at Troy and slaughtered in his sleep (469–73).

(ii) The *infelix* Troilus, no match for Achilles;[41] in a version apparently calqued upon both the (traditional) ambush of Troilus by Achilles and on the treatment of Hector's corpse. The boy is not on board his chariot, *amissis. . .armis*, and, specifically (477), without helmet (474–8).[42]

(iii) The women of Troy pray to Pallas,[43] almost as implacable an enemy as Juno would prove to be (cf. 2.162f.) (479–82).

(iv) Achilles drags Hector's body not round Patroclus' tomb, but three times round the walls of Troy.[44] Priam tries to ransom it against payment.[45] Aeneas sees only pathos (487) in the spectacle of old Priam's pleas (487), while we, more familiar with Carthaginian sadism in Roman historiography, note the more savage post-Homeric version of the story (483–7).

(v) Aeneas sees himself, along with Memnon and Penthesilea (two allies of the Trojans killed by Achilles). He is so overwhelmed to discover that the fame of Troy has reached even the unknown continent of Africa that his reading of the paintings is punctuated by

---

[39] Only rank bad Latin can make of these lines a general reflection on the human condition. Decisive is the repetition *sunt. . .sunt*, with *hic*, here in the temple, attached to the first member. The genitive is simple objective; Austin compares 2.784. After H. Williamson, *CR* 33 (1919), 30, cf. E.J. Kenney, *CR* 14 (1964), 13. Alas, many will remain unconvinced that here at least a plain answer to a non-problem is possible (cf. *EV* s.v. *lacrima!*).

[40] Cf. Johnson (n. 34), 105, R. Scarcia, *EV* 2, 932: the pictures are devoid of life, of substance, of real comfort; a sharp contrast to Demodocus' words (Virgil's formal model, *Od.*8.487ff.)

[41] No match for Achilles: cf. Horsfall, *GR* 34 (1987), 48ff.

[42] *Alambicco*, 51; cf. further *LIMC* 1.1.72f., Williams (n. 34), 145ff.

[43] Cf. E. Henry, *The vigour of prophecy* (Bristol 1989), 93, 97.

[44] *LIMC* 1.1.138, Eur. *Andr.*107f., Hyg. *Fab.*106, C. Robert, *Die griech. Heldensage* 2.3 (ed. 4, Berlin 1923), 1118, W.R. Paton, *CR* 27 (1913), 45.

[45] *Uendebat*: cf. *Il.*24.76, 119, 137, 146f. From whose viewpoint is *uendebat* meant to be seen? A pretty question.

wonder and tears. We should perhaps be readier to notice the Carthaginians' choice of scenes of special brutality and Greek victory, however well disposed the queen in person shows herself at the outset. What might the choice of scenes mean, we wonder, for Aeneas and for the Trojans in the long run? The choice of mythological variants serves as a precious indicator of the key in which these stories should probably be read (488–93).

Book 2: Points of view; symbolism and imagery

Points of view

It is not my intention to discuss here Virgil's 'cinematographic' technique.[1] Of more lasting importance seem the results of a strong reaction, particularly in Italy,[2] against a certain oversimplification (most clearly seen in the polar terminology "empathy–sympathy') inherent in ch. 3 ('The subjective style') of Otis' *Virgil*.[3] That interacts with an old concern of mine with the neglect shown towards books 2 and 3 as narrative delivered by the principal character in the poem's action.[4] Virgil (no surprise!) turns out to be a good deal more complex (or ambiguous) than appeared thirty years ago. Let me first cite summarily four cases which have recently attracted notice in work on bk. 2, before passing on to some other instances which unsettle even a reader of Virgil as old-fashioned as myself:

(a) At 2.556 *superbum*: as seen by Aen.? Hardly! Or by Aeneas' enemies (pride leading to destruction)? Or as seen by Virgil, in the light of an extended analogy with Pompey's evanescent oriental grandeur?[5] Virgil as author enters into the text with comment; he may likewise offer comment through the mouth of his narrator; he may even (and not only here) attribute to his narrator a comment more strictly proper to Troy's enemies (for the context, cf. 2.241f., 363, 554).

(b) 2.711 *longe seruet uestigia coniunx*: how far is Aeneas (the narrator) distancing himself (the husband) from his (first) wife in the last words which he addresses to her? (Lyne *FV*, 150f., 176).

(c) Contrast the change of perspective we are invited to recognise by Creusa's words at 2.776ff. (Lyne, *FV* 169f.): the divine role in Creusa's disappearance is introduced by C. herself.

---

[1] E.J. Kenney in *Creative imitation and Latin Literature* ed. T. Woodman and D. West (Cambridge 1979), 105, 116, Quinn, 94.

[2] Note already subtle observations in Austin's commentary e.g. at 2.428. A. La Penna *Dial.Arch.*1 (1967) 220ff., A. Perutelli, *Maia* 24 (1972), 42ff., Kenney (n. 1), 113f., G. Rosati, *ASNP* 1979, 539ff., A. Perutelli, *MD* 3 (1979), 69f., M. Bonfanti, *Punto di vista e modi di narrazione nell'Eneide* (Pisa 1985), 252ff., G. Senis, *EV* s.v. *Punto di vista*, Lyne, *FV* (1987), 217f. et passim, C. Lazzarini *SIFC* 3.7 (1989), 241ff., 248f., D. Fowler, *PCPhS* 36 (1990), 42ff.

[3] Though cf. already Heinze, 370ff.

[4] Lyne *FV*, 176, Kenney (n. 1), 113, Lazzarini (n. 2), 241ff., Mackie 45f., Highet, 34f., 196ff., Williams 246f., 262f.

[5] Fowler (n. 2), 47ff., A. Bowie, *CQ* 40 (1990), 475f.

(d) The poet and the reader may view the wolves of 2.355ff. very differently from the Trojan narrator (Lyne *FV*, 212f.).

Secondly, my own hunt through the text of bk. 2, stimulated by Lyne and Fowler in particular (n. 2):

(e) *ductores Danaum. . .instar montis equum. . .aedificant* (14–6). Who sees 'the horse as big as a mountain' (cf. Austin on 2.150)? The poet? The awestruck narrator Aeneas? Or the Greeks? Note *aedificant*: does Aeneas suggest Agamemnon's orders to Epeius: 'make it as big as a mountain'? Our judgement may refocus after reading 2.150 (a Trojan viewpoint) and 185 (a Greek viewpoint, but expressed by Sinon).

(f) Similarly, the view of the Greeks within as *delecta uirum. . .corpora* (18): is it the poet who tells us that they are elite troops? Or Aeneas after fighting them? Or does Aeneas express the Greek view: that lots were drawn (*sortiti*, 18), and it was the elite that actually went on board. I do not wish to suggest that such questions should actually be asked; it is perhaps more important to recognise simply that Virgilian narrative admits (often, even) a multiple, and elusive point of view. Fowler's "deviant focalisation' should at very least be in the plural! It is particularly rewarding to see how the Greeks are viewed in bk. 2; that is, how far poet permits Trojan narrator an insight (in itself in no way implausible) into the mentality of his old foes. That is important not only for how we approach scenes of combat in 7–12, but also for how we evaluate Virgil's reading of Homer.[6]

(g) While *exitiale* (31) clearly represents Aeneas' *post-factum* evaluation, which the poet shares, *stupet* (31) and *mirantur* (32) are subtler: they represent for an instant the wonder of a *pars* (31) of the Trojans, sharply corrected by 35 *et quorum melior sententia menti*. But is Aeneas consistently classed among the wise Trojans? Hardly, when we reach 105 *ardemus scitari* (cf. 145, 212 and 234 with Austin's note). Is Aeneas part of the astonished group at 63–4? We never know. Does 396 suggest that Aeneas too, on Coroebus' suggestion, puts on Greek armour? The interplay of first and third person verbs and the use of (e.g.) *cuncti* and *omnes* in 2 seems to require further analysis (cf. Mackie, 46). Aeneas is shown as part of a group of Trojans (from 25 to 464f.) or as observer of other Trojans (from 31(?) to 445ff.), then as alone (565, 624, 632f., 655, 669, 670(?), 671); then as part of his family (716; cf. 712, 743, 748) and finally as leader of his people (800). Sinon appears (67) *turbatus, inermis*: disguise and histrionics; that

---

[6] J. Griffin, *Homer on Life and Death* (Oxford 1980), 4f. and ch. 4.

is how the Trojans see him and how we do at first, but it is also how the Greeks planned it.

(h) The repeated references I find to a Greek point of view are confirmed by (e.g.) *instructis nauibus* or 256 *litora nota petens*: though Aeneas is his mouthpiece, the poet identifies easily with Troy's assailants (cf. 265f., while Aeneas is fast asleep (290), 328f., as reported to Aeneas by Panthus), 401 (Aeneas refers to the belly of the horse as *nota*—to the Greeks), 413ff. Lastly, 510 *nequiquam. . .inutile*: does Virgil comment through Aeneas on Priam? Does he also appear an easy victim to the Greeks? Is he, additionally, shown as being himself aware of the futility of his undertaking? Whether (Lyne, Fowler) or not we shackle 'multiple viewpoints' to the judgement of 'Two Voices' (or rather of the poet as critic of war, Aeneas, Augustus, Rome. . .), there is clearly a lot more to be done on the analysis of what some call, not unreasonably, 'deviant focalisation'.

Symbolism and imagery

There are four preliminary issues which need to be clarified:

(a) One might get the impression from (e.g.) J. Richmond, *GR* 23 (1976), 144 that the study of Virgil's symbolism and imagery was invented in 1950 (V. Pöschl, *Die Dichtkunst Virgils* (ed. 1, Wiesbaden 1950; Eng. tr. *The Art of Vergil*, Ann Arbor 1962). That is not so: cf. Pöschl's own bibliographies at *EV* 4, 863f. and in *Bibl. zur antiken Bildersprache* (ed. V.P., Heidelberg 1964), 425–39 passim. Cf. further R. Rieks, *ANRW* 2.31.2 (1981), 1022–7 and Suerbaum, 90, 193f. I discovered Pöschl's predecessors for myself on reading W.-H. Friedrich, *Phil.*94 (1940), 142ff. Nor should we linger over the quite mistaken impression (e.g. Pöschl, Eng. tr., 5) that ancient Virgil-critics were quite unaware of symbolism and imagery: cf. Lyne *WP*, 63ff., *Ind.Serv.* s.v. *imago, comparatio, metaphora*, Pöschl, *Bibl.*, 352, M. Mühmelt, *Griech. Grammatik in der Vergilerklärung* (Zetemata 37, München 1965), 115ff.; for the general background, M. McCall, *Ancient rhetorical theories of simile and comparison* (Cambridge, Mass. 1969), 252, n. 25 *et passim*.

(b) There seems to be no totally uniform and agreed English system of definition and terminology: cf. R. Wellek and A. Warren, *Theory of Literature* (ed. 3 New York 1956), 186ff. for a convenient survey. But— with the exception of Northrop Frye, *Anatomy of Criticism* (Princeton 1957), 84ff.—divergences of usage are not particularly significant. 'Image' is almost totally suppressed in Pöschl's article *Simbolistica critica* for the *EV*, and there is no article *Immagine*, while *Metafora* is sanely and briskly handled (though missing from Pöschl's article in the *EV* as well as from his book!). Seligson's translation of Pöschl (which is not and presumably was not intended as a precise reproduction in English of the German text) tends to render *Bild* as 'image' and *Symbol* as 'symbol'; no 'metaphor', remember. For those wanting to go further, cf. W.K. Wimsatt and M.C. Beardsley, *The Verbal Icon* (Lexington 1954), 128, T.S. Eliot, *Selected Essays* (ed. 2 1934, repr. London 1951), 243, W. Empson, *Seven Types of Ambiguity* (repr. London 1991), 25, and the still exciting and valuable pages of W.B. Stanford, *Greek Metaphor* (Oxford 1936, repr. New York 1972). This list does not pretend to satisfy the trained critic of modern literatures.

(c) The Untutored Midriff and the Poetic Tradition. In Pöschl, Knox,[7] Brooks,[8] Putnam[9] there is but the lightest dusting of annotation (cf. Richmond, 144). The implications of Virgil's metaphors are generally uprooted from the poetic tradition in which they have grown and the significance of his symbols is determined by the fancy (which may be well-informed, or may not; hence the citation from Housman in my title) of the investigator. Putnam unfortunately demotes discussion of sources to the (separated) notes. Solid facts relevant to the evaluation of the Golden Bough do exist (cf. Norden's comm. or the first chapter of my *Alambicco*), but they are not adduced by Brooks. We cannot always be sure that Virgil will consistently use a given image in an altogether traditional way (cf. (d) below): in practice, though, or so at least I have found, his imagery is rooted in his reading,[10] and the implications of that imagery can only therefore be comprehended after a close study of that image's history and use in other authors.[11] This is not archaic pedantry on my part;[12] however

---

[7] AJP 71 (1950), 379ff. = Commager 124ff. (with reduced annotation) still reads as a genuinely exciting, 'classic' discussion.

[8] R.A. Brooks, *AJPh* 74 (1953), 260ff. = Commager, 143ff.

[9] M.C.J. Putnam, *The poetry of the Aeneid* (Cambridge, Mass., 1965).

[10] This does not run contrary to a most interesting tradition of inventivity in the subject-matter of epic similes, M. Coffey, *BICS* 8 (1961), 63ff.

[11] Pöschl's *Bibliographie* is invaluable; *RAC* often helpful; J. Taillardat, *Les images d'Aristophane* (Paris 1962, corr. repr. 1965) unexpectedly useful because so well indexed. It is often helpful to translate into Greek—sometimes the commentators who have collected Virgil's 'sources' have done it for you—and then to proceed via *Lexicon der frühgr. Epos* ed. B. Snell, H. Erbse (Göttingen 1955–), W.J. Slater's Lexicon to Pindar, and even, unexpectedly, the *Theol. Wörterbuch z. neuen Testament* (ed. G. Kittel, G. Friedrich, Stuttgart 1933–78; note the Eng. tr., Grand Rapids, 1967–74). The *Sachregister* of O. Gruppe, *Griech. Mythologie* 2 (München 1906) repays study.

[12] Cf. Lyne, *FV*, 114ff., D. Fowler in *Homo Viator (Essays. . .Bramble)* (Bristol 1987), 185ff.

little I am in sympathy with much of the methods and conclusions of Fowler and Lyne, it is good to see that at the cutting edge of critical fashion in Virgilian studies today traditional analysis of sources counts for much.[13] A scrupulous attention to sources does not bring stability and order to Virgil's imagery, but at least if we stick to those sources, our research is no longer both aleatory and blindfolded!

(d) Consistency, flexibility and ambiguity. If 'reading' Virgil's imagery by the light of uninformed inspiration is a recipe for catastrophe,[14] almost the same may be said of any attempt to reduce the traditions of imagery to a code of unbending equivalences. I quote a few random examples; the point unfortunately needs to be made, but the need to expose misguided method hardly justifies prolonged expenditure of time and effort:

(i) The snake of 5.85–93. 'As much cause for uneasiness as for encouragement' (Putnam, *Poetry*, 72). But the snake represents the *famulus* or *genius* of Anchises.[15]

(ii) The shade of 7.36 (*fluuio succedit opaco*): 'a latent symbolism of war in his (sc. Aeneas') entering the dark river'.[16] Pleasant shade of a hot day (cf. NH on Hor. *Od*.2.3.10, e.g.); the Trojans have been rowing![17]

(iii) The simile of 2.355–8. Trojans compared to *lupi. . .raptores*: cf. Lyne, *FV*, 212–4 who is right to point out that the Trojans are not hungry, nor their children thirsty: for him, therefore, the simile implies that the wolves'/Trojans' heroism 'was at the expense of Aeneas' dependants'. The wolf frequently does have negative implications.[18] Here, Lyne admits,[19] wolves do show valour. As symbols, they are therefore ambivalent (and *furor* at 2.355 is, in the context, a desperation not, I would suggest altogether blameworthy; no more is *rabies*, 357). I can hardly believe that Virgil expects us to condemn even a

---

[13] A hallmark, as I am delighted to acknowledge, of the best work of G.B. Conte and his school.

[14] *GR* 23 (1976), 142ff. = McAuslan 24ff.: a collection of weak examples, energetically pilloried; my old friend John Richmond knows I think he goes too far in his scepticism!

[15] E. Küster, *Die Schlange*, *RVV* 13.2 (Giessen 1913), 62f., Wissowa, *RKR*, 176f., S.J. Harrison, *PLLS* 5 (1985), 104.

[16] K.J. Reckford, *AJP* 82 (1961), 255, followed by others.

[17] Pöschl, *Art*, 33 and, better, V. Buchheit, *Vergil über die Sendung Roms*, *Gymnasium Beiheft* 3 (1963), 173ff. for the implications of the symbolic landscape.

[18] H.D. Jocelyn, *PCPhS* 17 (1971), 52f.

[19] Cf. S. Rocca, *Etologia Virgiliana* (Genova 1983), 156.

wolf for wanting to find food for its own young; ambivalent too in Hom. (*Il.*16.156ff.) and Hor. (*C.*4.4.50). The point at issue changes: not so much the character of the wolf as the role of the narrative element in the Virgilian simile as potentially relevant (or not) to the ethical and moral evaluation of the narrative to which a given simile refers.[20] Negative evaluation is there for those who want to find it:[21] we have to decide whether its existence has been established by universally (or partially) valid methods.

(iv) 10.565–70. Aeneas compared to the giant Aegaeon (cf. 182, on bk. 10), who rages *Iouis. . .fulmina contra* (567): Virgil atypically follows (West on Hes. *Theog.*149) the *Titanomachy* as against Homer (*Il.*1.402–5, cf. the comm. of G.S. Kirk ad loc.) and Hesiod (*Theog.*617ff.), who make Briareus/Aegaeon (alternative names for one figure) an ally of Zeus against the Titans.[22] The simile has been a mainstay of criticism of Aeneas.[23] Such stories are old and confused: they contain perhaps an inherent ambivalence.[24] Is Aeneas portrayed through this simile as seen by the Latins?[25] No,[26] because he is so brutal in bk. 10. But is he really (cf. 200)? That depends on the standards by which he is judged. Certainly, the poet is parading his mythological erudition; the acute reader is expected to pick up the rarer version (*Titanom.* fr.3 Bernabé/Davies). The good Briareus (cf. *Il.*1.403–6) has changed sides and the ancient giant (so I have suggested that the Aen. of bk. 10 is a markedly archaic figure, 180) is fighting to the limits of his valour and strength against Zeus himself. The poet may be thought to concentrate more on the weaponry than on the divine authority arrayed against Aegaeon/Briareus. Had Virgil been seeking to deliver a ringing condemnation, less ambiguous means, I submit, lay open to him.

The excitement provoked by the apparent 'discovery' of Virgil's imagery ca. 1950 (Pöschl and Knox; see (i) above) still remained fresh when M.C.J. Putnam's *The poetry of the Aeneid* (Cambridge, Mass.)

---

[20] Cf. Lyne, *FV* 65, 119ff., 224ff. but also D.A. West, *JRS* 59 (1969), 43, *Phil.*114 (1970), 262, A. Traina, *RFil* 118 (1990), 497f.

[21] Cf. V. Stephens, *ICS* 15 (1990), 114.

[22] Preller-Robert, *Griech.Myth.*1 (ed. 4, Berlin 1894), 57, n. 2.

[23] Cf. even Harrison's comm. ad loc.; cf. (e.g.) R.A. Hornsby, *Patterns of Action* (Iowa City 1970), 109.

[24] J. Fontenrose, *Python* (Berkeley 1959), 473.

[25] Williams, 180.

[26] Hardie, 155.

appeared in 1965. However, by the time J.A. Richmond's general protest (cf. n. 14) appeared eleven years later, not all his examples appeared to be still ablaze with novelty. Study of Virgil's imagery has not exactly faded away (cf. Stephens, n. 21), but the best work on it recently[27] is limited in scope and concerned particularly with implicit links between simile and narrative. Lyne and I would, I think, agree that there is still a great deal that we do not really understand about Virgilian metaphors, images, similes, though I doubt we would then want to proceed in the same direction! After reading over a fair part of what has been written on the imagery of bk. 2, it was a curious experience to go back to the text itself to discover what had fallen out of focus and what sort of thing seemed not yet to have been clarified (or classified). Your perspective after reading a book of Virgil (retaining the order of the lines as printed! a crucial caveat), with, specifically, an eye to the use of figured language in its many aspects, is very different from that reached by the study of a particular use of imagery. I offer therefore a brief account of seven lines of thought which my latest re-readings of *Aen*.2 suggest:

(a) The effect upon the reader of an inherited metaphor is very different from that of a new coinage: the former is part of the *lingua poetica latina*, or even of that bilingual *koine* so dear to learned Romans. Inherited metaphors can often be worn-out, moribund, even dead. The Trojan horse is a case in point: as the hull of a ship, traditional;[28] traditional too is the transference of weaving language to shipbuilding;[29] note too the traditional language of woodworking;[30] equally traditional is the image of horse as womb.[31] Brilliant variation and supreme art raise Virgil above any risk of appearing flat and worn-out; it is only worth noting that the individual metaphors are visibly not new. *Exempli gratia* I add some other examples of inherited metaphors:[32] 62 *occumbere*, 91 *superis. . .oris*, 85 *demisere* with 398 *demittimus*, 265 *somno. . .sepultam*, 329 *fundit*, 606 *nubem* (cf. Austin on 608ff.)

---

[27] Lyne *FV* and *WP*; on which cf. A. Traina, *RFil* 118 (1990), 490ff. and 120 (1992), 490ff. also Horsfall, *CR* 38 (1988), 243ff. and *AR* 38 (1993), 203–10.

[28] Austin on 2.16, 19, Putnam, 205, n. 3.

[29] Enn. *Scaen*.65f. cited by Austin on 2.16; cf. further vv. 112, 186.

[30] *terebrare* 38 (cf. Lyne *WP*, 115), *compagibus* (51, where Austin cites Pacuv., *trag*.250).

[31] *uterum*, 20, 52, 258; cf. *aluus* 51, 401, *feta*, 238; see Austin on 2.20, Putnam, 205, n. 2.

[32] I presuppose consultation of Austin's commentary, in some respects dated, but still a rich source of fascinating information.

(b) A particularly rich nexus of terms belongs to the (Homeric in origin) use of physiological language in the description of emotion. Neglected by most of those (but not S.J. Harrison on *Aen.*10) who write on Virgil. R.B. Onians' *Origins of European Thought* (Cambridge 1951, repr. 1988) remains essential, though it does not solve all the problems. In bk. 2, cf. 120f. *gelidusque per ima cucurrit/ossa tremor*, 200, 367, 562 *pectora*; 173f. *salsusque per artus/sudor iit*.

(c) The varied richness of Virgil's imagery is inevitably underrated on account of the relative neglect with which certain metaphors, however striking, are treated, if they do not form part of those large complexes (serpents, flames) which have been the focus of study for over forty years. Cf. (e.g.) 416 *rupto turbine uenti*, 434 *diuellimur*, 475 *trisulcis* (interaction of serpent's tongue and trident), 649 *fulminis adflauit uentis* (thunderbolt as whirlwind), approved by Serv.: an unexpected widening, though, however 'correct', of our visual image of the 'bolt'.

(d) A few problems of method seem not to have been addressed amid the (often justifiable) enthusiasm raised by Pöschl, Knox and their followers. Snake-language used of the horse is, let us allow, of clear and certain significance (236 *lapsus*, 240 *inlabitur*). But just how far (and by what criteria?) are we expected to exclude *labor*-derivatives that really do not seem to fit the pattern?[33] Or, perhaps more seriously, Putnam, 21: 'the verb *condo* has a distinctly sinister side'. Thus, is passing, a forced interpretation of 7.303, of a type already noted (cf. n. 11). But are 2.24, 401 and 696 all then equally sinister? The same can hardly be said of 1.276f. *Mauortia condet/moenia* (except on a rabidly anti-Augustan reading of the poem!). The dogmatic evaluation of a single word remains open to various lines of attack!

(e) There are also occasions on which the outer limits of a complex of metaphors present delicate problems of demarcation: thus 229 *insinuat* (sc. *pauor*) is in truth a snake-word,[34] but (vd. supra) is the same (see (d) above) true of all *lab*-compounds? And after Knox, where, if anywhere, should we draw the line with words designating flame, fire, heat, spheres rich in burned-out metaphors? Verbal play may be a helpful guide.[35] These remarks should not be taken as in any sense indicating a general condemnation of imagery-study in Virgil;

---

[33] 14 *labentibus annis*, 97 *labes*, 169 *sublapsa*, 262 *lapsi*, 318 *elapsus*, 551 *lapsantem*, 695 *labentem*.

[34] Knox (n. 7), 384 = 128.

[35] 269 *serpit* (cf. *serpens*): Putnam, 25f., Knox (n. 1) 388 = 132.

restraint and careful judgement are applicable here as elsewhere and we would do well to remember that imagery is no more than a strand present in the texture of the book as a whole.

(f) It should be noted that Virgil is clearly attracted by expressions which point up an ambiguity between the literal and figured senses of a word, or even between different ends of the scale of literal senses: 196 *capti*: captured and 'taken in'; 214, 218 *amplexus*: the children are both embraced and throttled; 227 *teguntur*: hidden and protected (by Minerva); 265 burial in drink anticipates that in death; 430 *texit*: cover and protect; 514 *complexa*: cling to and (for protection) embrace (cf. 517); 553 *capulo tenus abdidit ensem*: the sword, I take it, is more commonly 'hidden' in the scabbard, rather than here, in the opponent's body; 606 just how literal is *nubes*, the 'fog of war'?

(g) Lastly—and here we pass into the realm of precise lexicographical enquiry, most of which has not yet been undertaken—we must face the problem of dead or moribund metaphors, cases, that is, where, formally, the presence of figured language exists, but where it appears likely that the metaphor has shrivelled away into an unremarkable term available to the poet from the Latin poetic language's wide range of synonyms, without any real, active figurative force:

2.1 *intenti*, 12 *horret*, 13 *fracti*, 39 *scinditur*, 62 *uersare*, 73 *compressus*, 169 *fluere*, 181 *remenso*, 251 *inuoluens*, 280 *expromere* (?), 303 *arrectis*, 316 *ardent*, 329 *fundit*, 343 *incensus* (in a burning city!), 360 *circumuolat*, 398 *conserimus*, 421 *fudimus*, 429 *confixi*, 507 *conuulsa*, 528 *lustrat*, 600 *hauserit*, 609 *undantem*, 624 *considere*, 639 *robore*, 653 *urgenti incumbere*, 706 *uoluunt*, 734 *ardentis*, 758 *edax*, 759 *furit aestus*. Enquiry into such a list (here, radically selective) could lead either to untimely condemnation of Virgil's imagery as frequently moribund or just as well to excessive admiration for its traditional riches. I can only suggest that there is still careful work to be undertaken, and that a great bulk of unexamined figured language exists, apart from those few striking complexes of images which have attracted scholars.

Book 3: Character and development

Virgil offers, deliberately, no clear indication of Aeneas' appearance[1] and only in passing hints at his age: 6.764 *longaeuo*, which refers to a period not more than ten years after the fall of Troy. The issue is not entirely frivolous: it was possible, according to ideas current in Virgil's Rome, even for a grown man (a middle-aged hero, if we want to press 6.764)[2] to change, for better or for worse.[3] That Virgil was familiar with the philosophers' views of character is very likely, and that in turn makes it easier to admit, if we find reason to, 'development', at least within ancient limits, in the poet's portrait of Aeneas,[4] though that 'development' need not of course be seen in terms of a Stoic 'improvement'.[5] In so far as there may still be an issue open for serious and useful discussion, it concerns, I think, whether such 'development' as there is (which is of course not to be equated with the *Charakterentwicklung* of the modern *Bildungsroman*)[6] comes from within Aeneas, or is induced by circumstances, or is even provoked by those who surround the hero. 'I am a part of all that I have met' said Ulysses (Tennyson, not Homer): that applies well to Aeneas. We shall see, I think, that to formulate these possibilities in a spirit of 'either'/'or' is a peculiarly unhelpful *modus operandi*. I do not find it easy to understand why Virgil should have been so narrow and selective in his view of the matter, particularly after reading Gill and Pelling on the open-minded curiosity that many ancient authors display about the sort of influences that can be exerted upon a grown man.[7] On Aeneas' first appearance

---

[1] Cf. M. Griffith, *CP* 80 (1985), 314ff.

[2] Pease on 4.11 and 619 is not reliable.

[3] Cf. C. Gill, *CQ* 33 (1983), 469ff. who distinguishes between the views of philosophers and biographers. See in particular, ib. 478f. and C. Pelling in (ed. C. Pelling) *Characterisation and Individuality in Greek Literature* (Oxford 1990), 224ff.

[4] Cf. E. Burck, *Gymn* 65 (1958), 137 = id., *Vom Menschenbild i.d. röm. Literatur* 1 (Heidelberg 1966), 296, T. Fuhrer, *GR* 36 (1989), 68f.; I am also indebted to Dr. Fuhrer for *viva voce* exegesis of the question.

[5] C.M. Bowra, *GR* 3 (1933–4), 8ff. = Harrison, 363ff., *From Virgil to Milton* (repr. London 1972), 63, V. Pöschl, *Art*, 54ff., Heinze, 277 (with Wlosok, pref., xi), G. Carlsson, *Eranos* 43 (1945), 119, n. 2, 124f.

[6] Fuhrer (n. 4) is right to insist that 'development' is a slippery term: we agree that some 'development' (in the ancient sense) is present in the text; we agree also that 'Romantic' development of the character is not present, cannot have been, and should not be sought!

[7] E. Kraggerud, *Aeneisstudien, SO* Suppl. 22 (1968), 23f., Burck (n. 4), W. Kühn, *Götterszenen bei Vergil* (Heidelberg 1971), 95f., Heinze, 271ff., W. Warde Fowler, *Re-*

(1.92ff.),[8] despite his groan, the chill of fear which slackens his sinews and the unvoiced prayer of 1.93, his first actual words are markedly heroic in tone: to death by shipwreck, the end of a warrior, in defence of his home's *moenia* (an end befitting his *pietas*), *ante ora patrum*, alongside his kin and comrades, and at the hands of a worthy enemy was on all counts preferable. Do we suppose Aeneas' followers heeded him, *talia iactanti* amid the storm? Perhaps not: contrast 1.208ff. Is Aeneas' journey then one of real inner development?[9] That is anachronistic language, I suspect, and best not used. But Book 3, given its reduced emotional temperature, has perhaps a certain value if we are seeking some indication of how the text invites us, on a balanced reading, to view Aeneas between the Troad and Sicily.[10] 'Balanced reading' is worth underlining: it is very easy to cite verses from the *Aen.* in support of one interpretation or another of Aeneas' character,[11] and rather less so to maintain clarity and equilibrium when confronted by Virgil's multiple, complex, ambiguous, understated, even conflicting hints or apparently explicit remarks on the topic.

    The Trojans are uncertain of their fated goal at the outset.[12] Anchises (3.9) leaves their course to fate, that fate which had tried them at Troy[13] and (58), confronted by the portent of the bush, does nothing to oppose their departure from Thrace. Helenus alone acknowledges a divine purpose behind the Trojans' wanderings (375). At 3.717 Virgil tells us that Aeneas was recounting the *fata. . .deum*:

---

ligious Experience of the Roman people (London 1922), 411, Carlsson (n. 5), 111ff., J.P. Poe *TAPA* 96 (1965), 321ff., F.A. Sullivan, *AJP* 80 (1959), 150ff., Büchner, 318.62ff., Pöschl (n. 5), 54ff., A. Wlosok, *Klio* 67 (1985), 221f. This is no more than a rough indication of what I have found most useful among the innumerable discussions of the topic. The nettle of 'growth' appears not to be grasped in C.J. Mackie's often useful *The characterisation of Aeneas* (Edinburgh 1988).

  [8] Mackie, 17ff., Highet, 189ff., H.-P. Stahl, *Arethusa* 14 (1981), 160ff., A. Wlosok, *Die Göttin Venus* (Heidelberg 1967), 13f.

  [9] Kühn (n. 7), 94. Aeneas as a good Stoic, developing (*proficiens*) in wisdom and virtue, has had a long run (Heinze, 278f., C.M. Bowra in Harrison, 370f.). But the traces of technical Stoic language are very scanty (3.182, 5.725, 6.105), and though Seneca could cite Aeneas to praise him (*Ep.*76.33), that does not prove the case. Cf. P. Cova, *EV* s.v. *Stoicismo*, D. Gall, *Creusa und Helena* (Mainz 1993), 19, n. 26 for further bibliography. Had V. really seen Aeneas as a *proficiens*, he was capable of making the point; make it, though, he did not. Aeneas' eventual compliance with the divine will, likewise, is not so regularly underlined (cf. 3.188) as to make it seem a programmatic statement of Stoic ethics (but cf. M.W. Edwards, *Phoen.*14 (1960), 154f.

  [10] Cf. Mackie 61–77, helpful at times.

  [11] I recognise the justification behind Mackie's polemic (n. 7), 1–5.

  [12] Horsfall, *Vergilius* 35 (1989), 12.

  [13] *exercite* recognised already by Bowra (n. 5, 1933).

in bk. 3, the gods, markedly, express their will by oracular speech (*for–fata*). It was (3.2) the gods who had destroyed Troy. Apollo (at Delos) gives the Trojans a scrap of information on their destined course (94ff.), promptly misunderstood (154, etc.). Jupiter forbids a settlement in Crete (171). The Harpies terrify the Trojans by deed and word (265f., etc.), but Apollo, Celaeno's source (251), also inspires Helenus (359, 434, 474) and will (395, 479) give further help, while Juno (380) limits what Helenus may reveal. It was a *deus* (i.e. the wind) who finally bore Aeneas (715) to North Africa. Notoriously, Bk. 3 is rich in manifestations of the divine will through portents and oracles: 5 *auguriis*; 24ff. (portent in Thrace at Polydorus' grave); 84ff. Aeneas consults Delian Apollo, whose oracle is forthwith misunderstood by Anchises (102ff.);[14] in Crete a mysterious plague,[14] to which no divine origin is attributed (but cf. 144), strikes the Trojans, and Anchises bids them leave (137ff.); at sea, the Penates appear, not to Anchises, but to Aeneas (147ff.), though (179f.) he promptly tells his father, who now perceives that he had misunderstood Apollo's message. In the Strophades (253ff.), Celaeno reveals more of the Trojans' future in Italy, and Anchises prays by way of antidote, 265f.; in Epirus, Helenus, a friendly voice (463), tells Aeneas what he may of the journey to Italy (374ff.; cf. 559, 684; 712ff.: the significant omission is Anchises' death), and reveals that (441ff.) more will be forthcoming from the Sibyl at Cumae; Helenus adds more specific sailing instructions of divine origin (479) to Anchises (475ff.); on first sighting Italy, Anchises sacrifices (525ff.), and the Trojans sight four horses, a *primum omen*, which is (539ff.) interpreted by Anchises.[15]

Aeneas is, and already knows that he is, a 'man of destiny'; conviction grows with further revelation (a process that, formally, begins at 2.293ff.). Large remarks about Aeneas' journey towards knowledge are justified in as much as the future is unfolded to him in stages. Slowness and error in the interpretation of what is revealed are typical of human reaction in such stories. The man of destiny[16] is well aware of future *labores* and *pericula* and the need for properly understood divine revelation in order to overcome them: cf. 443ff.; there is more to come and that too will be hard to grasp. From the

---

[14] R.B. Lloyd, *AJP* 78 (1957), 138ff., B. Grassmann-Fischer, *Die Prodigien in Vergils Aeneis* (München 1966), 39ff., E.L. Harrison, *PLLS* 5 (1985), 131ff.

[15] Horsfall (n. 12), 10f.

[16] 3.367f., 377, P. McGushin, *AJP* 85 (1964), 234.

very outset of his journey, Aeneas wishes to halt and build:[17] while at
85ff. Aeneas prays for a settled home and at 132ff. starts building
one in the wrong place, we come later to see a more decided and
commanding figure: cf. 289, 362f., 367f., 374f. At 364, Aeneas is
sure of his goal, yet needs detailed instructions from Helenus. We
discover that there is no one moment of decisive understanding and
no one overwhelming agent of revelation. Indirection is all, though
the attentive reader will note a decline in perplexity and acceleration
in the action after the encounter with Helenus.

When Aeneas is faced by so many manifestations of the divine
will and such complex intimations of destiny's intentions, he very
properly defers to his father's *auctoritas*, on several occasions.[18] This is
pietas rather than insecurity. The Trojans also react, as has often
been noted, with frequent displays of religious observance (19ff., 34ff.,
62ff., 84, 93, 118ff. 287f., etc.). It is singular that the Trojans' passage between Scylla and Charybdis, their meeting with Achaemenides,
and their escape from the Cyclopes, take place, by contrast in a
notably 'lay' atmosphere (but cf. 697). Aeneas' *pietas, erga patrem, erga
deos*, and *erga patriam* is therefore fully formed. In the face of 24ff.,
84, 132, 147ff., 235, 287ff., 343, 358, 374ff. Aeneas is hardly to be
dismissed as a mere future leader, still hidden by the long shadow
his father casts. Helenus hardly needs to remind us that Anchises
does give practical orders (9, 267, 472, 560f; cf. 440ff.); he is also
(480) *felix nati pietate*. He has a specially active role, as has been noted,
in the Trojans' relations with their gods and their destiny: in the
later part of the book, his role is perhaps deliberately reduced (558ff.,
610f.) in anticipation of his death. Cf. Aeneas' use of the first-person
singular after 688. We should not imagine that Aeneas' consultation
(58) of *delectos populi proceres primumque parentem* about the portent of
Polydorus' grave is to be taken as a sign of unreadiness for command;[19] the use of *refero* suggests a respectful, Roman procedure of
consulting the senate[20] Aeneas, it is perhaps sometimes also forgotten, has to face the hostility of nature: I mean not so much portents
as plague (137ff.), volcano (570ff.), giants (655ff.), storm (194ff.), rock
and whirlpool (410ff., 555ff.), not to mention human foes (273, 282f.,

---

[17] Horsfall (n. 12), 8ff., P. McGushin, *Lat.*24 (1965), 411ff., E.D. Carney, *Coll.
Lat.*196 (1986), 422ff.

[18] R.B. Lloyd, *TAPA* 88 (1957), 47ff.

[19] Horsfall (n. 12), 17.

[20] P. Willems, *Le sénat*. . .2 (Liège 1883), 175ff.

398, cf. 499). Confronted by danger, Aeneas is markedly more sure
of himself than when facing the unknown (cf. 88f., 494ff.). One might
also survey Aeneas' interaction with the other (numerous) humans
he meets in the course of Bk. 3.[21] Most significant by far, Aeneas
and Andromache.[22] Their imitation Troy[23] and overwhelmingly
affectionate, or affecting, even sentimental welcome (cf. 344f., 348)
has a specific programmatic function: Andromache herself sets Aeneas
on a par with Hector as a model for Ascanius,[24] and, perhaps even
more important, it is from the ruler of a 'second Troy' that Aeneas
first hears in any detail of the future that awaits him. Helenus acknowledges Aeneas' destined mission (374f.) to found (387; contrast
the disquieting destiny revealed at 255) a city in Italy, as goal of all
the preceding *labores* (393, cf. 459), a goal signalled by twin portents
(388ff., cf. 255ff.). Even Troy's arch-enemy Juno can be placated.[25]
The climax of Helenus' prophecy is the assertion *ingentem factis fer ad
aethera Troiam* (462). The contrasting destinies are spelt out—by Aeneas
himself (493ff.), who looks forward to the establishment of an
unam. . .utramque Troiam animis under Augustus.[26] Aeneas remains
uncertain of his mission's term (496 *semper cedentia*, 500 *si quando*),
despite the *signa* and their interpretation already vouchsafed him. After
earlier events in 3, that is hardly culpable. If Anchises is already *felix
nati pietate*, Aeneas himself is still acquiring certainty: in 3 he is both
formed and still unformed: if that suggests some informal pre-
romantic inner *Entwicklung*, we have seen no theoretical obstacle
to it, though Virgil clearly has not selected the 'inner growth' of
Aeneas as a central motif of the book: it is hinted, not drawn, latent
not explicit.

---

[21] Mackie (n. 7), 63f.
[22] A. Wlosok, *EV* s.v. *Andromaca*, M. Bonjour, *Terre Natale* (Paris 1975), 287, 502.
EV s.v. *Eleno* (P.V. Cova), R.E. Grimm, *AJP* 88 (1967), 151ff., A. König, *Die Aeneis
und die griech. Tragödie* (diss. Berlin 1970), 52ff.
[23] 3.302, 304, 306, 336, 349ff. 497; cf. their gifts, 469, 484ff.
[24] 343; cf. Horsfall, *Vergilius* 32 (1986), 17.
[25] 3.380, 435ff.; cf. D.C. Feeney, *CQ* 34 (1984), 179ff. = Harrison, 339ff.
[26] 3.500ff.; cf. M. Paschalis, *Phil.* 130 (1986), 52ff.

Book 4: Love, and ethics

The years of fervent partisan evaluation of 'Dido vs. Aeneas' as some kind of 'case' were, at times, quite fun for professional Virgilians, but of course gave off far more heat than light. Partisanship is not over,[1] but it is easier than it was to cite relatively sane and objective surveys of a violently emotive and undeniably difficult text.[2] The problems are at least relatively circumscribed in scale, and they are all susceptible (or so I believe) of passably balanced and systematic analysis, even if that analysis leaves us in the end less clear than we were at the start about what Virgil may be trying to tell us. In the case of bk. 4, I concentrate on issues and not on a single passage or group of passages, and do so with book 12 in mind: similarities between Dido and Turnus[3] represent ground well-trawled by Aeneas' critics. It may perhaps help, therefore, with the greater (in some ways) problems of 12 to suggest, in this smaller context, some outlines of what Virgil seems to be doing and of how it may be helpful to go about reading and assessing the text. *Sine ira et studio*, but even to readers who believe that such a text can only be read with passion and commitment, it may be possible to indicate some useful bibliography and some avoidable pitfalls.

History and irony

Present in Virgil's Dido-narrative (and we must include bk. 1) are numerous levels of irony, closely linked to the perception of that narrative as being in some sense a tragedy, and indeed open to useful analysis in Aristotelian terms.[4] Such analysis is not new but of late has been notably refined in detail.[5] It is hardly necessary to offer here a detailed summary of progress reached (see n. 4). Not only,

---

[1] D.P. Fowler, *JRS* 81 (1991), 32 (e.g.); n. 12 below.
[2] D.C. Feeney, *CQ* 33 (1983), 204ff., = Harrison, 167ff., E.L. Harrison, in *Vergilian Bimillenary Lectures*, *Vergilius* Suppl. 2 (1982), 1ff., id. *EMC/CV* 33 (1989), 1ff., A. La Penna, *EV* s.v. *Didone*, J. Moles, in *Homo Viator, Classical Essays for John Bramble* (Bristol 1987), 153ff., id., *GR* 31 (1984), 48ff. = McAuslan, 142ff., F. Muecke, *AJP* 104 (1983), 134ff., W.J.N. Rudd, *Lines of Enquiry* (Cambridge 1976), 32ff. = Harrison, 145ff., S. Skulsky, *AJP* 106 (1985), 447ff., J. Tatum, *AJP* 105 (1984), 434ff., A. Wlosok, *Res Humanae-res divinae* (Heidelberg 1990), 320ff., = *Studien zum antiken Epos* ed. H. Görgemanns and E.A. Schmidt (Meisenheim 1976), 228ff.
[3] Cf. Wlosok 321 = 229 with further bibliography.
[4] Cf. (n. 2) Wlosok, Muecke, Moles (1984), Harrison (1989).
[5] Cf. 103, 105f. for hints at tragedy present in the literary texture of bk. 1.

though, foreshadowing, editorial intrusion, tragic, and dramatic irony,[6] but also, as a constant presence, historical irony, in that, as we have seen (n. 5), Rome's opposition to Carthage is a theme strongly present in the text from 1.13 on, and therefore of necessity before our eyes in 1.297ff. and in bk. 4.[7] Virgil is eager to exploit the counterpoint of present love and future strife.[8] It seems to have become less dangerous to admit in public that Virgil may after all have intended there to be (even strongly) negative elements in his portrait of Dido.[9]

Aeneas' faults[10]

For centuries, Aeneas was normally evaluated by the moral standards, or by the code of gentlemanly conduct of the day, almost always to his discredit, and often with consequent damage to the seriousness with which the text was read (cf. already Aug. *Civ.*9.4 *ad fin.*). The 'case for the defence'[11] cannot even now be left to the dispassionate reader's good sense: however delicate and complex the moral and emotional issues, the urge to tilt the lance at Aeneas remains strong among scholars[12] and this section may lead its author to be branded as illiberal and antifeminist(not his intention!). Let us at least try to distinguish between Virgil's censure, Dido's (see in particular 4.305–30, 365–78) and ours. 'Ours', first. I take a single example from a vast selection: Lyne, *WP* 77–9, reads the wounded deer simile of 4.69ff. as implying a wound of love inflicted by Aeneas as hunter (and therefore as the man who courted Dido vigorously).[13] But how well does such a role square with the text? Was it Aeneas

---

[6] For the distinctions, cf. in particular Muecke (n. 2).

[7] The First Punic War was Naevius' subject-matter, the Second, Ennius': Virgil's repeated allusive evocation is therefore perhaps also (but unrecognisably) in the nature of a literary tribute.

[8] Horsfall, *PVS* 13 (1973–4), 1ff. = Harrison, 127ff., D.C. Feeney, *CQ* 34 (1984), 180ff., Muecke (n. 2), 151ff., who is shocked (136, n. 12) by my vigorous and hostile account of Dido's vices.

[9] Cf., for example, Moles' two articles. Note in particular 1.297ff., 522ff., 661f., 671f., 4.235, 560ff., 592ff. (which echoes the destruction of Troy: cf. *Il.*22.410ff.), 669ff. (destruction of Carthage anticipated in simile, cf. Lyne *WP*, 41f.). On the fulfillment of Dido's curse, in the *Aeneid* and later, cf. (with no sort of general agreement), Lyne, *FV*, 130, Horsfall, *Alambicco*, 81f., C. Murgia, *CP* 82 (1987), 50ff., J.J. O'Hara, *Death and the optimistic prophecy* (Princeton 1990), 94ff. For Dido's use of magic, vd. (e.g.) discussion and bibliography in La Penna (n. 2).

[10] Wlosok 327n. = 235n., for an admirable summary.

[11] Subtitle of John Sparrow's 6th. Jackson Knight Memorial Lecture, Exeter 1972.

[12] Cf. (e.g.) Lyne, *FV*, 155–7 or M.C.J. Putnam, *Atti*, 2, 241.

[13] *Cresia*, 4.70 makes a point generally missed, but not by Pascoli in his *Epos* (repr. Firenze 1958), ad loc.: the Cretans used poisoned arrows.

who took the initiative?[14] It does seem to be Dido who acts out the role of the active partner as understood by the elegists.[15] If explicit narrative and contemporary (elegiac) usage suggest that it is in fact Dido who is the active partner in the affair, then if 4.69ff. is meant to hint at Aeneas and not Venus/Amor as the hunter, it does seem a curiously feeble and unconvincing way of advancing an alternative point of view: a show of incompetence in terms of rhetorical strategy. If the poet underlines thunderously (he does!) Dido's role as seducer, I fail to see what he might be trying to achieve by hinting once (and ambiguously at that) at quite another moving force to the narrative. If we turn to Dido's own view of the matter, we do need to bear in mind that her rhetoric is not factually reliable at all points.[16] At one level she knows and has always known that Aeneas will leave her.[17] Granted[18] that Aeneas tells Venus, not Dido, that *Italiam quaero patriam. . .data fata secutus* (1.380, 382), he does not disguise from the queen that he intends to leave Tunisia (1.610). Nor is there any need to repeat here the messages given to Aeneas and repeated by him to Dido in bks. 2–3: his destiny includes an Italian wife, city and descendants.[19] So what was Aeneas, or Dido, to do? Virgil (deliberately) creates an impossible and unbearable situation. All are losers. How, lastly, does Virgil present Aeneas himself? Not a question suited to a brief summary: I indicate only some lines of thought. In bk. 4, *Aen.* says little (cf. Feeney, n. 2) and disappears from the narrative at 469 (cf. Mackie, 80). Let us be clear: he loves Dido (395); he weeps for her;[20] he feels for her, acutely (394). Once out of the cave, Aeneas' affair with Dido is very much public property (cf. 170, 193ff., 215ff., 224f., 260ff., 265ff.). Criticism is expressed by Fama, by Iarbas, by

---

[14] C. Saylor, *Vergilius* 32 (1986), 73ff., Cairns, 136ff.

[15] A situation not unparalleled: Cairns, 138, S.M. Treggiari in *The craft of the ancient historian, Essays in Honor of Chester G. Starr* (Lanham 1985), 331ff., S. Farron, *Vergil's Aeneid: a poem of grief and love* (*Mnem.* Suppl. 122, 1993), 91 et passim.

[16] Feeney (n. 2, 1983), 207f. = 170ff.; contrast the markedly unsympathetic and untypically obtuse pages of Highet, 72ff.

[17] Feeney (n. 2, 1983), 207, n. 24 = 172, n. 24 cites 4.298, 419f.

[18] E.L. Harrison (n. 2, 1982), 3ff.

[19] As Dido remembers, 432; Latium is a name she heard from Ilioneus.

[20] The *lacrimae* which do not divert him from his course (449) are his and his alone. To the case correctly advanced by (e.g.) D.A. West, *JRS* 59 (1969), 45, Williams, 183, Lyne *FV*, 164, Pöschl, 45ff. I add only that the internal logic of a multiple-correspondence simile requires that the tears be Aeneas'; for them to belong even in part to another character, an exceptionally awkward change of subject is required and that Virgil does not habitually leave to the reader's fantasy. It is surprising that Moles (n. 2, 1987), 158, and Mackie, 92 are both taken in by one of the least convincing articles on Virgil known to me, in McAuslan, 149ff.

Jupiter, by Mercury, and by Virgil in objective narrative, before ever
Dido lets fly (305ff.). Given that he was not in reality *ille Paris cum
semiuiro comitatu* (so Iarbas), did he have any choice but to become
Dido's lover (a topic on which Dryden's preface remains hilarious
and very fair)? Hardly her seducer (v. supra). His fault as a Roman
(a topic I am not disposed to omit, because it is critically out of
favour in some quarters) is not so much a breach of *fides* towards
Creusa or the unnamed *regia coniunx*, nor a reprehensible indulgence
in an extramarital act or acts, as the extended period given over to
dalliance, in the energy given not to his destined city but to hers.[21]
We may recall Anchises' expressed fear (6.694) for the harm that the
Libyae. . .regna might have done him: less often remembered are Aeneas'
dreams of Anchises (351ff.; cf. Otis, 267), which correspond to Dido's
of Sychaeus (457–9). When brought back to his duty by Mercury
(331), Aeneas has no choice: the full weight of his destiny returns to
his conscious mind.[22] *Pius* (393)[23] is crucial. Though Virgil does not
linger on Aeneas' tragedy, it is none the less real: if the reader cannot find it in the text, then that shows a failure in the care and
sensitivity employed in reading.

Culpa; hamartia

Cf. 133f. for the ample debt of *Aen.*4 to Greek tragedy; the precise
definition of the *hamartia* in the tragedy of Dido continues to elude
definition, not least because the meaning of *hamartia* itself continues
to perplex scholars.[24] If we were satisfied that 'error of fact' was
definition enough, then Dido's sense that Aeneas might, despite the
evidence to the contrary in bks. 2–3, be free to remain in Carthage,
might serve. But if *hamartia* refers to a flaw or weakness, then its
identification remains a legitimate matter for discussion, closely related to Virgil's two uses of *culpa* in reference to Dido:[25]

(a) 4.19 *huic uni forsan potui succumbere culpae.* The context leaves no

---

[21] I am most grateful to Prof. Treggiari for discussion of issues of sexual ethics
relevant to bk. 4.

[22] Cf. E.L. Harrison (n. 2, 1982); on 345ff., cf. Hardie, 372f., noting analogies
between Aeneas and Atlas.

[23] In *pius*, S. Farron in *Coll.Lat.*217 (1992), 260ff. discovers numerous unnecessary
difficulties.

[24] Moles (n. 2, repr. 1990), 143f., Rudd (n. 2), 162.

[25] Treggiari (n. 35), 59f., after E. Badian, *Phil.*129 (1985), 82ff.

doubt that Dido refers to her 'betrayal' of Sychaeus' memory, to her abandonment of the status of 'uniuira', as a *culpa*. Let us not forget that the *Aeneid* predates any certain Augustan legislation on remarriage: the traditional honour attached to the *uniuira* therefore stands unimpaired as an ideal by which Dido fails to stand.[26] Dido's lost *fama* or *species* is a very serious matter (91, 170, 221). We should note the analogous destruction of *pudor* (27, 55, 322). A queen's morality is judged by high standards.[27] Dido laments that (550f.) *non licuit thalami expertem sine crimine uitam/degere more ferae*.[28] She has just spoken to Anna, whose pressures in the end drive her decisively into Aeneas' embraces (note *soluitque pudorem*, 55). Breach of loyalty to Sychaeus involves sex (*thalami*, 18), repute (*crimine*, 555; *pudor* (27) is not, either, an entirely private matter) and emotional upheaval (*talis. . .curas*, 551). *More ferae* (551) is more intractable: Dido lost her innocence not in the royal *thalamus* but like a beast in a cave: her delusion of lost animal innocence (no nuptial chambers in the palace, no moral reproof, no emotional upheaval) has already (Virgilian irony) been undercut by events.

(b) 4.172 *coniugium uocat; hoc praetexit nomine culpam*. Betrayal of Sychaeus' memory, or an indecorous and unhallowed romp?[29] After the cave *regina* is also *concubina*.[30] We are not, it seems to me, obliged to interpret the two uses of *culpa* in the same way and if we look more closely at the criticisms which Virgil implies at Dido's expense, then the interpretation of *culpa* at 172 as 'sexual misdemeanour' acquires increased credibility. I have never quite been able to shake off thoughts of Cleopatra: perhaps the association (not to use a stronger word!) really was, as many have supposed,[31] present in the poet's mind. But Dido's markedly Sophoclean suicide is—in the fullest tragic sense—a fate out of all proportion to the tragic flaw; enriched understanding of the texture of allusion out of which Dido's disintegration and death is created serves not to exculpate her (or to inculpate

---

[26] Cf. (e.g.) E.L. Harrison (n. 2, 1989), 11. Note the *promissa* on 4.552. Monti's argument that the *facta impia* of 596 do not refer to the breach of *fides* (62ff.) does not carry conviction (*The Dido episode and the Aeneid* (*Mnem.* Suppl. 67, 1981), 62ff.)

[27] Tatum (n. 2), 448ff.

[28] K. Quinn, *Latin Explorations* (London, 1963), 55.

[29] *Pudor*, 27 refers to D. as *uniuira*; so too therefore 55. Cf. Cairns, 48f. and Moles' two useful discussions.

[30] Cf. Treggiari (n. 35), 51f. with further bibliography.

[31] Cf. 162ff. for allegory in general and n. 63 for Cleopatra.

Aeneas), but to deepen the grief aroused by her end.[32] She dies, she says (547ff.) because she has betrayed Sychaeus: readers will wish to supply more complex reasons. Note therefore that Virgil pulls the reader's head and heart in conflicting directions. We shall see more of how the poet creates a moral and emotional battleground within his audience both here in 4 and (more so) in 12.[33]

Coniugium

A serious attempt was made recently to argue that the reader of *Aen.*4 should suppose, or so Virgil suggests that Dido and Aeneas were married.[34] That had the merit of making scholars look closely at those indications in the text which make it altogether clear that in fact this was in no way Virgil's intention! The omens at the cave (166ff.) are hideous parodies of those appropriate at a wedding. The suggestion that Aeneas and Dido might be thought wed by consent will not work:[35] *conubium* did not, in Roman law, exist between them, for Dido was beyond doubt a foreigner, and Aeneas, in so many senses, already a Roman (Treggiari (n. 35), 44ff.). Nor could a mere consensual union ever have been enough for Augustus' distinguished ancestor. Dido, Anna, Juno and Venus talk about marriage (so Williams, n. 34). The hideous omens (supra) occur at the *conubiis* (168). That proves nothing: witness the explicit condemnation at 169–72 (cf. 221); *coniugium* is a word which Dido uses to conceal (*praetexit*, present) her *culpa* (on which cf. p. 127). Explicit comment thus reveals that all else is but self-delusion. At 338–9 Aeneas is, quite simply and factually, right.[36]

Fate and the gods (on whom see more fully 141ff.)

'Jupiter is better able to bear the blame than either Virgil or Aeneas' (Dryden). First, *fatum* and *fata*: Dido, *fati nescia* at 1.299, is (4.450)

---

[32] Foreshadowed already at 4.169 (cf. 451, 547) and developed in a markedly Sophoclean (cf. nn. 66, 67) manner.

[33] Moles (n. 2, 1984, repr.), 147, id. (n. 2, 1987), 160f., G.W. Williams, *Tradition and originality in Roman poetry* (Oxford 1968), 386f., E.L. Harrison (n. 2, 1989), 19ff., Wlosok, 336ff. = 243ff., Lyne *FV*, 173, Monti (n. 26), 55, Quinn (n. 28), 34, 44f.

[34] Monti (n. 26), 30ff., Williams (n. 33), 380, *JRS* 52 (1962) 43ff. Cf. the useful discussions by Moles (n. 2, 1984, repr.), 144ff. and (n. 2, 1987), 156, Rudd (n. 2), 153, Quinn (n. 28), 37f., E.L. Harrison (n. 2, 1982), 21, Feeney (n. 2, 1983), 204f. = Harrison 167f.

[35] S. Treggiari, *Roman Marriage* (Oxford 1991), 54ff.

[36] Feeney (n. 2, 1983), 207 = Harrison, 171f.

fatis exterrita: she recognises and dreads the will of heaven.[37] At 4.614 Dido suspects that the *fata Iouis* may have willed that Aeneas arrive in Italy. The *exuuiae* of Aeneas (651) were *dulces* to Dido, *dum fata deusque sinebant*; cf. *fortuna*, (653). At 4.696, Dido, by her suicide, anticipates the mortal span.[38] Aeneas too (cf. 3.717, his tale of the *fata diuum* to Dido) is equally a prisoner (4.340, cf. 225, 355) of the *fata*. While Venus feigns herself *fatis incerta* (4.110, 'fatally unsure'!) whether Jupiter favours an alliance between Trojans and Carthaginians. The *fatum* of Aeneas and Rome is, impartially, cruel towards both Aeneas and Dido (cf. 4.434 on Dido's view of her own *fortuna*).

Venus tells her son Dido's story (1.340), thereby 'fostering Aeneas' interest'[39] in the queen. She ensures the Trojans' safe arrival at Carthage,[40] fears for her son's safety there, in Juno's city[41] and sends Cupid to take Ascanius' place and fire Dido with love for Aeneas,[42] inducing her thereby to forget (or betray) Sychaeus (1.720). That does not make Dido into a paralysed puppet, innocent of responsibility. I have wondered whether Virgil intends us to suspect that she was not perfectly sober at the banquet (cf. 1.724, 728ff., 749). Does her experience predispose her to fall, anyway, for another exile?[43] Would the story, without divine intervention, have developed identically? The question is unhelpful: that is not how Virgil did things; in the version we have (the only one), the gods are, like it or not, present, and we can only read the text that we have. We are left with no clear answer about Dido's innocence. Attraction there was (613) before Cupid's intervention. The issue is one that Virgil does seem (deliberately?) to have left unresolved.

Juno (4.90ff.) knowns of Venus' fears for Aeneas' safety and consequent conquest of Dido. She proposes, as an end to rivalry, a marriage of the principals and an alliance between the peoples. Venus (knowing Aeneas' Italian destiny to be endangered thereby, 105f.)

---

[37] Moles (n. 2, 1987), 158 with bibliography, Muecke (n. 2) 150f.

[38] J. Ter Vrugt-Lentz, *Mors Immatura* (Groningen 1960), 71f.

[39] Cf. E.L. Harrison (n. 2, 1989), G.H. Gellie, in *Cicero and Virgil. Studies in honour of Harold Hunt* (Amsterdam 1972), 138ff.; for Venus in bk. 1, cf. further 103, 105.

[40] 411ff. in the manner of *Od*.7.14ff., Mackie, 30.

[41] 1.661, 672, confirmed by Juno's remarks at 4.96ff.; cf. Horsfall (n. 8), 5 = Harrison, 133f.

[42] Cf. E.L. Harrison (n. 2, 1989), 14, Moles (n. 2, 1987), 154, Rudd (n. 2, repr.), 163.

[43] E.L. Harrison (n. 2, 1989), 6, 10, Moles (n. 2, 1987), 154, Williams, 14f., Otis, 265, Mackie, 32, 78, D.C. Feeney, *The Gods in Epic* (Oxford 1991), 175. But cf. Horsfall (n. 8), 6 = Harrison, 134.

replies that she does not know if such a plan has Jupiter's approval
(110ff.); Juno is best placed to find out. Juno replies that she will; for
the moment *qua ratione quod instat/confieri possit* she will explain, and
outlines the plan for a hunt and a storm. Venus, after her tampering
with Dido's heart, can hardly object.[44] Virgil is at some pains not to
indicate (1.595–610) Aeneas' first reactions to the queen; at 610 he
does not say that he is called to Italy, but I do not see actual dis-
simulation in his imprecision. At 1.715, the false Ascanius embraces
his 'father' at dinner. When Dido asks for an account of Aeneas'
adventures, she calls him *hospes*. After the banquet, she leads Aeneas
about Carthage, dines with him, asks him anew of his adventures.
Not a word of Aeneas' thoughts or actions, though. With great skill
and art (artfulness, too!), Virgil suppresses half the impending affair
and discourages us from asking the sort of question Lyne (124f. above)
incautiously answers. Even Mackie (77ff.) offers no remark: if the
text says nothing about Aeneas' reaction to a certain development, is
that, or is it not, significant? Is he to be thought of as entirely *nescius*
(4.72), as application of the wounded deer simile might imply? We
might wonder whether any man could be that unaware of the effect
he has on a woman (and some conclude that therefore he is no hero
worth reading about!). Dido leads him *per moenia* (74), shows him
urbem. . .paratam (75), yet (88) *pendent opera*. For love, all is at a halt;[45]
for love, Dido breaks off her thread of speech. Virgil, I conclude
must deliberately suppress any reaction to such symptoms. Aeneas is
not blind, deaf, or impotent; no god has fired his passion; he has no
spouse; he is prisoner of destiny, but hardly of desire too, at least as
yet. No word of love, no room for blame (at least as yet; no universal
ethic imposes simultaneity of emotion in such situations); no father
to supervise.

Plot[46]

No intention here to retell the 'story' of bk. 4. Rather, Virgil man-
ipulates a brief sequence of action in such a way as to create an
unbearable human situation. Mercury brings Aeneas, in altered version,

---

[44] Monti (n. 26), 30, E.L. Harrison (n. 2, 1989), 13f., Cairns, 46, Horsfall, *Vergilius*
35 (1989), 19f., Moles (n. 2, 1987), 154.
[45] Horsfall (n. 8), 7 = Harrison, 135.
[46] Feeney (n. 2, 1983), 207 = Harrison, 172.

Jupiter's orders.[47] Aeneas is struck dumb: he (281) *ardet abire fuga dulcisque relinquere terras.* He is on fire (a particularly Didonian word) to leave (at once, without hesitation. Why? Cf. 282) and quit the *dulcis. . .terras* (reflecting the other side of his heart). Three rhetorical questions underline his problem and give him pause for thought. Orders to the fleet to prepare for sailing; *quae rebus sit causa nouandis/ dissimulent* (291f.): the balance of 291 shows that this secrecy is not aimed so much at Dido as (unsuccessfully) at town gossip (cf. 296f.). Aeneas himself, since *optima Dido* (Austin well compares *dulcis. . .terras*) has no idea of what is up, will try to find the right moment to break the news (293–4). That would not have been easy, nor (cf. 331ff.) a task suited to Aeneas' skills. We cannot, though, deny that he intended to do so. His men, significantly, are *laeti* at the orders. *At. . .regina* (Act 2 begins) *dolos. . .praesensit.* Virgil does not call Aeneas' action, objectively, *doli*; that, rather, is how Dido sees it (cf. 306 *tacitus*; simply untrue; vd. Feeney, l.c.), *omnia tuta timens* as she does (Feeney compares 419f.). Underlined (*eadem*) ring-composition brings back *Fama* to give Dido *furenti* (cf. 300–3 on her Dionysiac madness) the news of the fleet's preparations. And she does not yet know why. *Tandem* (which gives Dido's subjectively justifiable rage time to swell) she finds Aeneas: *his Aenean compellat uocibus ultro.* Crucial is *ultro*: Dido speaks first, while Aeneas, who has planned to offer an explanation, is forced instead into an anguished and halting defence.[48] Let us be precise: it is *eadem impia Fama*[49] who moves faster than Aeneas and thereby transforms an impossible situation into an inevitable tragedy.[50]

---

[47] B. Axelson, *Unpoetische Wörter* (Lund 1945), 57, Lyne, *WP*, 43ff.

[48] Of which Highet, 72ff. offers a conventionally hostile reading. Far preferable Feeney (n. 2, 1983); cf., on the echoes (*tacitus, dissimulent*) between 289ff. and 305ff., Highet, 74, 289, Feeney (n. 2, 1983), 207 = Harrison, 172.

[49] *Impia* because she announces things *impia*; cf. Serv. *ad Aen.*12.608: so A. Traina, *EV* 4, 95. But in what sense could Virgil describe Aeneas' flight, in objective narrative, as 'impious'? Might it have been so classified by the hearer-victim, Dido (cf. 4.596)? Or is the sense (cf. *Buc.*1.70, *G.*1.511, 2.537) rather 'hard, unpitying', as indeed Fama is towards both Aeneas and Dido?

[50] We may wonder just how far we might be expected to feel sympathy for Aeneas' censure of Dido's unhelpful use of overly emotive language (Feeney, n. 2, 1983, passim). The queen's hold upon our esteem is diminished, or so we may feel we are invited to conclude, by Virgil's attribution to her of (increasingly) violent and hysterical outbursts: cf. Quinn (n. 28), 53, E.L. Harrison (n. 2, 1989), 16ff. This is not for one moment to deny that Dido in the later stages of bk. 4 has moments of the greatest grandeur and dignity (cf. E. Fraenkel, *Glotta*, 33 (1954), 158 = *Kl.Beitr.*2 (Roma 1964), 140f., on 4.655f.) or that her status as great tragic heroine remains.

Footnotes

At 5.3, Aeneas looks shorewards and sees the flame of Dido's pyre: *quae tantum accenderit ignem/causa latet.* True, he does not and can not know the manner of her death. Mercury's third intervention[51] roused Aeneas as he slept, *rebus rite paratis*: fully ready to leave, he could thus (however little we may like him for it) slumber in dolorous counterpoint to Dido's perhaps most balanced (and therefore most obviously moving) speech (534–52) until Mercury's warning (not idle: cf. 590ff.) stirred him to hasty departure. Now, *duri magno sed amore dolores/polluto notumque furens quid femina possit/ triste per augurium Teucrorum pectora ducunt.* Not the reactions of Aeneas in particular, but of the Trojans in general,[52] as Virgil only makes plain *after* describing the reactions in question. *Polluto* is rare and very strong, given added prominence by its position, while *furens. . .femina* is pure familiar Dido (4.69, 283, 465, 548. . .). Virgil refers generally to the human experience of Aeneas' men without specifying the (unmistakable) queen. Bailey offers the translation 'lead the hearts of the Trojans through a sad path of augury' (*RiV*, 20): *augurium* is not just a grand word for 'conjecture'; the Trojans see the anomalous flames above the walls of Carthage, and that is a sign, apparently hostile to them, and certainly so intended by Dido (4.662); that *augurium* the Trojans must in the short term evaluate[53] and may find its immediate fulfilment (so SDan) in the storm (5.8ff.) or in the burning of their ships.

Upon Aeneas' encounter with the shade of Dido, I only glean where T.S. Eliot reaped,[54] but Virgil does comment extensively upon the earlier narrative and the coda is integral to a balanced evaluation of the whole.[55] Dido here too (6.456) is *infelix* (1.749, 4.68, 529, 596), on Aeneas' lips. She responds to Aeneas' attempt (two conative imperfects)[56] to assuage her wrath (*ardentem*) and fierce mien (*torua*

---

[51] E.L. Harrison (n. 2, 1982), 29ff.

[52] Who (cf. 1.700, 4.289, 295, 573ff.) did not much enjoy, according to Virgil, their stay in Carthage.

[53] Catalano, *EV* 1, 403.

[54] La Penna (*EV* s.v. *Didone*, 57) notes a lack of good modern discussion, but cf. R.G. Austin, *PVS* 8 (1968–9), 51–9, Mackie, 128ff., G.S. West, *TAPA* 110 (1980), 315 Tatum (n. 2), Skulsky (n. 2). But cf. above all, T.S. Eliot, *What is a classic?* (London 1945, etc.), 20f.

[55] The more recent articles cited in the preceding note are specially useful for determining the implications of the company in which Dido is found.

[56] Two conative imperfects: *lacrimasque ciebat* has aroused discussion (a summary, Mackie, 133, n. 1). If Aeneas is (455) in tears already and Dido emphatically not

tuentem), and to stir her to tears as he is himself already weeping, from love (455, cf. 4.395) with a stony and explicitly hostile (472) silence (6.471ff.), which answers Aeneas' oaken but anguished imperturbability at 4.441ff. She flees Aeneas, as Aeneas fled her[57] and it is to her first love Sychaeus that she returns, the great betrayal forgotten. At her departure, Aeneas (476) weeps again in pity.[58] Aeneas had somehow heard of Dido's suicide (perplexing only if you let such trivia bother you): her decision to die (4.475, cf. 451) is taken after their last colloquy. Aeneas nonetheless does in some sense know already that indeed *funeris heu tibi causa fui* (458, cf. 463f.). He swears that it was not by his own will (*inuitus*) but by divine command that he left Carthage:[59] love for his father and love for Italy make for easy compliance.[60] His presence in the underworld is equated morally with his departure from Carthage.[61] A part of Dido's tragedy is her inability to comprehend the divine imperative to which Aeneas bows. Much in the underworld, as has often been noted, is a reversal of the behaviour seen in bk. 4; 'reversal', though, should not carry us away: Dido's inability to understand a man *sub auctoritate constitutus* (*Matt.*8.9) remains unaltered: it is hardly a weakness, but no less tragic for being entirely comprehensible.

Sources

In despair, attentive readers of *Aen.*4 are reduced to drawing up lengthy lists of Dido's mythical and literary analogues.[62] Let us here distinguish at least between (i) alleged allegorical comparisons, notably

---

(469ff.), then it is very hard not to apply *ciebat* to Aeneas' efforts to move Dido. Austin is right to say that V. often uses *cieo* of the expression of the subject's own emotions. But not so at 3.68 or 9.766.

[57] 6.466, 4.314, Mackie, 133.

[58] Mackie 129f. is quite wrong here. Aeneas weeps in bk. 4, but not enough for Dido's tastes (369f.). We might wish to compare the departure of Creusa's ghost before Aeneas can speak, 2.790f.; cf. Feeney (n. 2, 1983), 210f. = Harrison, 176f. Highet, 138f., G. Lieberg in *Vergiliana*, 187f.

[59] The immediate contrast of *sed me iussa deum* determines the implication of *inuitus*. Cf. 4.361 *Italiam non sponte sequor*: the volition is not his own. Mackie, 88, 131 tries ill-advisedly to distinguish the two and to suggest that Aeneas is driven unwillingly to visit the underworld (131)! Orders, again: 5.731ff., 6.116, accepted with passionate enthusiasm, to the Sibyl's dismay.

[60] Skulsky (n. 2), 449f.

[61] 461, explicitly: *iussa deum. . .quae.*

[62] Muecke (n. 2), 144, with further bibliography, Pease, 12ff.

Cleopatra,[63] (ii) Dido in Naevius,[64] Varro,[65] and Ateius Philologus,[66] (iii) Homeric antecedents, female and male,[67] and antecedents in Greek tragedy and Hellenistic poetry.[68] Perhaps most important both for the suicide and for the encounter in the underworld is Ajax.[69] That is to set aside the figures beside whom Dido is found in the underworld (cf. nn. 53, 4), or those whom she has herself had displayed on the temple (cf. 107f.) which she has set up to Juno.

Evaluation

Dido thus becomes the most complex literary figure yet created. Always, Aeneas is simpler and plainer: his moral lapse is sketched tersely and his personal tragedy so discreetly that it escapes many readers. We, like Aeneas, are dazzled by Dido. The formidable plot-structure (cf. 130f.) creates a tragedy in which no-one is altogether blameworthy, or altogether innocent. Judgement is perhaps therefore irrelevant and critically unhelpful! Perhaps Aeneas has incurred heavier guilt because he at least survives, and because, with Dido on stage, there was—one speech apart—no need and no room for him. Perhaps only in bk. 6 do we realise that he too has suffered greatly. No winners and only one survivor. 'Less judgements than disentangling.'

---

[63] Pease, 24ff., Cairns, 57, La Penna 54, who rightly points to 191–4 and 261–4 as the closest points of contact.

[64] Wigodsky (22ff.) took the case against Naevius as far as it could go; cf. rather Horsfall (n. 8), 9ff. = Harrison, 139ff., E.L. Harrison (n. 2, 1989), 2f. La Penna, 52ff.

[65] On the problems of SDan *ad Aen.*4.682 (cf. Serv. *ad Aen.*5.4) *Varro ait non Didonem sed Annam amore Aeneae inpulsam se supra rogum interemisse*, cf. Horsfall (n. 8) 11 = Harrison, 141f., La Penna 52, G. D'Anna, *Virgilio* (Roma 1989), 159ff = *Rend. Linc.*30 (1975), 3ff., G. Brugnoli in G.B. and F. Stok *Ovidius παρῳδήσας*, (Pisa 1992), 26ff.

[66] *Testimonia*, 9, *GRF*, 137. Discussion: cf. preceding note.

[67] Helen: Knauer, 155, n. 3, Calypso and Circe: Knauer, 209ff., Arete: Knauer, 164, 174, Penelope, E.C. Kopff, *Phil.*121 (1977), 244ff.; Hector: Muecke (n. 2), 144, n. 50, Lyne *WP*, 42, *FV*, 20.

[68] For Hypsipyle (AR), Medea (Eur. and AR), Berenice, Ariadne (Catullus), cf. Muecke l.c., (n. 2) Skulsky, Tatum, E.L. Harrison (1989), J.C.B. Foster, *PVS* 13 (1973–4), 28ff., König, 164ff., Clausen, 40ff., W.W. Briggs, *ANRW* 2.31.2 (1981), 959ff. Monti (n. 26), 50ff., La Penna, 53; cf. 123 for *Aen.*4 as tragedy.

[69] Cf. most recently La Penna, 53f., Harrison (n. 2, 1989), 19f. (not forgetting Deianeira); for Alcestis, cf. Lyne, *WP*, 110. No doubt several more analogues will have been suggested by the time this list reaches the press.

Book 5

Structure and architecture

If what we think we see as structural elements in the *Aeneid* had in fact some significance in Virgil's conception of the poem's architecture, and if what seems to be the relationship of those elements is not mere guesswork on our part (an ever-brimming fountain of fun and publications for some Virgilians) but corresponds to something once present, if not in "Virgil's intentions", then at least, in the common and heartfelt reactions of the poem's first educated readers, the consequences are important—for our evaluation of VSD: the text is unfinished (evidently), was composed in little bits (not just because VSD says so, but because that is how it looks; cf. though ch. 1, n. 109), yet for all that appears to have some kind of overall structure and started from a prose summary (it must have done, if part or all that passes for architecture has some objective validity!). Analysis of the text (some statistics apart) in fact does suggest that VSD on how the *Aen.* was written is one of the very few reliable sections in that work.

We can create links between books on the basis of verbal and thematic echoes, but if that is done without proper caution (cf. 112f. on bk. 2) it unleashes a kind of thematic perpetual motion[1] and can lead to the dissolution—or so it might seem—of order and coherence in the *Aeneid*: exciting, or so it might appear and what some critics have wanted (or want), but, arguably, a reduction, at the same time, of the poem's claim—I am still thinking of Eliot!—to 'classic' status ('maturity of mind', 'maturity of language', 'gravity'; lessened, arguably, if the sense of the poem depends on continuous access to an *index verborum*). Nor should we let ourselves be overimpressed by 'architecture' which depends on selective definition of the contents of individual books or upon superficial and loaded descriptions of the individual books' general characters. That will permit one pretty diagram after another.[2] But can we ever hope that our chiasmi or Chinese boxes may become not playthings, not (alas, but perhaps just as well) certainties, but at least probabilities in our evaluation of how Virgil might have expected his epic to be perceived? Are there, in short, any external and independent criteria that can be applied?

---

[1] Cf., for example, *HSCP* 66 (1962), 205ff., and my remarks on bk. 2 (111ff.).
[2] Cf. E. Coleiro, *Tematica e struttura dell'Eneide di Virgilio* (Amsterdam 1983), 76ff.

Parallelisms with Homer look as though they might be helpful: common use of Posidon's speech (*Od.*5.282–5) links Juno's speeches in *Aen.*1 and 7.[3] *Aen.*1 and 7 both owe something to *Od.*7 too.[4] That certainty helps to confirm the many verbal and thematic parallels that have been detected between 1 and 7.[5] At the same time, though, the Games in 5[6] correspond to two distinct schemata of Homeric imitation that are wholly independent of any architectural analysis of the *Aen.* It is Knauer's great merit to have shown that such schemata really do exist, but they do not always serve to confirm our pretty diagrams. In the end, perhaps only detailed thematic parallelisms, confirmed by strong and repeated verbal echoes, have any real value as a criterion. By that, I do not mean the definition of books p, q, r and s as 'light' or 'dark', or the characterisation of c and d as 'tragic', while n and m are 'relaxed'.

It proved unexpectedly illuminating to examine the various 'architectural designs' of the *Aen.* from the point of view of one book (five): not a method that did much to encourage me to take 'architecture' very seriously as a critical tool.[7] Certainly 5 is less, shall we say, intense than 4 or 6. Though there appears to be a strong 'caesura' at the end of 4 (death of Dido), its effect is weakened by the opening of 5 (Dido's pyre still burning; cf. 132), which takes up story, themes and imagery from the end of 4.[8] Similarly[9] 5 and 6 are intimately linked by Palinurus' death,[10] while the end of 5 and the opening of 7 are connected by references to the Sirens and Circe.[11] Thus, though 4, 5 and 6 all end with a death (Dido, Palinurus, Marcellus), in no case is the 'caesura' strong. The geographical movement of the narrative separates 5 sharply from 4 and links 5 intimately to 3.[12] The classic statement that Anchises must die before Aeneas reaches Dido

---

[3] Knauer, 337 n. 1, W. Görler, *Würz.Jhb* 2 (1976), 165ff.

[4] Knauer, 230.

[5] Knauer, 335, Buchheit, 173ff., Worstbrock (218, n. 10), 37.

[6] Knauer, 156f. 220, 330, 334.

[7] J. Perret, *Virgile. L'homme et l'oeuvre* (Paris 1952, etc.), 112f.

[8] E.L. Harrison, *ANRW* 2.31.1 (1980), 365ff.

[9] Cf. n. 8: this is a notably useful discussion.

[10] Knauer, 137, n. 1; cf. Harrison l.c. again, who rightly insists that the interlocking of Misenus and Palinurus (who incorporates both Phorcys and Elpenor) is complex, not confused.

[11] Still cf. Harrison, l.c.; cf. Knauer l.c. (n. 10) for the complications introduced by Virgil's further layer of references to Naevius and the geographical-aetiological tradition.

[12] For an entirely contrary view, cf. Williams, 278f.

is Heinze's.[13] The threat to Aeneas' *pietas*, obligations and mission in 4 is wiped out in the scrupulous observance of 5; in that respect, the rites in 5 correspond to those on the shield in 8.[14] With reservations, then, the role of 1–4 as a 'unit' ('Carthage') is secure, as is that of 9–12 ('Turnus' or 'Warfare in Italy'), and the pursuit of correspondences between 5 and 8 (which could lead to the establishment of a 'chiastic' pattern) is quite helpful:[15] cf. Venus' plea to Neptune in 5 and arrival with Aeneas' armour in 8, his sea-journey in 5[16] and his river-journey in 8.[17] But at the same time Camps noted[18] strong links between 5 and 9: Nisus and Euryalus, burning of ships, the Trojan *matres* and Euryalus' mother. The first and last books of the second 'quartet' are therefore linked just as are the first books of the second and third 'quartets'.[19]

This is not the place to enter into two further problems: (i) the marked irregularity (which can be no accident; the poet labours the point) of the division into 1–6 and 7–12; the second prooemium is delayed until 7.37, the main sequence of the action until 7.286;[20] (ii) arguably more important, the structure and definition we are to assign to the sequence 5–8. Strong though the presence of 'Roman' elements is in 7,[21] I cannot label 7 (and no book of the *Aen.* do I know more intimately) sensibly and at the same time compatibly with 5, 6 and 8. Neither Aeneas nor *pietas* are important in 7, nor, for that matter, Gates of Janus and allusion to the Claudii aside, the Roman future. 'Quartets', therefore, are all very well but perhaps more problematic than is generally realised.

---

[13] Heinze, 147.

[14] Compare the Trojan genealogies and the *lusus Troiae* in 5 with the historical vision of the shield in 8. See Worstbrock, 98ff.

[15] The links between 5 and 11 (cf. Coleiro (n. 2), 87, G.E. Duckworth, *AJP* 75 (1954), 6f., W.A. Camps, *An introduction to Virgil's Aeneid* (Oxford 1969), 54f.)—both begin with a funeral (Anchises, Pallas) and end with a death (Palinurus, Camilla)—are unpersuasive: the common features are too common, mere matters of superficial definition, not of solidly structured narrative unity.

[16] Harrison (n. 8), 368f.

[17] For analogies between Evander and Acestes, cf. G.K. Galinsky, *AJP* 89 (1968), 167.

[18] W.A. Camps, *CQ* 4 (1954), 214f.

[19] Camps (n. 15), 56, *CQ* 9 (1959), 53ff.

[20] The issue is needlessly complicated in Camps (n. 18).

[21] Cf., for example, my remarks in *EV* s.v. *Anacronismi*.

Gods

'These first 300 lines (sc., of bk. 1) introduce half a dozen divine characters, and as many ways of regarding the gods, through different conventions of reading and understanding'.[22] Just so, though there are still those, as we shall see in passing, who try to reduce the gods of the *Aeneid* to a single theological or intellectual system, governed by one philosophical source or pattern of interpretation: that seems to me not to conform to Virgil's habitual indeterminacy of mind, or to his many-faceted intellectual curiosity.[23] I would be easier in mind offering, if that is true to the text, a picture of Virgil's gods that is, in some respects, confused and incoherent![24] We begin, very briefly, with deities reduced to metonymy: so *Baccho*, 5.77, *Uolcanus* 662.[25] A good deal more interesting is Somnus/*somnus* (838ff.): Pötscher rightly (n. 4, 132f.) draws attention to his wand, his capacity for flight, his movements (858), his denomination as *deus* (i.e. the Iliadic Hypnos): a personification conventional but not altogether colourless. The *Tempestates* of 5.772 have a grand history (*ILS* 3.6). What of (5.721) Nox/*nox* (cf. Pötscher (n. 4, 118ff.)? Or Aurora/*aurora* (5.65)? It may be enough to say that if they have attributes, or act, then they are in some sense personifications and merit the majuscule. The case of Iris is[26] more interesting: The Iris of 4.700f. seems 'any old rainbow', but[27] at 702 speaks, like a goddess. At 5.606, Juno despatches Iris, without any specific instructions,[28] but because her arrival at the Trojan fleet is in itself in accordance with orders, she is to be considered a personification (*uirgo*) rather than a meteorological phenomenon.[29] On

---

[22] D.C. Feeney, *The gods in epic* (Oxford 1991), 141; cf. Boyancé, 35ff., C.H. Wilson, *CQ* 29 (1979), 371: 'Vergil's divinities are each a rich tapestry of many different strands'.

[23] A main thesis of *Alambicco*. Cf. below, 151f.

[24] Cf. Boyancé 19ff. for a useful survey of earlier views. See too Feeney, 169; on Williams, cf. (e.g.) R.G. Mayer, *CR* 34 (1984), 31ff. Almost as hostile as Williams, R.G. Coleman, *GR* 29 (1982), 162 = McAuslan, 58. It is interesting to compare the essentially tedious unity of cosmological and eschatological thought that some have found in bk. 6; cf. 151.

[25] Cf. Bailey's index s.v. Ceres, Neptunus, Vulcanus, Bacchus, *EV* 2.519 (Calboli) W. Pötscher, *Vergil und die göttlichen Mächte* (*Spudasmata* 35, Hildesheim 1977), 131.

[26] *TLL* s.v. *iris*, 378.37ff., Feeney (n. 1), 175f., Williams, 21, Pötscher (n. 25), 123, W. Kühn, *Götterszenen bei Vergil* (Heidelberg 1971) 77ff., E.A. Hahn, *TAPA* 88 (1957), 62, G.K. Galinsky, *AJP* 89 (1968), 167ff., W. Fauth, *Gymn.*78 (1971), 67ff.

[27] Cf. 5.88f., Hahn, l.c. (n. 5).

[28] Kühn (n. 26), 78.

[29] Both the path and the goddess, Hahn (n. 5), l.c.

touchdown, *haud ignara nocendi*, she adopts the form of Beroe (618–21),[30] exactly in the manner of Allecto (7.419) and the Dira (12.861ff.). Her work accomplished, Iris departs ambiguously, much as she arrived (657f.): *tum uero* (659) the Trojan *matres* take the rainbow as the *monstrum* which really convinces them to act (Feeney (n. 1), 176): cf., closely enough. Allecto's self-revelation, to goad Turnus to action (7.445ff.). The sequence of action in 5 should be noted with care: Iris throws a torch (641ff.); Pyrgo pierces the goddess' disguise; the *matres* are in doubt at first (654–6), until Iris manifests her full divinity. Only then, *attonitae monstris* do they all set to burn the ships. That does not suggest that Iris merely represents what they are all thinking. They see something in what she says, but like Turnus (cf. 158ff.) need a forceful and explicit divine intervention before they will act,[31] For Virgil, then, Iris, very usefully, belongs to both pantheon and common meteorology, an ambiguity amply exploited. Another terminological extension Virgil employs to augment the complexity and majesty of his divinities is that offered by *numen* and *fatum*. *Numen*[32] has a wide range: at 1.8f. an equivalent to Juno, at 3.437 Juno's godhead, at 3.633 divinities in general; at 5.56, *numen* is the unspecific divine will (note the etymological link with *nuo*, the nod by which the god's judgement is declared) by which the Trojans return to Anchises' place of burial on the anniversary of his death while at 5.466 the *numina* are the divine powers who have abandoned Dares in the ring, an indication that the pugilist feels no longer inspired or upheld by a force greater than himself. As unnecessary to dismiss these *numina* as a mere 'trope' for giving up as it is to claim that *Musae* are a mere synonym for 'inspiration'. I do not wish to offer any reinterpretation of Virgil's conception of *fatum* in general;[33] note, however,[34] 5.656, 703 where *fata* (cf. *for, fari*) are synonymous with oracles, while at 784 they indicate precisely the *imperium* of Jupiter,[35] fate as the will

---

[30] A disguise challenged by Pyrgo (645), who notes the points of dissimilarity and prettily undercuts (cf. Feeney (n. 1), 176) the narrative convention of the concealed divine agent.

[31] So, well, Feeney (n. 1), 175f.; contrast Williams, 23f. on Allecto; cf. Coleman (n. 3) 161f. = 57f.

[32] Bailey, 60ff., Pötscher (n. 25), 101.

[33] Cf. Timpanaro (intro., n. 6), 389ff., Wilson, l.c. (n. 1). Why should Nautes, the poem's one character overtly and explicitly Stoic in his views, be called a pupil of Pallas? Cf. Pötscher (n. 25), 77f.

[34] Cf. Pötscher (n. 25), 69f.

[35] Cf. Pötscher (n. 25), 45.

of Jupiter opposed to the *ira* and *odia* of Juno, the struggle of the *Aeneid* raised not merely to an Olympian plane but to a combat of often unnamed hypostaseis.

At a level more perceptible to both participants and readers, and particularly close in both detail and language to contemporary Roman usage,[36] the divine world communicated with the human unmistakably but not unambiguously though portents. The great serpent which appears at Anchises' *tumulus* (5.84ff.) leaves Aeneas stunned:[37] he is *incertus geniumne loci famulumne parentis/esse putet* (95f.). That is a neat case of a character's point of view (uncertainty) undercut by the reader's knowledge; the first hypothesis is perfectly in keeping with Roman belief.[38] In this case, to the reader, the gods speak clearly. The serpent is explicitly *innoxius* (92) and the Trojans are *laeti*: no sense in saying that snakes in the *Aen.* must necessarily signify doom and evoke Laocoon. Roman beliefs and the text itself may be allowed more weight than a dogmatic application of rigid schematism in the interpretation of symbols (cf. 114ff.);[39] to see the death of Palinurus (cf. Laocoon) foreshadowed by this benign tutelary serpent does seem to me altogether fanciful. When Acestes fires his arrow and it bursts into flames, *hic oculis subitum obicitur magnoque futurum/ augurio monstrum; docuit post exitus ingens/seraque terrifici cecinerunt omina uates* (522–4).[40] Again, several points of view: the Trojans are frightened, as they should be, by a manifestation of the divine presence; Aeneas and Acestes are delighted (530f.); Aeneas was wrong, says Servius (on 524) because he thought of the shooting star of 2.694. But what was the *exitus ingens*, explicitly later in time? Most probably Segesta's alliance with Rome and their victory in the first Punic war. Why then the apparent incompatibility with 524? Interpretation is dominated by a desire to link the flaming arrow with the burning of the Trojan ships, but the *omina* are described as *sera* (cf. *post*). If Aeneas and Acestes react with at least a minimum of good sense to what the *uates* sing, then their joint delight suggests that the *uates* also spoke of

---

[36] Cf. the good, full study by B. Grassmann-Fischer, *Die Prodigien in Vergils Aeneis* (München 1966), with A. Wlosok, *Gnom.*44 (1972), 245ff.

[37] *obstipuit uisu*, 90; cf. Cic. *Diu.*2.50, Prop.1.3.28; reaction and language are correctly Roman.

[38] Wissowa, *RKR* (ed. 2), 176f.

[39] Galinsky 26, 170f., 177; *aliter*, E. Block, *The effects of divine manifestation* (New York 1981), 105, after Putnam, *Poetry*, 72f.

[40] *Attonitis haesere animis*; cf. Block (n. 18), 102f., Galinsky (n. 5), 178, Grassmann-Fischer (n. 15), 86ff.

a great historical *exitus ingens*. *Terrifici*, then, perhaps, not only because alarm is a normal and proper reaction when faced by a portent (i.e. proximity of the divine), but also because the seers have
talked, as they will do, of a great war to come in Sicily. The facts,
we know, were bloody enough; wrapped in prophetic alarmism well
might they rouse dismay, despite the happy outcome.[41]

Among the divinities of bk. 5, Anchises, whose returns to the land
of the living as a serpent (when he speaks after the manner of a
deity, 83–90) and as a prophetic vision to Aeneas bracket the book,
belongs only in as much as some details of the honours paid him
suggest strongly not Roman ritual but Greek hero-cult.[42]

The role of Italian divinities (as against Greek) in the *Aeneid* may
be assessed through sceptical use of Bailey 103ff. (cf. the devastating
critique at Boyancé 19f.). It is interesting, though, to see how far the
active participation of fully Italian deities in the action is limited:
Feronia at 8.564 hardly counts; Juturna in bk. 12 is much the most
significant example; there remains Portunus (241). An older generation of critics was shocked by this outrage against fair play;[43] but this
is *pietas* answered, not gamesmanship.

We may finally turn to the main struggle at the divine level, between Neptune and Venus against Juno and Iris. In Virgil, Neptune
is not (but see 7.23) a lifeless embodiment of the sea (cf. the play on
Hera-*aer* latent at 9.2) and its powers. He sends the storm (14) which
drives the Trojans back to Sicily; not even Jupiter could help Palinurus
steer against it. At 639f., he has four altars and *deus ipse faces animumque
ministrat*, as Iris/Beroe says (640); the connexion of Neptune with fire
and the apparent hostility to the Trojans might, as did much else,
have suggested to Pyrgo the imposture. Venus, *exercita curis* (779) is
moved to address a deeply felt complaint to Neptune at 781ff. (cf.
her fear, 1.257 and plea to Jupiter at 1.229ff.). She refers back in fact
to the storm Juno raised in bk. 1 (with Aeolus' help suggested at
791) and to Neptune's knowledge of those trespasses on his domain

---

[41] Cf. 6.86ff., *Buc*.4.35, D. Potter on *Or.Sib*.13.89ff.

[42] Cf. Williams on 5.42f., Bailey, 293ff., Boyancé 149f.; G.W. Williams (278ff.)
suggests that some details of the ritual are more appropriate to a funeral than to an
anniversary and that Anchises' funeral therefore belonged in origin before Aeneas'
visit to Carthage. At 6.338, there is a real problem, but the minor anomalies in
bk. 5 suggest that Virgil, having entirely omitted the burial of Anchises in bk. 3 now
enriches the narrative with some details appropriate to the other ceremony.

[43] H.A. Harris, *PVS* 8 (1968–9), 25, *Sport in Greece and Rome* (London 1972), 131,
W.W. Briggs, *Stadion* 1 (1977), 270f.

(792). Now the Trojan ships have been fired and she requires a safe passage for the Trojans as far as the Tiber. Neptune is used to such requests (801f.); it was he who had saved Aeneas from Achilles before Troy (cf. 180, 200, 204). His *cura*[44] towards Venus' son Aeneas remains unaltered (812) and, curiously, while Venus speaks of the Trojans in general, it is Neptune who dwells at length on Aeneas (804–13): he will reach the Tiber safely, with the loss only of Palinurus.[45] Venus is cheered and calmed; Neptune departs in lordly majesty[46] with an escort of marine deities.[47] Neptune does not refer to Juno herself (he is after all *Saturnius* too, 799, as is Jupiter himself, 4.372), but merely to the storm she raised in bk. 1, while Venus (781f.) harps on her rival's *grauis ira neque exsaturabile pectus*, as yet untamed by time, by *pietas*, by Jupiter's *imperium* or by the *fata*; Juno has devoured[48] Troy with her *odia*, both before and after the sack. Such language is familiar.[49] Juno acts in bk. 5 through the subaltern Iris (cf. Aeolus, Allecto), and this time too, despite the dimensions and complexity of the struggle,[50] she fails (146f.), as will Carthage in the end. Her malignity attains cosmic dimensions,[51] though in bk. 5, since she does not interfere directly, there is little chance of personality or characterisation emerging here at least.[52] Juno and her subalterns fail (partly) in the end because Jupiter (in general, though not always in detail) is against them.[53] Anchises appears to Aeneas *Iouis imperio* (726) and Jupiter himself *caelo tandem miseratus ab alto est.*[54]

It is not helpful to read the *Aeneid* as a theological treatise, far less as a guide to Virgil's own beliefs; it is not even prudent to look for coherence or consistency. Even the great 'theological statement' of

---

[44] 5.804; cf. Pötscher (n. 25), 117.

[45] Pötscher (n. 25), 116. A. Wlosok, *Die Göttin Venus*. . .(Heidelberg 1967), 112; cf. Knauer, 138 on the relationship of Neptune's help here and at 7.23 to Circe's in *Od.*12.

[46] 5.817–21; cf. Hardie, 299f.

[47] Cf. 183, 185 on 10.219ff. (both Homeric and Hellenistic); Virgil's *cete* are Homer's κήτεις (*Il.*13.227), but the cortège is Hellenistic in conception and flavour; cf. R. Thomas on *G.*4.333–86.

[48] Cf. Lyne, *WP*, 174 on *exsaturabile-exedisse* and *satur-Saturnia.*

[49] 1.668, 7.298; cf. Juno's agent Allecto, 7.327, and her protectorate Carthage at 10.14. On the theme on *ira* in bk. 1, cf. 103f.: note 1.4, 11, 25, 130, 251, 8.60 and compare 7.326, 445 of Allecto.

[50] Feeney (n. 1), 144f., 149, Pötscher (n. 25), 149, Buchheit, 59.

[51] Cf. D.C. Feeney, *CQ* 34 (1984), 179ff.

[52] Not that that is lacking, Feeney (n. 1), 134ff., etc.

[53] Feeney (n. 1), 143ff.

[54] 5.727; cf. Galinsky (n. 26), 171.

10.112f. has a significant rhetorical purpose and context: it is not doctrine but bluff.[55] Virgil's deities react kindly to patient and dispassionate analysis; perhaps more than any other aspect of the epic, they turn to clay, or lead, or concrete in the hands of those who approach them with convictions or preconceptions or with a single 'global' theory.

Not good enough, says R.G. Coleman:[56] the gods of the Hellenized literary-religious tradition 'were not capable of bearing the serious burden of causation that Virgil placed upon them'. For bk. 1, Feeney's analysis, already cited, constitutes a fully sufficient reply and I hope to have shown that the divine presence in bk. 5 is complex and varied enough to suggest that Virgil is not merely wheeling tinselly automata across his stage.

---

[55] Feeney (n. 1), 145, after E.L. Harrison, *ANRW* 2.31.1 (1980), 390. But cf. A. Wlosok, *Res humanae-res divinae* (Heidelberg 1990), 378ff. = *Gymn.*90 (1983), 198ff., in a fine and serious study of Virgil's Jupiter.

[56] Coleman (n. 24), 164 = 60.

Book 6: History and philosophy

History

Virgil makes plain the rhetorical intent of the 'Parade of Heroes' at
6.756–9 and 888–9. *Tua fata docebo* is taken up in the short term by
891–2 (contrast 3.458–60) but Anchises' prooemium identifies the
figures under review—for that is what it is; Aeneas and Anchises are
on the stand (754), and the heroes march past[1]—as Aeneas' own
descendants, of mixed Trojan-Italian stock, a recurrent motif (cf. 717,
756f., 762, 767, 788). Anchises *incenditque animum famae uenientis amore*
and proceeds at once to recount (how, we are not told) the wars
Aeneas himself must fight. Aeneas' own struggles therefore form
explicitly an integral part of the series of all Rome's struggles towards greatness, and it is the *famae uenientis amor* that fires Aeneas (by
clear implication) to face those struggles like a Roman. After showing Aeneas the future Augustus, Anchises adjures him *et dubitamus
adhuc uirtutem extendere factis?/ aut metus Ausonia prohibet consistere terra?* (806f.).
The revelation of future greatness is a direct inspiration to present
action, as we saw already at 717f. *iampridem hanc prolem cupio enumerare
meorum/quo magis Italia mecum laetere reperta.* The sequence 889f. (cf.
806f., 717f.) seems therefore to rule out the idea that Aeneas passes
through the *porta eburna* to strip him of awareness of his future (contrast the clear perplexity of 8.730). Venus leaves the shield with
minimal explanation (8.612ff.); Aeneas has his father beside him during
the whole parade. The situations are therefore fundamentally different,
and 'genealogical protreptic'[2] is not a form of discourse to be cast in
riddles. The parade does indeed contain problems;[3] for Virgil, history is not a matter of hard facts,[4] but is, like geography, malleable,
though far less so than mythology. The poet, like the orator, can
chose his *exempla*, and manipulate the emphasis they bear, to stimulate, provoke and allude.[5]

---

[1] Cf. 755, 845, 863, D.A. West in *Tria Lustra* (*Essays. . .Pinsent*) (Liverpool 1993),
284, 289.
[2] *Pace* H.C. Gotoff, *CP* 80 (1985), 37.
[3] J.E.G. Zetzel, *TAPA* 119 (1989), 273; much overstated by Feeney, *PCPhS* 32
(1986), 5–16, on which see now West (n. 1), 283ff.
[4] *Alambicco*, 84, 86f.
[5] Cf. Horsfall, *Vergilius* 37 (1991), 31ff.

Virgil's protreptic use of history is swiftly set in context:[6] we should compare *Buc.*4.26f. *at simul heroum laudes et facta parentis / iam lege et quae sit poteris cognoscere uirtus*. . ., Augustus' declaration of the intent of the statues in the Forum Augusti (Suet. *Aug.*31.5, *Edicta* fr.xiii Malcovati),[7] Sall. *Iug.*4.5 *cum maiorum imagines intuerentur uehementissume sibi animum ad uirtutem accendi*, Plb.6.53.10 (of the funeral processions of the aristocracy; cf. West (n. 1), 289) (Loeb trans.): 'for who would not be inspired by the sight of the images of men renowned for their excellence, all together and as if alive and breathing'; cf. further Cic. *Rep.*6.13, a place in the heavens for all those *qui patriam conseruauerint, adiuuerint, auxerint*, with the intent *quo sis, Africane, alacrior ad tutandam rem publicam*, those passages in the Scipionic *elogia* which refer to matching or surpassing the *gloriam maiorum*,[8] and the *carmina antiqua in quibus laudes erant maiorum*, sung by *pueri modesti*.[9] I concentrate deliberately on Roman usage, rather than on the amply-studied use of the historical *exemplum* in rhetoric.[10] Some years ago, I identified the main literary source of the Parade, aside from the Homeric *teichoscopia*, as Varro *Imagines*.[11] After Degrassi's discussion,[12] the Forum of Augustus, once touted, should never again have been mentioned as a possible source for Virgil (though unfortunately it sometimes still is); the statues of the Forum and the Parade may, though have in part a common visual source (cf. n. 11).

Virgil's Roman heroes are of course as yet incorporeal (751), but, just as the inhabitants of Elysium have retained their old kit, so, for example, Camillus is already shown (perplexingly, or challengingly) *referentem signa*. These heroes are therefore at least to Anchises, and

---

[6] Cf. Horsfall, *Prudentia* 8 (1976), 82ff., conveniently but ungratefully summarised at *HSCP* 92 (1989), 235ff.

[7] Cf. F.G.B. Millar, *JRS* 83 (1993), 3 on Tiberius, and on Augustus, Z. Yavetz in *Caesar Augustus* (ed. F. Millar and E. Segal, Oxford 1984), 18ff.

[8] Horsfall (n. 6), 84 with n. 101.

[9] Varro *de uita* fr.84 Riposati with J.N. Bremmer in *Sympotica* (ed. O. Murray, Oxford 1990), 138. Horsfall, *RFil* 122 (1994), 70ff.

[10] Cf. now W. Martin Bloomer, *Valerius Maximus* (London 1992), index, s.v. *exempla*, H. Roloff, *Maiores bei Cicero*, diss. Leipzig 1937, H.W. Litchfield, *HSCP* 25 (1914), 1ff.

[11] On the basis of a close link between Varr. *Imagines* ap. Symm. *Epist.*1.4 and *Aen.*6.841–3, 855—*Anc.Soc.* (Macquarie) 10 (1980), 20ff., though the strong visual element in the Parade had long been recognised (L. Delaruelle, *RevArch.*4.21 (1913), 153ff.) and some attempts have been made to identify extra-literary influences on the Parade (e.g. funeral processions: West (n. 1), 289): cf. Highet, 241f., Horsfall (n. 6), 82f., Feeney (n. 3), 5, T. Habinek, *HSCP* 92 (1989), 236f.

[12] *Epigraphica* 7 (1945), 88ff.

so, largely, if not entirely, to Virgil's readers historical and identifiable. The point needs unfortunately to be laboured for it bears very directly on the endlessly discussed question of the *somni*[13] *portae*: through that of horn *ueris facilis datur exitus umbris* (894), and through that of ivory *falsa ad caelum mittunt insomnia Manes* (896).[14] If Anchises tells his son three times that the function of the Parade is to stiffen his sinews (vel sim.) for the fight to come, then the most pessimistic interpreters of the *Aeneid* may feel that it is just like Virgil to send Aeneas through the gate of ivory to show that all of bk. 6 (and in particular the vision of Rome's future) comes under the general heading of *falsa insomnia*.[15] This is not, I suggest, a credible or correct reading of the text; certainly it is rank bad rhetoric and sheer clumsiness in handling the reader's expectations. Aeneas shows no recollection of the Parade in 7–12, and is indeed perplexed by the scenes on the Shield. That is not to say that he is deaf to his father, bored by the Parade and immediately brainwashed of its explicit lesson. How he reacts (if he reacts) Virgil does not tell us. Or is it we as readers who are meant to see all of *Aeneid* 6, or at least the Parade, as a dream or an illusion? Not entirely, for though I can see that Virgil might have wished to use the Gates as a metaphor[16] for distancing himself from a detailed and active belief in the traditional Hades/Elysium, he can hardly be telling us that Roman history did not happen, or that it all 'meant' naught but one long tale of woe and wrong, and given the long-recognised explicit co-existence of encomium and psogos in the Parade,[17] he can scarcely be suggesting that we are hereby instructed not to believe the (to some extent) mixed and complex interpretation he offers! I do not mean to revert to the old interpretation that Virgil is using a piece of folklore rooted in physiology to tell us the time of night! I note Tarrant's fine observation (n. 14) that our bodily existence (and Aeneas in the Underworld is massively corporeal, 292ff.,

---

[13] From *somnium*? Cf. Perutelli (n. 20).

[14] Of the most useful recent bibliography, I cite Habinek (n. 11), 253f., Zetzel (n. 3), 264 Feeney (n. 3), 15, Goold (n. 22), 122f., Gotoff (n. 2), 35ff., R.J. Tarrant, *CP* 77 (1982), 51f., E.C. and N.M. Kopff, *Phil.*120 (1976), 246ff., D.A. West, *The Bough and the Gate* (Exeter 1986) = Harrison, 224ff., F.E. Brenk, *Coll.Lat.*217 (1992), 277ff., Williams, 48 and the very useful summary at *EV* 2.962 (Setaioli), A. Thornton, *The Living Universe* (*Mnem.* Suppl. 46, 1976), 61 and even *Alambicco*, 103f.

[15] Thus (e.g.) A.J. Boyle, *Ramus* 1 (1972), 121f. and several of the discussions just cited. West (nn. 1, 14) stands at the opposite pole, of robust common sense.

[16] 'Enallage' says Zetzel (n. 3), 275; 'synecdochic', Williams, 48.

[17] So already Norden, 314; cf. Feeney (n. 3).

413f.) is less real (cf. Plat. *Phaed*.66 BC.) than that of a purer and more ethereal world. But is this quite the right moment, in terms of narrative strategy, for Virgil to offer us a philosophical allusion that gently deflates much of the Parade's explicit point? Some may think so. Aeneas does have to get out of the Underworld and narrative economy dictates all manner of advantages inherent in a short cut. He cannot leave by the gate of horn, for he is certainly not a *uera. . .umbra*. Does he come under *falsa. . .insomnia*? The phrase is in itself ambiguous (so e.g. Kopff (n. 14) with further bibliography): the adjective need not signify 'lying', though it can,[18] and I hope to have offered reason enough to make the reader pause before accepting without question that sense here. *Falsus* can also mean 'unreal' (of a deceiving appearance)[19] at *Aen*.1.407 (Kopff, 249f.) Venus *uera incessu patuit dea* and Aeneas protests that she deceives him, *falsis/ludis imaginibus*. There too we find a contrast *uera. . .falsis*. But here Aeneas is certainly not sent by the Manes (*mittunt insomnia Manes*); on his own two feet he strides through the Gate. Nor is he, having nearly sunk Charon's barque, in any sense a dream. Fine work has been done on analysing and distinguishing the various kinds of dream and vision in the *Aeneid*.[20] We need to distinguish the Gate's normal traffic (whether or not we claim to understand exactly what that is) from Aeneas, who in no way corresponds with it. Much has he seen and known: it may be that Virgil is telling us that parts of that experience are more solidly based in history or literature than others. But he hardly invites either Aeneas as hearer or us as audience to dismiss an entire book from our minds as predominantly illusion.

At this point we may return to look briefly at two of the problems in the Parade which have aroused particular interest in recent years:[21]

First, G.P. Goold has recently restated with elegance and ingenuity the case for regarding the Marcellus-section as an addition to a draft already complete.[22] I am one of those who 'have passionately

---

[18] *Aen*.6.430, *G*.1.463, Kopff (n. 14), 249, n. 21.

[19] Kopff (n. 14), 249, citing *Buc*.6.48, *Aen*.1.716, 3.302, 6.513.

[20] Cf. Kopff (n. 14), H. Steiner, *Der Traum in der Aeneis* (Bern 1952), P. Kragelund, *Dream and prediction in the Aeneid* (Copenhagen 1976), A.K. Michels, *CQ* 31 (1981), 140ff., A. Perutelli, *EV* s.v. *Somnium/insomnia*.

[21] My general account of its structure and purpose is unfortunately well-hidden in *Anc.Soc.* (Macquarie) 12 (1982), 12ff., but Feeney (n. 3) accepts in more accessible form many of my conclusions; likewise West, indirectly (n. 1).

[22] In *Author and audience in Latin literature*, ed. T. Woodman and J. Powell (Cambridge 1992), 110ff.

argued that the whole pageant was designed as we now read it' (Goold, 111f.; cf. n. 21). Virgil's public reading of bk. 6 (Goold, 111f.; cf. p. 19) is beset with problems of text and detail, though it probably did happen, some time between 23 and 19! Goold allows that the first draft contained the verses on the elder Marcellus (855–9). But Virgil's source for the notable prominence assigned him was already known to Servius and was in fact Augustus' own *laudatio funebris* for the younger Marcellus,[23] which developed, as was appropriate in that genre, the links within the *gens* that we find maintained in Virgil. If we are to believe in drafts, then let us at least take the addition in the second as running unbroken from 854 to 887. But there are also extremely close thematic links between the elder Marcellus and the larger context.[24] Were 854–87 an addition, the 'tacking on' is a work of genius, intensely meditated and hardly the swift cobbling of a deft *uates* bowing to court sentiment. The hypothesis seems therefore quite unnecessary.[25] Worse, if my suspicion about a link between *excudent alii...* and Augustus' account of Marcellus' education in the *laudatio funebris* (a necessary theme when death precludes the normal praise of a full career) is right,[26] then the coherent unit must begin not at 853 but at 847!

Secondly, a manner of 'reading' the Parade which has convinced me less and less since my old friend Denis Feeney first showed it me in typescript.[27] No question, the Parade contains figures good, bad and ambiguous. Some are already subject to their vices (*iam*, 816) or bear the instruments of their future cruelty (824): they are[28]—and this is theologically consistent and comprehensible—liable even now to the weaknesses of human existence. It is worth remembering that in his Forum —not a reply to the Parade, but a reworking of the

---

[23] Cf. SDan. *ad Aen.*1.712, Plut. *comp.Pelop. cum Marc.*1.7 = Aug. *orat.* fr.xiv Malc., Horsfall, *CQ* 39 (1989), 266f.

[24] *Spolia opima* (cf. now S.J. Harrison, *CQ* 39 (1989), 408ff., M.C.J. Putnam, ib. 35 (1985), 237ff.), war against Gauls, war against Carthaginians, strength of *gens*; cf. 846 and 857.

[25] Note though at Goold (n. 22), 121 a fine answer to D.R. Shackleton Bailey's discussion of the grammatical problem of 882f. at *HSCP* 90 (1986), 199ff.

[26] Cf. Horsfall (n. 23): to the bibliography collected there (nn. 1, 2) add Habinek (n. 11, 236) a position close to that of J. Griffin, *Latin poetry and Roman life* (London 1985), 169f. On *paci imponere morem* cf. now my note in *SO* 68 (1993), 38f. The text is certain, the Latinity hard, even harsh, and the political message unwelcome and unfashionable. Pacification required when peace does not obtain.

[27] On Feeney (n. 3), cf. also Zetzel (n. 3), 282, n. 79, West (n. 1).

[28] Cf. Anchises' explanation, 723, Zetzel (n. 3), 282.

same material—Augustus did not avoid difficult figures: Marius, Sulla, Lucullus.[29] That shows that rhetorical balance (on psogos, v. supra) and moral courage (in Virgil and Augustus). But a parade of riddles (Feeney, 5)? A parade to illustrate 'political life's intolerable demands on human nature' (Feeney, 16) and 'the evanescence of mortal aspirations'?[30] 'Poised ambivalence' (Feeney, 18)? But are the Gracchi, Drusi and Scipiones truly riddling, any more than 'the untroublesome names of the Decii and Camilli' (Feeney, 6)? The plurals, I repeat, point to the continuity of the *gens*. They generalise deliberately, excluding necessarily any precise prosopographical pedantry. Romulus, of course, was in truth an ambiguous figure, but he was present in both Forum and Parade. Merits outweigh defects. Whether the criticism of Ancus is justified (Feeney 9) is again quite another matter: a small error[31] or a large programmatic allusion to *populares* in the *gens Marcia*? At this point it is not difficult to re-read the whole Parade without Lucan in hand and without all the reference books required to enable you to extract doubts sufficient to justify Virgil's inclusion of each hero or group of heroes in his (to push Feeney's point a little further than he does himself!) Rogue's Gallery of Roman History. So too now West (n. 1). Elements of criticism are present, enough to set heroism and merit in high relief:[32] they were not intended to be overvalued out of all proportion.

Philosophy

I do not intend to offer a brief general introduction to 6.236–751, when A. Setaioli provides one ample and fully satisfactory, with rich bibliography in *EV* s.v. *Inferi*. Here I should like to concentrate on certain problems and issues of method which are likely to confuse the reader when first at grips with the vast, often selective and as often overexcited and underinformed (cf. F. Graf, *Gnom.*53 (1981), 545ff., 58 (1986), 360ff.) bibliography on Virgil's underworld. Many keys have been offered to unlock the text's 'mysteries'. None of them work; no single key is required, for you come to realise that only by long and patient tinkering with a complex combination lock can you

---

[29] *Inscr.It.*13.3, 17, 83, 18, 84.
[30] Feeney (n. 3), 16 and Tarrant there cited.
[31] Zetzel (n. 3), 273, Horsfall, *Alambicco*, 87.
[32] Feeney has written excellently on Virgil; my almost complete disagreement with (n. 3) does not diminish my general admiration.

begin to understand something of these 'mysteries'! So I only venture to suggest some parameters of prudence and imprudence in the reader's *modus operandi*:

(i) It is *prima facie* unlikely that Virgil changes his method of composition here and here alone in the *Aeneid*, and of that method we do now know, in detail, a good deal. Thus at *Alambicco*, 19ff., I offered a fairly full summary of what we can actually demonstrate to have been the poet's sources for the Golden Bough.[33] Patient enquiry leaves very few problems unsolved, though I should have made more of Norden's point that *cunctantem* (211)—no indication that Aeneas is after all not (or only in part) the man of destiny—is a *uox propria* of objects which naturally resist pressure. He cites *G*.2.236, Lucr.3.192f.; add *TLL* 4.1395.82ff. Again, it was clear that for circumstantial detail Virgil drew upon the rites of Eleusis (*Alambicco*, 25); but the idea is really quite old.[34] It is, though, essential at this point not to make the giddy leap to the conclusion that the whole of *Aen*.6 is in some sense an initiation ritual.[35] The technique, if you will, is that of a mosaicist: there is no place for large masses of unbroken colour! A few parallel cases may be cited:

(ii) The labyrinth on the doors of the temple at Cumae (6.27) has provoked a good deal of interest and even a pig-headed reactionary sceptic (*de me ipso loquor*) gladly acknowledges that some solid evidence exists for the connexion of labyrinths, real or apparent, with the Underworld (Plin. *Nat*.36.91).[36] The entrance to the oracular shrine at Ephyra certainly seems a labyrinth: if that is a scholar's reaction, it may well have been a believer's.[37] Pliny (l.c.) cites Varro: the link may therefore have been known to Virgil. Whether it was also of significance to him, I have no idea.

(iii) A good deal more serious is the issue of 6.640f. and 6.887:[38] Servius (in his notes on the passages cited and *ad Aen*.5.735), like

---

[33] Cf. West (n. 14).

[34] Boyancé, 161f., Zetzel (n. 3), 276, n. 52, G. Luck, *AJP* 94 (1973), 147ff.

[35] Cf. F. Graf, *Gnom*. 1986, just cited.

[36] R.J. Clark, *Catabasis* (Amsterdam 1979), 148f., M.C.J. Putnam, *AJP* 108 (1987), 175ff., M. Paschalis, *Vergilius* 32 (1986), 33ff.

[37] Cf. S. Dakaris, *AK Beiheft* 1 (1963), 52f. I am most grateful to Dr. Mary Mantziou for actually taking me there.

[38] Cf. Boyancé, 165, Clark (n. 36), 180ff., Norden, 23f., Thornton (n. 14), 66f., A. Wlosok, *Gnom*.53 (1981), 758 = *Res humanae-res divinae* (Heidelberg 1990), 361, cad. *Listy Fil*.106 (1983), 14f. = (1990), 386f.

Macrobius (*comm. ad Somn.Scip* 1.9.8) has little doubt: here we have a *gemina doctrina*, both a *poeticae figmentum* and a *philosophiae ueritas*. The *ueritas* is that these passages, or even all *Aen*.6 constitute an allegory for a journey of the soul through the cosmos.[39] Even easier if you take (v. supra) the Gates as indicating some sort of dream-journey on Aeneas' part. But that is not proved and cannot serve as a starting-point for a general reinterpretation. Nor, though Virgil certainly knew allegorical interpretations of Homer, intimately, even,[40] am I easy about reading the entire book as an allegory, when the only possible hints that we should do so flicker briefly towards its end.[41] Certainly Virgil was familiar with doctrines or accounts of the soul's skyward wanderings;[42] but this is, after all, Virgil: two or three (at most) allusions show that he is well aware of ideas of the soul's stellar wanderings, and that means that a new strand in the whole raiment is identified— but that is all.

(iv) We come therefore to another issue of method: that of how much consistency and uniformity we should try to restore to *Aen*.6. The hunt for inconsistencies in this book is an old game.[43] The full account by Zetzel (n. 3) suggests (274) that the concentration of inconsistencies is intended to afflict the reader with doubt as to the reality of the whole. It is above all[44] the conflict between 'static' and 'redemptive' views of the afterlife that worries careful modern readers. We are, I suspect, faced by two distinct issues: the minor discrepancy can very often be explained as a deliberate exercise of the techniques of Alexandrian scholarly poetry.[45] The concentration of discrepancies in this book reflects the great bulk of pre-Virgilian literature on the Underworld and the variations it inevitably manifests. Apparently discordant views of the afterlife are of course a more serious matter than doubt over the precise location of Theseus.[46] Virgil attempts a synthesis in narrative form of a wide range of sources:

---

[39] A. Wlosok, *PLLS* 5 (1985), 75f. = (1990), 392f.
[40] Cf. Hardie, 26ff. et passim, Wlosok (n. 39).
[41] Aliter, Thornton (n. 14), 63f.
[42] Cic. *Somn*.13, cf. A.F. Segal, *ANRW* 2.23.2 (1980), 1342ff.
[43] Butler, intro., 11ff., Setaioli, cit., 957 et passim, R.D. Williams, *GR* 11 (1964), 50 = Harrison, 193, B. Otis, *TAPA* 90 (1959), 165ff.
[44] Zetzel (n. 3), 267, Habinek (n. 11), 223ff.
[45] *Alambicco*, chs. 5–6, id., *Vergilius* 37 (1991), 31ff., Zetzel (n. 3), 270, n. 28, A.S. Hollis, *HSCP* 94 (1992), 269ff.
[46] F. Solmsen, *Proc.Amer.Phil.Soc* 112 (1968), 8ff. = *Kl.Schr*.3 (Hildesheim 1982), 412ff., id. *CP* 67 (1972), 31ff. = Harrison, 208ff. = *Kl.Schr*.3, 419ff.; for more recent discussion, cf. Zetzel (n. 3), Habinek (n. 11).

Homer, 'Orphic' and 'Pythagorean',[47] Plato, Stoics[48] and perhaps 'Syncretist'.[49] Virgil's narrative sequence (so Solmsen 1972 = Harrison, 211f.) reflects the chronological order of his sources, and to some extent the development of Greek eschatological thinking. It is easy enough now for the careful reader to take ten lines, or a hundred lines of *Aeneid* 6 and shuffle the constituent elements into heaps, relatively safe and neat, according to their texts of origin. If we can do it (usually!), it must have been far easier for Virgil's 'educated reader'. I doubt whether reader or poet necessarily needed to have Platonism and Stoicism' pre-syncretised' or whether Prof. Thornton's neat and orderly 'Picture of the Universe of an educated Roman in the first century B.C.' (n. 12, 20–34) is methodologically desirable.[50] It may be felt that 'my' *Aeneid* 6 is too untidy to be read or believed, but it reflects a view (not, I hope, entirely incredible or incoherent) of how the poet worked and composed. I welcome, let us be clear, attempts to establish links between Anchises' speeches at 724ff. and 756ff.[51] But the notion that Virgil might use a 'sandwich' technique, one of layering thin recognisable slices of diverse origins, is a secure and established technique of his (cf. 239ff. on *G*.4): no surprise to find it used again in more elaborate form.

(v) On one crucial point of detail, which has very wide implications, we must pause. I refer to the punctuation of 743–7, a problem which has generated a very large bibliography.[52] Habinek is perfectly right to insist that we should follow scrupulously not eschatological considerations but the precise pointers Virgil gives us in his (originally unpunctuated) text:

---

[47] Against Solmsen (n. 46, 1968), 9, n. 12 = 413, n. 12, cf. W. Burkert, *Lore and science in ancient Pythagoreanism* (Cambridge, Mass., 1972), 125ff. on the limited sense in which we are justified in using the terms 'Orphic' and 'Pythagorean', F. Graf, *Eleusis und die orphische Dichtung*, *RVV* 33, (Berlin 1974), 92. The relationship of *P.Bonon*.4 to *Aen*.6 is perhaps a little clearer than it used to be: Horsfall, *ZPE* 96 (1993), 17f.

[48] On Lucretian language, as against Epicurean thought, cf. Habinek (n. 11), 204.

[49] For the reconciliation of Platonic and Stoic ideas in Antiochus of Ascalon, cf. Boyancé, 151ff. and in *Hommages Dumézil* (*Coll.Lat*.45, 1960), 60ff. For Posidonius in *Aen*.6, cf. Norden, 20ff. and now Moreschini in *EV* s.v.

[50] E. Rawson, *Intellectual life in the late Roman republic* (London 1985), 312ff.

[51] Zetzel (n. 3), 282, Habinek (n. 11), 234f.; less convincing Clark (n. 36), 179ff., Thornton (n. 14), 61ff.

[52] Cf. Setaioli, *EV* s.v. *Inferi*, 961f., Habinek (n. 11), 228, n. 7, Clark (n. 36), 177f. and *SO* 50 (1975), 121ff.

ALIAE panduntur inanes
suspensae ad uentos ALIIS sub gurgite uasto
infectum eluitur scelus aut exuritur igni
QUISQUE suos patimur Manis[53] exinde per amplum
mittimur Elysium et PAUCI laeta arua tenemus
donec[54] longa dies perfecto temporis orbe. . .

The two first-person plural verbs which follow *patimur* cannot be
separated strongly from the first verb in the series, though a step in
the sequence is marked by *exinde*. A pause at *igni* and another at
Manis are therefore justified. Clark has raised the question of whether
pauci (in opposition to *has omnis* 748, which takes up 713–5) applies
only to *tenemus* or should be taken (perfectly correct Latin) with *mittimur*
as well. We should therefore ask if we can distinguish *Elysium* from
laeta arua. Surely not (cf. 638 *locos laetos et amoena uirecta* at the entrance to Elysium). And if that is so, the adjective applies necessarily
to both verbs.[55] We (all), says Anchises, suffer (taking up the previ-
ously listed punishments) our *Manes*: a few of us are then further
purified and return to the *pneuma*.[56]

There remains one further issue which, alas, needs to be clarified:
the necessity of avoiding anachronistic elements in our exposition of
the Virgilian Underworld. I have suggested (*Alambicco*, 24f.) that the
knowledge which Pliny displays of the importance of mistletoe in the
Celtic world (cf. *Aen*.6.205f.) was not yet available to Virgil. If that is
right (and we cannot be wholly certain), then there is no room for
'Baldurdash'[57] in Virgilian exegesis. So too J. Préaux[58] who uses the
Herbarius of Ps.Apul. and Martianus Capella to explain—inevitably,
the Golden Bough. Or take the *pii uates* of 662: poets are not priests
(*sacerdotes casti*, 661), especially in view of Virgil's notable emphasis
on poetry in Elysium.[59] But Boyancé cites the late c. 6 A.D. philosopher Olympiodorus in support (163) of an interpretation of the word
in the sense of seers, μάντεις (but what of 645 and 667?)! And do we

---

[53] Cf. Austin ad loc., Durry and Wistrand on 'Laud.Tur.' 2.69, S. Weinstock,
Divus Iulius (Oxford 1971), 291, n. 9, Nisbet on Cic. *Pis*.16.
[54] Cf. Plat. *Phaed*.114C, *Tim*.41D.
[55] Cf. Norden, 40, Austin on 6.748; cf. Plut. *Mor*.415B who distinguishes ὀλίγαι
(sc. souls) from ἐνίαις ('some', put more strongly by Virgil).
[56] Solmsen 1972 = Harrison, 218, Norden, 19f.
[57] West (n. 14) 4 = 228.
[58] J. Préaux in *Hommages* (n. 49), 151ff.
[59] Horsfall, *SCI* 12 (1993), 156ff.

need to follow the same learned exegete (172) back via Servius and
Martianus Capella to (?) Pherecydes[60] to explain 740 *panduntur suspensae
ad uentos*? Simpler to invoke Emped. fr.115.9ff. DK, Plat. *Gorg.*525C.[61]
Aeneid 6 is extremely learned and difficult, but at times has become
much more so, and in part needlessly so, since the poet's death.

---

[60] Pherec. fr.6DK.
[61] Cf. further Austin ad loc., Norden, 28 (should we not also think of Ixion?). . .

Book 7: Motivation and responsibility

The war in Italy, announced to the reader at 1.263f., 266 and to Aeneas in Helenus' prophecy,[1] is, like the battle between the bees (*G*.4.68 *discordia*) essentially a civil war. Both the Sibyl (6.86ff.) and, typologically, Anchises (6.826ff.: Pompey and Caesar) have prepared us for this characterisation, which becomes ever clearer from 7.39ff. on.[2] For Virgil, the outbreak of civil war calls for the analytical methods of the contemporary historian,[3] as he makes clear by dense allusion at 7.37ff. Above all, why? Whose fault was it? An old question, again one dear to historians.[4] So, the emphasis on *causae*.[5] Our reading of the text therefore becomes a particularly challenging exercise in the avoidance of analytical partiality and moral polemic.[6] Those who believe there is a simple answer (either way!) had best not read on.

The Trojans, from 2.289ff., have supernatural assurance that their flight and their foundation of a city once their goal is reached are alike destined (cf. bk. 1, 103). The most explicit confirmation at 7.120ff. Aeneas sends an embassy at once, as his father would have done (7.152), to bear gifts to Latinus, *pacemque exposcere Teucris* (155). Latinus receives the *oratores* with overwhelming benevolence (vd. infra). Despite what they have heard at 2.783 and 6.93, the Trojans ask very little of their new host (229f.), on their return to their homeland.[7] Unexpectedly, Ilioneus is offered (268ff.) a wife for Aeneas, who must only (264ff.) come to meet Latinus in person to ratify the accord. Even Juno knows (313f.) that Aeneas cannot be denied, in the end, a home and a wife. Virgil does not return to the Trojans until 7.493, and even then not quite to them in person, but to Ascanius' hounds, who start Silvia's pet stag.[8] The young Ascanius (whom we know to be a keen huntsman, 4.156ff.) fires an arrow; if the stag were even

---

[1] 3.458, 539f.; cf. 4.615, 5.731, 6.83ff., 890, 892.

[2] Buchheit, 102ff., Glei (introd., n. 1), 178ff., Camps, *Introduction*, 96f., E. Fraenkel, *JRS* 35 (1945), 3f. = *Kl.Beitr.*2 (Roma 1964), 150f., Schenk (181, n. 23), 190.

[3] Cf. P. Jal, *La guerre civile a Rome* (Paris 1963), 360ff., M. Pohlenz in *Epitymbion H. Swoboda* (Reichenberg 1927), 201ff., Horsfall, *GR* 38 (1991) 207.

[4] Cf. Pohlenz (n. 3).

[5] Cf. Horsfall (n. 3). For causes of Juno's anger, 1.8ff.; for causes of war, 6.93, 7.197, 482, 553, 10.90, 11.178, 361, 12.567.

[6] Cf. Feeney 171, citing Horsfall *GR* 34 (1987), 49.

[7] On this motif, cf. H.D. Jocelyn, *Sileno* 17 (1991), 77ff., Horsfall, *BICS* Suppl. 52 (1987), 99ff.

[8] Cf. R.J. Starr, *AJP* 113 (1992), 435ff.

now bathed, combed and garlanded (488ff.) one might charge Ascanius with imprudence or myopia, but the text hardly requires us to do so.[9] *Nec deus erranti*[10] *deus*[11] *afuit.* The stag is shot, and it does not seem credible or helpful to attribute to the Trojans the reprehensible violation of a bucolic paradise.[12] *Ceruum fortuito saucium* observes Macrobius correctly (5.17.2) of the impression created by Allecto's intervention. Silvia raises the alarm; Allecto *Tartaream intendit uocem*, and the *Troia pubes* (521) rushes to reinforce Ascanius. Where is Aeneas? Not, at least, there to try to prevent escalation. If we ask whether he could (or should) have, the answer is negative: such escalation, explicitly, was within Juno's powers (315ff.).

The elderly and peaceable Latinus has an unwed daughter, sought by the handsome and noble Turnus with the eager support of Amata. Latinus, by implication, is less eager: the gods are clearly against the match. Though we know that the *externus uir*,[13] whom Latinus' *uates* perceives as predicted by the bees who swarm on the sacred laurel is in fact Aeneas, Latinus does not; the portent must be 'read', both with our eyes and with his.[14] The crown of flames about Lavinia's head *canebant* (but who is the subject? the *uates* of 7.68 and his reverend colleagues?) as indicating Lavinia's fame, but war for her people (who are now, like the Trojans, forewarned). The king, *sollicitus*, consults the oracle of Faunus: no *conubia Latina*, no *thalami parati*. This is mystification, the more so as it is applied to past, not future. Turnus is Rutulian, not Latin, though the reference of the latter adjective can be extended;[15] king of the Latins Turnus can only become by succession to Latinus himself. Nor are there *thalami parati*: Amata dreams, Turnus boasts and blusters, but, in truth, he is not affianced to Lavinia at the moment of Aeneas' arrival.[16] Latinus is now told of the *externi generi* (98, which explains 68). His immediate reactions and actions Virgil suppresses, but Latinus greets the Trojans as known

---

[9] Cf. Lyne, *FV*, 198.

[10] Proleptic; cf. Fordyce, ad loc.

[11] *TLL* s.v., 890.27.

[12] Cf. S. Rocca, *Etologia Virgiliana* (Genova 1983), 147f., W. Wimmel, *Hirtenkrieg u. arkadisches Rom* (München 1973), 48; cf. id. *Collectanea* (Stuttgart 1987), 224ff., M.C.J. Putnam, *AJP* 91 (1970), 417f.

[13] 7.68f.; cf. Horsfall, *RFil*.119 (1991), 188ff., Schenk (181, n. 23), 296.

[14] Glei (introd., n. 1), 181, Grassmann-Fischer (140, n. 36), 64ff.

[15] Horsfall, *EV* s.v. *Laurentes*, ad init.

[16] Schenk l.c. (n. 13), Renger (181, n. 23), 21ff.; cf. Highet, 288, Heinze, 175, Cairns, 158, W. Warde Fowler, *Death of Turnus*, 42, n. 1.

(196) and welcome (202). He has worked out who the *generos externis. . .ab oris* must be (270). Aeneas will be his destined (272) and desired (*opto*, 273) son-in-law. Virgil offers a terse summary of Amata's reactions (343–5). At her Allecto then flings a serpent, which has recently attracted much attention[17] and she speaks, still *mollius et solito matrum de more*, with a fair dose of dishonesty (cf. n. 16), but no evident irrationality.[18] No effect on Latinus. However, by now the snake's poison is working (374f., cf. 348: but how did it enter her? Cf. Feeney, 165f.). Thereat, *ingentibus excita monstris*[19]/*immensam sine more*[20] *furit lymphata per urbem*. But was the madness already latent? Or is it all Allecto's doing?[21] Mad, Amata's intention is unaltered (388, 398, 402): judgement is again suspended. We do not yet know what Amata's madness is. The Dionysiac origins of the top, which is Callimachean in detail (*Epigr.*1.9f.) only become explicit at 385, though the careful reader will have noticed hints of Dionysiac frenzy (*uerbera*, *faces*) in Virgil's list of Allecto's attributes and powers.[22] Amata's Bacchic frenzy is not authentic; the god's *numen* is *simulatum* (385);—by whom? by Allecto? by Amata herself?[23] Madness (406) is unleashed; Latinus' palace is in upheaval (407); marriage ceremonies are necessarily postponed (388), with the queen and her followers cavorting in frenzy, real enough in itself, but not in origin genuine, through the forests (cf. 581).[24] Only after Allecto has worked on Turnus and on Ascanius' hounds does Virgil return to Latinus. In chiastic order, with respect to the preceding narratives, the victims of the rustic skirmish, the enraged Turnus and the pseudo-Bacchants' families all cry for war and besiege Latinus' palace. He resists (586) like a rock (586–90), but is powerless in the face of *caecum. . .consilium* and the will of Juno

---

[17] Cf. 228 on the *genitivus inhaerentiae*, Feeney, 164ff.

[18] Cf. Feeney, 165f.

[19] Allecto? Feeney, 167 suggests an etymological reference to Amata's own *ingenium* (cf. *ingentibus*), which just might be right.

[20] Cf. Glei (introd., n. 1), 184.

[21] Lyne, *FV*, 69.

[22] Feeney 167 and R.J. Rabel, *CJ* 77 (1981–2), 27ff. are quite wrong to have dispensed with G. Hirst, *CQ* 31 (1937), 65f. The link of tops and Dionysus is impregnable: cf., C.A. Lobeck, *Aglaophamus* 1 (Königsberg 1829), 699ff., B. Schmaltz, *Terrakotten aus dem Kabirenheiligtum* (Berlin 1974), 141, P. Wolters, G. Bruns, *Das Kabirenheiligtum bei Theben* 1 (Berlin 1940), inscr.2.22, pp. 23, n. 2, 123. The Stoic top of Chrysipp. fr.974 von Arnim = Cic. *Fato* 42f. is, in the circumstances, irrelevant association. Cf. Renger (181, n. 23), 39.

[23] Feeney, 167.

[24] Glei (introd., n. 1), 187f.

(590–1, 824). It is fate and the storm of events that sweep him away (594). The Latins (595f.) and Turnus (596f.) will pay. Latinus thinks that only death awaits him (598ff.). Has the king been feeble and inadequate?[25] To say so, by way of accusation, is surely to underestimate the scale of the forces opposed to Latinus. One might suppose that a younger king would have reacted with greater energy. But Virgil's Latinus is not young.[26] That is a choice useful to the plot, and again it hinders precise evaluation of blame! That activity is so often thwarted, on a careful scrutiny of the text, that the prudent reader might wish to conclude that moral judgement was actually being discouraged.

Thus, furthermore, if we try to examine the guilt, or blame which attaches to Turnus (and that is a theme hotly pursued of late in Germany) we will find (and that by now has become less surprising) an almost equally studied absence of objective judgement. He is the suitor of Lavinia, favoured by her mother, but not, I think it is clear, by her father. With the narrative focused on Latinus, Turnus' desired bride is removed from his grasp for reasons of fate and state.[27] While Turnus is asleep, at night (413f., 458), he is visited by Allecto. Hitherto, he is *audax* (409) and no more. Once again, Allecto sets to work to arouse passions not already explicitly present: they are, though, in retrospect, perfectly compatible with our expectations of how such a character might behave in such a crisis. Here, Allecto tells the sleeping Turnus that an *externus heres* has supplanted him in bed and throne, while his efforts as Latinus' ally (cf. 8.474) have gone for nothing. She urges an attack on the Trojans, and on Latinus too, if he does not change his tune. Turnus, still asleep, as he remains to 458, replies in memorably irreverent mockery: he is well aware of the threat and does not need advice from old women. Allecto at this point flies into rage, a movement which does not correspond closely to that of 376:[28] Turnus' eyes *deriguere*[29] and his limbs quiver. Allecto's

---

[25] Cairns, 66.

[26] Horsfall, *GR* 34 (1987), 49.

[27] 96ff., 253ff., 268ff.; a destiny acknowledged by Juno, 314. On Turnus' *audacia* here, cf. Buchheit, 102ff., Kühn (138, n. 26), 107ff.

[28] So rightly Feeney 168ff. against Fraenkel and current orthodoxy.

[29] Cf. *Gloss.*5.287.23 *stupuere obtuto*, Tib.Claud.Don.2.67.16 *usque adeo pererritus fuit, ut oculi eius vigorem solitum perdidissent*. Note Suet. *Ner.*49.4, of the dying Nero *exstantibus rigentibusque oculis*. Cf. *Il.*22.453 πήγνυται (knees, as a symptom of fear, Onians, 46, n. 6). More to the point, Eur. *HF* 1395 (of limbs), a text closely followed by V. in the Amata-scene, König, 123ff. See too *Aen.*3.260.

rage swells as Turnus tries to speak (449). Fully revealed not as Calybe but as an authentic Fury (452–5), she declares herself; note how her closing words take up Turnus' (444; 455; Highet, 78). At Turnus' chest, she flings her torch, and he wakes sweating, in terror (458–9). Only now does he *arma amens fremit. . .saeuit amor ferri et scelerata insania belli/ira super.* No explanations, but sudden crazed, perverse (*amor ferri*) battle-rage.[30] Turnus is compared to a cauldron of boiling water.[31] Not 'a simmering cauldron which is brought to the boil when a torch is placed beneath it' (Feeney, 170). The water is already *undantis* (463, which could just be proleptic): a rolling boil. Noisily, blazing kindling is heaped up on the outside. With the sudden access of heat, the water leaps and spurts and finally (466) boils over. 'Turnus' natural resentment. . .brought to a climax by the torch of Allecto'.[32] But by what means has the water already become *undans*? Allecto's torch (456f.) does not correspond precisely to the *flamma. . .uirgea* of 462–3, which is applied to a cauldron already seething. Are we to ascribe retrospectively a rolling boil of resentment to Turnus' pre-torch slumbers?[33] Is it therefore Turnus' 'fiery nature' that is to be extrapolated from the simile? The images of 320, 322 point in a different direction and here, until rudely awakened, he has been simply asleep (though involved in dialogue with Allecto). Can we really infer that the simile of the cauldron shows Allecto 'working with a potential in Turnus'?[34] The sequence seems to me altogether less clear: Turnus wakes in turmoil (the water already *undans*); he shouts; he seeks swords amid the sheets (460); he is filled with mad battle-lust. Does his anger fuel itself? Is it then Turnus in person who heaps kindling about the cauldron, after Allecto has set the fire going? Note 467, *ergo*, directly after the simile: Turnus' anger has reached a full boil within the palace, *tectis*; *ergo*, he gives orders to his subordinates for the defence of Italy; if needs be, he will fight both Aeneas and Latinus. Virgil leaves the question, as usual, unresolved. The development of Turnus' emotions and Allecto's precise role remain unspecified. I am not absolutely sure that I am right, any more than I am that both Lyne

---

[30] Cf., not Schenk (bk. 10 (ii), n. 23), 189f., but word by word, Hellegouarc'h (190, n. 23), and Jal (n. 3), 472f. et passim.

[31] Cf. M. von Duhn, *Gymn.*64 (1957), 64f., S.J. Harrison, *PLLS* 5 (1985), 99f. A. Perutelli, *Maia* 24 (1972), 46.

[32] Feeney 170, after Lyne, *FV*, 69.

[33] I do recognise that Lyne (*WP*, 63ff.) has shown several probable cases of similes used to expand the narrative. But here?

[34] Lyne l.c. (n. 32).

and Feeney are wrong: poetical indirection imposes critical caution.

Virgil continues (467–75) with a masterly account, rich in explanatory detail and credible motivation (cf. 400–3), of how, with Turnus berserk, all Ardea runs amok (note 340 :: 470, 472 :: 525f.). It remains to look back at 7.293–600 to examine those further elements of motivation or justification not explicitly covered hitherto:

The outbreak of war in Latium is an event, we remember, destined and predicted long since; Juno's intervention is prompted by the sight of Aeneas *laetus, moliri iam tecta. . .iam fidere terrae* (290). Resigned though she is to ultimate defeat (313f.) she is not yet ready (315) for Aeneas' triumph over her (310). Foreknowledge and Juno's malignity alike, therefore, render the war predictable and inescapable: a war that is both civil, and, in some respects once more Trojan (cf. bk. 10, p. 182; here cf. 321, 363, 430). Juno therefore turns to Allecto.[35] Allecto's powers (335ff.) are amply sufficient for the task in hand: she is, specifically, well able to set in motion a civil war (335–7), and Juno, threatened in *honos* and *fama* (332–3) gives her subordinate free rein. Note, though, 339–40: *sere crimina belli* (the accusations that lead to war)/, *arma uelit. . .iuuentus* (Allecto is to create the will for war). We have already seen that Allecto's precise effects upon Amata remain uncertain,—until she flies into Bacchic frenzy. With Turnus likewise: irresoluble indirection precedes the explosion of maddened battle-rage (note Serv. on 7.456 for an acute comment on Allecto's choice of methods). Turnus gives orders (468) and (472) *certatim sese Rutuli exhortantur in arma* (cf. 340!). In her third scene, Allecto casts a scent in the way of Ascanius' hounds and *subitam. . .rabiem* (cf. 493). . .*obicit* (479). In *rabiem*, we see both the wild excitement of the pack that has found, and the frenzy inspired by Allecto, which prompts them to start (494) a harmless (but eventually dangerous) pet. The stag's wounding *bello. . .animos accendit agrestis* (482; cf. again 340!). Allecto, as we have seen, guarantees Ascanius' aim: a shot to wound (498). Silvia calls for *auxilium*.[36] That might seem enough, but still *pestis enim tacitis latet aspera siluis* (505; cf. 3.215, 12.845): the angry (508; is this *ira* the work of the *pestis?*) rustics arrive, rudely armed.

---

[35] Allecto is a figure not yet understood in detail: Feeney, 163ff., König, 130f., Schenk (181, n. 23), 288f., Buchheit, 101f., Kühn (n. 27), 103ff., *EV*, s.v. *Alletto*. Much is still to be learned from A. O'Brien Moore, *Madness in ancient literature* (diss. Princeton, pub. Weimar 1924).

[36] 'Help' is feeble; the *duri agrestes* respond to a rustic 'declaration of emergency'; cf. W. Schulze, *Kl.Schr.* (Göttingen 1934), 176.

Uocat agmina Tyrrhus (508; cf. 478; again, Allecto rouses the will to fight).[37] Thirdly, *pastorale canit signum* (513),[38] but with all the force (514) of a hellish demon: that is enough for the *indomiti agricolae* of central Italy to rush to arms (520f.). The third intervention is far more elaborate, because on a far vaster scale: Allecto has immobilised Latinus, aroused Turnus, maddened Amata, and now set central Italy ablaze. The *agricolae* can recognise a call for *auxilium* or a *pastorale signum*: *ira* (508) and escalation are her work. At that point it is hardly necessary to go further. Allecto has accomplished irreversible (546f.) *discordia* (545, an elegant bow to Ennius): to her proposal of further geographical expansion of the conflict (cf. 516–9, 549), Juno replies 'enough': to go on (507f.) would be to risk Jupiter's intervention.

So who starts the war? Men (and women), gods (and dogs), all together. If we seek to blame Allecto beyond all others, we have then to think of Juno behind her. Virgil seems to me at all points to discourage us from reaching any simple answer.

---

[37] The stag's *imploranti* belongs to the same sphere as *auxilium*: Schulze l.c. (n. 36), *TLL* s.v., 646.7ff.

[38] Cf. Varr. *LL* 6.92, Prop.4.1.13, Gell.15.27.2.

Book 8

Historical[1] *allegory*

This is a short chapter: I do not believe its subject of central importance for our understanding of the *Aeneid*.[2] Historical allegory is all too often a blunt instrument used, and this is nothing new, to batter the text of Virgil into revealing its mysteries. The first exegetes of *Buc.*1 and 9 had no doubt that those poems should be read in autobiographical terms (cf. ch. 1, nn. 78, 79): so Servius and the Virgil-biographers. But Servius himself was averse, unlike others, to interpreting figures in *Buc.* in general as 'masks' for historical personages.[3] The possibilities for unfettered expansion that such exegesis offers are best seen in Philargyrius (mid-c. 5), for example in the opening notes to *Buc.*2, 3, 4.[4] Ancient statements that the principal intention of the *Aeneid* was *Romanae simul urbis et Augusti origo contineretur* (VSD 21) or that the poet's *intentio* was *Augustum laudare a parentibus* (Serv. *ad Aen.*1.1) should not[5] be taken as evidence for an overall allegorical reading of the poem; they reflect rather a crude rhetorical view of the poem's 'public voice', and, if dressed up in prettier language, represent a view of the text still maintained by quite numerous Virgilians, even serious ones. For there is in the poem an objectively real element of genealogical panegyric,[6] and in *Aen.*1, 4, 6 and 8 in particular, we find serious and intelligent readings of Roman history (cf. 105, 123f., 144ff.). Whetever view the critic takes of poet (court poet, even, in some ways!) and *princeps*, these elements are there in the text, and it is not enough to dismiss them with a remark to the effect that of course they had to be!

A distinction between small- and large-scale historical allegories should be maintained: Servius[7] not infrequently sees in the *Aeneid*

---

[1] Contrast bk. 6, n. 40.

[2] A. Novara, *Poésie virgilienne de la mémoire* (Clermont Ferrand 1986) was unfortunately not available to me.

[3] So *et multi uolunt*, Serv. *ad Buc.*7.21, 3.1.85.14f. Th.H.

[4] Cf. J. Griffin, *Latin poets and Roman life* (London 1985), 187 on the influence of Theocr.'s apparent portrayal of himself as Simichidas in *Id.*7, which left the scholiasts on 7.1 in no doubt.

[5] *Pace EV* s.v. *Allegoria*, E. Coleiro, *Tematica e struttura dell'En.* (Amsterdam (1983), 5ff., D.L. Drew, *Allegory of the Aeneid* (Oxford 1927), 98; cf. R.J. Starr, *Cl.Ant.*11 (1992), 159ff.

[6] Cf. Men.Rhet.370.10ff. Horsfall, *Prudentia* 8 (1976), 84.

[7] Cf. Camps, *Introduction*, 99ff., 137ff., Drew (n. 5). 98ff., E. Thomas, *Essai sur Servius* (Paris 1880), 243f.

precise references to historical actions by Augustus. And not to
Augustus alone: cf. (e.g.) Serv. *ad Aen*.2.557 *Pompei tangit historiam*.[8]
The hunt for references, above all to contemporary history, in the
Aeneid is far from over.[9] Some are merely silly, or comical.[10] Others
belong (e.g.) to an elaborate nexus of allusions unquestionably present
there in the text: I refer, for example, to the multiple and mutually
supporting reference to the second Punic war.[11] An allusion to the
Arae Perusinae at *Aen*.10.517ff., 11.81f. (for Aen.'s human sacrifice
cf. bk. 10, p. 179f.), to the joint discredit of *princeps* and poet is almost a commonplace.[12] The case would be more convincing if we
could be sure that the Arae had ever taken place.[13]

   The leap from a recognition of scattered allusions to Augustus in
the *Aeneid* (so Servius) to a reading of substantial parts of the text
(particularly books 5 and 8 as containing a dominant element of
historical allegory was first made by D.L. Drew,[14] and his heirs are
still busy.[15] Indeed the case Drew makes for a precise reference to
the events of 12–13 Aug., 29 BC in *Aen*.8.103, 179f, 269, 281[16] is
remarkably neat and I do not quite know how one could establish
convincingly that it is just not there! But allegory alone was never
quite sufficient and satisfying[17] and it was perhaps E. Zinn[18] who first

---

   [8] Cf. A.M. Bowie, *CQ* 40 (1990), 470ff. On 1.148ff., S.J. Harrison, *PCPhS* 30
(1988), 55ff.
   [9] Cf. *EV* (n. 5) for some bibliography.
   [10] Cf. Griffin (n. 4) 184, Camps (n. 7), 95, and cf. n. 13.
   [11] Cf. 102, 105f.
   [12] Cf. (e.g.) Glei (introd., n. 1), 218 with refs.
   [13] See E. Kraggerud, *SO* 62 (1987), 77ff.
   [14] Drew, 1927 (n. 5); note Pease, 47, n. 351 for some precursors.
   [15] Cf. Gransden's comm. to *Aen*.8, 16 et passim, Pease 47ff., V. Buchheit, *GB* 1
(1973), 25ff., Glei (n. 12), 24ff., G. Binder, *Aeneas und Augustus* (Meisenheim 1971),
passim.
   [16] Drew (n. 5), 15ff., cf. Camps (n. 7), 99f.
   [17] A. Powell in *Roman poetry and propaganda in the age of Augustus*, ed. A. Powell
(Bristol 1992), 141ff. has recently taken a complex step further. Virgil, we know
well, defends Aeneas in the text, almost systematically, from the mythological calumnies that had been heaped upon him (Powell, 143, cf. Horsfall, *Vergilius* 32 (1986),
1ff.). Augustus, in his autobiography (Powell, 147) was similarly concerned to defend
himself against the calumnies (and real embarassments) cast in his teeth during the
30's. So too (thus Powell, 148) Virgil is concerned, by suppression or apologia, to
answer, allegorically, the case against Augustus (a needless complication based on a
misunderstanding (cf. n. 38) of the relations between poet and *princeps*). Some of
those who see in Aeneas a brutal murderer have supposed that Virgil saw in Augustus
another such, and said so. For this negative allegory, which does not merit a serious
reply, cf. D. Gillis, *Eros and death in the Aen.* (Rome 1983), 141ff., S. Farron, *AC* 24
(1981), 103f., 25 (1982), 136ff., 28 (1985), 21ff.
   [18] Cf. Knauer, 356.

seriously applied the idea, familiar from biblical criticism, of typology to the interpretation of the *Aeneid*. Typology is a good deal more subtle and ingenious than some of its critics are prepared to allow.[19] Not only does Aeneas (so Knauer, 354) recapitulate and encapsulate the Homeric Aeneas, Achilles and Odysseus, as Turnus does both Paris and Hector, but (cf. 133f.) behind Dido we see Circe, Calypso, Arete, Alcinous, Medea (etc.!). At this point, students of *Aen*.8[20] fell upon the sequences of founder-heroes (Saturn-Evander-Hercules-Aeneas-Romulus-Augustus) and enemies (Cacus-Mezentius-Turnus-Catiline-Tarquin-Antony, etc.):[21] the historical vision of the *Aeneid* appeared thereby to acquire a goal in these sequences expanding towards an Augustan *telos*. The transference of the terminology and reasoning of biblical exegesis to the study of Virgil was itself sharply criticised.[22] Was this mode of thinking familiar in Augustan Rome, and therefore legitimately applicable to the poet's vision of history? The issue is of some importance and complexity:

(i) There is in Virgil[23] a cyclic view of history, but that neither means that the poet believes in a post-Augustan regression towards a second smoking den on the Palatine,[24] nor does it negate or exclude a simpler linear view:[25] Roman history begins with *Saturnia regna* and reaches its present climax in new *Saturnia regna*. Such hints as there are of a vision of the future[26] certainly do not point to a downwards cyclic path (however much some might want to read Tiberius as the second Cacus!). The poet's view of thematic links between characters is likewise, not exactly a mystery, and in part depends on a pretty point of terminology:[27]

---

[19] On typology, cf. Buchheit, 93, 102, 131f., 148f., Gransden, passim, Knauer, 354ff., Glei (introd. n. 1), 27f. A. Wlosok, *Res humanae-Res Divinae* (Darmstadt 1990), 74, 289f. Griffin (n. 4) offers a most amusing critique of typology's worst excesses. Cf. too the objections of A. La Penna, *Maia* 17 (1965), 355ff.

[20] Binder, Gransden: the existence of such ample and accessible recent discussions exempts me from the burden of entering into detail. The critics (n. 19) should not be forgotten. On the shield, begin from Hardie, ch. 8.

[21] Cf. further, n. 23.

[22] Cf. Buchheit (n. 15), Glei (introd. n. 1), 24ff., Griffin (n. 4), 185f., R. Rieks, *ANRW* 2.31.2 (1981), 813ff. It is interesting that both G.N. Knauer and A. Wlosok have an exceptional grounding in patristics.

[23] *Buc*.4.6, *Aen*.6.792ff., cf. 8.324ff., Binder, 281f.; cf. 214, n. 150.

[24] Pace P. Hardie in Powell (n. 17), 59ff.; contrast Horsfall (n. 6), 76f.

[25] A. La Penna introd. to PVM ed. E. Cetrangolo (Firenze 1967), lxxxiif.

[26] Cf. n. 24.

[27] Cf. Traina (n. 31).

(ii) Cicero sees both himself and his antagonists as belonging to more or less stable sequences of names,[28] a notion directly relevant to the interpretation of Virgil, but apparently not present in (e.g.) Binder.

(iii) Virgil has a number of ways of indicating links between characters in the *Aeneid* and those in earlier texts. First, by literary references unmistakable to the educated reader (thus Aeneas and Achilles in bk. 10; cf. 182).

(iv) By adopting the earlier character as exemplary in function.[29]

(v) By applying to the later character the earlier's name, without further qualification beyond e.g. *ille*. That belongs to the traditional language of both insult and of proverbs.[30]

(vi) By the use of the earlier character's name, qualified by *alter*; this is common Latin usage.[31] *Alter* refers to the second of the same series or type.

(vii) Use of the earlier character's name qualified by *alius* (a new variation upon *alter*). Perhaps only at 6.89, *alius. . .Achilles*: this means that he is not *Larisaeus* but Latin.[32]

Typology has, therefore, or so it seems, a real basis in language and usage.

In the last forty years or so, a good deal of attention has been paid to the theme, explicitly and strongly significant in bks. 6–12 of the war in Latium as a 're-run' of that before Troy (cf. bk. 10, 182). That is enough to confirm that the Homeric correspondences of Virgilian characters from *ille Paris* and *alius. . .Achilles* on are not elegant literary play, but have an active and continuous function in adding a further dimension, one that lends temporal and literary depth and resonance to Virgilian characters. *Iliad* and *Odyssey* serve explicitly and implicitly as source of models, not merely verbal, but at the level of conduct and ethical choice. Both that is, for the characters themselves, and for the reader in evaluation. Typology, therefore, seems to me a valid and useful concept for students of the *Aeneid*, though it should not be understood in a narrowly biblical sense, nor

---

[28] Griffin (n. 4), 191, with ample references.

[29] Cf. *Buc*.4.26f., 12.435, 439f., Horsfall, *Vergilius* 32 (1986), 17.

[30] Otto s.v. Callipides, Cecropides, Ladas, Melitides. . .So *Aen*.4.215 *ille Paris*, 9.742, 10.581, 11.404, 11.438.

[31] Griffin (n. 4), 191, A. Traina, *Poeti latini* 3 (Bologna 1989), 145ff. = *Mnemosynum. . .A. Ghiselli* (Bologna 1989), 550ff.

[32] So, well, Traina.

(*di meliora!*) should we imagine that Virgil had to talk to a multitude of rabbis before coming up with the idea.[33]

Which brings us to Aeneas and Augustus. The former, it is said, was conceived as a model for the latter.[34] Not an idea alien to the *princeps*' views of history, literature, or ethics.[35] Augustus did, objectively, find Aeneas exemplary, as we may judge from Aeneas' place in the Forum of Augustus and from Augustus' own interpretation placed on the statues in his Forum.[36] After, we note, the publication of the *Aeneid*. Provoked by the publication of the *Aeneid*? We shall never know. But we have some faint idea of how Augustus viewed the epic (194); how the poet viewed the principate is a more complex question (194f.), but an exemplary element in the Virgilian Aeneas would not be incompatible with the poet's view (nor that of his contemporaries) of the function of history and myth (cf. 206ff.). But let us be clear: allegorical, typological and exemplary readings only fit part of the epic: just as the Dido of bk. 1 has (unlike the Dido of bk. 4, 133f.) little of Cleopatra about her, and just as the Aeneas of bk. 12 has shed the mantle of Hector which weighs heavily on him elsewhere (cf. 204f.), so the Augustan Aeneas is far more vividly present to our minds in 5, the beginning of 6, and 8 than elsewhere. The ideas explored in this chapter may be accepted as useful keys—but only to a very limited number of difficulties in the poem.

I touch briefly on an ethical variant current in some allegorical interpretations of the *Aeneid*, to the effect that Aeneas displays (sometimes) certain virtues that were specially dear to Augustus or particularly valued during his principate.[37] I do not quite believe that we are compelled to see political expediency, or imperial policy, or hidden persuasion at work in Virgil's characterisation of Aeneas,[38] nor that among Virgil's principal sources in the 'composition' of Aeneas

---

[33] Griffin (n. 4), 193, cf. D. Thompson, *Arethusa* 3 (1970), 147ff., Glei (introd., n. 1), 27f.

[34] E. Wistrand, *Eranos* 82 (1984), 195ff.

[35] A. Wallace-Hadrill, *Hist*.30 (1981), 300ff., Suet. *Aug*.31.5, 89.2.

[36] The edict quoted by Suet. *Aug*.31.5; cf. Ov. *F*.5.563f.

[37] Cf. *RG* 34.2 *uirtus, clementia, iustitia* and *pietas* with Binder, 278f. In *Virgil's Augustan Epic*, Cairns (18ff.) goes a good deal further, with the help of philosophical treatises on the Good King. I expressed some doubts when Cairns first appeared (*CR* 40 (1990), 28f.); cf. now G.B. Conte, *Gnom*.63 (1991), 488f. On ideas about kings at Rome, cf. A. Erskine, *CQ* 41 (1991), 106ff.

[38] P. White, *Promised Verse* (Cambridge, Mass., 1993) compels reassessment of most conventional ideas about the relations of Aug. and Virgil.

we must count Augustus himself (or rather Augustus' own image of himself).[39] We shall have to return to the question of whether it is possible, without confessing to literary blindness and moral turpitude, to restore some credit to the public voice of the *Aeneid*. For the moment, I would only suggest that even embattled champions of that public voice do not find it necessary to read the whole epic as a kind of moral catechesis, a systematic presentation of values dear to the head of state. Excess has brought allegory and typology into disrepute; wide (and wild) generalisations have been tried, and they have failed. Only patience, good sense, and experience will reveal just how important (or unimportant) historical allegory is for bk. 8, or (a very different question) for the *Aeneid* as a whole.

Incompleteness

We do not, I believe, have the means to check VSD's account of Virgil's methods of composition (cf. ch. 1, 15–17); analysis of the indications offered by the text has not led to any sort of general agreement; the use of statistics and computer analysis for determining units of composition has not really started (cf. ch. 1, n. 109). In the circumstances, my aim here is only to indicate, for one book, the sort of 'evidence' that has been adduced to establish incompleteness, order of composition, and the like. As it is, the topic has become, I believe, a dead end: only a fresh start with completely new techniques, can rescue it from death by tedium.[40]

There are only three half-lines[41] in bk. 8; the rarer they are, the more finished, on the generally held view, the book's state (lines 41, 469, 536). If, that is, the books themselves were composed as units, which is far from certain on VSD's account (cf. 16). It is interesting that 8.41 and 536 are both found near other lines where signs of disorder have been detected.[42] Thus at 8.43–6,[43] Tiberinus' prophecy repeats Helenus' as Anchises (7.123ff.) repeats Celaeno (3.250ff.). Both portents are of prime importance, justifying thereby repetition.

[39] Cf. Powell (n. 17). 150f.

[40] Cf. in general, M. Geymonat, *EV* 2.286ff., Fordyce, index s.v. Inconsistencies, Camps, *Introduction*, 127ff., J. Sparrow, *Half-lines and repetitions* (Oxford 1931), 10.

[41] F.W. Lenz in *Vergiliana*, 158ff., M. Geymonat, *EV* 2, 287f.; cf. further ch. 1, nn. 145–7.

[42] Th. Berres, *Die Entstehung der Aeneis* (*Hermes*, Einzelschr. 45, 1982) was not found unconvincing by me alone, *CR* 37 (1987), 15ff.

[43] I have no wish to defend 8.46, omitted by MP; cf. Berres (n. 42), 315ff.; on the

Here, the sow is only found at 8.81ff. and the repetition is thus even more pardonable. The circumstantial detail of the sow's discovery[44] in bk. 3 corresponds closely to the actual circumstances in bk. 8. It becomes hard to condemn the repetition as infelicitous.[45] Both accounts depend on a long and complex literary tradition, which Virgil's readers can have been expected to know.[46] That 39 *hic tibi certa domus* is taken up by 65 *hic mihi magna domus* may be damned (Sparrow, 102) as 'pointless similarity' or defended as ring-composition framing the prophecy!

As for the neighbourhood of 8.536,[47] it has been claimed against 539 that there is no battle beside the Tiber: topography in Virgil's hands in surprisingly pliable, especially when you realise that Tiber and Numicus in some sense correspond to Simois and Xanthus.[48] Of the messengers at 8.547ff. we hear no more, though had Virgil been by nature a pedant, he might have linked them to the reinforcements of 10.238ff.[49] And at 8.541–5 critics from Mackail on have noted (i) that the altar of Hercules is not near Evander's 'palace' and (ii) that the *Troiana iuuentus* had not slept on the Palatine (as 546 makes plain). Do such observations indicate lack of finish or a poet genuinely not concerned with this level of accuracy in matters of detail? We are further invited to deplore 8.55, 'inconsistent' with 7.46.[50] Was primitive Latium peaceful or warlike? Both traditions preceded Virgil and he drew on both alike.[51] The poet has no scruple about ancient Fauni (8.314) and a recent Faunus (7.47–9).[52] At 8.366 Aeneas is lodged within Latinus' 'palace'; at 461ff., Evander and his hounds leave the king's *limen* to go to the *hospitis Aeneas sedem et secreta*. Are we to think (Eden) of huts round a courtyard? The realism of 455 *humili tecto* and the epic grandeur of 461 *limine ab alto* derive from distinct

---

repetition in general, cf. Berres (n. 42), 189ff., G. D'Anna, *Il problema della composizione dell'Eneide* (Roma 1957), 60ff., W. Moskalew, *Formular language and poetic design* (*Mnem.* Suppl. 73, 1982), 113.

[44] 3.384–9, passim:; cf. Grassmann-Fischer (ch. 5, n. 15), 55.

[45] Berres (n. 42), 198f. on the priority of bk. 8 is notably unconvincing; likewise Sparrow (n. 40), l.c.

[46] Horsfall, *Antichthon* 15 (1981), 146, *Vergilius* 35 (1989), 12, *Alambicco*, 99.

[47] Cf. Sparrow (n. 40), 44, 104, Moskalew (n. 43), 128.

[48] Cf. *EV* 5*.156, 3.142 (Horsfall), Buchheit, 179f.

[49] Cf. H.-G. Nesselrath, *Ungeschehenes Geschehen* (Stuttgart 1992), 74ff.

[50] Cf. Camps, *Introduction*, 134.

[51] Cf. *Alambicco*, 95, (n. 46, 1981), 148, id. *Vergilius* 37 (1991), 35 for V. and Apollonius' usage. Cf. now J. O'Hara, *Colby Quarterly* 30 (1994), 216.

[52] Cf. Eden ad loc., against Fordyce.

literary traditions,[53] though the two references are, here, perhaps a little close for comfort!

Repetitions of lines and groups of lines are of the most varied character.[54] We note 8.20–1 :: 4.285–6;[55] 8.49–50 :: 4.115–6;[56] 8.449–53 :: *G*.4.171–5 (simile in the *G*., but narrative in *Aen*.).[57] Of lesser moment, 8.171 :: 1.571;[58] 8.546 :: 6.899. *Lectas de more bidentis* (8.544, 6.36) Sparrow rightly (66, 103) classifies as 'ritual'.

The problems here noted do prompt a careful reading of the text and can have interesting implications, but whether they are in themselves intellectually rewarding I often venture to doubt.

---

[53] Cf. Camps, *Introduction*, 133, Horsfall, *Alambicco*, 93.

[54] Geymonat, *EV* 2, 288; cf. Austin on 2.505 with excellent bibliography.

[55] Moskalew (n. 43), 174; M. has collected useful material but is (too) eager to find significance where convenience or Homerising mannerism might be a fairer explanation, as is surely the case in the final two examples cited.

[56] Cf. Berres (n. 42), 190, n. 4.

[57] Oddly, not in W.W. Briggs, *Narrative and simile* (*Mnem.* Suppl. 58 (1980).

[58] Cf. Moskalew (n. 43), 128.

[59] Cf. Moskalew (n. 43), 176.

Book 9: Emotions and evaluations

In defence of offering here yet another discussion of the Nisus-Euryalus episode, I can only plead that after reading the bulk of the modern bibliography[1] I believe it necessary. It is very easy to use the text of Virgil to prove a case; it is also an almost irresistible temptation to forsake whole for part. I do not, though, propose to offer the fullest and widest-ranging analysis of the episode yet attempted, but rather, to indicate ways in which such an analysis might be undertaken, and how it might lead to conclusions rather more circumscribed than some of those current on the judgement or reactions that Virgil invites, or permits, us to reach. That this year's Virgil is not last year's may in some sense be true: that does not legitimate haste, partiality, inaccuracy, neglect of the poet's sources (or even his learned reading), or of the ancient scholia either to those sources or to Virgil himself!

At 9.176ff. Nisus and Euryalus are introduced quite as though we had never heard of them before: only as the action develops do qualities they had shown in bk. 5 reappear.[2] *His amor unus erat* (182; cf. 5.296 et passim, 12.391–4). Homosexual love, absent from Homer but not from Apollonius; a preference, perhaps, of the poet's own here (6). And an *amor* called *pius* (5.296) by Virgil; 'chaste', it has been claimed.[3] Both (249) are *iuuenes*, but Euryalus (181) is clearly much younger, though already (180) able to bear arms, in partial contrast with Ascanius (656). At 185, Nisus, on guard duty, enquires *dine hunc ardorem mentibus addunt/ Euryale, an sua cuique deus fit dira cupido?* To some extent Virgil answers his own question (354). And, notably, the gods are absent from the rest of the episode (apart from 406), in sharp contrast with that of Ascanius and Numanus Remulus (590–671),[4] which is to be seen as counterpoise and corrective. It would be wrong, though, to suppose that Virgil is inviting the reader to view the whole episode as emblematic of *dira cupido* or to contem-

---

[1] Cf. most recently E. Potz, *Herm.*121 (1993), 325ff. and S. Farron, *Vergil's Aeneid: a poem of love and grief* (*Mnem.* Suppl. 122, 1993), 1ff.; in F., the issue is considerably oversimplified. See now *Aen.*9 ed. P. Hardie (Cambridge 1994).

[2] Cf. Heinze, 217f., n. 2.

[3] Cf. M. Owen Lee, *Fathers and sons* (Albany 1979), 109f., B. Pavlock, *TAPA* 115 (1985) 218, Lyne, *FV*, 229, n. 33, A. La Penna in *L'Eneide* ed. M. Gigante (Napoli 1983), 312, J.F. Makowski, *CJ* 85 (1989–90), 1ff., Farron (n. 1), 12.

[4] Cf. R. Winnington-Ingram, *PVS* 11 (1971–2), 68, R.B. Egan, *Coll.Lat.*168 (1980), 157ff., G.E. Duckworth, *AJP* 88 (1967), 147f.

plate in depth a theological dilemma with a long history.[5] Though *dira cupido* appears at times to dominate, it is, as will emerge, only one of the comments which Virgil offers upon his narrative.[6] Nisus' proposal is not in violation of Aeneas' parting orders (9.42),[7] for no kind of pitched battle is intended. Nisus reveals ambition, restlessness, power of observation. At least he is awake: the Rutuli are both drunk and asleep. He will be satisfied with fame; for Euryalus (vd. infra) he wants rewards. His proposal, to go and fetch Aeneas, is both dangerous and in the tactical situation of the moment urgently necessary. Euryalus too (cf. 194f.) is struck by *laudis amor*[8] and answers the *ardentem* Nisus (again, no criticism necessarily implied):[9] he will not be left behind:[10] the lovely boy values honour high and life low; we are here in the company of Lausus and Pallas.[11]

Nisus glows with pride for his right-thinking beloved. It would be quite wrong (*nec fas*) for him to return in glory (*ouantem*), but alone (208), Jupiter or some other deity permitting (but they do not; intimations of doom cluster as thickly here as they do about Dido) (209). If he dies, he wishes Euryalus to survive to see to his friend's funeral rites (whether his body is, or, if fortune forbids, is not there) and to look after his own old mother: both corpses are dishonoured (465ff.), and Euryalus' mother, whose laments (500) are a risk to morale, has to be led away from the scene.[12] Nisus is told not to fuss or to waste more time. They see that they are relieved on guard-duty, seek out the Trojan commanders, who are even now discussing *quisue Aeneae iam nuntius esset* (228)[13] and ask for an urgent hearing. Virgil seems to aim at a sequence of studiously correct military behaviour. Nisus asks that they be heard fairly, despite their youth. He explains the plan,

---

[5] Feeney, *Gods*, 180, Otis, 349, P.G. Lennox, *Herm.*105 (1977), 335, Duckworth (n. 4), 135.

[6] For some creditable attempts at a balanced reading of the episode, cf. Heinze, 216ff., Potz (n. 1), Lennox (n. 5) 331ff., Klingner, 563ff., Pavlock (n. 3), 207ff. = ead., *Eros, imitation and the epic tradition* (Ithaca 1990), 87ff.

[7] 9.42. R.A. Hornsby, *Patterns of action* (Iowa City 1970), 65ff. unfortunately misunderstands the matter.

[8] At *G.*3.112, *Aen.*5.138, 394, 7.496 not a reprehensible reaction.

[9] Cf. 6.5, 8.163, 9.652.

[10] A significant contrast with a certain reluctance to volunteer shown by both sides in *Il.*10: R.R. Schlunk, *The Homeric scholia and the Aeneid* (Ann Arbor 1974), 63.

[11] R. Glei (intro., n. 1), 206f., La Penna (n. 3), 305, Klingner (n. 6); W.R. Johnson, *Darkness visible* (Berkeley 1976), 62 growls 'sentimental', not unreasonably.

[12] For such *Schrecklichkeit*, cf. 8.196f., 12.509f., Glei (n. 11), 326.

[13] Cf. R.G.M. Nisbet, *PVS* 18 (1978–80), 50ff. = Harrison, 378ff.

based on careful observation and knowledge of the terrain (contrast 245 and 605!). They will return with Aeneas and with rich booty besides: see below for the difficult 240–3; their slaughter of the sleeping Latins and fatal rapacity in the campsite on their outward journey is neither envisaged nor excluded by the language used. Aletes[14] declares that Troy's gods have not forsaken her *cum talis animos iuuenum et tam certa tulistis/pectora*. That gently anticipates Virgil's own *makarismos* (446ff.). In Nisus' speech there was no trace of the *quae posco* threatened at 194: Aletes, after tears, handshakes, embraces, unprompted talks of *digna. . .praemia* (251f.). The *pulcherrima. . .(praemia)* will come of the gods; Aeneas and Ascanius, *integer aeui*[15] will see to the rest. The sequel to Ascanius' killing of Numanus Remulus shows that the description hardly fits. Perhaps we are meant to realise as much at once: the issue is of some importance if *integer aeui* is intended as an anticipatory comment on the speech that follows, follows indeed with impatient immediacy (*exipit Ascanius* postponed): with a mighty oath, he places all his *fortuna* and *fides in uestris gremiis* and lists quite unprompted (263–74) the gifts they will receive:[16] on 267 Servius well notes that Ascanius offers Turnus' horse, as yet unavailable, as he knows (267–8). Hector offers Dolon (*Il.*10.306) the best pair and chariot at the Achaean ships, ἃ οὐκ ἔχει (schol. T).[17] Not enough for Dolon, who (321ff.) asks Hector to specify that Achilles' own are those meant. A mercenary element is therefore traditional in the episode's literary history, but Ascanius, in his catalogue of rewards for Nisus, goes almost to the point of parody, including a *crater* which was a gift from *Sidonia Dido* and therefore arguably ill-omened.[18] At 275, Ascanius turns to his contemporary (ib.) Euryalus, hailed as *uenerande puer*, an unparalleled expression: from now on, he will be Ascanius' closest companion in peace and war. Not a word of gifts. Euryalus replies that he will not be *dissimilis* to *tam fortibus ausis* so long as *fortuna secunda/haud aduersa cadat*. Intimations of doom continue to cluster thick. He asks *super omnia dona* (which he has not been offered to his face) for one thing, that Ascanius look after his aged mother, of whom he will not take his leave, *quod nequeam lacrimas perferre parentis*. The

---

[14] *annis grauis atque aeui maturus*; cf. *GR* 34 (1987), 51.
[15] Cf. 2.638; the sequel to Ascanius' killing of Numanus Remulus will show that the description hardly fits; cf. 590ff., 638ff.
[16] Pavlock (n. 3), 208f., (n. 6), 89ff., Schlunk (n. 10), 66ff.
[17] Cf. (Eur.) *Rhes.*184ff.; cf. Pavlock (n. 6), 92.
[18] Glei (n. 11), 284, C. Murgia, *CP* 82 (1987), 52f.

Trojan command weeps and Iulus is moved by the *patriae pietatis imago*.[19]

Analogies with the Mezentius-Lausus episode have been explored with some success (cf. n. 11): it is above all important to realise that however formally self-contained an episode may be, it will never prove bereft of links (thematic, 'ideological', linguistic, imagistic. . .) to other episodes and contexts. On our skill and judgement depends how far we pursue such links and what conclusions we draw from them. Of course Ascanius responds with particular alacrity to the claim of *pietas*: whatever happens, she will be another Creusa to me in all but name (and 501 shows that the promise, reinforced by an oath (300) is to be read seriously). Ascanius' declarations to Euryalus, valid *tibi. . .reduci rebusque secundis* (301) will likewise (sc. if you do not return), he concludes in tears, hold good for your mother and *genus*.

At this point, we pass to the arming scene.[20] The Trojan leaders accompany Nisus and Euryalus to the camp gate; Iulus in particular *ante annos animumque gerens curamque uirilem*[21] *multa patri mandata dabat portanda*, but they were carried away by the wind. A symbol of the whole mission's failure? A criticism of Ascanius' behaviour so far?[22] Drawing on Homer and Catullus, *inter alios*, Virgil, who has already hinted repeatedly that the messengers will not survive, adds a parting note, that they did not hear Ascanius' last words to them. Tragic, but clearly, as Virgil has been at pains to establish, not futile. Some form of equilibrium is maintained: youth, courage and *pietas* have been amply displayed and compensate for much.

Nisus and Euryalus at once reach the Latin camp, *multis tamen ante futuros exitio*. Their behaviour in 314–66 has been criticised on two scores: its brutality (the Rutuli are asleep) and its cupidity.[23] Some explanation is called for:

At one level, the Latins and Rutuli are arrogant, unsoldierly,

---

[19] 9.294; cf. 10.812, Egan (n. 4), 161ff.

[20] 9.303ff.; cf. *Il*.10.254ff. Aletes makes a present of a *galea*, sensibly, as befits his years.

[21] 9.311; cf. 255: his behaviour has indeed been irreprehensible, except perhaps in the abundance of gifts offered to Euryalus.

[22] Cf. M. Di Cesare, *The altar and the city* (New York 1974), 162f., cf. id. *RSC* 20 (1972), 411ff., G.J. Fitzgerald in *Cicero and Virgil. Studies in honour of H.A.K. Hunt* (Amsterdam 1972), 123.

[23] M.C.J. Putnam, *Poetry of the Aeneid* (Cambridge, Mass., 1965), 50ff., Lee (n. 3), 111, Pavlock (n. 3), 213f., 216, Glei (n. 11), 213, Fitzgerald (n. 22), 118, Di Cesare (n. 22), 163, Farron (n. 1), 4 et passim, etc.

incompetent in the field, and we are therefore well-prepared[24] to evaluate Numanus' polemic bluster at its true worth. It is the Trojans, not the Italians, who embody military energy, and their messengers' path lies through the drunken disorder of the Italians' camp (320ff.).[25] Nisus says that it is time for action (*audendum dextra*, 320); Euryalus can watch their rear while he will *uasta dabo et lato te limite ducam*. Is the massacre necessary, we might want to ask? Could not the Trojans have slipped through their enemies' camp without disturbing the drunkards and sleepers, instead of indulging in unsportsmanlike(!) slaughter?[26] No, first because the Doloneia contains the exact model for such a massacre (10.479ff.). Second, because, however little he (or we) may like it, Virgil is a poet of war and slaughter.[27] Thirdly, because such scenes are not governed by philosophical theories of clemency, or by the Geneva convention. Virgil, as we shall see, has his own unmistakable way of saying 'too much'. So the massacre begins.[28] Serranus had better have gambled until dawn; so he might have survived. At this point, Virgil comments, explicitly enough:[29] Euryalus has become like a lion in the sheepfold: (340) *suadet enim uesana fames. . .fremit ore cruento*[30]*. . .(342) nec minor Euryali caedes; incensus et ipse/perfurit*. No general declaration, but blood-lust has distracted Euryalus from the needs of his mission and has driven him beyond what the occasion requires. Euryalus, however, continues (343–51), up to Rhoetus, awake, after heavy drinking (350), and cowering behind his *crater* (346). Virgil comments again on Euryalus (350) *hic furto feruidus instat*.[31] The adjective is loaded enough (cf. Aeneas at 12.748 and in his aristeia at 10.788), and *furtum* is very strong language.[32] It is Nisus

---

[24] Cf. 236, 316f., 326, 336, 338, 350; cf. *Il*.10.417ff., 471, 474; Winnington-Ingram (n. 4) remains an excellent discussion.

[25] Cf. B. Tilly, *Arch.Class*.8 (1956), 164ff.

[26] Cf. Lee (n. 3), 111.

[27] Cf. *Aen*.10 ed. S.J. Harrison, xxi, id., *PVS* 19 (1988), 48ff. Passionate dissent from R. Thomas, *Vergilius* 38 (1992), 138ff.

[28] *Il*.10.483, 488: Homer gives the scale and speed of the undertaking precedence over his taste for specific and often excessively gory detail: cf. B. Fenik, *Typical battle-scenes in the Iliad* (*Herm*. Einzelschr. 21, Wiesbaden 1968), 32. For Virgil's tolerance of gore, cf. Harrison (bis), n. 27.

[29] Lennox, in his defence of Nisus (n. 5), 336–9, takes insufficient note of Virgil's ample indications.

[30] Cf. 1.296, Glei (n. 11), 207. The simile derives in outline from the corresponding context in Homer (*Il*.10.485ff.). Cf. Schlunk (n. 10), 77f.

[31] Cf. Farron (n. 1), 4.

[32] 6.568, ambush at 11.515, 2.258, Sinon opens the horse (cf. 2.18), 6.24, Pasiphae's contraption.

who calls a halt (cf. Lennox, 337): *sensit enim nimia caede atque cupidine
ferri* (354; cf. 185, 342). The way is clear and the enemy punished
enough (*poenarum exhaustum satis est*, 356: understatement, we may feel)
and dawn is near.[33]

Much booty they leave behind (357–8), but whether we are justified
in judging all those characters in the *Aeneid* who desire, or strip, or
wear the arms of others by the standards of the text alone, or by
strict Roman usage is quite another matter (not to mention the distinct
Homeric ethic). There is indeed a preliminary question to be asked:
whether the issue as a whole in the *Aen.* required any overall judgement, or whether the poet invites or requires us to make any such
judgement (consistent to cover all instances, or variable?). Are all
characters and all actions of this kind to be judged by one and the
same standard? Do we know when Homer is our yardstick and when
Livy? The question of Euryalus' spoils has acquired a particular
importance, but has not always been studied with all the attention
due to literary and antiquarian precedent (on bk. 10, cf. further 205).

At 240ff., Nisus, to the assembled Trojan leaders, declares *si fortuna
permittitis uti/quaesitum Aenean et moenia Pallantea,/mox hic cum spoliis ingenti
caede peracta/adfore cernetis*. We have, first, a major difficulty of language.[34] I incline to believe that *quaesitum* is indeed an unparalleled use
of the supine, depending on the motion implied in *permittitis uti*: such
an extension of usage seems compatible with the poet's habitual
pushing of the language to (and beyond) its limits. Who then will
return *cum spoliis*? That is left unspecified, perhaps deliberately so.
The speaker hopes it will be himself, his young friend, and Aeneas,
but perhaps prefers not to say so explicitly. At this point the acquisition of *spolia* envisaged is, let us be clear, not necessarily that which
actually ensues.

Before they leave the Trojan camp, Euryalus is given a sword by
Ascanius and Nisus a lionskin by Mnestheus and a helmet by Aletes
(303–7). *Galeae enim sunt explorantum.*[35] Here the lionskin is described

---

[33] Cf. Schlunk (n. 10), 70ff.: see *Il.*10.251, but as S. notes, the change of light is
crucial to Virgil's plot (373–4). That may possibly have been suggested by Homer's
scholia.

[34] Cf. Henry ad loc., Lennox (n. 5), 337ff.; *contra*, Potz (n. 1), 330f., Perret, *note
complémentaire* ad loc. P. Heuzé *REL*, 63 (1985), 94ff., *EV* s.v. *Supino*, 1083, LHS,
381, KS 2.1.721ff., Ernout-Thomas, 261. I suspect that the subject of *adfore* is left
(deliberately) unclear.

[35] Cf. Serv. on 9.305, schol. A and T. on *Il.*10.258, with Schlunk (n. 10), 69f.

as *exuuiae*, a trophy of the hunt (cf. 11.577, 2.473). The word is more often used of arms stripped from the vanquished. The Trojans leave behind much booty, but not enough. Nisus had revelled in the slaughter, and now Euryalus appropriates *nequiquam* (364) the *phalerae* and *cingula* of Rhamnes[36] and the *galea* of the absent Messapus. *Excedunt castris et tuta* (ironical!) *capessunt*. It is the helmet, not gift but loot, which betrays Euryalus (373ff.); that leads to his death, and to Nisus'. The Rutuli return *praeda. . .spoliisque potiti* (450); they recognise (457f.) the *phalerae* (of Rhamnes) and the helmet of Messapus. So how are we to judge the stripping of the corpses and the wearing of arms acquired not by gift but by force? In the ethic of Homeric warfare, there would be little problem.[37] In Virgil, though, the wearing, or even the desire to wear, another man's armour ends badly.[38] Has the ethic of battle changed? Have warriors become more civilised?[39] It is curious that (since Warde Fowler!) commentators have paid so very little attention to Roman usage in the disposal of the armour of the defeated.[40] To wear an enemy's armour with intention to deceive (2.389) is reprehensible.[41] You can dedicate your victim's arms to the gods in a *tropaeum*;[42] you can hang them in a palace or temple;[43] you can burn them in large quantities;[44] if you are a general and you kill the enemy's general, that, in Roman usage, is a very special case.[45] Only in the gravest emergency can you remove dedicated arms from a temple and use them.[46] Arms acquired in war seem therefore to belong, in the Roman view, to the gods or to the victor's house, in a wide sense. In the *Aeneid*, two incompatible ethics coexist: Aeneas grants the dead Lausus his *arma* (10.827); Mezentius' he offers (11.4–

---

[36] On its history (cf. *Il*.10.266ff.), cf. Pavlock (n. 3), 216, (n. 6), 100f.

[37] R. Hornsby, *PQ* 45 (1966), 347ff., R.S. Shannon, *The arms of Achilles* (*Mnem.* Suppl. 36 (1975), 25f. J. Griffin, *Homer on life and death* (Oxford 1983), 36, C.W. Macleod comm. *Il*.24, 20, n. 2. Cf. further, 205.

[38] So Hornsby (n. 37), Duckworth (n. 4), 148.

[39] Hornsby (n. 37), 356.

[40] R.O.A.M. Lyne, *CQ* 33 (1983), 194, n. 19. E. Henry, *The vigour of prophecy* (Bristol 1989), 22, Warde Fowler on *Aen*.8.562, R.G. Basto, *AJP* 105 (1984), 336f., C. Saunders, *Vergil's primitive Italy* (New York 1930), 139f., S. Reinach, *Cultes, Mythes et Religions* 3 (Paris 1908), 223ff. = *Rev.Arch*.1908, 42ff., G.C. Picard, *Les trophées romains* (BEFAR 187, Paris 1957).

[41] Cf. Front. *Strat*.3.2.3, Liv.27.28.9, Carthaginian, predictably! Called *dolus* at §4.

[42] 11.5ff. (cf. 10.422, 542, 775), Reinach (n. 40), 225, Picard (n. 40), 122, 125.

[43] 7.183ff. (cf. 2.504, 5.393), Reinach (n. 40), 225, Picard (n. 40), 122.

[44] 8.562, 11.193ff., Reinach (n. 40), 229f., Picard (n. 40), 119f.

[45] Cf. 148, n. 24.

[46] Liv.23.14, etc., Reinach (n. 40), 226.

11) perhaps to Mars (cf. 10.542). He at least has understood the Roman usage.[47] At 2.396, at Coroebus' suggestion, Aeneas is armed as a Greek, in captured equipment: *uadimus immixti Danais haud numine nostro*. A fatal error (cf. 2.402, 410, 413), that he would not make in Italy. Does Homeric usage come into the question at all? I am in no hurry to judge.

Let us return briefly to the text. A patrol led by Volcens is returning from Latinus' city to the Trojan camp (373); *sublustri*[48] *noctis in umbra*, Messapus' helmet gives Euryalus away. Volcens is wide awake and impeccably efficient (375–80). In the dark wood,[49] Euryalus is impeded by his booty and loses his way.[50] Nisus escapes, realises that he is alone and, like Aeneas in bk. 2, returns (391) to the forest, where the noise leads him to the fight about Euryalus, given away *fraude loci et noctis*.[51] Can Nisus save his beloved? Or shall he rush upon the enemy in pursuit of a *pulchram. . .mortem* (401)?[52] As a hunter he prays to the Moon/Diana, kills Sulmo, with bloody and unHomeric detail, and while the enemy *trepidant*, kills Tagus too. Volcens, to avenge his men, turns on Euryalus (422ff.). That brings Nisus out of ambush: *mea fraus omnis* he cries, *nihil iste nec ausus/nec potuit*[53]. . .*tantum infelicem nimium dilexit amicum*. Inevitably, Volcens stabs Euryalus.[54] Nisus (438) makes for Volcens, whom his men seek in vain to protect; dying, he kills his enemy (443), and over Euryalus' body himself dies.[55] The authorial intrusion into the epic text (446ff.)[56] that follows creates some difficulties for those who see Nisus and Euryalus as inept teen-age murderers.[57] Nisus and Euryalus take their place in Virgil's noble

---

[47] Cf. *EV* s.v. *Anacronismi*, Schlunk (n. 10), 61f., Nisbet (n. 13), F.H. Sandbach, *PVS* 5 (1965–6), 26ff. = (much altered) Harrison, 449ff.

[48] *habens aliquid lucis* Serv.

[49] Of much symbolic importance, according to Fitzgerald (n. 22), 125.

[50] *Aen*.2.737, 9.385: on analogies with *Aen*.2 in general, cf. Lennox (n. 5), 339.

[51] Cf. 11.522, and Liv.9.2.9, with my remarks, *PBSR* 50 (1982), 47.

[52] Cf. *G*.4.218, *Aen*.11.647, G. Arrigoni, *Camilla* (Milan 1982), 55ff.

[53] *Fraus* in battle: cf. 11.708, 717, 552. Nisus claims the typical behaviour of Rome's enemies (Farron (n. 1), 4ff.), and especially the Carthaginians. Why? Was killing his enemies while they slept really *fraus*? Or does he inflate his guilt in the hope of saving Euryalus' life? At all events, not an objective moral evaluation. Potz (n. 1), 332 well cites Tac. *Ann*.1.50f.: Romans neatly slaughter drunken and torpid Germans.

[54] On possible erotic implications in the simile at 9.433ff., not inappropriate in the context, cf. Lyne, *FV*, 229.

[55] 9.445 *placidaque ibi demum morte quieuit*: ring-composition with 9.187 (Nisus' ambition) *aliquid. . .inuadere magnum nec placida contenta (sc. mens) quiete est*.

[56] Heinze, 370ff.

[57] Analysed with exceptional delicacy by Klingner, 561ff.: the immortality which

series of youths valiant but doomed: Marcellus, Pallas, Lausus.[58] The wary and unpartisan reader[59] realises that we have, like it or not, to reach some form of moral equilibrium: beyond any reasonable doubt, Virgil pulls us in conflicting directions, compelling us to share both admiration and some degree of condemnation for the victims' methods. The most sensitive and intelligent reader of such an episode is, I believe, the one who comes nearest to understanding exactly where the point of equilibrium lies.[60]

Virgil bestows on the young heroes is anchored in familiar symbols of the permanence of Rome herself; cf. Hor. *C.*3.30.8. Cf. too Lee (n. 3), 111, Quinn, 206, Fitzgerald (n. 22), 126, Farron (n. 1), 10f.

[58] Hornsby (n. 37), 356, di Cesare (n. 22), 170. The thought of Marcellus should have given pause to those who see in Nisus and Euryalus an outdated or superseded mode of heroism: with 6.882, cf. 10.825, 11.42.

[59] Glei (n. 11), 207f., di Cesare (n. 22), 166, Johnson (n. 11) 62, Winnington-Ingram (n. 4), 68.

[60] On the lament of Euryalus' mother, cf. Egan (n. 4), 164ff., La Penna (n. 3), 320ff.

Book 10

Battle-scenes

Given that battle is the principal subject-matter of *Aen*.9–12, it is most remarkable that so little attention has been paid to Virgil's techniques of structure and arrangement. Heinze's discussion (193ff.), for all its many merits, precedes modern understanding of Homer's techniques: Fenik (203 n. 75) marked a notable step forward, and in details such as the stripping of armour (204–5) comparable progress has been made. For the *Aeneid*, P.-J. Miniconi *Etude sur les thèmes guerriers*...(Paris 1951) did not mark a real advance, while P. Jal, *La guerre civile* (Paris 1963) has much to offer readers of Virgil;[1] the technicalities of warfare have been even more neglected.[2] But the subject as a whole is entirely serious, however unfashionable, and its neglect imposes fundamental limitations on our understanding of how Virgil has re-worked his Homeric material. Thus we have already seen that the moral issue raised by the stripping of the dead in bk. 9 is often imperfectly evaluated, while the one article (176 n. 37) specifically on 'The armor of the slain', often cited as it is, does not collect adequately the Homeric or Roman *comparanda*! Inevitably, Virgil does not tell us which set of *comparanda* we should apply, and the two sets of parallel material differ in their implications. Worse still, both Homer and Virgil offer moral comment (as should never have been questioned!).[3] There is negative authorial comment both in Homer[4] and in Virgil, though it might be questioned (cf. Barchiesi 42f., n. 56) whether 'Schuld' was the most felicitous term to use of Hector's stripping of Sarpedon's corpse.[5]

Homer intervenes to condemn Achilles' human sacrifice at *Il*.23.176. Not so Virgil. Conway, cited with approval by Renger,[6] pointed out that Virgil reduces the number of victims from 12 to 8 and does not actually describe the moment of death. Nor is Aeneas (11.98) present

---

[1] Cf. H. Raabe, *Plurima mortis imago* (München 1974), T. Krischer, *PLLS* 2 (1979), 143ff., Nisbet (171, n. 13), M.M. Willcock, *PCPhS* 29 (1983), 87ff., S.J. Harrison (174, n. 27), Horsfall, *GR* 34 (1987), 48ff.

[2] Cf. 177, n. 47.

[3] Against Klingner, 578f., n. 1 and A. Barchiesi, *La traccia del modello* (Pisa 1984), 42, n. 56, cf. Knauer, 301ff.

[4] *Il*.17.205 οὐ κατὰ κόσμον; cf. *Aen*.10.501–5, Barchiesi (n. 3), 40, 42.

[5] An act implied in Homer, not narrated, Barchiesi (n. 3), 40f.

[6] R.S. Conway, *CR* 46 (1932), 201, C. Renger, *Aeneas und Turnus* (Frankfurt 1985), 68, n. 6.

when they are killed, as killed they clearly are (11.81f., cf. *Il.*23.175ff.).[7] But no word of explicit condemnation, either. By what terms are we to judge Aeneas? The apparent contemporary parallel is illusory and irrelevant.[8] *Minime Romano sacro* comments Livy (22.57.6);[9] but Pliny[10] suggests that Roman usage had been different.[11] The Aeneas of bk. 10 is 'archaic'.[12] His sacrifice of eight youths is not laudable, or admirable, or justifiable, without indecorous verbal gymnastics, but it is an act not incompatible with a vision of Aeneas as an archaic Roman warrior-hero.

Discussion of Virgilian battles has become notably judgemental in tone (174, n. 27). The precedents for those judgements are, however, most imperfectly understood and that in turn means that the general context of Virgilian battlefield ethics (and its sources) has yet to be evaluated in the detail it requires.[13] Out of the scattered but ample bibliography, I offer an anthology of discussions of individual aspects of Virgilian battle-scenes, with specific reference to instances in which Virgilian usage differs, however slightly, from Homeric:

(i) Virgil has declined every chance to create a category of developed minor figures in whom the reader may take a lively interest.[14]

(ii) Virgil avoids combats whose outcome is not clear: his warriors are unevenly matched.[15]

(iii) Virgil tends to abbreviate (necessarily) the leisurely conventions of the full-scale Homeric battle.[16] Pallas' combat with Turnus is, though, exceptionally full in detail.

(iv) It has been pointed out[17] that Pallas (10.486) tears Turnus'

---

[7] Cf. E. Henry, *The vigour of prophecy* (Bristol 1989), 167.

[8] Cf. 163, 206; E. Kraggerud, *SO* 62 (1987), 77ff., Renger (n. 6), 65f., H.-P. Stahl, *Arethusa* 14 (1981), 158f.; S. Farron *AC* 28 (1985), 21–33; rather better, Glei (introd., n. 1), 218f.

[9] F. Schwenn, *Die Menschenopfer bei den Griechen u. Römern, RVV* 15.3 (Giessen 1915), 156.

[10] *Nat.*30.12, with Schwenn, l.c.

[11] So too Varr. ap. Serv.Dan. *ad Aen.*3.67, Schwenn (n. 9), 174. Other examples can be cited (Schwenn (n. 9), 140ff., passim).

[12] H.-J. Schweizer, *Vergil und Italien* (Aarau 1967), 55ff.

[13] Cf. T. Taylor, *The anatomy of the Nuremberg trials* (London 1993), 3ff. for the legal and diplomatic history of the 'rules of war' in modern times.

[14] Horsfall (n. 1), 50, Willcock (n. 1) 89, 96.

[15] Horsfall (n. 1), 53, cf. 5.809, 10.438, 459, 811.

[16] Harrison, *Aen.*10, xxxi with n. 24, id., *PVS* 19 (1988), 55f.

[17] Barchiesi (n. 3), 33f., M. Bonfanti, *Punto di vista...nell'En.* (Pisa 1985), 48f., P. Schenk, *Die Gestalt des Turnus* (Königstein 1984), 103f.

spear from his own body; this reverses Patroclus over the body of Sarpedon (*Il*.16.503–5: victor tugs spear from victim's body).

(v) Aeneas to Lausus (10.811f.): a reversal of the Homeric pre-battle taunt;[18] Pallas to Turnus too (449–51). Compare the tone of Mezentius' address to Rhaebus (861–6) and to Aeneas himself (878–82). Modesty does not save Pallas or Mezentius; Homeric vaunters often survive.[19]

(vi) The death-wound not intended for the victim.[20]

(vii) On the Virgilian *aristeia*, cf. Harrison, xxvii, Willcock (n. 1) *passim*.

But this brief list should be taken as indicating that most of the work still remains to be done.

Poetic sources

Aeneid 10 was not chosen as starting point for such a survey because its poetic sources were notoriously rich and complex: on examination, however, the book does reveal the range of those sources as amply as one could wish and provides sufficient examples of Virgil's techniques of allusion and conflation.

(a) The central nexus of Homeric allusion in *Aen*.10 is specially elaborate and of major thematic and structural importance.[21] It is noteworthy how very little substantial progress has been made since Knauer:[22] if Pallas[23] corresponds to Patroclus, then Patroclus' last victim, Sarpedon, must in some sense correspond to Halaesus; Achilles honours the body of Hector in *Il*.24, and Aeneas honours that of Lausus; contrast[24] Turnus' despoiling of Pallas' corpse, which in turn corresponds to Hector's stripping of Sarpedon's.[25]

---

[18] Krischer (n. 1), 147.

[19] Krischer (n. 1), 147ff.

[20] Bonfanti (n. 17), 56f., Harrison on 10.343f., 781f.

[21] Knauer, 296–308. Those unnerved by the density and elaboration of his text might start from *GRBS* 5 (1964), 62ff. or *ANRW* 2.31.2 (1981), 870ff. as an introduction to his method. But for the serious enquirer, there is no choice.

[22] K.W. Gransden, *Virgil's Iliad* (Cambridge 1984), 141ff. is not very helpful. The most convenient summary in English is Harrison (comm.), xxviii–xxxi.

[23] Aeneas' relationship to Pallas is, as we have known for a long time, grounded not only in *Il*., but in Roman concepts of *hospitium*; cf. Harrison on 494–5, C. Renger, *Aeneas und Turnus* (Frankfurt 1985), 54ff., P. Schenk, *Die Gestalt des Turnus* (Königstein 1984), 101ff. On Sarpedon, cf. Harrison, xxx, but see already Knauer, 298, n. 3, 306.

[24] Cf. A. Barchiesi in *L'Eneide* (ed. M. Gigante, Napoli, 1983), 349ff.

[25] Cf. further Schenk (n. 23), 103f., A. Barchiesi, (n. 3), 30ff.

In the light of ample recent discussion in (at least) English, German
and Italian, I prefer not to summarise afresh the overall scheme of
allusion. That Aeneas often acts in bk. 10 as *alter Achilles*[26] is not here
advanced as a moral justification, but when his actions upon an Achillean model seem to modern stomachs violent or even repugnant,
their Homeric antecedents do nevertheless confer upon them a peculiar and distinctive literary flavour. They are heralded (cf. (c). 1
below) by the Sirius simile, drawn from Achilles' terrible return to
battle after the death of Patroclus,[27] and they belong to an age already of complex morality, but prior to the development of systems
of ethical theory. The function of Homeric analogy in *Aen.*10 does
not, I think, have the primary function of condemning both Aeneas
and Achilles as (in Virgil's eyes) war-criminals. Cf. further 203ff. on
bk. 12. In becoming more explicitly Achillean, Aeneas' heroic stature is enlarged and altered; moreover—not unimportant for a proto-
Roman—he passes to the side of the victors. The Achillean Aeneas
is not to be condemned out of hand as a Philosophically Correct
modern hero regrettably regressed into ethical primitivism.[28] Aeneas
never was—except perhaps briefly at Carthage—a second Paris (cf.
4.215); as cousin, admirer, imitator of Hector (cf. 122, n. 24), Aeneas
had but a short and bloody future; his transformation into Achilles,
prepared for by Turnus' un-Achillean defeat, despite his vaunts, 9.742,
in bk. 9,[29] is a pre-requisite of his role as (victorious) founder of the
gens Iulia.

(b) Further large-scale debts to Homer:

(1) The council of the gods takes the place of a scene, of closely
similar length, between Patroclus and Achilles at the beginning of
*Il.*19 (Knauer, 296), while the content derives (Knauer, 294) in
important respects from *Il.*20.4–31.[30]

(2) Virgil's secondary catalogue (10.163–214) corresponds not only
to Homer's minor catalogue (the Trojans, *Il.*2.816–77) but also,

---

[26] Cf. Barchiesi (n. 25), 36ff., Schenk (n. 23), 85, Renger (n. 23), 53, Mackie,
162ff., W.S. Anderson, *TAPA* 88 (1957), 26f., T. Van Nortwick, *TAPA* 110 (1980),
303ff. Cf. bk. 8, 165.

[27] Van Nortwick (n. 26), 308f.

[28] Cf. (e.g.) Otis, 222, R.D. Williams, *Aeneas and the Roman hero* (London 1973),
28ff., G.K. Galinsky, *ANRW* 2.31.2 (1981), 999ff. S. Farron *AC* 20 (1977), 204–8.

[29] Cf. Anderson (n. 26), 26, Van Nortwick (n. 26), 304.

[30] Cf. Knauer 283; compare too the placing of a council at the beginning of *Il.*4
(1–72) and for that matter (Knauer, 330) at the beginning of *Il.*8 (1–52).

perhaps more significantly, to that of Achilles' Myrmidons (16.168–97, Knauer, 297, Harrison, comm., 101).

(3) Aeneas with his fleet of Etruscan allies encounters his former fleet transformed (10.215–50, Knauer, 297).[31]

(c) Subordinate allusions to Homer. It may also be helpful to note some of the more interesting smaller Homeric imitations in *Aen*.10:

(1) From the shore, Aeneas appears to the waiting Rutulians like a bloody comet or like the star Sirius (270–4): cf. not only the Diomedes-simile at the beginning of *Il*.5 (4–7), but, much more to the point (because thematically so significant), *Il*.18.205–6 (Achilles finally returns to combat, Knauer, 298). At the same time, Aeneas recalls (cf. 8.680) Augustus at Actium (Glei, introd., n. 1, 218).

(2) Aeneas' severe words of consolation to Lausus (10.829). Cf. Achilles to Lycaon, *Il*.21.106–8 (Knauer, 307). Note that Aeneas' taunts to Magus (10.531–4) owe much to Achilles' words to Lycaon (21.99–102), as do those addressed to Tarquitus (10.557–60; cf. *Il*.21.122–7).[32]

(3) For Orion and *Od*.11, cf. n. 40 below.

(4) Aeneas raises the body of Lausus (831) as does Achilles that of Hector (*Il*.24.589).[33]

(5) Mezentius' address to his horse (861ff.). There are several Iliadic instance of animals mourning in Homer;[34] Glenn draws attention (cf. (e) below) to Polyphemus' reference to his ram, *Od*.9.447ff.

(d) Iliadic 'history': not enough attention has been paid to Virgil's use of the *Iliad* (as well as *Od*. and AR) as an historical record, a chronicle of events to which reference may be made; 10.471 is a splendid example.[35]

---

[31] Harrison, comm., 131, citing *Od*.4.364ff., 5.333ff., *Il*.13.27ff. Cf. further E. Fantham, *CP* 85 (1990), 113ff., Moschus, *Europa* ed. W. Bühler, 156.

[32] Cf. Highet, 205, Knauer, index s.v. *Listen*, Renger (n. 23), 57.

[33] M. Bonfanti, *Punto di vista...nell' En.* (Pisa 1985), 63. Harrison xxxi correctly notes that the parallel is not in Knauer. But let us be clear: Knauer has transformed our understanding of Virgil's *modus operandi* and we play like dwarves on the shoulders of a giant (Bernard of Chartres, *PL* 199.900C).

[34] J. Glenn, *AJP* 92 (1971), 140ff., *Il*.8.184ff., 17.437ff., 19.397ff., Harrison on *Aen*.10.860.

[35] Gransden (n. 22), 142, Knauer, 299, Horsfall, *GR* 34 (1987), 53f., *Vergilius* 32 (1986), 17, *Alambicco* 69, 84–6, H.-D. Reeker, *die Landschaft in der Aeneis* (Hildesheim 1971), 166ff. I shall be writing further on this topic (cf. 187f.).

(e) When we say 'Virgil used Homer' (or Hesiod, or Callimachus, or Apollonius, or Aratus), we understand by 'Homer' not only the text itself, but the entire inherited apparatus of scholiasts and imitators which the original text had acquired. Though R.R. Schlunk's *The Homeric Scholia and the Aeneid* (Ann Arbor 1974) raised more problems of chronology than it answered,[36] the central theme of indebtedness is settled and certain.[37] For *Aen*.10, cf. Schlunk, 32f. on the comparison of Aeneas to Sirius (267–77) (cf. (c) 1 above). Zoilus had doubts about *Il*.5.4,[38] not imitated by Virgil. Schol.A on *Il*.5.4 notes too (not that Virgil needed to be told!) that the fire about Diomedes created terror for the Trojans (cf. *Aen*.10.267, *tamen*, 276). An arguably rich source of detail in Virgil's portrait of Mezentius is his own, as well as Homer's, Cyclops.[39]

(f) The epic cycle. We have seen (114) that Virgil's Aegaeon (565–70) conforms to a version known from the *Titanomachy*. Not that Virgil read that text! Cf. Call. *Aet*.59.6Pf., *LIMC* 4.1.482 (E. Simon).[40] Equally unconvincing is Virgil's supposed use of the *Aethiopis* (Antilochus saves Nestor) as a source for 10.789–832 (Lausus seeks to defend his father).[41] It is quite uncertain that Virgil had access to *Aethiopis* (or *Titanomachy*!) and Fraenkel cannot show convincingly that Virgil went beyond his beloved Pindar (*Pyth*.6.28ff.) to Pindar's sources.[42]

(g) Greek tragedy. Capaneus (A. *Septem* 425) and Parthenopaeus (ib. 531f.) might have had something to do with Virgil's conception of Mezentius as *contemptor deorum*.[43] Even less convincing is the comparison[44] of 10.904–6 with Eur. *Alc*.365–8 and *Orest*.1052–3. But Soph.

---

[36] N.G. Wilson, *Gnom* 48 (1976), 716f., E.C. Kopff, *CJ* 71 (1976), 279f.

[37] Cairns, 181, A. Wlosok, *Res humanae—res divinae* (Heidelberg 1990), 398f. for two random examples.

[38] Schol.A, *Il*.5.4; cf. Schol.A, *Il*.18.206, Schol. T., *Il*.5.7.

[39] J. Glenn, *AJP* 102 (1981), 43ff., Hardie, 266f., Glenn (n. 34), 129ff.

[40] For Pallas and Troilus (*Aen*.1.474–8), cf. Knauer, 305f. That Virgil got his Troilus from the *Cypria* is unlikely. Possibly from Sophocles' lost *Troilus* (vd. *LIMC* 1.1.72f.). That Achilles had to 'pay' for the killing of the young Troilus presupposes a version in which the effect of 'unfair' slaughter is augmented by sacrilege (altar of Thymbraean Apollo): A. Lesky, PW s.v. *Troilos* 605.11ff. For Orion (10.763–8), cf. perhaps, rather than *Od*.11.572–5, Eratosthenes, *Catasterismi* ch. 32 Robert (Hyg. *Astr* 2.34, Schol.Germ. *Arat*. p. 163.13, etc.), E.W. Leach, *Areth*.4 (1971), 83ff.

[41] So E. Fraenkel, *Phil*.87 (1932), 244f. = *Kl.B*.2 (Roma 1964), 175.

[42] Cf. *EV* s.v. *Pindaro* (Setaioli), *Alambicco*, 45, 47, A. Hollis, *HSCP* 94 (1992), 273. On V. and the epic cycle, cf. *Alambicco*, 47, Horsfall, *JHS* 99 (1979), 46f.

[43] Against F.A. Sullivan, *CP* 64 (1969), 225f., cf. Glenn (n. 34), 129ff.

[44] Cf. Glenn (n. 34), 138ff.

Aj. is quite another matter; the text is anyway well-known to Virgil.[45]
With Mezentius' *hybris*, cf. *Aj.*762ff., 770ff.; with Mezentius' appeal
to his right hand (773), cf. *Aj.*772.[46]

(h) Hellenistic Greek poetry. Phanocles has long been recognised
as the main source for the story of Cycnus (10.189–93).[47] For the
affinity between 10.22–4 and Moschus, *Europa* 115ff. cf. Harrison's
note on 21–50 (but not Fantham).[48] Apollonius' Idas may be counted
among possible antecedents for Mezentius as *contemptor diuom*. More significant, the debt of 209–11 to AR 4.1610–6 (and 212 to 1.542–3)[49].

(i) Archaic Latin poetry. Two cases of particular interest from
Ennius. The debt of 394–6 to Enn. *Ann.*483–4Sk was noted by Serv.:
the horror of battle as a literary inheritance. The detail of Mezentius'
revolting conduct at 8.485ff. may owe something to Enn. *Thy.*297
Joc. (cf. 8.487), though the hint of necrophilic eros detected in the
language of 8.485f. is quite the poet's own.

(j) From more recent Latin poetry, Harrison lists (index rerum,
s.v. Vergil, imitations or use of other authors) Catullus, Egnatius,
Lucretius. Flosculi and turns of phrase, not large-scale imitations.

On the prose sources of the *Aeneid*, I have said enough to try my
own and my critics' patience. The tortures inflicted by Mezentius at
8.485ff. derive in part from Cic. *Hort.* fr.112 Grilli = Arist. fr.60
Rose. The aition of the Vinalia Rustica, kernel of the characterisation
of Mezentius as *contemptor divom* is already at Cato *Orig.* fr.12P (La
Penna *EV* s.v. *Mezenzio*, 512f., H.C. Gotoff, *TAPA* 114 (1984), 196,
203). Mezentius himself is solidly rooted in the annalistic version of
the Aeneas-legend. But fr.11P is not Cato and cannot be (*BICS* 52
(1987), 22, n. 133). This has long been known and to suggest otherwise is merely to muddy the waters. For literary stereotypes of the
cruel tyrant (Mez.), cf. P.M. Martin in *Présence de Virgile, Caesarodunum*
13 bis (1978), 163ff., A. La Penna, *EV* 3, 513f., *Maia* 32 (1980), 10f.

---

[45] Cf. 134, n. 69.
[46] Sulllivan (n. 43), 221f.; aliter, Glenn (n. 34), 130ff.
[47] Cf. Horsfall, *Athen* 66 (1988), 50, *Alambicco* 109, 119.
[48] Fantham (n. 31), 104ff.
[49] Cf. Harrison on 209–11, Fantham (n. 31), 116 on AR 1.1310–25.

Book 11: Rhetoric[1]

Many modern readers will react with an instinctive shudder to the word 'rhetoric', which may seem to carry the suggestion of a windy and probably dishonest prolixity. Dishonest? In the *Aen.*, Virgil knows it[2] and some of his characters are copious and compulsive liars. But that is incidental. It is the infinitely skilled use of rhetoric that makes his speeches such a delight to an audience attuned to the highest standards of late republican oratory. Those speeches vary greatly in their formality but reveal a complete mastery of technique.[3] *Orator an poeta* is a silly schoolroom debating point raised à propos of Virgil by Florus, an old dilemma and a false one, as Homer well knew![4] Epic presupposes speeches, speeches presuppose the orderly arrangement of ideas and their skilled expression. A *Uergilius uates rhetoris arte carens* would have been unreadable in 19 B.C. As it was, though we know nothing for certain (6, 9) about the poet's actual rhetorical training, he exerted an immediate effect on the rhetorical schools.[5] The criticism which Heinze and others[6] levelled at Norden[7] for his 'discovery' of analogies between the 'rules' of Menander Rhetor and (e.g.) the

---

[1] Cf. G. Highet, *The speeches in Vergil's Aeneid* (Princeton 1972); id., *HSCP* 78 (1974), 189ff. (both contain wearing statistics and much formal detail, along with abundant fine and sensitive observations). *EV* s.v. *Figure retoriche* is more useful that (ib.) *Retorica, Discorsi* or *Dialoghi*. Heinze 403–35 remains admirable. Cf. also A.J. Keith, *CJ* 19 (1923–4), 554ff. (taunts), M.L. Clarke, *GR* 17 (1948), 14ff., S. Lundström, *Acht Reden in der Aeneis* (Uppsala 1977).

[2] Highet (n. l.; I cite 1972 unless otherwise stated), 283f., H. Hine in *Homo Viator* (ed. M. Whitby, etc., Bristol 1987), 175, D.C. Feeney, *CQ* 33 (1983), 216 = Harrison, 186, F. Stok, *Percorsi dell' esegesi virgiliana* (Pisa 1988), 32ff. *Uerba uendebam* Augustine makes Virgil say (*Serm.*105.7.10; cf. H. Hagendahl, *Augustine and the Latin classics* ? (Göteborg 1967), 416.

[3] Cf. D.A. Russell, *Criticism in antiquity* (London 1981), 156ff. If Virgil did not use a handbook to remind himself of the approved arrangement of formal speeches (which he knew admirably; for a small and significant detail, cf. my note, *CQ* 39 (1989), 266f.) then he had learned the content of such manuals by intimate study of those texts whose usage the manuals distilled and dried out. Cf. further, n. 8.

[4] Highet, 277ff., *EV* s.v. *Floro*, Feeney, l.c. (n. 1).

[5] For Seneca Rhetor, cf. *EV* 4, 765f., for Ps. Sall., cf. 247f.; Quint. (cf. 9.2.48f. on 11.383ff.) uses V. freely as a source of examples of rhetorical usage (cf. 10.1.27ff. on poetry in the orator's education). See the useful summary in *EV* s.v. *Quintiliano* (Winterbottom). For Macrobius on Virgil as rhetor, cf. Highet, 4; for Tib. Claud. Donatus, cf. R.J. Starr, *Class.Ant.*11 (1992), 159ff.; the rhetorical analysis in Serv. is often far better than Highet (7f.) is prepared to allow. Note Aug. *Ep.*16.4 *Mantuani rhetoris* (with Hagendahl (n. 2), 424). For Virgil in rhetorical education, cf. 251.

[6] Heinze, 433f., Highet (n. 1), 11f.

[7] Norden, comm., index *Rhetorisches* s.v. *Reden, Rhetorisches disponiert.*

lament for Marcellus is quite misconceived:[8] Menander analyses poetic usage to lay down principles of rhetorical arrangement. In Virgil,
the choice of words, along with the rhythm, movement, elaboration,
order, figures, and energy of a speech are neither a tedious inheritance from the epic tradition nor a weary bow to a public over-
nourished on the glories of Cicero, but an essential element in the
poet's technique of characterisation and an indispensable mechanism
both for the expression of ideas and for the development (or destruction) of human relationships.

(i) Venulus, 243–95, reporting Diomedes, 252–93. Diomedes,
placido. . .ore, begins with a solemn *makarismos*, in tricolon: the Latins
have a long tradition of peace and have therefore no business to
begin a war, above all a war against an unknown opponent, whom
Diomedes knows they cannot beat. His *miseratio* of their intentions
implies a coming refusal of their request. The *exordium* anticipates all
the main lines of argumentation on which his majestic refusal rests.
A *narratio* (255–77) of 'ancient history' follows. Virgil uses *Iliad, Odyssey*
and Nostoi-stories as a source of those experiences and prejudices
which colour his character's behaviour and language.[9] Diomedes speaks
as one of the victors (cf. 255–7, 266, 268) crushed by common (*omnes*)
misfortune, by the length, the cost, the toll of ten years' war as a
prelude to the nightmare journey homewards and the Greeks' yet
more catastrophic arrival at their destinations. The compressed history offered (a *percursio*) is shortened and varied by two *praeteritiones*
(256, 264) and three rhetorical questions. The range of time varies
from the events of *Iliad* 5 (275–7) to (271) the present. The *Leitmotif*
of richly deserved punishment, both human (259f.) and divine, for
various outrages (cf. 274 *demens*) is unmistakable (255, 257f., 260, 273f.,
276f.). Even Priam, the Greeks' chief victim, would pity them (259);
to Venulus, Diomedes offers not troops but tragedy: shipwreck, exile,
doomed wandering, adultery, murder, separation, metamorphosis.
Explicitly emotive words are used sparingly. From one of the very
greatest warriors among the victorious Greeks, the bare facts are more
than enough. Virgil has surabundance of material at his disposal and

---

[8] Menander analyses poetic usage to lay down principles of rhetorical arrangement: cf. Men. Rhet. ed. D.A. Russell and N.G. Wilson, xxxiiiff., A. Hardie, *Statius
and the Silvae* (Liverpool 1983), 93, Horsfall, *SCI* 11 (1991–2), 126.
[9] Horsfall, *Vergilius* 32 (1986), 16f., *Alambicco*, 69f., 84, 86.

narrates with extreme allusive brevity.[10] Diomedes' *dextra* had wounded
Venus (277); Clytemnaestra's *dextra* killed Agamemnon (267). Weather
(259f.), geography (257, 260, 262ff.), men (268; cf. 260: Nauplius
implied), monsters (263) and gods (269, 277) are all now against those
who fought against Aeneas and his men. Climactic and most fully
narrated is Diomedes' own tragedy, his loss of his homeland (269f.)
and the metamorphosis of his men (272ff.).[11] Only for his men does
Diomedes burst into open lament (273f.). So the great warrior pleads
(278 *ne. . .ne*) with Venulus, to urge him not to take up arms again,
above all not against the Trojans: with them he has no quarrel, and
however glorious a conqueror he is, he does not dwell in pleasurable
recollection (*memini laetorue*) on old *mala*.[12] It is the vanquished Aeneas
to whom they should bear gifts. There follows eloquent testimony to
Aeneas' valour and character (282–92), not exactly true to the 'facts'
in Homer:[13] Aeneas is as great a warrior as Hector. The two of
them delayed the Greeks' victory for ten years; two more like Aeneas
and the Greeks would have been defending their own homeland.
Diomedes speaks as one who fought Aeneas: *experto crede*. Above all,
Aeneas is *pietate prior* and has therefore implicitly the gods' favour:
the Latins should make peace while they can. Beware—he ends
menacingly—of a clash of weapons.[14] This is a measured, orderly
plea (240f. *et responsa reposcit/ordine cuncta suo*); it is not Homeric, nor
does it seek to be.[15] At times the passion of remembered experience
fires Diomedes' exposition, but he is represented as pleading with
grave authority, with all the peculiar weight of a repentant victor.
Virgil warns us in advance (227–30) what Diomedes' response has
been: the messengers arrive (226) *maesti*. The Latins are already shaken
by three days of funeral rites (210) and many groups have already
denounced Turnus and his war before Venulus' arrival (215ff.), while
others still look to Amata's support for him and to his battlefield
credentials (222ff.). Latinus, who has collapsed, *ingenti luctu* (231), lis-
tens to Venulus *haud laeta fronte* (238).[16] There is no call to analyse
the whole debate in such detail here, but I draw attention to:

---

[10] 262ff.; cf. Horsfall, *Vergilius* 35 (1989), 21.
[11] Already in Ibycus, Callimachus, Timaeus: cf. Bömer on Ov. *Met*.14, p. 150.
[12] On *mala*, Forbiger comments *belli Troiani labores*.
[13] Cf. nn. 2 (lies; cf. Highet in particular); 9 (Homer and the facts).
[14] Cf. Dido at 4.629 for similar language.
[15] Cf. Heinze, 414f.
[16] Cf. Highet 1974, 220 for such indications.

(ii) The ample stage-setting that Virgil offers us. Latinus' response to Venulus' news is introduced with a simile (297–9), which clearly takes up that of 7.586–90 (again, Latinus). The Latins' war-fever here is for the moment not out of control, and the venerable Latinus, in regal array (238) and enthroned (301) comments on the news with relative brevity[17] and scrupulously in accordance (305–9) with the facts as recently expounded. As Servius notes (on 312), he keeps his (justifiable) inculpation of Turnus to an anonymous (and disingenuous) minimum (*nec quemquam incuso*). The relative absence of formal rhetorical figures and the slow pace[18] and gloomy tone, the two formal proposals (316–23; 324–9 *sin.* . .; 330–4 *praeterea*. . .) for restoring temporary calm to the situation whatever the Trojans' decision are admirably suited to an elderly and enfeebled ruler,[19] whose grasp on authority is slipping.

(iii) At this point, though, the debate takes fire.[20] Drances rises to make trouble (*his onerat dictis atque aggerat iras*), having been introduced in a detailed character sketch, necessary because a major speech by a minor character for whose complexity and significance the context has hardly prepared us.[21] We do not yet have the sort of very detailed analysis (cf. 244–8) of all Virgilian speeches (let alone of Drances'!) which will permit us to talk with assurance about his choice of words, manipulation of stylistic levels, use of metrical and rhythmical effects, application of grammar and syntax to rhetoric and characterisation, use or avoidance of particular figures in certain speeches and contexts, and so forth. Drances' whole speech, as has to some extent been recognised, provides a dazzling formal contrast to Turnus' (343–75).[22]

---

[17] 302–35; cf. Highet, 57.

[18] The broken rhythm of 309 (cf. 313), numerous unelaborated dicola (303, 305–7 (bis), 311, 315. . .), absence of syntactical elaboration and of bold effects, whether of language, grammar, metre, or rhetoric, the ponderous and conventional introduction to his alternative policies (314f.), the slow formal sequence of *est antiquus ager*. . .*(316)*. . .*haec omnis regio* (320). The concluding suggestion (330ff.) draws upon Roman ritual and Homeric gift-exchange; *pacis* (332) is smothered by formality. Latinus' concluding plea (335) is confined to a single line: its climax is the phrase *rebus*. . .*fessis* (cf. 3.145); the order of noun and adjective could have been reversed but the adjective gives colour to the entire speech.

[19] Cf. Highet, 65.

[20] Cf. 336–41, A. La Penna in *Vergiliana*, 287f., and in *EV* s.v. *Drance*. Cf. Heinze, 377f., and already *Aen*.11.122f., 220.

[21] For the closely comparable introduction to Numanus Remulus, cf. 9.593–7. Turnus (376–7) is a simpler matter.

[22] For the rhetorical structure of the whole and for Drances' exposition of policy, cf. Highet, 58f.; for Drances and Thersites, cf. N. Postlethwaite, *GR* 35 (1988), 123ff.,

While Gransden, in his commentary, is right to look (14f.) hereabouts
for links between the *Aeneid* and late republican oratory, the cases he
cite point rather (cf. 247f.) to the influence of Virgil on early c. 1
A.D. rhetorical schools and the precise instances of *loidoria* cited do
not really belong to the minutely-studied lexicon of late-republican
abuse,[23] though Turnus' loathing of Drances is expressed by a variety of devices (cf. n. 22) which, in variety and malignity go far beyond the crude pleasures of insulting language! Drances has already
been called *lingua melior* (338), *saeuus* (220), and (122), a man of hatred and abuse. Heinze (426) thinks that Turnus' speech, and Drances',
come closest to the formal rhetoric of senate or courtroom. And what
if they do? As tours-de-force, they are magnificent. The Roman public
that revelled in a good speech[24] will hardly have done so less because it was in hexameters! Turnus' reply has attracted much admiration,[25] and even a little detailed analysis (cf. 244–8, Highet, 59ff.,
210ff.). Diversity of age, talents and character prepare us for a different
style and manner. Drances, as intended (342, 354, 376), has roused
Turnus to *uiolentia*, beneath which lies a mutual loathing (336ff.) inherited (Highet, 210f.) from that between Thersites and (notably)
Odysseus in *Il.*2 (cf. especially 241ff.). Heinze (426, with n. 2) is perhaps
sorry that competent rhetorical *dispositio* triumphs over angry disorder. I am perhaps more interested in how Virgil uses formal means
to let hatred and contempt gleam through. Between the death of
Cicero and the battle of Actium, political abuse had, if anything,
coarsened:[26] Virgil here lends art to rage.

　　(iv) It is hard not to add something to my detailed analysis (244–8)
of 378–91: *pulsus ego* (392; cf. the abrupt *quid cessas?*, 389) takes up
Drances' *pulsus abi* (366) and indeed 392 is enclosed by the polyptoton
pulsus. . .pulsum. Though Cicero is much attached to the superlative
of *foedus* (392), it is apparently never used elsewhere—except here—

Highet, 248ff. For the incomplete conclusion, cf. Highet (n. 1, 1974), 200f. Note the
fine point of Drances not naming the Turnus he loathes at 347, Highet, 58, n. 17.
For the physical threats implied by the text at 348, 408f. (cf. 399), cf. Highet, 1974,
215f., Highet, 61.

　　[23] *mussare* (345), cf. Sall. *Hist.*1.77.3, 3.48.8; *fugae fidens* (351), cf. Opelt (n. on 11.390,
247f.), 164, Ps. Cic. *in Sall.*3.10; *uiolentia* (354), J. Hellegouarc'h *Le vocabulaire latin des
relations et des partis politiques.* . .(Paris 1963), 309; *caput. . .et causa* (361), Opelt, 163,
*Aen.*12.600, *Bell.Hisp.*33.3.

　　[24] A.-M. Guillemin *Le public et la vie littéraire à Rome* (Paris 1937), 16f., Cic. *Brut.*198f.,
*de or.*3.150.

　　[25] Heinze, 426, Heyne.

　　[26] N. Mackie, *Coll.Lat.*196 (1986), 302ff.

as a direct insult. But the question that begins at (392) *aut quisquam* lasts four lines, of irreproachably regular structure (so too 396–8). The tension between dignified defence and hatred for the coward who questions his *uirtus* returns in 399. Another abrupt question, taking up Drances' charge (362), and another insult, *demens* (cf. Opelt, 142), given added weight by its setting within hyperbaton at line-end. Thereupon Turnus returns to the systematic rebuttal of Drances' allegations.[27] The Trojans have lost before: are the Myrmidons' chieftains now (after Troy's fall) afraid of Phrygian (derogatory) aims? Are Diomedes and Achilles still fearful? Turnus knows, and we know, that Diomedes is not afraid, but ruefully respectful (cf. Gransden ad loc.) The Aufidus (and note the artful intertwined order Myrmidons-Diomedes-Achilles-Aufidus)—heavy irony—flows backwards in terror.[28] Lastly,[29] an answer to Drances' claim of intimidation:[30] Turnus raises his sword-arm and Drances flinches (408; cf. 348, Highet, 61), but the threat is feigned, as a climax of Turnus' contempt: if Drances can live with his cowardice, he will not die by Turnus' hand. Turnus' answer to Latinus follows in unbroken sequence. Language and movement are properly adapted to the addressee. At 424, the speaker permits himself a double rhetorical question and only in the climax (438–42) do rhythm and grammar once more reflect emotion: 440, 441, 442 all have pauses at 1S and 442 in addition a bucolic diaeresis.[31] The rest of Turnus' address is measured and mannerly.[32] I would say that only minute analysis can reveal Virgil's variation and artistry, the play between characters, the weight of argument and reply, the expression of emotion, the debt both to Homer and to late republican oratory. The detailed analysis offered elsewhere and here lightly sketched is, I fear, slow work and slow reading, but it represents a grossly undervalued aspect of Virgil's technique, to which Heinze and Highet only in part provide satisfactory guidance.

---

[27] With *nunc. . .nunc*, Serv. appropriately compares 4.376ff.

[28] Cf. Gransden *ad loc.*

[29] For the colloquial initial *uel*, cf. Highet 61, n. 21, Hofmann-Ricottilli, 362.

[30] An *artificis scelus*, a sort of secondary object of *fingit*; cf. Highet, 62.

[31] So only at 57, 550, 682 and here in bk. 11.

[32] Cf. Highet, 62f.

Book 12: Justice and judgement

Of simple solutions to the great problem (or problems) of *Aen.*12 Alessandro Barchiesi remarks: "they tell us much about the ideology of their creators, and very little of the way in which Virgil's text is built up".[1] After prolonged immersion in the bibliography,[2] I should only have put it more strongly: you notice, for example, both that some readers of *Aen.*12 maintain exactly the same position with equal fervour and unaltered arguments after twenty-five years[3] and that the whole issue is (more than ever, strangely enough) heavily politicised, with the result that scholarly discussion is even now obscured by raised voices and intemperate language.[4] It used to be thought that what has been called 'The two-voices school', or, quite inaccurately, 'The Harvard school' was in some way inspired by opposition to American policy in Vietnam.[5] Chronologically, that will not stand,[6] though the force of anti-war sentiment in America and particularly in American universities gave 'Bivocalism' a snug ideological niche. Strangely, one of the Bivocals' father-figures, R.A. Brooks, was in fact Assistant Secretary of the Army in the early days of the Vietnam War.[7] Indeed the further you labour through the bibliography, the more you realise that Bivocalism has a long and rather respectable history *ante litteram.*[8] A new name and a small joke, to defuse the issue and to restore accuracy. No sign of disrespect. Indeed, quite

---

[1] *La traccia del modello* (*Biblioteca di MD*, Pisa 1984), 106: cf. K. Toll, *Helios* 18 (1991), 6.

[2] I have notes on rather over 130 books and articles; brief study of the notes here will reveal what I found most helpful; much, though, is too polemical or partisan to clarify some of the complex issues at stake.

[3] Thus A.J. Boyle, *Ramus* 1 (1972), 81ff. with (ed. id.) *Roman Epic* (London 1993), 92f. or M.C.J. Putnam, *Poetry of the Aeneid* (Cambridge Mass., 1966), 201 with id., *Apeiron* 23 (1990), 17f.

[4] *GR* 37 (1990) 106f., 38 (1991), 241, *Vergilius* 38 (1992), 138: for some extreme examples; I have no wish to increase the heat of the debate.

[5] E.g. K. Galinsky, *Classical and modern interactions* (Austin 1992), 75, G.W. Williams, *What is happening to interpretation of Virgil's Aeneid?* (Todd Memorial Lecture, Sydney 1982), 2, J. Farrell, *Vergilius* 36 (1990), 75.

[6] Prof. W.V. Clausen kindly permits me to print as an appendix (313–4) to this chapter his account of the historical origins of the mis-named 'Harvard School'. 'Bivocals' might be better.

[7] K.J. Reckford in R.A. Brooks, *Ennius and Roman tragedy* (New York 1981), 2.

[8] E.A. Hahn, *TAPA* 56 (1925), 185–212, C.M. Bowra, *GR* 3 (1933), 8–21, = Harrison, 363–77, W.F. Jackson Knight, *Roman Vergil* ch. 7, *passim*, F.H. Cowles, *CJ* 29 (1933/4), 357ff.

the reverse. For let us be clear: in his fundamental text,[9] Adam Parry speaks almost apologetically of Virgil's "private voice of regret". Now it would be mere intellectual hebetude or idle perversity to deny this "voice"'s existence and no attempt will be made to question Virgil's doubts about glory, strength of feelings for victims and vanquished, repeated expressions of criticisms at the expense of heroes and victors, and the like. Parry stated the matter with commitment and elegance[10] and repetition (or expansion) is unnecessary. The question then arose of where, if anywhere, to stop, as the "private voice" acquired volume and authority through repetition and meditation in the helpful context of a nurturing *Zeitgeist*. Why stop at all, indeed? It is now a widely held view that the *Aeneid* is actually a poem (even, the key poem) of the opposition, given a top-dressing of sycophantic propaganda to keep Virgil's bosses happy, both sceptical, at very least, of Augustus and Rome and almost continuously hostile to Aeneas, who emerges as a brutal, bloodthirsty murderer. I am not quite alone[11] in suspecting that such a reading of the text is almost exactly as degrading a parody of an extremely complex original as the complete vindication of Aeneas in a spirit of righteous triumphalism.[12] To return to Barchiesi (n. 1.): "(some of the interpretations proposed) turn out simple and straightforward because they make light of the objective complexity of Virgil's text"; "l'oggettiva complessità" is just right:[13] a straightforward solution will be almost necessarily misleading or insufficient. "Bivocalism" was never quite enough: it implied an "either. . .or. . ." polarity in the end incapable of doing justice to the original.[14] R.O.A.M. Lyne's "Further voices" (Oxford 1987) seemed therefore, in conception, a very promising notion,[15] though in the

---

[9] Commager 121 = *Arion* 2 (1963), 79.

[10] Cf. Barnes, 281 and, variously, P. Hardie, *The epic successors of Virgil* (Cambridge 1993), 19ff., A.J. Boyle, *The Chaonian dove* (*Mnem.* Suppl. 94, Leiden 1986), 85ff., M.C.J. Putnam in *Atti* 2, 245–7, S. Farron, *AC* 24 (1981), 97, K. Quinn, *Texts and contexts* (London 1979), 67.

[11] Cf. P. Hardie, *Cosmos and Imperium* (Oxford 1986), 154, Toll (n. 1), 4, R. Gaskin, *Coll.Lat.*217 (Bruxelles 1992), 295.

[12] P. Schenk, *Die Gestalt des Turnus* (Königstein 1984), 394, C. Renger, *Aeneas und Turnus* (Frankfurt 1985), 105; further bibliography at A. Wlosok, *Res humanae—res divinae* (Heidelberg 1990), 419, n.

[13] This was the presupposition of my *L'epopea in alambicco* (introd., n. 2).

[14] Which is why it is not even enough to view Virgil as a sort of ethical Manichaean, though it would not be anachronistic to do so (H. Dörrie, *RAC* s.v. *Dualismus*, 336ff.), struggling to harmonise his two voices.

[15] However flawed in the detailed execution, *CR* 38 (1988), 243–5. A. Traina, *RFil.*118 (1990), 490–9.

end too many of those voices seemed to be saying exactly the same thing! The *Aeneid* is most certainly—at least in part—a poem about the *respublica* (cf. n. 30) and therefore, even if you are not a convinced follower of reception-theory,[16] you soon realise that, almost inevitably, modern reactions—and that remains true even in our own post-ideological era—will be at least to some degree politicised. Those who in reaction attempt a reading in terms of ancient, not modern values incur the label of 'New Augustans' and occupy ground perhaps rather more pregnable than they suspect (introduction, p. xi; vd. infra, n. 21 and 206ff.).

In a delightful passage, L.P. Wilkinson[17] invites us to "imagine the scene at Atella in the summer of 29. Octavian. . .on the eve of celebrating his triple triumph is sitting for the fourth successive day listening to the *Georgics* being read. . .". It is not altogether an idle fantasy to reapply the invitation to the first reading, twelve years later (ch. 1, n. 131), of the edited *Aeneid*. Augustus, Varius, Maecenas, Horace were surely present; perhaps even Propertius. We have no idea who the readers were. But we do know a little of Augustus' reactions to *tuae. . .Aeneidos* and its *felix. . .auctor*, as Ovid sourly called them (*Tr.*2.533) (cf. 21, n. 101, 252, n. 30), and Peter White has reminded us recently of Maecenas' active part in the first debates on literary and rhetorical problems raised by the new epic;[18] Horace, in *CS* and *Carm.*4, fell eagerly upon the *Aen.* as a source for themes and language.[19] But what if Bivocalism in its crudest form had in truth been from the very first that very mode of reading the poem best suited to all the text's manifold and complex implications and indications, and even to the author's (unrecoverable!) intentions? This "attack on Augustan propaganda"[20] rolls on, for several days, and we might wonder whether the entire audience missed the point (because they preferred to out of embarrassment, or because of their intellectual incapacity!), whether they sat in silent perplexity or rage, or whether indeed Augustus snarled at Varius that a sound man

---

[16] Cf. Glei (introd., n. 1), 17ff., Wlosok (n. 12), 417, n. 28 for some interesting caveats; even to Jauss, not quite all new interpretations are necessarily valid or legitimate.

[17] *The Georgics of Virgil* (Cambridge 1969), 110f.

[18] *CPhil.*86 (1991), 138. No answer from C.O. Brink, in *Homage to Horace* (Oxford 1995), 276ff.

[19] Cf. Buchheit, 171, n. 92 (e.g.).

[20] S. Farron's phrase. *AC* 23 (1980), 53; cf. id., 24 (1981), 97, 25 (1982), 136, Boyle (n. 10), 110, P. Burnell, *GR* 34 (1987), 186f. Contrast Gaskin (n. 11), 311,

would have burned the text after all, while as it was a decade at
(e.g.) Tomi might help a witless editor to think straighter, only to be
begged off by an emollient Horace. That scene, though, does not
square with the known facts here summarised: however Lucan and
the critics cited by way of example in n. 10 read the *Aeneid*, such a
reading should be recognised as the product of tormented critical
and historical development: extreme Bivocalism is clearly anti-historical, though to many modern readers that matters not one bit!

This is not the prelude to a wallow in New Augustanism:[21] I shall
consider "Augustan values" as only one of seven possible sets of criteria
by which Virgil might have expected the *Aeneid* to be judged and we
shall see (206ff.) that, though these values are particularly popular as
starting-points for an 'objective' or 'historically valid' critique, their
proponents do come up with sharply conflicting answers. That, if
you view the emotions which *Aen*.12 still inspires *sine ira et studio*, is
quite funny: far more important (and in itself an ample justification
for the minute historical study of the relevant texts) is the discovery
of developments, ambiguities and inconsistencies in Roman views of
war, peace, mercy, justice, revenge and empire. Nothing new here
to historians; Latinists seem to have taken longer to recognise the
problem and what it might imply.

We must assume (for we cannot prove it) that the *Aeneid* ends in
pretty much the way Virgil wanted it. A difficult, complex, allusive,
challenging end: we should have expected nothing less. The last line
repeats 11.831 (death of Camilla); Virgil had in mind the deaths of
Patroclus (*Il*.16.856f.) and Hector (22.361f.); he both omits and adds:
note γοόωσα > *gemitu*, while the misunderstood *indignata* (cf. 215) is a
highly significant addition. Nor does Virgil leave the ending quite as
abrupt and open as might at first sight appear: we do, after all, know
pretty much what happens next, from the *Aeneid* itself.[22] Critics of
Aeneas have, for that matter, wondered why he could not have spared

---

S.F. Wiltshire, *Vergilius* Suppl. 2 (Vergilian Bimillenary Lectures 1982), 134.

[21] A term not always clearly understood, whether by friends or by foes: cf.
K. Galinsky, in (ed. K.G.) *The interpretation of Roman poetry* (Frankfurt 1992), 9, 16ff.,
contra, R. Thomas, *Vergilius* 36 (1990), 66.

[22] Cf. *Aen*.1.264–6, 2.783f., 6.763–5, 7.99, 12.834ff., G.E. Duckworth *Foreshadowing
and Suspense* (diss. Princeton 1933), 34, C. Springer, *CJ* 82 (1986/7), 310ff., W. Kühn,
Götterszenen bei Vergil (Heidelberg 1971), 166f., R. Jenkyns, *JRS* 75 (1985), 74,
G. Thome, *Gestalt und Funktion des Mezentius* (Frankfurt 1979), 278. S. Farron, *AC* 25
(1982), 136–41 is not recommended. F. Cairns, *Virgil's Augustan Epic* (Cambridge
1989), 212–4 overestimates the importance of *Od*. for the end of the *Aen*.

Turnus, who (12.937) offers him Lavinia (and, by implication—
cf. 209f.—the succession to Latinus' throne.)[23] The question is perhaps not quite as theoretical or as trivial as might at first sight appear. Turnus' surrender has (cf. 210) to be evaluated as a clever,
even a dangerous piece of rhetoric and not as necessarily honest and
factually reliable statement. Real heroes (a title Turnus' admirers would
hardly wish to see denied him) do not, upon rejection or defeat, go
off to live in respectable retirement, deprived of their bride and of
their (second) throne. Virgil is still nearer Homer than Trollope, and
from Lavinium to Ardea is an easy walk: the 'peaceful solution' that
Virgil 'rejected' is palpably absurd. It is at this point hardly relevant
that Turnus may be 'in love' with Lavinia, and (more clearly) Lavinia
with Turnus.[24] Turnus' ardent suit (7.55f.), abetted by Amata (7.56f.)
is likewise not to the point: Virgil has gone to the greatest lengths to
tell us, explicitly (cf. 210) that Lavinia is Aeneas' destined bride by
divine dispensation; if Turnus seems to forego his claim, that hollow
and senseless offer should be seen in its context: Turnus had never,
exactly, kept a strict regard for truth;[25] now, as he pleads for his life,
we cannot assume that he speaks as a committed convert to veracity.

There are three ancient texts which show that the Romans themselves found at least a degree of difficulty in the ending of the *Aeneid*
(and that in turn suggests that the topic was rather more widely
discussed).[26] These three texts should be seen in the context of a
taste for debate on (apparently or really) controversial literary topics,[27] which in turn fits admirably into a wider context of enthusiastic
discussion of apparently insoluble ethical or literary problems.[28] Rec-

---

[23] R.A. Hornsby, *Patterns of action* (Iowa City 1970), 139, W.S. Anderson, *Art of the Aeneid* (Englewood Cliffs 1969), 99, Thome (n. 22), 321.

[24] R.O.A.M. Lyne, *GR* 30 (1983), 55–60, = McAuslan, 157–62.

[25] Highet, 284ff., Buchheit, 102ff., H.J. Schweizer, *Vergil und Italiien* (Aarau 1967), 26ff.

[26] I find it remarkable that though St. Augustine (by far the most intelligent ancient reader of the *Aen.* whose remarks survive!) criticises Aeneas' conduct towards Dido (*Civ.*9.4), there is no word of reproach at the expense of *Aen.*10 or 12: cf. H. Hagendahl, *Augustine and the Latin classics* 2 (Göteborg 1967), 423, with 1.321ff., for a full list of the relevant passages.

[27] For Hom., cf. Plut. *Quomodo adulescens* 8, H.-I. Marrou, *Hist. de l'éducation* 1 (ed. 6, Paris 1981), 253f.; for the place of Hom. in Greek education, cf. R. Pfeiffer, *History of classical scholarship* 1 (Oxford 1968), 69f., W.J. Verdenius, *Homer, educator of the Greeks* (*Med.kon.Ned.Akad.Wet.Lett.*33.5, Amsterdam 1970), 6ff. Before Virgil, cf. Ateius Philologus, *An amauerit Didun Aeneas*, test. 9, *GRF*, O. Ribbeck, *Prolegomena* (Leipzig 1866), 188f., Horsfall, *JHS* 99 (1979), 35, n. 65; cf. too Florus' *Uergilius orator an poeta.*

[28] Almost the whole of Cic. *Off.*3 contains 'problems' of this kind; on the antecedents

ent debate on *Aeneid* 12 shows how relatively little progress has been made: the conceptual step from an *aut. . .aut. . .*dilemma to the complex analysis of a complex problem has apparently proved too hard for many. So:

(i) Serv. on 12.940 *omnis intentio ad Aeneae pertinet gloriam: nam et ex eo quod hosti cogitat parcere, pius ostenditur, et ex eo quod eum interimit, pietatis gestat insigne: nam Euandri intuitu Pallantis ulciscitur mortem.*

(ii) TCD on 12.947–9 *recte immotus est; praestabat quippe interfectori Pallantis negare uitae beneficium quam inultam relinquere familiaris mortem. ecce seruata est in persona Aeneae pietas, qua uolebat ignoscere, seruata religio Pallanti, quia interfector eius non euasit.*

(iii) Lact. *Inst.*5.10.1–11, in particular §9 *quisquamne igitur hunc putet aliquid in se uirtutis habuisse, qui et furore tamquam stipula exarserit et manium patris per quem rogabatur oblitus iram frenare non quiuerit? nullo igitur modo pius, qui non tantum non repugnantes, sed etiam precantes interemit.*[29]

The careful reader might even feel free to say that Virgil had here invited an ethical reaction: that much is indicated by the poet's lexical choice in 12.930–52, lines particularly rich, as we shall see, in terms which have acquired moral weight, resonance and associations through fairly frequent use in significant contexts earlier in the poem (cf. 211–5). The two pagan critics just cited, along with Lactantius, had noticed as much: battle-lines are indeed already drawn up in an almost modern manner (cf. Wlosok, n. 29), and the Christian ethic is as irrelevant (or relevant, depending on your view of the limits of 'reception-theory') to the end of the *Aeneid* as is the dominant liberal outlook of academics in the period 1965–85. It may be as well to add that a complex (complex, I stress, not ambiguous) end is not just suitable but positively essential to a poem not 'merely' epic but actual and political in character. The *Aeneid* is *inter alia* about the state, Rome, justice, morality, government, the ethics of war and punishment.[30] By Virgil's day, that was how the *Iliad* was often read,[31] not

---

of Sen. *Contr.*, cf. J. Fairweather, *Seneca the Elder* (Cambridge 1981), 104ff.

[29] Wlosok (n. 12), 440–4, = *2000 Jahre Vergil* (*Wolfenbütteler Forschungen* 24, 1983), 65–7. We must recall that Lact. writes in the context of an attack on Virgil, not on Aeneas. Note sections 5–6 on the same chapter for Aen. and human sacrifice.

[30] Boyle (n. 10), 85, D.J. Stewart, *Antioch Review* 32 (1972–3), 649–64, Toll (n. 1), 3ff., Wiltshire (n. 10), 118ff., Perret (ed. Budé) 3.259. It might, in particular, be appropriate to compare the debates about Julius Caesar's rule and death; cf. *Philosophia Togata* ed. M. Griffin, J. Barnes (Oxford 1989), index s.v. Julius Caesar. Assassination.

[31] Verdenius (n. 27), 14f., P. Hardie, *JHS* 105 (1985), 15ff., Cairns (n. 22), *passim*,

indeed as a gigantic ethical 'puzzle',[32] but as a text deserving of close discussion because rich in references both implicit and explicit to conduct both deplorable and praiseworthy. We shall see very shortly that the philosophers' discussions of anger are firmly anchored in examples derived from Homer: we know, of course, that Virgil's *Iliad* is not merely the Greek words of any given passage, but the entire tradition of imitation and exegesis (both scholarly and philosophical) dependent therefrom. It is becoming increasingly clear that Virgil knew well the main lines of philosophical exegesis of *Iliad* and *Odyssey*.[33]

In the *Aeneid*, the choice of starting-point for an ethically defensible reading of the end of bk. 12 is a good deal more complex than might appear from a reading of some of his critics,[34] though the ethical 'solution' will appear in the end a good deal simpler, I suspect, than the emotional one. Virgil was in practice well able to indicate his sources when he wished to do so,[35] or to hint at the 'key' in which he wished a given passage to be read,[36] but I do not believe that to have been the case at the end of bk. 12, nor have I read any convincing demonstration that one particular 'key' was necessarily to be preferred to all others. It is not my wish or intention to complicate the issue, but I find seven 'keys' in which it is not *prima facie* unreasonable to try to read the end of the *Aeneid*. They are none of them clearly mandatory or wildly unlikely and if I and others[37] have not forced the sources, they provide conflicting solutions. Those 'keys' are: (i) Homer; (ii) Plato; (iii) Aristotle; (iv) Stoicism; (v) Epicureanism; (vi) traditional Roman values; (vii) 'the Augustan ethic'. They must all be surveyed, briefly, and we might start with the two

---

Philodemus, *De bono re* (ed. T. Dorandi, Napoli 1982), 29.5ff., O. Murray, *JRS* 55 (1965), 161ff.

[32] *Il.*24 ed. C.W. Macleod, 6f., N.J. Richardson, *CQ* 30 (1980), 271, J. Griffin, *Homer on life and death* (Oxford 1980), 118.

[33] Wlosok (n. 12), 392–402 = *Filologia e forme letterarie. Studi. . .Della Corte* 2 (Urbino 1987), 517–27, Hardie (n. 11), 340ff. *et passim*, R.R. Schlunk, *The Homeric scholia and the 'Aeneid'* (Ann Arbor 1974), 1ff.

[34] It is a great merit of G.K. Galinsky's vigorously polemical paper, *AJP* 109 (1988), 321ff. that the author does attempt a defence of his position along several distinct lines of ethical evaluation.

[35] Cf. ch. 7 of my *L'epopea in alambicco*.

[36] Many of the demonstrations of allegorical interpretation offered by Hardie (n. 11) are at least to some degree correct; so that, we must conclude, was how Virgil thought!

[37] Some strictures will be unavoidable; several presentations of the 'evidence' are insufficient, and, upon examination, inexcusably partisan.

that provide a pretty clear-cut answer; that very simplicity may be enough to diminish their credibility as solutions!

(iv) *Stoicism*.[38] While Aeneas' refusal to relent in the face of Turnus' plea is itself in keeping with the Stoics' objection to pity,[39] that in itself is evidently an argument absent from the text of the *Aeneid*. More to the point, anger is vigorously deplored by the Stoics, in frequent polemic with the Peripatetics; it is not even a necessary or desirable quality for the warrior.[40] Were the *Aeneid* an epic written overwhelmingly in one single philosophical key[41] and were its hero clearly to be judged by Stoic values, then this chapter could end here. "There is considerable evidence that, to many Romans, Stoicism as a moral philosophy seemed like a rationalisation of (or a poor substitute for) Rome's own traditional ideals".[42] Hence much apparent Stoicism in the *Aeneid* but remarkably little explicit, thought-out Stoic language and ethical values in the text.[43] Had Virgil wished to construct a Stoicising epic, he was clearly competent to do so, and it is therefore clearly of some moment that in practice he did not. To invoke Stoic ethics in condemnation of Aeneas[44] seems methodologically infelicitous; other possibilities should be investigated before the hero is condemned as a failure or a brute.

(vi) *'Traditional Roman values'*. I refer to the heavily elaborated and romanticised history of the whole period covered by Livy's first decade. Study of anachronisms in the *Aeneid* shows that late republican antiquarian work on the life and conduct of the period was of real importance to Virgil.[45] Several attempts have recently been made[46] to associate Aeneas with patterns of behaviour attributed to 'old Roman heroes' in late republican historiography; such stories were

---

[38] A.L. Motto, *Seneca sourcebook* (Amsterdam 1970), Cairns (n. 22), 78f., Wlosok (n. 12), 430–2, Galinsky (n. 34), 337–9, Putnam (n. 3, 1990), 13ff., M. Erler, *Grazer Beitr.*18 (1992), 113f., id., *MH* 49 (1992), 191, R.O.A.M. Lyne, *CQ* 33 (1983), 189f.

[39] Galinsky (n. 34), 339.

[40] Cic. *TD* 4.43, 49, *Off.*1.62, Sen. *Ira* 1.9.1, 12.5, 17.1.

[41] Lyne (n. 38), on which cf. Galinsky (n. 34), 337.

[42] Griffin in Griffin/Barnes (n. 30), 8.

[43] Cf. 151f. on bk. 6; cf. too Griffin in Griffin/Barnes (n. 30), 11f. on the dichotomy of philosophy and conduct.

[44] So e.g. Putnam and Lyne (n. 38).

[45] Cf. *EV* s.v. *Anacronismi* (Horsfall), id. *L'epopea in alambicco*, 136ff., *Athen.*78 (1990), 524.

[46] Burnell (n. 20), 191f., Lyne (n. 38), 188f., Renger (n. 12), 78–81, Thome (n. 22) 273, 328 (on Horatii), G.W. Williams, *Technique and ideas* (New Haven 1983), 223.

also on occasion subjected to ethical comment in philosophical texts.[47]
We have seen (180) that Aeneas' human sacrifice might have been
explicable (I do not say justifiable) in such terms. The same might be
said of the duty to vengeance (i.e. to kill Turnus in order to avenge
Pallas), strongly present if not in Livian narrative (Burnell (n. 46),
189f.) then in the *Leges XII Tabularum*,[48] an accumulation of texts of
very mixed date. Vengeance, however, is equally inherent in Homeric
values.[49] But Aeneas, though overall perceptibly less barbarous than
the *Iliad*'s fiercest bloodletters, is nevertheless not to be burdened
with an irrelevant and inappropriate degree of moral sensibility. In
war, he is not a gentle philosopher who takes up the sword only
with doubts and reluctance; the Virgilian revision of Homeric values
has led too many critics into sentimentalising excess.[50] The Homeric
Aeneas was unsuccessful in war when fighting superior opponents
(who was not?), but Virgil is careful to improve the record[51] in order
to present a militarily credible hero, whose flashes of Homeric χάρμη,
when he drinks delight of battle with his peers, surprise and disconcert
the modern reader (cf. 179ff. on bk. 10), perhaps more than they
should.[52] The post-war Western academic ethic, particularly in the
Vietnam period, has been overwhelmingly anti-militarist[53] and that

---

[47] Cf. Cic. *Off*.1.35 (the Romans spared those *qui non crudeles in bello, non immanes
fuerunt*), 36–8 *passim*, *TD* 4.49f., VM 9.10.1, Sen. *Ira* 1.11, 12 (*ira* absent in the great
commanders).

[48] Renger (n. 12), 78ff.

[49] E.g. *Il*.9.633, 13.659, 14.483, 15.116, 16.398, 22.271, 347, 24.736, *Od*.1.46,
R.J. Bonner, G. Smith, *The administration of justice from Homer to Aristotle* 1 (Chicago
1930), 19ff.

[50] G.K. Galinsky *ANRW* 2.31.2 (1981), 996, 1000; not 'civilised' of Aeneas to act
as he does in bk. 12; M.C.J. Putnam, *Essays on Latin lyric, elegy and epic* (Princeton
1982), 337 = *Arethusa* 5 (1972), 61, C.M. Bowra, *From Virgil to Milton* (London 1972),
84, R.D. Williams, *Aeneas and the Roman hero* (London 1973), 55, id. *The Aeneid* (London
1987), 95, K. Quinn, *Virgil's Aeneid* (London 1968), 20, Thome (n. 22), 322f.

[51] Cf. Horsfall, *Vergilius* 32 (1986), 17, *CQ* 29 (1979), 372f.

[52] Cairns (n. 22) 82, S.J. Harrison, *Aen*.10, xxi; with the needlessly polemical reaction of R. Thomas, *Vergilius* 38 (1992), 139. But it is hardly impermissible to
suggest that Virgil's readers had reactions different from ours to (e.g.) the ethics of
warfare. For robust common sense, cf. H.-P. Stahl, *Arethusa* 14 (1981), 159f. We
may note in particular the inexplicable agitation to which *Aen*.12.554ff. reduces some
modern critics—Quinn (n. 50), 264, M.O. Lee, *Fathers and sons* (Albany 1979), 99,
Boyle (n. 10), 102, Putnam (n. 3, 1966), 174. Cf. rather H.-P. Stahl in *Between
republic and empire* ed. K.A. Raaflaub and M. Toher (Berkeley 1990), 191.

[53] But note the extraordinary merits of J. Keegan, *The face of battle* (Harmondsworth
1978) as an attempt to understand the fighting man of earlier ages from the inside.
R. MacMullen, *Changes in the Roman Empire* (Princeton 1990), 225ff. deserves mention
in the same breath.

may have led to misunderstandings, even grave ones, of (e.g.) *Aen*.10–12. Anchises invites Aeneas to measure himself by the standards set by his descendants (6.806, 888f., etc.) and it might therefore be appropriate at times at least to see what happens if we try to apply some of those criteria ourselves, to see how Aeneas fares by the criteria the poet has himself set. Tentative, experimental historicism to be sure, and only one key, of course, out of many. The results, moreover prove unexpectedly controversial. But that should not discourage us from trying to identify elements of 'archaic Roman man' in Aeneas.[54]

Perhaps (ii) *Platonism*[55] is to be taken more seriously. Plato is well aware of the risks inherent in the θυμοειδές,[56] but the term carries rather too many senses (cf. *Rep*.440E) and thus provokes a degree of self-contradiction: no surprise therefore to find τὸ θυμοειδές also as the moving spirit of noble causes (*Rep*.440DE)[57] and even ὀργή as potentially the ally of reason against desire.[58] No chance, then, to invoke Plato as an outright enemy of anger and of action prompted by anger on all occasions.[59] Anger indeed never was a clear-cut issue[60] and a scrupulous Platonist would—both at Rome and today—have found texts both to justify and to condemn Aeneas' *ira*.

(iii) *Aristotle*. Something markedly Aristotelian has been noted in the characterisation of Turnus,[61] and further detailed enquiry is called for. Aristotle[62] was no enemy to anger, or at least to a degree thereof,

---

[54] For elements of criticism in the *Heldenschau* cf. 144–9 above; for the crucially important 6.852–3, cf. 206 below.

[55] Putnam (n. 3, 1990), 10–2 takes too narrow and partial a view of the evidence; cf. Galinsky (n. 34) 328–30 for a sharply different conclusion. Better, turn to the experts: F.M. Cornford, *CQ* 6 (1912), 261f., T.M. Robinson, *Plato's Psychology* (*Phoen*. Suppl. 8, Toronto 1970), 44f., T. Penner in (ed. G. Vlastos) *Plato* 2 (Notre Dame 1978), 111–6, M.M. Mackenzie, *Plato on punishment* (Berkeley 1981), 133–224.

[56] *Rep*.441A, C (with reference to Homer), 554C, 572A.

[57] Robinson (n. 55), 45.

[58] *Rep*.440AB, 441A, E; cf. *Tim*.70A, *Leg* 731BC, on the noble θυμός, in violent opposition to injustice.

[59] Galinsky (n. 34), 330 well cites Cic. *Acad*.2.135: Plato's complex position was perceived at Rome.

[60] Bowra (n. 50), 16f., Wlosok (n. 12), 433, Galinsky (n. 34), 326ff., Erler *GB* (n. 38), 107ff., Cairns (n. 22), 58ff., 75ff., Schenk (n. 12), 110ff., 201ff., A. Thornton, *The living universe* (*Mnem*. Suppl. 46, Leiden 1976), 159ff.

[61] Gaskin (n. 11), 308, Galinsky (n. 34), 334f. in particular on *odiis* (12.938), alleged by Turnus against Aeneas (cf. 214), and replaced with *ira* by Virgil. Particularly relevant is *EN* 3.7.7f. on the rash man. Miss M.E. Hubbard stressed the importance of *EN* for the characterisation of Turnus to me *viva voce* about ten years ago; there is a lot more work to be done.

[62] Cf. Galinsky (n. 34), 330ff., Erler *GB* (n. 38), 114f., Cairns (n. 22), 78f., S.R.L. Clark, *Aristotle's man* (Oxford 1975), 93f., D. Charles, *Aristotle's philosophy of action* (London

as critics from Panaetius (n. 40) to Putnam (n. 62) have insisted. The ample bibliography dispenses me from detailed discussion and I cite only three passages of particular interest: (i) *EN* 3.8.10ff. on the relationship between anger (θυμός) and courage (ἄνδρεια) in the fighting man; (ii) ib. 4.5.3 cause, object, manner, moment and duration of anger; if anger is fully appropriate, it can even be shown by the equable man; (iii) ib. 7.6.1f. even unrestraint in anger is less disgraceful than unrestraint in desires. Anger and bad temper are more natural than desire for excessive pleasures.

A good deal more surprising is (v) *Epicureanism*.[63] Here again (cf. n. 31), the philosopher turns repeatedly to the analysis of anger through Homeric instances[64] and while anger is, in general, a κακόν (*Philod. Ira* 1.6), a are its consequences (1.22), nor is it (in polemic with the Peripatos) a necessary characteristic of the fighting man (32.16ff.), there is a natural anger[65] which is positively an ἀγαθόν (38.18): that is the anger which derives from a good (38.18), not a bad (38.1) διάθεσις.[66] Whence the surprising line of defence advanced on Aeneas' behalf by Michael Erler (n. 63): so long as he does not act from love of war and vengeance, deplorable even in Homer[67]—and e.g. 12.313ff. suggests that he certainly does not. Philodemus modifies for a Roman public his school's strict dogma,[68] and his insistence on the διάθεσις from which anger arises should lead us to look aside from endless analyses of Aeneas' *furor* and *ira* to the questions of why he is fighting in bk. 12 and to what end. I am not wholly convinced that Virgil is here following his (ch. 1, nn. 15, 16, 50) old teacher, and other possible philosophical allegiances for bk. 12 are here sug-

---

1984), 178f., W. Fortenbaugh, *Aristotle on emotion* (London 1975), 31ff., id. in *Articles on Aristotle* ed. J. Barnes, etc. 4 (London 1979), 133ff., J. Fillon-Lahille, *REA* 72 (1970), 60ff. Note A.'s use of Homeric examples, *EN* 3.8.2, 4, 10, 7.1.1, *Rhet.*2.2.6, 2.3.16, 17. Putnam (n. 3, 1990), 13 is seriously misleading: Aristotle's extremes are ὀργιλότης ('wrathfulness', *iracundia*) and ἀοργησία ('wrathlessness', *lenitudo*); the mean (*EN* 2.7.10, 4.5.1ff.) is called πραότης, rendered 'gentleness' by Putnam in the wake of H. Rackham, the Loeb translator, and indeed by LSJ. But such a mean means very little to English ears; rather the 'good temper' of Ross and Burnet, and perhaps even better 'even temper' or 'equability'.

[63] Galinsky (n. 34), 335–7, *ICS* 19 (1994), 191ff. Erler *GB* (n. 38), 103ff., *MH* (ib.), 187ff. We now have a new text, with comm. and Italian translation, of Philodemus, *de ira* ed. G. Indelli (Napoli 1988).

[64] The use of Homeric instances is very marked: 8.31, 16.21, 29.24, 44.21ff.

[65] ὀργή, not θυμός, 45–6 *passim*, cf. Erler *GB* (n. 38), 117f.

[66] Cf. already Arist. *Rhet.*2.2.9 πῶς ἔχοντες ὀργίζονται αὐτοὶ καὶ τίσι καὶ διὰ ποῖα.

[67] *De bono rege* 28.23ff. and *De ira* 44.23ff. both cite *Il.*9.63f.

[68] Thus Prof. Erler in correspondence; cf. *id.*, *GB* (n. 38), 117, n. 54, *MH* (ib.), 171ff.

gested, but Prof. Erler has done Virgilian studies a notable service by inviting us to look carefully at Aeneas' διάθεσις,[69] an eminently plausible and (cf. 214—effective) line of justification.

Philodemus naturally leads us to take a closer look at (i) *Homer* himself: for the moment, I should like to consider the relevance of Iliadic[70] models to the ethical debate:[71]

(i) the breach of treaty (*Aen.*12.215–317),[72] indebted to *Il.*4.1ff. Agamemnon comments (4.160ff.) on the sacred character of the 'treaty' (3.265ff.) and on the gods who will eventually punish the breach.[73] (ii) Turnus receives a wound that does not remove his power of speech; so too Hector (*Il.*22.328f.). But Hector's wound is mortal, while Turnus is simply immobilised (926–7); whence the need for a second blow and Aeneas' moments of doubt (938–41; cf. 211f.).[74] (iii) Turnus pleads for his life, in vain: all similar pleas on the battlefield in the *Iliad* are likewise to no effect, while Priam secures the return of Hector's body. But that is altogether exceptional and the very nature of the request is entirely different.[75] For Aeneas to have spared Turnus would have been a violent reversal of code and expectations. Turnus pleads by his *miseri. . .parentis* (for Aeneas too had had a father); he invokes Daunus' *senecta* and pleads to be allowed to return home, alive or dead (932–6).[76] (iv) The issue of the return of Turnus' body is a mere rhetorical flourish: Aeneas had already (10.827–8) returned

---

[69] On which, cf. M. Erler, *GB* (n. 38), 119f., Indelli on *Ira* 2.15, A. Grilli in *Syzetesis* (*Studi M. Gigante*) (Napoli 1983), 93ff.

[70] For *Od.*, cf. n. 22, G.N. Knauer, *ANRW* 2.31.2 (1981), 887. On *Aen.*12 and *Il.*, cf. A. Traina, *EV* s.v. *Turno*, Barchiesi (n. 1), 91–122, Galinsky (n. 34), 340–8; K.C. King, *MD* 9 (1982), 31–55 is acute, but overly ideologised.

[71] The bibliography is particularly vast, but Virgilian scholars have usually been more assiduous in their pursuit of specific models, than in their study of the *Iliad*'s code of behaviour (but see Barchiesi (n. 70), 96). Those who write on *Aen.*12 should re-read the *Iliad* more often!

[72] An outrage to Aeneas (12.313–7, cf. 494–6) and in Roman eyes: cf. Galinsky (n. 50), 993, n. 27, (n. 34), 323, citing Serv. on 12.949, *ad rupti foederis ultionem*, Schenk (n. 12), 173f., W.R. Johnson, *CJ* 60 (1964–5), 362, Gaskin (n. 11), 297, Stahl (n. 52, 1990), 188f.

[73] Cf. G.S. Kirk's comm. on 4.158f., with further bibliography.

[74] Cf. Traina (n. 70), 333, Barchiesi (n. 1), 108f.

[75] Cf. Barchiesi (n. 1), 110–2, with good bibliography, C. Phillipson, *International law and custom* 2 (London 1911), 259f., T.D. Seymour, *Life in the Homeric age* (London 1907), 613, B. Fenik, *Typical battle-scenes* (*Hermes Einzelschr.* 21, Wiesbaden 1968), 82f., J. Gould, *JHS* 93 (1973), 80f. Prisoners might once have been spared, even by Achilles (6.43, 11.112, 21.99), but that was business.

[76] Compare 12.43f.: Latinus' plea to Turnus in similar terms rejected outright, Galinsky (n. 34), 341.

Lausus' corpse, unstripped.[77] Turnus envisages the possible return of his own corpse, *spoliatum lumine* (936), a phrase which Virgil reverses brilliantly in Aeneas' *spoliis indute meorum* (947).[78] Turnus' prayer reflects Hector's (22.253ff., cf. 338ff.). However, neither Turnus nor the reader is invited to imagine that Aeneas would ever refuse to yield his corpse for burial, even though Turnus' wearing of Pallas' baldric reflects Hector's abuse of Patroclus' armour. Threats and brutal vaunts aside (e.g. *Il*.21.122, 184), actual refusal to return a body for burial[79] is a wilful and cruel reversal of the 'norm' in the *Iliad* (Achilles after Patroclus' death, leading up to Achilles and Hector's corpse) and may even (15.350) be threatened as a punishment.[80] We realise now that the roles of Hector and Achilles are divided between both Aeneas and Turnus, but have not (yet) found reason to condemn the victorious Aeneas because, as victor, for however brief a space, he is perforce Achillean.[81] (v) The plea 'by your father' is perhaps more complex and rewarding. Virgil has in mind both Hector to Achilles (failed: 22.338–343; cf. 421) and Priam to Achilles (24.486–506; cf. 467, 507: successful). Thus he creates an ambiguous expectation; there are no 'unwritten rules' inherited from Homer to influence the issue.[82] (vi) Aeneas hesitates (12.938–40): that is a startling novelty and we have no literary presuppositions as to where it may lead us.[83] Aeneas weighs

---

[77] Harrison notes a similar generous act on Achilles' part, *Il*.6.416f.

[78] Barchiesi (n. 1), 117.

[79] Not present at 15.348–51 (e.g.) or 11.452–4, where vd. Hainsworth's comm.

[80] Cf. *Il*.7.78 and 82, 334f. and 408. On Hector's corpse (24.114f., 135f.) Achilles' obduracy reflects in part the length and bitterness of the fight (cf. 17.125f.) over Patroclus' corpse), cf. Griffin (n. 32) 44–9, C. Segal, *The theme of the mutilation...Mnem.* Suppl. 17, Leiden 1971), 30, J. Redfield, *Nature and culture in the Iliad* (Chicago 1975), 183–6, N.R.E. Fisher, *Hybris* (Warminster 1992), 180f. (who does not distinguish between the cruel boast and the actual, calculated denial). Contrast the many unburied lesser warriors of the *Il.*, Griffin (n. 32), 137f. Cf. further S. Farron, *AC* 29 (1986), 69–83.

[81] Aeneas, we have seen (n. 22), will not live long after the end of the *Aen.*; so already, and repeatedly, Achilles (*Il*.24, ed. C.W. Macleod, 10, M. Edwards, comm. on *Il*.17–20, 7f.). On the use of both Achilles and Hector as models for both Turnus and Aeneas, cf. Traina (n. 70), 328, King (n. 70), 31–55, J.K. Newman, *Augustus and the new poetry* (*Coll.Lat*.88, Bruxelles 1967), 239–59, T. Van Nortwick, *TAPA* 110 (1980), 303–14.

[82] Cf. Traina (n. 70), 334, Barchiesi (n. 1), 111–7; note (Barchiesi, 113) that the physical details of Turnus' plea (930f., 936, 939) point to Priam before Achilles: cf. Richardson on *Il*.22.338, citing 15.659–66, 24.485–92, *Od*.11.66–8.

[83] In contrast to fervid anglo-saxon rhetoric, cf. the sober evaluation of Traina (n. 70), 334 with sufficient bibliography. Dr. W.R. Barnes draws my attention to Menelaus' inclination to mercy at *Il*.6.73ff. See too now A. Traina, *Poeti Latini* 4 (Bologna 1994), 75ff.

Turnus' affecting plea; Virgil will have had in mind Achilles' delayed reaction (24.509–17) to Priam's. (vii) Pallas' *balteus*, markedly absent from the scene of Turnus' arming (12.81ff.) strikes Aeneas' eye (*apparuit*, 941: what, only now?) as he inclines ever more to mercy. Turnus had stripped it roughly from its young owner,[84] but there is no sign in bk. 10 that he put it on. In considering the armour stripped by Nisus and Euryalus (176), we had occasion to note that Roman and Greek usage in respect of spoils differed sharply. Homeric custom is not quite unambiguous: normally, in the *Iliad*, victor strips victim as a matter of routine.[85] But note both the σέβας shown by Achilles towards Eetion's (unstripped) corpse (6.417) and 17.201–6, where Hector puts on the ἄμβροτα τεύχεα of Achilles, which he had stripped οὐ κατὰ κόσμον from Patroclus. The armour was not a gift of the gods to him.[86] Who *actually* stripped the armour from Patroclus' corpse, however? That remains a real problem,[87] which, however, does not lessen the impropriety of the entirely mortal Hector's conduct. In Homeric terms, Turnus has done nothing worthy of censure or punishment, though (cf. 176) Roman views were very different. The case of Hector and Achilles' armour is not really comparable: it was not fitly stripped (for Eetion represents earlier usage), nor was its stripping Achilles' motive in killing Hector.[88] In Homer, therefore, its real importance lies in providing a pretext for the creation of a new and wondrous set of armour: as Achilles says to Iris, he cannot for the moment fight ἔχουσι δὲ τεύχεα κεῖνοι (18.188). Nor can he bury Patroclus without his τεύχεα, 18.335: that is perhaps the closest link between Achilles' *armour* and Hector's death.[89] In Homer, therefore, the armour is less significant to the Patroclus-Hector-Achilles plot than might be supposed at first sight, while the role of Pallas' baldric in the *Aeneid* is a remarkable *coup de théâtre*. (viii) If we begin to wonder about links between Aeneas' *ira* and Achilles' μῆνις,[90] we should

---

[84] 10.495f. (but no sign that Turnus puts it on). For the scenes on the baldric, cf. n. 130.

[85] Cf. n. 80: a sign of disrespect to be shown to an enemy's corpse, but far short of non-return or mutilation (cf. *Il*.7.78–80, 16.559).

[86] So Edwards' comm. *ad loc.*, comparing 10.439–41.

[87] Cf. Edwards on 17.126–39.

[88] Cf. 22.323; it is not ever spelled out that Achilles saw the armour as he dealt the death-blow, though it is implied (321).

[89] Not, despite 17.693, 18.131f., in the forefront of Achilles' thoughts.

[90] Cf. J. Griffin, *JHS* 106 (1986), 43, Fisher (n. 80), 151, Redfield (n. 80), 11–7 *et passim*, Galinsky (n. 34), 342–4.

do well to pause long enough to recognise that while anger, however expressed, is a fundamental element in Achilles' very nature, *ira*, which is anyway a term with its own set of (very different) resonances,[91] is by no means a continuous or inherent feature of Aeneas', but rather one which Virgil attributes to him in precise and particular circumstances, which will receive (214) more detailed discussion.

The last set (vii) of criteria by which Aeneas' behaviour might reasonably be judged we may loosely call '*Augustan values*'. What their bearing upon the end of bk. 12 might be has itself become a matter for academic controversy:[92] if the spiritual heirs of Timagenes and the latter-day admirers of the *princeps* are still, after two millenia, at loggerheads, that is amusing, even significant, but I question whether it really advances our understanding of the end of the *Aeneid*. Too often, the evidence has been excerpted or surveyed in part and with partiality, to prove a case. It was therefore particularly welcome to see G. Thome's remarks[93] on the two faces of Rome's Janus-head: she notes coolly (n. 93) what can only have been 'forgotten' in the heat of controversy, that (e.g.) both Julius Caesar and Augustus, while they exalted *clementia* as a key element of their public images and exercised it with deliberate policy upon an ample scale, were likewise capable—both of them—of acts of savage cruelty (but see 163, 180 on the alleged "*Arae Perusinae*"). Ancient historians will note with mirth and pity that the point ever needed to be made.[94] It would be as easy (Thome, 325) to assemble a case, based on philosophical texts, against *ultio*,[95] but *ultio* is likewise a key element in the policy of Octavian/Augustus, both against his adoptive father's assassins and against the Parthians.[96] *Pax* itself is a strikingly ambiguous term: a golden idyll or the result of bloody conquest: *paci imponere morem* (6.852) represents imperial menace towards the independently-minded.[97] Much the same, of course, might be said about *gloria*.[98] No need to con-

---

[91] H. Kleinknecht, *Theol.Wörterbuch* (112, n. 11) 5 (1954), 391f.

[92] E.g. Galinsky (n. 34), 340, n. 52 on Burnell, ib., 337, n. 48 on Lyne.

[93] Thome (n. 22), 342, cf. E. Potz, *Gymn.*99 (1991), 260f.

[94] Cf. P.A. Brunt, *Roman imperial themes* (Oxford 1990), 314ff.

[95] Cf. Cic. *TD* 4.21, 44, Sen. *Ira* 2.1.4, 3.2.3, etc.

[96] Cf. Renger (n. 12), 78ff., Stahl (n. 52, 1990), 202f., Wlosok (n. 12), 428ff., P. Zanker, *Il Foro di Augusto* (It. trans. Roma 1984), 21f.

[97] Horsfall, *SO* 68 (1993), 38f., Brunt (n. 94), 315, S. Weinstock, *Divus Julius* (Oxford 1971), 267, and *JRS* 50 (1960), 47f., E. Gruen in Raaflaub/Toher (n. 52), 414, Brunt (n. 94) index s.v. 'peace as *victoriis parta*'.

[98] *Aen.*7.4 *si qua est ea gloria* maintains a position of entire uncertainty; see

tinue: while 'Augustan values' are not always the safe stronghold
against critical disquiet that their proponents might wish, it will emerge,
as we might be now expect, that alleged failures in *pietas*, *clementia*
and the like are not unanswerable charges to be laid at the door of
the murderous barbarian Aeneas.[99] A failure of *pietas*, then,[100] or rather
a conflict of various orders of *pietas*, brought to violent and in many
ways unexpected resolution? Duty to the memory of Pallas, to Evander,
to the claims of the *respublica*, even to his own son's interests against
the claims of pity: we have seen (197) how Servius and TCD answered the question.[101] The poet's technique is not the lexicographer's;
because Virgil does not call Aeneas *pius* after v. 311, that does not
mean that he views his hero as *impius*: read, and re-read, v. 945.
Fuller discussion is superfluous. Or a failure of *clementia*?[102] Key texts
contain what Lyne (192) calls the 'exclusion clause': *quibus **tuto** ignosci
potuit* (*RG* 3.2) or Cic. *Off*.1.35 *conseruandi ii **qui non crudeles in
bello, non immanes** fuerunt*. So too *parcere subiectis* (6.853). Despite
the gestures of 12.930[103] and the plea of 932ff., Turnus' total submis-
sion is not to be thought of as beyond question: he begins, after all,
with the words *equidem merui nec deprecor*, to which Aeneas' reactions
at the sight of Pallas' baldric function as a kind of ring-composition,
in full explanation of *merui*. Does Turnus' previous conduct, we might
further wonder, lead us to take his plunge into subjection as entirely
reliable and credible?[104] "So Aeneas' last act is the killing of a
defenceless Italian after the war is over",[105] inexcusable, if true by
the criteria of Cic. *Off*.1.35 *tum ii qui armis positis ad imperatorum fidem
confugient, quamuis murum aries percusserit, recipiendi*.[106] The 'option' of a
Turnus spared at the war's end gives rise, we have seen, to complexities worthier of Plautus (196), while Turnus' claim to clemency

---

J. Hellegouarc'h, *Le vocabulaire latin des relations et des partis politiques* (Paris 1963), 380f.,
Brunt (n. 94), 290ff.

[99] Cf. notably S. Farron, *AC* 24 (1981), 97ff., Burnell (n. 20), Lyne (n. 38), *passim*.

[100] Burnell (n. 20), 194–7, Farron (n. 99), 97; for an anthology of Putnam's more
extreme expressions, cf. Wlosok (n. 12), 414, n. 21 = *Würz.Jhb*.8 (1987), 18, n. 21.

[101] Cf. *Cic.Off*.3, *passim* for apparent conflicts of *officium*; on ideas of pity, cf. P.H.
Schrijvers, in *La présence de Virgile*, *Caesarodunum* 13 bis (1978), 483–95.

[102] Farron (n. 98), 98ff., *AC* 29 (1986), 69–72, J. Pomathios, *Le pouvoir politique*
(*Coll.Lat*.199, Bruxelles 1987), 206f.

[103] Farron (n. 102), 71f., Barchiesi (n. 1), 108f.

[104] Cf. Stahl (n. 52, 1990), 195ff.

[105] Farron (n. 99), 106.

[106] Lyne (n. 38), 188, W.V. Harris, *War and imperialism* (Oxford 1979), 174f., 263f.

is (as he clearly knows) not strong.[107] In practice, wars, especially civil wars, as this one was (155) did not all end a blaze of general *clementia*.[108] With Octavian's victories at Actium and Alexandria, *Furor impius* ends safely in chains (1.294). The *furiae* of 12.946 are at one level anything but impious, as we shall see (211), and as Virgil lets Aeneas explain (947–9). The poet is not, therefore[109] inconsistent, hypocritical, or concerned to condemn Aeneas by criteria he has himself laid down earlier in the poem (cf. above on 6.852–3). But that does not quite mean that Virgil, and I myself, for suggesting as much, are to be damned as imperialistic *Staatsschweine*: what I called 'Bivocalism' (192) is actually a phenomenon reaching far beyond the *Aeneid*,[110] and inherent, for example, in writing about the *imperium Romanum* itself:[111] the 'case against', after all—in terms of sufferings caused to the subject nations—rests in large measure (for the late republic at least) upon evidence provided by Cicero and Caesar themselves. The very high price to be paid for glory was not a notion limited to Virgil.[112] Though *pro patria mortuus* (or the like) is a curiously rare consolatory (or condemnatory) theme in epitaphs,[113] the theme of rule as a costly burden demanding huge effort and endless sacrifice from *princeps*, administrators, soldiers and the families of all the above, is widespread.[114] The deaths of Pallas, Nisus, Euryalus, Lausus and Camilla are all, in a sense, allegorical of all those others who die young in Rome's wars. Aeneas has to decide how to react to Turnus' plea; such decisions are part of the *onus* of rule and *clementia* is not always the right, or even the politic answer.

We have, therefore, seven possible ancient 'keys' to the problem, sets of ethical criteria which might be applied to condemn (or to

---

[107] Renger (n. 12), 99ff.

[108] Stahl (n. 52, 1990), 202f., Wlosok (n. 12), 428, Brunt (n. 94), 314–6, Hellegouarc'h (n. 98), 263, P. Jal, *La guerre civile à Rome* (Paris 1963), 144–6.

[109] *Aliter*, Boyle (n. 10), 87.

[110] So, most appropriately, Thome, n. 93 above.

[111] Brunt (n. 94), 288–323, 433–46; cf. further, H. Strasburger, *JRS* 55 (1965), 40–53.

[112] Cf. Jenkyns (n. 22), 75.

[113] Prof. S. Panciera confirms that R. Lattimore's remarks, *Themes in Greek and Latin epitaphs* (Urbana 1962), 152, 240 remain valid, but adds Germanicus, *ob rem p. mortem obisset*, on the Tabula Siarensis (cf. J. Gonzalez, *ZPE* 55 (1984), 59, line 18).

[114] Tac. *Ann.*1.4.3, 11.1 with Goodyear's notes, Binder, 60ff., Hardie (n. 11), 375, P. McGushin, *AJP* 85 (1964), 240f., F. Christ, *die röm. Weltherrschaft* (Stuttgart 1938), 134f., 146f., W. Gernentz, *Laudes Romae* (Rostock 1918), 90f., J. Béranger, *Principatus* (Geneva 1973), 185f., = *MH* 5 (1948), 193f., *TLL* s.v. *patrius* 769.11ff. (Tessmer), s.v. *moles* 1340.83ff. (Lumpe).

acquit) Aeneas on a charge of homicidal mania. We have not come up with a reason to prefer one system above all the others and we have discovered that the seven 'keys', when applied, have strikingly varied effects, or are, when operative, markedly ambiguous in their practical application.[115] If, then, we have at least some doubts about the appropriateness of employing modern ideologies or ethical sensibilities for the evaluation of the *Aeneid* (cf. 200) and if ancient criteria turn out too polyvalent or ambivalent for comfort or for arrival at a decisive answer, we are left with little but the text of *Aen*.12 itself and in conclusion I should like to look at half a dozen sometimes neglected details in the last lines of the poem. These lines are particularly dense and difficult: modern 'readings' which appear to rest upon a rather partisan 'pre-selection' of the textual evidence tend, I sometimes suspect, to tell us rather more about ourselves or about our own age than about Virgil.

But first, a word about Turnus, who has had until now rather less than his due share of attention. I am not sure that it is good thinking or helpful strategy to use his vices in mitigation of Aeneas',[116] but we should perhaps look briefly at Turnus' conduct and character (as perceived by Aeneas and by us) in so far as they are relevant to Aeneas' decision to kill him and to our reactions to that decision. Is Turnus a Tragic Hero or an Enemy of the State? The obligation to choose is itself an illusion;[117] the categories are neither mutually exclusive not severally sufficient, nor is this the place to summarise the many recent analyses of the criticisms that Virgil voices of Turnus (see n. 117). I dwell only on two details, which do not seem to have been viewed quite as clearly as they should.

First, Turnus' motives are palpably confused:[118] he claims repeatedly

---

[115] The end of *Aen*.12 is, these days, quite often seen as morally ambiguous: cf. Williams (n. 46), 224f., Burnell (n. 20), 186f., K.W. Gransden, *Virgil's Iliad* (Cambridge 1984), 216. Note the sane remarks of W.S. Anderson (n. 23), 98ff. My own discussion should not be read as attributing moral uncertainty to the poet. The text is so dense, however, that we may at times find it within ourselves.

[116] Cf. Galinsky (n. 34), 326, Boyle (n. 10) 124, Gaskin (n. 11), 299.

[117] See Traina (n. 70), 324; cf. 331 on the change from *superbus* to (930) *humilis* in the course of bk. 12, Schweizer (n. 25), 44–6, Wlosok (n. 12), 284 = *Gymn*.80 (1973), 134f. The 'case against Turnus': Traina (n. 70), 326f., Cairns (n. 22), 75ff., Galinsky (n. 34), 323–5, Thome (n. 22), 290, Potz (n. 93), 253ff., R. Rieks, *Affekte und Strukturen* (*Zetemata* 86, München 1989), 175–95, Wlosok (n. 12), 427, Erler *GB* (n. 38), 108f., Hornsby (n. 23), 139, Stahl (n. 52, 1990), 174ff., Schenk (n. 12), *passim*, a condemnation more comprehensive than helpful.

[118] Gaskin (n. 11), 298ff., Stahl (n. 52, 1990), 195, Renger (n. 12), 20.

to be fighting 'for Italy' (or for the kingdom he hopes to inherit as Latinus' future son-in-law.[119] He is also fighting for Lavinia,[120] with Amata's support (7.56f.) but (cf. 156) against the will of the gods. There is never, *de facto*, an engagement, whatever Turnus may claim[121], and it is ethically quite irrelevant that Lavinia's emotions (and even Turnus') may have been touched. Love, patriotism, or ambition; or, perhaps, indecision or vacillation; confusion, certainly, and possibly a hint of disingenuousness (dishonesty might be too strong). A realistic complexity (call it confusion, if you are feeling honest) of motivation, fascinating in its elaboration and utterly unhomeric. Secondly, and not unhomeric at all, the sympathy that accrues to Turnus from his role as clear military inferior,[122] and as inevitable loser in the much-delayed[123] final battle. From the outset of bk. 12, Turnus' death is anticipated by the lion's wound at v. 5 (cf. *metuentem* 21, *mortem*, 41),[124] but Virgil interweaves his characteristic feeling for the loser with undiminished commitment to the detailed portrayal of Turnus' viti-ated character and unhallowed cause:[125] note even the inconsistency, very human but very weak, between the proud declaration 931 *equidem merui nec deprecor* and his plea for life four lines later.[126] Turnus has in any case vowed his life away[127] and formally it is no longer his to 'ask back'. Long before the Rutuli realise that *impar ea pugna* (216; cf. 220f.) the outcome of the final combat has been implied to the reader (cf. n. 124): a paradox, since that same combat (cf. n. 123) is de-layed, awkwardly, even, and repeatedly. Just as the Iliadic Aeneas was no match for Achilles, so in the *Aeneid*, despite a lot of blood shed, Turnus, unlike Hector, is never built up as an authentic,

---

[119] Son-in-law as successor: 7.423f.; cf. 7.52f., 98f., 268ff., 343f., 359f., 433, 578f., 12.27ff., Stahl (n. 52, 1990), 195f. Turnus as 'champion of Italy': 7.436, 469, 9.137, 11.116, 12.14f., 359ff. Renger (n. 12), 30 and Schenk (n. 12), 311f., 367, n. 59 are disappointing.

[120] Turnus as the fighting lover: 9.136ff.; cf. 9.600, 10.78, 12.17, 80. Oversexed, Cairns (n. 22), 75. Note the implied criticism offered by Aen., 12.190–4.

[121] Cf. not so much Schenk (n. 12), 296 as Schweizer (n. 25), 22–34, Highet, 287–9, Horsfall, *Alambicco*, 102, and far more fully, *RFil*.119 (1991), 188f.

[122] Jenkyns (n. 22), 73f., Williams (n. 46), 220f., Horsfall, *GR* 34 (1987), 53f., Traina (n. 70), 328f.

[123] Traina (n. 70), 332f., D.A. West, *GR* 21 (1974), 21ff., Heinze, 178ff.

[124] Cf. Traina (n. 70), 331, Barchiesi (n. 70), 104f.

[125] Cf. *uiolentia* 9, *arma impia* (31), *nostro. . .sanguine* (35f.); for bibliography, cf. n. 117.

[126] If I cite Traina (n. 70, 334) yet again, it is because his terse objectivity is so rare and admirable. The same point is made more polemically by e.g. Stahl (n. 52, 1990), 195.

[127] Cf. Renger (n. 12), 87ff., Galinsky (n. 34), 324, Wlosok (n. 12), 366, 382, 427.

unchallengeable warrior of the first rank and as such a serious, dangerous opponent for the new model Aeneas, in the sense of that martial equality apparent between (e.g.) Hector and Ajax.[128] Tension and drama are by no means lacking in the *Aeneid*, but they are of an altogether unhomeric nature: we have (by and large) learned not to seek Homeric merits in Virgilian combat.

At that point, we may turn to some details of the final combat:

(i) The gods. Virgil delays Turnus' reaction to the apparition of the Dira: first Juturna (869–86; note in particular 877–8 *nec fallunt iussa superba/magnanimi Iouis*), who departs powerless to help her brother; then Aeneas comments on Turnus' new delay (889–93) and only now does Turnus respond: *di me terrent et Iuppiter hostis* (895). Jupiter, note; the Dira works precisely to his command (849, 851) and it was Jupiter (854) who sent the Dira to warn Juturna.[129] We were never told the outcome of Jupiter's weighing the fates of Aeneas and Turnus,[130] but Juno knows, on hearing Jupiter's declaration (793–806 *ulterius temptare ueto*) that though there are negotiable elements in determining the future settlement in Latium, Turnus' life is not one of them; that is necessarily forfeit. Turnus' breaches of the treaty and of his own *deuotio* have suggested to some that the withdrawal of divine favour and protection is an actual punishment for his transgressions.[131] If that is what Virgil really meant, then the point might have been rendered more explicitly, without difficulty. The ethical argument should be conducted on more solid foundations. As it is, Aeneas puts into effect a decision already agreed between the Olympians.

(ii) The belt; some problems. At Turnus' plea for his life, Aeneas is still *acer* (938), but, *uoluens oculos* (939),[132] he stays his hand. That suggests that *acer* is to be understood antithetically, almost as 'though

---

[128] Boyle (n. 10), 108. Horsfall (n. 122), 48ff., and particularly 53f.

[129] The Dirae are not Furies, though there are similarities of form and genealogy. Both belong within a much wider grouping of comparable divinities (Keres, Moirai, Eris, Discordia, Apate, Hecate). The case against identifying Dirae and Furies was made, neatly and decisively, by W. Hübner, *Dirae im röm. Epos* (Spudasmata 21, Hildesheim 1970), 38, 110; cf. Horsfall, *AR* 38 (1993), 209f. Too often, they are identified without due care and with much resultant confusion.

[130] *Aen.*12.725–7; cf. West (n. 123), 23f.; further bibliography in F. Giancotti, *Victor tristis* (Bologna 1993), 96, n. 87.

[131] Cf. Wlosok (n. 12), 380f. = *Gymn.*90 (1983), 200f., Stahl (n. 52, 1990), 194, Thome (n. 22), 283ff., Thornton (n. 60), 148, Hardie (n. 11), 147f., W. Suerbaum, *Altspr.Unterricht* 24 (1981), 77.

[132] Cf. W.S. Anderson, *CSCA* 4 (1971), 58–65.

acer'. Turnus' plea begins to move him more and more (*magis cunctantem flectere sermo coeperat*) when the belt catches his eye (941 *apparuit*). Virgil is lavish with indications of its effect: *NOTIS...bullis*[133]...*Pallantis PUERI*[134]...*saeui monimenta doloris*[135]...*SPOLIIS indute MEORUM*[136]... *POENAM SCELERATO ex sanguine sumit.*[137] The scene of the Danaids is incised on gold plaques (10.499), that is, stitched to the baldric; the *bullae* (cf. 9.357) draw the eye to the scene between them. Just what the scene on the baldric[138] tells us is far from clear: I should like to believe that Conte is right and that it underlines the untimeliness of Pallas' end.[139] Pallas certainly had been no match for Turnus (10.438): that makes Turnus' rejoicing (500) particularly untimely and his hybris provokes prolonged explicit authorial comment; that unhappy moment in which Turnus *ouat spolio* (10.500) leads him to his death.[140] It is not boasting over a militarily inferior victim, so much as impiety (the belt was not for Turnus to wear; it belonged to the gods: cf. 176); it was moreover an outrage and an affront to Aeneas, not merely personal, but involving Aeneas' formal commitments as head of state (relations with Pallas and with Evander, ruler of Rome; sense of *fides*, of alliances personal and national, etc.). The baldric is enough to turn Aeneas from the brink of pardon to the *furiae* and *ira*: in part at himself; not only had he failed to protect Pallas, but

---

[133] The narrative does not make it quite clear how the *bullae*, or indeed the baldric as a whole, could have acquired the accumulated emotivity implied by *notis*.

[134] Cf. Barchiesi (n. 1), 117, Giancotti (n. 130), 112f., Traina (n. 70) 334. Compare 8.514, 11.42f., 51, 57 to form some idea of the intensity of the emotive effect here. For the level of the relationship between Evander and Aeneas, cf. 10.515-7.

[135] Cf. Giancotti (n. 30), 114; the *dolor* is that felt by Aen., on hearing of Pallas' death (10.510ff.): cf. 3.486, 4.498, 5.538.

[136] For *meorum*, cf. 4.342, 6.717; *spoliis* reminds us that Turnus did not return the belt at 11.91f., and therefore, in theory, Aeneas 'knew' that Turnus still had it! More to the point, Turnus (contrast 10.423, 541f., 11.5f., 224 and perhaps above all, 10.827, where Aeneas returns Lausus' body untouched) wears a belt due to the gods by Roman usage (cf. 176), if not to Evander.

[137] Vengeance is explicitly due, whether by Homeric (203ff.) or by archaic Roman (cf. 200) usage. In the context, Turnus' *scelus* is necessarily that (though there are several others!) of killing Pallas, whom Aeneas had promised (11.45f.) to protect. The *nefas* of 10.497 is of course the scene on the belt, while that of 7.597 is Turnus' contribution to the outbreak of war. Association between the two (Barchiesi (n. 1), 39, Giancotti (n. 130), 109f., n. 98) is idle.

[138] Cf. Traina (n. 70), 330, Giancotti (n. 130), 109f., n. 98, Harrison on 10.497-9, S. Spence, *Vergilius* 37 (1991), 11ff. M.C.J. Putnam, *ICS* 19 (1994), 171ff.

[139] *Gnom.*63 (1991), 192, *Rhetoric of Imitation* (Ithaca 1986), 185ff., Barchiesi (n. 1), 38.

[140] Cf. *Il.*18.131f., 17.201f.; see Traina, 330, Harrison (*Aen.*10), 199f. and notably the detailed analysis by Barchiesi (n. 1), 43-56.

he had come close to a far greater error, that of sparing Turnus' life.

(iii) 946f. *furiis accensus et ira/terribilis*.4.697 *subitoque accensa furore* (Dido) is often cited (parallelism between Aeneas' chief victims!) but not the far closer parallel of 7.392 *furiisque accensas pectora matres*. There, not *Furiis*, for only Allecto is at work, and therefore perhaps not here, either.[141] The idea that the Erinyes of Pallas drive Aeneas to exercise vengeance has a superficial charm, but it is unfortunately a by-product (Foster, n. 141) of the misbegotten identification between Dira and Furiae. Though Farron (*EV* s.v. *Furie*) points to two other cases (3.331, 12.668) where there is potential confusion between Furiae personified and *furiae* (the mental state),[142] we should probably here concentrate on Aeneas' mental state and not on vengeance personified. Is Turnus therefore the victim of Aeneas' homicidal mania? To put it mildly, say the more radical Bivocalists.[143] Aeneas' champions naturally cite those passages where *ira* and *furiae* are exercised in a just cause[144] and invoke the (presumably—cf. 164) righteous anger of Hercules (8.219) in the face of (8.205) *furiis* (perhaps, rather than *furis*) *Caci mens effera. Furiae* can therefore be displayed in a righteous cause;[145] Virgil does not commend the cause explicitly here, and those who question whether his hero can really end up branded as a homicidal maniac may feel he does not need to again, explicitly. Or is this *ira*, are these *furiae* simple, old-fashioned battle-rage?[146] Could Aeneas really not have killed Turnus without it? Was he really so good and gentle that he could not otherwise have taken another man's life? That is not borne out by the text.[147] The placing of *furiis accensus et ira terribilis* provides a more convincing answer: it is the climax of Aeneas' reaction to the sight of Pallas' *balteus* and should therefore be interpreted in that particular context before all else. *Furiae* and *ira* are therefore

---

[141] But cf. J.C.B. Foster, *LCM* 2 (1977), 127, accepted by Wlosok (n. 12), 435; cf. Renger (n. 12), 96–8.

[142] TCD 2.640.25 is not decisive either way, *pace* Wlosok (n. 12), 435; on *furor*, cf. J. Korpanty, *Klio* 67 (1985), 248ff. Against fallacious distinctions between *furor* and *furia*, cf. R. Thomas, *AJP* 112 (1991), 261.

[143] Putnam (n. 3, 1990), 27–30; *aliter*, Cairns (n. 22), 82–4 (but see Thomas, l.c., n. 142), Thornton (n. 60), 159–63, Stahl (n. 52, 1990), 198, Wlosok (n. 12), 425ff., E. Kraggerud, *Aeneisstudien, SO* Suppl. 22, 1968), 22f.

[144] 10.714 *iustae. . .irae*, 8.494, *furiis. . .iustis*, 8.500f. *iustus. . .dolor. . .merita. . .ira*, all of Etruria's reaction to the tyrant Mezentius.

[145] Cf. 10.68 the *Cassandrae furiis* which drove Aeneas to Italy.

[146] Thornton (n. 60), 160, Potz (n. 93), 250.

[147] Cf. 200 for the inappropriateness of certain modern standards of conduct, applied to Aeneas.

the outcome of a relationship deeply rooted in *pietas* and the context thus renders it unnecessary to label them as 'righteous'. Given the context, I think 'homicidal mania' need not trouble us further.

(iv) *Ira*. We have seen that anger did not evoke a consensus of condemnation among the philosophers (199ff.): Cic. *TD* 4.49 presupposes a (Peripatetic) defence of anger in the Roman warrior.[148] So too Hercules (*TD* 4.50): an *exemplum* often debated between the schools; violently enraged in a good cause (*Aen.*8.219f., 228, 230) but only successful after (232) a pause for *ratio* (cf. 8.299, Cic. *TD* 4.50 *neque enim est ulla fortitudo quae rationis est expers*).[149] The fight of Hercules and Cacus is not, we are coming to realise, a simple typological anticipation of that between Aeneas and Turnus.[150] The emotional issue in bk. 12 is immeasurably more complex, and Aeneas' anger, moreover, is quite different from Turnus': in *Aen.*9–12, Virgil is at pains to show it as a reaction to the circumstances of war and to the behaviour of others.[151] A different *diathesis*, Philodemus would have called it (cf. 202f.). The general condemnation of anger found in many modern studies of bk. 12[152] is 'ideologically correct' in its proponents' moral environment but runs foul of too many difficulties in too many ancient texts and theories.

We should also note that *odiis* (938) are attributed by Turnus to Aeneas, but the text elsewhere offers no support to the allegation that Aeneas was consumed by hatred for his victim. Were 'hatred' an objectively attested feature of Aeneas' behaviour, the detail would be of notable importance, given the prominent place of hatred in ancient anger-theory,[153] but, as it is, *odium* belongs to Turnus' rhetoric, and we have no reason to elevate it into a charge to be discussed, proved, or in some way justified.

(v) *immolat* (949), most often, the technical language of religious usage; from 'sacrifice' to 'kill', the passage is simple, but of course

---

[148] Cf. Hor. *Carm.*1.16.10, 3.2.12, Thornton (n. 60), 160–2, Bowra (n. 50), 16. It is not constructive to cite Hor. *Ep. passim* against Aeneas (thus Putnam (n. 3, 1990), 18ff.); we have realised that Stoic criteria will indeed condemn Aeneas on almost any charge!

[149] G.K. Galinsky, *The Herakles Theme* (Oxford 1972), 144f., id., *AJP* 87 (1966), 41f. Wlosok (n. 12), 430–5, Putnam (n. 3, 1990), 30.

[150] Cf. Glei (introd., n. 1), 325.

[151] Erler *GB* (n. 38), 107–10, Stahl (n. 52, 1990), 182ff., Cairns (n. 22), 74f.

[152] Putnam (n. 3, 1990), 22ff.

[153] Arist. *Rhet.*2.4.31, Philod. *Ira* 11.8, Cic. *TD* 4.16, 21, Sen. *Ira* 1.14.1, 15.2, 20.4, etc. Cf. further, n. 61.

'kill' altogether lacks the resonances of *immolat*! At 10.519, *inferias quos immolat umbris*, Aeneas' human sacrifice is couched discreetly in sacral language; that the verb is here re-used does not convert the death of Turnus into another act of human sacrifice (cf. Farron, n. 154). At 10.541, the verb is used of Aeneas' killing of the priest(!) Haemonides in his passionate outburst of battle-rage at the news of Pallas' death, though that rage is no obstacle to Serestus dedicating, very properly, Haemonides' *spolia* to *rex Gradiuus*. Again, a 'significant echo', in the view of Aeneas' critics, by which the death of Turnus is yet further reduced to the level of his 'anti-Augustan fury' in bk. 10.[154] Others read the rest of the line: *immolat et poenam scelerato ex sanguine sumit* (visibly, theme and variation, a phrase coined by James Henry) and even (which is probably going too far) raise the death of Turnus to the level of hieratic execution.[155]

(vi) Victim of an inexplicable neglect is 952 *indignata*, normally rendered mechanically into English as 'indignant'. Traina (n. 70, 334) sees an allusion to the common epigraphic use of *indigne*, in reference to those who die before their time (cf. 6.426ff.). But cf. *TLL* s.v. 1186.47–9 (Bulhart): 'fere i.q. dedignari, cum indignatione recusare, nolle', citing Forbiger's paraphrase at 11.831 (Camilla), *inuita*. This is by no means a rare sense of the word: cf. Lucr.3.1045 *tu uero...indignabere obire*, Ov. *M*.6.555, 12.354. The sense of righteousness implicit in 'indignant' seems therefore to give way to an element of plaint or protest ('non decet', if we turn to the word's origin!); thus, 'reproachful' might seem a more suitable rendering. Even after death, Turnus' *anima* retains the hope that a plea for life might have been effective.

The reader who sought here a comprehensive doxography to *Aen.*12 will, alas, be sent empty away: bits and pieces of descriptive bibliography do already exist (e.g. Burnell (n. 20), 186–8) and bigger in Virgilian studies certainly does not mean better. The reader who came to this chapter convinced of the validity of a particular 'reading' of the end of the *Aeneid* will, I hope, depart with some sense of

---

[154] Boyle (n. 10), 131, n. 86, S. Farron, *AC* 20 (1977), 208, 28 (1985), 29 'metaphorically a human sacrifice', King (n. 11) 44ff. Putnam, *Essays* (n. 50), 306f. = *AJP* 91 (1970), 426f.

[155] Note the curious notion of Lee (n. 52), 103, that the repetition of *Pallas* means that the enraged Aeneas strikes twice! Cf. further, Stahl (n. 52, 1990), 199, Renger (n. 12), 60ff., 94f., Wlosok (n. 12), 323 = *Studien zum ant. Epos*, ed. H. Görgemanns, E.A. Schmidt (Meisenheim 1976), 231, Traina (n. 70), 334.

misgiving: I know of no critical account that quite convinced me and trust only that I have been able to convey my sense of unease. The reader who scanned these pages in the hope of learning where exactly I stand on the spectrum between fanatic Bivocalism and jingoistic triumphalism will, I am confident, depart frustrated and annoyed: these pages were not written with the intent of revealing a novel and long-awaited answer to an extremely complex series of problems, though a sharp eye will perceive that on certain very pertinent issues I do venture at a legitimate position to be taken. No less disappointed will be the reader who, after some threadless wanderings through the labyrinthine bibliography, turned to a big book for the answer. I do not give it, because it is not there. But the reader not rendered dizzy by these convoluted disclaimers will find, unless I have made a hash of things, enough hints at how one might go about evaluating the death of Turnus with some degree of balance (I dare not say, objectivity!), to make a next reading of bk. 12 perhaps a more confusing, and, I would hope, a richer and more interesting experience.

The conscientious reader of this chapter will not conclude that I attribute moral ambiguity or confusion to the text: thus there is an ethical or moral problem to which, or so I have tried to argue, a reasoned answer is offered by the poet. By what criteria, though? In the end, by none of my seven, I fear, but perhaps only by the inner logic of the text, as left us by Virgil, carefully read, and so far as possible, without any sets of ethical criteria, whether ancient or modern! Emotional reactions, whether old or new, are quite another matter. Who was the first reader of the *Aeneid* to weep for Turnus at the end of bk. 12? That is a question of reception-history that I cannot answer to my own satisfaction. I think I know whether or not Virgil wants me to *plorare Turnum mortuum*, to plunder St. Augustine's phrase, or not, but I know too that I may be wrong and that, anyway, is not the sort of question to which the serious reader wants a prefabricated response. Response, or responses? On the page, the *Aeneid* ends with Turnus' departure from this life, climax to an abrupt reversal of expectation; certainly the text does not end there. For the reasonably acute and sensitive reader, Aeneas remains right, as he always was, and Virgil tells us why, or so I have suggested, in much explicit detail, but there is no general resolution of issues and tensions (contrast *Il.*24!), such as to leave us (or Aeneas) emotionally at ease or content.

CHAPTER FIVE

STYLE, LANGUAGE AND METRE

N.M. Horsfall

Introduction

It might seem an irresistible temptation to offer, in place of a critical introduction to this vast and refractory topic ('impossible' according to kind and sceptical friends), yet another essentially mechanical bibliography by topics, re-sorting and up-dating material already available in *EV*, Maurach,[1] *ANRW*, Lunelli[2] and the commentators. But the topic is not quite as moribund as might at first sight appear. It has not all yet been said and there is not a dissertation or 'Programm' on every aspect and detail of the subject.[3] The computer (see above all 232ff.) has made a real contribution to progress and it can probably make many more (see 219). At the outset, I dreaded having to pen a re-statement of things known and am instead delighted to find I can offer some sort of orientation in a reviving field of study. It is perhaps inevitable that the odd receives more attention than the standard:[4] the attentive reader of Virgil is so often startled by anomalies that 'Latin poetic language'[5] is neglected, relatively, and the richly eccentric criteria for in- and ex-clusion practised by the *EV* mean that too often, especially for seekers after the latest research (particularly after Lunelli, ed. 2, 1980, a work amply informed and admirably indexed) systematic progress becomes aleatory. I have tried to break the topic down into manageable compartments and to offset fragmentation by adding some specimens of detailed analysis by way of appendix. To each compartment I offer a brief critical guide, but the reader seriously interested in Virgil's style, language or metre has

---

[1] G. Maurach, *Enchiridion Poeticum* (ed. 2, Darmstadt 1989).

[2] A. Lunelli, *La Lingua poetica latina* (ed. 2, Bologna 1980).

[3] Often only to be found in the stacks of the very best research libraries. Often also surprisingly unhelpful. I fell with joy upon 'The sentence structure of Vergil' (1911): it did not last. I have tried hard not to cite rare items.

[4] Maurach (n. 1), 96ff.; far more detailed W. Görler, *EV*, 2.262ff. (1985), id., *Würz.Jhb*.8 (1982), 69ff. id., in *Vergilius* Suppl. 2 (1982), 48ff.

[5] Cf. nn. 20, 26, 50, 52 below.

necessarily to become a self-taught expert. There are no short cuts, no general guide. Slow reading of a good commentary can help; after digesting Coleman (*Buc.*), Thomas and Mynors (*G.*), Austin (*Aen.*1.2.6), Harrison (10), Williams (3, 5), Page (still, for all of Virgil), and above all Norden, you begin to know what to look for. Terminology is a real difficulty. Some phenomena have never been classified or labelled,[6] for others we use a bewildering range of terms of the most mixed origin, Latin and Greek, Icelandic (Kenning), English (homodyne), French (Enjambement), German (inevitably; much of the hard work was done in Germany). If you are exploring a phenomenon of grammar, syntax, morphology, rhetoric, prosody or metre, the undertaking itself can be relatively easy, if you have the right technical term to start from. But that can be hard to find: Servius, and the *Index Servianus* (J.F. Mountford and J.T. Schulz, Ithaca 1930) may help. Then indices to the commentaries; A. Sidgwick (Cambridge 1903) offers minimal exegesis but an excellent index. That to Henry's *Aeneidea* is in some ways even better.[7] For problems of grammar, syntax, morphology the two volumes of LHS are indispensable,[8] though of course some German is required. There is now (München 1979) a *Stellenregister* which can save a lot of time and effort. For rhetorical figures, you have almost more in the way of handbooks and guides.[9] If the technicalities seem overwhelming, then you have to remember that specialists in many cases use language that goes back to the Alexandrian commentators on Homer; it has to be mastered. If it proves hard to baptise your particular problem, then often enough the hunt for the right name itself proves rewarding. If the technicalities do in the end seem overwhelming, then it may be as well to turn back to a good general introduction to poetic usage, not so much the chapters on style in Jackson Knight or Quinn, nor Worstbrock, nor ch. 5 of Palmer's *Latin Language*[10] as Wilkinson

---

[6] *Maia* 41 (1989) 251.

[7] J. Henry, *Aeneidea*, 4 vols. (London et alibi, 1873–89).

[8] M. Leumann, *Lat.Laut- und Formenlehre* (München 1977); J.B. Hofmann, A. Szantyr, *Lateinische Syntax und Stilistik* (München 1965, 1972).

[9] H. Lausberg, *Handbuch der literarischen Rhetorik* (München 1960, 1973); two vols., excellent index, *EV* s.v. *Figure retoriche, Tropi*; cf. the useful glossary in H.C. Gotoff, *Cicero's Caesarian Speeches* (Chapel Hill 1993). Görler (1985) is a useful starting point for a wide range of stylistic enquiries.

[10] L.R. Palmer, *The Latin Language* (London 1954), 95ff., W.F. Jackson Knight, *Roman Vergil* (London 1966), 225ff., K. Quinn, *Virgil's Aeneid* (London 1968), 350ff., F.J. Worstbrock, *Elemente einer Poetik der Aeneis* (Münster 1963).

(though he only treats a small part of the topic), Marouzeau (still a masterpiece of insight, elegance and good sense), or Lunelli.[11]

Language

Though the *EV* does not offer us an article 'Lessico', the study of Virgil's vocabulary is less comatose than that of some of the other topics touched on in this chapter. Modern research starts from Cordier's book (1939), in several ways not satisfactory.[12] The growth of *ThLL*, the proliferation of computer-based author-lexica, the notable concentration of work on the fragments of Latin poetry in the last few years,[13] the existence of the IBYCUS programme, the presence of many Virgilian words (though hardly ever the ones you want!) in the *EV* make something of a fresh start easier. To the classic study of B. Axelson, *Unpoetische Wörter* (Lund 1945), G. Williams offered a vigorous challenge.[14] To Axelson, 'high' poetry, especially epic, filtered out 'unpoetic language' from a sense of stylistic decorum, while to Williams, the individual poet's choice and the subject-matter in hand were decisive. In 1985, there appeared an energetic defence of Axelson's explanation,[15] which does not, however, deny that subject-matter may play a significant role. R.O.A.M. Lyne, *Words and the Poet* (Oxford 1989), 1–19 *et passim*[16] changes the debate's starting-point and is concerned in particular to isolate significant usages of words that we might call 'ordinary', or, more precisely, 'prosaism, colloquialism, neutral words'.[17] We should never let ourselves forget the tensions between a word's acquired connotations (cf. Lyne, (supra),

---

[11] Lunelli (n. 2), who prints Italian translations of papers by Kroll, Janssen and Leumann with ample updating of the annotation, L.P. Wilkinson, *Golden Latin Artistry* (Cambridge 1963), J. Marouzeau, *Traité de stylistique latine* (Paris 1946).

[12] A. Cordier, *Études sur le vocabulaire épique dans l'"Énéide"* (Paris 1939): see F.H. Sandbach, *CR* 54 (1940), 198f., A. Ernout, *RPh* 3.14 (1940), 143ff.

[13] After Morel, Büchner (1982); soon Blänsdorf (1994); cf. *Supplementum Morelianum* (A. Traina, M. Bini, Bologna 1986), *Index Morelianus* (M. Bini, Bologna 1980), *The fragmentary Latin poets* ed. E. Courtney (Oxford 1993); another commentary is expected from A.S. Hollis.

[14] *Tradition and Originality in Roman poetry* (Oxford 1968), 743ff.; cf. D.T. Benediktson, *Phoen.*31 (1977), 341ff., Görler (n. 4, 1985), 262f. Cf. already A. Ernout, *RPh* 3.21 (1947), 55ff. = *Philologica* 2 (Paris 1957), 66ff., L.P. Wilkinson, *CQ* 9 (1959), 188.

[15] P. Watson, *CQ* 35 (1985), 430ff.

[16] Cf. my remarks in *AR* 38 (1993) 203–10 and those of A. Traina, *RFil.*120 (1992) 490ff.

[17] Lyne, (supra) 7; cf. *EV* s.v. *Parlato*.

39 on the use of *conlabor* for the collapse of buildings) and the context in which the word is found: love-scenes, battle-scenes, narrative, oratory all evoke a different chemistry of reaction. Lyne only begins to explore characterisation by vocabulary in the *Aen.*; there is much more to be done (see below on 11.381 *distinet*). It is when Axelson's categories do not quite work that they become specially interesting.

At this point one might offer a very rough and provisional classification (in no sense a hierarchy!) of the main categories into which Virgilian vocabulary may be broken down:

(1) words and expressions of high poetry. First, inheritances from Homer: cf. Harrison's note on 10.216.[18] Greek epic, let us be clear, moulds much in the inherited diction of Latin poetry. On 'formulae', cf. W. Moskalew, *Formular Language and Poetic Design in the Aeneid.*[19] Secondly, words which belong, provably, to the language of early Latin poetry, epic and tragic; here we have long been at the mercy[20] of Norden's intuitions and Cordier's enthusiasms. About 240 words in the *Aen.* belong clearly to this category.[21] Thirdly, words which look as though they ought to be 'Homeric' or 'archaic', though we cannot quite prove the point! Fourthly, what one might call neotericisms, which may cover exclamations, apostrophes, parentheses, grecisms real or apparent, accumulated plays of erudition, recognisable echoes of neoteric poets (e.g. elements in *Buc.* of recognisably Catullan origin, Nisbet 2f.), literary attitudinising, epanalepsis, some spondeiazontes, metrical plays such as variation in the prosody of a repeated word.[22] Often not really to be distinguished from the general inheritance of Hellenistic poetry, filtered, or not filtered, through Roman heirs of the early/mid-c. 1 B.C.

(2) Prosaisms, unpoetic expressions. Whatever stand we take on the discussion of Axelson's contribution to our understanding of Virgil's lexicon, the careful reader of Virgil (and of Axelson, Lyne, etc.) realises swiftly that the poet had an amazing 'nose' for the character and

---

[18] Cf. Harrison on 10.216 *noctiuago*, with full bibliography, Worstbrock (n. 10), 172ff., S. Mariotti, *Livio Andronico* (ed. 2, Urbino 1986), 21ff., Ennius *Annales* ed. O. Skutsch, 66f. A. Traina, *Vortit barbare* (Roma 1970), index s.v. composto.

[19] *Mnem.* Suppl. 73 (1982); not entirely persuasive.

[20] Cordier (n. 12), 155ff., Görler (n. 4, 1985), 263, Lunelli-Janssen (n. 11), 93f., Lunelli-Leumann (n. 11), 153ff., *EV* s.v. *Arcaismi*, Enn. *Ann.* ed. Skutsch, 13f., R.B. Steele, *AJPh* 15 (1894), 164ff. on Serv. and Virgilian archaisms.

[21] Görler l.c. (n. 20), Cordier (n. 12), 146f., 162f., Skutsch (n. 18), 777.

[22] *EV* s.v. *Neoterismi*, R.G.M. Nisbet, *PVS* 20 (1991), 1ff., F. Cupaiuolo, *EV*, 1.572ff., Lyne, (p. 219), index s.v. Catullus, F. Klingner, *Virgil* (Zürich 1967), index s.v. Lyrismus.

resonance of the individual word; if we suspect him with good reason of a given prosaism, there has to be a reason why. Prosaisms (Lyne, (p. 219), 8–11) may often belong to colloquial Latin but are characterised above all by their presence in prose authors (not *any* prose authors, and specially not those with pretensions to stylistic grandeur). Words, above all, of the unadorned almost toneless clarity of daily business: *gemo, conlabor, uxorius*.

(3) Flat, colourless, neutral words. Lyne, 13: they may belong to any genre of prose or poetry and bear no tonal quality of their own: *sol, uir, herba. agricola, arator* (ib., 145), *tacitus, laetus, uulnus*. Such words may acquire interest through use in an unusual context (*ardentis spectant socios*, Lyne, (p. 219), 23f.). Thus *gladius, expugno* (Lyne, (p. 219), 34), *neco* (ib. 106), *scutum* (ib. 101), *pilum* (ib. 105) *aedifico, trucido*, etc. (125f.: a useful list).

(4) Colloquialisms. Often not identifiable with certainty, and a category to be employed with particular caution (*EV* s.v. *Parlato, Volgarismi*); this is not the moment to enter current debate on the right language to use when discussing categories of spoken Latin. An element predictably more prominent in the impressionist evocation of shepherds' language in *Buc.* (cf. Coleman's index s.v. colloquialisms, and see below on *Buc.*9.56ff.). Their frequent presence in the *Aen.* is therefore the more significant as indication of the poet's manipulation of tone (to which the reader is required to react). Lyne points to *agitator, deludere, lassus, porto*; add *proluit, gyro*, and for *G.*, cf. 1.388–9 and 3.256 *fricat*. Diminutives (cf. *EV* s.v.) are far commoner than Axelson supposed (cf. Ernout's rev., n. 14). Milani expands the list of possible leaps of lexical level (*EV* s.v. *Volgarismi*) and adds a list of exclamations (1.135, 2.289, 7.545, 4.569) which colour speeches in the *Aen.*

(5) Apparent Virgilian innovations: exceedingly hard to identify on account of all that we have lost. But cf. Cordier (n. 12), 144, 248, 276, *EV* s.v. *Hapax* (Salemme), Görler (n. 4, 1985), 263. With little confidence I repeat (Cordier (n. 12), 144) *debellator, dedignor, derigesco, desolo, detono, improperata, infabricata, subuoluere, suburgere* (ex. grat.).

(6) Synonyms. The study of Virgil's synonyms for 'kill', 'die', 'ship', 'woman', 'man', 'shield', 'Trojan' is a particularly fruitful way[23] towards the understanding of his lexicon. But it should not be supposed that the choice of synonyms is necessarily significant: their existence is

---

[23] Cordier (n. 12), 134, 156, 164.

also an indication of the resources of the language available to the poet seeking variation: a classic case is the wood of the Trojan horse: variously *abies, acer, robur, pinus,* not to mention anatomical details and metaphors. But we do need a full analytical index.[24]

(7) Technical language. For *G.,* cf. 90, 225f. there are degrees of technicality not always borne in mind (beware *EV* 2.692f.): Varro writes for rich farm-owners and his language is perforce not ripely rustic. Contrast, oddly, Calp.Sic., who splashes about authentic rusticisms to good effect (J. Moore-Blunt, *AC* 46 (1977), 192ff.). A good deal of work has been done towards identifying legal, sacral, constitutional, military, astronomical, nautical registers in the *Aen.,* though *EV* s.v. *Tecnicismi* is not a safe overview.[25]

Prosody and morphology; metre and rhythm; sounds and alliteration

It is particularly unhelpful to study the forms and prosody of Virgil's lexicon in terms of 'normal' and 'exceptional'. Thus *abiete* (2.16) and *ariete* (2.492) as trisyllables, *steterunt* (ib. 774) as anapaest, *dehinc* as monosyllable (1.131). Variation in the quantity of the first syllable of *Italia* (-*us*), and *Lavinius, alueo* as disyllable (6.412), a list which could be vastly extended with the help of a shelf full of good indices s.v. *prosody.* So too with morphology: *aquai* (7.464), *caelicolum* (gen.pl.3.21), *Thymbre* (2 dec.voc., 10.394), *imbri* (abl., 4.249), *currum* (gen.pl., 6.653), variation between *Achilli* and *Achillis* (gen.), 12.519 *potentum* gen.pl., *mi* for *mihi*, pres.pass.infin. in *-ier*, impf. in *-ibam* for *-iebam*, syncopation like 1.201 *accestis*, 8.274 *porgite*, or *implessem* (4.605), *-ēre* or *-ĕrunt* for 3rd. person pf.plur. in *-ērunt*. Again, the tip of an iceberg; still clucks of disapproval in older books (I suspect because if we had known the dodges, composition would have been too easy!), and they are quite out of place: such phenomena form and had always formed an integral part of the development from poet to poet of the Latin poetic language, though this is not to suggest that there is a linear develop-

---

[24] Cf. F.S. L'Hoir, *The rhetoric of gender terms* (*Mnem.* Suppl. 120, 1992), Lyne, (p. 219) 100ff. on arms (cf. too F.H. Sandbach in *Oxford Readings in Vergil's Aeneid* (ed. S.J. Harrison), 449ff.), dying: Lyne (p. 219), 108–11, killing: Lyne, 106–8, J.N. Adams, *Glotta* 68 (1990) 230ff., 69 (1991), 94ff., Cordier (n. 12), 156f., 164f., *EV* s.v. *Sinonimi* is unhelpful.

[25] H.D. Jocelyn, *PLLS* 2 (1979), 115ff., Horsfall (n. 6), *EV* s.v. *Tecnicismi*, Cordier (n. 12) 103ff., 138ff., 166f. Horsfall, *Alambicco*, 111ff. *CR* 32 (1982), 187, *Athen.*68 (1990), 523ff.

ment from poet to poet in the liberty with which such conveniences are employed.[26] Grecisms, archaisms and novelties all play a part in the adaptation of Latin to the exigencies of a subtle and melodious form.

It is here assumed that the reader has a working knowledge of the Latin hexameter: S.E. Winbolt, *Latin Hexameter Verse*,[27] written for young composers of Latin verse prior to fossilisation, is perhaps the fullest introduction in English to the Virgilian hexameter; for the niceties, the appendices to Norden are essential.[28] For a good survey of the problems involved, with ample bibliography, see *EV* s.v. *Esametro* (F. Cupaiuolo).[29] The effects Virgil achieves[30] vary widely in their degree of intensity (cf. 8.452, 596 for some extreme cases). Many 'effects' claimed by modern editors seem, however, to be merely unconvincing subjective fantasy. We need always to remember a fundamental point, one obvious if you have read Wilkinson and Marouzeau with care, that effects of metre and sound are highly complex: each word—to leave aside for the moment any questions arising out of its semantic 'colour'—has its prosody, its accent, its sequence of sounds, its length, its musicality, its place in the hexameter and its relationship to its neighbours, while each hexameter is a yet more complex accumulation of all these variables in a sequence of words determined within the (surprisingly flexible) limits of metre by factors of prosody, rhythm, euphony.[31] At the end of this chapter I offer some brief notes on how in practice these elements interact: analysis of Virgilian sound-effects, carried to a high degree of refinement by J. Soubiran and his équipe in frequent articles in *Pallas*, is not at all played out, but it should not be forgotten that standards have risen. (Particularly neglected is the play of long and short words).[32] On the occasionally burning topic of metrical ictus and word-accent, I think

---

[26] Lunelli-Leumann (n. 11), 150ff. (= M. Leumann, *Kl.Schr.* (Zürich 1959), 141ff., Lunelli-Janssen (ib.), 88ff., Lunelli-Kroll (ib.), 25, Quinn (n. 10), 375ff., but E. Bednara, *De sermone dactylicorum Latinorum quaestiones, ALL* 14 (1906), 317ff., 532ff. remains fundamental. For morphology in particular cf. Görler (n. 4, 1985), 263f., Jackson Knight (n. 10), 262ff.

[27] London 1903.

[28] *Aen.*6, 363ff.; all refs. are to reprints of the 3rd. ed.

[29] The commentaries of Austin and Williams (I do not refer to his unhappy 3-vol. 'replacement' of Page) may serve as introductions to many of the principal anomalies and difficulties.

[30] On onomatopoea, cf. Marouzeau (n. 11), 26ff., Wilkinson (n. 11), 56ff., and *CQ* 36 (1942), 121ff.

[31] Worstbrock (n. 10), 159.

[32] Marouzeau (n. 11), 92ff.; this is a serious topic; read *Buc.*1.83, *Aen.*6.853, 11.344!

we are in a brief golden age of general agreement: *PSI* 1.21 (*CPL* 11) confirms that if we leave the beat of the hexameter to take care of itself and give precedence to the word-accent in our reading, we have at least a hint of ancient usage on our side.[33]

Discussion of sound and alliteration plunges too often into a *uolutabrum* of excited sentimentality. It was my first explorations of the ancient verdicts on the effects of individual letters[34] that discouraged me from such amiable wallowings in uncritical company. If the ancient critics are so loud in their condemnation of the letter r (and of f for that matter), then *G.*4.71 *Martius ille aeris rauci canor increpat* must have carried onomatopoea to the verge of the disagreeable, if not beyond. And why the accumulation of r's in 7.10 if the sound was so disliked? Assonance ('a certain closeness of sound between two or more words, even when not necessarily in immediate sequence'),[35] alliteration, rhyme, rhythm work together (3.575f. *euulsaque uiscera montis/erigit eructans!*), and it is therefore necessary to insist that the student of Virgil gets into the regular habit of reading long passages aloud with the most scrupulous attention to prosody, metre and pronunciation. For pronunciation, Allen's *Vox Latina* is warmly recommended;[36] G.B. Nussbaum, *Vergil's Metre* (Bristol 1986) is subtitled 'A practical guide for reading Latin hexameter poetry'. On Virgilian alliteration, most commentators offer overenthusiastic guidance. But more careful enquiries exist.[37] The reader convinced that (s)he can explain every case of Virgilian alliteration encountered should question ear or honesty! We must never forget that we do not know with any precision how Virgil's fabled readings of his own work sounded. I do not find it easy to suggest, ninety years after Roiron's large book on *L'imagination auditive de Virgile* (Paris 1908), what progress (precise, concrete, objective) might be made in this field, except perhaps for a reassessment of c. 1 B.C.–A.D. theories (both Greek and Latin) on sounds in general and in particular.

---

[33] Wilkinson (n. 11), 124, W.S. Allen, *Accent and Rhythm* (Cambridge 1973), 345.

[34] W.S. Allen, *Vox Latina* (Cambridge 1965), Marouzeau (n. 11), 17ff., Wilkinson (n. 11), 9ff., *ThLL* (the first article for each letter so far covered).

[35] *EV* s.v. Assonanza, ad init., R.G. Austin, *CQ* 23 (1929), 46ff.

[36] Cf. too G.P. Goold, in *Author and Audience in Latin literature*, ed. T. Woodman and J. Powell (Cambridge 1992), 112f.; cf. also A. Traina, *L'alfabeto e la pronuncia del latino* (Bologna 1973).

[37] *EV* s.v. Alliterazione, Wilkinson 1942 (n. 30), A. Cordier, *L'alliteration latine* (Paris 1939). For statistics, W.M. Clarke, *Lat.*35 (1976), 276ff., N.A. Greenberg, *Lat.*39 (1980), 585ff.; for rhyme, cf. id., *TAPA* 103 (1972), 49ff.

Grammar and syntax; oddities and ambiguities

Much, even too much, attention has recently been devoted[38] to VSD 44:

M. Vipsanius a Maecenate eum suppositum appellabat nouae caco-
zeliae repertorem, non tumidae nec exilis, sed ex communibus uerbis
atque ideo latentis.

Four main problems may be distinguished:

(i) The name of the critic: the *Vipranius* of the mss. is hotly defended by Jocelyn (69–71): however, he does not take into account
either (i) the (?) grammarian Vipsanius of Isid. *Etym.*1.22.2[39] or (ii) if
Vipsanius is correct and if M. Vipsanius Agrippa is meant, that the
discourtesy involved in the use of an unloved *nomen* (Sen. *Contr.*2.4.13)
is marked and presumably belongs to a tradition of vituperation current
among Virgilian scholars for two thousand years.[40] Agrippa was not
absent on campaign between 31 and 21:[41] the remark could apply to
Buc., *G.*, or *Aen.* (Jocelyn, 73f., 111). It should also be remembered
that Agrippa was no unlettered *miles gloriosus*.[42]

(ii) Cf. Jocelyn, 74–6 for the hypothesis that this remark is an answer
('smuggled in by M.') to a favourable judgement which had entered
Virgil in a grammarians' list or catalogue of poets and their achievements. That might be right, though I wonder if there were serious
critics who ventured to exclude Virgil from his due place. On the
other hand, Agrippa's humble origins were a matter of extreme
delicacy:[43] that might have made him reluctant to jeer at Virgil as a
nurseling only given status and respectability by Maecenas. The remark is too close to the brick dropped by the rhetor Latro (Sen.cit.)
for comfort. A literary interpretation lends unity to the passage and
should perhaps therefore be preferred.

(iii) *cacozelia*: cf. Jocelyn 77–109: 'a strong tendency to associate
the fault with attempts at stylistic elaboration' (id., 108): a conclusion
amply documented for the *G.* Virgil, according to the criticism

---

[38] H.D. Jocelyn, *PLLS* 2 (1979), 67ff., L.P. Wilkinson, *CQ* 9 (1959), 183f.,
W. Görler, *Entr.Hardt* 25 (1978), 175ff., S. Costanza, *Sileno* 16 (1990), 53ff., Lyne,
Words, 18, n. 66.

[39] Schanz-Hosius 1 (ed. 4), 590: cf. Peter White, *Promised Verse* (Cambridge, Mass.
1993), 265, no. 55.

[40] Costanza (n. 38), 54, Bowersock ap. Görler (n. 38), 203.

[41] M. Reinhold, *Marcus Agrippa* (Geneva NY, 1933), 89, against Bowersock l.c.

[42] Cf. my comm. on Nep. *Att.*12.1.

[43] Sen. *Contr.*2.4.13, Reinhold (n. 41), 7.

reported in VSD, and on Jocelyn's reading, avoided the proper language (or jargon) of agriculture and used instead *uerba communia* (almost 'non-technical language'), creating thereby a kind of discord between theme and the language strictly appropriate (though we might wonder about the rules of decorum as applied to technical terms; cf. 222).

(iv) The language of the remainder of the critique has been studied amply by students of Virgil's vocabulary in terms of other contemporary analyses of the language of poetry, both Latin and Greek.[44] The antithesis (8) *tumida-exilis* (fat or bloated—lean or meagre) presupposes a *via media*, which, to judge from the context, is itself necessarily defective (Jocelyn 71–4 with nn. 57–9). In *latentis*, Jocelyn sees an allegation of obscurity (116, though he does not elucidate this use of *lateo*, which (cf. *ThLL*) does not seem obviously paralleled). *Latenter*, however, is a favourite term in Serv. to indicate 'allusively'.[45] The detailed case advanced by Jocelyn for the accusation as being one of obscurity arising out of an avoidance of specialist *uerba* (as against *communia*) remains the reigning exegesis of this extremely difficult and important passage, but I wonder if the sense noted for *latenter* might not support a meaning of 'allusive' (instead of calling a spade a spade; cf. Jocelyn, 116, 117) for *latentis*: not so much obscurity as whimsical indirection in the face of the precise detail so much cultivated in the didactic tradition (cf. n. 6).

The little work on Virgilian grammar and syntax in recent years has perhaps unfortunately tended to focus our attention on the extremes and anomalies. We are now, thanks above all to the work of W. Görler, splendidly well-informed on the wildest leaps of Virgil's verbal gymnastics, but that should not lead us to think that we have therefore reached a full and deep understanding of his style. Far from it. I was recently asked to explain the grammar of *Aen*.3.60f.: *omnibus idem animus, scelerata excedere terra, / linqui pollutum hospitium et dare classibus Austros.* Three infinitives, but why is one of them, with no metrical reason, passive? *Linqui* is also a first-foot self-contained spondee (rather rare). To a modern ear it is also cumbrous in sense.

---

[44] Jocelyn (n. 38), 109ff., Görler (n. 38), 175ff., Wilkinson (n. 11), 186f., Brink on Hor.*AP* 46–9 and 240–3; cf. Maecenas' remark on Virgil ap. Sen. *Suas*.1.12 with Costanza (n. 38), 73ff.

[45] *ThLL* 7.2.998.64ff., *Ind.Serv.* s.v., cf. H. Erbse, index to *Il.* scholia, s.v. λανθάνω. The use of λανθάνειν at Arist. *Rhet*.1404b18 ('be unobtrusive') squares (pace F. Marx, Costanza, etc.) far less well with the general sense of this passage.

Does the passive infinitive ever acquire that sense of duty or obligation present in the gerundive? Cf. *Aen*.9.192, 7.429. How common indeed is the passive infinitive in Virgil?[46] Does it suggest a collective decision? Is not 8.216 extremely similar? The material has been roughly collected (Ott), but the real work has yet to be done. 3.60f. is no oddity, but a passage where we do not yet understand the tonal quality of an apparent stylistic anomaly. The real, serious, startling oddities are not all that rare: they are an aspect (Görler 1982, 69) of Virgil's astonishing ability to force simple words to work overtime. *Callida iunctura* said his friend Horace (*AP* 47f.); note too Macr.6.6.2 (Virgil) *uarie modo uerba modo sensus figurando multum Latinitati leporis adiecit.* Thus (and I keep the most dramatic *iuncturae* to a minimum, since the material is ready to hand and potentially misleading if over-privileged), enallage and hypallage.[47] So 6.2 *Euboicis Cumarum adlabitur oris* and 6.268 *ibant obscuri sola sub nocte per umbram*: the adjective, from its 'expected' position is shifted to qualify a dependent noun. Further examples, variously classified, pullulate: 'exchange' of direct and indirect objects: 3.61 (two oddities in one verse!) *dare classibus Austros*, 4.683 *date uulnera lymphis* (some editors, disconcerted, repunctuate), 10.906 *me. . .concede sepulchro*; cf. the limbs leaving the soul at 4.385. Subject and object are likewise inverted (1.9f. *tot uoluere casus* (0). . .*insignem pietate uirum* (S), *G*.3.251) and verbs of separation encourage a particular virtuosity or ingenuity (3.418; the sea which rips Italy from Sicily: is this a joke?). How profoundly is the reader called upon to analyse 3.72 *terraeque urbesque recedunt*? Of course literally it is the Aeneadae who recede, but that is not, as Görler notes, how the traveller sees it. At 8.3 *atque acris concussit equos atque impulit arma* each verb is separated from its 'obvious' noun. So too *excudent* and *ducent* at 6.847f. The alert reader (and Serv. is much exercised by many of the cases here cited) is torn between wonder and exasperation. We may likewise marvel at Virgil's, use of verbs (both simple and compound) normally intransitive in a transitive sense: 1.67 *nauigat*, 4.609 *ululata*, 7.580f. *nemora. . .insultant*, *G*.3.33 *triumphatas gentes*. Such bravura passages are not puzzles, but challenges. The master chef concocts a remarkable dish from plain ingredients. The chalcenteric reader

---

[46] Cf. Ott's reverse index (n. 83, vol. 8); with patience, all the passive infinitives could therefore be listed. Warmest thanks to Prof. Cynthia Kahn (Univ. of Arizona) for raising this problem.

[47] Görler (n. 38, 1978), 194, n. 2, (1982, *Vergilius*), 61.

might start from Lunelli-Kroll, 27, n. ** to explore the poetic origins, Greek and Latin, of Virgil's acrobatics.

The student of Virgil seriously interested in questions of grammar
will be almost necessarily self-taught: to return for a moment to my
learned skirmish over the *genitiuus inhaerentiae*: (n. 16, 204) just how
rare is this usage? We do not know. No-one has collected the figures,
but this genitive does have a long history in Latin poetic usage, is
therefore a form of pleonasm inherent in the Latin poetic language
and one expects to find it in Virgil. No surprise that it turns out to
be less rare than we thought. Nor is the question one of unrelieved
tedium: on it turns the presence (or otherwise) of a disagreeable and
remarkable metaphor in *Aen.*7. If such phenomena could be explained
by reference to a computer or a large book, they would be a good
deal less exciting as challenges to the reader's 'nose' or memory. At
3.61, there was bibliography to help. Here, at 7.352, there is not. It
all still depends on memory and observation.

This chapter does not attempt to provide the shortest grammar of
Virgilian Latin yet offered. Enough bibliography is spread about, I
hope, to get even the stickiest enquiry under way. To return (again!)
to *Aen.*3.61: why could not *linqui* be middle, given that Virgil uses
many passive verbs in a middle sense?[48] Because Virgil's experiments
with a Latin middle fall into certain fairly well-defined categories,
after Greek precedents.[49] Virgil's Latin belongs not only to the development of the 'Latin poetic language' from Livius Andronicus on,
but it is also, often enough, Greek in its very nature, in metre, morphology,[50] grammar and syntax. If you do not have a sound working
knowledge of poetic Greek usage from Homer to the Alexandrians,
your reading of Virgil is unfortunately but inevitably much at risk.
Greek is an essential element of the 'Latin poetic language' from the
first: so, *exempli gratia* the history of. . .*que*. . .*que*, 11.349, *lumina*. . .*ducum*,
5.285, *Cressa genus*, 6.467 *torua tuentem*, 6.49 *maiorque uideri*, 1.319
dederatque comam diffundere uentis, 10.138 *molli circulus auro* (in place of
the huge compound epithets beloved of archaic Latin) all of clearly
Greek origin. But that is not all: 'Calco semantico'[51] is missing from
the *EV*, but Virgil is very partial to the calque.[52] *Mixta deo mulier*

---

[48] See the criticisms of R. Thomas, *Vergilius* 38 (1992), 136f.
[49] *EV* s.v. *Grecismi*, section 2 and Lunelli (n. 2), index, s.v. id.
[50] Görler, *EV* 2, 264.
[51] Cf. Lunelli-Kroll (n. 11), 13, n. 12.
[52] Calques are part of the old 'Latin poetic language': Traina (n. 18), index
s.v. *calco*.

(7.661) looks strange Latin; literally translated, though, it is perfectly normal Greek idiom. So too *sate sanguine diuom, desistere pugnae* (gen.). E. Steiner, *Das Bedeutungslehnwort. . .*(diss. Königsberg 1921) remains indispensable. If you are truly baffled by a phrase in Virgil's Latin, try turning it literally into Greek (advice often offered by a distinguished Horace specialist).

No surprise that Virgil's text is rich in ambiguities[53] of grammar, lexicon, syntax, though nowhere as rich as has been claimed.[54] (a) of lexicon: 10.768, 11.641 *armis*: shoulders or weapons? 12.85 *lacessunt* literal or metaphorical or both? 5.350 *casus* (literal and metaphorical perhaps, and a joke too). So too *mensas* (3.257, 7.116), 5.673 *inanem* (literal or metaphorical or both?) 6.273 *faucibus* (narrows? or jaws? or both?) 9.677 *pro turribus* (in front of? in place of?) 4.384: Quinn and Serv. are equally bemused; like Quinn, I have no objection to a polyvalent explanation. *Buc.*2.24 *Actaeo*: 'Attic' or (transliterated) 'on the shore'? The poet is not muddled or incompetent, but he is compulsive in setting challenges to the reader, and instinctively indirect in his expression. (b) of syntax and grammar. Is the subject of *meruit* (10.492) Evander or Pallas? Are we perhaps blind to the implications of word-order? At 2.4 does *ut* depend on *dolorem* (3) or on *fando* (6)? The question only arises in a modern—usually over-punctuated— text. 1.4 *saeuae. . .iram* might seem (Quinn (n. 10), 406) equally slippery, but unity of sense seems to attach it firmly to what precedes. But Quinn (408) is perfectly right to see syntactial ambiguity in both *uobis* and *pugna* at 12.265. Only the translator or public reader is forced to make an explicit decision; the rest of us should be disposed to hedge our bets intelligently. There are many other cases[55] where we would do well to refrain from insisting that X goes with Y, not Z. But by no means always. Thus (e.g.) at 4.124 rhythm links *dux* firmly to *Troianus*, not *Dido*; no reader would ever naturally insert an unsignalled sense-pause after the third foot. Does *tenuis* (5.740) refer to *fumus*,

---

[53] Quinn (n. 10), 394ff., Dolç, *EV* s.v. *Ambivalenza*, G.B. Townend, *CQ* 19 (1969), 330ff. and *PVS* 9 (1969–70), 76ff.

[54] Unfortunately many of the passages cited by Quinn and Dolç are only ambiguous by courtesy of those determined to find confusion even where none exists: e.g. 4.449, 2.75, 2.646, 2.255 (cf. *CQ* 1986, 212), 6.743, 1.462); because the plain sense of a verse has been disputed, that does not mean it is necessarily ambiguous. When an ideological stance drives a Virgilian to seek out ambiguities, it is hard to remain calm or silent, Horsfall, *CR* 1988, 243f.

[55] Townend (n. 53, 1969), 333 for the substantially unpunctuated text available to Serv.; marks of punctuation were later added to codd. PMG.

Anchises or *auras*? The common pattern of adjective at caesura and noun at line-end points firmly to the last explanation.

The difficulties raised by Townend's two articles are challenges to the fineness of the reader's ear and to the depth of our knowledge of grammar and usage. At *G*.3.501, *aret. . .pellis* seems confirmed beyond reasonable doubt by the technical parallels Mynors now cites. At *Aen*.7.37f. *tempora rerum* or *status rerum*? The latter; pause after 5th. foot is rare but *s.r.* is an historiographical commonplace particularly appropriate in the context.[56] At 6.122–3 *Thesea magnum* or *magnum Alciden*? Despite the same rare pause at issue, see J.B. Carter, *Epitheta Deorum* (suppl. to Roscher's *Lexicon*): Hercules, not Theseus is truly *magnus*. Or (Townend) is the adj., like the verb, to be taken with both? For the particular case of adverbs at line-end, I refer to Townend's discussion. The reader who wants to explore these problems more fully, making use of the statistics now available for frequency of pauses at given metrical sedes should remember that Ott's data reflect Mynors' punctuation and that (see Townend) is not to be taken as definitive. When you read Virgil aloud—and if you do not, better not read Virgil at all—you have to decide exactly where to pause; at line-end the skilled reader can slur if (s)he genuinely believes in an authorial ambiguity. At *G*.3.501, that is less easy.

Lastly, a few words on syntax. 'Virgil concentrates on cutting down the incidence of the small, fussy, unproductive word'.[57] The remark is true enough and much cited:[58] out goes *esse* in situations numerous and diverse;[59] out too many prepositions;[60] constructions which facilitate the omission of conjunctions are embraced and developed (*amor. . .cognoscere, cura struere, uenturum excidio*);[61] favoured stylistic mannerisms ('theme and variation', 'general and particular', 'hysteron-proteron')[62] further aid the creation of a compact and sinewy man-

---

[56] Goold (n. 36), 116, with n. 24; but this has long been known: Horsfall, *Alambicco*, 106.

[57] K. Quinn, *Latin Explorations* (London 1963), 199, cf. Maurach (n. 1), 106f.

[58] Görler (n. 4, *Vergilius* 1982), 49, (n. 4), 1985, 265, e.g.

[59] Quinn (n. 10), 383f., Görler (n. 4, *Vergilius* 1982), 49, (n. 4, 1985), 247.

[60] Quinn, (n. 10), 387f., Görler (n. 4, *Vergilius* 1982), 49, Lunelli-Kroll (n. 11), 9.

[61] Quinn (n. 10), 381. Such means towards economy of expression and acceleration of the verse's movement tend to be Greek in origin. Notorious is the poet's predilection for simple, as against compound verbs: Lunelli-Jansen (n. 11), 128, F. Bömer, *Gymn*.64 (1957), 4ff., Görler (n. 4, 1985), 265f.

[62] Quinn, 426, Görler (n. 4, 1985), 274, A.S. McDevitt, *CQ* 17 (1967), 316ff.

ner of writing. Startling above all is the prevalence of parataxis over subordination whenever possible:[63] often, that is, given the alternatives here listed. That is not to deny that subordination exists, even subjunctives dependent on subjunctives,[64] but subordination is rare, and its stylistic impact, case by case, has yet to be explored.[65] Virgil knows very well how to construct a long period or sequence thereof; in *G*.3.1–24 Mynors prints nine strong pauses and the poet can go five lines without. Two conjunctions (*si*), one part of *esse*, one preposition and four subjunctives. Fraenkel's remark on the debt of the Virgilian period to the Ciceronian[66] is often quoted, but it is above all the lack of elaborate subordination in the poet that strikes the reader and it would be helpful to have detailed comparisons with Sall. *Hist.* and with the early books of Livy, the prose classics of Virgil's prime years; with the Lucretian period, Virgil has broken. We are still waiting for a widely-based and thoughtful analysis of the Virgilian sentence.

Sentence-structure and relation to verse and rhetoric

We have seen (section 4) that the syntax of the Virgilian period is in general less elaborate and less syntactically complex (the poet's reluctance to subordinate is[67] well-known) than the length and majesty which his sentences often attain might suggest at first. How Virgil's syntax and metre interact is a relatively unexplored topic (n. 66). If one looks at some long Virgilian periods (e.g. *G*.1.5–23, 4.67–85, *Aen*.1.261–6, 2.254–9, 10.362–8, 11.346–51, 12.270–6), then it swiftly becomes clear that there is a lot more work to be done. The reader, on looking at the complex Virgilian sentence and at certain repeated (even frequent) stylistic effects, may then also want to understand the poet's word order better.[68] The distribution of words in the line

---

[63] Norden, 376, Worstbrock (n. 10), 130, Görler (n. 4, 1985), 274f., Quinn (n. 10), 425, n. 1, 428ff.; for indirect speech, A. Perutelli, *MD* 3 (1979), 69ff.

[64] Lunelli-Janssen (n. 11), 110f., Norden, 379, n. 1 citing 10.362–8 and 12.270–6, Görler (n. 4, 1985), 273, 274.

[65] Cf. Norden, 376f. and section 6 below on colon-length.

[66] *Att.Acc.Virg.Mantova* NS 19/20 (1926/7; pub. 1928), 224ff.; cf. Wilkinson (n. 11), 191f., Jackson Knight (n. 10), 399f.

[67] Worstbrock (n. 10), 148ff., Wilkinson (n. 11), 189ff., Marouzeau (n. 11), 232ff., Quinn (n. 10), 414ff., Norden, 376ff.

[68] Worstbrock (n. 10), 159ff., Görler (n. 4, 1985), 275f., Quinn (n. 11), 418ff.,

is affected by certain familiar and convenient patterns,[69] by certain characteristic ways of achieving emphasis, by a desire for some types of striking juxtaposition, by the traditional tendency of words of a certain shape and character to gravitate to certain points in the line. Such forces are easier to understand (i) if you write Latin hexameters yourself (but even to mention that delightful exercise dates the author terribly!) and (ii) if you read widely and wisely for comparison in (e.g.) Ov. *Met.*, where the disposition of words appears far more repetitive and mechanical.

Just how much speeches and narrative differ (for characterisation by vocabulary in V., p. 244ff.) is beginning to emerge, though some of the obvious places where an enquirer might look for help[70] will prove disappointing, and analysis at the moment is perhaps handicapped by the desire for meticulous classification of all the figures used.[71] It would, I think, be illuminating to know if the 'spoken' *Aeneid* differs from the narrative metrically, in colon-length, in pauses, in enjambement, in placing of words, and as I yet I do not think we do.[72] The status of the orator in the *Aen.* is ambiguous but it is not enough to analyse the means speakers use (cf. *Aen.*1.131–41, 198–207, 229–53, 257–96, a remarkable sequence) predominantly (or exclusively) as techniques of characterisation.[73]

Development

The idea that Virgil 'developed' intellectually or spiritually is old and familiar.[74] That has provoked in turn occasional attempts at defining Virgil's development as a writer, an undertaking in some sense hopeless from the outset in as much as he writes in three distinct genres, each

---

Norden, 391ff., Lunelli-Kroll (n. 11), 33f., 63f., Wilkinson (n. 11), 215ff., Marouzeau (n. 11), 291ff. (with the critique of L. de Neubourg, *Glotta* 56 (1978), 102f., a strongly-worded defence of formal considerations as against verbal effects.

[69] Bibliography, de Neubourg (n. 68), 120, n. 40.

[70] G. Highet, *The speeches in Vergil's Aeneid* (Princeton 1972), 280ff. here dissapoints; not much joy in *EV* s.v. *Retorica*, either.

[71] Cf. *EV* s.v. *Figure retoriche, Tropi* (Calboli).

[72] Much is to be hoped for from the study by H. Gotoff (UNC, Chapel Hill; in press).

[73] Characterisation: Highet (n. 70), 16ff., Lyne (p. 219) 125, et passim. Status of the orator: EV s.v. Oratores, H. Hine in *Homo Viator. Classical Essays for John Bramble* (ed. M. Whitby, etc. (Bristol 1987), 178ff.

[74] F. Klingner, *Virgil* (Zürich 1967), index s.v. Virgil, Zur Einheit des Lebenswerkes.

with sharply differentiated language, style and metre. Hence a number of largely infelicitous and imprecise attempts to explain how Virgil alters.[75] At two points the evidence might seem to favour such an enquiry: (a) lines from the *G.* re-used in the *Aen.*[76] and (b) the more extended reworking that involves certain passages from *G.*4: here imprecise analysis (cf. p. 87 above) has led to unfortunate conclusions about an alleged 'second edition' of *G.*4. But the sum total of the evidence is quite insufficient to provide a basis for any sort of overall analysis or safe conclusions. It might seem therefore that the whole undertaking was necessarily fruitless: Virgil, from the first, is master of a bewildering range of levels, tones, modes, genres and manners of writing. That is to say that in the *Aen.* he can adopt the manner of elegy, bucolic, tragedy or Alexandrian erudition; in the *G.* he may don the mantle of Pindaric lyric or ethnography; in the *Buc.*, that of political allegory or Jewish prophecy. Such changes go far beyond any mechanical adaptation of 'colour' from the great variety of sources that the poet uses;[77] ancient critics even noted a *color comicus* in *Aen.*1 and 4.[78] It becomes, therefore, even more interesting—I hardly mention the importance that a solidly-based analysis might in theory have for studies of the order of composition of books or parts of the *Aen.*—and even more difficult to establish the existence, or otherwise, of certain technical constants, a difficulty augmented in many cases either by the non-availability of statistics, or by an abundance thereof either sorted too crudely to be useful or of generally discredited application. Thus (i), on Jackson Knight's figures for homodyne and heterodyne fourth foot,[79] see Allen (n. 33), 338. Homodyne refers to coincidence of word accent and metrical beat, heterodyne to the clash thereof.[80] Or, (ii), enjambement (absence of pause at line-end), more strongly felt when an 'indifferent' word (*quantus, ipse*) stands in the last foot. An increasingly evident feature of the late books, it has

---

[75] F.W.H. Myers, *Essays classical* (London 1897), 137, Jackson Knight, 330f., A. Salvatore, pref. to ed. of *Aen.*1, Naples 1947, H. Schultz, Χάριτες *Friedrich Leo. . . dargebracht* (Berlin 1911), 359ff. For three disyllables at line end, cf. Harrison on 10.301f.

[76] W.W. Briggs, *Narrative and simile from the Georgics in the Aeneid* (*Mnem.* Suppl. 85, 1980).

[77] Harrison, *Aen.*10, p. 285, Klingner (n. 74), index s.v. Lyrismus, Epopea. My *Alambicco* contains much discussion of non-epic elements in the *Aen.*

[78] W.S. Anderson, *Vergilius* 26 (1980), 10ff., *Arethusa* 14 (1981), 115ff.

[79] *Accentual symmetry in V.* (Oxford 1939), table at end; Allen (n. 33), 338.

[80] Jackson Knight's theory is not well-regarded by linguists (Allen, n. 79); however, (cf. Wilkinson (n. 11), 93, 120) Virgilian 'counterpoint' does seem deliberate and successful on occasion.

been claimed.[81] Adequate figures have not hitherto been employed
and even the statistics here offered are weakened because Ott's collections do not take account of the effect of proclitics, enclitics,
anaphora, anastrophe, parenthesis and hypermeter. Technical terms,
alas, to save space.[82] I use Ott's figures for colon-end (any mark of
punctuation stronger than a comma; as printed in Mynors' text):

Work	(i) colon-end at line-end	(ii) as percentage of line-total	(iii) colon-end elsewhere	(i) as percentage of all colon-ends
Buc.	400	48.19	155	72.07
*G.*1	149	28.99	50	74.87
*G.*2	167	30.81	58	74.22
*G.*3	178	31.45	56	76.07
*G.*4	164	29.03	70	71.00
G.	658	30.07	243	73.76
*Aen.*1	266	35.19	106	71.89
*Aen.*2	267	31.14	142	65.28
*Aen.*3	258	35.93	98	72.47
*Aen.*4	245	34.80	123	66.58
*Aen.*5	312	35.82	114	73.76
*Aen.*6	310	34.41	142	68.58
*Aen.*1–6	1658	35.03	725	69.57
*Aen.*7	250	30.60	84	74.85
*Aen.*8	234	32.01	85	73.35
*Aen.*9	261	32.02	154	62.89
*Aen.*10	310	34.18	174	64.05
*Aen.*11	308	33.66	115	72.81
*Aen.*12	324	34.11	135	70.28
*Aen.*7–12	1687	32.81	747	69.30

Now that we have all of Ott at our disposal[83] progress sometimes
becomes easier. Not always. Gransden again claims[84] a greater freedom in the use of synaloepha in the later books of the *Aen.* Though
Ott unfortunately does not distinguish between synaloepha of short
syllables, of long syllables and diphthongs and of words in -m, nevertheless, if his statistics are recast in terms of the percentage of lines
per book in which there is synaloepha, the results are disconcerting.[85]

---

[81] Gransden, *Aen.*11, 31 and n. on 471.
[82] Cf. *EV* s.v. and s.v. *Pause di senso*, *Esametro*; also Worstbrock (n. 11), 21, Harrison
on 10.29, with further refs.
[83] W. Ott, *Materialen z. Metrik und Stilistik* (20 vols., Tübingen 1973–85).
[84] Gransden (n. 81), 25; cf. *EV* s.v. *Elisione*.
[85] Critics of the Helen-episode have of course noted the excess of synaloepha, 39

Work	Elisions	Line-total	Percentage
Buc.	226	829	27.26
*G.*1	246	514	47.85
*G.*2	255	542	47.04
*G.*3	248	566	43.81
*G.*4	293	566	51.76
G.	1042	2188	47.62
*Aen.*1	361	756	47.75
*Aen.*2	455	782 (see n.)	58.18
*Aen.*3	417	718	58.07
*Aen.*4	382	705	54.18
*Aen.*5	431	871	49.48
*Aen.*6	453	901	50.27
*Aen.*1–6	2499	4733	52.79
*Aen.*7	448	817	54.83
*Aen.*8	375	731	51.29
*Aen.*9	417	818	50.97
*Aen.*10	416	908	45.81
*Aen.*11	526	915	57.48
*Aen.*12	528	952	55.46
*Aen.*7–12	2710	5141	52.71

It will be noted that no book in 7–12 is as rich in synaloepha as 2 and 3, and none in 1–6 as poor as 10!

We have long known that Virgil's hexameters become more spondaic.[86] Taking, of course, only the first four feet in the line the overall statistics are (and I have not made allowance for half-lines!):

Work	Feet	Dactyls	Percentage
Buc.	3316	1633	49.24
G.	8752	3855	44.04
*Aen.*1–6	18932	8277	43.71
(less Helen episode)			
*Aen.*7–12	20564	8797	42.77

---

in 22 verses: G.P. Goold, *HSCP* 74 (1968), 147, cf. Norden, 454. The passage is, I hope, purged from all my statistics. They do suggest that the brilliant forger went a lot too far. There may possibly be similar concentrations of synaloepha in V., but I very much doubt it; certainly they have not been cited in defence of these lines. For elision-statistics in general, note the caveats as summarised at *Ciris* ed. R.O.A.M. Lyne, 16f.

[86] G.E. Duckworth, *Vergil and classical hexameter poetry* (Ann Arbor 1969), 138.

But if we break down our figures by foot and book no sort of consistent pattern emerges:

Work Percentage of dactyls per foot:	First	Second	Third	Fourth
Buc.	65.54	52.29	40.24	38.67
*G.*1	63.23	45.53	36.77	30.74
*G.*2	62.73	46.86	36.53	25.46
*G.*3	65.90	45.23	42.40	29.15
*G.*4	60.88	44.96	39.82	28.67
G.	63.19	45.63	38.69	28.49
*Aen.*1	59.50	46.88	40.50	26.43
*Aen.*2 (less Helen episode)	58.69	48.20	40.02	29.41
*Aen.*3	63.15	44.30	39.10	29.25
*Aen.*4	61.52	50.21	41.49	25.46
*Aen.*5	60.53	46.99	39.70	29.51
*Aen.*6	60.07	46.05	39.82	28.36
*Aen.*1–6	60.19	46.82	39.86	27.99
*Aen.*7	61.28	48.09	36.87	29.35
*Aen.*8	56.04	49.45	37.31	26.65
*Aen.*9	60.69	45.36	40.67	24.72
*Aen.*10	63.93	46.84	39.51	29.86
*Aen.*11	59.15	44.36	39.98	26.07
*Aen.*12	57.32	43.37	42.15	22.97
*Aen.*7–12	59.44	45.88	39.38	26.39

The marked variations by book may have some as yet unexplored consequences for our understanding of the poet's methods of composition; I do not pretend to know. That there is an increase in 'unpoetic language' in the later books of the *Aen.* is well-known;[87] that is a consequence of the changed subject-matter; in comparison with 1–6 it is relatively unvaried (and the poet therefore needs more synonyms) and it tends to butchery (particularly in 9–12), passing thereby into the lexical sphere that the poet shares with the literate soldier. I conclude, therefore, that we have yet to make significant progress beyond the imprecise generalities (n. 75) offered on this topic of 'development' in the days of our great-grandparents.

---

[87] Axelson (p. 219) 144, Watson (n. 15), 437f., Lyne (p. 219), passim.

Part Two

To offset a swift introduction to a large and complex range of problems, I thought it might prove helpful to offer some analysis of four brief and carefully selected passages:

(i) *Buc.*9.56–65. Here we already have Coleman's commentary, quite often helpful on questions of this kind; rather less so Clausen's. Note also R.G.M. Nisbet, *PVS* 20 (1991), 1–13 'The style of Virgil's *Eclogues*'. 56 **caussando** (perhaps the better orthography), 'by your protests' (*TLL* s.v. 705.80); a verb used in tragedy (Pacuv.23, Acc. 418) and Lucr. (1.398), but rare in both prose and verse before V. Form and *sedes* echo *cantando* (52): for such sequences of initial molossi cf. 1.72, 76, 78, 3.25–41, 4.35–51, 5.37–51 (for such questions, W. Ott's *Metr.Analyse z. Verg.Buc.* (Tübingen 1978) is indispensable). **in longum ducis:** the phrase is new (*TLL* s.v. *duco* 2152.53, s.v. *longus* 1642.81), apparently, but not surprising: cf. LHS 276, *in abruptum, in aduersum*, Serv. *ad Aen.*8.55. **amores** thrown into relief by word-order: *n.a.* would more obviously mean 'my beloved', or 'my tale of love' (*Buc.*8.23, 10.54), but here the sense is clearly 'my desire' (sc. to hear); cf. v. 32 *incipe si quid habes*, hitherto postponed, and *Aen.*2.10 *sed si tantus amor casus cognoscere nostros*. A challenging phrase. Note the typically high proportion of end-stopped lines (233f.). 57 **et nunc:** cf. 3.56 **omne. . .aequor:** hyperbaton (so Quint. uses the term, 8.6.65, but there is little agreement, Platnauer, infra, 1951, 104ff.) followed by a light pause at 5tr.; the proclitic *et* avoids any disagreeable irregularity at line-end. The noun refers to any flat surface of water: river for V., sea for Theocr. **tibi:** the final i is not of course lengthened before str- (see H.M. Hoenigswald, *TAPA* 80 (1949), 276f.); rather, this prosody (38 times in V., against 141 with the i short) reflects the original orthography *tibei* (NW 2, 349ff., *TLL* s.v. *ego* 255.19ff.); the 'ethic' dative. **stratum silet:** the significant silence underscored by alliteration (perhaps suggested by Theocr.2.38) and central position; for the use of *sternere*, cf. *Aen.*5.763, 821, 8.89. All surfaces, made flat, keep silent (cf. *Aen.*1.164): *stratum* is a real participle and there is no doubling of adjectives (not really at *Aen.*5.24), as for special effect at *G.*1.407 and *Aen.*6.283 (with Austin's note). 58 **aspice:** separated off by commas in printed texts; this gives a false impression, e.g. of 57 as end-stopped, which it is not, as the hyperbaton *omnes. . .aurae* shows. *Aspice* is, rather, parenthetic, a signal of intimate dialogue and a gift to the performer (cf. *Buc*.2.66, 4.50, 52, 8.105, *TLL* s.v. 830.57ff., Cic. *poet.* fr.32.2, 33.28, *epigr.funebre Q. Enni* 1). **omnes. . .aurae:** anaphora of the adj.; *aura* is a mild word (cf. *Aen*.2.728, Hor. *C*.1.2.48), common in Cic.'s poetry, Lucr., Cat. **uentosi murmuris:** for adjs. in -osus see below on 11.390. 'Every last breath' had belonged to the *uenti qui murmurabant*. V.'s enallage here gives augmented prominence to the original *murmur*. *ceciderunt*, like *stratum silet*, is given prominence by a central position, enclosed by two pairs of nouns and adjs; cf. Varr. *Men*.471 *aduersi uenti ceciderunt* (but hardly therefore colloquial here).

59 **hinc adeo:** the particle (cf. *TLL* s.v. 615.77) increases mildly the force of the adverb. **media. . .uia:** the middle part of the journey: cf. Lucr.5.905, 6.576, *G*.3.423, *Aen*.5.738. **namque** unelided (so 31 times in V., against 34 elided). Clearly *atque* was viewed differently (and *atque* and *neque* too differ, J. Richmond, *Glotta* 43 (1965), 97ff., ib. 50 (1972), 96f.) Unfortunately, the figures currently in use for the elision of *atque* (M. Platnauer *CQ* 42 (1948), 91ff., id. *Latin elegiac verse* (Cambridge 1951), 78ff. are altogether unreliable. **sepulcrum. . . Bianoris:** the name (mysterious) is delayed and thus given prominence. 60 **incipit apparere:** cf. *G*.1.404, Hor. *Epd*.10.9; perhaps first here of a place coming into sight. Note the 'Greek' caesura at 3tr., very common in *Buc*. (F. Cupaiuolo, *EV* 1, 575); followed by bucolic diaeresis (pause after dactylic fourth foot, Cupaiuolo, l.c.). **hic. . .hic:** V. elegantly puts the second *hic* one *sedes* earlier in the line, where it is followed by pause at 5tr. In 59–61 there are also two enjambed lines; Lycidas' urgency finds expression through an accumulation of these apparently trivial phenomena of metre. **densas. . .frondes:** the adj. explains why the leaves are being stripped.

61 **agricolae:** already in Cat. and Lucr.; when exactly does V. use *a.* and when *colonus*? I do not think we know. **stringunt:** the verb is technical (Cato, Varro, *G.*, Colum.); was it, for Cat.66.50, a prosaism? **Moeri:** NW 1.292, Cat.4.13, *Buc*.1.36, 8.77, 78 for the Greek vocative. Here Lyc. employs urgent prosphonesis before the climactic *canamus*. 62 **hic:** but Lyc. had not finished; the anaphora is triple. **haedos:** the synonyms *h., caper, capella* have not, it seems, been clearly distinguished. **tamen:** in first place, cf. 10.31, KS 2.2, 99, LHS 496. The parataxis (which V. uses to characterise direct speech, Hof.-Ric., 249ff.) is deceptively simple (cf. n. on *G*.4.409): *tamen. . .*converts the imperative into—effectively—a concessive clause, 'even if. . .still. . .'; perhaps a semi-colon would be more appropriate at the caesura.

63 **aut si...veremur:** the verb found in old tragedy, Lucr., Cic. *carm.*; in sense and level apparently not distinguished from *timeo*. On the other hand, *pluuiam*, on account of its romance descendants, *pluie, pioggia, llover* will have had a more modest resonance than would *imbrem*, familiar in Enn. and Lucr. For the run of three monosyllables at the beginning of the verse, cf. *EV* 3, 571, *Buc*.6.49. **colligat:** cf. Quint. 10.1.109 (a trans. of Pindar); the word has a Lucretian flavour, 4.1065 *collectum umorem et saepe.*

64 **cantantes...cantantes:** cf. n. on 56 *caussando* for the initial molossi; the part. takes up the underlined final *canamus* of 61. **licet:** with the verb not the participle (cf. LHS 385, *TLL* s.v. 1366.32ff.). **usque:** adv.; spoken usage (cf. Plaut. *Capt* 269 with Lindsay's note, LHS 253). **minus...:** paratactic (cf. on 62 *tamen*): the sense might be that of a *quia sic* in prose. The parenthesis is also characteristic of spoken language (cf. Hof.-Ric.262ff.). **laedet:** cf. 1.50; a word much favoured by Lucr. Note the Greek caesuras both here and in v. 65 (also 60 (where see n.), 62!).

65 **cantantes** repeated in the same sense, but *eamus* is in a different *sedes* and no longer jussive but dependent on *ut*. **ego te:** juxtaposition of pronouns for emotive effect, Hof.-Ric.240. **fasce:** for *onus*, first here; cf. *TLL* s.v. 307.25, Serv. and Schol.Med. here, *G*.3.347, 4.204. The use of *f.*, 'a bundle', normally of e.g. sticks for a live goat or goats is perhaps a mild rustic joke. **leuabo:** *TLL* s.v. 1230.74, cf. *G*.2.400, Hor. *Epd*.13.17.

   (ii) So much has been said about the various essential differences between the Aristaeus and Orpheus stories in *G*.4 (e.g. Otis, 194f., 197; cf. 86–9) that I thought it would prove useful to compare in detail short passages from both. First *G*.4.405–14 (where we are told to expect a cool, objective, Homeric manner of narrative).

405 **uerum ubi:** common in *G*. and *Aen*.; perhaps 'invented' and here surely felt as (an exact metrical) equivalent of the Homeric ἀλλ' ὅτε (*Od*.4.460); **ubi...tum:** possibly archaic in flavour, Bennett, *Verb*, 86. **correptum...tenebis:** given the sense of *tenere*, the verb is often found thus with a part. ('keep caught'): cf. *G*.3.352, *Aen*.2.802, 4.331, 6.722, 7.250. *Corripio* already in Lucr., Cat., Cic. *carm*. **manibus uinclisque:** not to be understood as some sort of hendiadys (cf. 396, 399, 439). For the metrically necessary (and archaic) syncopation of *uinculis* into *uinclis*, cf. Leumann-Lunelli, 161f., *EV* s.v. *sincope*. 406 **uariae...species...ferarum:** cf. *variae comitum facies, Aen*.5.822, *talis erat species*, 6.208, *formae magnorum...luporum*, 7.18. I had thought

that V. might have in mind a Greek compound epithet, but there seem to be no suitable candidates. **eludent:** *TLL* s.v. 430.14: perhaps first here in high poetry; the object is omitted (LHS, 34f.; contrast *Aen.*11.695). **atque ora:** 'of beasts unusual', says Mynors oddly: cf. *TLL* s.v. 1088.32ff., from Acc. (*trag.*686) on.

407 **subito:** 'Lower' than *repente*, but common in poetry (Axelson, 32f., Ross (infra, *Aen.*11.390), 70ff.) **sus:** for all its brevity and farmyard air, no stranger to high poetry: Enn. *Ann.*96 Sk., Lucr.5.25, 970, etc., Horsfall, *CJ* 74 (1978–9), 319, *Maia* 41 (1989), 253, n. 7. The alliteration is marked, but I should not like to have to define its effect. **horridus:** 'bristly' (*TLL* s.v. 2991.39), rather than 'nasty, brutal, rough' (which is post-classical of animals, *TLL* 2994.32ff.). **atraque tigris:** adjs. and nouns are patterned abba. On *a.* Serv. comments *id est saeua:* cf. J. André, *Etude sur les termes de couleur...*(Paris 1949), 50, *TLL* 1018.40ff., *EV* s.v. (Zaffagno, who cites analogous explications from Serv.). Black stripes are hardly relevant!

408 **squamosusque draco:** for adjs. in *-osus* cf. below on 11.390; V. has also *squameus* (*ter*); the context reinforces the claims that have been made for Greek and epic associations in many such adjs. *draco* in Enn. (*Sc.*274V), and Cic. *carm.*: cf. Lucr.5.905, *Aen.*2.225 and *EV* s.v. *serpenti*; more monstrous and fabulous than other snakes, at least to begin with. **fulua ceruice:** a common use of noun + adj. in abl. (of description) as equivalent to an Homeric compound adj.: cf. PVM ed. Mackail, 515, Leumann-Lunelli, 169f., Görler 1985, 268. The adj. is conventional: Lucr.5.901, Lygd.6.15, André, 133, Horsfall, *RFil* 119 (1991), 216. **leaena:** Cat.60.1, 64.154, Verg. *Buc.*2.63.

409 **acrem...sonitum dabit:** for the adj. used of fire, cf. *TLL* s.v. 361.53ff., Lucr.5.906 *acrem..flammam*, 1.650, 3.477, 6.850, *G.*1.93; of sound, *TLL* 360.45, Acc. *trag.*238(?), Lucr.1.275, 3.958. 'Normally the phrase (sc. *sonitum dare*) is absolute' (Thomas): yes: Enn. *Ann.*411 Sk., Lucr.6.110. What is odd here is less the idiom (*TLL* s.v. 1687.22ff.) than the situation; it is Proteus who will emit the sound of fire. **atque ita uinclis excidet:** cf. Prop.4.7.96, *TLL* s.v. *excido*, 1236.30. Again (cf. *Buc.*9.62) an unobtrusive and economical parataxis: 'by means of transformations, P. will escape the bonds'. Cf. Görler 1985, 274, Quinn, 430f., Janssen-Lunelli, 110f., Worstbrock, 130ff., *EV* s.v. *ipotassi*. 410: the energetic verb is run-on. **tenuis:** qualifying *aquas* not Proteus: cf. *acrem* above and *TLL* 2.347.61, *G.*3.335, 1.92 with Serv.'s n. **dilapsus abibit:** *d.*: cf. Naev. *trag.*51, Lucr.5.311, etc. (traditional

poetic lexicon); contrast *abibit*, first here in the sense of 'mutari in' with the hint of 'penetrare, sedem mutare' or the like; *TLL* 1.71.44. **411 quanto. . .magis. . .tam. . .magis:** the conventional *tanto magis. . .quanto magis* is prosy, and there are a lot of variations which attract the poets: KS 2.2.483f., 485, n. 27 trag.inc. fr.160, Lucr.4.81, 250, Verg. *Aen.*7.787f., *quanto* is separated from *magis*, *ille* from *uertet*, *formas* from *omnis*; the dense texture of the line provokes expectation and may suggest the complexity of the struggle. **formas se uertit in omnis:** cf. *Aen.*7.328, Prop.4.2.47, *TLL* s.v. *forma* 1068.13.

412 **tam tu, nate. . .:** *tu* contrasted with *ille*; alliteration; *tu* reinforced by apostrophe (cf. 396, 531); the climax of Cyrene's advice has arrived. **contende. . .uincla:** the original and literal sense of the verb: *TLL* 662.66, Enn. *Ann.*369 Sk, Naev. *trag.*36. **tenacia:** for adjs. in -ax, cf. n. on *Aen.*11.391 below.; *t.* in comedy, Cat.17.26.

413 **donec:** consecutive lines begin with *sed, tam, donec*; 411f. and 413 contain two sets of correlatives. Not prosy so much as unconcealedly elaborate in thought and expression. *donec* with the fut. is unusual (KS 2.2.378f., LHS 629, *TLL* 1995.13ff., *EV* 3.994, Liv.Andr. fr.7 Mariotti, *Aen.*1.273). **talis. . .qualem:** trag.inc.50, Lucr.5.194, *Buc.*5.46, *Aen.*6.208, but cf. above all Homer's τοῖος ἐὼν οἷον. . . *Od.*4.421. **mutato corpore.** For the history of the abl. abs., see Bennett, *Cases*, 368ff. (Enn., early tragedy), *EV* s.v. *ablativo assoluto*. For the phrasing, cf. *Buc.*8.70, *Ciris* 198 (with Lyne's note).

414 **uideris:** generic subjunctive, like Homer's ἴδησθε (Kühner-Gerth, 2, 425, Goodwin, *Moods and tenses*, 207f.) in the line just cited: cf. Woodcock, 114ff. Ernout-Thomas, 335, LHS, 561f.; because Proteus is Proteus, *qualem*, used of his original state is necessarily indefinite ('however you may have seen it'). The few commentators who pause on *u.* make heavy weather of it. **incepto. . .somno:** the vb. in poetry from Enn. on, *TLL*, 916.38. **lumina cum tegeret:** cf. Cat.50.10 *nec somnus tegeret quiete ocellos*, 51.11f. *gemina teguntur lumina nocte*. The same idiom in Gk., S. *El.*780. But here in V., it is not sleep that covers the eyes, but P. himself: for this sort of hypallage in V., cf. Görler (n. 4 *Vergilius* 1982), 58ff. (*Würz.Jhb.* 1982), 76f., 1985, 269.

Secondly, by way of (rather obvious) contrast, *G.*4.490-8: **restitit:** vb. in Enn. and Lucr.; light pause at 1d, which places marked emphasis on the run-on word, is quite common. (Winbolt, 13ff., cf. vv. 493, 515, 525). 490-2 have no pause at line-end, but there is most artful variation in where the pauses do fall. **suam:** for the rhythm, cf. Norden, 431. **luce sub ipsa:** cf. Enn. *Ann.*484 Sk., Lucr.3.1011, Varr.Atac. *carm.* fr.11 Morel, 24 Büchner, *G.*3.551, *Aen.*4.692 for this sense of *lux* as contrasted with the darkness of death. *Ipsa* is in itself an unexciting word; it occurs, then, at line-end rarely and for special effect (Norden, *Aen.*6, 400–1).

491 **immemor:** Catullan (64.58, 135); cf. *TLL* s.v. 447.27: in the sense of *incautus* (i.e. as a synonym of *incautum*, 488), or more specifically, 'forgetful of an instruction given on this occasion', anticipating *foedera*, 492, but perhaps belonging to the same set of rules as the *legem* of 487. Given that we do not hear elsewhere of such an instruction, it would in fact be very much in V.'s manner to allude to it here before telling the reader a little more about it two lines on. **heu:** applies in particular to *immemor*, as it does to *non tua* at 498. In high poetry from Enn. *Trag.* on. The word-order (exclamation postponed) is peculiarly Virgilian (though cf. Hor. *Epd.*16.11; see *TLL* s.v. 2673.27ff.): cf. *Aen.*3.709, 4.541, 7.594, etc. **uictusque animi:** for this 'genitive of reference', cf. Löfstedt, *Syntactica* 1, 143, *Aen.*4.203 *amens animi* with Austin and Pease, 5.73 *aeui maturus*, 202 *furens animi* with Williams, 10.686 *animi miserata* with Harrison. The rhythm (weak elision at 2 1/2; two secondary caesuras) throws into relief *heu* and *respexit.* **respexit:** a Lucretian word (3.854, 4.1159); already at *Buc.*8.102. **ibi:** for the strong pause at 5tr., cf. Austin on 1.99 *ubi ingens*, Norden, 389, n. 6, 9.351 *ibi ignem*, where (as at *Buc.*2.4) *ibi* also stands first in the sentence. When an adverb precedes and is separated from its verb, it receives particular emphasis, Marouzeau, *TSL*, 329f. For the elision betwen fifth and sixth feet, cf. Norden, 456. A remarkable accumulation of metrical and rhythmic effects.

492 **effusus labor:** the verb is found in Ennius, but in this sense appears (*TLL* s.v. 226.51) first in *Rhet.Her.***immitis. . .tyranni:** the adj. (which indicates that here at least the noun cannot be neutral!) in poetry from Cat. on (64.245, *TLL* s.v. 467.27, Lyne on *Ciris* 420); only here does V. use the noun of a deity, common though such usage is in Gk. . .**rupta. . .foedera:** cf. Lucr.2.254, *TLL*, s.v. *foedus* 1007.32ff. Virgil employs language appropriate to a formal accord between powers: cf. D.O. Ross, *Style and language in Catullus* (Cambridge, Mass., 1969), 84f. for a likely fount of inspiration. For the run-on dactylic word, cf. n. on 490. Note the very marked alliteration of r (growling and rumbling) and f.

493 **fragor:** Lucretian; 6.129, 136, *TLL* s.v. 1233.62. **stagnis. . . Auernis:** not *Auerni* (*stagna Auerni*, *tr.inc.*250): A. is commonly used as

adj. too (cf. *Aen*.6.118 *lucis. . .Auernis*), at least from Lucr.6.738.

494 **illa:** a notably economical means of indicating change of speaker: cf. *Buc*.10.31, *G*.4.446; commoner *ille autem*. **quis. . .quis:** not at all the same as the repeated *quis* of e.g. *Buc*.9.19; here there is anaphora of the interrogative pronoun to indicate that a single power has destroyed both Orpheus and Eurydice; cf. *G*.4.315, *Aen*.12.500. **inquit:** used by Lucr. and Cat.; six times in *Buc*., but in *G*. only here and at 4.446. **miseram:** far worse than (Lucr.4.1076, Cat.8.1 et saepe) lovesick. **et:** such postposition is neoteric: Norden, 402, *TLL* s.v. 897.55ff., *CLE* 55.6, *Buc*.1.34, Varr.Atac. fr.6. **perdidit:** from Enn. *trag*.73; cf. Lucr.4.814, Cat.51.16 et saepe. **Orpheu:** for the effect of empathy, cf. Kroll-Lunelli, 25f., Norden on *Aen*.6.18.

495 **quis tantus:** cf. *Buc*.1.26 *quae tanta*. **furor:** hardly (*EV*) the state of mind of one contemplating suicide! V. refers explicitly (vd. 488) to the folly caused by love (cf. *Buc*.10.21f., *TLL* s.v.1630.45). **en iterum:** the interjection here first with advb. (or adj., numeral or the like, *TLL* s.v. 548.2); it introduces something new, or worse; cf. *EV* 2.995–6. The advb. indicates precisely 'a second time': cf. *Buc*.4.36; already in *fr.trag*. **crudelia. . .fata:** an adj. dear to Catullus; cf. also *Buc*.5.20 **retro. . .uocant:** the advb. possibly at Pacuv.333 and in Lucr.; notable interlocking word-order.

496 **conditque:** Catullan (64.231); cf. *TLL* s.v. 151.69. **natantia lumina:** cf. Lucr.3.480 *nant oculi*, *Aen*.5.856; *lumina* of the eyes in early tragedy, Enn., Lucr., Cic. *Arat.*, and Cat. (51.12, etc.). The rhythm (caesura at 2S, Greek caesura in 3rd. foot, bucolic diaeresis) is evocative of the slow drift into death: cf. the similar language and effects at *Aen*.2.9, 4.81, 5.856, with Norden 433f.

497 **uale:** cf. Greek χαῖρε, *EV* 5*, 420f. **feror:** as often of involuntary motion: cf. *Aen*.4.376, *EV* 2,493; the admirable forger of *Aen*.2.588 knew this well. **ingenti. . .nocte:** cf. Lucr.5.650 *ingenti caligine noctis*; Szantyr (*TLL* s.v. 1539.48f.) classifies under 'ea quae vehementia sua imprimis sensus afficiunt', but might not 'without limits' (night as a vast enveloping cloak) be a more alarming notion? On *ingens*, there is an article in *EV*, but Henry 3, 39–45 remains unsurpassed. **circumdata:** the partic. already seen as convenient by Lucr. (5.468, 6.1036); so too Virg.: cf. *Aen*.11.496, 12.416.

498 **inualidas:** *in umbrae tenuitatem redactas* Serv.; cf. *G*.3.128, 189, *TLL* s.v. 119.18, and apparently a word brought into high poetry by V. (cf. *EV* s.v. *Neologismi*, 699f.), who seems to have enjoyed coining compound adjs. The hyperbaton. . .*palmas* is striking; likewise the

alliteration (but what exactly does it convey?) **tendens:** *manus. . . tendebam,* Enn. *Ann.*48f. Sk., *TLL* 10.1.142.38. **heu:** Enn. *Ann.,* Cat., *Buc.*; cf. *EV* 2,994f. **non tua:** in tension with the cognate *tibi*; in apposition with the unexpressed subject of *tendens*; still within the hyperbaton of noun and adj.

(iii) *Aen.*11.378–91. Lastly, a short piece from Turnus' violent reply to Drances in the war council: Virgil's rhetoric at its best. Cf. Highet 59ff., 210f. and 190f. above. Enraged, Tu. replies first, without exordium, to the most wounding taunt, 351 *fugae fidens.*

378 **larga:** given emphasis by particle, adverb, prosphonesis and hyperbaton; typically *est* is omitted; Görler 1985, 274, Quinn, 383f., Harrison on 10.106. The adj. (Lucr.1.412, Cic. *Arat.*394, Cat.66.92) receives negative connotation from the delayed *copia fandi*; it has already been used of Drances, in V.'s own introduction, 338 *largus opum.* **semper:** suggested by *Il.*2.796, Iris to Priam who 'always' likes words; 391 is very similar. See too *Buc.*6.15, *Aen.*4.569, 9.775, 11.732f. For the form of the voc. *Drance,* cf. NW 1.295. **copia fandi:** close to *copia uerborum* (Cic. *ND* 1.8, etc., *TLL* s.v. *copia* 902.36ff., 903.39ff.) and similar expressions denoting the orator's fluency; the gerundive gives a briefer and more energetic turn of phrase.

379 **tum cum:** in V. juxtaposed only here, in Turnus' urgent words. Marked alliteration, perhaps in expression of contempt. **bella manus poscunt:** the flat, plain words of a warrior's rhetoric; cf. Tu. again at 7.444. For *manus* in the sense, near enough, of *robur,* cf. *Aen.*11.16, 289, 12.348. **patribusque uocatis:** the formal language of government; *TLL* s.v. 676.60ff. for 'senators'. For the elders of a non-Trojan people, cf. *Aen.*7.176, 727, 12.211 *TLL* s.v. 678.60, Horsfall, *Athen.*78 (1990), 524. *Uoco* is technical: Mommsen, *Staatsrecht* 3 (ed. 3), 915, n. 4.

380 **primus ades:** climactic as signalled by the strong pause at 2S; *adsum* common in V. with the adj. used adverbially (so 2.182 *improuisi aderunt,* 7.506, 10.443; cf. Görler 1985, 270). Note the ironic transference of words appropriate to the warrior first in the fight: 7.577 *Turnus adest,* 5.497, 9.38, 49, 696. *sed non*: repetition with variation of the previous sentence's content; paired monosyllables as in the previous line, tending to a staccato effect in the reading. Four words ending, and one beginning with s: a hiss of contempt? **replenda est. . .uerbis:** cf. 7.502, *montis gemitu. . .replebat,* Lucr.5.992.; the conceit of 'filling a building with words' is common enough: cf. *Buc.*6.48, *G.*3.94, 4.461, 515, *Aen.*2.769. **curia:** again a technical term of pub-

lic life transferred back to primitive Latium, *TLL* s.v. 1483.60, *Aen*.7.174, 11.234.

381 tuto tibi: the adj. (cf. 1.243, 8.323 *latuisset tutus*) can be used in the sense of Eng. 'in safety'; not, therefore, predicative. **magna uolant:** cf. 10.547 *dixerat ille aliquid magnum* (cf. Harrison's note, S. Timpararo *Nuovi Contributi* (Bologna 1994), 276; a use of 'big' already familiar in Gk.); here the adj. (cf. *TLL* s.v. 136.2, Hor. *C*.4.6.1) clearly is predicative. **uolant:** cf. Enn. *Ann*.409Sk, *Var*.18, 10.584 *dicta uolant* (a metaphor in e.g. Pindar, D. Steiner, *The Crown of Song* (London 1986), 107); the dat. *tibi* (cf. 10.584 *Ligeri* is not 'of agent', which V. uses with pass. verbs) but 'ethic' (e.g. Ernout-Thomas, 72). **distinet:** Lucretian (5.203, in a different sense), but much used by Caesar and in the Caesarian corpus (*TLL* s.v.1522.73ff.). Cf. Lyne, *WP*, 125 et passim: military language is often used to characterise Aen.; so too here of Tu.

382 agger moerorum: for the orthography, cf. Harrison on 10.24 (an archaic formula ?). The *agger* is strictly the mound at the base of the wall (cf. 10.24, 9.43 *tutos seruarent aggere muros*, *TLL* s.v. 1307.64; but *agger* is not always (cf. Serv. on 10.24) used so strictly and the genitive may therefore well be *inhaerentiae* (cf. 228 above). **nec inundant** (with ellipse of a word to indicate 'yet'!): a striking and gory expression (*TLL* s.v. 250.20, Prisc. *Gramm*.2.394.9): cf. 10.24 *inundant sanguine fossae*, 12.280f.; the verb (in Cic. and Liv.) is normally used of the liquid and not the container, but V. may have been moved to stretch Lat. usage by Homeric antecedents (Harrison on 10.24, G.B. Conte, *RFil*.111 (1983), 150ff.). The ditch below the *agger* is not (yet) lapping over with blood; from Enn. on, warfare (with its technicalities and gory detail) lay within the subject-matter (and lexicon) of epic.

383 proinde: used by Naev. (*trag*.63 Ribb.) and Lucr. (3.1053); only twice in V. (again at 11.400). To intensify an imperative: KS.1, 201. **tona:** Gk. βροντᾶν (whence in Lat., Cic. *Orat* 29); cf. 4.510 *tonat ore deos*. This 'derisive' use of the imperative is not rare: cf. Pease on 4.381.

eloquio: first in Aug. poetry to avoid *eloquentia, elocutio* (cf. *TLL* s.v. 412.28ff., Lunelli-Leumann, 161f.) **solitum tibi:** for the omission of *est* cf. n. on 378; the parenthesis is typical of spoken language: Hofmann-Ricottilli (ed. 2), 262, *EV* 3, 973f. For this use of the neuter participle, cf. 5.6 *notumque furens quid femina possit*, Ernout-Thomas, 281, LHS, 153, KS 1, 228. **meque timoris argue tu:** V. is fond

of antithetic juxtaposition of pronouns: cf. 11.505f. *me sine. . .tu. . .serua,*
12.810 *tu me, Buc.*5.4, etc. **argue:** cf. *TLL* s.v. 552.36, Cat.64.322
perfidiae. . .nulla arguet aetas.

384 **Drance:** this is not to be classified as *prosphonesis* (the rhetorical
use of the apostrophe on which see Kroll-Lunelli, 25, Norden 122),
but the insulting use of the name in direct address clearly is an
authentic phenomenon of Latic rhetoric: Cic. *Cat.*1.13, 20, Gotoff,
123, *Aen.*10.649, 11.363 I do not know that we have a name to use
or a discussion to help, just as in the case of the derisive imperative.
quando: heavily ironical. **stragis acervos:** the acc. is unproblematic
('heaps': cf. 10.245, 509; already in Acc. *trag.*323 and Cat.64.359);
stragis (on which Baffi in *EV* sheds fitful light) quite the reverse: cf.
Lucr.1.288 *dat. . .stragem,* 6.1263 *confertos ita aceruatim mors accumulabat,*
*G.*3.556 *cateruatim dat stragem.* Is *s.* here used in a concrete ('slaughtered bodies') or in an abstract ('slaughter') sense? Or is the distinction artificial? *Teucrorum* may be the key to the problem: KS 2.1.416f.,
LHS, 65f., Bennett, *Cases,* 81, Shackleton Bailey, *Propertiana,* 223. The
phrase is a good deal easier to digest if the genitives are of different
types (thus 'heaps of bodies of Trojans' is undesirable). In which case,
cf. 373 *sternamur:* if *sternere* is felt in *strages,* then the sense of 'slaughter' is indicated and *Teucrorum* becomes virtually an objective genitive.
stragis then indicates the nature of the heaps (genitive of description
or quality).

385 **tua dextra dedit:** for the spelling of the noun, cf. *TLL* s.v.
916.60ff.; cf. 10.610, 11.339, 735 (where d. is used again with sar-
casm of the failed warrior). *dedit:* cf. *TLL* s.v. *do,* 1686.16, Lucr.1.288
amnis dat. . .stragem, 5.1329, *G.*3.247 *stragemque dedere, Aen.*12.453.
passimque: cf. 2.364; here in ironic exaggeration. Turnus' contempt-
uous rage finds expression in alliteration of t and s.

385f. **tropaeis/insignis agros:** cf. the trophies honestly won at
11.172 (Pallas) 224 (Turnus); already at Acc. *trag.*148. The verb perhaps first here and at 7.790; apparently a back-formation from *insignitus*
(*TLL* s.v. 1908.45, Enn. *Ann.*330Sk.).

386 **possit:** the verb thrown before the subject, the dependent clause
before the main verb, for sharp emphasis and to avoid self-contained
spondaic fourth foot: cf. Austin on 1.1. The subjunctive depends on
another subjunctive, *experiare,* an instance which seems to have es-
caped the hunters: Görler 1985, 274, Norden 379, n. 1. The verb
(TLL s.v. 1669.43) is Ennian (*Ann.*187Sk.). **uiuida uirtus:** the adj.,
dear to Lucr.(1.72, 178; cf. *Aen.*10.609), is cognate with *uiuo,* not di-

rectly with *uirtus* (*pace* Harrison on 10.609), which is related to *uir*, though some sort of association may have been felt within this striking alliterative expression.

387 **licet:** in Enn. and Lucr.; cf. 11.348f., 6.400 for the paratactic construction **longe. . .quaerendi:** adverb (cf. 6.378f.) and verb enclose the phrase; *sunt* as so often omitted. The gerundive helps V.'s quest for speed and density of expression, reducing the need for syntactical elaboration. **scilicet:** as often with ironic tinge; cf. 4.379, 6.526, 11.371, 12.570.

388 **nobis:** a real plural; Turnus invites Drances to fight alongside him. Two invitations to Drances, running from caes. to caes. in the following line, with a terse three-word peak (cf. 4.629): the foe is here; molossic words at 1–2S and 3S–4 bring Turnus to a weighty climax. **circumstant:** cf. Enn. *Scaen.*30, *Aen.*7.585, *TLL* s.v. 1174.33. For these *muri*, cf. J. Carcopino, *Virgile et les origines d'Ostie* (ed. 2, Paris 1968), 290f.

389 **imus:** not, I think, *imus* for *eamus*, or even *ibimus*; Tu. here answers the gibes of 368ff., 371ff., beginning 'we march together. . .', but before he can say (e.g.) 'and you will win glory alongside me', he sees that D. has not moved. **aduersos:** common in V. as both noun and adj. (though I do not think we have a study of the Virgilian synonyms for 'enemy'; cf. *hostis, hostilis, inimicus*); *adu.* from LA *trag.*21; cf. *Aen.*9.761, 10.412, 11.370 *aduersum. . .hostem.* **quid cessas?:** not, strictly, anacoluthon, for the construction is complete at *aduersos* and V. is close to the manner of normal speech; the short question, though, is also a rhetorical weapon (cf. *Aen.*4.325, 369, 6.52, 11.392; cf. the run of three in Cic. *Cat.*1.20). For the verb, cf. Enn. *Scaen.*214, *Aen.*6.51, 2. **an tibi. . .erit?** We may be invited to think of a suppressed question: 'why do you hesitate? (will you never march?) and will you always talk and run?'. **Mauors:** not an authentic archaism (*pace EV* 1.288): see Wissowa *RKR*, 142, n. 4. Recognised as a poeticism by Festus; from Enn. *Ann.*99Sk. Tu. takes up D.'s taunt at 373: *Mauors* is used in the transferred sense of 'courage'.

390 **uentosa in lingua:** cf. Kroll-Lunelli 63 and Wilkinson *GLA*, 216f. for the patterning of nouns and adjs. For adjs. in *-osus*, cf. Ross (n. on *G.*4.492), 53ff., Leumann-Lunelli, 164, Axelson, 61, Watson, 439f., Harrison on 10.141: the termination is no sign of the old lexicon of high poetry, but is perhaps developed to provide Latin equivalents of certain endings in the Greek poetic vocabulary. V.'s choice of insults is of particular interest: cf. here I. Opelt, *Die lateinischen*

Schimpfwörter (Heidelberg 1965), 164, Cic. *Fam*.11.9.1, PsSall. *Rep*.2.3.6
uirtus in lingua; literally, cf. Cat.64.59. **pedibusque fugacibus istis:**
the adj. from Plaut. on, but rare in republican Latin; here cf. PsCic.
in Sall.10, PsSall. *in Tull*.5 *pedes fugaces*, PsSall. *Rep*.2.9.2 *pedes fugaces*,
Rutilius Lupus (late Augustan) 1.18 *pedes ad fugam* (citing a lost speech
of Lycurgus), R.G.M. Nisbet, JRS 48 (1958), 31, A. La Penna, *EV*
s.v. *Drance*, 139, and in *Vergiliana*, 387, R. Syme, *Sallust* (Berkeley
1964), 348f. Rutilius Lupus uses Lyc. and influences the PsSall. corpus (so already Ruhnken in his comm. on Rut.), while Virgil, as
Prof. Nisbet suggests to me *per litteras*, draws on a tradition of Greek
invective (as old as *Il*.1.225), though I do not think we can exclude
that political rhetoric of the c. 1 A.D. drew on Virgilian language.

CHAPTER SIX

VIRGIL'S IMPACT AT ROME: THE NON-LITERARY EVIDENCE

N.M. Horsfall

This chapter abbreviates, amplifies and updates my contribution 'Aspects of Virgilian influence in Roman Life' to 'Atti del convegno mondiale scientifico di studi su Virgilio' 1981 2 (Milano 1984), 47–63. For Virgil's popular *fortuna*, no adequate and recent survey exists, or so it seems, apart from 'Aspects', and it was high time that a good deal of antique pedantry and tralatician error, my own included, was cleared up.[1]

The Aeneas-legend, if my analysis of its history[2] is correct, was, prior to Virgil, a political plaything of the Iulii Caesares. It was the Aeneid which transformed it into a truly national story. Equally successful was Virgil's first venture into bucolic poetry in Latin; not so the *G.*, as we shall see.

It may be necessary to jettison (cf. p. 7) the stories in Tacitus (*Dial.*13.2 *caruit neque apud populum notitia*: a theatre audience, on hearing some lines of Virgil, rises to honour the poet) and VSD (11: on a rare visit to Rome, Virgil flees from a mob of fans *in proximum tectum*). Tributes to fame and *verecundia* should at very least awaken disquiet. Two details, however, remain unquestionable:

(i) Virgil's fame in his own lifetime and immediately after his death. Thus Velleius (2.36.3) *inter quae nostri aevi eminent princeps carminum Vergilius*. . .Cfr. Hor. *Ep.*2.1.245–7, Prop.2.34.59–80, Ov. *Tr.*4.10.51, *Am.*1.15.25f., 3.15.7, *AA* 3.338. *RA* 396. Suet. *Cal.*34 may be read as a protest; cf. Pers.1.96.

(ii) VSD 26: *Bucolica eo successu edidit ut in scaena per cantores crebro pronuntiarentur*. Serv. *ad. Buc.*6.11 cannot be quoted in support.[3] Cf. however Macr.5.17.5 (pantomime of Dido), Suet. *Ner.*54 (pantomime

---

[1] Cf. J. Tolkiehn, *De Homeri auctoritate in cotidiana Romanorum vita*, *Jhb.klass.Phil.*, Suppl. 23 (1896), 222–289. For V. it seems that nothing similar has ever been attempted, with any seriousness.

[2] *Roman Myth and Mythography*, *BICS* Suppl. 52 (1987), 12–24; cf. now E. Gruen. *Culture and national identity in republican Rome* (Ithaca 1992), 6ff.

[3] Cf. 17 and M. Bonaria, *Romani Mimi* (Roma 1965), 190.96, G. Wille, *Musica Romana* (Amsterdam 1967), 226.

of Turnus), Aug. *Serm*.241.5 (PL 38.1135–6) *pauci nostis in libris, multi in theatris*.[4] And note also Virgil readings and discussions at dinner (Juv.6.434ff., 11.180ff.): delectable confirmation is provided by Habinnas' slave at Petr.68.4,[5] just as the comparison of Cicero and Publilius Syrus mocks the fashion for too-serious assessments of 'Homer vs. Virgil' (Quint.l0.1.106, Horsfall (n. 5), 79).[6] We should not forget that public readings of Virgil continued into the late Empire and beyond.[7] This accumulation of testimonia leads us in an unexpected direction and serves to destabilise current wisdom (to wit, that the ample presence of Virgil citations and reminiscences in graffiti, inscriptions, etc. reflects the study of the poet at school). *Pauci nostis in libris, multi in theatris*, said Augustine (supra); compare Ovid on the crowd at the festival picnic on Anna Perenna's day: *illic et cantant quidquid didicere theatris*.[8] Thus St. Jerome remarks (Ep.21.13.9) that some *sacerdotes* left gospels and prophets aside *comoedias legere, amatoria bucolicorum versuum verba cantare, tenere (= 'memorise') Vergilium*. These irreverends are not necessarily just well-schooled; they may perhaps also (almost worse!) have learned their *Bucolics* from frequent visits to theatre performances. The evidence does seem to point to some form of chanting or singing.[9]

Virgil became a school text in his lifetime.[10] In the early c. 5 A.D., Orosius still says that the story of Aeneas' arrival in Italy *ludi litterarii disciplina nostrae quoque memoriae inustum est* (1.18.1). Nothing new: Quintilian lays down (1.8.5) that school reading should begin with Homer and Virgil, at the outset imperfectly understood; no matter: *neque enim semel legentur*.[11] You begin very young so that *teneris ebibitus animis non facile oblivione possit aboleri* (Aug. l.c., n. 11). This is not the place to examine just how Virgil was read at school.[12] The master

---

[4] Cf. Flor. *Verg*.1.6 *uersus concinuntur*, Owen's note on Ov. *Trist*.2.519, Wille (n. 3), 225–7.

[5] Cf. my discussion of this inept cultural imitation at *GR* 36 (1989), 78.

[6] Cf. too Juv.6.436–7 and *CIL* 6.1710 for a wry footnote.

[7] H.-I. Marrou, *MEFR* 49 (1932), 99, S.F. Bonner, *Education in ancient Rome* (London 1977), 123, Ven.Fort.3.18.7f., 7.8.26. The origins of the *sortes Vergilianae* I hope to clarify in a note in the 1992 SHA Colloquium.

[8] F.3.535, Stat. *Silv*.1.2.172f., Suet. *Galba* 13, Wille (n. 3), 127.

[9] Accompanied? Cf. Wille (n. 3), 226.

[10] Cf. Suet. *Gramm*.16 on Caecilius Epirota.

[11] Cf. Aug. *Civ.Dei* 1.3 *quem. . .paruuli legunt*.

[12] Bonner (n. 7), 213f., Horsfall, *Aspects*, 47f., H.-I. Marrou *Histoire de l'Education dans l'Antiquité* 2, (ed. 6, Paris 1964, often repr.), *passim*; avoid the English translation.

praelegebat the text;[13] the pupils chanted the text, once mastered, back again.[14] Group chanting was at Rome[15] and remained even in my youth the best way to memorise a text. Virgil was read very slowly:[16] that explains (thus Marichal, n. 16) the preponderance of Aen.1–2 among the Pompeii graffiti. Those who persevered might, surprisingly, come to love Virgil,[17] notwithstanding such exercises as the prose paraphrase of Virgil, the metrical reworking and the Virgilian declamation.[18] The survivors had memorised the text amazingly well, in some cases.[19]

School and theatre are complementary, not exclusive. The Virgil-graffiti, always executed in that fluent cursive hand which reveals at least study with a *grammaticus*,[20] bear testimony either to schoolday memories of Virgil (or indeed to schoolboy scribblings), or, as seems not usually recognised, to the impact of public performances. The frequency with which the opening lines of books are cited has also been noted,[21] but it does not lend decisive support to a case for school as against theatre: first lines of performances are hardly remembered less often than first lines of set books! At Pompeii, it must be reiterated, the find-spots of graffiti do point to a predominantly school-centred authorship,[22] but this is not exclusively true (witness Virgil in gladiatorial barracks, ironmonger's shop, brothel).[23] The Virgil-graffiti have little bearing on current discussion of literacy and educational levels in the Roman world.[24] Knowledge of Virgil, or

---

[13] Macr.1.24.5, Bonner (n. 7), 225f.: reading and exposition.

[14] Macr. l.c., *SHA* Clod.Albin.5.2.

[15] Cf. my remarks in *Literacy in the Roman world*, *JRA* Suppl. 3 (1991), 62.

[16] Horsfall, *Atti*, 48, R. Marichal, *REL* 35 (1957), 82.

[17] Aug. *Conf*.1.13.21f.; cf. Marichal (n. 16), 82, Horsfall, *Atti*, 50.

[18] Prose paraphrase, Aug. *Conf*.1.17.27, cf. 1.13.20; declamation, Serv. *ad Aen.* 10.18, 532, Ennod. *Declam.*, *MGH* AA 7 (ed. F. Vogel, 1885), 324, no. CDLXVI, cf. *Anth.Lat.*255R; metrical reworkings in hexameters (*PSI* 142) or iambi (Serv. *ad Aen.*10.272).

[19] Aug. *de an.* 4.7.9, PL 44.529, *CSEL* 60 (1913, = *Opera* 8.2), 389.3ff., R.P. Hoogma, *Der Einfluss Vergils auf die CLE* (Amsterdam 1959), xii. Such feats attracted disproportionate attention: R. Blum, *Die antike Mnemotechnik* (*Spudasmata* 15, Hildesheim 1969), 130ff.

[20] H. Solin, *Enc.Virg.* s.v. *Epigrafia*, A. Petrucci in *Virgilio e Noi* (Genova 1981), 51ff.

[21] Marichal (n. 16), 82, Horsfall, *Atti*, 51, etc. See too H. Solin in *Neue Forschungen in Pompeji* (Recklinghausen 1975), 250.

[22] Petrucci (n. 20), 53, Solin (n. 20), 333f., *Scr.Civ.*5 (1981). 310f., *Cron.Erc.*3 (1974), 98f.

[23] Horsfall, *Atti*, 50, after D. Joly, *Caesarodunum* 13 bis (1978), 97: cf. Horsfall (n. 15), 68, n. 63.

[24] Cf. Solin and Petrucci (n. 22), W.V. Harris, *Ancient Literacy* (Harvard 1989), 261.

love for him, was not the exclusive privilege of an educational elite.[25] The writer of a Virgil graffito is not necessarily the man who re- members the verse, nor is the calligraphy necessarily learned at school.[26] You do not even have to be literate to remember a verse from the theatre and to ask a friend to write it on a wall! I have tried elsewhere (cf. n. 25) to show how a Roman of but very modest education could partially but still passionately enjoy his Virgil. At this point let us survey the various contexts in which a knowledge of Virgil is certain (or has been loudly claimed):

(i) Conversation.

Distinguished Romans of the late Republic cite Homer and Sophocles with suspicious frequency;[27] deathbeds are particularly eloquent.[28] Apposite quotation enters the biographical tradition, and the artful parodist never quite knows when to call a halt.[29] Suetonius places Virgil on the lips of Augustus (brilliantly credible), Nero and Domitian.[30] A report in Greek of an untimely quotation by a praetorian tribune in 199 A.D. (Dio 76.10.2) is particularly interest- ing in view of parallel testimony from Vindolanda and Masada (see 254 infra).

(ii) Graffiti from Pompeii and elsewhere.

In 1981, I cited 62 (at most 64) graffiti of Virgil from Pompeii: it is not certain that the *G.* are present at all;[31] 17 citations from *Buc.*[32] and 46 from *Aen.* are strikingly out of proportion to the works' lengths.[33] *Buc.* were the Pompeians' favourite love poetry (Solin notes that about half the graffiti derive from the homosexual *Buc.*2); for *Aen.*4 and 6 virtually no appetite; 17 citations of 1.1, 15 of 2.1.[34] Away from Pompeii, no full list exists.[35]

---

[25] Cf. *Alambicco*, 57–60.

[26] There are other possibilities, Horsfall (n. 15), 63f.

[27] W. Kroll, *Die Kultur der ciceronischen Zeit* 2 (repr. Darmstadt 1963), 119, J. Kaimio, *The Romans and the Greek language* (Helsinki 1979), 191.

[28] A. Ronconi, *SIFC* 17 (1940), 16, Pelling on Plut. *Ant.*77.7.

[29] R. Syme, *Emperors and Biography* (Oxford 1971), 61f., *HA Papers* (Oxford 1983), 108, *Ammianus and the HA* (Oxford 1968), 127.

[30] Suet. *Aug.*40, *Ner.*47.1, *Dom.*9.1.

[31] On a possible citation of 1.163, see *Atti* 61, n. 61 and Solin (n. 20), 333.

[32] Add *CIL* 4.8222 and the unpublished graffito cited by Solin, l.c., from Castellamare di Stabia.

[33] Horsfall, *Atti* 51, Solin l.c.

[34] Cf. Solin (n. 21), 250.

[35] Cf. *CLE* 1785–6, 2293, Solin (n. 20), 333, Marichal (n. 16), 81f. I am glad to be able to add a tile from Kesztök, *Ann.Epigr.*1983, 772, bearing *Aen.*9.1–2 (*vidi*).

(iii) Inscriptions.
Note the ample discussions by H. Solin in *EV* s.v. *Epigrafia* and *Carmina Latina Epigraphica*. Epigraphic echoes of Virgil have recently become a major area of study[36] and new material continues to come to hand.[37]

(iv) Wall-paintings.
Only one from Pompeii is unquestionably Virgilian in origin, a wounded Aeneas from bk. 12;[38] a Virgilian inspiration has been claimed, wishfully, for many others.[39] A fragmentary painting from Oxford, Kent[40] bears the words *bina manu* (1.313, 12.165) and could have represented a Virgilian scene. Note the probable illustration of *Buc.*4 on the ceiling recovered from under Trier cathedral.[41]

(v) Mosaics.
Aeneas, Dido and Virgil from Sousse,[42] the sequence of Dido-scenes from Low Ham, Somerset,[43] Dares and Entellus from Vaucluse,[44] and, possibly a (lost) scene from Halicarnassus.[45]

(vi) Sarcophagi.
Of the material collected by Canciani in *LIMC* s.v. *Aineias*, only 161 (= Helbig, *Führer*, 3 (ed. 4), 66–9, no. 2162 (B. Andreae) is securely Virgilian (Aeneas and Dido leaving for the hunt). *LIMC* 167/180 (sacrifice of the sow; marriage of Aeneas and Lavinia) does not derive necessarily from the *Aeneid*. The same is true of *LIMC* 162 (a c. 3

---

[36] *Enc.Virg.* s.v. *Epigrafia* and *Carmina Latina Epigrafica* (Solin), L. Gamberale and others in *Atti del convegno virgiliano di Brindisi nel bimillenario della morte* (Perugia 1983), 199ff., M. Massaro, *AION* 4–5 (1982–3), 193ff., P. Cugusi, *Aspetti letterari dei CLE* (Bologna 1985), 165ff.

[37] *Ann.Epigr.*1981, 874, 1982, 370, 1987, 266, 1989, 75, 185, 231.

[38] *LIMC* s.v. *Aineias*, 174, on which see the useful paper by D. Joly, *Hommages M. Renard* 1 (Coll.Lat.101, 1969), 482–5.

[39] My scepticism in *Atti* 54–7 follows that expressed by G.E. Rizzo, *BASM* 1.5 (1930), 6ff. F. Canciani, *Enc.Virg.* s.v. *Enea*, 233 and in *LIMC* 1, cit., p. 396 is insufficiently rigorous. The same might be said (cf. M.I. Davies, *LIMC* s.v. *Antenor*, 17, 18!) of G.K. Galinsky, *Aeneas, Sicily and Rome* (Princeton 1969), *passim*. *LIMC* 175 was identified in passing as a 'wounded Aeneas' by K. Bulas, *AJA* 54 (1950), 115; this unconvincing whim, lent authority by Canciani, l.c., does not survive dispassionate examination of the extensive bibliography, Helbig, *Führer* 2 (ed. 4, 1966), p. 855 (B. Andreae).

[40] *LIMC* 207, = *JRS* 16 (1926), fig. 68.

[41] E. Simon, *Die konstantinischen Deckengemälde in Trier* (Mainz 1986), 23f.; cf. Constantine's polemic use of the same text, (?) at the council of Antioch, 325 A.D., A. Wlosok, *Res humanae- Res divinae* (Heidelberg 1990), 444, cf. 60f. above.

[42] *LIMC* 158, = K. Dunbabin, *Mosaics of Roman North Africa* (Oxford 1978), 269, 12.

[43] *LIMC* 159.

[44] H. Lavagne, *Caesarodunum* 13 bis (1978), 133ff.

[45] *Atti*, 62, n. 98 and (with extreme scepticism), *LIMC* 160.

A.D. relief of Aeneas' arrival in Italy).[46] That the *Tabula Iliaca Capitolina* reflects Virgil's text is possible.[47]

(vii) *Instrumentum domesticum.*

Two silver spoons.[48] Macr.5.17.5 talks of the Dido story as *tamquam unico argumento decoris* for painters, sculptors and embroiderers, an assertion not borne out by the surviving material.[49] Of the two high-relief cups from late antique Gaul claimed as illustrating G.4,[50] the Orpheus is unspecific and the marine deities inconclusive. It is worth noting that slaves might bear names inspired by the *Aeneid*.[51]

(viii) Coinage.

Cf. *Expectate ueni* (after 2.283) on coins of Carausius.[52]

(ix) Gems.

LIMC 176: the wounded Aeneas receives first-aid? But cf. the doubts expressed by E. Zwierlein-Diehl, *Ant. Gemmen in deutschen Sammlungen* 2 (Berlin) (München 1969), 155, no. 404.

(x) Papyri.

In 1981, I referred to recent publications by W. Cockle (now *POxy* 50.3554) and H. Maehler; the flow continues:[53] C. Gallazzi, *ZPE* 48 (1982), 75–8 (P. Narmuth. inv. 66.362); first half of c. 2 A.D.; *Buc*.8.53–62), D. Hagedorn, *ZPE* 34 (1979), 108 identifies *POxy* 10.1315 as *Aen*.11.1 = 4.129; for the elusive P. Strasb. 2, cf. for now *CLA* 833 (vol. 6, 38); on a wooden tablet from Vindolanda (ca. 100 A.D.)

---

[46] Rizzo (n. 39), 18.

[47] Horsfall, *JHS* 99 (1979), 32.

[48] *CLE* 1786, Horsfall, *Atti*, 48f.

[49] Embroidery: *LIMC* 215, highly doubtful. Canciani, *LIMC*, p. 396 notes that Macr.'s statement is not really borne out by the surviving evidence. On the gladiatorial helmet from Pompeii, see *Atti* 57f.; M. Gigante, *Virgilio e la Campania* (Napoli 1984), 92 has not noticed that his (and Comparetti's) view has now been answered in detail. For the (undoubtedly Virgilian) scene on a cuirass from Beth Shean, cf. G. Foerster, *Atiquot* 17 (1985), 139ff.; I was glad to be able to identify the scene's origin: *Atti*, 61, n. 71.

[50] G. Faider-Feytmans and J. Hubaux, *Mél. Grégoire* 2 (Bruxelles 1950), 253ff.

[51] L. Vidman, *Anc.Soc.*2 (1971), 162ff.

[52] N. Shiel, *PVS* 12 (1972–3), 51ff., P. Webb in H. Mattingly and E.A. Sydenham, *Roman Imperial Coinage* 5.2 (London 1933), 510.554 and 528.771.

[53] For recent bibliography, cf. Cotton and Geiger, *infra*, Petrucci (n. 22), M. Gigante in *La Fortuna di Virgilio* (ed. M.G.) (Napoli 1986), 28ff., *Enc.Virg.* s.v. *Papiri* (Petrucci), A. Grillone, *Atti del convegno...delle Georgiche* (Napoli 1977), 401ff., B. Baldwin, *AJPh* 97 (1976), 361ff. = *Studies on late Roman and Byzantine History, Literature and Language* (Amsterdam 1984), 149ff.

Aen.9.473: see A.K. Bowman and J.D. Thomas, *JRS* 76 (1986), 122 and *Britannia* 18 (1987), 130ff. Similarly, from a military context, Masada Pap. 721 (73/4 A.D.) of *Aen*.4.9, H. Cotton and J. Geiger, *Masada II: the Latin and Greek Documents* (Jerusalem 1989), 32f. For palaeographical and educational aspects, cf. Petrucci, Gigante and Baldwin in n. 53.

(xi) The Byzantine world.

Virgil and the Greek East is an unexpectedly rewarding topic that is now receiving due attention.[54] For the *G.* and the *Geoponica*, cf. R.H. Rodgers, *GRBS* 19 (1978), 277ff. Both V. himself and even Serv. have a place in the early Byzantine antiquarian tradition (Lydus and Malelas.[55] On the *G.* and the great mosaic of the Imperial Palace, see J. Trilling in *Dumb. Oaks Papers* 43 (1989), 60–3. R. Stüpperich[56] fails to handle adequately (229) the Virgilian statues from the Baths of Zeuxippus, known to us from Christodoros' descriptions in *Anth.Pal.*2: Virgil himself (and Apuleius!), Aeneas, Creusa, Dares and Entellus (cf. the Vaucluse mosaic), apart from figures such as Panthus and Thymoetes, not so exclusively Virgilian. The problem of dating remains unresolved: the statues might be Severan, could well be Constantinian and need only be earlier than Christodorus (late c. 5). Lydus, Malelas and the statues bear witness to Virgil as a central element in a culture still actively bilingual but under imminent threat.

---

[54] Baldwin (n. 53), 155–6 = 368–8 and *AuA* 28 (1982), 81ff. = *Studies* (n. 53), 445ff. B. Hemmerdinger *Byz.Forsch.* 1 (1966), 174ff., A. Garzya, *Enc.Virg.* s.v. *Bizantina, letteratura*.

[55] Baldwin (n. 54), and Horsfall, *Messana* forthcoming.

[56] *Ist.Mitt.*32 (1982); for the reference to Trilling's paper, I am grateful to Prof. E. Kitzinger.

VIRGIL: THE LITERARY IMPACT

W.R. Barnes

OVID, *Metamorphoses*

Virgil is everywhere in Ovid;[1] a new index is needed.[2] Homer also is in the *Met.*, with the criticism of Homer,[3] which will have influenced Ovid's reading of Virgil.[4] Ennius is there behind Virgil, in some places significantly.[5] But the epithet for Ovid among modern scholars, even in the *Met.*, is Callimachean, not Virgilian.[6] The poem is a poem of many genres.[7]

Genre. Ovid's response to Virgil first presents itself as a matter of generic preference in poetry.[8] Announcing in *Amores* 1.1 in the manner of Roman admirers of Callimachus that he will not write hexameter verse on arms and battles but elegiac verse on love, he begins with his failure to write a poem like the *Aeneid*, and ends with his Muse taking the crown that Octavian might take in the *Georgics*.[9] In

---

[1] So, a little differently, F. Bömer in *Ovid* (ed. M. von Albrecht, E. Zinn, Darmstadt 1968), 198 (= *Gymn.*66 (1959), 285). Bibliography on Ovid and Virgil: *ANRW* 2.31.1 (1980), 59ff. (Suerbaum), 2.31.4 (1981), 2204ff. (Hofmann), *EV* s.v. *Ovidio*. On Ovid's "sources" and "models" in general, *ANRW* 2.31.4.2200ff. (Hofmann), F. Bömer, *Gymn.* 81 (1974), 511ff.

[2] The standard index remains A. Zingerle, *Ovidius. . .2* (Innsbruck 1871). A mass of material in Bömer's commentary, but until an index appears, cf. his notes to 12.76, 14.102f.

[3] M. Lausberg, *Boreas* 5 (1982), 112ff.

[4] Ovid as 'il primo critico di Virgilio', R. Lamacchia, *Maia* 12 (1960), 310ff. Popular or scholarly criticism of Virgil is another matter, but cf. J.C. McKeown, *PLLS* 2 (1979), 172 on *Am.*3.12.38.

[5] P.E. Knox, *Ovid's Metamorphoses. . .(PCPhS* Suppl. 11 1986), 69ff. On allusions to Virgil and to Ennius behind Virgil see also Bömer (n. 1, 1974), 503ff. and his n. on *Met.*9.48f.; on the practice of 'double' allusions in general, S. Hinds, *The metamorphosis of Persephone* (Cambridge 1987), 151, n. 16.

[6] Ovid as 'Callimachean': cf. E.J. Bernbeck, *Beobachtungen zur Darstellungsart in Ovids Metamorphosen* (München 1967), 126f., 130f. Ovid as 'Hellenistic' or 'Callimachean' in his response to Virgil: Bömer (n. 1, 1959/1968), 198, R. Lamacchia, *AR* 14 (1969), 4, n. 5. But detail seems to be lacking.

[7] 'An anthology of genres', E.J. Kenney, in his introduction to A.D. Melville's trans. (Oxford 1986), xviii.

[8] O.S. Due, *Changing Forms* (Copenhagen 1974), 45ff.

[9] Cf. J.C. McKeown Ovid, *Amores* 2 (Liverpool 1989) on 1.1–2. V. Buchheit, *Gymn.*93 (1986), 257ff., with further bibl., 257, n. 2.

the *Remedia Amoris* he compares himself to Virgil as a writer of elegy to a writer of epic (395f.).[10] But in the *Metamorphoses* he announces something new, which he writes in hexameter verse;[11] a poem which he later describes, with whatever irony, in terms that Virgil had used for the second half of the *Aeneid* (*Tristia* 2.63f.). Virgil himself had passed from the rejection of heroic epic in the *Bucolics* to the post-ponement of it in the *Georgics* to the writing of it in the *Aeneid*; Ovid perhaps alludes to a significant passage in the *Georgics*.[12] The *Aeneid* had its Alexandrian, "Callimachean", elegiac features; Ovid takes po-etic advantage of that generic complexity.[13] He himself brought to the *Metamorphoses* certain features of sentence and verse structure, and certain motifs and themes, from elegy.[14] The generic character of the *Metamorphoses*, as a whole and in its parts, is more overtly complex than that of the *Aeneid*, and description of it continues.[15] Ovid's re-sponse to Virgil in the poem is only one feature, or rather two or three, of that complexity. What follows will focus on Ovid's response to Virgil; larger questions lie beyond. Callimachus may not have said quite as much about long poems in hexameter verse on heroic sub-jects as has been thought; and his Roman admirers' allusions to his principles may need to be reconsidered.[16]

The prooemium in its implication of adherence to Callimachus' principles resembles and perhaps echoes *Buc.*6.[17] (Whether that ad-herence is partial, whether *perpetuum* indicates a departure, and whether it is ironical, are three further questions.)[18] The opening sequence of the poem, from Chaos to Cosmogony to Deucalion and Pyrrha and then a series of mythological stories, resembles the sequence of Silenus' song in *Buc.*6.[19] The Daphne story is in a prominent position in both

---

[10] Other explicit references to Virgil and to the Aeneas-legend are common enough in Ovid's earlier poetry (e.g. *Am.*1.15.25f., *Ars* 3.337f.) but need a little caution (like Prop. 2.34.65f.; R.F. Thomas, *PLLS* 5 (1985), 71, n. 2).

[11] V. Buchheit, *Herm.*94 (1966), 83f., E.J. Kenney, *PCPhS* 22 (1976), 46f., Knox (n. 5), 9.

[12] Thomas (n. 10), 61ff., *AJP* 99 (1978), 449f.

[13] Hinds (n. 5), 133f.

[14] Elegiac theme and variation, as in 1.489f.; caesurae, Knox (n. 5), 84ff., motifs and themes, H. Tränkle, *Herm.*91 (1963), 459ff.

[15] Cf. S.E. Hinds' review of Knox (n. 5), *CP* 84 (1989), 266ff.

[16] Knox (n. 5), 9f. with n. 12, A. Cameron, *TAPA* 122 (1992), 305ff.; but notice Knox (n. 5), 71 on "the invention of the Augustan poets".

[17] Knox (n. 5), 10.

[18] Contrast Knox (n. 5), 10.

[19] ib. 10ff.

the *Metamorphoses* and *Buc*.6; the Io story echoes Calvus and, perhaps
by coincidence, *Buc*.6.[20] Behind *Buc*.6 is Gallus; which prompts caution.[21] The prooemium also echoes the invocation of *Georgics* 1.40;[22]
the echo, with the allusion through Virgil to Callimachus and at the
head of a sequence from Chaos, evokes the Hesiodic tradition of
Silenus' song (cf. Call. fr.2 Pf). Ovid begins the *Metamorphoses* then
with the Virgil who had declined to write heroic epic in *Buc*.6, and
so refers the poem to the Alexandrian, neoteric tradition.[23]

But the prooemium also indicates that the poem will present a
continuous sequence of events from the beginning of the world down
to the poet's own time; the poem will differ then from other collective poems and from Silenus' song.[24] Silenus' cosmogony has universal pretensions, but Ovid's pretensions appear to be those of universal history.[25] (Ovid's adherence to Callimachus' principles seems at
least to that extent to be partial.) Universal histories in the first century came down to Rome;[26] and in the *Metamorphoses* the sequence
comes down through the events of the *Aeneid* to a celebration of Rome
and Augustus that uses some of the forms of the *Aeneid*.[27] That presents the question of the relation of Ovid's history to Virgil's history.
Not the question, whether the poem is an epic, but at most, what
sort of epic. The opening sequence of the poem does not treat the
generic pretensions of epic very seriously. (If *perpetuum* does indicate
a departure from Callimachus' principles, which seems likely in the
context of *ab origine mundi. . .ad mea. . .tempora*, it is ironic.)

The opening sequence from Chaos to the second emergence of
life has indeed some pretensions to a higher dignity[28] and adapts the
Aeneid in 200ff. But these pretensions are at least ambiguous.[29] Then
the Apollo-Daphne story (452ff.) is programmatic and exemplary for
the poem,[30] and not least for Ovid's treatment of generic identity

---

[20] P.E. Knox, *TAPA* 120 (1990), 183ff., Due (n. 8), 27f.
[21] M. von Albrecht, in *Virgilio e gli Augustei* (Napoli 1990), 214f., D.O. Ross, *Back-grounds to Augustan poetry* (Cambridge Mass. 1975), 39.
[22] Due (n. 8), 95.
[23] Knox (n. 5), 10ff.
[24] H. Herter in *Ovid* (n. 1), 350ff. (= *AJP* 69 (1948), 138ff.).
[25] Silenus' song: Knox (n. 5), 11. Ovid: W. Ludwig, *Struktur und Einheit der Metamorphosen Ovids* (Berlin 1965), 74ff.
[26] Ludwig (n. 25), 78ff.
[27] W. Kraus, *Ovid* (n. 1), 105, 108f. (= PW 18.2.1938, 1940).
[28] Hinds (n. 15), 269f.
[29] D.C. Feeney, *Gods in Epic* (Oxford 1991), 189f., Due (n. 8), 70ff.
[30] W.S.M. Nicoll, *CQ* 74 (1980), 174ff., Knox (n. 5), 14ff.

and hierarchy. The Apollo-Cupid story with which it begins itself programmatically evokes differences of literary genre in its reworking of the theophany of *Amores* 1.1;[31] Apollo's heroic pretensions are wounded as the poet's epic ambitions are wounded. Then the erotic assumes heroic forms. Cupid's anger motivates the action, as Juno's does in the *Aeneid*; he shoots like Apollo himself in the *Iliad*; Apollo's passion is described in a simile using material from the *Georgics* in epic form (492ff.); the pursuit is described in a simile combining similes from the final great pursuits of the *Iliad* and the *Aeneid*.[32] But it is not all Virgil, or all epic. For Daphne and her father there is the narrative of Callimachus' hymn to Artemis, for Apollo's wooing pastoral and elegiac (perhaps Gallus and Euphorion),[33] and the invocation form of the hymn. A number of works and genres are appropriated by the erotic; and several works and genres, including amatory poetry itself, are deflated.[34] Not always deflated; for example, *Georgics* 1.430 in 484. But even the original programmatic idea of the Apollo who turned the poet from epic is perhaps deflated when it is Apollo who is reduced from heroic pretensions;[35] even if the episode can be thought an aition in this detail as well (450f., 557ff.). Generic hierarchy matters less here than the interest of a variety of ways of presenting the world, or seeing it, in a variety of literary forms and works which may bear on one another. Generic relations in the Polyphemus-Galatea story have been explained as a dialogue evoking themes of authority running through the poem;[36] but the explanation has yet to be applied elsewhere. In the Apollo-Daphne story the epic voice does not have the last word.[37] But a treatment of a story may be reworked for humour without reference to other genres, such as a *pièce de resistance* of Alexandrian, neoteric narrative, Virgil's Orpheus and Eurydice.[38]

Style. Ovid's diction and style resembles Virgil's in some respects, differs in others.[39] Some differences are the interrelated features of

---

[31] Nicoll (n. 30).
[32] On Daphne's appeal to her father, see Knox (n. 20), 197ff.
[33] Knox (n. 5), 14ff.
[34] Cf. also A. Primmer, *WSt*.10 (1976), 210ff.
[35] Nicoll (n. 30), 175f.
[36] J. Farrell, *AJP* 113 (1992), 235ff.
[37] Primmer (n. 34), 219.
[38] C. Neumeister, *Würz.Jhb*.12 (1986), 169ff.
[39] E.J. Kenney in (ed.) J.W. Binns, *Ovid* (London 1973), 116ff.

style and verse of a more rapid narrative.[40] Others, including the absence, the rarity, and the replacement of some features of Virgil's high style, may amount to a rejection of that style as a general style, for an eclectic style of many styles, in the neoteric tradition.[41] But Ovid also imitates neoteric elements in Virgil's style.[42]

In his use and adaption of particular words, phrases, ideas, and episodes from Virgil Ovid reduces or "profanes" the language and ideas.[43] The terms "profane" and "profanation" are perhaps a little colourful;[44] but much of the material is from religious or related contexts. The profanation is humorous in the weighing of *felix* in *Fasti* 3.597f., and perhaps in *beatos* in *Met.*11.539f.;[45] if the latter is indeed profanation, with the change of perspective in *funera quos maneant*. Some observations might be put a little differently. The collocation *memor ira*[46] may have been used by Livy in 9.29.11 before it was used by Virgil in *Aen.*1.4, and may derive (it has been suggested) from Roman tragedy.[47] The phrase still refers to memory in *Ep.*21.9; and the strengthening of the expression in *Met.*12.583 is not peculiar to Ovid's use of other poets' language, and not a profanation in itself. Variations of the idea used by Ovid of Venus need to be noticed in *Met.*4.190 and especially 14.477f. The phrases *pone metum* and *potiere petitis* in *Met.*14.110 do not reduce Virgil's original context, Aeneas' meeting with the Sibyl, by Ovid's use of them in erotic contexts elsewhere, since he also uses them without erotic significance.[48]

Humour. Ovid's humour in general has received more attention in the course of the century.[49] It is often identified and even measured, but not with much agreement.[50] Its subjects, modes, and forms have

---

[40] Kenney (n. 39), *passim.*

[41] Knox (n. 5), 27ff.

[42] A particular instance in J.J. O'Hara, *HSCP* 93 (1990), 335ff.

[43] Bömer (n. 1, 1959/68), 173ff.

[44] Kenney (n. 39), 118f.

[45] Bömer (n. 1, 1959/68) 178f. On profanation and humour, cf. ib., 199f.

[46] Bömer (n. 1, 1959/68), 182ff.

[47] Austin on *Aen.*1.4 (on the chronology cf. P.G. Walsh in *EV* s.v. *Livio*) cf. 15 above; on Ovid and the Roman stage, cf. H. MacL. Currie, *ANRW* 2.31.4 (1981), 2701ff.

[48] Bömer (n. 1, 1959/68), 194f., G.K. Galinsky, *Ovid's Metamorphoses* (Oxford 1975), 225f.

[49] Survey in E. Doblhofer, *Phil.*104 (1960), 64ff.

[50] For example, on Polyphemus in the Polyphemus-Galatea story, see M. von Albrecht in *Ovid* (n. 1), 435f. (= *Der altspr. Unterricht* 6.2 (1963), 70f.), B. Otis, *Ovid as an epic poet* (ed. 2, Cambridge 1970), 287, Farrell (n. 36), 235ff.; on Orpheus-Eurydice, cf. the views collected by Neumeister (n. 38), 181, n. 48.

been described to some extent;[51] the terms used are not often examined.[52] His literary humour has been analysed as an end in itself,
and has been described as a game and no more than a game, or as
a feature of narrative as an end in itself.[53] A more didactic purpose
has been found, the reduction of the actions and values of heroic
warriors, and the elevation of other sensibilities and emotions, especially those of care and pity, in newer, sometimes neoteric and elegiac
colours.[54] But even in the Apollo-Daphne story, which is programmatic for the reduction of heroic pretensions by love, heroic epic is
by no means the only literary mode absorbed by the erotic. In the
Orpheus-Eurydice story love and pity, or at least the treatment of
them in Virgil's forms, are themselves the object of humour.[55] The
treatment of the *Aeneid* in the *Metamorphoses* is not everywhere humorous or subversive (see under *History* on Dido, Turnus, and Numa).

Ovid's History and Virgil's. (History in the sense of interpretation.) Ovid's
response to Virgil's history may be seen in his treatment of the Aeneas
story itself at that point in his chronology, in his treatment of Roman
legend and history in some places in Virgil's terms, in his treatment
of other stories in Virgil's terms; and finally in historical and philosophical perspectives that are perhaps longer and broader than Virgil's.

    In the opening sequence of the poem Jupiter, consulting the gods
about the destruction of the human race, is explicitly compared with
Augustus in a simile (200ff.) which is apparently adapted from Virgil
*(Aen.*1.148ff.). It is perhaps not quite certain whether the simile refers
to the assassination of Caesar or to an attempt on Augustus.[56] Allusions to Augustus' victory at Actium have been found in Apollo's
victory over Python and earlier in the Gigantomachy.[57] At the end
of the poem Augustus will restore order after the wars following the

---

[51] Cf. Doblhofer (n. 49), von Albrecht (n. 50), 405ff. (= 47ff.), J.M. Frécaut, *L'esprit
et l'humour chez Ovide* (Grenoble 1972; literary humour, 114ff., *Met.*, 237ff.).

[52] Briefly, cf. N.M. Horsfall, *CJ* 74 (1979), 330; on the range of the term 'parody',
cf. S. Döpp, *RhM* 134 (1991), 330, M. Steudel, *Die Literaturparodie in Ovids 'Ars Amatoria'*
(Hildesheim 1992), 11ff.

[53] Humour as an end in itself: Neumeister (n. 38); a game, Bömer (n. 1, 1959/
1968), 199ff. (but on 'game', cf. also J. Latacz, *Würz.Jhb.*5 (1979), 134ff.); narrative
as an end in itself: Galinsky (n. 48), ix, 4f., 245ff.

[54] So Otis (n. 50), 354ff., Latacz (n. 53), 154f.

[55] Seriousness is found by C. Segal, *TAPA* 103 (1972), 473ff.

[56] See Bömer *ad loc.*, Due (n. 8), 71f.

[57] Buchheit (n. 11), 80ff. and especially 90ff.

assassination of Caesar (15.832ff.). But analogies posited by the phrase "vom Chaos zum Kosmos" used of Books 1 and 15 seem rather tenuous,[58] and the idea cannot be said to run through the poem (Augustus in Book 15 imposes order only on a recent political disturbance, not on the events of the whole poem). The simile is a compliment to Augustus[59] which has a certain piquancy against its background in the *Aeneid*: the statesman, Augustus, now faces two different disturbances, the indignation of his supporters as well as the crimes of his enemies.

After the Apollo-Daphne story explicit references to Roman legend and history are few until Troy.[60] But Ovid uses patterns of Virgil's history in other contexts, in which some differences have been interpreted as subverting Virgil's history. In the Cadmus story he uses Virgil's pattern of Aeneas' search for a new home for a foundation that turned out badly.[61] He develops that pattern, it is suggested, from within the *Aeneid*, with allusions to the war in Latium and to Carthage.[62] Other patterns of allusion have been interpreted less seriously, in Perseus' fight with Phineus (5.1ff.) and Hercules' with Achelous (9.1ff.), both in the pattern of Aeneas' conflict with Turnus for Lavinia.[63]

The Trojan War was a significant point in Greek and Roman universal history;[64] it also brought Ovid to the material of the *Iliad*, the *Odyssey*, and the Aeneas legend, in Ennius' version as well as Virgil's.[65] Ovid integrates the events of the *Iliad* with the events before and after, the events of the Aeneas legend with those of the *Odyssey*, and the events of both with the legends of Italy.[66] The object of such integration, here and elsewhere in the poem, is an appearance of

---

[58] E. Zinn in (ed. H. Oppermann) *Römertum* (Darmstadt 1967), 176 (= *AuA* 5 (1956), 19f.), citing R. Pfeiffer, Buchheit (n. 11) 84f.; Jupiter in bk. 1 and Augustus in bk. 15 are compared by R. Heinze, *Ovids elegische Erzählung, Ber. Akad. Leipzig* 71.7 (1919), 11, n. 1 = *Vom Geist der Römertums* (Stuttgart 1960), 315f., n. 8.

[59] Knox (n. 5), 17ff., 76ff.

[60] Galinsky (n. 48), 252.

[61] P. Hardie, *CQ* 40 (1990), 224ff., especially 226f.

[62] Hardie (n. 61), 227ff.; on Carthage as a type for Rome, cf. Plb. 38.21, 22.

[63] Perseus and Phineus: Bömer, comm. on *Met.*4–5, 186f., 230f., Hercules and Achelous: G.K. Galinsky, *WS* 6 (1972), 93ff., especially 116.

[64] Ludwig (n. 25), 76ff.

[65] Knox (n. 5), 69f.

[66] Ludwig (n. 25), 60ff., Latacz (n. 53), 147ff., J.D. Ellsworth, *Mnem.*41 (1988), 333ff., L.P. Wilkinson in *Ovidiana* (ed. N.I. Herescu, Paris 1958), 239 (Picus in the *Aen.*: 7.48f., 170ff., 187ff.).

coherent continuity;[67] which might seem to Ovid's audience more
historical at this point in his chronology than earlier in the poem.[68]
On the other hand this integration also shifts the focus in the Aeneas
story itself, for example in the correlation of the Achaemenides and
Macareus stories, and in Macareus' tales of Circe.[69] Ovid's treatment
of the Aeneas legend has been the subject of much attention.[70] He
presents a shadow of Virgil's interpretation at intervals, not without
differing from that interpretation, but not always, perhaps, entirely
seriously.

Ovid does not anticipate a Roman empire. Aeneas hears from the
oracle on Delos only where he should go (13.677ff., *Aen*.3.90ff.); although Ovid does repeat Virgil's theme that the Trojans are returning to their ancient mother (677ff., 705f.). At Actium he refers to the
present importance of the place, much more explicitly than Virgil
(13.715, in a curious context; *Aen*.3.278ff., an allusion to Augustus'
games); but that is the exception that proves the rest. In the underworld Aeneas sees only his ancestors, not his descendants, and learns
of nothing after the war in Italy (14.116ff.; *iura locorum*, 118, if it
includes the cycle of rebirth, conceals it). Ovid also reduces Virgil's
aura of the event here (120ff. reduces *Aen*.6.128f., if less aggressively
than *Ars*.1.453f., and 123ff., 130ff. seems to reduce *Aen*.6.65ff.). In
the war in Italy Ovid finally eliminates even the motive of power in
Italy, for something different from, or additional to, Virgil's motives,
the mere will to win (14.569ff.; *iam* 569).[71]

His treatments of Dido and Turnus are complex in their brevity,
and evoke Virgil's, without perhaps differing significantly. In the visit
to Carthage he reduces Juno's and Aeolus' storm to a single word,
uento (14.77). But his use of the phrase *Phrygii. . .mariti* for Aeneas (79,
Dido's perspective), from Juno's use of the phrase in the *Aeneid* (4.103),
evokes the several ironies of Virgil's treatment of Juno's actions at
Carthage. *Incubuit ferro* (14.81) has much force after *incubuitque toro*
(*Aen*.4.650); and *deceptaque decipit omnes* (81) evokes at least two interpretations of events.[72] Turnus is something of an Aeneas on the other

[67] R. Coleman, *CQ* 21 (1971), 464ff.
[68] Notice the genealogy in 11.754ff.
[69] Achaemenides and Aeneas: Galinsky (n. 48), 232. Achaemenides and Macareus
as experiments in perspective: W. Schubert, *JAC* 4 (1989), 115ff.
[70] Döpp (n. 52), 327ff., with bibl., 329, n. 6.
[71] *Lauinia uirgo* (570): *Aen*.7.72, 11.479.
[72] *decepta* is not necessarily pejorative; but it could be referred to Ovid's own

side, in language and ideas that might be referred to the *Aeneid*, to Tibullus, and to other passages in the *Metamorphoses*.[73]

The gods' interest in the Trojans runs through Ovid's treatment, if only in the background in most places: in references to the plague on Crete (13.706f.),[74] the Harpies (709f.), Dodona (716f.),[75] Helenus (720ff.), the burning of the ships in Sicily (14.85; *Iris Iunonia* even after Ovid's treatment of the storm, 14.77), as well as in the transformation of the ships in Italy (530ff.).

The voyage presents a series of occasions for stories of metamorphosis, like Medea's flight to Corinth in 7.350ff. The first stories, those told on Delos, evoke, by Ovid's usual repetition and variation of themes,[76] stories of the Trojan War (the women victims of the Greeks, the Memnonides). The metamorphosis of the Trojan ships has something of the divine resonance of Virgil's version.[77] Ovid's version of the Diomedes story, like Virgil's, integrates events of the Trojan war and the Returns with the Aeneas legend; but Ovid's Diomedes even after his sufferings in this version does not offer Venus as a reason for not fighting Aeneas (14.460ff., 510ff.; cf. *Aen.*11.275ff.). The other stories seem to have little if any relation to the historical significance of the migration in Virgil's version.[78] The function of the migration as a whole in the composition of the *Metamorphoses* is to make the transition from Troy and the Greek and Eastern world to Italy. The migration has historical resonance and consequences, at intervals, perhaps not always altogether seriously and even a little subversively. But history is only one focus of Ovid's treatment of it.

The lineaments of history appear more distinctly in Book 15, some of them the lineaments of Virgil's history. Numa is the inheritor of

---

earlier reworking of Virgil's subject, *Her.*7.69 (an important feature of Ovid's treatment of Virgil in the *Met.*). *Omnes* is interesting: it might include Aeneas (*Aen.*6.463f.).

[73] 14.573f.—*Aen.*8.470f. (with both passages, notice *Met.*15.440); 574f. *barbarus ensis* (if that is the right reading: see Bömer)—Tib. 2.5.48 (a reversal of a reversal); 576ff., the bird that rises from the ashes—13.604ff., the Memnonides (repetition of a theme: see Coleman (n. 67), 464ff.)

[74] Galinsky (n. 48), 223.

[75] See Bömer *ad loc.*

[76] Coleman (n. 67), 464ff.

[77] But see R. Lamacchia, (n. 6), 9ff. Ovid's treatment of the metamorphosis as such should be compared not only with Virgil's version in *Aen.*9.77ff. but also with the appearance of the nymphs in *Aen.*10.219ff.

[78] Possible relations of these stories to the Aeneas-story: J. Fabre, *REL* 64 (1986), 172ff. and (on Polyphemus-Galatea) Farrell (n. 36), 263.

Aeneas' burden in the *Aeneid* (15.1f.). His visit to Croton presents
him as a founder like Aeneas.[79] Myscelus, of whom he hears in Croton
(19ff.), migrated to Italy as another founder like Aeneas.[80] Myscelus'
migration evokes not only Virgil but also perhaps, behind Virgil,
Ennius and the migration of poetry to Italy.[81] Pythagoras also had
migrated to Italy (60ff.).[82] Myscelus perhaps evokes, behind the appearance of Hector to Aeneas in *Aen.*2, the appearance of Homer to
Ennius in the *Annales*; Pythagoras' speech in the *Metamorphoses* evokes
the pattern of Anchises' speech in *Aen.*6 and behind that the pattern
of Homer's Pythagoreanism followed by the history of the *Annales*.[83]
That is the history of literature, but it is literature of history, which
in the *Annales* began with the migration of poetry.

But Pythagoras' speech, although its doctrines inspire Numa (479ff.),
remains difficult to take entirely seriously against the background of
Roman ideas about vegetarianism.[84] An apparent echo of Virgil on
Cassandra (73f., *Aen.*2.246f.), following immediately the first reference
to vegetarianism, is therefore not certainly serious either. His veg-
etarian doctrines have been interpreted as the vehicle to urge an
end to bloodshed of any kind, and an echo of Virgil on bees (80;
*G.*4.169) as an allusion to an ideal society;[85] but Ovid's context is not
imitation but consumption. On the other hand Pythagoras' teaching
of the rise and fall of cities (420ff.) appears to be serious, and to cast
a light which is not Virgil's on his report of Helenus' prophecy of
Rome, which begins by echoing Virgil's Helenus (439ff.; *Aen.*3.374).

Ovid's treatment of the apotheosis of Caesar (15.746ff.) echoes
Callimachus' compliments to Berenice;[86] but there is more history
here than appears to be there. The apotheosis of Caesar is one of a
series from Aeneas to Romulus and eventually to Augustus, and the
translation of Aesculapius also bears on it; Ovid touches on the relation of the Julii to Venus as a goddess of the Roman people.[87] He
adapts Venus' anxiety (760ff.) and Jupiter's prophecy (807ff.) from

---

[79] Numa and Pythagoras: V. Buchheit, *Herm.* 121 (1993), 77ff. (Numa and Aeneas, 91ff.).
[80] ib., 90ff.
[81] Knox (n. 5), 70, P. Hardie, *Epic Successors of Virgil* (Cambridge 1993), 102f.
[82] As Virbius and Aesculapius do; on the theme, see Coleman (n. 67), 473f.
[83] See Hardie (n. 81), 106.
[84] See Coleman (n. 67), 462f., 472f.
[85] Buchheit (n. 79), 93ff.; on *G.*4.169, 95, n. 100.
[86] Knox (n. 5), 75ff.
[87] Feeney (n. 29), 205ff.

Aeneid 1 (227ff.) and the omens (782ff.) from *Georgics* 1 (466ff.); he narrows the focus of Venus' and Jupiter's interest from the Roman people to Caesar and Augustus.[88] Virgil already shifts the focus a little between Venus' complaint *(Aen.*1.227ff.) and Jupiter's reply (257ff.). Ovid's list of Caesar's achievements (752ff.) and Jupiter's prophecy of Augustus' achievements (822ff.) have similarities with Jupiter's prophecy in *Aen.*1.286ff. (whoever is the subject there); but such lists are a larger type.[89]

The themes of Virgil's history with which, among others, the poem ends—foundation, a transition from Greece to Rome, the achievements of the Julii, the restoration of order after civil war—do not run through the poem. The order that Augustus restores at the end of Book 15 at most frames the poem with the references to that order in Book 1. The *Metamorphoses* has a wider and longer perspective than the *Aeneid* in some respects;[90] it might be said to incorporate the *Aeneid* within itself (and not only in the treatment of the Trojan migration). It is tempting to look for an idea in the poem as a whole that might bear on this part of it. Some have found that idea in Ovid's interest in the emotions, especially in love. But it remains true that no particular idea, political or philosophical, has been identified and defined as informing the poem as a whole.[91]

Bibliography

For bibliographies on Ovid and Virgil see n. 1, for indexes, n. 2. Only an outline of the relation is possible in the restricted format of S. Döpp, *Virgilischer Einfluss im Werk Ovids* (München 1968). Aspects of it are described by Bömer (n. 1, 1959/68) on Ovid's games of language and thought (still an excellent introduction; cf. Lamacchia (n. 4)), by Kenney (n. 39) on style, by Knox (n. 5) on genre, by Galinsky (n. 48) under a number of headings, and by others on particular episodes ("Ovid's *Aeneid*": Lamacchia (n. 6)). A more ambitious account is in Otis (n. 50).

---

[88] ib., 213f.
[89] See Bömer on 15.752–4.
[90] On *Met.* as 'Weltgedicht' cf. M. von Albrecht in (ed. E. Burck) *Das röm. Epos* (Darmstadt 1979), 125ff.
[91] J. Barsby, *Ovid* (*GR* Survey 12, Oxford 1978), 33f., 35.

LUCAN

"*Et quantum mihi restat ad culicem*"[1] should perhaps be left in its slight obscurity[2] for another description of Lucan's relation to Virgil, "eine Art Gegen-Virgil",[3] a simplification of the relation and of the poem, but not untrue in itself.

Virgil's subject was arms and the man who had made the first beginning of Roman history, Lucan's is wars and a people that turned on itself (*Aen.*1.1ff., *BC* 1.1ff.).[4] Lucan's war is the war that Virgil's Anchises had wanted to avert (*BC* 1.3, *Aen.*6.833). The cause was not divine anger but human passion (*Il.*1.8, *Aen.*1.8ff., *BC* 1.8).[5] Virgil opens the *Aeneid* with disturbance in nature and a restoration of order which he compares with a restoration of order in the state, anticipating the order that was the end of his history (*Aen.*1.148ff., 291ff.); Lucan enlarges upon his prooemium with a description of a fall of the state which he compares with a dissolution of the cosmos (*BC* 1.72ff.).[6] Virgil had looked beyond the civil wars to the events that he represented as restoring order, Lucan denies the restoration: *Aen.*1.291ff., *BC* 1.668f. (*Aen.*1.294ff.), 669f. (*Aen.*1.241).[7]

Lucan's thoughts on the war in his prooemium echo Virgil's thoughts on the wars that followed the assassination of Caesar in *Georg.*1.489ff., where Virgil refers back, without specifying the connexion, to the war of Caesar and Pompey (490 *iterum*, 491 *bis*);[8] and Lucan's account of the signs that accompanied the war in 1.522ff. echoes Virgil's account of the signs that accompanied the assassination, *Georg.*1.466ff.[9] Virgil's later invocation of Octavian in *Georg.*1.24ff. places the fears of 498ff. in the past (cf. 4.559ff.). Lucan declares that

---

[1] From a story in the Suetonian Life (in C. Hosius, *M. Annaei Lucani Belli Civilis Libri Decem* ed. 3 [Leipzig 1913], 332, 6), known in some form to Statius (*Silv.*2.7.73f.).

[2] See A. Rostagni, *Suetonio De poetis e biografi minori* (Torino 1944), 144f., H.-J. van Dam, *P. Papinius Statius. Silvae Book II* (Leiden 1984), 486, n. 22 (but respect might be ironical).

[3] A. Thierfelder, *Archiv für Kulturgeschichte* 25.1 (1934), 1ff. = W. Rutz (ed.), *Lucan* (Darmstadt 1970), 50ff., here 63.

[4] See W.D. Lebek, *Lucans Pharsalia* (Göttingen 1976), 32ff.

[5] G.B. Conte, *Maia* 18 (1966), 44f., 50f. = Rutz (n. 3), 342f., 350f.

[6] See Lebek (n. 4), 48ff., M. Lapidge, *Herm.*107 (1979), 344ff.

[7] See E. Narducci, *La provvidenza crudele* (Pisa 1979), 41f.

[8] *BC* 1.1 *per Emathios...campos*, *Georg.*1.492 *Emathiam et latos...campos*. On Lucan and the *Georgics* see E. Paratore, *ASNP* 2.12 (1943), 40ff.; on the prooemium 51ff., and L. Thompson, R.T. Bruère, *CP* 63 (1968), 1ff.

[9] Paratore (n. 8), 42f., R. Badalì, *Atti del convegno virgiliano sul bimillenario delle Georgiche* (Napoli 1977), 121ff.

the wars were not too high a price to pay for Nero, 1.33ff., and invokes Nero as Virgil had invoked Octavian, 45ff. He has been taken to mean what he says, and his thought has been defined as the same as Virgil's;[10] if he is not taken to mean what he says[11] he may be understood to use the earlier *Georgics* (1.466ff.) against the later *Georgics* (1.24ff.) and the *Aeneid*.

Lucan's subject (or one of his subjects) is the destruction of Virgil's construction of Roman history from Homer. Homer had anticipated the day when Troy would fall (*Il.*4.164f. = 6.448f.); Virgil had described the day when it came (*Aen.*2.324ff.) and then the day when Rome began to rise (*Aen.*7.144f.); Lucan describes the day when Rome fell (*BC* 7.195f.).[12] So Lucan marks an end in Roman history by evoking Virgil's ends in Trojan history and his beginnings in Roman history: Caesar's vision of Roma in 1.186ff. evokes Aeneas' visions of Hector in *Aen.*2.270ff. and of Venus in 2.589ff.,[13] the fall of Rome in Book 2 evokes the fall of Troy in *Aen.*2,[14] Pompey's flight from Italy evokes both Aeneas' flight from Troy and his first arrival in Italy.[15] Events that present degeneration evoke events that had anticipated greatness: Curio and the story of Hercules and Antaeus in 4.581ff.,[16] Sextus Pompeius' consultation of Erictho in 6.419ff.,[17] Caesar's visit to Troy in 9.961ff.[18] Lucan may appeal occasionally to Virgil's authority, as perhaps in 1.22f. (*Aen.*4.229ff.);[19] but his effect is usually to destroy that authority. Some episodes and ideas in the *Bellum Civile* have been said not to reverse those of the *Aeneid* but to heighten or

---

[10] Paratore (n. 8), 50f.; similarly with reference to the *Aeneid* ("at the outset. . .not an anti-*Aeneid*, but. . .a new *Aeneid*,. . .the suffering and death which issued in the present benign dispensation"), R. Mayer, *Lucan. Civil War VIII* (Warminster 1981), 5 (cf. R. Mayer, *AJP* 103 (1982), 311f.). But such an interpretation is difficult even in the first book, or the first three books (see C. Martindale, *GR* 31 (1984), 69f.).

[11] On the invocation see now D.C. Feeney, *The Gods in Epic* (Oxford 1991), 298ff.

[12] See G.B. Conte in *Mnemosynum. Studi in onore di Alfredo Ghiselli* (Bologna 1989), 95ff. On *Il.*4.164f. = 6.448f. and the fall of Rome see P. Hardie in A. Powell (ed.), *Roman Poetry and Propaganda in the Age of Augustus* (London 1992), 59f.

[13] And much else from epic, oratory, and history; see J. Masters, *Poetry and civil war in Lucan's* Bellum Civile (Cambridge 1992), 1, n. 4.

[14] See E. Fantham, *Lucan. De Bello Civili. Book II* (Cambridge 1992), 8f. Marius and Sulla in 2.67ff., among other functions, supply the want of fighting for the assimilation.

[15] See Fantham (n. 14) on 691–2, 728–30.

[16] F.M. Ahl, *Lucan* (Ithaca, NY 1976), 88ff.

[17] Masters (n. 13), 179ff.

[18] O. Zwierlein, *Herm.*114 (1986), 460ff., esp. 469ff.

[19] Interpreted differently by Thompson, Bruère (n. 8), 3; but Virgil had not quite said that Rome had now subdued the whole world.

surpass them; not only an "anti-*Aeneis*" then but also an "*über-Aeneis*".[20]
But even in some of these instances Lucan's use of Virgil implies a
rejection of Virgil's larger idea, as when the fall of Troy becomes
the fall of the Roman world, or a simile used of Turnus who eventually fails is used of Caesar who eventually succeeds.[21] Virgil's own
uncertainties and unease in the *Aeneid* become elements in Lucan's
anti-*Aeneid*. Not his unease about his gods,[22] nor his sympathy for
individual suffering,[23] but rather his allusive or ambiguous treatment
of particular events, persons, and ideas.[24]

Phrases such as "anti-*Aeneid*" and "*über-Aeneid*" are simplifications
if used of the poem as a whole; they have been described as a manner
of speaking *pars pro toto* which has restricted perception of other relations.[25] But it is not simply a question of quantity; Lucan's response
to Virgil is of special significance in some of the more important
events, structures, and ideas of the poem (for example, the fall of
Rome, the consultation of Erictho, the battle of Pharsalus, and the
visit to Troy). In that context other relations may be significant specifically as they bear on Lucan's relation to Virgil.[26]

Lucan may be described as an anti-Virgil then in political terms.
He may be described as an anti-Virgil also in poetic terms;[27] as it

---

[20] M. von Albrecht in *Lucain, Entretiens Hardt* 15 (Vandoeuvres-Genève 1970), 281ff.,
M. Lausberg, *ANRW* 2.32.3 (1985) 1614.

[21] Von Albrecht (n. 20), 283f.; on the simile in 7, 568ff. see also Lebek (n. 4),
246ff. The simile in 1.205ff., which reworks that in *Aen.*12.4ff., (von Albrecht 286ff.,
Lebek 120f.), contains an interesting obscurity (212, *per ferrum*). So Aeneas' banquet
with Dido becomes Caesar's with Cleopatra, O. Zwierlein, *AuA* 20 (1974), 54ff. (see
esp. 65f.).

[22] With reference to Lucan, S. Timpanaro, *Maia* 19 (1967), 372, n. 4 = *Contributi
di filologia e di storia della lingua latina* (Roma 1978), 327ff., here 331, n. 4; but Lucan's
avowed uncertainty now seems more than a development of Virgil's position (see
Feeney (n. 11), 274ff.).

[23] With reference to Lucan, Narducci (n. 7), 35f.; but Lucan's indignation at a
general catastrophe seems very different (e.g. 7.617ff.). But see further Narducci
145ff.

[24] See Narducci (n. 7), 43ff., D.C. Feeney, *PCPhS* 212 (1986), 1ff., esp. 7f., 16ff.
P. Hardie, *The Epic Successors of Virgil* (Cambridge 1993) examines the successors'
exploitation of Virgil's "energies and tensions" (xi), but in Lucan's case seems not to
discover anything quite so pointed.

[25] P.H. Schrijvers, *Crise poétique et poésie de crise. La réception de Lucain aux XIXe et
XXe siècles, suivi d'une interprétation de la scène 'César à Troie' (La Pharsale, 9.950–999)*
(Amsterdam 1990), 21, who refers to Ovid.

[26] On Ovid between Lucan and Virgil see now Feeney (n. 11), 292ff.

[27] So, in effect (before the phrase was used by Thierfelder, n. 3), E. Fraenkel,
Vorträge der Bibliothek Warburg 1924–1925 (Leipzig 1927), 233 = *Kleine Beiträge zur
klassischen Philologie* 2 (Roma 1964), 238ff. = Rutz (n. 3), 20ff.

has been argued that he uses Homer, and the interpretation of Homer, against Virgil, for style, or rather stylistic level, and for content.[28] But he can be seen also to react against, and to rework, not the *Aeneid* alone, but the genre, or traditions in the genre,[29] in his response to the conventions, such as, notoriously, the representation of the gods in the action,[30] and in his use of the forms, for example, of the narrative of battle,[31] and in his style, both in general[32] and in the particulars of diction and rhythm.[33] Every poet of any originality developed the genre; and Lucan was apparently more original than most. But he may himself follow at least in some respects another tradition in the genre.[34]

On a front that is wider still Lucan engages with writers of prose, not merely as sources[35] but at least with Caesar as a historical and political authority;[36] an anti-Caesar then, in political terms. The question remains, whether Lucan's poetics issue in his politics or his politics in his poetics;[37] it divides descriptions of him.[38]

Bibliography

Lucan's relation to Virgil is described well and briefly by von Albrecht (n. 20) and more fully, especially with reference to Virgil's myth of Rome, by Narducci (n. 7; later descriptions in *ANRW* 2.32.3, 1538ff., *EV*, *Lucano*,

---

[28] Lausberg (n. 20), 1611ff.

[29] G.B. Conte, *Memoria dei poeti e sistema letterario* ed. 2 (Torino 1985), 75ff. On Lucan's use of elegy in epic see U. Hübner, *Herm.*112 (1984), 227ff.; on didactic, M. Lausberg, *Würz.Jhb.*16 (1990), 173ff.

[30] Feeney (n. 11), ch. 6, esp. 264ff. (the conventions), 269ff. (Lucan's practice).

[31] J.C. Bramble in *CHCL* 2.543; for example, 7, 617ff.

[32] K. Seitz, *Herm.*93 (1965), 204ff.

[33] Diction: Bramble (n. 31), 541f. Rhythm (necessarily compared with Virgil's in the first instance): G.E. Duckworth, *TAPA* 98 (1967), 88ff. (relatively like Virgil's in use of dactyls and spondees), Hosius (n. 1), 388ff. = D.R. Shackleton Bailey, *M. Annaei Lucani De bello civili libri X* (Stuttgart 1988), 286ff. (very different in use of elision and some line endings).

[34] Bramble (n. 31), 485ff.

[35] See n. 13. Caesar and Cleopatra: M.G. Schmidt, *Caesar and Cleopatra. Philologischer und historischer Kommentar zu Lucan. 10.1–171* (Frankfurt am Main 1986), 122ff., 136ff. Lucan's causation and the historians': Narducci (n. 7), 70f. Work on sources: W. Rutz, *ANRW* 2.32.3 (1985), 1460ff.

[36] Masters (n. 13), ch. 2, esp. 17f.

[37] Narducci (n. 7), 38f., J. Masters in J. Elsner, J. Masters (ed.), *Reflections of Nero* (Chapel Hill 1994), 151ff.

[38] Schrijvers (n. 25), 12ff.

with a useful bibliography). Much has been observed in treatments of other aspects of the poem, by Lebek on composition and structure (n. 4), Lausberg on Homer (n. 20), Feeney on the gods (n. 11), and Masters on the self-conscious poet (n. 13), and in studies of episodes and themes by Hübner (n. 29), Zwierlein (n. 18), and Conte (n. 12). A systematic index of Lucan's reference to Virgil is lacking (see von Albrecht (n. 20), 281f.).

VALERIUS FLACCUS

Valerius' response to Virgil must be described from his poem itself alone; there are no stories to determine expectations.[1] His subject is defined correctly enough as Greek myth rather than Roman history;[2] but if his primary source is Apollonius his primary model is Virgil,[3] and he adumbrates a history that is not Apollonius'[4] but Virgil's, at least in one or two of its most important ideas.[5]

Valerius' scene in heaven at the Argonauts' departure (1.498ff.) is more grandiose than Apollonius' (1.547ff.).[6] Jupiter wants his reign to be more active than Saturn's (500); this theodicy may be referred to Virgil's in the *Georgics* (1.121ff.), although Jupiter's purposes are not the same in both (Valerius' Jupiter apparently wants the labours by which he gained his kingship to be a model for all activity, 561ff.). Jupiter has planned a series of ruling powers through the ages, Asia, Greece, then others (531ff.). The ordering of history in a series of empires had become familiar in Greek and Roman historiography;[7] but Valerius' series differs from the historians', in that power passes from Asia to Greece at Troy (551ff.). The causes of conflict are Herodotus' (1.1–5); but Valerius' fall of Asia is Virgil's fall of Troy (542, *Aen.*2.324; and Homer's, of course, *Il.*4.164f., 6.448f.). Virgil had described the fall of Troy as a transfer of power from Troy to Argos by Jupiter (*Aen.*2.324ff.; and as an overturning of Asia, 3.1ff.). The purpose of Valerius' history in the series of empires is not the

---

[1] Valerius' life: E. Burck in id. (ed.), *Das römische Epos* (Darmstadt 1979), 209.

[2] Valerius' choice of subject: Burck (n. 1), 211f.

[3] "Fonte" and "modello", P. Venini in *EV*, s.v. *Valerio Flacco*, "Vorlage" and "Vorbild", Burck (n. 1), 213; but Apollonius may also be a model (e.g. Valerius 5.329ff., Apollonius 4.662ff.). On Valerius and Apollonius, P. Venini, *RIL* 105 (1971), 582ff. (bibliography, n. 1); on Valerius and the scholia on Apollonius, F. Bessone, *MD* 26 (1991), 31ff.

[4] One of Apollonius' histories is the perspective of the *aitia* and the foundation legends; but see also R. Hunter, *The* Argonautica *of Apollonius* (Cambridge 1993), ch. 6. For a possible relation between Valerius and Apollonius compare D.C. Feeney, *The Gods in Epic* (Oxford 1991), 328ff. with Hunter 162ff.

[5] Virgil as both model and point of reference in history: W. Schetter. *Phil.*103 (1959), 302, n. 1.

[6] The most recent discussion: M. Wacht, *Juppiters Weltenplan im Epos des Valerius Flaccus, AAWM* 1991, 10 (Stuttgart 1991).

[7] See A. Momigliano, *ASNP* 3.12.2 (1982), 533ff. = *Settimo contributo alla storia degli studi classici e del mondo antico* (Roma 1984), 77ff., esp. 85ff., J.M. Alonso-Núñez, *Athen.*62 (1984), 640ff.; on the empires and Valerius see L. Alfonsi in K. Gaiser (ed.), *Das Altertum und jedes neue Gute. Festschrift für W. Schadewaldt* (Stuttgart 1970), 125ff.

purpose of Virgil's history; it is a testing for selection (558ff.).[8] (A hint of that idea in Silius, 3.573f.; but the principal purpose of the war there is testing in preparation, 575ff.).[9] An empire to last for ever is finally in view in Valerius' history (560); but it is not identified as Rome's empire, at least in the council in heaven.[10] Valerius' differences from Virgil are of some interest in themselves;[11] but they are apparently not significant in the rest of the poem.

Valerius refers to Virgil's history elsewhere in the poem. He alludes to the theodicy of *Georgics* 1 in the scene of revelation and exhortation before the Argonauts' departure (1.235f., *Georgics* 1.145f.; 246f., *Georgics* 1.121f.).[12] He alludes quite often to the Trojan War, which is eventually to follow from the expedition,[13] a perspective that appears in Apollonius' treatment of the story only fleetingly;[14] but the poem does not often look beyond the *Iliad* to the *Aeneid* and Roman history.[15] In the poem as a whole Valerius follows Virgil's reference of his subject to history rather than his history itself. In the context of Jupiter's plan of empires analogies between the Argonauts' expedition and Aeneas' migration have been suggested;[16] but they do not extend far (the Argonauts do not found anything), even if they might be further justified by echoes in *Arg*.1.244ff. and 249 of *Aen*.2.601ff. and 1.203,[17] and by the assimilation of the structure of the *Argonautica* to that of the *Aeneid*;[18] the Argonauts' war with Perses does not have the same consequences as Aeneas' war with the Latins, and the *Argonautica* echoes from the *Aeneid* only that combination of warfare with seafaring in a hero's exploits that starts in the *Odyssey* (1.12; 13.91). The prooemium represents Vespasian as surpassing the Argonauts (1.7f.; cf. 1.1) and the Julii (8f.), making this latter point

---

[8] See W. Schubert, *Jupiter in den Epen der Flavierzeit* (Frankfurt am Main 1984), 38f.

[9] See W. Kissel, *Das Geschichtsbild des Silius Italicus* (Frankfurt am Main 1979), 42ff., Schubert (n. 8), 58ff.

[10] See Wacht (n. 6), 11ff.

[11] See Wacht (n. 6), 13, n.45.

[12] See E. Lefèvre in M. Korn, H.J. Tschiedel (ed.), *Ratis omnia vincet* (Hildesheim 1991), 178ff.; on his interpretation see below, n. 29.

[13] W. Barnes, *Herm*.109 (1981), 360ff.

[14] See AR 1.553ff. and compare Valerius, 1.255ff.

[15] See 2.570ff., 6.55f. W.C. Summers, *A Study of the Argonautica of Valerius Flaccus* (Cambridge 1894), 56f., casts his net wide.

[16] S. Wetzel, *Die Gestalt der Medea bei Valerius Flaccus* (Diss. Kiel 1957), 11f., E. Burck, *Vom römischen Manierismus* (Darmstadt 1971), 28, id. (n. 1), 231, n. 67.

[17] On 1.244ff. see E. Pollini, *Maia* 36 (1984), 58f.

[18] See Schetter (n. 5), B.E. Lewis, *Mnem*.40 (1987), 420ff.

with reference to the *Aeneid* (1.286ff.);[19] but it does not represent him as finally fulfilling Jupiter's intentions (Jupiter wanted the seas open so that nations might compete for power, 1.556ff.).[20] If Virgil's history is a frame in which Valerius' treatment of the story has a significance that Apollonius' does not it is a rather remote frame. Some formulations of the leading ideas in the poem explicitly or implicitly exclude a relation to Virgil's history, at least in the *Aeneid*.[21]

Valerius casts or colours his events and persons from Virgil's in particular episodes and other parts of the poem, and in the structure of the whole,[22] to an extent of which it may be said quite truly that he takes the patent of his nobility in the genre largely from Virgil.[23] He composes from Virgil and from other models at the same time, especially Homer, whom he also uses in Virgil's terms;[24] the accumulation is sometimes elaborate,[25] and sometimes perhaps not altogether coherent.[26] But it remains a question whether or to what extent he uses Virgil only as a repertory of events, persons, images, and appropriate treatment, and to what extent he uses Virgil for more than his own immediate context;[27] when, for example, he adapts Evander for Alcimede and Aeson in 1.317ff.[28] The farewell has its significance for the theme of parents and children in Book 1; but it is not evident that the reference to Virgil is significant. The assimilation of the structure of the *Argonautica* to that of the *Aeneid* cannot apparently be related to the historical ideas of the poem (as has been noticed above).

---

[19] As the compliment is also a legitimation of Vespasian's rule it is appropriate that Valerius' prooemium follows and outdoes Virgil's prooemium in *Georgics* 1; see W.-W. Ehlers, *MH* 42 (1985), 338f. and also E. Lefèvre, *Das Prooemium der Argonautica des Valerius Flaccus, AAWM* 1971, 6, 47f.

[20] Cf. Lefèvre (n. 19), 55f.; see further Burck (n. 1), 211.

[21] J. Adamietz, *Zur Komposition der Argonautica des Valerius Flaccus* (München 1976), 22ff., Burck (n. 1), 230ff.

[22] A survey of events and persons in Venini (n. 3); on the structure of the whole see Schetter (n. 5), Lewis (n. 18).

[23] "Patent of nobility": O. Fuà, *GIF* 38 (1986), 273.

[24] On Valerius, Virgil, and Homer see O. Fuà, *AAT* 122 (1988), 23ff.; and also P. Schenk, *Die Zurücklassung des Herakles, AAWM* 1986, 1 (Stuttgart 1986), J.J.L. Smolenaars in Korn, Tschiedel (n. 12), 57ff.

[25] For example, in Jason's first meeting with Medea, 5.329ff., on which see Adamietz (n. 21), 72ff. and with more detail Wetzel (n. 16), 57ff.

[26] So A. Perutelli, *MD* 7 (1982), 123ff.

[27] A minimalist assessment apparently in M.J. Barich, *Aspects of the Poetic Technique of Valerius Flaccus* (Diss. Yale 1982), *DA* 43 (1982), 1135–A.

[28] A.J. Gossage in D.R. Dudley (ed.), *Virgil* (London 1969), 85f.; cf. AR 1.250ff.

It is then a further question whether Valerius may be said to represent the same order in the world as Virgil. He has been thought
to characterize his events and persons as different from Virgil's, and
Jason in particular as different from Aeneas.[29] In that interpretation
Jason is an anti-Aeneas, but the poem is not an anti-*Aeneid*.[30] But in
the same year in which Lucan was described by Thierfelder as "eine
Art Gegen-Virgil"[31] Valerius was described by Mehmel as a poet
"der revoltiert, womöglich ohne es zu wissen, gegen das Klassische
Virgils";[32] especially with reference to the form of the poem and to
the relations of men and gods in it.[33] Here then is an anti-*Aeneid*; but
the poet may not have known it.[34] Many of Mehmel's arguments no
longer stand;[35] and indeed his account of Virgil, especially perhaps
of Virgil's men and gods, is too simple to determine a definition of
Valerius' response.[36] But a somewhat similar conclusion was reached
from Valerius' treatment of Virgil's language by Nordera.[37] In the
terms of her time she described Valerius' style as baroque rather
than classical, closer to Statius' style than to Virgil's.[38] She was inclined to attribute the characteristics she found in Valerius' style,
and in his subject, to a compulsion on a successor "di ricercare ad
ogni costo nel mutamento la sua originalità";[39] at the same time like
Mehmel she found a certain pessimism in Valerius' treatment of the
relations of men and gods.[40] But she too like Mehmel thought that

---

[29] On Jason in 1.240ff. see Lefèvre (n. 12), 177ff.; a similar interpretation is pursued
through the poem by E. Lüthje, *Gehalt und Aufriss der Argonautica des Valerius Flaccus*
(Diss. Kiel 1971). But the scene in 1.188ff. might perhaps be interpreted differently.
On Jason's trespass on Neptune's domain see Feeney (n. 4), 330ff.; *omine dextro* (245)
might refer to the signs of the sacrifice as they were read by Idmon (227ff.; cf.
Lefèvre 178).

[30] See Lüthje (n. 29), 373.

[31] A. Thierfelder, *Archiv für Kulturgeschichte* 25.1 (1934), 1ff. = W. Rutz (ed.), *Lucan*
(Darmstadt 1970), 50ff., here 63f.

[32] F. Mehmel, *Valerius Flaccus* (Diss. Hamburg 1934), 135.

[33] Mehmel (n. 32), 41ff., 55ff., 89ff.

[34] Valerius wanted to write like Virgil and thought that he did so, Mehmel
(n. 32), 132.

[35] On the form of the poem see Schetter (n. 5), 297ff., esp. 306, H.-O. Kröner,
Herm.96 (1968), 733ff.; on the gods Feeney (n. 4), 328ff., esp. 335ff. (although he
does not discuss Mehmel) and for another view M. Wacht in Korn, Tschiedel
(n. 12), 101ff. (perhaps exaggerating Aeneas' confidence in his gods).

[36] "Nur augenblickliche Leiden und Schwierigkeiten" from Virgil's gods, 95.

[37] R. Nordera in *Contributi a tre poeti latini* (Bologna 1969), 1ff.

[38] 84ff., 90f.

[39] 9; cf. 90.

[40] 9f.

Valerius may not have been entirely aware how much he differed from his model.[41] Her observations need some revision in detail;[42] some differences of language and tone from Virgil's follow from differences of subject that are not significant in themselves.[43] Moreover, her description of the formal and aesthetic qualities of Valerius' style needs a more particular account of Valerius' thought in the action of the poem; Medea is not necessarily a more tragic or more dreadful subject than Dido.[44] Since Nordera Valerius' relation to Virgil has been described in terms of genre by Pederzani;[45] a tone of pathos in Valerius' style as it was analysed by Nordera is described as more elegiac than epic.[46] But here again the effect is not Valerius' own intention; he set out to write like Virgil.[47] But the question is not whether the poet knew that this was a revolt or an apostasy, but still whether and then in what respects it is to be called a revolt, and whether it is to be referred specifically to Virgil. Moreover, a pessimistic Valerius can no longer be defined by reference to an optimistic Virgil.

Venus acts on Lemnos in *Arg*.2 like Allecto in *Aen*.7 and then in Colchis as Juno's agent in *Arg*.7 like Allecto again and also like Cupid in *Aen*.1; these similarities have been referred to certain similarities between her actions and Juno's in the *Aeneid*, as a reading of Virgil that exploits a tension in Venus' actions in the *Aeneid*.[48] But that tension is not present in the *Argonautica*; the characterization of Venus is less complex. It is also less significant for the poem as a whole.

Valerius' language and style[49] both accept and resist the influence of Virgil's. Variation from Virgil's language was examined by Nordera,

---

[41] 91.

[42] W.-W. Ehlers, *Lustrum* 16 (1974), 136f.

[43] In 1.48 Pelias naturally emphasises the disturbing character of his vision, as Nordera herself recognizes, 37.

[44] Nordera's view of the subject of the poem: 9f., 80f.

[45] O. Pederzani, *MD* 18 (1987), 101ff.

[46] Pederzani (n. 45), 111ff.; but on elegiac and epic elements in the poem see also Feeney (n. 4), 327f. (in a discussion of genre in the poem, 318ff.).

[47] 103, 111, 126, 127.

[48] P. Hardie in A.J. Boyle (ed.) *The Imperial Muse. Flavian Epicist to Claudian* (Bendigo 1990), 5ff. Further details of Valerius' use of Virgil in the Lemnos episode in F. Bornmann in *Studia Florentina A. Ronconi oblata* (Roma 1970), 41ff., H.M. Poortvliet, *C. Valerius Flaccus Argonautica Book II. A commentary* (Amsterdam 1991).

[49] A description in Burck (n. 1), 246ff.; a survey of scholarship in M. Scaffai, *ANRW* 2.32.4 (1986), 2436ff.

because that was more interesting for the description of Valerius'
style; but those echoes that might be considered mechanical or un-
conscious may be equally significant in the matter of Virgil's influence.[50] Valerius' word order, often noticed as a characteristic of his
style, differs from Virgil's.[51] His metrical practice also differs from
Virgil's, and rather resembles Ovid's, more or less, in some features;[52]
but a comprehensive description with reference to the other epic poets
after Virgil and Ovid is lacking.[53]

Bibliography

The commentary of P. Langen, *C. Valeri Flacci Setini Balbi Argonauticon libri
octo* (Berlin 1896–1897), is supplemented for Valerius' relation to Virgil by
H. Stroh, *Studien zu Valerius Flaccus* (Augsburg 1905). New commentaries on
single books are appearing (see Korn, Tschiedel (n. 12), 7f.). The forms and
contexts of Valerius' use of Virgil are described well by P. Venini, *EV*, s.v.
Valerio Flacco. Scholarship on Valerius in the years 1938–1982 is surveyed in
useful detail by Scaffai (n. 49), 2359ff. The section on Valerius' models is
short (2400ff.); most work on Valerius and Virgil has been incidental to the
description of Valerius. Much of Mehmel's vigorous analysis (n. 32) has
been revised or rejected, one point at a time, but it has not been replaced
by anything comprehensive. His radical position is now best represented by
Nordera (n. 37), a more conservative position by Adamietz (n. 21).

---

[50] Nordera (n. 37), 6ff.; on Valerius' variation of Virgil's language see also
M. Korn in Korn, Tschiedel (n. 12), 50ff.

[51] M. Schmidt; see Scaffai (n. 49), 2436f.

[52] On dactyls and spondees and certain accentual patterns see G.E. Duckworth,
TAPA 98 (1967), 88ff. Ovid's influence in matters other than verse rhythm has not
been described in detail. Too little and too much in the index of Summers (n. 15),
37ff.; comparisons (Hercules-Hesione and Perseus-Andromeda, Io) in E. Frank, *RIL*
105 (1971), 320ff., E. Burck, *WS* 10 (1976), 221ff., M. von Albrecht *Würz.Jhb.* N.F.
3 (1977), 139ff. (= *BAGB* 38 (1979), 46ff.); on Medea see K.W.D. Hull, *Proc. Leeds
Philos. & Lit.Soc.*16.1 (1975), 13f.

[53] Cf. Summers (n. 15), 49ff.; some more recent figures for Valerius in R.W.
Garson, *CQ* 18 (1968), 376ff.

STATIUS, *Thebaid*

Statius refers to the relation of the *Thebaid* to the *Aeneid* in two places in the poem itself, with an explicitness that is striking in an epic, and to that relation or to Virgil in several places in the *Silvae*. In *Theb*.10.445ff., 12.816ff. he expresses deference, and he is sometimes taken at his word;[1] but he can be interpreted as implying ambition.[2] In *Silv*.4.4.51ff. he describes a reverence like Silius'.[3] Elsewhere in the *Silvae* he is less deferential; each of those references has its own context,[4] but they indicate at least what he could say. The *Thebaid* itself is one genre, the *Silvae* another; and Statius' own confidence may have grown.[5]

The *Aeneid* then is the declared model (for the episode at 10.445ff.) and point of reference for the *Thebaid*; and in practice Statius uses Virgil's bricks and mortar, his paint and paper, his furniture, and part of his floor plan.[6] But his first two words, *fraternas acies*, announce a subject like Lucan's, *cognatasque acies* (*BC* 1.4), and his epilogue (12.810ff.) expresses ambitions like Ovid's;[7] and two or three of his "sources" and "models" are of some significance in the form and especially in the thought of the poem.[8] "Despite his veneration, Statius stands farthest from Virgil, closest to Seneca and Lucan."[9] So Tisiphone's signal in *Theb*.1.114ff. has an effect in nature like Allecto's in *Aen*.7.511ff.; but she is perhaps as much like Seneca's Fury at the

---

[1] G. Aricò, *Ricerche Staziane* (Palermo 1972), 57ff., G. Williams in J.D. Bernard (ed.), *Vergil at 2000* (New York 1986), 218ff.

[2] See W. Schetter, *Untersuchungen zur epischen Kunst des Statius* (Wiesbaden 1960), 150f. On 10, 445ff. see also B. Kytzler, *Herm*.97 (1969), 210f., and on 12.816ff. P. Hardie, *The Epic Successors of Virgil* (Cambridge 1993), 110f.

[3] See K.M. Coleman, *Statius. Silvae IV* (Oxford 1988), on 54; and A.J. Gossage in D.R. Dudley (ed.), *Virgil* (London 1969), 69 and n. 13.

[4] On *Silv*.2.7.33ff., 79f. see H.-J. van Dam, *P. Papinius Statius. Silvae Book II* (Leiden 1984), 470, Hardie (n. 2), 110; on 4.7.25ff. see Coleman (n. 3) on 27; in 5.3.61ff. he gives the measure of his father's love for him.

[5] F. Vollmer, *P. Papinii Statii Silvarum Libri* (Leipzig 1898), 11, n. 4.

[6] A survey by P. Venini in *EV*, s.v. *Stazio*.

[7] J. Henderson, *PCPhS* 37 (1991), 38f., n. 50, Hardie (n. 2), 110.

[8] On Statius' use of "sources" and "models" in general see P. Venini, *RIL* 95 (1961), 371ff., 103 (1969), 461ff.; for an analysis of a single book in detail, J.J.L. Smolenaars, *Statius. Thebaid VII. A Commentary* (Leiden 1994), xviff., xxviff., 396ff. On Antimachus see D.W.T.C. Vessey, *Phil*.114 (1970), 118ff., P. Venini, *Athen*.50 (1972), 400ff., P. Carrara, *Prometheus* 12 (1986), 146ff. On Hellenistic epic see O. Zwierlein, *RhM* 131 (1988), 75ff. (on the brothers in art see now also I. Krauskopf, *LIMC*, s.v. *Eteokles*, esp. 34ff.).

[9] D.W.T.C. Vessey in *CHCL* 2.559.

beginning of *Thyestes*,[10] and the thoughts she inspires in Eteocles and
Polynices in 1.128f. are those that Lucan describes in *BC* 1.124.[11]
Between Statius and Euripides the differences have usually been of
more interest than the similarities;[12] but the social and political significance of Thebes for Athens that is now found in Athenian tragedy
has recently been adduced in a description of the implications of the
Thebaid.[13] Statius uses Homer with Virgil; Tisiphone is also like Apollo
in *Il*.1.43ff.[14] But his use of Homer, both the *Iliad* and the *Odyssey*, in
episodes and especially in composition and structure, has been explained as evasion of engagement with Virgil, who might have been
oppressive.[15]

The characteristics of the *Thebaid* have been described in some
detail in episodes and in aspects of the poem during the last forty
years;[16] and descriptions have included comparison with the *Aeneid*
and especially with models in it.[17] The function and coherence of
Statius' reworkings of Virgil in their new context have been demonstrated.[18] The characteristics that have been identified are often those
of Statius' style, manner, and interests in general rather than those
of a response to Virgil in particular;[19] and if Statius seems to compete with Virgil he competes with Homer and with others in the
same way.[20] The terms "mannerism" and "mannerist" have been used,
sometimes with reference to Statius' relation to Virgil in particular.[21]

---

[10] Vessey (n. 9), 574, D.C. Feeney, *The Gods in Epic* (Oxford 1991), 347f. with
n. 116.

[11] On Statius and Seneca and Lucan see P. Venini, *RFil.* 95 (1967), 418ff. (on
Tisiphone 419ff. and F. Caviglia, *P. Papinio Stazio. La Tebaide—Libro I* (Roma 1973).
on 128, 129–130); E. Narducci, *La provvidenza crudele* (Pisa 1979), 149ff., esp. 152ff.

[12] D. Vessey, *Statius and the Thebaid* (Cambridge 1973), 69, 308; on Statius and
Euripides' *Phoenissae* see P. Venini, *RIL* 95 (1961), 391ff.

[13] Henderson (n. 7), 52ff., and in A.J. Boyle (ed.), *Roman Epic* (London 1993),
168f.

[14] H. Juhnke, *Homerisches in römischer Epik flavischer Zeit* (München 1972), 52f.

[15] Juhnke (n. 14) 123, 183f., 301ff.; see also 180f., on dissimilation of the *Aeneid*
in the *Thebaid*. Some discussion in Caviglia (n. 11), 27f., and criticism in Smolenaars
(n. 8), xxxiiff.

[16] Published work starts especially with G. Krumbholz, *Glotta* 34 (1955), 93ff.,
231ff., and Schetter (n. 2).

[17] E.g. Krumbholz (n. 16), 94ff.

[18] E.g. B. Kytzler, *Der altspr. Unterricht* 11.1 (1968), 50ff.; (n. 2), 209ff.

[19] E.g. brevity and ingenuity on the one hand, and expansion on the other, Williams
(n. 1), 212ff.

[20] See Kytzler (n. 2), 209ff.

[21] See Schetter (n. 2), 122ff., E. Burck, *Vom römischen Manierismus* (Darmstadt 1971),
Vessey (n. 12), 7ff.; with reference to Virgil in particular, Schetter 122, Burck 20,

But the analogies identified with other periods and relations in art and literature seem usually to have remained peripheral to the description of the *Thebaid* itself.

The characteristics that have been described are often largely formal and aesthetic,[22] or if not necessarily that have sometimes been said to have no more than formal and aesthetic significance.[23] But the *Thebaid* has been seen to differ from the *Aeneid* in its representation of men and gods, as an epic of ruling powers destroyed by human desire for power encouraged by the gods of both the upper and the lower worlds, from an epic of a ruling power founded by human virtues at the will of or at least with the concurrence of the gods.[24] It has been called with reference to those differences "eine >Anti-Aeneis<".[25] The differences might be attributed both to the influence of Seneca and Lucan and of the schools, and to the poet's own perception of the political events of the first century.[26] The last book of the poem has been thought to describe a return to *pietas*;[27] but the effect of the book has also been thought to be less than that of the rest of the poem, or indeed ambiguous.[28]

The differences in moral and other themes between the poems have not been identified in the text in much detail.[29] But in any case they will be described otherwise if the *Aeneid* is described otherwise;[30] and it is now fairly widely said that the *Aeneid* itself contains, if not an anti-*Aeneid*, at least other versions of an *Aeneid*, unease about the power the poem celebrates, about the foundation and history of that power and about the divine forces that are supposed to be the source of it. So the treatment of some themes in the *Thebaid* that

---

Vessey 8, 11f. Reservations and restrictions in Schetter's review of Burck, *Gnom.* 47 (1975), 558ff.

[22] For example, the exaggerated structuring of some battle narrative, Schetter (n. 2), 111ff.

[23] So Schetter (n. 2), 124f.; see the comments of H. Langerbeck, *RFil.* 92 (1964), 447ff.

[24] So E. Burck, in G.E. Mylonas, D. Raymond (ed.), *Studies Presented to David Moore Robinson* (St. Louis 1953), II 701ff. = E. Burck, *Vom Menschenbild in der römischen Literatur* (Heidelberg 1966), 311ff.

[25] Burck (n. 21), 92; *Das römische Epos* (Darmstadt 1979), 306.

[26] Burck (n. 21), 99ff.; cf. Burck, *Epos* (n. 25), 306ff.

[27] Vessey (n. 12), 59f., 307ff.

[28] Burck, *Epos* (n. 25), 339ff., Feeney (n. 10), 362f., 389ff., Hardie (n. 2), 46ff.

[29] See Burck (nn. 24, 25); detail for *Theb.*1 in D.E. Hill in A.J. Boyle (ed.), *The Imperial Muse. Flavian Epicist to Claudian* (Bendigo 1990), 98ff.

[30] For Burck's reading of the *Aeneid* see (n. 24), 702f. (= 312), (n. 21), 94; Hill's reading is similar (n. 29).

were identified as differences between the poems has now been interpreted as exploitation of "the energies and tensions called up but
not finally expended or resolved in the *Aeneid*".[31]

The duel between Eteocles and Polynices, once described as very
different from that of Aeneas and Turnus,[32] is interpreted as an
exploitation of the same idea, that distinctions between antagonists
are effaced by violence.[33] In *Theb*.4.397ff. a Bacchant at Thebes
describes a vision of the conflict of a pair of bulls, which anticipates
the duel. Eteocles and Polynices are described in terms of a pair of
bulls in several places in the *Thebaid*,[34] as Aeneas and Turnus are
described at the beginning and the end of *Aeneid* 12 (103ff., 715ff.);
and Statius in 4.397ff. seems to echo Virgil in 12.715ff. The image
of the bulls stresses the shared blood between them, and between
the brothers, and might therefore be said to convey the idea of the
common character of the antagonists in violence. But it is not evident that Statius exploits the idea as one he reads in Virgil. The shared
blood of the brothers is an element in his own story already; and
what Virgil stresses in his context is the different origins of Aeneas
and Turnus, 12.708, 723. Statius' next lines, 401f., seem to echo
Aen.6.834f. But the Bacchant's exhortation to Eteocles is actually a
fair definition of a distinction between the brothers,[35] just as, indeed,
Anchises' exhortation to Caesar has a point against the background
of the original historical circumstances. At the same time Statius might
be understood to refer the pairing of Aeneas and Turnus to the pairing
of Caesar and Pompey in a "combinatorial" allusion to Virgil;[36] that
might make an interesting reading of the *Aeneid* in terms other than
those of distinctions effaced by violence. The duel of Eteocles and
Polynices itself is a climax in the composition of the *Thebaid* as the
duel of Aeneas and Turnus is the climax of the *Aeneid*;[37] and a few
features of Statius' duel have been identified more or less certainly
as reworkings of Virgil's.[38] One, the pairing of Tisiphone and Megaera

---

[31] Hardie (n. 2), xi; cf. P.R. Hardie in J.H. Molyneux (ed.), *Literary Responses to Civil Discord* (Nottingham 1993), 57ff. Compare Schetter (n. 2), 122 (with P. Venini, *Athen*.42 (1964), 210f.), 124.
[32] Burck (n. 24), 702f. (= 312), (n. 21), 91f.
[33] Hardie (n. 2), 22ff.
[34] See B. Kytzler, *WSt*. 75 (1962), 146.
[35] On the characterization of Eteocles and Polynices: Burck, *Epos* (n. 25), 327f.
[36] On "combinatorial imitation": P. Hardie in Boyle (n. 29), 3ff.
[37] P. Venini, *P. Papini Stati Thebaidos Liber XI* (Florence 1970), xix.
[38] Tisiphone-Megaera, *Theb*.11.57ff.: the two Dirae and Megaera, *Aen*.12.845ff.

throughout the action, which might perhaps be thought to refer to a tradition in art more clearly than to the *Aeneid*,[39] conveys the idea of distinctions effaced; but the actions of the Furies who lead Eteocles and Polynices to kill each other are not the same, in their effects on each of the antagonists as a pair, as the actions of the Dira and the furies, or Furies, which bring it about that Aeneas kills Turnus. Eteocles and Polynices may certainly be said to embody the idea that distinctions between antagonists are effaced by violence; or rather, perhaps, in their case, by the desire for power, as Polynices' character, in Statius' treatment of him, deteriorates with the desire for power.[40] But it is not evident that Statius makes specific reference to Virgil in his treatment of that idea.

The larger structure of the *Thebaid* has been the subject of debate;[41] features of it have been attributed to imitation of the forms of the *Aeneid*, such as the relation of the first six books to the next six, and the introduction of Hypsipyle's account of Lemnos. But the *Thebaid* may be said to begin at the point that the *Aeneid* reaches in Book 7;[42] and some features of the treatment of *Theb.*1–6 have been explained as the elaboration of a theme of delay in *Aen.*10–12.[43]

Statius' style and diction and his practice in particular use of Virgil's language are examined by Legras;[44] but they need fresh attention.[45] In his metrical practice Statius "steers something of a middle course between Virgil and Ovid";[46] but with Valerius he is more like Ovid than Silius is in some respects.[47] But all three make much less use than both Virgil and Ovid of exotic line endings.

(see also Krauskopf (n. 8), 34ff., esp. 37). Polynices-Adrastus, *Theb.*11.149ff.: Turnus-Latinus, *Aen.*12.1ff. Eteocles, *Theb.*11.251ff.: Turnus, *Aen.*12.103ff. Creon, *Theb.*11.262ff.: Latin opponents of Turnus, *Aen.*11.215ff., 336ff. Pietas-Tisiphone, *Theb.*11.472ff., 482ff.: Juturna-Dira, *Aen.*12.222ff., 869ff. (see also Venini (n. 37) on 458, 474ff., 482).

[39] See Krauskopf (n. 8), 37.
[40] See Burck, *Epos* (n. 25), 328.
[41] See Vessey (n. 12), 317ff., Burck, *Epos* (n. 25), 311ff.
[42] Hardie (n. 2), 62f.
[43] Feeney (n. 10), 339f.; versions of the theme appear in the *Iliad*.
[44] L. Legras, *Etude sur la Thébaïde de Stace* (Paris 1905), 311ff.
[45] See Burck, *Epos* (n. 25), 344ff.
[46] M. Dewar, *Statius. Thebaid IX* (Oxford 1991), xxxiv.
[47] G.E. Duckworth, *TAPA* 98 (1967), 90f. (cf. 92ff.).

Bibliography

The external forms of Statius' relation to Virgil are described well by
P. Venini, *EV*, s.v. *Stazio*. The material must be found in the commentaries
(listed by Venini, to which add now Dewar (n. 46) and Smolenaars (n. 8),
and in the collections of a hundred years ago (also listed by Venini). Statius'
relation to Virgil must be read with reference to his relation to Euripides,
Seneca and Lucan, Homer, and probably Ovid (mentioned but somewhat
neglected for the last sixty years). For an analysis in detail of *Theb.*7 see
now Smolenaars (n. 8); see also the running description of "les sources" in
Legras (n. 44) and the analysis of his relation to Homer, with occasional
reference to Virgil, in Juhnke (n. 14; criticised by Smolenaars (n. 8),
xxxiif.). Statius' relation to Virgil has seldom been interpreted in much detail; but Burck (nn. 21, 24, 25) has been influential and Hardie (nn. 2, 31)
will stimulate.

STATIUS, *Achilleid*

Statius refers the *Achilleid* to the *Iliad* as explicitly as he refers the *Thebaid* to the *Aeneid* (*Ach*.1.3ff.).[1] His particular terms are more specific. He will tell what Homer had not told; he will tell the whole life. The *Odyssey* was thought to supply stories that the *Iliad* had omitted;[2] but to tell the whole life was to do what Aristotle had praised Homer for not doing.[3] Statius' description of his subject (1.1f.) may contain a light echo of Virgil;[4] but the style of his first verse and his election to tell what Homer had not told have been defined as "Alexandrian".[5] The generic character and affiliations of the poem have been an object of some interest recently,[6] but that interest has been pursued without much assessment of Statius' relation to Virgil in particular.[7]

Some imitations have been observed on the larger scale of episodes and structure. The narrative begins from the moment when Thetis sees Paris' ship on its way back from Sparta, and because she has heard of the future asks Neptune for a storm (1.20ff.); as in the *Aeneid* Juno sees the Trojans off Sicily and asks Aeolus for a storm (1.34ff.).[8] Neptune refuses, but promises the storm that in the *Aeneid* Juno recalls (*Ach*.1.91ff., *Aen*.1.39ff.).[9] Then in *Ach*.2 as in *Aen*.2 characters tell of events from before the moment when the narrative began,

---

[1] See H. Juhnke, *Homerisches in römischer Epik flavischer Zeit* (München 1972), 162ff., E. Burck, *Das römische Epos* (Darmstadt 1979), 352f.

[2] Schol. Hom. *Od*.4.245 (Q).

[3] See S. Koster, *Würz.Jhb* 5 (1979), 190f., G. Rosati, *Maia* 44 (1992), 233, n. 3.

[4] So O.A.W. Dilke, *Statius. Achilleid* (Cambridge 1954), *ad loc*. But Statius specifies and elaborates only the second of Virgil's subjects, *uirum*; see S. Jannaccone, *P. Papinio Stazio L'Achilleide* (Firenze 1950), *ad loc*.

[5] V. Tandoi, *AR* 30 (1985), 167.

[6] See Koster (n. 3), 189ff., Rosati (n. 3), 233ff., and also G. Aricò, *ANRW* 2.32.5 (1986), 2931f., 2959ff.

[7] 1.147 is identified as an echo of Propertius' reference to the *Aeneid*, 2.34.66, by Koster (n. 6), 201, n. 34 (cf. Aricò (n. 6), 2936, n. 54); it might seem to count against Koster's description of the poem as an epic on comic and elegiac themes.

[8] See Aricò (n. 6), 2933f., and for more detail of Statius' other allusions to Virgil here, and of the reworking of the *Iliad* and of his own *Thebaid*, see L. Legras, *RÉA* 10 (1908), 48ff., H.M. Mulder in P. de Jonge *et al*. (ed.) *Ut pictura poesis. Studia latina P.J. Enk septuagenario oblata* (Leiden 1955), 120ff.

[9] The storm that does not happen is described as "eine antivergilische Pointe" by Burck (n. 1), 354, n. 7 (with a reference to Statius' second use of the idea in 1.684ff.). *Dabo tollere fluctus*, 1.92, responds to *da pellere luctus*, 74 (on the text in 74 see Dilke (n. 4), *ad loc*.) as *fluctusque. . .tollit*, *Aen*.1.103, responds to *et mulcere dedit fluctus et tollere vento*, 66; *Aen*.1.79f. responds to 65f. with the same syntax more ironically.

Ulysses of the judgment of Paris and the abduction of Helen, and of the earlier abductions (2.49ff.),[10] and Achilles of his education by Chiron (94ff.).[11] So Statius doubles Virgil's device, with two stories shorter than Aeneas'. The combination of Thetis' appeal to Neptune in *Ach*.1 when the Trojans are already returning with this device in *Ach*.2 defines a beginning *in medias res* like Virgil's in the *Aeneid*. But the correspondence between *Ach*.2 and *Aen*.2 is a correspondence of books in the same place in the sequence, not necessarily a correspondence of a planned *Achilleid* as a whole with the *Aeneid* as a whole.[12]

Some imitations on a smaller scale evoke Virgil's treatment of events and persons later in the war. Achilles will be Virgil's destroyer of Troy, *Ach*.1.529f., *Aen*.12.545 with 3.1f.; Ulysses and the Greeks have already the qualities that Virgil describes, *Ach*.1.846f., *Aen*.2.43f.[13] Statius' imitations of Seneca's *Troades* also evoke events later in the war, but with more irony.[14] Other imitations of the *Aeneid* imply a significance in episodes in the poem like a significance in episodes in the *Aeneid*. Statius' treatment of Achilles on Scyros echoes Virgil's of Aeneas at Carthage.[15] But neither Statius' anticipations of Virgil's history nor his treatment of Virgil's themes seems to express a response to Virgil's thought.

Bibliography

It used to be said that there are few imitations in the *Achilleid*. That is certainly not true; see Mulder (n. 8) and Fantham (n. 14). It is still said that he reworks the forms of the tradition more freely in the *Achilleid* than in the *Thebaid* (Mulder 128, Aricò (n. 6) 2962). But an index has not been made; recourse must be had to the commentaries of Jannaccone and Dilke (n. 4). Thetis' interview with Neptune and some other parts of the poem are analysed in detail by Mulder. Other elements in the poem are described by Aricò (Euripides, 2943ff.) and by Rosati (elegy, especially Ovid's *Heroides* (n. 6), 255ff.).

---

[10] Jannaccone (n. 4) on 50; cf. 1.63ff.
[11] Dilke (n. 4) on 87.
[12] See M. von Albrecht in *Lucain, Entretiens Hardt* 15 (Vandoeuvres-Genève 1970), 282 with n. 4 on such correspondences in Lucan and Virgil and in Silius and Virgil.
[13] Qualities that Statius' character in the text cannot know, but which Statius' reader knows from Virgil, Rosati (n. 3), 242f.
[14] E. Fantham, *CQ* 29 (1979), 457ff.
[15] Mulder (n. 8), 126ff.; on Statius' use of Euripides see Aricò (n. 6), 2943ff.

SILIUS ITALICUS

Silius revered images of Virgil, and his tomb, and celebrated Virgil's birthday more seriously than his own; Pliny's description of Silius' life in retirement and of his enthusiasm for Virgil, which Martial confirms, may well suggest a certain dilettantism, even if he was the Italicus whom the grammarian and philosopher Cornutus addressed flatteringly as a poet in a work on Virgil.[1] But there is enough matter to consider within the poem itself.[2]

Silius treats the historical tradition of the Second Punic War in the terms and the forms of epic.[3] His principal point of reference in the historical tradition is Livy,[4] in the epic Virgil. Virgil himself had anticipated the Punic Wars, and especially the second (*Aen.*4.622ff., 10.11ff.); the events of the *Punica* are a continuation and a consequence of the events of the *Aeneid*.[5] The idea is perhaps implicit in the prooemium (1.17–20);[6] it is then made more explicit in the exposition of the events leading to the attack on Saguntum, in Juno's monologue (1.42ff.) and in Hannibal's oath in terms of Dido's curse (1.114ff.).[7] The mythological (or Virgil's) causes of the war are

---

[1] Plin. *Ep.*3.7; Mart.11.48.50 (49); 12.67; Cornutus *ap.* Char.125. 16K. On Pliny's letter: G. Laudizi, *Silio Italico* (Galatina 1989), 14ff. The cult of Homer in the Hellenistic world: C.O. Brink, *AJP* 93 (1972), 549ff.; of other poets: F. Cairns, *Tibullus: A Hellenistic Poet at Rome* (Cambridge 1979), 218, 220.

[2] Silius refers to Virgil at 8.595f. Dilettantism within the poem: M. von Albrecht, *Silius Italicus* (Amsterdam 1964), 187ff.

[3] The relation of the genres in the poem: E. Burck, *Historische und epische Tradition bei Silius Italicus* (München 1984), M. Wilson in A.J. Boyle (ed.), *Roman Epic* (London 1993), 218ff., and on the battles P. Venini, *RIL* 106 (1972), 532ff., K.-H. Niemann, *Die Darstellungen der römischen Niederlagen in den Punica des Silius Italicus* (Bonn 1975). On Greek and Roman theory and practice: D.C. Feeney, *The Gods in Epic* (Oxford 1991), 252ff.

[4] Silius and the historical tradition, most recently: H.-G. Nesselrath, *Herm.* 114 (1986), 203ff. On "sources" and "models" notice W. Kissel, *Das Geschichtsbild des Silius Italicus* (Frankfurt am Main 1979), 221, n. 35.

[5] See E. Burck in id. (ed.), *Das römische Epos* (Darmstadt 1979), 290f.

[6] *Irarum* (17) in Silius' immediate context refers to human not divine anger; *tantarum causas irarum. . .aperire* echoes Luc.1.67f., introducing an account of human causes. But *tantarum. . .irarum* and *causas irarum* also echo *Aen.*1.11 and 25, referring to Juno's hostility, and *causas aperire is* followed by *superasque recludere mentes* (19); and later Hannibal puts on Juno's anger (38f.). On the prooemium, J. Küppers, *Tantarum causas irarum* (Berlin 1986), 22ff. (on this point, 30f., 39). *Pun.*1, 26f. makes *Aen.*1, 15f. specific with reference to the *Iliad*.

[7] 42ff.: *Aen.*1.6, 27 (*spretae*), 68; 9.599, 635; 7.313f. (J. Delz, *MH* 26 (1979). 114f.): *Aen.*4.626ff. The exposition: Küppers (n. 6), 61ff. Hannibal's oath: F.Ahl-M.A. Davis-A. Pomeroy, *ANRW* 2.32.4 (1986), 2495f.

integrated with the historical (or the historians') causes (1.60ff., 77ff., 107f.; Liv.21.1.3–5).[8]

Juno's hostility to the Trojans in the *Aeneid* will continue to the Second Punic War; she does not abandon her hostility entirely in her negotiation with Jupiter in *Aen*.12.791ff.[9] Virgil anticipates what Ennius had described. So Silius describes what Virgil had anticipated. Juno's negotiation with Jupiter in *Pun*.17.341ff. evokes her negotiation in *Aen*.12,[10] and marks the continuation of her hostility; Silius may imply the further continuation of her hostility.[11] As Juno's hostility had continued from the *Iliad* to the *Aeneid*, and Venus complained to Jupiter that the Trojans continued to suffer (*Aen*.1.240f.), so she complains in the *Punica* (3.559ff.) and implies that Hannibal threatens to undo Jupiter's promise in the *Aeneid* (*Pun*.3.563f., *Aen*.1.279). So far, Silius and Virgil; beyond lies the question of Silius and Ennius. Silius treated the Second Punic War on a larger scale than Ennius;[12] and in detail few allusions or echoes have been identified with any security from scepticism.[13] A relation between the two poems in the treatment of Juno's hostility and placation seems to remain a matter of speculation.[14]

Dido's curse, and Hannibal's oath, are depicted on Hannibal's shield (2.422ff.).[15] Dido's sister Anna, as Anna Perenna, carries out Dido's behests in encouraging Hannibal before Cannae (8.41ff.).[16] The story of Anna herself (8.50ff.) continues from the *Aeneid* in a reworking of Ovid's treatment (*Fast*.3.545ff.); Anna's account of Dido's death (8.116ff.) reworks the *Aeneid*.[17] Anna's meeting with Hannibal (ending

---

[8] Küppers (n. 6), 44f., 61ff.

[9] D.C. Feeney, *CQ* 34 (1984), 179ff., *Gods* (n. 3), 146ff.

[10] von Albrecht (n. 2), 168ff.

[11] Jupiter anticipates the Third Punic War (371ff.; cf. 7.492f.); see Feeney, *Gods* (n. 3), 303 on *turbata* (604).

[12] A. Klotz, PW 3A 1, 83.

[13] See R. Häussler, *Das historische Epos von Lucan bis Silius und seine Theorie* 2 (Heidelberg 1978), 149ff.; scepticism from O. Skutsch, *The* Annals *of Quintus Ennius* (Oxford 1985), 17f., H.D. Jocelyn, *LCM* 13 (1988), 131ff., 14 (1989), 62. Silius honours Ennius in the poem in 12.390ff.

[14] See Häussler (n. 13), 193f., 199f.

[15] See Küppers (n. 6), 154ff. More recently: P. Venini in *Studi di filologia classica in onore di Giusto Monaco* (Palermo 1991), 1191ff.

[16] On the episode: C. Santini, S*ilius Italicus and his View of the Past* (Amsterdam 1991), 5ff., Ahl-Davis-Pomeroy (n. 7), 2496ff. On the authenticity of verses 144–223: J. Delz, *Silius Italicus. Punica* (Stuttgart 1987) lxivff., against G. Brugnoli, *GIF* 44 (1992), 203ff. (unsound).

[17] Santini (n. 16), 9f., 39f. Silius, Virgil, and Ovid: von Albrecht (n. 2), 154ff.

in 8.224ff.) brings Virgil's, and Ovid's, events into the historical tradition.[18]

The continuation of events from the *Aeneid* in the *Punica* is an incidental idea in the treatment of other episodes and stories that begin from Trojan origins: the Nereids' visit to Proteus and his story (7.409ff.),[19] Dasius' story of the Palladium (13.30ff.).[20]

A more comprehensive account of the relation between the poems was proposed by von Albrecht, referring in part to the continuation of events[21] but principally to certain typological and anti-typological relations between events and between persons in the two poems. (The terms "Typologie" and "typologisch" are not used by von Albrecht, but rather "Spiegelung".)[22] "Silius lässt die vergilische Romidee und seine Aeneasgestalt auf eine Vielzahl von Helden und Geschehnisse ausstrahlen."[23] So Hannibal is a Turnus and an anti-Aeneas, the Romans a whole people of Aeneas figures, Saguntum another Troy, Rome another Troy or an anti-Troy, especially in *Pun.*12.[24] Silius does not achieve the depth, complexity, and coherence of Virgil's use of Homer's patterns;[25] but some such relation appears in his treatment of the fall of Saguntum, the siege of Rome, and the storm that keeps Hannibal from Italy.[26]

The *Punica* is not indeed a mirror image of the *Aeneid* (to use von Albrecht's metaphor); but the differences in thought and in themes described by von Albrecht do not declare independence.[27] The toils of the war differ from those of the foundation; they serve perhaps to test (3.573f.), certainly to harden for empire (575ff.). *Pun.*3.582f. reworks *Aen.*1.33 in these new terms (575ff.), but as an allusion to the

---

[18] Santini (n. 16), 59ff.

[19] Cymodoce (428f.) may be identified with Cymodocea, *Aen.*10.225, even if the name appears elsewhere in lists of Nereids (Hom. *Il.*18.39, Hes. *Th.*252, Virg. *Aen.*5.826); the episode as a whole is of course an instance of Silius' use of the *Georgics*.

[20] See Serv. *ad Aen.*2.166, who refers to Varro; F. Canciani, *EV*, s.v. *Palladio* 940.

[21] von Albrecht (n. 2), 173f.

[22] E.g. 168, n. 8, 188.

[23] 21.

[24] 172ff.

[25] On Virgil and Homer: G.N. Knauer, *Die Aeneis und Homer* (Göttingen 1964), 345ff. On Silius' poetic achievement in this see H. Juhnke, *Homerisches in romischer Epik flavischer Zeit* (München 1972), 225, n. 167.

[26] On the storm: Burck (n. 3), 129ff., Ahl-Davis-Pomeroy (n. 7), 2514ff.

[27] von Albrecht (n. 2), esp. I. Teil ("Grundlinien und Grundtendenzen"); see 184.

Aeneid implies only a comparison between the acquisition of the empire and the foundation of the people.[28] But the elements of an anti-*Aeneid* (as it is likely enough to be called) have been discovered. Silius has been thought to present more plainly than Virgil an Aeneas who breaks faith.[29] The events of the poem have been placed in Roman history between those of the *Aeneid* and those of the *Bellum Civile*;[30] "the Rome of the 'Punica' moves, inexorably, towards the Rome of the 'Pharsalia'".[31] Silius in a number of passages expresses the conventional idea that the defeat of Carthage brought moral decline at Rome, and makes allusions to moral failing even in his own time.[32] These comments and allusions seem incidental to the events he is describing (e.g. 10.657f., 14.682ff., which is also a compliment to Domitian); he does not relate the loss of chastity (13.823f., very early) and other crimes among Roman women (13.831ff.) to his history (844ff. is perhaps another allusion to Domitian). He does not refer his pessimism to the *Aeneid*. His characterization has been thought to anticipate the collapse of the republic;[33] but his representation of Roman politics during the Punic War is not obviously more pessimistic than Livy's. He makes much reference to Lucan;[34] but it has not been shown to define his response to Virgil in particular detail.[35] His reference to the Civil Wars in *Pun*.13.853ff. is more striking in some respects than Virgil's in *Aen*.6.826ff.: what Scipio sees of the future beyond the Punic War, at a high point in the structure (such as it is) of the vision,[36] is Marius and Sulla and then Pompey and

---

[28] See further Kissel (n. 4), 44f. (with E. Burck, *Gnom*.53 (1981), 132), W. Schubert, *Jupiter in den Epen der Flavierzeit* (Frankfurt am Main 1984), 59f.

[29] Ahl-Davis-Pomeroy (n. 7), 2498f.; but 8.50–53 are a more complex allusion to the *Aeneid* than they indicate; see, for a start, F. Spaltenstein, *Commentaire des Punica de Silius Italicus (livres 1 à 8)* (Geneva 1986), *ad loc.*

[30] Kissel (n. 4), esp. 221f. (cf. Küppers (n. 6), 23, n. 95), Ahl-Davis-Pomeroy (n. 7), 2501ff., 2555ff.; contrast von Albrecht (n. 2), 164ff.

[31] Ahl-Davis-Pomeroy (n. 7), 2502. "Silius' epic functions as a kind of aetiology for Lucan's poem", Hardie (282, n. 31), 66; cf. 69.

[32] Lists (complementary) in Häussler (n. 13), 208, n. 65, Feeney, *Gods* (n. 3), 302, n. 202.

[33] Kissel (n. 4), esp. 221f. (see Burck (n. 28), 133ff.), Ahl-Davis-Pomeroy (n. 7), 2502, 2536ff. (whose arguments can be pruned).

[34] Collected but not much analysed by K. Meyer, *Silius und Lucan* (Diss. Würzburg 1924). See Häussler (n. 13), 161ff.

[35] See Ahl-Davis-Pomeroy (n.7), 2502; von Albrecht (n. 2) 164ff. stresses Silius' and Lucan's Stoicism.

[36] Juhnke (n. 25), 292.

Caesar.[37] But Silius does not relate this vision of the future to Scipio's present.

Silius' range of reference is wider than Livy and Virgil.[38] He honours Homer in the poem more highly than Virgil.[39] He makes much use of the epics,[40] including some parts of them that Virgil had used already. In particular episodes in which he uses both Homer and Virgil the extent and the detail of his use of Homer is sometimes at least underestimated by von Albrecht, as appears from Juhnke's more elaborate analysis;[41] but the conclusion reached by Juhnke concerning Silius' relation to Virgil and Homer is no more than that Silius' use of Homer was a solution to a problem "in Sinne einer Entlastung von jenem Druck vergilischer Grösse".[42]

Silius' language and style have not been much studied in relation to Virgil's, or indeed in any respect. Some material was collected by Groesst.[43] In one small semantic and contextual field (phrases of the kind *haec ubi dicta dedit, his dictis*) variation from Virgil's style has been observed, except for purposes which might be described as the marking of effective speech.[44] Silius' use of Virgil's language was examined as evidence for the textual tradition of Virgil by Ussani;[45] which might prompt reconsideration of the range of Silius' variation of particular phrases. Silius' verse rhythms, as determined at least by sequences of dactyls and spondees and some effects of accent, are more like Virgil's than any other epic poet's after Virgil;[46] but at the verse end they are much less various than Virgil's,[47] in which respect Silius' rhythms are like the other epic poets'.

---

[37] See Kissel (n. 4), 182f.

[38] See for example, E.L. Bassett, *CP* 50 (1955), 1ff., 54 (1959), 10ff., 58 (1963), 73ff., M. Billerbeck, *Herm*.111 (1983), 326ff.; and also P. Venini, *MIL* 36.3 (1978), 123ff., esp. 219ff.

[39] 13.778ff.; Juhnke (n. 25), 289ff.

[40] See Juhnke (n. 25).

[41] E.g. Hannibal's farewell to his wife and son, 3.62ff.: von Albrecht (n. 2) 146f., Juhnke (n. 25), 193ff.

[42] Juhnke (n. 25) 302; cf. 49f.

[43] J. Groesst, *Qua tenus Silius Italicus a Vergilio pendere videatur* (Diss. Halle 1887), 52ff. (cf. 30ff., 44ff.).

[44] S. Lundström, *„Sprach's" bei Silius Italicus* (Lund 1971).

[45] V. Ussani jr., *Mem.Linc.*, 8.3 (1950), 87ff.

[46] G.E. Duckworth, *TAPA* 98 (1967), 88ff., esp. 91, 98ff.

[47] M.L. Arribas Hernáez, *Emerita* 58.2 (1990), 231ff.; figures 253.

Bibliography

Allusions to and echoes of Virgil (and other authors) in the *Punica* are noted most fully in (it must be said) the commentary of G.A. Ruperti (Göttingen 1795–1798), as edited by N.E. Lemaire (Paris 1823), which is supplemented but not superseded by F. Spaltenstein, *Commentaire des Punica de Silius Italicus* (Genève 1986–1990); there is no Juhnke (n. 25) for Virgil in the *Punica*. The collection by Groesst (n. 43) is a classification into various categories. The most complete description of Silius' relation to Virgil is still von Albrecht (n. 2). A survey of work bearing on Silius' relation to Virgil in C. Santini, *EV*, s.v. *Silio Italico*.

CHAPTER EIGHT

THE TRANSMISSION OF VIRGIL'S WORKS IN ANTIQUITY AND THE MIDDLE AGES

M. Geymonat (Translated by the Editor)

The publication of Virgil's poems and the earliest phase of their diffusion in Rome and in the Empire

For its age and its riches, the tradition of Virgil is comparable only—and that is no accident; cf. n. 45 below on Virgil as the Pagans' bible in late antiquity—with that of the Bible and of a few other important Christian works. Of *Buc.*, *G.* and *Aen.* we have over 1000 mss. (cf. n. 63): a notable quantity, but only a tiny part of the innumerable rolls and codices that must have been produced in the 1500 years between the poems' publication and their first printed editions. It is a paradox that the intense reading of Virgil itself led not only to the production, but also to the loss of very many copies: as lacunae appeared and as the script became illegible in a ms., it was swiftly enough replaced. The disused text was either destroyed or reused after washing, as a palimpsest (cf. 307 below); so too many imperial buildings were used as quarries for later constructions!

Numerically, the largest part of our Virgil mss. consists of humanist copies, but we do also have seven splendid late antique productions, three of which are almost complete, which have passed without break from the patrician palaces of Rome to later mediaeval libraries, and thence to modern collections. There are moreover more than thirty mss., complete or fragmentary, copied in France, Germany or Italy between the end of the c. 8 and the beginning of the c. 10: in the case of (e.g.) Horace, Lucretius and Ovid, we have no earlier mss. The epigraphic and papyrological evidence, some of which belongs to the first century after Virgil's death, is discussed elsewhere (252–5).

To the question of how Virgil's works were circulated from the outset, there is no altogether simple answer. We have seen already that there is good evidence for the circulation and performance of individual *Eclogues* (28, 249f.); Virgil himself suggests as much, quoting the incipits of *Buc.*2 and 3 at 5.85–7, and referring to 6 by its title, *Varus* at vv. 11–2. The success of *Buc.* individually, and as a collection, is demonstrated by numerous echoes in contemporary authors.[1] But in the context of contemporary Roman literature, the *Buc.* were a text so strongly innovative that there was no shortage of jealous critics opposed to Virgil: thus e.g. Bavius and Maevius are probably to be identified as *obtrectatores* (*Buc.*3.90f.).[2] That could have been a scathing answer, for example, to a poetaster who had had fun at the expense of 2.23 (certainly earlier than *Buc.*3): there Serv. notes: *sane hunc versum male distinguens Vergiliomastix vituperat 'lac mihi non aestate novum, non frigore: defit', id est semper mihi deest!* We should perhaps also bear in mind the possibility of adjustments effected when the collection was brought together, such as the hypothetical addition of 2.45–55 (which do not gybe with the symmetry of the poem as a whole: 1–5, 6–18, 19–44, 56–68, 69–73); when they are added (cf. 33f.), *Buc.*2 + 8 (181 verses) = *Buc.*3 + 7 (the same).

The *G.* too had their jealous and mocking critics (cf. 65 n. 15 for some statistics in support of their unpopularity in general): e.g. the man who *recitante eo ex Georgicis [1.299]: 'nudus ara, sere nudus' subiecit: 'habebis frigore febrem'* (VSD 43) or C. Melissus, Maecenas' learned and witty secretary, who wrote a pamphlet *de apibus* (cited by Serv. on *Aen.*7.66; cf. 9 on M.'s description of Virgil's voice) to make fun of the topic (cf. *EV* 3.461f.). The first 'publication' of *G.* was of course oral, by means of the reading at Atella (13, 87), and their rapid diffusion[3] is, as we have seen, one of the factors which makes it quite impossible to lend credence to the silly tale in Servius about a revised edition of *G.*4 (cf. 86–9 for detailed discussion and bibliography).[4]

The tradition of the *G.* soon enough conformed to that of *Buc.* and *Aen.*, but there are traces of an independent phase: mediaeval and humanist mss. of *G.* alone are rare but may have been more numerous in late antiquity[5] and the grammarians Julius Hyginus (Augustan) and Valerius Probus (late c. 1 A.D.) claim to have consulted

---

[1] Cf. n. 61 for Hor. *Epd.*16; G. D'Anna in *Virgilio e gli Augustei* (Napoli 1990), 89ff., for Tib., V. Gigante Lanzara, ib., 113ff. for Prop.; cf. too *EV* s.v.

[2] So already W. Kroll, *Studien. . .*(Stuttgart 1924), 117–38; cf. *EV* s.v. *obtrectatores* (Görler).

[3] R. Starr, *CQ* 37 (1987), 213–23 collects some interesting material.

[4] For the little story reported, not without irony (*ea res uerane an falsa sit non laboro; quin tamen melius suauiusque ad aures sit 'ora' quam 'Nola', dubium id non est*) by Gell.6.20, about *G.*2.224f. see ch. 1, n. 48. Important as an indication of how and why people played, in the days before crossword puzzles, with the text of Virgil.

[5] See not so much **A** (see 306f. below; note that this typeface (**A**) is used only for sigla of the mss. of Virgil), of which we have only pages containing *G.*, but which

copies of the *G. ex domo atque familia Uergilii* and corrected *ipsius manu* (cited by Gellius 1.21.2 and 13.21.4), though Gellius' text does not require us to believe that these mss. were necessarily of *G.* alone, nor do we have to suppose that they were autographs; it is enough to suppose that we are talking about old mss. (of individual books, or even of *G.* entire): old, containing interesting variants and sought after on the second-hand market, like the ms. of (or including) *Aen.*2 *emptum in sigillariis uiginti aureis, quem ipsius Uergilii fuisse credebatur.*[6]

The *Aeneid* was published by Varius, perhaps in 17 B.C.,[7] two years after Virgil's death: time enough for the final revision which the poet was not able to carry out in person (20f.). VSD (chs. 23–4) tells us a good deal about the composition of the *Aen.* and some details may even be true (p. 16f.), though there are passing hints to suggest (pp. 234–6) that this section is in the end no more reliable than the rest! Other details of the poem's history in VSD (e.g. 34 on 6.164–5) are (20) clearly absurd. But, to be sure, VSD 30 is right to mention the poem's great and immediate fame; he cites Propertius' excited anticipation (2.34.65f.; cf. 15, 18) and might have added the evidence of Hor. *CS* 37–8, performed in early June 17, but certainly composed earlier: as a close friend of Virgil's, Horace would not have had to wait for the 'official publication'.

We have seen that the story of Virgil's 'last voyage' to Greece and of his testamentary dispositions regarding the unfinished text of the

---

included originally *Aen.* as well, as the sumptuous eastern book of the c. 5 (*CLA* 1708). From this C.H. Roberts published (*Antinoopolis Papyri* 1 (London 1950), 75–7) some fragments from the end of *G.*2 and the beginning of *G.*3 (2.527–3.25) as well as a brief *argumentum* to bk. 3. Each page was at least 41 x 27.5 cm and contained 25 lines; huge margins (9–10 cm!); a commentary might once have been intended. On the quantity of writing material necessary for copying individual works of poetry, and on the size of the earliest *uolumina* of *Buc.*, cf. J. Van Sickle, *Arethusa* 13 (1980), 5–42.

[6] In this case (Gell.2.3.5f.) surely a fake; Sebastiano Timpanaro too has doubts, in this case: *Per la storia della filologia virgiliana antica* (Roma 1986), 41. In other passages in the *Noct.Att.* (9.14.7) and in individual notes of SDan. (*G.*1.12, *Aen.*2.37) there is still talk of an *idiographum*, of *antiquissimi libri*, of *antiqua exemplaria*, but see the sharp critique of L. Gamberale in *Atti. . .Convegno. . .Bimillenario delle Georgiche* (Napoli 1977), 359–67. Timpanaro's defence of Gellius' good faith (op.cit. 33–42) should be noted; J.E.G. Zetzel, *Latin textual criticism in antiquity* (New York 1984), 61f. is readier with accusations of lucrative fraud. On the antiquarian book-trade in the Roman world, cf. R.J. Starr, *Phoen.*44 (1990), 148ff.

[7] The date is given by Jerome in his additions to Eusebius' *Chronicon*, conveniently available in *EV* 5**, 436, no. 70. On this edition, contrast 23 and H.D. Jocelyn, *Sileno* 16 (1990) 263–78. Jocelyn's attempt to reinstate Tucca may not be found entirely persuasive (cf. Timpanaro, cit., 18, n. 7 et passim).

poem bristle with irresoluble difficulties (20–3). We cannot be quite
sure that it was Augustus who insisted on publication at all costs
(22f.). That it was Varius, and not Varius and Tucca who undertook
the necessary work of revision is very likely.[8] Varius left the half-lines
as they were, though others tinkered with them (23f.); these half-
lines, particularly frequent in bk. 2,[9] seem to confirm what we are
told in VSD 24 about Virgil's technique of composition (17). It may
be legitimate to wonder whether the *tibicines* may not originally have
been more numerous and whether the poem's first editor did not
perhaps flout the order *nihil addere*, with some supplements that were
not in the poet's ms. (or mss.), of the type which Messalla, cited by
Sen. *Suas*.2.20, suspected had been inserted at 11.290: '*haesit*' Messalla
*aiebat hic Uergilium debuisse desinere: quod sequitur 'et in decimum uestigia
rettulit annum', explementum esse*.[10] It has been suggested that at least
some of the hemistichia have an artistic effect and value,[11] of which
the poet could not have been unaware: thus at 4.361 SDan. already
noted: *et oratorie ibi finiuit, ubi uis argumenti constitit*. We might wish to
compare, from (e.g.) bk. 2, verses 66, 346, 640, 787. Such unfinished
verses indicate a narrative or dramatic pause and mark, with their
alteration of the rhythm, a change of scene or the end of a rhetorical development; the effect must have been greater in the standard
means of performance of Virgil—aloud. We might therefore be reluctant to exclude the possibility that in a final revision the poet too
might have saved at least some of the hemistichs: an unprecedented
and unimitated deviation from the epic tradition (cf. Sparrow 25f.).

The problem of repetitions[12] is more complex: such repetitions

---

[8] To defend the place of Tucca because he was mentioned in V.'s will alongside
Varius (cf. G. Marconi, *RCCM* 3 (1961), 342–80, R. Scarcia, ib. 5 (1963), 303–
21, *EV* 5.307f.) is hazardous, given the state of our *testimonia* about that document
(cf. 21–3)!

[9] *Aen*.2 is after all one of the most worked-up and formally finished books, but
see vv. 66, 233, 346, 614, 623, 640, 720, 767, 787.

[10] At *Ep*.94.28 Seneca rounds off the terse *audentis fortuna iuuat* with *piger ipse sibi
obstat*. For other ancient supplements, cf. Serv. on 2.787 and 8.41; in the mss., cf.
M at 11.391, **P** at 3.661, and **R** at 5.595 and 10.490. There are, inevitably, many
more examples in the mediaeval and humanistic mss. Among the hexameters which
have given rise to most doubt from this point of view, note (e.g.) 12.218, whose end,
non uiribus aequis is repeated shortly afterwards at 12.230 and may be repeated from
5.809, 10.357, 431.

[11] So notoriously J. Sparrow, *Half-lines and repetitions* (Oxford 1931, repr. New York
1977); cf. F. Lenz in *Vergiliana*, 166f.

[12] Cf. W. Moskalew, *Formular language and poetic design. . .(Mnem.* Suppl. 73, 1982),
EV s.v. *Ripetizioni* (Briggs).

cannot always be assigned to a precise formal wish to imitate Homeric repetitions. There are cases in which a whole half-line recurs with a precise function, in the same metrical *sedes* (thus *iamque propinquabam/ propinquabant* at the beginning of 2.730, 5.159, 9.371, 11.621) as there are also instances in which whole verses or groups of verses are repeated, as at 1.311 and 3.230,[13] at 3.65 and 11.35, at 9.104–6 and 10.113–5.[14] Cases in which a particular word is repeated after a brief interval bother a modern ear, but it is not at all clear that this sort of *tic* was equally unpleasant to an ancient poet or to his audience.[15] It is possible that 'three years' (cf. 20) of revision might have weeded some cases out, but we have no means of being sure. We may recall (thus Favorinus ap.Gell.17.10.2f.) that the poet worked at his verses as did the she-bear in giving form to her cubs (cf. ch. 1, n. 107).

We may also imagine, with some justification, that the autograph copy of the *Aeneid* was full of alternative readings, and it is conceivable that some of them may have penetrated into the first edition.[16] But after Varius finished his task, what, physically, happened to the autograph text? Could it have been deposited in the Palatine library, to be consulted by the learned? It does seem, though, that it early ceased to be available.[17] Might it have been hidden away in the imperial archives, or even destroyed, as a sort of belated bow to Virgil's 'last wishes', and to remove lingering questions about what the poet might really have written here or there?[18] In any case, I do not think that any of the variant readings, preserved in both direct[19] and indirect traditions, going back to a very early stage in the trans-

---

[13] Though transmitted by **M** and **P**, this verse is not annotated by Serv. and is expelled by many modern editors.

[14] In **R**, these instances seem yet more numerous, because it depends, clearly, on an exemplar which contained numerous interlinear and marginal annotations; as a result, see e.g. the repetition of 6.311–310–312 after *G.*4.472 (cf. 87 n. 128).

[15] So (e.g.) 8.317, 322 *componere*, 9.605, 610 *fatigare*, 10.382, 393 *discrimina*. But ancient taste and modern are very different: see Austin on *Aen.*2.505, with ample bibliography.

[16] Ribbeck, Jachmann (*RhM* 84 (1935), 224) and Pasquali (*ASNP* 12 (1943), 74–6 suspected, in particular that 9.85 was no more than a duplication of what followed (86–7).

[17] Timpanaro (n. 6), 36f., 56, 184. Suet. *Cal.*34.2 relates that Caligula was on the point of removing portraits and *scripta* of both Virgil and Livy *ex omnibus bibliothecis*: more than Augustus ever managed to do for Ovid! When Quint. (1.7.20) and Plin. (*Nat.*13.83) refer to the spelling and to the texts of V., it is not quite clear that they refer exclusively to non-poetic texts.

[18] So Horsfall *CR* 37 (1987), 178. ['I can as easily believe. . .' I wrote: let that be a warning against attempts at gentle irony. Ed.]

[19] The idea was G. Funaioli's (*Il valore del Mediceo nella tradizione manoscritta di*

mission of Virgil, and which some have wished to claim as author variants, can really be brought right back to the pretty clearly mucky autograph ms. of the epic.[20]

On the other hand, I do believe it probable that all our most ancient mss. descend *recta uia* from Varius' edition[21] and that the hypothesis of an archetype of some centuries later is not to be taken seriously.[22]

The obvious reason for the swift diffusion of Virgil, and in particular of the *Aen.* throughout the Empire was its rapid adoption in schools as a fundamental text (250f.). Caecilius Epirota, a freedman of Atticus, who founded a school at Rome while Virgil was still alive (? ca. 26) was the first to hold public lessons on the text (Suet. *Gramm.*16); thereafter many critics, professional and amateur, competed to take possession of this cultural heritage—and to draw some personal advantage from it, like the instructor paid by the people of Brindisi who *legebat barbare insciteque Uergilii septimum* (Gell.16.6.3). Evidence for the use of Virgil in schools is provided by the graffiti of the Basilica degli Argentari (Rome) and of the Great Palaestra (Pompeii), spaces used for teaching and by pupils.[23] From then on, Virgil was read, copied and recopied, committed to memory times without number (whence many errors of citation), and the whole process of comprehension and contamination went on uninterrupted

---

V. (1932), in *Studi di letteratura antica* 2.1 (Bologna 1947), 375); with reference to these instances, S. Mariotti has remarked that the hypothesis serves only to save us from the difficulty of choosing between variants accepted by serious scholars (or at least acceptable to their judgement), between which there is no real basis for choice (in *La critica del testo* (Convegno, Lecce 1984; pub. Roma 1985), 102f.). The fact is, says Mariotti, that these variants are much closer in form, sound, and appearance than in sense; we can no longer establish what the reason—whether palaeographical or psychological—for the passage from one to the other. For two instances, cf. F. Boldrer, *MD* 27 (1991), 145–57; on 12.605, not so much F. Giancotti, *Victor Tristis* (Bologna 1993), 123–47 as Timpanaro (n. 6), 99ff.

[20] An idea decisively rejected by Timpanaro (n. 6, 183–95); it had already been severely criticised by A. La Penna, *RFil.*107 (1979), 5–11, and more fully by Zetzel (n. 6), 27–147.

[21] The lack of an archetype 'if not for all Virgil, at least for entire books of the *Aeneid*' was already maintained by G. Pasquali, *Storia della tradizione e critica del testo* (ed. 2 Firenze 1962), 21: it is not in fact impossible to explain all the errors common to all our mss. by the vicissitudes of horizontal transmission.

[22] In particular the hypothesis of a c. 4 archetype, advanced by E. Courtney, *BICS* 28 (1981), 26 does not convince (cf. Timpanaro (n. 6), 181f.). It would be quite incredible to suppose that at the height of the Empire, Virgil had been reduced to a single exemplar!

[23] Cf. *EV* s.v. *Epigrafia* (Solin), Petrucci (n. 46), 53ff.; but it is possible to overestimate the influence of Virgil-at-school: cf. 252. On graffiti, cf. 252.

for centuries (306). Cheap editions for schools, more numerous for the early books,[24] which were certainly those most often read, were full of trivialisations and mechanical errors, which could be picked out without much difficulty; we cannot, though, rule out that precisely on account of its naive and 'casual' character this sort of 'vulgate' may have preserved old forms of spelling and some correct readings, such as, I believe, *noris* at 4.423. The formulation of easy didactic 'glosses' to school-texts began early; in the East, they were represented by a simple Greek translation, of which we have interesting fragments in many of the surviving Virgil papyri.[25]

Different, but not without their own peculiar features and indeed errors were, from the first decades of the transmission on, the luxury editions, made for men of letters, and personages of high rank, who might take delight in discovering arcane details and learned allusions and in discussing the latest textual variants. Defined as *optimi* or *antiquissimi* (cf. n. 6), these mss. already bristled with variant readings few years after the poet's death: this was the delicate period through which every work of literature passed after its drafting and publication, down to the age of printing. The 'learned' tradition of Virgil was by definition contaminated. Every new copy inclined to take a particular line, with its own peculiar features and variants, but was straightaway compared with other texts of the same kind, so that branches which should have diverged tended instead to intertwine. In every copy, the tradition as a whole tended to re-form, with new variants, resulting from happy errors of transcription, reminiscences and conjectures aimed at improving verses and passages which seemed infelicitous—touches by the restorer often ingenuous but sometimes surprisingly felicitous.[26]

The very formal imperfection of the *Aen.* challenged from the first decades of the transmission on the skill of men of learning, even earlier than it did the imagination of imitators, who were keen to fill real or imagined lacunae. VSD 42 provides two striking cases, though the language used ('Nisus (mid-c. 1 A.D.) used to say that he had heard from older men') indicates a degree of detachment: the first

---

[24] On the learning of Virgil in class, cf. 250f.; R. Marichal, *REL* 35 (1957), 81f.

[25] Cf. Petrucci (n. 46), 56ff., M. Gigante in *La fortuna* (n. 63), 23–42, *EV* s.v. *Papiri* (Petrucci) and 254f.

[26] Favoured by the amateurish enthusiasm and fake learning of the non-experts; thus Quint.9.4.39: *quae in ueteribus libris reperta mutare imperiti solent, et dum librariorum insectari uolunt inscientiam, suam confitentur!*

story (that the order of books two and three had been reversed by Varius) reflects, as Servius makes plain (ch. 1, n. 149) a literal-minded urge to bring order of narration into line with chronological order. It is very hard indeed to see what we are really being told here: certainly nothing of real value about the work of Varius. VSD adds to Nisus' version of what he had heard that Varius did that the editor had removed the four verses placed before *Aen*.1.1 (*ille ego*. . .). We now have two minute examinations of the problem by Gamberale (ch. 1, n. 150): Virgil could never have written the lines, and they are necessarily post-Ovidian, though not by much. It is easier to suppose that their author wished to guarantee the authenticity of *Buc.-G.-Aen.* (as against the growing *Appendix*) than that there was some sort of anti-Augustan motive entailed in removing the Augustan, classic opening *arma uirumque*.[27] SDan. (who here probably goes back to Donatus) uses turns of phrase which explicitly express doubt (*hi uersus circumducti dicuntur et extra paginam in mundo* and *sane quidam dicunt uersus alios hos a poeta hoc loco relictos, qui ab eius emendatoribus sublati sint*) when transmitting other extra-canonical verses at 3.204 and 6.289; the serious critic recognises ingenious attempts at interpolation by someone who clearly knows Ovid too.[28]

More serious is the case of the Helen-episode, *Aen*.2.567–88; Serv. and SDan. (Goold, n. 29, 130ff.) both tell us that it is agreed that they had been removed (*praef.*, 1.2.22 Th.-H. *constat esse detractos, sublatos* at 2.592), or omitted (SDan. on 2.566 *versus qui a Tucca et Vario obliti sunt*). But we have learned that the scholiastic evidence is of very limited evidential value (Goold), that the language is too rich in mannerisms and oddities, which suggest not a great epic poet, but rather the exceedingly skilled imitator or even parodist, that the style is in some ways more Virgilian than Virgil himself, and that the lines were already known to Lucan.[29] An extremely ingenious attempt was made to show that the structure of Homeric imitation links the episode to its context unbreakably, but the multiplicity of Homeric texts in Virgil's mind here seems to invalidate that gallant defence.[30]

---

[27] On the 'pre-prooemium' cf. Gamberale, just cited, who supersedes earlier discussions.

[28] M.L. Delvigo, *RFil*.117 (1989), 297–315, Goold (n. 29), 132f.

[29] On Lucan, cf. G.P. Goold, *HSCP* 74 (1968), 165f.; despite Goold, cit., 101–68 and (especially on these verses as a sort of parody), C.E. Murgia, *CSCA* 4 (1971), 203–17, believers in authenticity are not extinct.

[30] [The elegant arguments of G.B. Conte, *The Rhetoric of imitation* (Ithaca 1986),

From the beginning, the grammarians toiled to defend Virgil from interpolators and imitators:[31] for example, Julius Hyginus (the fragments are in *GRF* 528–33) a younger contemporary of the poet, freedman of Augustus and Palatine librarian, cited by Serv. to defend the reading *uelati limo* at 12.120;[32] his pupil and freedman Julius Modestus, who worked *inter alia* on the spellings with -u- and with -y- in words of Greek origin; Celsus, cited in some interesting scholia to *G.* and probably to be identified with Cornelius Celsus, the Tiberian encyclopaedist, whose books on medicine survive; Annaeus Cornutus, arbiter of literary taste in the age of Seneca and Nero, and originator of certain polemic shafts at the poet's expense (e.g. on the excessive realism shown in the embrace of Venus and Vulcan, 8.405f. or on the vulnerability of the episode of the cutting of Dido's lock at the end of *Aen.*4 to rationalistic criticism). Greatest of them all was surely Valerius Probus of Berytus; he had, it appears, minimal effect on our texts of Virgil, and may never have produced an edition of the poet, but worked on his text with conscientious intelligence.[33] It may conceivably be thanks to Probus that later scholarship at Rome worked on *Buc.*, *G.* and *Aen.*, equally, consigning the *Appendix* appropriately to outer darkness.[34] Suet. *gramm.*24 says of Probus *multa exemplaria contracta emendare ac distinguere et adnotare curauit*; clearly, then he used a number of mss. believed, presumably, to be old and worthy of respect, but the language used of his activity as editor or critic remains exceedingly problematic: *emendare* probably entailed the careful removal or errors of transcription; *distinguere*, punctuation in accordance

---

196–207 I have tried to take to pieces in a review of D. Gall, *Ipsius umbra Creusae*, in *CR* forthcoming. Ed.]

[31] In most of these grammarians, see *EV*; e.g. on Apronianus, Asper, Haterianus, Carminius, Celsus, Cornutus, Philargyrius, Gallus, Gaudentius, Nisus, *scholia non Serviana*, Urbanus (Geymonat). It will be helpful to consult also Timpanaro and Zetzel (n. 6), as well as O. Ribbeck, *Prolegomena* (Leipzig 1866).

[32] See Timpanaro (n. 6), 59f.; not wholly convincing to Horsfall, *CR* 37 (1987), 179. On Hyg., cf. too F. Boldrer, *MD* 29 (1992), 183–98.

[33] [Did Probus really 'edit' V. in a modern sense? See Timpanaro (n. 6), 19f., L. Lehnus, *EV* s.v. *Probo*, 284f., Zetzel (n. 6), 41–54, M.L. Delvigo, *Testo virgiliano e tradizione indiretta* (Pisa 1987), 12–18, H.D. Jocelyn, *CQ* 34 (1984), 464–72, 35 (1985), 149–61, 466–74. The use of critical signs suggests at least a work of extensive revision. Geymonat in *La fortuna* (n. 63, 1986), 115–21 has a rather more modern Probus. Ed.]

[34] [See Geymonat in *La fortuna* (n. 63, 1986), 116; but it is not certain that P.'s role was decisive in the definition of the corpus. Ed.] *G.*, we see, was hardly edited alone (294, 307); for *Aen.* in isolation, cf. Par.7906 **p**, late c. 8, and, for that matter, the commentary of Tib.Claud. Donatus (n. 55).

[35] Cf. Serv. on 5.871 for Probus on the division between bks. 5 and 6.

with the rhetoric and syntax of the verse;[36] *adnotare* perhaps the habit of inserting in the margin diacritical signs in the Alexandrian tradition. If the *Notae Probianae*[37] do in fact reflect his scholarly method, then we have some more solid indication of how he went about his work of improving the texts available of certain 'classic' authors, beyond the few references in Servius. In later works of grammar and Virgilian exegesis, references to Probus' work are frequent, and the renown of his name helped preserve a commentary to *Buc.* and *G.* which bears his name; it contains some interesting notes, along with much material of scant value.[38] But a careful examination of our best mss.—**M** and **P** in particular—show that they depart markedly from the text of Probus, and omit altogether the diacritical signs.

Other distinguished grammarians did much for Virgilian studies: Gellius, for example, whose *Noctes Atticae* preserve so much valuable information on the composition and earliest reception of the poems of Virgil[39] and Aemilius Asper (late c. 2-mid-c. 3), who also worked on Terence and Sallust; of Asper's ample and authoritative commentary on *Buc.*, *G.* and *Aen.*, more than 150 fragments have been preserved by indirect transmission,[40] not to mention scraps of a Virgilian grammar, copied at the end of the c. 5 on some leaves of a palimpsest of Corbie and now at Paris (Th.-H. 3.2.533–40). But the most important name in this phase is undoubtedly that of Aelius Donatus, active in the mid-c. 4: he influenced strongly both his pupils (amongst whom are to be numbered Servius and Jerome) and the whole of late-antique Roman culture.[41] We can follow the traces of his most important Virgil commentary far into the middle ages, but to us there have come down directly the dedicatory letter (Götte-Bayer, 212), a *vita* pretty clearly not in substance by him (3f.), and the preface to the *Buc.*, a sort of methodical and didactic *accessus*.[42]

From the period which immediately precedes Donatus we have

---

[36] Cf. Jocelyn (n. 33), 467ff.

[37] For the *notae*, see above all Jocelyn (n. 33), 149–61.

[38] On Ps.Prob., cf. the interesting book by M. Gioseffi, *Studi sul commento a Virgilio dello Pseudo-Probo* (Firenze 1991).

[39] *EV* s.v. *Gellio* (Gamberale) gives an idea of how much remains to be done!

[40] Note the very useful ed. by A. Tomsin, Paris 1952.

[41] [On Ael.Donatus, cf. *EV* s.v. (Brugnoli), Goold (n. 29), 117–21, Kaster, (n. 55), 169f. et passim, and, in general, D. Daintree, *GR* 37 (1990), 65–79. Ed.]

[42] Conveniently available in Bayer-Götte, 228ff. Geymonat (*EV* 2.772) suggests that some notes on *Aen.*12 (Th.-H.3.2.523–4) happily recovered by K. von Barth (1624) from some palimpset leaves now lost, may derive from Don.'s commentary.

another exegetic text of great importance, copied at the end of the c. 5 in the margins of our ms. **V** (cf. 307, the so-called *Scholia Veronensia*, published for the first time by Angelo Mai in 1817 (cf. n. 54), and aimed at a public of particular intelligence and culture). The *Schol.Ver.*, in their exact analyses of the poetic text, transmit to us many fragments of archaic Latin poetry and interesting information on points of detail regarding the work of the major grammarians of the first centuries of the Empire (Cornutus, Asper, Probus, Haterianus and others), whose views are quoted in detail and are properly compared; there are also references to Greek literature, not only Homer, Hesiod and Theocritus, but also Antimachus, Callimachus and even Zenodotus.[43]

Devotion to Virgil in late antiquity and its swift decline in the early middle ages

To acquire a fully legitimate position across the vast spaces of the Roman empire, Christian culture assumed, from the c. 3 A.D. on, an attitude of syncretistic tolerance and of substantial continuity towards the classical tradition and Rome's glorious past. To this end, the Christians sought to take advantage precisely of Virgil, whom they interpreted as a kind of pagan prophet of the coming of Christ (cf. ch. 2, nn. 146, 147). Constantine's *Oratio ad Sanctorum coetum*, delivered by the emperor himself perhaps at an Easter between 325 and 337, was composed originally in Latin (and retains some Latinisms in the commentary) and cites almost the whole of *Buc.*4, verse by verse; it survives in the Greek translation and reworking by Eusebius of Caesarea, who quotes it as an appendix to his life of the emperor.[44]

Bucolics, *Georgics* and, above all, *Aeneid* remained central to a Latin education (cf. ch. 6, n. 12) well beyond the fall of the empire in the West. Twenty years after Julian the Apostate's nostalgic attempt at a pagan restoration (361–3), the powerful Roman families of the Nicomachi and Symmachi headed an idealistic revival, whose principal notion of true culture was Augustan: this movement led at the time to an exceptional flowering, particularly in Italy, of work on

---

[43] See *EV* 4.710f. (Geymonat).

[44] For texts, translations, discussions, see J. Quasten, *Patrologia* 2 (ital.trans., Casale Monferrato 1983), 329.

Virgil,[45] and the appeal to Virgil acquired an almost exemplary force when, at the end of the 5th. century (cf. 305f. below on codices **MP**), the last members of the Roman aristocracy had to convert to Christianity, even if some of them remained secretly pagan.

F is the first and certainly the most beautiful of the late antique codices of Virgil to survive; it derives from the world of Symmachus (cos. 391), nostalgic admirer of classical literature, or might be very slightly later. Its history in the Middle Ages is unknown (Cassiodorus' Vivarium has been suggested). At least, by the late c. 15, it was in the hands of the poet Giovanni Pontano (vd. *EV* s.v.) and, after the death of the humanist Fulvio Orsini (1600), passed into the papal library (now cod.Vat.lat.3225). The 75 surviving leaves contain slightly under 1500 lines of *G.* and *Aen.* (though in origin the ms. included *Buc.* too) and fifty splendid miniatures, which illustrate the main episodes; they too were once far more numerous. The placing of the illustrations on the page may derive from a c. 3 A.D. roll, but the richness of the colours and the sumptuous gleams of gold guarantee that commission and execution were linked to some element of Rome's highest élite.[46]

Our other chief witnesses to the text are some decades later:[47] three almost complete codices (**MPR**) and three extremely fragmentary (**AGV**), all in a capital script perhaps more suited to slabs of stone than to parchment books: in mediaeval library catalogues this script was indeed called 'litterae Virgilianae' (cf. *EV* 1, 832). Careful collation of these mss. has not led to the establishment of any precise relationships between them, and at this period it is proper to speak of Virgil as an 'open recension', in which the place of the individual witnesses cannot be fixed. A few words on each of these capital mss.:

---

[45] [See not so much E. Türk, *REL* 41 (1963), 327–49 as A.D.E. Cameron, *JRS* 56 (1966), 34–7, id., *Entr.Hardt* 23 (1976), 22ff., R.A. Markus in (ed.) J.W. Binns, *Latin literature of the fourth century* (London 1974), 11, B.W. Sinclair, *Maia* 34 (1982), 261–3, P. De Paolis, *LEC* 55 (1987), 299f., F. Paschoud, *Roma Aeterna* (Roma 1967), 107f., H. Bloch in (ed.) A. Momigliano, *Conflict between Paganism and Christianity* (Oxford 1963), 210. For the interesting and significant case of the *sortes Vergilianae*, cf. my note in *HA Colloquium* NS 3 (1992) (Macerata), forthcoming. Ed.]

[46] For full bibliography on the capital mss., see *EV* s.v. *codices* (Geymonat); for palaeographical descriptions, see E.A. Lowe, *Cod.Lat.Ant.* (11 vols. with supplement, Oxford 1934–71), R. Seider in *Studien z.ant.Epos* ed. H. Görgemanns and E.A. Schmidt (Meisenheim am Glan 1976), 129–72; see too A. Petrucci in *Virgilio e noi* (Genova 1982), 62–7, A. Pratesi, *Scr.Civ.*9 (1985), 5–33; on **F**, see now D.H. Wright, *The Vatican Vergil* (Berkeley 1993), on **R.**, C. Bertelli, *Vergilius Romanus* (Zürich 1985).

[47] A very different dating is found in many older works.

M: the most distinguished of the surviving late antique mss. of Virgil. It was acquired at the end of the c. 16 by Francesco I, Grand Duke of Tuscany, and from then on was called Mediceus (Florence, Bibl.Med.Laur., plut.39.1). Aimed at the literary *otium* of a member of the senatorial aristocracy, and in a handy format, and originally divided into two volumes copied by different scribes, the Mediceus was prepared at Rome in the first months of 494 and was corrected in the April of that same year by the consul Turcius Rufius Apronianus, as the subscription to *Buc.* relates (*legi et distincxi emendans*).[48] It survived the middle ages almost unharmed in the Benedictine monastery of Bobbio, near Piacenza; only the first gathering (*Buc.* to 6.47) is missing. In the late c. 15 it was brought to Rome, was admired at the papal court and was handled by humanists such as Pomponius Laetus (who introduced some corrections in red ink) and Petrus Bembus (who removed a leaf, which has remained at the Vatican, where it is preserved at the end of **F**). From the Renaissance on, **M** had a profound influence on all editions of Virgil (of which *EV* s.v. *Edizioni* unfortunately does not offer a critical history); only with Ribbeck's critical edition (Leipzig 1859–68) were the other main codices too evaluated satisfactorily, but **M** remains of exceptional importance and for some passages is indeed the only ancient witness we have (*G.*2.1–91, 118–38, *Aen.*11.757–782).

P: cod.Pal.Lat.1631 in the Vatican library, a manuscript of notable dimensions and fine parchment, copied carefully in the last years of the fifth century in an Italian scriptorium, probably the one in which **R** was copied half a century later (? Ravenna, ? Milan, ? the imperial scriptorium itself). Its name comes from the Palatine library of Heidelberg, where it arrived in the second half of the c. 15 (from the monastery of Lorsch, NE of Worms). From Heidelberg, it passed, with the whole Palatine library, to Rome.[49] A manuscript to confer distinction on its first possessors, it was also read with care and attention both in late antiquity (the period of its first three correctors) and in the Carolingian period, date of its (direct or indirect) descendant Guelferbytanus Gudianus Lat. 2° 70, **γ** copied in the late c. 9 at Lyon, which bears witness at least in part to readings lost in **P**. **P** still

---

[48] Zetzel (n. 6), 217f.

[49] H. Trevor-Roper *The plunder of the arts in the seventeenth century* (London 1970), 22f. [Prof. Julian Brown pointed out to me that the facsimile of **M** published by P.F. Foggini (Florence 1741) is the oldest complete facsimile of any whole ms. Ed.]

contains 90% of the Latin text along with interesting and authoritative
readings, in part already discussed in the ancient scholiasts and grammarians. Archaic spellings (e.g. *olli* for *illi*, *quoi* for *cui*, *equom* for *equum*,
etc.) are also frequent; this has led to the suggestion that **P**'s original
was a particularly old copy, perhaps in a semi-cursive hand.[50]

R is a luxury codex of an almost square format, written in careful
and mannered capitals, with ample use of red ink. The Romanus
(now cod.Vat.Lat.3867) contains 19 illustrations, full-page (though
smaller in *Buc.*), in an orientalising style, which has lent support to
the view (e.g. G. Cavallo; vd. *EV* 1.834) that it might derive from
Ravenna. Though it is clearly later, **R** repeats letter-forms from **P**,
which might lead one to think that they are both products of a single
workshop (wherever that may have been; vd. supra on **P**). As for
chronology, **R** may well belong to the later c. 6; that seems to be
the inference from some abbreviations of *nomina sacra*, such as *DS* for
deus, *DO* for *deo* and the insertion, at *Aen.*6.242 , of a verse from the
Latin translation (by Priscian) of Dionysius Periegetes.[51] **R** originally
contained 412 leaves, of which 309 survive; they transmit some ³/₄ of
the whole text and for *Buc.*3.72–4.51 are our only ancient witness.
Certainly, **R** was more complete in the Carolingian period, when it
was in northern France and both *Buc.* and *Aen.*9.537–10.379 + 10.854–
12.819 were copied from it in the Fleury ms **a**, now divided between
Bern (172) and Paris (Lat.7929); from **a**, we can to some extent reconstruct the faint letters and lost leaves of **R**. Of our late-antique
mss., **R** is perhaps the least accurate, with errors, even trivial ones,
that disfigure almost every page, omissions, repetitions, glosses that
have slipped into the text, all clear proofs that the showy wealth of
the man who ordered **R** was certainly not matched by an adequate
cultural level.

A (Augusteus) was long maintained to belong to the Augustan
period, but recent palaeographical studies have shifted the date considerably later, probably to the first half of the c. 6, on the basis of
the artificial and mannered character of the hand, the so-called 'elegant capital'. Once more, **A**'s large size and heavy parchment identify it as a de luxe copy, more to admire than to read and it is no
chance that in our surviving fragments there is no trace of ancient
corrections (while errors are certainly not wanting!). The seven surviving leaves, four at the Vatican (cod.Vat.Lat.3256) and three at

---

[50] R. Marichal, *REL* 35 (1957), 1–4.
[51] E. Norden, *RhM* 56 (1901) 473–4 = *Kl.S.* (Berlin 1966), 437f.

Berlin (Lat.fol.416, bought at auction in 1862) preserve 284 verses, all from *G*.; an eighth leaf was still legible in the early c. 18, when a drawing was made of it for the work that founded modern Latin palaeography:[52] it shows the four initial verses of a page from the *Aen*.(4.302–5), but all trace of the fragment has since been lost.

G: the Sangallensis consists of a dozen fragments in the library of St. Gall, in Switzerland (no. 1394). They contain just under 400 verses, which include parts of *G*.4 and *Aen*.1–6; there is also a leaf containing the *explicit* of *Buc*. and the *incipit* of *G*. The size of the pages and the sumptuous 'elegant capital' hand bear witness to the wealth and power of the man who commissioned and first owned **G**. He certainly wished to demonstrate an emphatic devotion to Virgil, symbol of Rome: possibly a Romanised barbarian of the early c. 6? Even, it has been suggested, Theodoric himself. **G** remained almost unharmed until the Carolingian period (to which some corrections should be attributed) and thereafter was used as a sort of hoard of large strong parchment: some leaves were washed and re-written in the c. 12 and c. 13; others were used to rebind and repair yet later mss. It has therefore been possible recently to rediscover some small fragments of **G**, which even contain important readings, such as *lauris* at *Aen*.6.658, or traces of writing on leaves to which such fragments had long been glued.[53]

V: 51 palimpsest leaves in the Chapter Library at Verona (XL 38), on which, in the early c. 8 some chapters of Gregory the Great's *Moralia in Iob* were copied, in that Merovingian hand characteristic of Luxeuil (probably by a scribe at that time active in northern Italy). Of the text of Virgil, some 1300 verses (from *Buc*., *G*. and *Aen*.) are preserved. The hand is a rustic capital of the late c. 5 (Pratesi thinks between 475 and 490, *Atti* 2.220ff.), with only thirteen verses of the text per page. A text written for a patron of the middle Po area (? a Mantuan), possibly a *grammaticus* eager to consult the copious and striking commentary in its margins, the so-called *scholia Veronensia*: to decipher these marginal notes, powerful reagents were used in the early c. 19, and they have burned and in part ruined the pages and the poet's text.[54]

---

[52] J. Mabillon, *De re diplomatica* ed. 2 (Paris 1709), 635.

[53] On **G** and **V**, see M. Geymonat, *MIL* 29 (1966), 289–438 and *SCO* 14 (1965), 86–99.

[54] On **V**, see Geymonat (n. 53, 1966), 326ff.; on Cardinal Mai and the use of reagents, see S. Timpanaro, *Aspetti e figure della cultura ottocentesca* (Pisa 1980), 225–71.

The period of our oldest mss. is still one of major and important commentaries to Virgil. At the end of the c. 4, or more probably at the beginning of the c. 5 was composed the largest commentary to the whole of Virgil to survive, that of Servius,[55] a pupil of Aelius Donatus and a character treated with much respect in the (very slightly later)[56] *Saturnalia* of Macrobius,[57] itself another important witness to the abundant 'Virgilian literature' of the period. Servius' commentary,[58] to *Aen.*, then to *Buc.* and *G.* (with a lacuna between *Buc.*1.37 and 2.10) has survived in numerous mss. and independent fragments from the c. 8 on, as well as in the margins of some mediaeval mss. of Virgil; it is already often cited in authors of the c. 6 and c. 7 such as Priscian and Isidore of Seville (thus an important source for the

---

[55] [On the date of Serv., see Cameron (n. 45), 29f., G. Brugnoli, *EV* 4.805., R.A. Kaster, *Guardians of language* (Berkeley 1988), 356–9, id. *HSCP* 84 (1980), 255, n. 104, P. Bruggisser, *MH* 41 (1984), 173, id. *Romulus Servianus* (Bonn 1987), 4–6. The late date suggested by (e.g.) N. Marinone (n. 56), 26 is quite unconvincing. C. Murgia, *Herm.*116 (1988), 496, n. 5 propounds that Serv. uses past tenses when speaking of pagan sacrifices (while his sources used the present). If this were true, it would be interesting, but cf. nn. on *Aen.*1.292, 335, 2.104, 134, 148, 202, 3.21, 118, 231, and notably 6.224. Murgia, l.c. proposes a mid-c. 4 date for Tib. Claud. Donatus since at 8.279 and 9.627 he speaks of pagan sacrifice as still current; he must therefore be earlier than Theodosius' laws of 391–5 (apart for apparent rivalry with Ael.Donatus); but mechanical repetition of the same prohibitions down to the late 430's suggests that this dating criterion will not work (cf. e.g. Lidia Storoni Mazzolani, *Sant'Agostino e i pagani* (Palermo 1987), 112–36). There is not much more to offer: cf. *EV* s.v. (Brugnoli), who suggests a date in the late c. 5, unpersuasively. M. Squillante Saccone, *Le Interp.Verg. di TCD* (Naples 1985), 11f. is properly cautious. I agree with her inclination to make of TCD, Serv. and Macr. contemporaries, more or less. At 2.643.1f., the author threatens a work on Virgilian geography, which squares nicely with the interests of Serv. and Macr. Cf. now on other aspects of TCD, R.J. Starr, *Class.Ant.*11 (1992), 159–74, *Vergilius* 37 (1991), 3–10, *CJ* 87 (1991), 25–34. Ed.]

[56] [A.D.E. Cameron (n. 45), 25–38, S. Pancicra *Epigrafia, e ordine senatorio* 1 (Roma 1982), 658–60, P. De Paolis, *Lustrum*, 27–9 (1985–7), 113–25, Kaster (n. 55, 1980). Marinone's preface, ed. Macr. *Sat.*, ed. 2, Turin 1977), 14–27 could not yet take account of the epigraphic evidence. Thus 394–409 for Serv. and 405–20 for Macr. are very likely dates of composition. Ed.]

[57] On Macr. in general, cf. Marinone, cit., 9–58, De Paolis (n. 56), 107–254, *EV* s.v. *Macrobio*.

[58] [There is no easy way of starting work on Serv.: 'state of the art' is C.E. Murgia, *HSCP* 91 (1987), 303–31, vs. S. Timpanaro *MD* 22 (1989), 123–82, repr. in *Nuovi contributi* (Bologna 1994), 405–58. See *EV* s.v. (with large bibl.), Kaster (n. 55, 1980), 219–62 (Serv. as idealised by Macr.), E. Fraenkel, *JRS* 38 (1948) 131–43 and ib. 39 (1949), 145–54 = *Kl.Beitr.*2 (Roma 1964), 339–90. E. Thomas, *Essai sur Servius* (Paris 1880) is still very useful, and G.P. Goold, *HSCP* 74 (1970), 101–68 reaches far beyond the problems of the Helen-episode. For Servius' comm. on *Buc.*, *G.* and *Aen.*, it is still simplest to use the ed. of G. Thilo (3 vols. Leipzig; various reprints). The faults of the Harvard ed. of Serv. on *Aen.*1–2 were detailed by Fraenkel, *cit.*; thereafter we have only Serv. on *Aen.*3–5 (Oxford 1965). Ed.]

history of the text). Ancient explanations of the text of Virgil were not works neatly separated and well-defined, but rather collections which did not, individually, form organic wholes. Each contained abundant inherited material and we should not therefore be surprised in the individual notes in Servius (which after all come from a variety of sources), if Virgil is not always cited from the same text and with the same variant readings, or if textual discussions (which are usually introduced in general terms (*ut aliquibus uidetur, quidam legunt, alibi,* etc.) retain but seldom an exact indication of their origin, but even in these cases there do occur surprising chronological inversions, as at *Aen.*10.539: *'insignibus armis' Asper* [c. 3] *sic legit et utitur Sallustii exemplo qui ait 'equo atque armis insignibus'* [Hist.2.63 Maur.]; *Probus uero* [early c. 2] *'insignibus albis' dicit legendum, ut albas uestes accipiamus, quae sunt sacerdotibus congruae, sicut Statius de Amphiarao dicit* (*Theb.*4.218, 6.331). See Timpanaro (n. 6), 90–4.

At an uncertain period between the end of the c. 6 and the beginning of the c. 8, when that ample 'Virgilian literature' which had for centuries been at the heart of the highest Roman culture was being drastically cut down, a compiler, unknown but probably Irish,[59] inserted in his copy of Servius a lot of other material which derived from a further authoritative commentary, perhaps even from the great Virgil commentary, now lost (cf. 302), of Aelius Donatus. This is the so-called Servius Auctus (or Danielinus, because it was first published in the edition of Pierre Daniel); it has come down to us incomplete (the commentary to *Buc.*1–3 is, for example, missing) and in a small number of mss.[60]

Yet further late-antique Virgil commentaries were put together at this period, specially by the learned Irish. The most important collection is the 'Scholia Bernensia', a series of annotations[61] to *Buc.* and *G.*, which derive from the c. 5 commentaries of Philargyrius, Gaudentius and Gallus and are preserved in the two redactions of an *Explanatio in Bucolica* and in the margins of some Carolingian mss. of Virgil, notably Bernensis 172.

Even in the worst period of crisis, between the c. 6 and the c. 8, the knowledge of Virgil remained the most solid bulwark to defend

---

[59] Goold (n. 58), 102–5; cf. ib. 105–17 for the working methods of SDan. in general.
[60] C.E. Murgia, *Prolegomena to Servius* 5 (UCPCS 11 1975), 9–40, 141–58.
[61] Ed. H. Hagen (Leipzig 1867). See *EV* 4.711–7 (Geymonat-Daintree).

the language and culture of Rome. At least some part of the serious
work of Virgilian exegesis undertaken in the schools of the Empire
was reworked and arranged differently at this period: thus the *Liber
grandis glossarum* attributed to the Gothic bishop Ansileubus, like, for
that matter, other larger collections (*Abstrusa, Abolita* etc.), turn out to
be an alphabetical rearrangement of annotation to *Buc., G.* and *Aen.*![62]

The renewal of interest in Virgil from the Carolingian period to the Renaissance

The transmission of the text of Virgil continued uninterrupted and
on a large scale even during the Middle Ages.[63] From that period,
our oldest fragments are two scraps from Munich (CLM 29216/7;
formerly 29005/18, *EV* 1, 836; **m** in our editions), recovered from
the binding of a Tegernsee ms. and written in north Italy in the late
c. 8 (perhaps a copy of the *Aen.* for personal use) and some leaves
now at Paris (Lat.7906; **p** in the edd.) copied in two columns, in a
tiny hand, in western Germany in the last years of the c. 8. This
witness preserves for us the beginning of the *Aen.*(1.1–128) and
*Aen.*3.682–5.734 (*EV* 1.837): the text of Virgil breaks off brusquely in
mid-page and in mid-phrase, probably at the point where the precious original (? late antique in capitals) did so too.

Unlike other Latin texts which reached the Carolingian world in
a single copy, Virgil was recopied repeatedly from various exemplars
and in various places, enjoying particular favour at the imperial court
in northern France. To this decidedly rich tradition a notable quantity of c. 9 and c. 10 mss. bears witness. Some of them are closely
related to capital mss. which have actually survived, as we have seen
(305 and 306) in the cases of **R** and **a** and in that of **P** and **γ**. Even
a c. 10 ms. **n** (Neap.Vind.6), our oldest ms. from south Italy, seems
to derive directly from a capital ms. now lost; **n** however preserves
many of its original's good readings.

---

[62] See *EV* 2.772 (Geymonat),

[63] See R.A. Kaster, *The tradition of the text of the Aen. in the ninth century* (New York
1990), L.D. Reynolds in *Texts and transmission* (ed. 2 Oxford 1986), 433–6, L. Holtz
in *Lectures médiévales de Virgile* (Rome 1985), 9–30 and in *La fortuna di Virgilio* (Napoli
1986), 125–49, B. Munk Olsen in *Lectures*, 31–48 and *Catalogue des manuscrits classiques
latins copiés du IXe au XIe et XIIe siècles* 2 (Paris 1985), 673–826, 3.2 (Paris 1989), 138–
53, G. Alessio, *EV* 3.432–43.

Attempts have been made, on the basis of certain similarities in the text, to divide into three groups (**br, dfhot, aeuv**) a dozen mss. copied in northern France during the ninth century.[64] But these groups break down and re-form differently when we take into account the work of their contemporary correctors, who often vary from book to book. So Mynors has well observed (OCT, p. x): *habebimus enim fere semper adnotationes istius formae, puta: «altera lectio» wxy²z²; lectio altera w²x²y, z, quod nihil novi nos docebit.* Nor should we think that variants other than those we can already observe in the text in the capital mss. showed up during the Carolingian period. Only seldom, therefore, do modern editions accept variants for which the evidence is of this period (e.g. *Buc.*1.12 *turbatur* **n** (but thus too Serv. and Quint.1.4.28), *Aen.*9.657 *aspectus* in all Carolingian mss., except **a** and **γ** but so too Tib.Don., 10.805 *arce* **e**). Clearly corrupt verses are almost absent from the text of Virgil: normally in the tradition, both direct and indirect, we are faced with two readings only, both of which appear almost equally plausible and are certainly of ancient origin, but of them one at least is a learned emendation or the happy outcome of an error.

Even during the last centuries of the Middle Ages, Virgil remained at the centre of education in letters and learning, and between the time of Dante and the first printed edition were produced more than ° of our surviving mss. of the corpus. A good part of these mss. are smooth, clean, elegant work: to read Virgil was a mark of the civilised and cultured man, but did not require a prolonged commitment to exegesis (as was the case in the late antique and Carolingian periods), and it is no chance that at this period some exceptionally large mss., which had lasted nearly a thousand years largely unharmed, were dismembered. (so **G**; cf. 30).

A sign of love for the poet and of a new way of approaching Virgil is to be found in a series of new cycles of miniatures;[65] they are more numerous for the *Aen.* but are surprisingly refined too for *Buc.* and *G.*: I am thinking of the fine illustrations in Bodl.Rawl. *G.*98 (Lombard, c. 15, of *G.* alone) or of the illustration by Simone Martini at the beginning of *Buc.* in Ambr.A.49 inf. (now S.P. 10/27), once the property of Petrarch. The poet, in a famous letter of his

---

[64] Cf. Kaster, cited in the preceding note.
[65] Cf. *AAVM* 57 (1989), 95–133 (Geymonat), A. Wlosok in (e.g.) *The two worlds of the poet* (ed. R.M. Wilhelm, H. Jones, Detroit 1992), 408–32, *EV* 3.443–50 (Cadei).

old age (16.1) relates how his father, to drive him back to his neglected legal studies, wanted to burn a copy of Virgil that he had!

The very numerous humanist editions of Virgil led at this point to a great expansion in the reading and knowledge of Virgil. They had the merit of revising the text in the light (*inter alia*) of a renewed knowledge of Greek (thus in the Ascensian edition of 1500 we find the palmary correction of *Hylax* for the *Hylas* of the mss. at *Buc.*8.107). But the c. 15 editions were also guilty of fixing certain errors in the 'vulgate' text: above all that of printing in the text the 'Helen episode' (cf. 300).

What is important in this period is the rediscovery and careful study of some of the old mss.: e.g. **M**, brought to Rome ca. 1467, some of whose precious readings were introduced into the Venice ed. of 1472 as derived *ex ipsis propriis Maronis exemplaribus*, and **R**, collated almost in its entirety by G.P. Valerianus for his *Castigationes et Varietates Vergilianae lectionis* (Rome 1521). We must not forget new editions of explanatory material hitherto ignored, like Ps.Probus' commentary on *Buc.* and *G.* (pub. by G.B. Egnatius, Venice 1507), or the first complete edition of Tiberius Donatus (Naples 1535) and above all the old additions to Servius (309) which Pierre Daniel revealed to the world in his epoch-making edition of Virgil (Paris 1600). By this point, it is safe to say that Virgil had well and truly passed into the hands of the great scholarly tradition of modern Europe.

APPENDIX

'*An Interpretation of the Aeneid*' was published in *Harvard Studies* in 1964, but written fifteen years earlier, in 1949. I had spent the summer of that year at the American Academy in Rome, and there met, and became friends with, a witty, charming woman, Isobel Licht, who for many years taught Latin at the Brearley School in New York City. That fall, she invited me to come and speak about the *Aeneid* to 'my girls'. I was flattered, for it was the first time I had been asked to speak anywhere for money (I was paid twenty dollars); and so I sat down, in my youthful innocence, and wrote '*An Interpretation of the Aeneid*'. I was then teaching at Amherst College, and remote, in every sense of the word, from Harvard.

The other works identified by Johnson as being central to the Harvard school (a designation he seems to have invented) are: R.A. Brooks, '*Discolor aura*: Reflections on the Golden Bough', *AJP* 74 (1953) 260–80; A. Parry. 'The Two Voices of Virgil's *Aeneid*', *Arion* 2 (1963) 66–80; and M.C.J. Putnam, *The Poetry of the Aeneid* (Cambridge, Mass., 1965). Michael Putnam I met in 1957, when I was visiting associate professor at Harvard; R.A. Brooks only once, socially, in 1959 or 60, after I had been appointed to the Harvard faculty. But Adam Parry— or Milman, as he then called himself—and I were colleagues at Amherst in the mid fifties. Since our studies were adjacent, we saw each other almost every day and talked, usually about literature (we were young and serious), often about the *Aeneid*, a poem that concerned us both. Similarities of tone or attitude between his essay, though it was written several years later, and my lecture are therefore owing, at least in part, to our conversations then (those many years ago). The mild-minded pessimism of the Harvard school—the so-called Harvard school—reflects the mood of the fifties: it had little or nothing to do with the dissent and anguish of the sixties, though this has been suggested [S.J. Harrison. *Oxford Readings in Vergil's Aeneid* (Oxford, 1990) 5].

I revised '*An Interpretation of the Aeneid*' and gave it once again as a lecture, at Deerfield Academy in the mid fifties, and then put it away. Finally, in 1964, I decided to publish it, not alone, however, but with a longer, intricate article on the textual transmission of the pseudo-Virgilian *Culex*. I hoped to show, by such a collocation, that technical and literary scholarship were not incompatible. I doubt that anybody noticed, except a few friends to whom I explained my intention. But, to my surprise, certain phrases in '*An Interpretation of the Aeneid*' acquired a modest notoriety.

What do I think of this interpretation now, looking back? It is extreme; more right than wrong, yet in need of qualification.

W.V. Clausen

INDEX

Please note that this index contains separate sections for *Aeneid, Bucolics, Georgics*; **Virgil: life, Style, Metre and Language** and **Text and Transmission**.

Actium in Ov. 262, 264; see *Aeneid*
Aeneas in Ovid 263f.
Aeneas-legend 249

Aeneid
accuracy of details 168
Achilles 107, 142, 164, 165, 204, 205f.
Actium, Aug. at 183
Aegaeon 114, 184
Aeneas and Achilles 142, 164, 165, 182, 183, 204ff.; and Aegaeon 114, 184; and Augustus 163, 166; and Creusa 109; and Hector 122, 162, 166, 182, 188; and Latinus 165.; first appearance in *Aen.* 118f.; 'comforted' in Juno's temple 106; as narrator, place in own narrative, 110f.; too ready to halt 120; development of character 118–22; and father 121; and Andromache 122; and Dido 123ff.; as suitor 124f.; love for Dido 125; tears in 4 125 n. 20; *pius* in 4 126; reactions to Dido 130; Dido and gods 133; flight 131; reaction to Dido's pyre 132; with Dido in 6 133; faults in 4 124; in Underworld 146; corporeality of 147; and *somni portae* 144, 146f.; savagery, alleged 84, 207ff.; and Pallas' belt 212, 213; human sacrifice by 179f. and see human sacrifice; reasons for killing Turnus 212; criticised in 12(?) 193; hesitation at end of 12 204f.; option of sparing Turnus 195f.; when judged by Roman standards 126; criteria (Virgilian) for evaluation 182, 201, 208, 216; bloodthirstiness of, and Homer 200; as builder 121; and courage 121f.; as man of destiny 120; in father's shadow(?) 121; and gods 121; intentions 131; *pietas* 103, 121; and rancour of Juno 103; suffers (undeservedly) 102f.; viewpoint 110f.

Aeolus 103f.
Alexandrianism 258; see *Buc., G.*
alius 165
Allecto 139, 157ff., 159, 160
allegory 102 (of *labores*), 150f. (in 6), 162ff.
alter 165
Amata 156ff.
anti-historical readings of 12 195
anachronism in readings of 6 153f.
anachronistic evaluations of *Aen.* as warrior 200
ancient views of purpose 162
anger, evaluations of 214; anger 192ff., 214; how motivated 202f., 214; Turnus' 159; in bk. 12 199; and *pietas* 214; justified 213; and courage 202
Anchises and Aen. 121; and Dido 126; death of 136f.; tomb of 140f.; in bk. 6 144ff.; view of Roman history ib.
Andromache 122
annalists 185
Apollo 120
Arae Perusinae 163, 180, 206; see sacrifice
architecture of epic 135f.
Aristotle 201f.
arma 102
armour, stripping of, 179; see spoils
Ascanius 172f.; as hunter 155f., 160
augurium 132
Augustus and Aeneas 163, 166; Aug., reactions to *Aen.* 193, 194; in *Aen.* by allegory 163; and Virgil's view of history 145; ambivalence of 206; his age as telos 164; 'Augustan values' 166f., 195, 206ff.
Aurora 138
authorial intrusion 177f.; authorial additions 147f.
auxilium 160

Bacchus and madness 157f.
Belidae 106
baldric see Pallas
battlefield ethics in V. 180
battle-rage 200, 213

battle-scenes 179ff.
belt see Pallas
blame, in Virgilian narrative 155–61
blood-lust 174
body, return of 203f.
books, characterisation of 135; ends
    of 136; in 'trios' or 'quartets' 137
booty 174ff.; see *spolia*
Bough, Golden 150
breach of treaty see treaty
brutality in war 171, 173f.
burial see corpse

'caesuras' at book-ends 136
Callimachus 105
Carthage 102, 105, 106–8, 137, 142;
    destruction of 106; Juno's
    temple 106–8; wars with
    Rome 124; sadistic natives 107
catalogue of Etruscans 182f.
Cato 185
causae 155; causes of war 155ff.
characters, links between 165;
    groupings of 164f.
chronology of composition 14, 20;
    date of 'publication' 21
civil war 155, 160
clementia 206–8
combat, unequal 210f.; of uncertain
    outcome 180; abbreviated ib.
complexity of 12 195
composition of *Aen.* 15ff., 135
condere 116
corpse, return of 203f.; plea
    for 204; stripping of 203ff.
cosmos, soul's voyage through 150f.
council of gods in 10 182
courage and anger 202
cruelty 206
criteria for judgement 201, 192–216
    passim
cupido of warrior 170

Danaids 212
deaths, at book-end 136
deities, Italian in *Aen.* 141
destruction, threatened, of text 22f;
    see Text and Transmission
deviant focalisation 110f.
diathesis 202f., 214
Dido 123ff.; tragedy 123, 134;
    irony, historical 123f.,
        dramatic 124; hamartia 126;
    culpa 126f.; not *uniuira* 127; loss of
    fama, pudor, etc. 127; as *fera* 127;

not invariably veracious 125;
    possibly inebriated 129; innocence
    doubtful 129; awareness of Aen.'s
    destiny 125 and Anchises 137;
    antecedents 164; and
    Cleopatra 166; banquet 130; in
    cave 127, 128; *coniugium* 127, 128;
    and fate 128f.; and gods 128f.;
    supposedly married 128; negative
    features 124; relations with Aen.
    public 125f.; silences in relations
    with Aen. 131; Sophoclean 127;
    sources 134; suicide 127, 132; as
    suitor 125; and Turnus 123; in
    Underworld 132; wound 124.
Diomedes 183, 184, 186ff.
Dionysus see Bacchus
Dira 211
Discordia 155
divine inspiration of warrior 170f.
Doloneia, V.'s imitation of 172, 174
doom, intimations of 171, 172f.
Donatus, Tib. Claudius, and
    rhetoric 186
Drances 189–91, 244–8
dreams in *Aen.* 147, 159;
    dream-journey 151

ekphrasis 105 n. 34
Eleusis 150
Elysium 153
enemies of Rome 164
encomium 148f.
end of bk. 12 195ff.
Ennius 105, 185
Epic cycle 184
Epicureanism and bk. 12 202f., and
    bk. 6 152; see *Buc., G.*, Life
ethics of warfare 176; ethical
    reaction, invited 197; ethical and
    emotional 'solutions' 198; ethical
    problems, taste for 196
exemplary view of characters 166
Euryalus see Nisus
externus 156, 158

Fama 131
fatum, fata, Fate 139, in 4 128ff., of
    Aen. 103, weighing of 211, of
    cities 102
focalisation 105 n. 34, 110f.
Forum of Augustus 145, 148f., 166
foundation of cities 102; of
    Carthage 106; founder-heroes
    164

Furiae, *furiae* 157ff., 208, 211
  n. 129, 213
furor 208
furtum 174

Games and Homer 136
genealogical panegyric 162,
  protreptic 144
gens, strength of 148
gifts, dangerous 175f., 177
glory, doubts about 193, 206f., 208
gods and Troy 120; and Dido 128f.;
  in *Aen.* 138ff.; council of,
  in 10 182; booty due to 176f.;
  in 12 211
Golden Bough 112, 150
Greek viewpoint in 2–3 110f.
guilt, Trojans' in 7(??) 156

half-lines 167f.; see Text and
  Transmission
'Harvard School' 192, 313f.
hatred 214
Hector 102, 107, 122, 166, 181, 188,
  203, 205
Heldenschau see Parade of Heroes
Helenus 120f.
Helen-episode see Text
Hellenistic sources 184
Hercules and Cacus 214; his
  anger 213f.
heroism, Roman, and Aeneas 199f.
history, malleable in V. 144;
  protreptic 145; exemplary ib.; in
  Aen. 162ff.; cyclic view 164; linear
  view ib.
Homer, and architecture of *Aen.* 136;
  allegorical interpretations of
  Hom. 151; reworking of 179;
  technique of allusions to 181f.;
  combat-patterns reversed 181;
  minor allusions to 183; 'history'
  from ib., 188; how conceived by
  V. 184; scholia to ib.; ethical
  readings of 197f., 202; complexity
  of *Il.* as viewed by V. 198; *Il.* in
  ancient discussions of anger 198;
  Homeric values and *Aen.* 200;
  norms of conduct and *Aen.* 203ff.;
  and bk. 12 203f.
homosexuality 170
Horn, Gate of 147
human sacrifice 163, 179f., 200, 206,
  215

Iarbas 126
ille ego verses see Text
imagery 111f., 115f.
immolare 214f.
imperium Roman, cost of 208
implorare 161 n. 57
incompleteness 167f.
inconsistencies 151f., 168f.
indignata 215
initiation 150
insomnia 147
intrusion by V. 177f.
Iris 138f., 141f.
Italy as Trojans' homeland 155f.
Ivory, Gate of 146f.

Julius Caesar, ambivalence of 206
Juno 141f.; anger of 103; and
  Aeolus 103f.; and Trojans'
  wanderings 120; and Dido 129f.;
  and subalterns 142; and
  Allecto 157f., 160; and
  *Aen.*12 211
Jupiter 139f., 141f.; and Dido 129,
  131; in *Aen.*10 143; and
  *Aen.*12 211

'keys' to read *Aen.*12 198ff.

labor ('glide') 116
labyrinths 150
lacrimae rerum 107 n. 39
lacunae see Text
Latinus 188f.; and Trojans 155,
  156ff.
Lausus, Aeneas and 183; Lausus,
  Pallas, Nisus, Euryalus 171
Lavinia 155, 156ff., and
  Turnus 176, 210
line, last of epic 195
links between books 135ff.
life, pleas for 203
literary problems, ancient taste
  for 196

madness 157f.
Maecenas, reactions to *Aen.* 194
makarismos 172, 174f.
Manes in 6 153
Marcellus-episode 147f., 178 n. 39
matres, Trojan 139
Memnon 107
Menander Rhetor 186f.
Mercury 106, 126, 130f., 132
metaphor 111ff.; traditional character
  of, in V. 112f., 115; not rigidly

applied 113; complexes of 116;
  moribund, or not 117
metonymy 138
Mezentius 173, 183, 184, 185
mistletoe 153
multiple viewpoints 111
mythology, deviant versions 107

Naevius 105, 134
Neptune 141f.
New Augustans xi, 194f.
Nisus and Euryalus 170ff.
nostoi 187f.
Numanus Remulus 177
numen 139

odia 142, 214
Olympiodorus 153f.
oracles in bk. 3 120
oratory 186ff.; late republican, and
  V. 190
order, victory of 103
Ovid and Aen. 194

Palinurus 142
Pallas 107, 142, 181; belt or
  baldric 205, 211f.; and
  Turnus 205, 212; and
  Aeneas 212
Parade of Heroes 144ff.;
  sources 145; intent 144; rhetorical
  function 144f., 146; encomium and
  psogos 146; as Rogues'
  Gallery 148f.
Paris and Aeneas 182
Patroclus 181
pax 148 n. 26, 206
Penthesilea 107
persons, second and third in Aen.'s
  narrative 110
perspectives 109
Philodemus 202f.
physiological language 116
pietas 173, 207, 214
Pindar 184
Plato 152, 201f.
points of view 109ff.
politics and reactions to Aen. 194
portents 119f., 140f., 156
private voice 193
proem: alleged ambiguity in 104
projected revision of 21
prose sources of Aen. 185; prose
  sketch of Aen. 16, 18
psogos 148f.
Punic War, Second 163

repetitions 169
're-run' theme 160, 165, 188, 191
res publica as theme of Aen. 103, 194,
  197
revelations of divine will 120
revenge 200, 206
Rhesus 107
rhetoric, studied by V. 6; from
  V. 251, cf. 186; in Serv. 186;
  and characterisation 189;
  expertise 186ff.; ambiguity and
  rhetoric 104
rituals, Greek and Roman 141
Rome 103; history 103;
  values 199ff.
Rutuli, characterised 171, 173

sacrifice, human 163, 180, 200, 206,
  215
sacrifice, Turnus' death as 214f.
Sarpedon 181
Saturnia regna 164
shade 113
Segesta 140
Sicily, history of 140f.
Silvia 155f., 160; her stag 155f.; its
  death 156
deer-simile 124, 130; 1.148ff. 103ff.;
  cauldron-simile 159f.
Sirius and Aeneas 182ff.
snakes 113; as metaphors 116
somnus 138; somni Portae 146f.
Sophocles 127, 184f.
soul in cosmos 151
speeches 186ff.
spoils 175f., 205 (Roman and Greek
  usage), 215; spolia opima 148 n. 24
Stoicism: Aen. to be read
  through? 118f., 199; and bk.
  6 152; and bk. 12 199; reaction
  to Aristotle on anger 202
structure 135ff.
subject of Aen. 101
Sychaeus 126–9 passim
symbolism 111ff.
syncretism in Underworld 152

Tempestates 138
Tiber 113
title (Aeneid) 101 n. 1, 105 n. 27
topography of Latium 168
tops 157
transformation of Trojan ships 183
treaty, breach of 203
Troilus 107

Trojan War 187f.; depicted 106–8;
  Horse 109, 115
Trojans' Italian origin 155f., religious
  observance 121; sufferings 102;
  uncertain travellers 119
Troy as *superba* 109
trophies 175f.
Turnus and Dido 123; and
  Lavinia 156ff.; *Schuld* of 158;
  slumbers 158ff.; as orator 190f.;
  should have been spared 195f.,
  207f.; honesty of 196; apparent
  surrender ib.; relations with
  Lavinia, Amata 196; and Achilles,
  Hector 206; and Pallas 205, 212;
  as tragic hero 209; as enemy of
  state ib.; motives of 209f.;
  characterisation of ib.; vices ib.;
  plea for life 210; *devotio* ib.;
  militarily inferior to Aen. 210;
  sympathy for ib.; and Lavinia ib.;
  Turnus' death 212
typology 163f.
tyrant, type of 185

ultio 206
Underworld 149ff.; as allegory 150f.;
  as illusion 146f.; and labyrinths
  150; consistency in 151f.; and
  reality of bodily existence 146f.;
  sequence of scenes 152
unfinished state of text 167f.

Varro and Dido 137; *Imagines* 145
vaunts of combatants 181
vengeance 200; see revenge
Venulus 187f.
Venus 106, 129f., 141f.
viewpoints 105 n. 34, 109ff.
Virgil's perception of *Aen.* 18
vituperation 190f.
voices, two 192, 313f.; further 193f.
Volcens 177

war in Latium, destined 160;
  bloodthirstiness in 174
warfare, ethics of 176; technicalities
  of 179
warriors, rewards for 171f.; minor,
  absent in V. 180
wolves 109, 113f.
wound, non-fatal 203

Allecto in VF 277
amicus, sense of 8

Ansileubus 310
anti-*Aeneid* 281, 290
Apollo, temple of, on Palatine 96, 97
Appendix Vergiliana 9–11
architecture as metaphor for
  composition 17
Asconius 7, 12
Asinius Pollio 12; see *Buc.*
Augustus and V.: readings 13, 17,
  19, 87; correspondence 2, 15, 18;
  and composition of *Aen.* 18f.;
  destruction of *Aen.* 22; publication
  of *Aen.* 23; bequests to 22; in
  Ov. 264. See also Life, *Buc.*, *G.*,
  Aen.

Ballista 9
Bavius and Maevius 294
bear-cubs, licked into shape 15f., 22,
  294
biography and hagiography 2; of
  ancient poets 1f.; inventions in 13

Bucolics
Alfenus see Varus
allegory 12, 43, 58f.
Amaryllis 43f.
Arcadia 45f., 56
archaic Latin, influence of 41
Aratus 40
arrangement of book 31ff.
Asinius Pollio 28, 29, 60
Augustus see Octavian
'autobiography' 30

Brundisium, peace of 28
Bucolics see title; chanted by
  priests 250

Calvus see Licinius
Catullus 41f.
changes in structure 32
characters, Theocritean practice 42ff.,
  consistency 42ff., social status 44
Christianising interpretation 59ff.
chronological references in poetry,
  difficulty of 28f.
chronology, internal, suggested criteria
  for 30f.; of composition and
  publication 11ff., 28ff.; imprecision
  of ancient sources 28f.; a 'first'
  collection? 30, 31f.
coherence of themes and attitudes 57
colloquialisms 41
comedy 41
composition, order of 30

confiscations 45
Conon 39f.
Constantine 59f.
correspondences, numerical, and chaos
    ungovernable 34; of theme,
    internal, 32
Corydon 39, 43
countryside, Italian elements in 47

Daphnis 37, 44, 55, 56f., 58
dedicatees 4, 12

'Easterners' and 'Westerners' in
    Buc.4 61
'Eclogues' 28
Epicureanism 54
eros 54
Erucius 45

Gallus, Cornelius 46, 55f., 58
genre of pastoral 35f., 40f.; interplay
    of generic and Roman
    elements 46f.; hierarchy of
    genres 55, 56
geographical setting 45ff.

Hor. Epd.16 and Buc.4 61

internal allusions 30

Julius Caesar and Buc.5 29f.; see
    Daphnis

language of shepherds 47, 48
landscape idealism and realism 46f.
Licinius Calvus 41
line-totals, significant 33
Lucretius 42

Marcellus 60
Mantua 45
Meliboeus 44
metapoetic element 55ff.

names and characters 42ff.
Neoterics 42, 49f.
numerology and interpretation 33f.;
    and text 294
Numitorius 27

obtrectatores 59
Octavian as writer of tragedy 29; in
    Buc.1 32, Buc.4 60; honours paid
    in 35 30
order of poems, original 31f.

pastoral at Rome before V.? 36f.; in
    general 34; farewell to 32; origins
    of 34f.; codification of 35f.
patronage 29

Peloponnese 34f.
Philitas 35
Pollio see Asinius
Polyphemus in Theocr. 39
prooemium to collection 31f.
puer in Buc.4 60f.

recusatio 32
riddles 40

Sicily and pastoral 34f.
Siro 58
song 54f.
structure 33
style, metre, language see s.v.

theatre, performance in 27
themes, dominant 54ff.
Theocritus 36, 37ff., 39–41; allegory
    in 58; geographical setting 45;
    names and characters in 42ff.;
    dialect 47; text of 36, 38; corpus
    of 38
title 27; alternative systems of
    titulature 293

Varus, Alfenus 29, 32, 58

Byzantium, V. at 255

Callimachus 96, 99; see Buc., G.,
    Aen.
Catalepton 10f.
coins, Virgilian scenes on 254
confiscations 93f.; see Buc.
conversation, Roman, V. in 252
Cornelius Gallus; see Gallus

Daphne 258ff.
Dido in Ov. 264; in Sil. 258f.
Diomedes in Ov. 265
discussion of Virgilian topics 250
Donatus, Aelius 3f.; see Life, Text
Donatus, Tib. Claudius 308

education, V. in Roman 250ff.
epic, anticipation of 73
Epidius 6
Epicureanism 54; see Buc., Aen., Life
Eros 19
Etruscan elements in V. (?) 5 n. 37

fame of V. 249
Furies in Stat. 283; see Aen.

Gallus, Cornelius 4, 12, 14, 86ff.,
    259; see Buc., G.
gems, Virg. scenes on 254

Georgics
Actium 93
activities of farmer 68
aetiology 79, 85
agricola 67–9
agriculture, Italian, at time of *G.* 69
Alexandrianism 79
Antonius, M. 60, 93
Aratus 80
Aristotle 77
arithmetical balances 74; exactitude in structure 91
Augustus/Octavian in 36–29, 93f.
'Augustan agricultural policy' 69
autopsy, poetical 71f.
autourgia and *poikilia* 68f.

bear, female, and cubs 73
bees, battle of 85
Brundisium, treaty of 93
Britanni and dating of *G.* 63

Callimachus 80, 96, 99
Cato the elder 79, 81
centrality 96
chronology of *G.* 63–5; and military history 63; and Varr. *RR* 63, 64f.; in ancient sources 63; 'late additions' 64, 73
Cicero, V., and Alexandrian meteorology 80
Cicero and Cato in V. 81
civil wars 93
colonus 67–9
countryside, attachment of readers to 70f.; idealisation of 71, 81; and town 70
contemporary references in *G.* 93

'descriptive' and 'didactic' 76
development of V. and *G.* 97
'digressions' 73, 75ff.
divinities in proem 99

Egypt 87f.
epyllion 85
Eratosthenes 79f.
errors in *G.* and their origin 72
erudition 79f.
excursus see digression; didactic role of 76

famine 69
farming, types of, envisaged 68
farms, size of 68
fossor 67

Gallus, C. Cornelius 86–9
Greek prose sources 77

haste 72
Hesiod 67, 78; and autopsy 71; and Perses 67; and didactic 78
historical context of *G.* 93
Homer and *G.* 84–6; and development of V. 85

'ideological' content 69f., 77
imitation and adaptation, techniques of 78
immortality and poetry 96, 98
invocations, typical language of 99
Italy, love of 84; depiction of in *G.* 93; contemporary realities of 69f.

latifundia 68
laudes Italiae 74, 76f.
Lucretius 82f.; and excursus 76; and autopsy 71

Maecenas and *G.* 64, 65, 97, 99; invoked 99; speech in Dio 69
mathematical balances 99
metaphrasts 77
meteorology, V.'s sources 80

Neoterics 83f., 90
Nicander 80

observation, precise 71f.
Octavian 94 (see also Augustus)
omissions 72
order of composition 73, 75
Orpheus 87f.

panegyric, traditional language of 96–8; commonplaces in 63, 64
Philitas 80f.
Pindar 96–8
Po Valley 71
poikilia, literary and the small farm 68; see also *variatio*
Pompeius Sex., defeat of 64, 69, 93f.
pride, Augustan poetic 96–8
prooemia 96–100
'propaganda' 69f.

readers of *G.* 65f., 70; readers, intended and imagined audience 65f.

'second edition' 86–9
selectivity 72
similes 83
slaves 68

structure 74f.
style, metre, language see s.v.

Theophrastus 77
title, '*Georgics*' 80
transitional character of *G.* 72f.
town and country 70
triumph, poetic and literal 97

variatio 74; see also *poikilia*
Varro, *RR* 63, 64f., 84
veterans 65f.; their allotments, ib., 68f.; as farmers 66
victory, metaphors for 96–8
uidi 71f.

women on farm 67
work-force envisaged 67–9

graffiti V. in 251f.
Greece, scholarly travel in 21

Homer: V.'s use of develops 14; see further *G.*, *Aen.*; ancient comparisons of V. and Hom. 250
Horace, *Epd.*16 and *Buc.*4 61; H. echoes in *Aen.* 15
Hyginus 294

inscriptions, Virgilian citations in 253
instrumentum domesticum, Virg. on 254

Julius Caesar and Daphnis 58; see *Buc.*, *Aen.*
Juno in Silius 288
Jupiter in Ov. 262, 266f., in VF 273f., in Sil. 288

labor limae 16, 20
liber, Augustan, size of 64
liberalitas, sense of 8

Virgil: life
admirers 7
Alban kings, alleged poem on 11
Andes 5
appearance of PVM 6
astrology, alleged interest 9
Augustus, relations with 18
autobiography, poetic, in V. 4

burning of *Aen.*, intended 22

chronology, problems of absolute 13
composition, alleged methods of 15ff.; speed of 15
confiscations 13
Cremona 5, 10

date of birth 5

education 6
Epicureanism 7f.
estate 21ff.

further studies 7f., 9

Georgics, chronology of 13

health and habits 6f.
heirs 21ff.
homes 8

kin 9

last wishes 22f.
last voyage 20
Lucretius, synchronism with 5f.

Mantua 5
Milan 6
miracles 7

Naples 7f.
name 5 n. 37; plays on 5, 7
nickname 7

obtrectatores 16, 18, 21, 23, 294
orator, V. as 9

parents 5, 9
place of birth 5
pederasty, alleged 6f.
philosophy, study of 11, 20
portraits 6

rank 8
reader of own poetry 17f., 19

Sicily 8
sources: methods of poetic biography 1f.; chronology of sources 2, 3; confusion in 23; 'facts' and inventions 4, 6; 'autobiography' in text, 4, 12, '*liber amicorum*' 2f., 15, Melissus 12, Servius 4, VSD 3f.
speaking names in biography 7, 9, 13

toga virilis 5
tomb 7, 21

verecundia 22, 23
Vergilius, in Hor. 2

wealth of poet 8
will 21ff.
See also s.v. Augustus, confiscations, Donatus Ael., Epicureanism, performances, readings, Suetonius

Livy and *Aen.*, relative chronology 15, 261

Lucan: style and Virgilian tradition 271; response to epic genre ib.; theme of *BC* 268; order and dissolution, ib.; and V.'s view of civil wars, ib.; Nero 269; and V.'s view of history 269; Homer 269; view of future 269; Roman history, end of ib.; Virgilian history, evocation of, ib.; and ideologies of *Aen.* 270f.; response to V., ib.; and prose sources 271

Maecenas and *G.* 12, 97; chronology of V.'s relations with 11f., 225; *Symposium* of 2; cf. further 4, 13, 17, 19 and s.v. *Aen.*, *G.*, Life
Macrobius 308
Marcellus-episode 19, 148; see *Aen.*
Melissus C. 294
memorisation of V. 250f.
miracles in poetic biography 5
Montanus, Julius 17f.
mosaics, Virgilian scenes on 253

Naples 7f.
Nisus (grammarian) 24, 299f.
Nola 7

obtrectatores 7; see *Buc.*, Life
Octavia 19, 148
Octavian see Augustus
Octavius Musa 11
oratory and V. 9; see *Aen.*, Life, rhetoric
opuscula of poet in *vita* 9
Ovid: Aen.'s voyage 265; apotheosis 266; attitude to V. 257f.; and *Buc.*6 258f.; and Callimachus 258, 260; and Calvus 259; complexity 258; cosmogony ib.; Dido 264; Ennius 266; epic, deflation of 260; epic ambitions ib.; erotic and epic, interplay 261f.; foundations 267; generic multiplicity 257; 'history' in, 262ff.; history, universal 259; history, perspective of 267; and Homer 257; humour 260, 261f.; integration of multiple strands 263f.; irony 259; perspective, historical 262, 267; 'profanation' 26; prophecy 266;

Pythagoras, ib.; Roman empire in 264; sensibility 262; style, and V., 260f.; Turnus 264; vegetarianism 266; Venus 266f.

Palatine library 297
Pan.Mess. and *Aen.* 15
papyri 254f., 299
Parthenias 7
Parthia 97
pastoral, departure from 72f.
performances of V. 17, 249, 294
Philodemus 2; see *Aen.*
Pliny the elder 22
Pliny the younger 19
Plotius Tucca 2, 11, 22f., 296
poetical autobiography 4
Pollio see Asinius
Pompeii 251–3
Propertius on *Aen.* 15, 18

Quintilius Varus 2, 7, 12

readings of V. 250
recitations by V. 19, 148
Rhetoric and V. 9; see Life, *Aen.*, Style, oratory

sarcophagi, V. on 253f.
Servius 308; reliability of on biography 12f., 14, 86f., cf. 86; allegory 56f.; Orpheus 14
Silius Italicus: reverence for V. 287; and epic tradition ib.; continuity of *Aen.* and *Punica* ib.; causes of war 287f.; Juno 288; Ennius ib.; and V.'s view of Carthage ib.; Dido and Anna 288f.; Hannibal and Turnus 289; typological relationship to V. ib.; and Lucan's 'history' 290; and moral decline ib.; and civil war ib.; pessimism ib.; and Homer 291; more Homeric than Virgilian ib.; style and language ib.
Siro 7, 10, 11
stage, V. on 249f.
Statius *Achilleid* and Homer 285; *Aen.* 7–12 283; anti- *Aeneid* 281; Eteocles and Polynices 282; explicit references to V. 279; Furies 283; generic affiliations 285; gods, Virgil's 281; Greek tragedy 280; Homer ib.; imitations, small-scale of V. 286; influence of Neronian literature 281; Lucan and

Ovid 279; mannerism 280f.;
scenes imitated from V. 285f.;
reworked 280; Seneca 279f.; style
and V. 283; Turnus 282, 289

Style, metre, language
Agrippa see Vipranius, Vipsanius
alliteration 224
ambiguity 229
ambivalence 229
archaisms 220

Buc. colloquialisms in 50; dialogue
in 54, 55; levels of language
in 47; metre and prosody 51ff.;
metrical patterns, variation in 52;
structure of hexameter in 52;
synaloepha in 52f.; syntax, neoteric
influence on 49f.

calque 228f.
colloquialisms 50, 90, 221
colon-end and line-end 234
compound epithets 228
connotations and contexts 219f.
criticism of V.'s style 229

development of style(?) 232ff.
didactic stilemes 66f.
digressions in *G.*, style of 75f., 90f.
diminutives 47

economy of language 230f.
elevation of 'ordinary' words 219f.
elision; see synaloepha
enallage 227
enjambement 233f.
Ennius 90
epicisms 90
euphony 223
euphuism 76

figured and literal senses of a
word 117
figures of speech 187

generic diversity in V. 233
genitivus inhaerentiae 228
G.: style of 75f., 90f.; of agricultural
instruction, 66f.; of precepts, 66f.
grammar 226ff.
Grecisms: and ms. tradition 48; of
syntax and usage 48f.
Greek names, words, declension of 48

hexameter 223
high poetic language 220
Homerisms 220

homodyne and heterodyne 233
hypallage 227

ictus and accent 223f.
infinitives, passive 226f.
innovations 221
intransitivation 227
inversion of object and subject 227
iunctura, callida 227

kakozelia 225f.

language of poetry 219; of *G.* 89–91
lateo, latenter 226
Latin poetic usage 220
lexical change in *Aen.* 236
lexicon 219
line-end: see colon-end; line-ends,
irregular, in *Buc.* 53
line-structure 232
literal and figured senses of a
word 117
Lucretius and *G.* 90

metaphors in *G.* 91; range of, in
V. 96–8
metaphrasis 91
metre 223; see also *Buc.*
metrical effects 223
'middle' verbs 228
morphology 222f.

neotericisms 90, 220
neutral words 221
normalisation of hexameter 52

onomatopoea 223

parataxis 231
patterns 231f.
pronunciation 224
periodic structure 231
prosaisms 220f.
prosodical anomalies in *Buc.* 53
prosody 222f.
punctuation 229f.

'recipe'-style 89f.
repetition in *Buc.* and Theocr. 49
rhyme 224
rhythm 223, 224; in *Buc.* 52;
compared with predecessors, ib.

sentence-structure 231f.
separation, verbs of, 227
sounds 223f.
speech and narrative, differences
between 232
spoken Latin 47, 221

spondees and dactyls, ratios of, 235f.
synaloepha 234f.; see also *Buc.*
synonyms 221f.
syntax 226ff., 230f.
style, of digression in *G.* 75f.;
  'standard' and anomalies 217, 226

technical language 47, 226
Theocritus, metre of 51; differences
  from V. 51; ancient views
  thereon 51f.

unpoetic expressions 220f.

variation in repetition 49f.
verbs and nouns, transposition of 227
Virgil, style of, development 72f.,
  232ff.; freedom, in *Buc.* 52
vocabulary 219
vocative, use in *Buc.* 50
voices of narrator and of
  characters 53f.
vulgarisms 48, 50f., 221, 237ff.

words, natural position for 232
word-order, interwoven 50

Suet.-Donatus *vita* 1–3; on
  patronage 12, 18; use of *dicitur,
  traditur*, etc. 3, 15, 19; see further
  Life
Sulpicius Carthaginiensis 22
syllabus, V. in school 250f.
Terence, *vita* of 21

Text and Transmission
Aen., intended burning of 22, early
  fame, and transmission 293, 305;
  publication of 295
archetype 297
Asper, Aemilius 302
author-variants 297
autograph text of *Aen.* 22ff.; *Buc.*,
  transmission of 293

Celsus 301
Carolingian mss. 310
Christians, and V. 303f.
Cornutus 301
critics, early 293, 294

defence of text 301
citations, by Serv. 309, reliability
  of, ib.
Donatus, Aelius 3f., 302
Donatus, Tib. Claudius 308

errors in citation, 298f.

Gellius, A. and V. 302
G., transmission of 294f.; *G.*4, '2nd.
  ed.' 86–9
glossators 310

half-lines or hemistichia 19f., 23f.,
  296
Helen-episode 300
Hyginus 301

ille ego., 24, 300
interpolations 24, 296, 300

lacunae 299
'learned' editions 299
litterae Virgilianae 304
'luxury' editions 299

Macrobius 308
MSS, capital, 304–7; alleged antiquity
  of V.'s mss. 295, 299
Middle Ages, late 311f.
miniatures 304, 306, 311
Modestus, Julius 301

Notae Probianae 302

order of books, alleged change in 24,
  300

pagan revival, V. and 303f.
papyri 254f., 299
Petrarch 311–2
Probus, Valerius 29f., 301f.
PsProbus 302

repetitions 296f.
richness of transmission 293

Scholia Bernensia 309,
  Veronensia 302
scholarship of c.1 AD 301; c.2 302,
  Renaissance 312
Servius 308, Servius Danielis 309,
  312

tibicines 16
transmission, early, rapidity of 294

unfinished text, as stimulus 299

'vulgate' text, 299

theatre, V. in 17, 249f.
Troy in Ov. 263ff.
Turnus in Ov. 264f.

Valerius Flaccus: and *Aeneid* 274, 275;
  Allecto 277; anti- *Aeneid* 276;

Apollonius 273; conscious revolt against V. 277; empires, sequence of 273; history in 273f.; Homer 273, 274, 275; Jupiter 273, 274; pessimism 276f.; style 276f., 277f.; Troy 273, 274; Venus 277; Virgil, use of 275; Virgilian history 274f.

Varius Rufus 2, 7, 11, 13, 21, 22f, 24, 200; see Life

Varro Atacinus 18

'Vipranius' 225

Vipsanius Agrippa M. 225

Virgil, attitude to *Aen.* 18

Virgil, love for, diffusion of 251f.

wall-paintings, V. on 253

wills, preservation of 22

ADDENDA

It was from the first intended that the *Companions* should be updated as and when possible, but it would not be in the spirit of *Companion to the study of Virgil* to offer at this point a distillation of five years' worth of *Vergilius* and *Ann.Phil.* bibliographies; since 1995 I have in fact still been working largely on Virgil and thus add a consciously selective list account of approaches and material which have come to my notice, which seem truly helpful and which bear on issues raised in *Companion*. To the friends who have sent me books and articles over this period, I am particularly grateful, as I am to Barbara Boyd, for her list (incorporated above) of the typographical slips present in my last pre-computer book.

xi] One reviewer of *Companion* mysteriously supposed that the short chapter-bibliographies represented the *summa summarum* of my own scholarly reading, by chapters; they are of course intended to help the reader get started on those topics where the learned bibliography is unusually vast and complex.

xiii] *Aen.*3: see P.V. Cova, *Il libro terzo dell' Eneide* (Milano 1994) (cf. my review in *Vergilius* 42 (1996), 143ff.)
*Aen.*7: commentary, Nicholas Horsfall, *Mnem.* Suppl. 198 (2000)
*Aen.*9: commentary, J. Dingel (Heidelberg 1997) (cf. my rev. in *Vergilius* 45 (1999), 123ff.)
*Aen.*11. I am now engaged on a commentary, similar to that on bk. 7.
*Aen.*12: commentary in A. Traina, *Virgilio. L'utopia e la storia* (Torino 1997). Exceptional

xiv] K. Galinsky, *Augustan culture* Princeton 1996
The Cambridge companion to Virgil ed. C. Martindale (Cambridge 1997)
P. Hardie *Virgil, GRNSC* 28 (1998)

id. (ed.) *Virgil* 4 vols. (London 1999) reprints a large number of articles
(ed.) H.-P. Stahl, *Vergil's Aeneid: Augustan epic and political context* (London 1998)

1ff.] S. MacCormack *The shadows of poetry. Vergil in the mind of Augustine* (Berkeley 1998), 1ff. retells the life of Virgil at length, as though doubt had never been voiced. The *Vitae* may now be consulted in an ample ed. by G. Brugnoli and F. Stok (Rome 1997)

19] It is extraordinary that Sen. *Cons.Marc.* 2.4 has apparently not been cited as proof of the romanticised character of this text: we know, explicitly, that Octavia detested such poetry and such occasions.

23] On incompleteness and V.'s methods of writing, see now the brilliant monograph by H.-C. Günther, *Überlegungen zur Entstehung von Vergils Aeneis* (Gottingen 1996); a few points of dissent expressed at *RFil.*125 (1997), 468ff.

65ff.] On addressees, cf. now P. Bing, *MD* 31 (1993), 102f., A. Schiesaro, ib., 136f.

71, n. 38] After Thomas, see now M. Leigh, *MD* 33 (1994), 181ff.

92] On identification of plants, see now G. Maggiulli, *Incipiant siluae* (Roma 1995)

96ff.] On the proem to *G.*3, see, more amply E. Kraggerud in Stahl, 1ff.; on Pindar and Callimachus here, cf. R. Thomas in *Style and tradition. Studies on honor of Wendell Clausen* (Stuttgart 1998), 103ff. Very differently, R. Krieger Balot, *Phoen.* 52 (1998), 83ff.

105, n. 34] On ecphrasis in general, cf. M.C.J. Putnam, *Virgil's epic designs* (New Haven 1998). The obloquy my reading of the pictures in Juno's temple has attracted reaches its climax in A. Barchiesi in *Style and tradition,* cit., 138, n. 223; but see now S. Casali, *CQ* 49 (1999), 208, n. 15 and M. Fernandelli, *MD* 42 (1999), 108, n. 37.

123, n. 2] On Dido and magic, see now E. Kraggerud, *Pap.Norwegian Inst.Ath.* 4 (1999), 103ff.

137, n. 20] See too, with caution, S. Kyriakidis, *Narrative structure and poetics in the Aeneid. The frame of book 6* (Bari 1998)

146, n. 14] Add R.G. Mayer, *PVS* 21 (1993), 53ff.

155ff.] Strong dissent with several positions taken in this section is expressed in Horsfall, *Aen.*7

163] On the Shield, cf. A.G. McKay in Stahl, 199ff., S.J. Harrison, *JRS* 87 (1997), 70ff., R.T. Scott in *Ultra terminum vagari. Scritti in onore di Carl Nylander* (Roma 1997), 301ff.

163, n. 15] For an extreme case, see M. Alessio, *Studies in Vergil, Aeneid Eleven* (Laval 1993)

186, n. 1] See now P. Hardie in Stahl, 243ff., Andrew Laird, *Powers of expression, expressions of power* (Oxford 1999), E. Fantham, *AJP* 120 (1999), 259ff.

193, n. 10] M.C.J. Putnam has collected his *Aeneid* papers in *Virgil's Aeneid* (Chapel Hill 1995); cf. too D. Quint, *Epic and Empire* (Princeton 1993), 65ff.

198, n. 34] Cf. now K. Galinsky, *ICS* 19 (1994), 191ff.

201, n. 62] M.R. Wright in (eds. S.M. Braund, C. Gill) *The passions in Roman thought and literature* (Cambridge 1997), 170ff.

202, n. 63] Cf. D.P. Fowler in *The passions*, 30ff.

203, n. 70] For *Aen.*12 and the Homeric scholia, cf. W.R. Barnes, *PCPS* Suppl. 22 (1999), 60ff.

209, n. 117] On Turnus, cf. R. Thomas in Stahl, 271ff.

211, n. 129] See too W. Hübner, *Eranos* 22 (1994), 23ff.

214, n. 150] On Hercules and Cacus, see L. Morgan in Stahl, 175ff.

217ff.] J.J. O'Hara *True names* (Ann Arbor 1996) at last gives V.'s etymologies their due, while M. Paschalis, *Virgil's Aeneid. Semantic relations and proper names* (Oxford 1997) should be used with extreme caution. On V.'s style, see the admirable summary by J.J. O'Hara in Martindale, 241ff. Horsfall on *Aen.*7 pays particular attentions to questions of style and language. On V.'s solution to the problem of multiple actions and multiple participants, cf. the remarkable discussion by E.A. Schmidt in *Hyperboreus* 3 (1997), 57ff.

217, n. 4] See now also W. Görler in *Aspects on the language of Latin poetry*, *PBA* 93 (1999), 269ff.

296f.] O. Zwierlein, *Die Ovid- und Vergil-Revision in tiberischer Zeit* 1-(Berlin 1999) has advanced the theory that our text of V. is heavily interpolated, largely thanks to the late-Augustan/Tiberian poet Iulius Montanus; his pupil, R. Cramer, has likewise applied the axe to *G*.4: *Vergils Weltsicht* (Berlin 1998). So Virgilian studies are to be haunted by Jachmann's ghost, though the informed reader is unlikely to yield to panic.

304ff.] For a less conventional view of the dating of the capital mss., cf. my *Aen*.7, xxx[f.].